HOLT McDOUGAL

GEORGIA

COORDINATE ALGEBRA

Edward B. Burger
David J. Chard
Paul A. Kennedy
Steven J. Leinwand
Freddie L. Renfro
Tom W. Roby
Bert K. Waits

HOLT McDOUGAL

 HOUGHTON MIFFLIN HARCOURT

Authors

Edward B. Burger, Ph.D., is Professor of Mathematics at Williams College and is the author of numerous articles, books, and videos. He has won several of the most prestigious writing and teaching awards offered by the Mathematical Association of America. Dr. Burger has made numerous television and radio appearances and has given countless mathematical presentations around the world.

Freddie L. Renfro, MA, has 35 years of experience in Texas education as a classroom teacher and director/coordinator of Mathematics PreK-12 for school districts in the Houston area. She has served as a reviewer and TXTEAM trainer for Texas Math Institutes and has presented at numerous math workshops.

David J. Chard, Ph.D., is the Leon Simmons Dean of the School of Education and Human Development at Southern Methodist University. He is a past president of the Divison of Research at the Council for Exceptional Children, a member of the International Academy for Research on Learning Disabilities, and has been the Principal Investigator on numerous research projects for the U.S. Department of Education.

Tom W. Roby, Ph.D., is Associate Professor of Mathematics and Director of the Quantitative Learning Center at the University of Connecticut. He founded and directed the Bay Area-based ACCLAIM professional development program. He also chaired the advisory board of the California Mathematics Project and reviewed content for the California Standards Tests.

Paul A. Kennedy, Ph.D., is a professor and Distinguished University Teaching Scholar in the Department of Mathematics at Colorado State University. Dr. Kennedy is a leader in mathematics education. His research focuses on developing algebraic thinking by using multiple representations and technology. He is the author of numerous publications.

Bert K. Waits, Ph.D., is a Professor Emeritus of Mathematics at The Ohio State University and cofounder of T^3 (Teachers Teaching with Technology), a national professional development program. Dr. Waits is also a former board member of the NCTM and an author of the original NCTM Standards.

Steven J. Leinwand is a Principal Research Analyst at the American Institutes for Research in Washington, D.C. He was previously, for 22 years, the Mathematics Supervisor with the Connecticut Department of Education.

Georgia Reviewers

Michelle Genovese
Sandy Creek High School
Tyrone, GA

C. Mark Henderson
Starr's Mill High School
Fayette County Board of
    Education
Fayetteville, GA

Steve Martin
Carrollton High School
Carrollton, GA

Ashley McAfee
McIntosh High School
Peachtree City, GA

Judy Riddell
Math Department Chair
Northgate High School
Newnan, GA

Susan S. Roach Ed.S.
Instructional Coach,
    Mathematics
Newnan High School
Newnan, GA

Kimberly Snell, Ed.S
Mathematics Teacher
Campbell High School
Smyrna, GA

Melanie Tomlinson
East Coweta High School
Coweta County, GA

Contributing Authors

Carmen Whitman
Pflugerville, TX

Linda Antinone
Fort Worth, TX

Field Test Participants

Len Zigment
Mesa Ridge High School
Colorado Springs, CO

Vicky Petty
Central Middle School
Murfreesboro, TN

John Bakelaar
Peebles Middle School
Jackson, MS

Carey Carter
Alvarado High School
Alvarado, TX

Reviewers

UNIT 1

Relationships Between Quantities

Reasoning with Equations and Inequalities

UNIT 2

Linear and Exponential Functions

UNIT 3 CONTINUED

Describing Data

UNIT 5

Transformations in the Coordinate Plane

Connecting Algebra and Geometry Through Coordinates

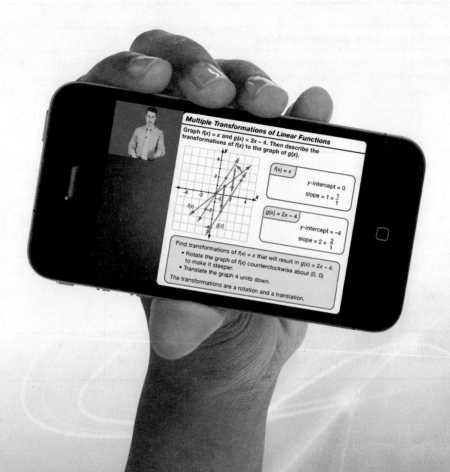

Common Core Georgia Performance Standards

Correlation for Holt McDougal Coordinate Algebra

Standard	Descriptor	Page Citation
Number and Quantity: Quantities*		
Reason quantitatively and use units to solve problems		
MCC9-12.N.Q.1	Use units as a way to understand problems and to guide the solution of multi-step problems; choose and interpret units consistently in formulas; choose and interpret the scale and the origin in graphs and data displays.*	SE: 6–11, 32–38, 39–44, 45–51, 92–97
MCC9-12.N.Q.2	Define appropriate quantities for the purpose of descriptive modeling.*	SE: 13–18, 20–26, 39–44
MCC9-12.N.Q.3	Choose a level of accuracy appropriate to limitations on measurement when reporting quantities.*	SE: 45–51
Algebra: Seeing Structure in Expressions		
Interpret the structure of expressions		
MCC9-12.A.SSE.1	Interpret expressions that represent a quantity in terms of its context.*	SE: 6–11
MCC9-12.A.SSE.1a	a. Interpret parts of an expression, such as terms, factors, and coefficients.*	SE: 6–11
MCC9-12.A.SSE.1b	b. Interpret complicated expressions by viewing one or more of their parts as a single entity. For example, interpret $P(1 + r)^n$ as the product of P and a factor not depending on P.*	SE: 19
Algebra: Creating Equations*		
Create equations that describe numbers or relationships		
MCC9-12.A.CED.1	Create equations and inequalities in one variable and use them to solve problems. Include equations arising from linear and quadratic functions, and simple rational and exponential functions.*	SE: 6–11, 13–18, 20–26, 32–38, 39–44, 62–68, 70–76, 92–97, 98–103, 108–113, 114–120, 121–127
MCC9-12.A.CED.2	Create equations in two or more variables to represent relationships between quantities; graph equations on coordinate axes with labels and scales.*	SE: 20–26, 133–138, 140–146, 147–153, 158–163, 203–209, 274–279, 280–286, 287–294, 516–521
MCC9-12.A.CED.3	Represent constraints by equations or inequalities, and by systems of equations and/or inequalities, and interpret solutions as viable or non-viable options in a modeling context. *For example, represent inequalities describing nutritional and cost constraints on combinations of different foods.**	SE: 13–18, 20–26, 86–91
MCC9-12.A.CED.4	Rearrange formulas to highlight a quantity of interest, using the same reasoning as in solving equations. *For example, rearrange Ohm's law V = IR to highlight resistance R.**	SE: 77–81

SE = Student Edition
* = Also a Modeling Standard

Standard	Descriptor	Page Citation
Algebra: Reasoning with Equations and Inequalities		
Understand solving equations as a process of reasoning and explain the reasoning		
MCC9-12.A.REI.1	Explain each step in solving a simple equation as following from the equality of numbers asserted at the previous step, starting from the assumption that the original equation has a solution. Construct a viable argument to justify a solution method.	SE: 12, 13–18, 20–26, 62–68, 69, 70–76, 77–81
Solve equations and inequalities in one variable		
MCC9-12.A.REI.3	Solve linear equations and inequalities in one variable, including equations with coefficients represented by letters.	SE: 13–18, 20–26, 27, 62–68, 69, 70–76, 77–81, 86–91, 92–97, 98–103, 108–113, 114–120, 121–127
Solve systems of equations		
MCC9-12.A.REI.5	Prove that, given a system of two equations in two variables, replacing one equation by the sum of that equation and a multiple of the other produces a system with the same solutions.	SE: 147–153
MCC9-12.A.REI.6	Solve systems of linear equations exactly and approximately (e.g., with graphs), focusing on pairs of linear equations in two variables.	SE: 132, 139, 133–138, 140–146, 147–153, 158–163
Represent and solve equations and inequalities graphically		
MCC9-12.A.REI.10	Understand that the graph of an equation in two variables is the set of all its solutions plotted in the coordinate plane, often forming a curve (which could be a line).	SE: 188–193, 214–220, 314–320
MCC9-12.A.REI.11	Explain why the x-coordinates of the points where the graphs of the equations $y = f(x)$ and $y = g(x)$ intersect are the solutions of the equation $f(x) = g(x)$; find the solutions approximately, e.g., using technology to graph the functions, make tables of values, or find successive approximations. Include cases where $f(x)$ and/or $g(x)$ are linear, polynomial, rational, absolute value, exponential, and logarithmic functions.*	SE: 27, 133–138
MCC9-12.A.REI.12	Graph the solutions to a linear inequality in two variables as a half-plane (excluding the boundary in the case of a strict inequality), and graph the solution set to a system of linear inequalities in two variables as the intersection of the corresponding half-planes.	SE: 164–170, 171–176, 177

Standard	Descriptor	Page Citation
Functions: Interpreting Functions		
Understand the concept of a function and use function notation		
MCC9-12.F.IF.1	Understand that a function from one set (called the domain) to another set (called the range) assigns to each element of the domain exactly one element of the range. If f is a function and x is an element of its domain, then f(x) denotes the output of f corresponding to the input x. The graph of f is the graph of the equation y = f(x).	SE: 203–209, 280–286, 287–294
MCC9-12.F.IF.2	Use function notation, evaluate functions for inputs in their domains, and interpret statements that use function notation in terms of a context.	SE: 202, 203–209
MCC9-12.F.IF.3	Recognize that sequences are functions, sometimes defined recursively, whose domain is a subset of the integers. *For example, the Fibonacci sequence is defined recursively by $f(0) = f(1) = 1, f(n+1) = f(n) + f(n-1)$ for $n \geq 1$ (n is greater than or equal to 1).*	SE: 230–235, 308–313, 332–335
Interpret functions that arise in applications in terms of the context		
MCC9-12.F.IF.4	For a function that models a relationship between two quantities, interpret key features of graphs and tables in terms of the quantities, and sketch graphs showing key features given a verbal description of the relationship. Key features include: intercepts; intervals where the function is increasing, decreasing, positive, or negative; relative maximums and minimums; symmetries; end behavior; and periodicity.*	SE: 188–193, 247–252, 254–261, 264–269
MCC9-12.F.IF.5	Relate the domain of a function to its graph and, where applicable, to the quantitative relationship it describes. *For example, if the function h(n) gives the number of person-hours it takes to assemble n engines in a factory, then the positive integers would be an appropriate domain for the function.* *	SE: 188–193, 214–220, 240–246, 247–252, 254–261, 280–286, 314–320
MCC9-12.F.IF.6	Calculate and interpret the average rate of change of a function (presented symbolically or as a table) over a specified interval. Estimate the rate of change from a graph.*	SE: 254–261, 262–263, 264–269, 348–351
Analyze functions using different representations		
MCC9-12.F.IF.7	Graph functions expressed symbolically and show key features of the graph, by hand in simple cases and using technology for more complicated cases.*	SE: 214–220, 280–286, 295, 314–320
MCC9-12.F.IF.7a	a. Graph linear and quadratic functions and show intercepts, maxima, and minima.*	SE: 214–220, 280–286
MCC9-12.F.IF.7e	e. Graph exponential and logarithmic functions, showing intercepts and end behavior, and trigonometric functions, showing period, midline, and amplitude.*	SE: 314–320
MCC9-12.F.IF.9	Compare properties of two functions each represented in a different way (algebraically, graphically, numerically in tables, or by verbal descriptions). *For example, given a graph of one quadratic function and an algebraic expression for another, say which has the larger maximum.*	SE: 352–357

SE = Student Edition
* = Also a Modeling Standard

Standard	Descriptor	Page Citation
Functions: Building Functions		
Build a function that models a relationship between two quantities		
MCC9-12.F.BF.1	Write a function that describes a relationship between two quantities.*	SE: 203–209, 280–286, 287–294
MCC9-12.F.BF.1a	a. Determine an explicit expression, a recursive process, or steps for calculation from a context.	SE: 203–209, 280–286, 287–294
MCC9-12.F.BF.1b	b. Combine standard function types using arithmetic operations. *For example, build a function that models the temperature of a cooling body by adding a constant function to a decaying exponential, and relate these functions to the model.*	SE: 279, 347
MCC9-12.F.BF.2	Write arithmetic and geometric sequences both recursively and with an explicit formula, use them to model situations, and translate between the two forms.*	SE: 321, 230–235, 308–313
Build new functions from existing functions		
MCC9-12.F.BF.3	Identify the effect on the graph of replacing f(x) by f(x) + k, k f(x), f(kx), and f(x + k) for specific values of k (both positive and negative); find the value of k given the graphs. Experiment with cases and illustrate an explanation of the effects on the graph using technology. *Include recognizing even and odd functions from their graphs and algebraic expressions for them.*	SE: 222–229, 296, 297–303, 358–359, 466

Common Core Georgia Performance Standards

Standard	Descriptor	Page Citation
Functions: Linear, Quadratic, and Exponential Models*		
Construct and compare linear, quadratic, and exponential models and solve problems		
MCC9-12.F.LE.1	Distinguish between situations that can be modeled with linear functions and with exponential functions.*	SE: 430–433
MCC9-12.F.LE.1a	a. Prove that linear functions grow by equal differences over equal intervals, and that exponential functions grow by equal factors over equal intervals.*	SE: 240–246, 357
MCC9-12.F.LE.1b	b. Recognize situations in which one quantity changes at a constant rate per unit interval relative to another.*	SE: 240–246, 274–279, 314–320, 341–347
MCC9-12.F.LE.1c	c. Recognize situations in which a quantity grows or decays by a constant percent rate per unit interval relative to another.*	SE: 314–320, 323–330
MCC9-12.F.LE.2	Construct linear and exponential functions, including arithmetic and geometric sequences, given a graph, a description of a relationship, or two input-output pairs (include reading these from a table).*	SE: 230–235, 322, 323–330, 341–347
MCC9-12.F.LE.3	Observe using graphs and tables that a quantity increasing exponentially eventually exceeds a quantity increasing linearly, quadratically, or (more generally) as a polynomial function.*	SE: 341–347
Interpret expressions for functions in terms of the situation they model		
MCC9-12.F.LE.5	Interpret the parameters in a linear or exponential function in terms of a context.*	SE: 214–220, 243, 254–261, 264–269, 280–286, 314–320, 323–330

SE = Student Edition
* = Also a Modeling Standard

Standard	Descriptor	Page Citation
Geometry: Congruence		
Experiment with transformations in the plane		
MCC9-12.G.CO.1	Know precise definitions of angle, circle, perpendicular line, parallel line, and line segment, based on the undefined notions of point, line, distance along a line, and distance around a circular arc.	SE: 444–449, 452–458, 459–465
MCC9-12.G.CO.2	Represent transformations in the plane using, e.g., transparencies and geometry software; describe transformations as functions that take points in the plane as inputs and give other points as outputs. Compare transformations that preserve distance and angle to those that do not (e.g., translation versus horizontal stretch).	SE: 444–449, 450–451, 452–458, 459–465, 467–473
MCC9-12.G.CO.3	Given a rectangle, parallelogram, trapezoid, or regular polygon, describe the rotations and reflections that carry it onto itself.	SE: 484–490
MCC9-12.G.CO.4	Develop definitions of rotations, reflections, and translations in terms of angles, circles, perpendicular lines, parallel lines, and line segments.	SE: 444–449, 452–458, 459–465, 467–473
MCC9-12.G.CO.5	Given a geometric figure and a rotation, reflection, or translation, draw the transformed figure using, e.g., graph paper, tracing paper, or geometry software. Specify a sequence of transformations that will carry a given figure onto another.	SE: 452–458, 459–465, 467–473, 478–483, 491–497

Common Core Georgia
Performance Standards

Standard	Descriptor	Page Citation
Geometry: Expressing Geometric Properties with Equations		
Use coordinates to prove simple geometric theorems algebraically		
MCC9-12.G.GPE.4	Use coordinates to prove simple geometric theorems algebraically. For example, prove or disprove that a figure defined by four given points in the coordinate plane is a rectangle; prove or disprove that the point (1, √3) lies on the circle centered at the origin and containing the point (0, 2).	SE: 509–515
MCC9-12.G.GPE.5	Prove the slope criteria for parallel and perpendicular lines and use them to solve geometric problems (e.g., find the equation of a line parallel or perpendicular to a given line that passes through a given point).	SE: 509–515
MCC9-12.G.GPE.6	Find the point on a directed line segment between two given points that partitions the segment in a given ratio.	SE: 516–521
MCC9-12.G.GPE.7	Use coordinates to compute perimeters of polygons and areas of triangles and rectangles, e.g., using the distance formula.*	SE: 508, 516–521

SE = Student Edition
* = Also a Modeling Standard

Standard	Descriptor	Page Citation
Statistics and Probability: Interpreting Categorical and Quantitative Data*		
Summarize, represent, and interpret data on a single count or measurable variable		
MCC9-12.S.ID.1	Represent data with plots on the real number line (dot plots, histograms, and box plots).*	SE: 370–378, 379–385, 394–401, 402–405, 406–407
MCC9-12.S.ID.2	Use statistics appropriate to the shape of the data distribution to compare center (median, mean) and spread (interquartile range, standard deviation) of two or more different data sets.*	SE: 394–401, 402–405
MCC9-12.S.ID.3	Interpret differences in shape, center, and spread in the context of the data sets, accounting for possible effects of extreme data points (outliers).*	SE: 394–401, 402–405
Summarize, represent, and interpret data on two categorical and quantitative variables		
MCC9-12.S.ID.5	Summarize categorical data for two categories in two-way frequency tables. Interpret relative frequencies in the context of the data (including joint, marginal, and conditional relative frequencies). Recognize possible associations and trends in the data.*	SE: 379–385, 386–393
MCC9-12.S.ID.6	Represent data on two quantitative variables on a scatter plot, and describe how the variables are related.*	SE: 412–419
MCC9-12.S.ID.6a	a. Fit a function to the data; use functions fitted to data to solve problems in the context of the data. Use given functions or choose a function suggested by the context. Emphasize linear and exponential models.*	SE: 412–419, 420, 421–428
MCC9-12.S.ID.6b	b. Informally assess the fit of a function by plotting and analyzing residuals.*	SE: 412–419, 421–428
MCC9-12.S.ID.6c	c. Fit a linear function for a scatter plot that suggests a linear association.*	SE: 412–419, 420, 421–428
Interpret linear models		
MCC9-12.S.ID.7	Interpret the slope (rate of change) and the intercept (constant term) of a linear model in the context of the data.*	SE: 429, 412–419, 421–428
MCC9-12.S.ID.8	Compute (using technology) and interpret the correlation coefficient of a linear fit.*	SE: 420, 421–428
MCC9-12.S.ID.9	Distinguish between correlation and causation.*	SE: 412–419, 421–428

Mastering the Standards
for Mathematical Practice

The topics described in the Standards for Mathematical Content will vary from year to year. However, the way in which you learn, study, and think about mathematics will not. The Standards for Mathematical Practice describe skills that you will use in all of your math courses. These pages show some features of your book and the **Explorations in Core Math for Common Core GPS** workbook that will help you gain these skills and use them to master this year's topics.

1 Make sense of problems and persevere in solving them.

Mathematically proficient students start by explaining to themselves the meaning of a problem... They analyze givens, constraints, relationships, and goals. They make conjectures about the form... of the solution and plan a solution pathway...

In your book

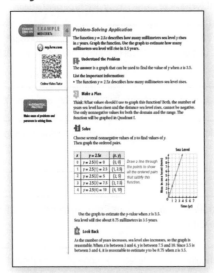

Problem Solving Applications in your book describe and illustrate a four-step plan for problem solving.

In *Explorations*

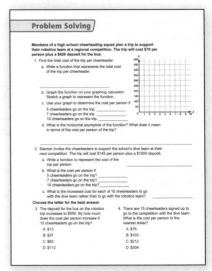

Problem Solving in *Explorations* provides an opportunity to practice and refine your problem-solving skills.

2 Reason abstractly and quantitatively.

Mathematically proficient students… bring two complementary abilities to bear on problems…: the ability to decontextualize—to abstract a given situation and represent it symbolically…and the ability to contextualize, to pause… in order to probe into the referents for the symbols involved.

In your book

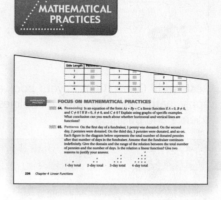

In *Explorations*

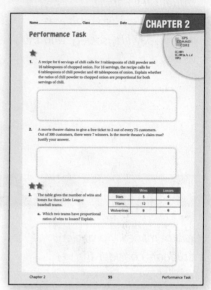

Focus on Mathematical Practices exercises in your book and **Performance Tasks** in *Explorations* require you to use logical reasoning, represent situations symbolically, use mathematical models to solve problems, and state your answers in terms of a problem context.

3 Construct viable arguments and critique the reasoning of others.

Mathematically proficient students… justify their conclusions, [and]… distinguish correct… reasoning from that which is flawed.

In your book

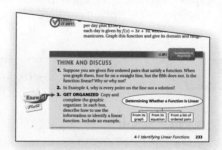

In *Explorations*

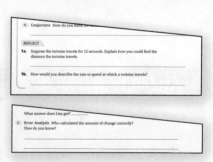

Think and Discuss in your book and **Reflect and Error Analysis** in *Explorations* ask you to evaluate statements, explain relationships, apply mathematical principles, make conjectures, construct arguments, and justify your reasoning.

4 Model with mathematics.

Mathematically proficient students can apply... mathematics... to problems... in everyday life, society, and the workplace...

In your book

In *Explorations*

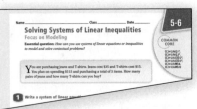

Real-World Connections in your book and **Focus on Modeling** in *Explorations* apply mathematics to other disciplines and real-world contexts such as science and business.

5 Use appropriate tools strategically.

Mathematically proficient students consider the available tools when solving a problem... [and] are... able to use technological tools to explore and deepen their understanding...

In your book

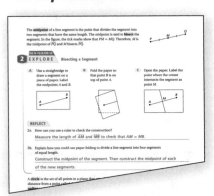

In *Explorations*

Hands-On Tasks and Technology Tasks in your book and Explore in *Explorations* use concrete and technological tools, such as manipulatives or graphing calculators, to explore mathematical concepts.

6 Attend to precision.

Mathematically proficient students... communicate precisely... with others and in their own reasoning... [They] give carefully formulated explanations...

In your book

83. **Write About It** Explain why the FO
    binomials at a time.

In *Explorations*

Key Vocabulary

Precision refers not only to the correctness of calculations but also to the proper use of mathematical language and symbols. **Write About It** in your book and **Key Vocabulary** in *Explorations* help you learn and use the language of math to communicate mathematics precisely.

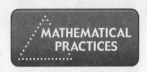
7) Look for and make use of structure.

Mathematically proficient students… look closely to discern a pattern or structure… They can also step back for an overview and shift perspective.

In your book

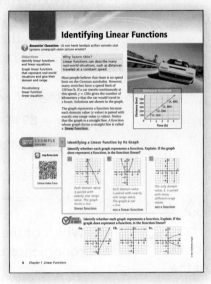

In *Explorations*

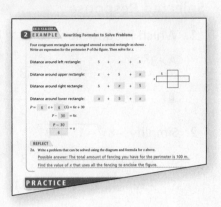

In both your book and Explorations, you will study regularity in mathematical structures, such as expressions, equations, operations, geometric figures, tables, graphs, and diagrams. Understanding the underlying structures of mathematics allows you to generalize beyond a specific case and to make connections between related problems..

8) Look for and express regularity in repeated reasoning.

Mathematically proficient students… look both for general methods and for shortcuts… [and] maintain oversight of the process, while attending to the details…

In your book

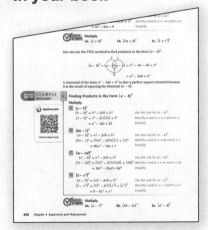

In *Explorations*

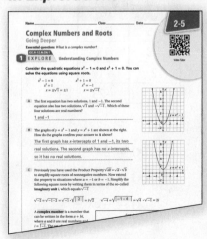

In both your book and *Explorations*, examples group similar types of problems together, and the solutions are carefully stepped out. This allows you to look for patterns or regularity and make generalizations while noticing variations in the details.

Review Test
Grade 8 - Part 1

Selected Response

1. Which is equivalent to $(3^{-4})^6$?

   (A) 3^2 (C) $\dfrac{1}{3^{24}}$

   (B) -12^6 (D) $\dfrac{1}{3^{10}}$

2. Simplify $-8\sqrt{-15+31}$.

   (F) -44.5 (H) 8

   (G) -32 (J) 31

3. A passenger plane travels at about 7.62×10^2 feet per second. The plane takes 1.23×10^4 seconds to reach its destination. About how far must the plane travel to reach its destination?

   (A) 9.37×10^6 feet

   (B) 9.37×10^8 feet

   (C) 8.85×10^8 feet

   (D) 8.85×10^6 feet

4. Which describes the linear function in the table?

x	f(x)
−5	25
−3	13
2	−17
3	−23

   (F) $f(x) = \dfrac{1}{6}x + 5$

   (G) $f(x) = \dfrac{1}{6}x - 5$

   (H) $f(x) = -6x + 5$

   (J) $f(x) = -6x - 5$

5. A remote-control airplane descends at a rate of 3 feet per second. After 6 seconds the plane is 89 feet above the ground. Which equation models this situation and what is the height of the plane after 12 seconds?

   (A) $y - 89 = -3(x - 6)$; 71 feet

   (B) $y - 3 = 89(x - 6)$; 537 feet

   (C) $y - 89 = -6(x - 3)$; 35 feet

   (D) $y - 6 = -3(x - 89)$; 237 feet

6. Which of the following is *not* a congruence transformation?

   (F) A dilation with scale factor 1

   (G) A reflection across the y-axis

   (H) A translation 5 units down

   (J) A dilation with scale factor 2

7. In the gift shop of the History of Flight museum, Elisa bought a kit to make a model of a jet airplane. The actual plane is 20 feet long with a wingspan of 16 feet. The finished model will be 15 inches long. What will be the wingspan of the model?

   (A) 6 inches   (C) 18.8 inches

   (B) 12 inches   (D) 21.3 inches

8. What is the value of n?

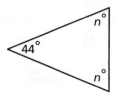

   (F) $n = 11.7°$ (H) $n = 68°$

   (G) $n = 18°$ (J) $n = 118°$

9. Melanie is making a piece of jewelry that is in the shape of a right triangle. The two shorter sides of the piece of jewelry are 12 mm and 9 mm. Find the perimeter of the piece of jewelry.

Ⓐ 36 mm   Ⓒ 32 mm

Ⓑ 34 mm   Ⓓ 30 mm

10. What is the distance, to the nearest tenth, from $S(4, -1)$ to $W(-2, 3)$?

Ⓕ −2.0 units   Ⓗ 2.6 units

Ⓖ 0.0 units   Ⓙ 7.2 units

11. Which is the best estimate of $\sqrt{285}$?

Ⓐ 12.83   Ⓒ 20.88

Ⓑ 16.88   Ⓓ 20.93

12. Harry and Selma start driving from the same location. Harry drives 42 miles north while Selma drives 144 miles east. How far apart are Harry and Selma when they stop?

Ⓕ 20,736 miles

Ⓖ 22,500 miles

Ⓗ 1,764 miles

Ⓙ 150 miles

Mini-Tasks

13. In Hannah's science report, she says that the average distance between the Sun and Earth is about 9.3×10^7 miles. Show how to write this number in standard notation.

14. A summer theater pass costs $24.75. Every time the pass is used, $2.75 is deducted from the balance. Write an equation to represent this situation, and graph your equation.

15. Describe a possible situation that could be modeled by the graph.

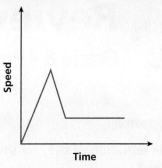

16. Dilate the figure by a scale factor of 3 with the origin as the center of dilation. Graph the new figure on a coordinate plane, and list the vertices of the image. Show your work.

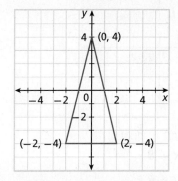

17. Identify the number $\sqrt{\dfrac{100}{121}}$ as *rational* or *irrational*. Explain your reasoning.

Performance Task

18. Is the following a function? Why or why not?

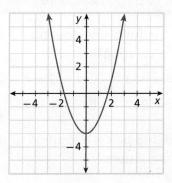

Selected Response

1. What is the equation of the line shown in the graph?

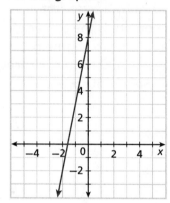

- Ⓐ $y = -5x + 8$
- Ⓑ $y = 6x + 8$
- Ⓒ $y = -6x + 8$
- Ⓓ $y = 5x + 8$

2. What is the solution of
$-4c + 10 + 8c = 86$?

- Ⓕ $c = -8$
- Ⓗ $c = 24$
- Ⓖ $c = 19$
- Ⓙ $c = 76$

3. Which of the following equations has exactly one solution?

- Ⓐ $c + 2 = c + 2$
- Ⓒ $c + 2 = c - 2$
- Ⓑ $c = -c + 2$
- Ⓓ $c - c = 2$

4. Which ordered pair is a solution of the system of equations?
$y = 3x + 1$
$y = 5x - 3$

- Ⓕ $(2, 3)$
- Ⓗ $(1, 2)$
- Ⓖ $(0, 1)$
- Ⓙ $(2, 7)$

5. A bicyclist heads east at 18 km/h. After she has traveled 19.2 kilometers, another cyclist sets out from the same starting point in the same direction going 30 km/h. How long will it take the second cyclist to catch up to the first cyclist?

- Ⓐ 2.6 hours
- Ⓒ 1.6 hours
- Ⓑ 2.1 hours
- Ⓓ 1.1 hours

6. Which of these functions is *not* a linear function?

- Ⓕ $f(x) = 3 - \dfrac{x}{3}$
- Ⓖ $f(x) = 3^x + 4$
- Ⓗ $f(x) = 3^3 - 3x$
- Ⓙ $f(x) = 3(4 - x) + 3$

7. Which function has the greatest rate of change?

- Ⓐ $y = 11x - 8$
- Ⓑ A fitness club charges a $200 membership fee plus monthly fees of $25.
- Ⓒ $y = -8x$
- Ⓓ $\{(-1, -2), (1, 2), (3, 6), (5, 10), (7, 14)\}$

8. You buy hats for $12, and sell them for $8 each. What does the graph of the profits look like?

- Ⓕ A curve that goes up
- Ⓖ A line that goes down
- Ⓗ A curve that goes down
- Ⓙ A line that goes up

9. An artist is creating a large conical sculpture for a park. The cone has a height of 19 feet and a diameter of 28 feet. What is the volume of the sculpture to the nearest hundredth?

Ⓐ 278.41 ft³   Ⓒ 3,897.79 ft³

Ⓑ 1,241.33 ft³   Ⓓ 11,693.36 ft³

10. A cylindrical barrel has a radius of 4.2 meters and a height of 3 meters. Tripling which dimension(s) will triple the volume of the barrel?

Ⓕ Height

Ⓖ Radius

Ⓗ Both height and radius

Ⓙ Neither height nor radius

11. Which equation best models the data in the scatter plot?

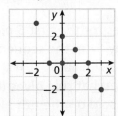

Ⓐ $y = -x + 1$ Ⓒ $y = x + 1$

Ⓑ $y = -x - 1$ Ⓓ $y = x - 1$

Mini-Tasks

12. Write and graph a function that converts x days to y hours.

13. Solve $h - 8 = 3h + 3$.

14. Solve the system using any for 15 minutes method.
$2x - 5y = -22$
$x + 3y = 11$

15. Rewrite the equation $2y + 3x = 4$ in slope-intercept form. Then find the slope and y-intercept.

16. Find the slope of the line that passes through the points $(-3, 6)$ and $(4, 2)$.

17. Gloria drives her daughter to school in the morning and then comes back home. She stays home until she has to go to pick up her daughter from school, and then they both return home again. Make a graph of distance versus time to demonstrate this situation. Explain your graph.

18. Describe the correlation in the scatter plot and explain what it means in the given situation.

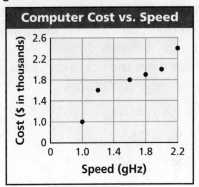

19. Use the graph to identify the slope and y-intercept. Then explain what each means in the context of the problem.

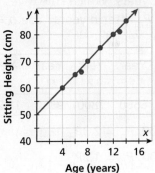

Performance Task

20. Ashley reads at a rate of 2 pages/minute for 15 minutes and then takes a break for 15 minutes. She then resumes reading at the same rate. Adam reads at the same rate the entire time. The equation for the number of pages y he reads in x minutes is $y = 0.7x$. Sketch a graph of each function. How are these functions alike? How are they different? Using the graphs, explain why Adam will read fewer pages than Ashley during a 30-minute reading period.

Selected Response

1. A movie theater charges $8.50 for a ticket. To help the local animal shelter, the theater agrees to reduce the price of each ticket by $0.50 for every can of pet food a customer donates. Which equation gives the ticket cost y for a customer who contributes x cans?

   Ⓐ $y = 8.5 - 0.50x$

   Ⓑ $y = 9x - 0.5$

   Ⓒ $y = 8.5 + 0.50x$

   Ⓓ $y = -9x - 0.5$

2. The population of a Midwestern suburb is growing exponentially. The chart shows its population for four consecutive years. Which rule gives the population P_n after n years? Use $n = 1$ to represent Year 1.

Year	Year 1	Year 2	Year 3	Year 4
Population	6500	7800	9360	11,232

   Ⓕ $P_1 = 7800, P_n = 2.3P_{n-1}$

   Ⓖ $P_1 = 6500, P_n = 1.2P_{n-1}$

   Ⓗ $P_1 = 6500, P_n = 2.3P_{n-1}$

   Ⓙ $P_1 = 7800, P_n = 1.2P_{n-1}$

3. Which is the graph of $\begin{cases} y < -3x + 2 \\ y \geq 4x - 1 \end{cases}$?

   Ⓐ 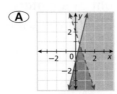 Ⓒ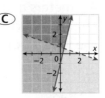

   Ⓑ 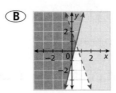 Ⓓ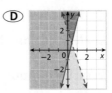

4. Ticket sales for the first 5 nights of a new play form the sequence 400, 399, 396, 387, 360, ... If this pattern continues, what rule gives the number of tickets sold on the nth night?

   Ⓕ $a_n = a_{n-1} - 3^{(n-1)}$

   Ⓖ $a_n = a_n - 3^{(n-1)}$

   Ⓗ $a_n = a_n - 3^n$

   Ⓙ $a_n = a_{n-1} - 3^n$

5. How could you translate the graph of $y = -x^2$ to produce the graph of $y = -x^2 - 4$?

   Ⓐ Translate the graph of $y = -x^2$ down 4 units.

   Ⓑ Translate the graph of $y = -x^2$ up 4 units.

   Ⓒ Translate the graph of $y = -x^2$ left 4 units.

   Ⓓ Translate the graph of $y = -x^2$ right 4 units.

6. Which represents a price that increases at a constant rate per ounce for ordered pairs in the form (ounces, price)?

Ⓕ (8, 0.50), (12, 1.00), (24, 1.50), (32, 2.00)

Ⓖ (8, 0.60), (12, 0.90), (24, 1.80), (32, 2.40)

Ⓗ (8, 0.80), (12, 1.20), (24, 1.60), (32, 2.00)

Ⓙ (8, 0.40), (12, 0.80), (24, 1.60), (32, 3.20)

7. A micrometer used in a factory measures thickness to one hundredth of a millimeter. This micrometer is used to measure the diameter of a ball bearing that is about 1.7 cm across. What is a reasonable value and error for the measurement of the bearing's diameter?

Ⓐ 2.25 cm $\pm$ 0.05 cm

Ⓑ 1.715 cm $\pm$ 0.005 cm

Ⓒ 2.354 cm $\pm$ 0.005 cm

Ⓓ 1.6713 cm $\pm$ 0.0005 cm

Mini-Tasks

8. Kristi rides her bike to school and has an odometer that measures the distance traveled so far. She subtracts this distance from the distance to the school and records the distance that remains. What are the intercepts of the function represented by the table? What do the intercepts represent?

Time traveled (min)	Distance remaining (ft)
0	5,000
2	3,750
4	2,500
6	1,250
8	0

9. How many terms are in the algebraic expression $2x - 9xy + 17y$?

10. Solve $y = \frac{5}{8}b + 10$ for b.

11. Solve $-0.25 + 1.75x < -1.75 + 2.25x$.

12. Solve $\begin{cases} -7x + 5y = -5 \\ -9x + 5y = 5 \end{cases}$ by elimination. Express your answer as an ordered pair.

13. Write an exponential function to model a population of 390 animals that decreases at an annual rate of 11%. Then estimate the value of the function after 5 years (to the nearest whole number).

Performance Task

14. A doctor's office schedules 10-minute and 20-minute appointments. The doctor also makes hospital rounds for four hours each weekday.

Part A: If the doctor limits these activities to at most 30 hours per week, write an inequality to represent the number of each type of office visit that can be scheduled in one week. Use x to represent the number of 10-minute appointments and y to represent the number of 20-minute appointments. Use minutes for all times. Graph the inequality.

Part B: Is the point (36, 4) in the shaded area of the graph? What does that mean?

Part C: If the doctor can have only 19 20-minute appointments next week, how many 10-minute appointments can be scheduled? Express the answer as an inequality and explain its meaning in words. Show the steps you use to find the inequality.

Benchmark Test

Coordinate Algebra - Part 2

Selected Response

1. Which graph shows a rotation of △RSQ 90° about the origin?

   Ⓐ
   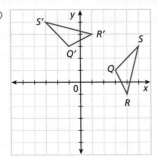

   Ⓑ
   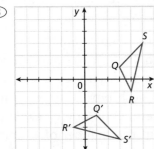

   Ⓒ
   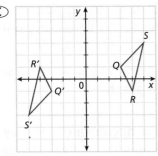

   Ⓓ
   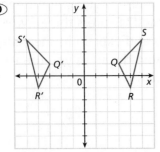

2. Which shows a box-and-whisker plot of the data 7, 9, 11, 12, 13, 15, 12, 17, 18, 12, 9, 7, 12, 15, 18, 10?

   Ⓕ
   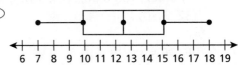

   Ⓖ
   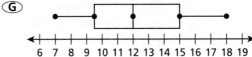

   Ⓗ
   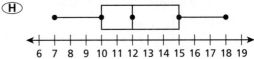

   Ⓙ
   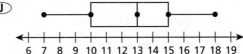

3. Point G is the midpoint of $\overline{AB}$, and point H is the midpoint of $\overline{DE}$. Which transformation(s) will create an image of the regular hexagon ABCDEF that coincides with itself?

   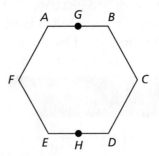

   Ⓐ Reflection across $\overline{AE}$

   Ⓑ Rotation of 90 degrees about the center of the hexagon

   Ⓒ Rotation of 270 degrees about the center of the hexagon

   Ⓓ Reflection across $\overline{GH}$

4. The data set shown by the box-and-whisker plot includes a single outlier and no duplicate data values.

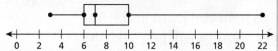

Which statement describes the effect on the range and interquartile range of the data set when the outlier is removed?

Ⓕ The interquartile range increases but the range decreases.

Ⓗ The range and interquartile range both decrease, but the interquartile range decreases more.

Ⓖ The range decreases but the interquartile range increases.

Ⓙ The range and interquartile range both decrease, but the range decreases more.

5. Look for a pattern in the data set. Which kind of model best describes the data?

Population Growth of Bacteria	
Time (hours)	Number of Bacteria
0	2,000
1	5,000
2	12,500
3	31,250
4	78,125

Ⓐ Cubic

Ⓑ Exponential

Ⓒ Quadratic

Ⓓ Linear

Mini-Tasks

6. Find the coordinates of the image of the point $(-5, 7)$ when it is reflected across the line $y = 11$.

7. What is the coefficient of x in the expression $(5a)x - 17x^2 + 14a$?

8. Consider the following box plots.

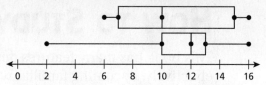

Which data set has the greater median? Which has the greater interquartile range?

9. Identify a single transformation that is equivalent to reflecting the figure across line n and then reflecting the image across line m.

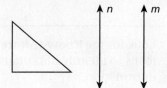

Performance Task

10. The PGA tour is for male professional golfers; the LPGA tour is for female professional golfers. Earnings for the top 50 golfers on each tour in 2010 are modeled by the functions in the table and the graph.

Compare earnings as a function of rank for the PGA and the LPGA.

PGA Earnings, 2010

Rank	Earnings (thousands of $)
1	4.95
10	3.53
20	2.87
30	2.41
40	1.88
50	1.61

LPGA Earnings, 2010

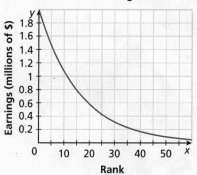

HOW TO STUDY COORDINATE ALGEBRA

This book has many features designed to help you learn and study effectively. Becoming familiar with these features will prepare you for greater success on your exams.

Learn

The **vocabulary** is listed at the beginning of every lesson.

Look for the **Know-It-Note** icons to identify important information.

Study the **examples** to apply new concepts and skills. Examples include stepped out solutions.

Test your understanding of examples by trying the **Check It Out** problems. Check your work in the Selected Answers.

Practice

Use a **graphic organizer** to summarize each lesson.

Refer to the examples from the lesson to solve the **Guided Practice** exercises.

If you get stuck, use the internet for **Homework Help Online.**

Complete **Test Prep** exercises to prepare for standardized tests.

Go beyond the lesson with **Challenge and Extend** problems.

Develop your math skills with **Focus on Mathematical Practice** exercises.

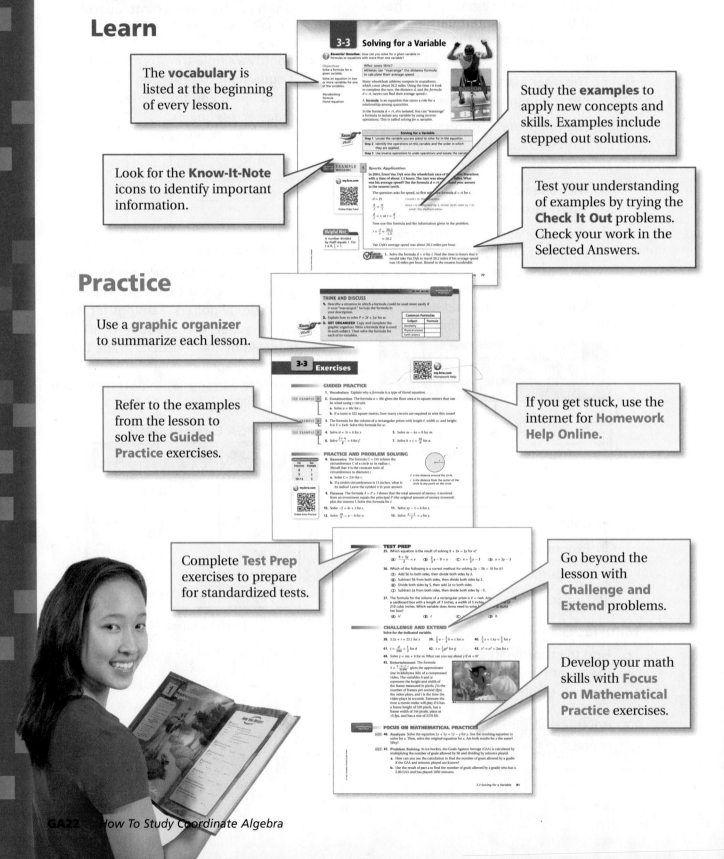

Focus on Problem Solving

The Problem Solving Plan

Mathematical problems are a part of daily life. You need to use a good problem-solving plan to be a good problem solver. The plan used in this textbook is outlined below.

UNDERSTAND the Problem

First make sure you understand the problem you are asked to solve.

- **What are you asked to find?** Restate the question in your own words.
- **What information is given?** Identify the key facts given in the problem.
- **What information do you need?** Determine what information you need to solve the problem.
- **Do you have all the information needed?** Determine if you need more information.
- **Do you have too much information?** Determine if there is unnecessary information and eliminate it from your list of important facts.

Make a PLAN

Plan how to use the information you are given.

- **Have you solved similar problems?** Think about similar problems you have solved successfully.
- **What problem solving strategy or strategies could you use to solve this problem?** Choose an appropriate problem solving strategy and decide how you will use it.

SOLVE

Use your plan to solve the problem. Show the steps in the solution, and write a final statement that gives the solution to the problem.

LOOK BACK

Check your answer against the original problem.

- **Have you answered the question?** Make sure you have answered the original question.
- **Is the answer reasonable?** The answer must make sense in relation to the question.
- **Are your calculations correct?** Check to make sure your calculations are accurate.
- **Can you use another strategy or solve the problem in another way?** Using another strategy is a good way to check your answer.
- **Did you learn anyting that could help you solve similar problems in the future?** Try to remember the types of problems you have solved and the strategies you applied.

Are You Ready?

my.hrw.com
Assessment and Intervention

 **Vocabulary**

Match each term on the left with a definition on the right.

1. constant

2. expression

3. order of operations

4. variable

A. a mathematical phrase that contains operations, numbers, and/or variables

B. a mathematical statement that two expressions are equivalent

C. a process for evaluating expressions

D. a symbol used to represent a quantity that can change

E. a value that does not change

Order of Operations

Simplify each expression.

5. $(7 - 3) \div 2$

6. $4 \cdot 6 \div 3$

7. $12 - 3 + 1$

8. $2 \cdot 10 \div 5$

9. $125 \div 5^2$

10. $7 \cdot 6 + 5 \cdot 4$

Add and Subtract Integers

Add or subtract.

11. $-15 + 19$

12. $-6 - (-18)$

13. $6 + (-8)$

14. $-12 + (-3)$

Add and Subtract Fractions

Perform each indicated operation. Give your answer in the simplest form.

15. $\frac{1}{4} + \frac{2}{3}$

16. $1\frac{1}{2} - \frac{3}{4}$

17. $\frac{3}{8} + \frac{2}{3}$

18. $\frac{3}{2} - \frac{2}{3}$

Evaluate Expressions

Evaluate each expression for the given value of the variable.

19. $2x + 3$ for $x = 7$

20. $3n - 5$ for $n = 7$

21. $13 - 4a$ for $a = 2$

22. $3y + 5$ for $y = 5$

Career Readiness Biologists

Biologists study living things and their relationship to the environment. Most biologists specialize in one area, such as botany (the study of plants) or zoology (the study of animals). They use many different kinds of math, including algebra, probability, and statistics. For example, a biologist may use equations, graphs, and proportions to study populations. Biologists usually have at least a bachelor's degree. Many biologists work in scientific research, in medicine, or in colleges.

Relationships Between Quantities

Online Edition

my.hrw.com

Access the complete online textbook, interactive features, and additional resources.

Multilingual Glossary

Enhance your math vocabulary with this illustrated online glossary in 13 languages.

Homework Help

Get instant help with tutorial videos, practice problems, and step-by-step solutions.

Portable Devices

On the Spot

Watch video tutorials anywhere, anytime with this app for iPhone® and iPad®.

eTextbook

Access your full textbook on your tablet or e-reader.

Chapter Resources

Scan with your smart phone to jump directly to the online edition.

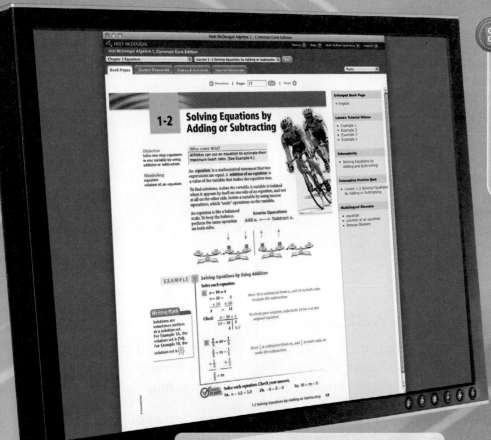

The online edition of your textbook is enhanced with videos and interactive features for every lesson.

COMMON CORE GPS Unit Contents

Module 1 Creating Expressions and Equations

MCC9-12.A.CED.1, MCC9-12.A.REI.1, MCC9-12.A.SSE.1, MCC9-12.N.Q.2

Module 2 Choosing Appropriate Units

MCC9-12.A.CED.1, MCC9-12.N.Q.1, MCC9-12.N.Q.2, MCC9-12.N.Q.3

1 Creating Expressions and Equations

COMMON
CORE GPS

Contents

MATHEMATICAL PRACTICES
The Common Core Georgia Performance Standards for Mathematical Practice describe varieties of expertise that all students should seek to develop. Opportunities to develop these practices are integrated throughout this program.

1 Make sense of problems and persevere in solving them.

2 Reason abstractly and quantitatively.

3 Construct viable arguments and critique the reasoning of others.

4 Model with mathematics.

5 Use appropriate tools strategically.

6 Attend to precision.

7 Look for and make use of structure.

8 Look for and express regularity in repeated reasoning.

Unpacking the Standards

my.hrw.com
Multilingual Glossary

Understanding the standards and the vocabulary terms in the standards will help you know exactly what you are expected to learn in this chapter.

 MCC9-12.A.SSE.1

Interpret expressions that represent a quantity in terms of its context.

Key Vocabulary

expression (expresión)
A mathematical phrase that contains operations, numbers, and/or variables.

What It Means For You

Variables in formulas and other math expressions are used to represent specific quantities.

EXAMPLE

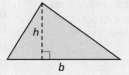

$A = \frac{1}{2}bh$

A = area of the triangle

b = length of the base

h = height

 MCC9-12.A.CED.1

Create equations … in one variable and use them to solve problems.

Key Vocabulary

equation (ecuación)
A mathematical statement that two expressions are equivalent.
variable (variable)
A symbol used to represent a quantity that can change.

What It Means For You

You can write an equation to represent a real-world problem and then use algebra to solve the equation and find the answer.

EXAMPLE

Michael is saving money to buy a trumpet. The trumpet costs $670. He has $350 saved, and each week he adds $20 to his savings. How long will it take him to save enough money to buy the trumpet?

Let w represent the number of weeks.

cost of trumpet	=	current savings	+	additional savings
670	=	350	+	$20w$
320	=	$20w$		
16	=	w		

It will take Michael 16 weeks to save enough money.

Variables and Expressions

Essential Question: How can you use variables to write an expression that represents a quantity in terms of its context?

Objectives
Translate between words and algebra.

Evaluate algebraic expressions.

Vocabulary
variable
constant
numerical expression
algebraic expression
evaluate

Why learn this?
Variables and expressions can be used to determine how many plastic drink bottles must be recycled to make enough carpet for a house.

Container City, in East London, UK, is a development of buildings made from recycled shipping containers.

A home that is "green built" uses many recycled products, including carpet made from recycled plastic drink bottles. You can determine how many square feet of carpet can be made from a certain number of plastic drink bottles by using *variables*, *constants*, and *expressions*.

A **variable** is a letter or symbol used to represent a value that can change.

A **constant** is a value that does not change.

A **numerical expression** may contain only constants and/or operations.

An **algebraic expression** may contain variables, constants, and/or operations.

You will need to translate between algebraic expressions and words to be successful in math. The diagram below shows some of the ways to write mathematical operations with words.

| Plus, sum, increased by | Minus, difference, less than | Times, product, equal groups of | Divided by, quotient |

COMMON CORE GPS
MCC9-12.A.SSE.1

EXAMPLE 1 Translating from Algebraic Symbols to Words

Give two ways to write each algebraic expression in words.

my.hrw.com

Online Video Tutor

A $x + 3$
the sum of x and 3
x increased by 3

B $m - 7$
the difference of m and 7
7 less than m

C $2 \cdot y$
2 times y
the product of 2 and y

D $k \div 5$
k divided by 5
the quotient of k and 5

 CHECK IT OUT! Give two ways to write each algebraic expression in words.

1a. $4 - n$ **1b.** $\dfrac{t}{5}$ **1c.** $9 + q$ **1d.** $3(h)$

Ray Roberts/Alamy Photos; (sky), PhotoDisc/Getty Images

To translate words into algebraic expressions, look for words that indicate the action that is taking place.

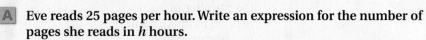

Add	**Subtract**	**Multiply**	**Divide**
↑	↑	↑	↑
Put together, combine	Find how much more or less	Put together equal groups	Separate into equal groups

 **EXAMPLE** 2
MCC9-12.N.Q.1

Translating from Words to Algebraic Symbols

my.hrw.com

Online Video Tutor

A Eve reads 25 pages per hour. Write an expression for the number of pages she reads in *h* hours.

h represents the number of hours that Eve reads.

$25 \cdot h$ or $25h$ *Think: h groups of 25 pages.*

B Sam is 2 years younger than Sue, who is *y* years old. Write an expression for Sam's age.

y represents Sue's age.

$y - 2$ *Think: "younger than" means "less than."*

C William runs a mile in 12 minutes. Write an expression for the number of miles that William runs in *m* minutes.

m represents the total time William runs.

$\dfrac{m}{12}$ *Think: How many groups of 12 are in m?*

 **CHECK IT OUT!**

2a. Lou drives at 65 mi/h. Write an expression for the number of miles that Lou drives in *t* hours.

2b. Miriam is 5 cm taller than her sister, who is *m* cm tall. Write an expression for Miriam's height in centimeters.

2c. Elaine earns $32 per day. Write an expression for the amount that she earns in *d* days.

To **evaluate** an expression is to find its value. To evaluate an algebraic expression, substitute numbers for the variables in the expression and then simplify the expression.

 EXAMPLE 3
MCC9-12.A.SSE.1a

Evaluating Algebraic Expressions

my.hrw.com

Online Video Tutor

Evaluate each expression for $x = 8$, $y = 5$, and $z = 4$.

A $x + y$

$x + y = 8 + 5$ *Substitute 8 for x and 5 for y.*

$\quad\quad = 13$ *Simplify.*

B $\dfrac{x}{z}$

$\dfrac{x}{z} = \dfrac{8}{4}$ *Substitute 8 for x and 4 for z.*

$\quad = 2$ *Simplify.*

 CHECK IT OUT!

Evaluate each expression for $m = 3$, $n = 2$, and $p = 9$.

3a. mn **3b.** $p - n$ **3c.** $p \div m$

COMMON CORE GPS

EXAMPLE 4

Recycling Application

Prep. for MCC9-12.A.CED.1

Approximately fourteen 20-ounce plastic drink bottles must be recycled to produce 1 square foot of carpet.

a. **Write an expression for the number of bottles needed to make c square feet of carpet.**

The expression $14c$ models the number of bottles needed to make c square feet of carpet.

b. **Find the number of bottles needed to make 40, 120, and 224 square feet of carpet.**

Evaluate $14c$ for $c = 40$, 120, and 224.

c	$14c$
40	$14(40) = 560$
120	$14(120) = 1680$
224	$14(224) = 3136$

To make 40 ft² of carpet, 560 bottles are needed.
To make 120 ft² of carpet, 1680 bottles are needed.
To make 224 ft² of carpet, 3136 bottles are needed.

Helpful Hint

A *replacement set* is a set of numbers that can be substituted for a variable. The replacement set in Example 4 is {40, 120, 224}.

CHECK IT OUT!

4. To make one sweater, sixty-three 20-ounce plastic drink bottles must be recycled.

   a. Write an expression for the number of bottles needed to make s sweaters.

   b. Find the number of bottles needed to make 12, 25, and 50 sweaters.

MCC.MP.6 | MATHEMATICAL PRACTICES

THINK AND DISCUSS

1. Write two ways to suggest each of the following, using words or phrases: addition, subtraction, multiplication, division.

2. Explain the difference between a numerical expression and an algebraic expression.

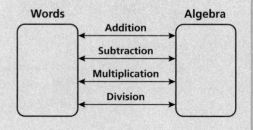

3. GET ORGANIZED Copy and complete the graphic organizer. Next to each operation, write a word phrase in the left box and its corresponding algebraic expression in the right box.

Words — Addition — Algebra
Subtraction
Multiplication
Division

GUIDED PRACTICE

1. **Vocabulary** A(n) ____?____ is a value that can change. (*algebraic expression*, *constant*, or *variable*)

SEE EXAMPLE 1

Give two ways to write each algebraic expression in words.

2. $n - 5$ 3. $\dfrac{f}{3}$ 4. $c + 15$ 5. $9 - y$

6. $\dfrac{x}{12}$ 7. $t + 12$ 8. $8x$ 9. $x - 3$

SEE EXAMPLE 2

10. George drives at 45 mi/h. Write an expression for the number of miles George travels in h hours.

11. The length of a rectangle is 4 units greater than its width w. Write an expression for the length of the rectangle.

SEE EXAMPLE 3

Evaluate each expression for $a = 3$, $b = 4$, and $c = 2$.

12. $a - c$ 13. ab 14. $b \div c$ 15. ac

SEE EXAMPLE 4

16. Brianna practices the piano 30 minutes each day.
    a. Write an expression for the number of hours she practices in d days.
    b. Find the number of hours Brianna practices in 2, 4, and 10 days.

PRACTICE AND PROBLEM SOLVING

Independent Practice	
For Exercises	See Example
17–24	1
25–26	2
27–30	3
31	4

my.hrw.com

Online Extra Practice

Give two ways to write each algebraic expression in words.

17. $5p$ 18. $4 - y$ 19. $3 + x$ 20. $3y$

21. $-3s$ 22. $r \div 5$ 23. $14 - t$ 24. $x + 0.5$

25. Friday's temperature was 20° warmer than Monday's temperature t. Write an expression for Friday's temperature.

26. Ann sleeps 8 hours per night. Write an expression for the number of hours Ann sleeps in n nights.

Evaluate each expression for $r = 6$, $s = 5$, and $t = 3$.

27. $r - s$ 28. $s + t$ 29. $r \div t$ 30. sr

31. Jim is paid for overtime when he works more than 40 hours per week.
    a. Write an expression for the number of hours he works overtime when he works h hours.
    b. Find the number of hours Jim works overtime when he works 40, 44, 48, and 52 hours.

32. **Write About It** Write a paragraph that explains to another student how to evaluate an expression.

Write an algebraic expression for each verbal expression. Then write a real-world situation that could be modeled by the expression.

33. the product of 2 and x 34. b less than 17   35. 10 more than y

36. The air around you puts pressure on your body equal to 14.7 pounds per square inch (psi). When you are underwater, the water exerts additional pressure on your body. For each foot you are below the surface of the water, the pressure increases by 0.445 psi.

   a. What does 14.7 represent in the expression $14.7 + 0.445d$?

   b. What does d represent in the expression?

   c. What is the total pressure exerted on a person's body when $d = 8$ ft?

37. Geometry The length of a rectangle is 9 inches. Write an expression for the area of the rectangle if the width is w inches. Find the area of the rectangle when the width is 1, 8, 9, and 11 inches.

38. Geometry The perimeter of any rectangle is the sum of its lengths and widths. The area of any rectangle is the length ℓ times the width w.

   a. Write an expression for the perimeter of a rectangle.

   b. Find the perimeter of the rectangle shown.

   c. Write an expression for the area of a rectangle.

   d. Find the area of the rectangle shown.

$\ell = 14$ cm

$w = 8$ cm

Complete each table. Evaluate the expression for each value of x.

39.

x	$x + 12$
1	
2	
3	
4	

40.

x	$10x$
1	
5	
10	
15	

41.

x	$x \div 2$
12	
20	
26	
30	

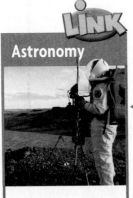

A crater on Canada's Devon Island is geologically similar to the surface of Mars. However, the temperature on Devon Island is about 37 °F in summer, and the average summer temperature on Mars is −85 °F.

42. Astronomy An object's weight on Mars can be found by multiplying 0.38 by the object's weight on Earth.

   a. An object weighs p pounds on Earth. Write an expression for its weight on Mars.

   b. Dana weighs 120 pounds, and her bicycle weighs 44 pounds. How much would Dana and her bicycle together weigh on Mars?

43. Meteorology Use the bar graph to write an expression for the average annual precipitation in New York, New York.

   a. The average annual precipitation in New York is m inches more than the average annual precipitation in Houston, Texas.

   b. The average annual precipitation in New York is s inches less than the average annual precipitation in Miami, Florida.

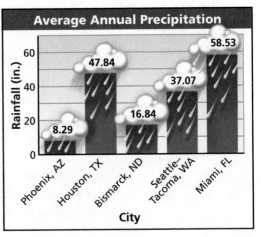

Average Annual Precipitation

Phoenix, AZ: 8.29
Houston, TX: 47.84
Bismarck, ND: 16.84
Seattle–Tacoma, WA: 37.07
Miami, FL: 58.53

Rainfall (in.)

City

44. Critical Thinking Compare algebraic expressions and numerical expressions. Give examples of each.

Write an algebraic expression for each verbal expression. Then evaluate the algebraic expression for the given values of x.

	Verbal	Algebraic	$x = 12$	$x = 14$
	x reduced by 5	$x - 5$	$12 - 5 = 7$	$14 - 5 = 9$
45.	7 more than x	▪	▪	▪
46.	The quotient of x and 2	▪	▪	▪
47.	The sum of x and 3	▪	▪	▪

TEST PREP

48. Claire has had her driver's license for 3 years. Bill has had his license for b fewer years than Claire. Which expression can be used to show the number of years Bill has had his driver's license?

Ⓐ $3 + b$ Ⓑ $b + 3$ Ⓒ $3 - b$ Ⓓ $b - 3$

49. Which expression represents x?

Ⓕ $12 - 5$ Ⓗ $12(5)$

Ⓖ $12 + 5$ Ⓙ $12 \div 5$

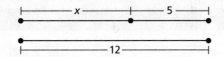

50. Which situation is best modeled by the expression $25 - x$?

Ⓐ George places x more video games on a shelf with 25 games.

Ⓑ Sarah has driven x miles of a 25-mile trip.

Ⓒ Amelia paid 25 dollars of an x dollar lunch that she shared with Ariel.

Ⓓ Jorge has 25 boxes full of x baseball cards each.

CHALLENGE AND EXTEND

Evaluate each expression for the given values of the variables.

51. $2ab$; $a = 6$, $b = 3$ **52.** $2x + y$; $x = 4$, $y = 5$ **53.** $3x \div 6y$; $x = 6$, $y = 3$

54. Multi-Step An Internet service provider charges \$9.95/month for the first 20 hours and \$0.50 for each additional hour. Write an expression representing the charges for h hours of use in one month when h is more than 20 hours. What is the charge for 35 hours?

FOCUS ON MATHEMATICAL PRACTICES

H.O.T. **55. Reasoning** Are there any values of x and y for which $x + y$ is equal to $x - y$? If so, give an example.

H.O.T. **56. Patterns** $x + 2$ is an odd number. Write an expression for each of the next 4 odd numbers. Is $x + 75$ even or odd? Explain.

H.O.T. **57. Error Analysis** One insect crawled for 5 minutes at a rate of 2.5 inches per minute while another insect crawled the same amount of time at a rate of 2.5 inches per second. Kevin used the variable t for the time (in minutes) each insect crawled, wrote the expression $2.5t$ for each insect's distance, and found that each insect crawled the same distance. Explain Kevin's error.

Model One-Step Equations

You can use algebra tiles and an equation mat to model and solve equations. To find the value of the variable, place or remove tiles to get the *x*-tile by itself on one side of the mat. You must place or remove the same number of yellow tiles or the same number of red tiles on both sides.

Use with Solving Equations by Adding or Subtracting

Use appropriate tools strategically.

MCC9-12.A.REI.1 Explain each step in solving a simple equation as following from the equality of numbers asserted at the previous step, starting from the assumption that the original equation has a solution. Construct a viable argument to justify a solution method. *Also* **MCC9-12.A.REI.3**

KEY	REMEMBER
+ = 1 − = −1 + = x	+ + − = 0

Activity

Use algebra tiles to model and solve $x + 6 = 2$.

MODEL		ALGEBRA
	Model $x + 6$ on the left side of the mat and 2 on the right side of the mat.	$x + 6 = 2$
	Place 6 red tiles on both sides of the mat. This represents adding −6 to both sides of the equation.	$x + 6 + (-6) = 2 + (-6)$
	Remove zero pairs from both sides of the mat.	$x + 0 = 0 + (-4)$
	One x-tile is equivalent to 4 red tiles.	$x = -4$

Try This

Use algebra tiles to model and solve each equation.

1. $x + 2 = 5$ **2.** $x - 7 = 8$ **3.** $x - 5 = 9$ **4.** $x + 4 = 7$

1-2

Solving Equations by Adding or Subtracting

 Essential Question: How can you use addition or subtraction to solve equations?

Objective
Solve one-step equations in one variable by using addition or subtraction.

Vocabulary
equation
solution of an equation

 Animated Math

Who uses this?

Athletes can use an equation to estimate their maximum heart rates. (See Example 4.)

An **equation** is a mathematical statement that two expressions are equal. A **solution of an equation** is a value of the variable that makes the equation true.

To find solutions, *isolate the variable*. A variable is isolated when it appears by itself on one side of an equation, and not at all on the other side. Isolate a variable by using inverse operations, which "undo" operations on the variable.

An equation is like a balanced scale. To keep the balance, perform the same operation on both sides.

Inverse Operations
Add x. ⟷ **Subtract x.**

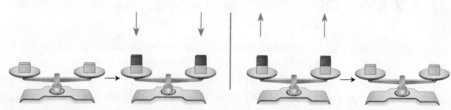

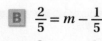 **EXAMPLE 1**
MCC9-12.A.REI.3

my.hrw.com

Online Video Tutor

Solving Equations by Using Addition

Solve each equation.

A $x - 10 = 4$

$$x - 10 = \quad 4$$
$$\underline{+\,10 \quad +\,10}$$
$$x = \quad 14$$

Since 10 is subtracted from x, add 10 to both sides to undo the subtraction.

Check $\dfrac{x - 10 = 4}{14 - 10 \;\big|\; 4}$
$\qquad\qquad 4 \;\big|\; 4 \checkmark$

To check your solution, substitute 14 for x in the original equation.

B $\dfrac{2}{5} = m - \dfrac{1}{5}$

$$\dfrac{2}{5} = m - \dfrac{1}{5}$$
$$\underline{+\,\dfrac{1}{5} \qquad +\,\dfrac{1}{5}}$$
$$\dfrac{3}{5} = m$$

Since $\frac{1}{5}$ is subtracted from m, add $\frac{1}{5}$ to both sides to undo the subtraction.

Writing Math

Solutions are sometimes written in a *solution set*. For Example 1A, the solution set is {14}. For Example 1B, the solution set is $\left\{\dfrac{3}{5}\right\}$.

 CHECK IT OUT!

Solve each equation. Check your answer.

1a. $n - 3.2 = 5.6$ **1b.** $-6 = k - 6$ **1c.** $16 = m - 9$

© Duomo/CORBIS

Solving Equations by Using Subtraction

Solve each equation. Check your answer.

A $x + 7 = 9$

$$x + 7 = 9$$
$$\underline{-7 \quad -7}$$
$$x \quad = \quad 2$$

Since 7 is added to x, subtract 7 from both sides to undo the addition.

Check $x + 7 = 9$

$$\begin{array}{c|c} 2 + 7 & 9 \\ \hline 9 & 9 \checkmark \end{array}$$

To check your solution, substitute 2 for x in the original equation.

B $0.7 = r + 0.4$

$$0.7 = r + 0.4$$
$$\underline{-0.4 \quad -0.4}$$
$$0.3 = r$$

Since 0.4 is added to r, subtract 0.4 from both sides to undo the addition.

Check $0.7 = r + 0.4$

$$\begin{array}{c|c} 0.7 & 0.3 + 0.4 \\ \hline 0.7 & 0.7 \checkmark \end{array}$$

To check your solution, substitute 0.3 for r in the original equation.

 CHECK IT OUT!   **Solve each equation. Check your answer.**

2a. $d + \dfrac{1}{2} = 1$ **2b.** $-5 = k + 5$ **2c.** $6 + t = 14$

Remember that subtracting is the same as adding the opposite. When solving equations, you will sometimes find it easier to add an opposite to both sides instead of subtracting. For example, this method may be useful when the equation contains negative numbers.

Solving Equations by Adding the Opposite

Solve $-8 + b = 2$.

$$-8 + b = 2$$
$$\underline{+8 \qquad +8}$$
$$b = 10$$

Since −8 is added to b, add 8 to both sides.

 CHECK IT OUT!   **Solve each equation. Check your answer.**

3a. $-2.3 + m = 7$ **3b.** $-\dfrac{3}{4} + z = \dfrac{5}{4}$ **3c.** $-11 + x = 33$

Student to Student   *Zero As a Solution*

Ama Walker
Carson High School

I used to get confused when I got a solution of 0. But my teacher reminded me that 0 is a number just like any other number, so it can be a solution of an equation. Just check your answer and see if it works.

$$x + 6 = 6$$
$$\underline{-6 \quad -6}$$
$$x = 0$$

Check $x + 6 = 6$

$$\begin{array}{c|c} 0 + 6 & 6 \\ \hline 6 & 6 \checkmark \end{array}$$

Fitness Application

A person's maximum heart rate is the highest rate, in beats per minute, that the person's heart should reach. One method to estimate maximum heart rate states that your age added to your maximum heart rate is 220. Using this method, write and solve an equation to find the maximum heart rate of a 15-year-old.

Age	added to	maximum heart rate	is	220.
a	+	r	=	220

$$a + r = 220$$

Write an equation to represent the relationship.

$$15 + r = 220$$

$$\underline{-15 \qquad -15}$$

$$r = 205$$

Substitute 15 for a. Since 15 is added to r, subtract 15 from both sides to undo the addition.

The maximum heart rate for a 15-year-old is 205 beats per minute. Since age added to maximum heart rate is 220, the answer should be less than 220. So 205 is a reasonable answer.

 4. What if...? Use the method above to find a person's age if the person's maximum heart rate is 185 beats per minute.

The properties of equality allow you to perform inverse operations, as in the previous examples. These properties say that you can perform the same operation on both sides of an equation.

Properties of Equality

WORDS	NUMBERS	ALGEBRA
Addition Property of Equality You can add the same number to both sides of an equation, and the statement will still be true.	$3 = 3$ $3 + 2 = 3 + 2$ $5 = 5$	$a = b$ $a + c = b + c$
Subtraction Property of Equality You can subtract the same number from both sides of an equation, and the statement will still be true.	$7 = 7$ $7 - 5 = 7 - 5$ $2 = 2$	$a = b$ $a - c = b - c$

MCC.MP.3   MATHEMATICAL PRACTICES

THINK AND DISCUSS

1. Describe how the Addition and Subtraction Properties of Equality are like a balanced scale.

2. GET ORGANIZED Copy and complete the graphic organizer. In each box, write an example of an equation that can be solved by using the given property, and solve it.

Properties of Equality

(+)   (−)

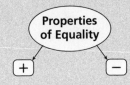

GUIDED PRACTICE

1. **Vocabulary** Will the *solution of an equation* such as $x - 3 = 9$ be a variable or a number? Explain.

Solve each equation. Check your answer.

SEE EXAMPLE 1

2. $s - 5 = 3$

3. $17 = w - 4$

4. $k - 8 = -7$

5. $x - 3.9 = 12.4$

6. $8.4 = y - 4.6$

7. $\frac{3}{8} = t - \frac{1}{8}$

SEE EXAMPLE 2

8. $t + 5 = -25$

9. $9 = s + 9$

10. $42 = m + 36$

11. $2.8 = z + 0.5$

12. $b + \frac{2}{3} = 2$

13. $n + 1.8 = 3$

SEE EXAMPLE 3

14. $-10 + d = 7$

15. $20 = -12 + v$

16. $-46 + q = 5$

17. $2.8 = -0.9 + y$

18. $-\frac{2}{3} + c = \frac{2}{3}$

19. $-\frac{5}{6} + p = 2$

SEE EXAMPLE 4

20. **Geology** In 1673, the Hope diamond was reduced from its original weight by about 45 carats, resulting in a diamond weighing about 67 carats. Write and solve an equation to find how many carats the original diamond weighed. Show that your answer is reasonable.

PRACTICE AND PROBLEM SOLVING

Independent Practice	
For Exercises	See Example
21–30	1
31–40	2
41–48	3
49	4

my.hrw.com

Online Extra Practice

Solve each equation. Check your answer.

21. $1 = k - 8$

22. $u - 15 = -8$

23. $x - 7 = 10$

24. $-9 = p - 2$

25. $\frac{3}{7} = p - \frac{1}{7}$

26. $q - 0.5 = 1.5$

27. $6 = t - 4.5$

28. $4\frac{2}{3} = r - \frac{1}{3}$

29. $6 = x - 3$

30. $1.75 = k - 0.75$

31. $19 + a = 19$

32. $4 = 3.1 + y$

33. $m + 20 = 3$

34. $-12 = c + 3$

35. $v + 2300 = -800$

36. $b + 42 = 300$

37. $3.5 = n + 4$

38. $b + \frac{1}{2} = \frac{1}{2}$

39. $x + 5.34 = 5.39$

40. $2 = d + \frac{1}{4}$

41. $-12 + f = 3$

42. $-9 = -4 + g$

43. $-1200 + j = 345$

44. $90 = -22 + a$

45. $26 = -4 + y$

46. $1\frac{3}{4} = -\frac{1}{4} + w$

47. $-\frac{1}{6} + h = \frac{1}{6}$

48. $-5.2 + a = -8$

49. **Finance** Luis deposited $500 into his bank account. He now has $4732. Write and solve an equation to find how much was in his account before the deposit. Show that your answer is reasonable.

50. **///ERROR ANALYSIS///** Below are two possible solutions to $x + 12.5 = 21.6$. Which is incorrect? Explain the error.

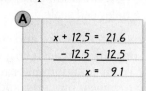

A

$x + 12.5 = 21.6$
$\underline{-12.5 \quad -12.5}$
$x = \quad 9.1$

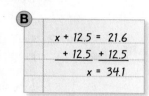

B

$x + 12.5 = 21.6$
$\underline{+12.5 \quad +12.5}$
$x = \quad 34.1$

Write an equation to represent each relationship. Then solve the equation.

51. Ten less than a number is equal to 12.

52. A number decreased by 13 is equal to 7.

53. Eight more than a number is 16.

54. A number minus 3 is –8.

55. The sum of 5 and a number is 6.

56. Two less than a number is –5.

57. The difference of a number and 4 is 9.

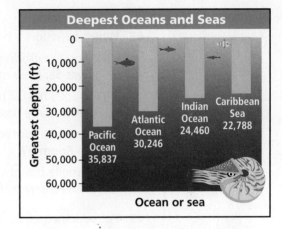
58. **Geology** The sum of the Atlantic Ocean's average depth (in feet) and its greatest depth is 43,126. Use the information in the graph to write and solve an equation to find the average depth of the Atlantic Ocean. Show that your answer is reasonable.

59. **School** Helene's marching band needs money to travel to a competition. Band members have raised $560. They need to raise a total of $1680. Write and solve an equation to find how much more they need. Show that your answer is reasonable.

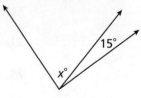

Deepest Oceans and Seas

Greatest depth (ft)

Pacific Ocean 35,837 · Atlantic Ocean 30,246 · Indian Ocean 24,460 · Caribbean Sea 22,788

Ocean or sea

60. **Economics** When you receive a loan to make a purchase, you often must make a down payment in cash. The amount of the loan is the purchase cost minus the down payment. Riva made a down payment of $1500 on a used car. She received a loan of $2600. Write and solve an equation to find the cost of the car. Show that your answer is reasonable.

Geometry The angles in each pair are complementary. Write and solve an equation to find each value of x. (*Hint:* The measures of complementary angles add to 90°.)

61.

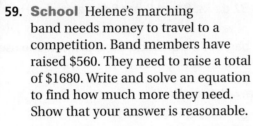

63° $x°$

62.

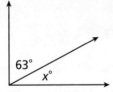

$x°$ 42°

63.

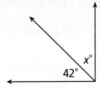

15° $x°$

64. *Rates* are often used to describe how quickly something is moving or changing.

  a. A wildfire spreads at a rate of 1000 acres per day. How many acres will the fire cover in 2 days? Show that your answer is reasonable.

  b. How many acres will the fire cover in 5 days? Explain how you found your answer.

  c. Another wildfire spread for 7 days and covered a total of 780 square miles. How can you estimate the number of square miles the fire covered per day?

65. Statistics The range of a set of scores is 28, and the lowest score is 47. Write and solve an equation to find the highest score. (*Hint:* In a data set, the range is the difference between the highest and the lowest values.) Show that your answer is reasonable.

H.O.T. **66. Write About It** Describe a real-world situation that can be modeled by $x + 5 = 25$. Tell what the variable represents in your situation. Then solve the equation and tell what the solution means in the context of your problem.

H.O.T. **67. Critical Thinking** Without solving, tell whether the solution of $-3 + z = 10$ will be greater than 10 or less than 10. Explain.

TEST PREP

68. Which situation is best represented by $x - 32 = 8$?

     Ⓐ Logan withdrew \$32 from her bank account. After her withdrawal, her balance was \$8. How much was originally in her account?

     Ⓑ Daniel has 32 baseball cards. Joseph has 8 fewer baseball cards than Daniel. How many baseball cards does Joseph have?

     Ⓒ Room A contains 32 desks. Room B has 8 fewer desks. How many desks are in Room B?

     Ⓓ Janelle bought a bag of 32 craft sticks for a project. She used 8 craft sticks. How many craft sticks does she have left?

69. For which equation is $a = 8$ a solution?

     Ⓕ $15 - a = 10$ Ⓖ $10 + a = 23$ Ⓗ $a - 18 = 26$ Ⓙ $a + 8 = 16$

70. Short Response Julianna used a gift card to pay for an \$18 haircut. The remaining balance on the card was \$22.

    a. Write an equation that can be used to determine the original value of the card.

    b. Solve your equation to find the original value of the card.

CHALLENGE AND EXTEND

Solve each equation. Check your answer.

71. $3\frac{1}{5} + b = \frac{4}{5}$ **72.** $x - \frac{7}{4} = \frac{2}{3}$ **73.** $x + \frac{7}{4} = \frac{2}{3}$ **74.** $x - \frac{4}{9} = \frac{4}{9}$

75. If $p - 4 = 2$, find the value of $5p - 20$.   **76.** If $t + 6 = 21$, find the value of $-2t$.

77. If $x + 3 = 15$, find the value of $18 + 6x$.   **78.** If $2 + n = -11$, find the value of $6n$.

MATHEMATICAL PRACTICES

FOCUS ON MATHEMATICAL PRACTICES

H.O.T. **79. Reasoning** Compare the equations $w + 3 = 65$ and $3 = w + 65$. How are the solutions related?

H.O.T. **80. Make a Conjecture** Consider the equation $8 = 8$.

    a. How can you obtain the equation $3 = 3$ by using the Subtraction Property of Equality? How can you obtain the equation $3 = 3$ by using the Addition Property of Equality?

    b. Is the Subtraction Property of Equality ever *needed* to solve an equation? Explain.

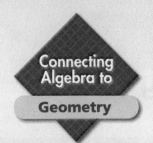

Area of Composite Figures

Review the area formulas for squares, rectangles, and triangles in the table below.

Squares	Rectangles	Triangles
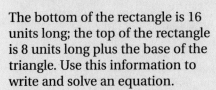 s	ℓ w	h b
$A = s^2$	$A = \ell w$	$A = \frac{1}{2}bh$

A *composite figure* is a figure that is composed of basic shapes. You can divide composite figures into combinations of squares, rectangles, and triangles to find their areas.

Example

Find the area of the figure shown.

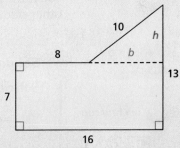

Divide the figure into a rectangle and a right triangle. Notice that you do not know the base or the height of the triangle. Use b and h to represent these lengths.

The bottom of the rectangle is 16 units long; the top of the rectangle is 8 units long plus the base of the triangle. Use this information to write and solve an equation.

$$\begin{aligned} b + 8 &= 16 \\ -8 \quad &\ -8 \\ \hline b &= 8 \end{aligned}$$

The right side of the figure is 13 units long: 7 units from the rectangle plus the height of the triangle. Use this information to write and solve an equation.

$$\begin{aligned} h + 7 &= 13 \\ -7 \quad &\ -7 \\ \hline h &= 6 \end{aligned}$$

The area of the figure is the sum of the areas of the rectangle and the triangle.

Area of rectangle
↓   Area of triangle
↓

$$A = \ell w + \frac{1}{2}bh$$
$$A = 16(7) + \frac{1}{2}(8)(6)$$
$$A = 112 + 24$$
$$A = 136 \text{ square units}$$

Try This

Find the area of each composite figure.

1.
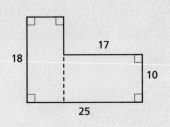

2.
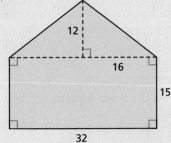

3.
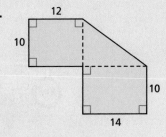

1-3

Solving Equations by Multiplying or Dividing

? *Essential Question:* How can you use multiplication or division to solve equations?

Objective
Solve one-step equations in one variable by using multiplication or division.

Who uses this?

Pilots can make quick calculations by solving one-step equations. (See Example 4.)

Solving an equation that contains multiplication or division is similar to solving an equation that contains addition or subtraction. Use inverse operations to undo the operations on the variable.

Remember that an equation is like a balanced scale. To keep the balance, whatever you do on one side of the equation, you must also do on the other side.

Inverse Operations
Multiply by x. ⟷ Divide by x.

 **EXAMPLE 1**
MCC9-12.A.REI.3

 my.hrw.com

Online Video Tutor

Solving Equations by Using Multiplication

Solve each equation. Check your answer.

A $-4 = \dfrac{k}{-5}$

$(-5)(-4) = (-5)\left(\dfrac{k}{-5}\right)$ — *Since k is divided by −5, multiply both sides by −5 to undo the division.*

$20 = k$

Check $\quad -4 = \dfrac{k}{-5}$ — *To check your solution, substitute 20 for k in the original equation.*

$$\begin{array}{c|c} -4 & \dfrac{20}{-5} \\ \hline -4 & -4 \ \checkmark \end{array}$$

B $\dfrac{m}{3} = 1.5$

$(3)\left(\dfrac{m}{3}\right) = (3)(1.5)$ — *Since m is divided by 3, multiply both sides by 3 to undo the division.*

$m = 4.5$

Check $\quad \dfrac{m}{3} = 1.5$ — *To check your solution, substitute 1.5 for m in the original equation.*

$$\begin{array}{c|c} \dfrac{4.5}{3} & 1.5 \\ \hline 1.5 & 1.5 \ \checkmark \end{array}$$

 CHECK IT OUT! Solve each equation. Check your answer.

1a. $\dfrac{p}{5} = 10$ **1b.** $-13 = \dfrac{y}{3}$ **1c.** $\dfrac{c}{8} = 7$

 **EXAMPLE** 2
MCC9-12.A.REI.3

Solving Equations by Using Division

Solve each equation. Check your answers.

A $7x = 56$

$$\frac{7x}{7} = \frac{56}{7}$$

$$x = 8$$

Since x is multiplied by 7, divide both sides by 7 to undo the multiplication.

Check

$$\begin{array}{c|c} 7x = 56 \\ \hline 7(8) & 56 \\ 56 & 56 \checkmark \end{array}$$

To check your solution, substitute 8 for x in the original equation.

B $13 = -2w$

$$\frac{13}{-2} = \frac{-2w}{-2}$$

$$-6.5 = w$$

Since w is multiplied by −2, divide both sides by −2 to undo the multiplication.

Check

$$\begin{array}{c|c} 13 = -2w \\ \hline 13 & -2(-6.5) \\ 13 & 13 \checkmark \end{array}$$

To check your solution, substitute −6.5 for w in the original equation.

 Solve each equation. Check your answer.

2a. $16 = 4c$ **2b.** $0.5y = -10$ **2c.** $15k = 75$

Remember that dividing is the same as multiplying by the reciprocal. When solving equations, you will sometimes find it easier to multiply by a reciprocal instead of dividing. This is often true when an equation contains fractions.

 EXAMPLE 3
MCC9-12.A.REI.3

Solving Equations That Contain Fractions

Solve each equation.

A $\dfrac{5}{9}v = 35$

$$\left(\frac{9}{5}\right)\frac{5}{9}v = \left(\frac{9}{5}\right)35$$

$$v = 63$$

The reciprocal of $\frac{5}{9}$ is $\frac{9}{5}$. Since v is multiplied by $\frac{5}{9}$, multiply both sides by $\frac{9}{5}$.

B $\dfrac{5}{2} = \dfrac{4y}{3}$

$$\frac{5}{2} = \frac{4y}{3}$$

$$\frac{5}{2} = \frac{4}{3}y$$

$\frac{4y}{3}$ is the same as $\frac{4}{3}y$.

$$\left(\frac{3}{4}\right)\frac{5}{2} = \left(\frac{3}{4}\right)\frac{4}{3}y$$

The reciprocal of $\frac{4}{3}$ is $\frac{3}{4}$. Since y is multiplied by $\frac{4}{3}$, multiply both sides by $\frac{3}{4}$.

$$\frac{15}{8} = y$$

 Solve each equation. Check your answer.

3a. $-\dfrac{1}{4} = \dfrac{1}{5}b$ **3b.** $\dfrac{4j}{6} = \dfrac{2}{3}$ **3c.** $\dfrac{1}{6}w = 102$

EXAMPLE **4**
MCC9-12.A.CED.2

my.hrw.com

Online Video Tutor

Aviation Application

The distance in miles from the airport that a plane should begin descending, divided by 3, equals the plane's height above the ground in thousands of feet. If a plane is 10,000 feet above the ground, write and solve an equation to find the distance at which the pilot should begin descending.

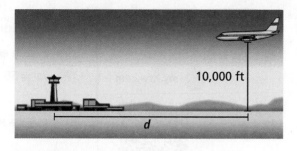

10,000 ft

d

| Distance | divided by 3 | equals | height in thousands of feet. |

$$\frac{d}{3} = h$$ *Write an equation to represent the relationship.*

$$\frac{d}{3} = 10$$ *Substitute 10 for h. Since d is divided by 3, multiply both sides by 3 to undo the division.*

$$(3)\frac{d}{3} = (3)10$$

$$d = 30$$

The pilot should begin descending 30 miles from the airport.

Caution!

The equation uses the plane's height above the ground in *thousands* of feet. So substitute 10 for *h*, not 10,000.

4. What if...? A plane began descending 45 miles from the airport. Use the equation above to find how high the plane was flying when the descent began.

You have now used four properties of equality to solve equations. These properties are summarized in the box below.

Know it!
Note

Properties of Equality

WORDS	NUMBERS	ALGEBRA
Addition Property of Equality You can add the same number to both sides of an equation, and the statement will still be true.	$3 = 3$ $3 + 2 = 3 + 2$ $5 = 5$	$a = b$ $a + c = b + c$
Subtraction Property of Equality You can subtract the same number from both sides of an equation, and the statement will still be true.	$7 = 7$ $7 - 5 = 7 - 5$ $2 = 2$	$a = b$ $a - c = b - c$
Multiplication Property of Equality You can multiply both sides of an equation by the same number, and the statement will still be true.	$6 = 6$ $6(3) = 6(3)$ $18 = 18$	$a = b$ $ac = bc$
Division Property of Equality You can divide both sides of an equation by the same nonzero number, and the statement will still be true.	$8 = 8$ $\frac{8}{4} = \frac{8}{4}$ $2 = 2$	$a = b$ $(c \neq 0)$ $\frac{a}{c} = \frac{b}{c}$

THINK AND DISCUSS

1. Tell how the Multiplication and Division Properties of Equality are similar to the Addition and Subtraction Properties of Equality.

2. **GET ORGANIZED** Copy and complete the graphic organizer. In each box, write an example of an equation that can be solved by using the given property, and solve it.

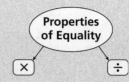

Properties of Equality
× ÷

1-3 Exercises

my.hrw.com
Homework Help

GUIDED PRACTICE

Solve each equation. Check your answer.

SEE EXAMPLE 1
1. $\frac{k}{4} = 8$
2. $\frac{z}{3} = -9$
3. $-2 = \frac{w}{-7}$
4. $6 = \frac{t}{-5}$
5. $\frac{g}{1.9} = 10$
6. $2.4 = \frac{b}{5}$

SEE EXAMPLE 2
7. $4x = 28$
8. $-64 = 8c$
9. $-9j = -45$
10. $84 = -12a$
11. $4m = 10$
12. $2.8 = -2h$

SEE EXAMPLE 3
13. $\frac{1}{2}d = 7$
14. $15 = \frac{5}{6}f$
15. $\frac{2}{3}s = -6$
16. $9 = -\frac{3}{8}r$
17. $\frac{1}{10} = \frac{4}{5}y$
18. $\frac{1}{4}v = -\frac{3}{4}$

SEE EXAMPLE 4
19. **Recreation** The Baseball Birthday Batter Package at a minor league ballpark costs $192. The package includes tickets, drinks, and cake for a group of 16 children. Write and solve an equation to find the cost per child.

20. **Nutrition** An orange contains about 80 milligrams of vitamin C, which is 10 times as much as an apple contains. Write and solve an equation to find the amount of vitamin C in an apple.

PRACTICE AND PROBLEM SOLVING

Solve each equation. Check your answer.

21. $\frac{x}{2} = 12$
22. $-40 = \frac{b}{5}$
23. $-\frac{j}{6} = 6$
24. $-\frac{n}{3} = -4$
25. $-\frac{q}{5} = 30$
26. $1.6 = \frac{d}{3}$
27. $\frac{v}{10} = 5.5$
28. $\frac{h}{8.1} = -4$
29. $5t = -15$
30. $49 = 7c$
31. $-12 = -12u$
32. $-7m = 63$
33. $-52 = -4c$
34. $11 = -2z$
35. $5f = 1.5$
36. $-8.4 = -4n$

Solve each equation. Check your answer.

37. $\frac{5}{2}k = 5$ **38.** $-9 = \frac{3}{4}d$ **39.** $-\frac{5}{8}b = 10$ **40.** $-\frac{4}{5}g = -12$

41. $\frac{4}{7}t = -2$ **42.** $-\frac{4}{5}p = \frac{2}{3}$ **43.** $\frac{2}{3} = -\frac{1}{3}q$ **44.** $-\frac{5}{8} = -\frac{3}{4}a$

45. Finance After taxes, Alexandra's take-home pay is $\frac{7}{10}$ of her salary before taxes. Write and solve an equation to find Alexandra's salary before taxes for the pay period that resulted in $392 of take-home pay.

46. Earth Science Your weight on the Moon is about $\frac{1}{6}$ of your weight on Earth. Write and solve an equation to show how much a person weighs on Earth if he weighs 16 pounds on the Moon. How could you check that your answer is reasonable?

47. ///ERROR ANALYSIS/// For the equation $\frac{x}{3} = 15$, a student found the value of x to be 5. Explain the error. What is the correct answer?

Geometry The perimeter of a square is given. Write and solve an equation to find the length of each side of the square.

48. $P = 36$ in.   **49.** $P = 84$ in.   **50.** $P = 100$ yd   **51.** $P = 16.4$ cm

Statistics

American Robert P. Wadlow (1918–1940) holds the record for world's tallest man— 8 ft 11.1 in. He also holds world records for the largest feet and hands.

Source: Guinness World Records 2005

Write an equation to represent each relationship. Then solve the equation.

52. Five times a number is 45.

53. A number multiplied by negative 3 is 12.

54. A number divided by 4 is equal to 10.

55. The quotient of a number and 3 is negative 8.

56. Statistics The mean height of the students in Marta's class is 60 in. There are 18 students in her class. Write and solve an equation to find the total measure of all students' heights. (*Hint:* The mean is found by dividing the sum of all data values by the number of data values.)

57. Finance Lisa earned $6.25 per hour at her after-school job. Each week she earned $50. Write and solve an equation to show how many hours she worked each week.

58. Critical Thinking Will the solution of $\frac{x}{2.1} = 4$ be greater than 4 or less than 4? Explain.

59. Consumer Economics Dion's long-distance phone bill was $13.80. His long-distance calls cost $0.05 per minute. Write and solve an equation to find the number of minutes he was charged for. Show that your answer is reasonable.

60. Nutrition An 8 oz cup of coffee has about 184 mg of caffeine. This is 5 times as much caffeine as in a 12 oz soft drink. Write and solve an equation to find about how much caffeine is in a 12 oz caffeinated soft drink. Round your answer to the nearest whole number. Show that your answer is reasonable.

Use the equation $8y = 4x$ to find y for each value of x.

	x	$4x$	$8y = 4x$	y
61.	−4	$4(-4) = -16$	$8y = -16$	
62.	−2			
63.	0			
64.	2			

© Bettmann/CORBIS

Real-World Connections

65. **a.** The formula for the mean of a data set is mean $= \dfrac{\text{sum of data values}}{\text{number of data values}}$. One summer, there were 1926 wildfires in Arizona. Which value does this number represent in the formula?

   b. The mean number of acres burned by each wildfire was 96.21. Which value does this number represent in the formula?

   c. Use the formula and information given to find how many acres were burned by wildfires in Arizona that summer. Round your answer to the nearest acre. Show that your answer is reasonable.

Solve each equation. Check your answer.

66. $\dfrac{m}{6} = 1$ 67. $4x = 28$ 68. $1.2h = 14.4$ 69. $\dfrac{1}{5}x = 121$

70. $2w = 26$ 71. $4b = \dfrac{3}{4}$ 72. $5y = 11$ 73. $\dfrac{n}{1.9} = 3$

Biology Use the table for Exercises 74 and 75.

Average Weight			
Animal	At Birth (g)	Adult Female (g)	Adult Male (g)
Hamster	2	130	110
Guinea pig	85	800	1050
Rat	5	275	480

74. The mean weight of an adult male rat is 16 times the mean weight of an adult male mouse. Write and solve an equation to find the mean weight of an adult male mouse. Show that your answer is reasonable.

75. On average, a hamster at birth weighs $\dfrac{2}{3}$ the weight of a gerbil at birth. Write and solve an equation to find the average weight of a gerbil at birth. Show that your answer is reasonable.

H.O.T. 76. **Write About It** Describe a real-world situation that can be modeled by $3x = 42$. Solve the equation and tell what the solution means in the context of your problem.

TEST PREP

77. Which situation does NOT represent the equation $\dfrac{d}{2} = 10$?

   Ⓐ Leo bought a box of pencils. He gave half of them to his brother. They each got 10 pencils. How many pencils were in the box Leo bought?

   Ⓑ Kasey evenly divided her money from baby-sitting into two bank accounts. She put $10 in each account. How much did Kasey earn?

   Ⓒ Gilbert cut a piece of ribbon into 2-inch strips. When he was done, he had ten 2-inch strips. How long was the ribbon to start?

   Ⓓ Mattie had 2 more CDs than her sister Leona. If Leona had 10 CDs, how many CDs did Mattie have?

78. Which equation below shows a correct first step for solving $3x = -12$?

   Ⓕ $3x + 3 = -12 + 3$ Ⓗ $3(3x) = 3(-12)$

   Ⓖ $3x - 3 = -12 - 3$ Ⓙ $\dfrac{3x}{3} = \dfrac{-12}{3}$

79. In a regular pentagon, all of the angles are equal in measure. The sum of the angle measures is 540°. Which of the following equations could be used to find the measure of each angle?

    Ⓐ $\frac{x}{540} = 5$ Ⓒ $540x = 5$

    Ⓑ $5x = 540$ Ⓓ $\frac{x}{5} = 540$

80. For which equation is $m = 10$ a solution?

    Ⓕ $5 = 2m$ Ⓖ $5m = 2$ Ⓗ $\frac{m}{2} = 5$ Ⓙ $\frac{m}{10} = 2$

81. Short Response Luisa bought 6 cans of cat food that each cost the same amount. She spent a total of $4.80.

    a. Write an equation to determine the cost of one can of cat food. Tell what each part of your equation represents.

    b. Solve your equation to find the cost of one can of cat food. Show each step.

CHALLENGE AND EXTEND

Solve each equation. Check your answer.

82. $\left(3\frac{1}{5}\right)b = \frac{4}{5}$ **83.** $\left(1\frac{1}{3}\right)x = 2\frac{2}{3}$ **84.** $\left(5\frac{4}{5}\right)x = -52\frac{1}{5}$

85. $\left(-2\frac{9}{10}\right)k = -26\frac{1}{10}$ **86.** $\left(1\frac{2}{3}\right)w = 15\frac{1}{3}$ **87.** $\left(2\frac{1}{4}\right)d = 4\frac{1}{2}$

Find each indicated value.

88. If $2p = 4$, find the value of $6p + 10$.   **89.** If $6t = 24$, find the value of $-5t$.

90. If $3x = 15$, find the value of $12 - 4x$.   **91.** If $\frac{n}{2} = -11$, find the value of $6n$.

92. To isolate x in $ax = b$, what should you divide both sides by?

93. To isolate x in $\frac{x}{a} = b$, what operation should you perform on both sides of the equation?

H.O.T. **94. Travel** The formula $d = rt$ gives the distance d that is traveled at a rate r in time t.

    a. If $d = 400$ and $r = 25$, what is the value of t?

    b. If $d = 400$ and $r = 50$, what is the value of t?

    c. What if...? How did t change when r increased from 25 to 50?

    d. What if...? If r is doubled while d remains the same, what is the effect on t?

FOCUS ON MATHEMATICAL PRACTICES

H.O.T. **95. Problem Solving** Teo did not know how many ounces of liquid his rice cooker cup would hold. He used the cup to put an entire 32-oz container of broth into the cooker, filling the cup $5\frac{1}{3}$ times. How much liquid does the cup hold?

H.O.T. **96. Communication** Suppose a and b are any nonzero numbers. Solve the equations $\frac{1}{a}x = b$ and $\frac{1}{b}x = a$ for x. Are the solutions the same? Provide an example that supports your answer.

H.O.T. **97. Number Sense** Write four equations that each have a solution of 0 and that are solved by using a different property of equality.

Technology TASK

Solve Equations by Graphing

You can use graphs to solve equations. As you complete this activity, you will learn some of the connections between graphs and equations.

Use with Solving Equations by Multiplying or Dividing

Use appropriate tools strategically.

MCC9-12.A.REI.11 Explain why the *x*-coordinates of the points where the graphs of the equations $y = f(x)$ and $y = g(x)$ intersect are the solutions of the equation $f(x) = g(x)$; find the solutions approximately, e.g., using technology to graph the functions, make tables of values, ….* *Also* **MCC9-12.A.REI.3**

Activity

Solve $3x - 4 = 5$.

1 Press **Y=**. In Y_1, enter the left side of the equation, $3x - 4$.

Y= 3 **X,T,θ,n** **—** 4 **ENTER**

In Y_2, enter the right side of the equation, 5.

Y= 5 **ENTER**

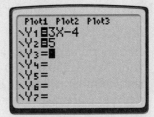

2 Press **GRAPH**. Press **TRACE**. The display will show the *x*- and *y*-values of a point on the first line. Press the right arrow key several times. Notice that the *x*- and *y*-values change.

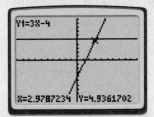

3 Continue to trace as close as possible to the intersection of the two lines. The *x*-value of this point 2.9787…, is an approximation of the solution. The solution is about 3.

4 While still in trace mode, to check, press **3** **ENTER**. The display will show the *y*-value when $x = 3$. When $x = 3$, $y = 5$. So 3 is the solution. You can also check this solution by substituting 3 for *x* in the equation:

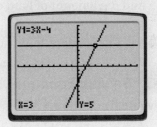

$$\begin{array}{r|l} \textbf{Check} \quad 3x - 4 &= 5 \\ \hline 3(3) - 4 & 5 \\ 9 - 4 & 5 \\ 5 & 5 \checkmark \end{array}$$

Try This

1. Solve $3x - 4 = 2$, $3x - 4 = 17$, and $3x - 4 = -7$ by graphing.

2. What does each line represent?

3. Describe a procedure for finding the solution of $3x - 4 = y$ for any value of *y*.

4. Solve $\frac{1}{2}x - 7 = -4$, $\frac{1}{2}x - 7 = 0$, and $\frac{1}{2}x - 7 = 2$ by graphing.

Ready to Go On?

 1-1 **Variables and Expressions**

Give two ways to write each algebraic expression in words.

1. $4 + n$ **2.** $m - 9$ **3.** $\dfrac{g}{2}$ **4.** $4z$

5. Grapes cost $1.99 per pound. Write an expression for the cost of g pounds of grapes.

6. Today's temperature is 3 degrees warmer than yesterday's temperature t. Write an expression for today's temperature.

Evaluate each expression for $p = 5$ and $q = 1$.

7. qp **8.** $p \div q$ **9.** $q + p$

10. Each member of the art club will make the same number of posters to advertise their club. They will make 150 posters total. Write an expression for how many posters each member will make if there are m members. Find how many posters each member will make if there are 5, 6, and 10 members.

 1-2 **Solving Equations by Adding or Subtracting**

Solve each equation.

11. $x - 32 = -18$ **12.** $1.1 = m - 0.9$ **13.** $j + 4 = -17$ **14.** $\dfrac{9}{8} = g + \dfrac{1}{2}$

Solve each equation. Check your answer.

15. $b - 16 = 20$ **16.** $4 + x = 2$ **17.** $9 + a = -12$ **18.** $z - \dfrac{1}{4} = \dfrac{7}{8}$

19. When she first purchased it, Soledad's computer had 400 GB of hard drive space. After six months, there were only 313 GB available. Write and solve an equation to find the amount of hard drive space that Soledad used in the first six months.

20. Robin needs 108 signatures for her petition. So far, she has 27. Write and solve an equation to determine how many more signatures she needs.

 1-3 **Solving Equations by Multiplying or Dividing**

Solve each equation.

21. $\dfrac{h}{3} = -12$ **22.** $-2.8 = \dfrac{w}{-3}$ **23.** $42 = 3c$ **24.** $-0.1b = 3.7$

Solve each equation. Check your answer.

25. $35 = 5x$ **26.** $-30 = \dfrac{n}{3}$ **27.** $5y = 0$ **28.** $-4.6r = 9.2$

29. A fund-raiser raised $2400, which was $\dfrac{3}{5}$ of the goal. Write and solve an equation to find the amount of the goal.

PARCC Assessment Readiness

Selected Response

1. Give two ways to write the algebraic expression $p \div 10$ in words.

  Ⓐ the product of p and 10; p times 10

  Ⓑ the quotient of p and 10; p divided by 10

  Ⓒ the quotient of 10 and p; 10 divided by p

  Ⓓ p subtracted from 10; p less than 10

2. Julia wrote 14 letters to friends each month for y months in a row. Write an expression to show how many total letters Julia wrote.

  Ⓕ $14y$ Ⓗ $14 - y$

  Ⓖ $14 + y$ Ⓙ $\dfrac{14}{y}$

3. Solve $p - 6 = 16$. Check your answer.

  Ⓐ $p = 22$ Ⓒ $p = 10$

  Ⓑ $p = -22$ Ⓓ $p = -10$

4. Solve $\dfrac{q}{5} = 41$. Check your answer.

  Ⓕ $q = 8\frac{1}{5}$ Ⓗ $q = 205$

  Ⓖ $q = 36$ Ⓙ $q = 46$

5. Salvador's class has collected 88 cans in a food drive. They plan to sort the cans into x bags, with an equal number of cans in each bag. Write an expression to show how many cans there will be in each bag.

  Ⓐ $88 - x$ Ⓒ $88 + x$

  Ⓑ $88x$ Ⓓ $\dfrac{88}{x}$

6. Evaluate the expression xy for $x = 6$ and $y = 3$.

  Ⓕ 9 Ⓗ 18

  Ⓖ 24 Ⓙ 21

7. Evaluate the expression $a \div b$ for $a = 24$ and $b = 8$.

  Ⓐ 3 Ⓒ 16

  Ⓑ 4 Ⓓ 192

8. Evaluate the expression $2m + n$ for $m = 7$ and $n = 9$.

  Ⓕ 25 Ⓗ 23

  Ⓖ 18 Ⓙ 32

9. The range of a set of scores is 23, and the lowest score is 33. Write and solve an equation to find the highest score. (*Hint*: In a data set, the range is the difference between the highest and the lowest values.)

  Ⓐ $h - 33 = 2 \cdot 23$ The highest score is 79.

  Ⓑ $h + 23 = 33$ The highest score is 10.

  Ⓒ $h + 33 = 23$ The highest score is -10.

  Ⓓ $h - 33 = 23$ The highest score is 56.

10. The time between a flash of lightning and the sound of its thunder can be used to estimate the distance from a lightning strike. The distance from the strike is the number of seconds between seeing the flash and hearing the thunder divided by 5. Suppose you are 17 miles from a lightning strike. Write and solve an equation to find how many seconds there would be between the flash and thunder.

  Ⓕ $\dfrac{5}{t} = d$, so t is about 0.3 seconds.

  Ⓖ $t = \dfrac{d}{5}$, so t is about 3.4 seconds.

  Ⓗ $t - 5 = d$, so t is about 22 seconds.

  Ⓙ $\dfrac{t}{5} = d$, so t is about 85 seconds.

11. If $4x = 32$, find the value of $35 - 5x$.

  Ⓐ -5 Ⓒ -3

  Ⓑ 3 Ⓓ 5

Mini-Task

12. Fatima enrolled in a traveler rewards program. She begins with 10,000 bonus points. For every trip she takes, she collects 3000 bonus points.

  a. Write a rule for the number of bonus points Fatima has after x trips.

  b. Make a table showing the number of bonus points Fatima has after 0, 1, 2, 3, 4, and 5 trips.

  c. When Fatima has collected 20,000 bonus points, she gets a free vacation. How many trips does Fatima need to take to get a free vacation?

2 Choosing Appropriate Units

Contents

MATHEMATICAL PRACTICES The Common Core Georgia Performance Standards for Mathematical Practice describe varieties of expertise that all students should seek to develop. Opportunities to develop these practices are integrated throughout this program.

1 Make sense of problems and persevere in solving them.

2 Reason abstractly and quantitatively.

3 Construct viable arguments and critique the reasoning of others.

4 Model with mathematics.

5 Use appropriate tools strategically.

6 Attend to precision.

7 Look for and make use of structure.

8 Look for and express regularity in repeated reasoning.

Unpacking the Standards

Understanding the standards and the vocabulary terms in the standards will help you know exactly what you are expected to learn in this chapter.

 MCC9-12.N.Q.1

Use units as a way to understand problems and to guide the solution of multi-step problems; …

Key Vocabulary

unit analysis/dimensional analysis
(análisis dimensional) A process that uses rates to convert measurements from one unit to another.

What It Means For You

Keeping track of units in problem solving will help you identify a solution method and interpret the results.

EXAMPLE

Li's car gets 40 miles per gallon of gas. At this rate, she can go 620 miles on a full tank. She has driven 245 miles on the current tank. How many gallons of gas g are left in the tank?

$$620 \text{ mi} = 245 \text{ mi} + \frac{40 \text{ mi}}{1 \text{ gal}} \cdot g \text{ gal}$$

Distance   Distance

Distance

 MCC9-12.A.CED.1

Create equations … in one variable and use them to solve problems.

Key Vocabulary

equation (ecuación)
A mathematical statement that two expressions are equivalent.

variable (variable)
A symbol used to represent a quantity that can change.

What It Means For You

You can write an equation to represent a real-world problem and then use algebra to solve the equation and find the answer.

EXAMPLE

Michael is saving money to buy a trumpet. The trumpet costs $670. He has $350 saved, and each week he adds $20 to his savings. How long will it take him to save enough money to buy the trumpet?

Let w represent the number of weeks.

cost of trumpet	=	current savings	+	additional savings
670	=	350	+	$20w$
320	=	$20w$		
16	=	w		

It will take Michael 16 weeks to save enough money.

Rates, Ratios, and Proportions

Essential Question: How can you use units to understand problems and guide the solution of proportions?

Objectives

Write and use ratios, rates, and unit rates.

Write and solve proportions.

Vocabulary

ratio   proportion
rate   cross products
scale   scale drawing
unit rate   scale model
conversion   dimensional
  factor   analysis

Why learn this?

Ratios and proportions are used to draw accurate maps. (See Example 5.)

A **ratio** is a comparison of two quantities by division. The ratio of a to b can be written $a:b$ or $\frac{a}{b}$, where $b \neq 0$. Ratios that name the same comparison are said to be *equivalent*.

A statement that two ratios are equivalent, such as $\frac{1}{12} = \frac{2}{24}$, is called a **proportion**.

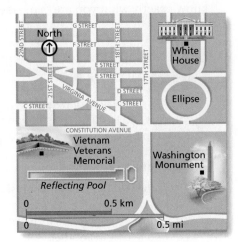

 EXAMPLE
MCC9-12.N.Q.1

1 **Using Ratios**

The ratio of faculty members to students at a college is 1:15. There are 675 students. How many faculty members are there?

$$\frac{\text{faculty}}{\text{students}} \rightarrow \frac{1}{15}$$

Write a ratio comparing faculty to students.

$$\frac{1}{15} = \frac{x}{675}$$

Write a proportion. Let x be the number of faculty members.

$$675\left(\frac{x}{675}\right) = 675\left(\frac{1}{15}\right)$$

Since x is divided by 675, multiply both sides of the equation by 675.

$$x = 45$$

There are 45 faculty members.

 my.hrw.com

Online Video Tutor

 **Reading Math**

Read the proportion $\frac{1}{15} = \frac{x}{675}$ as "1 is to 15 as x is to 675."

 1. The ratio of games won to games lost for a baseball team is $3:2$. The team won 18 games. How many games did the team lose?

A **rate** is a ratio of two quantities with different units, such as $\frac{34 \text{ mi}}{2 \text{ gal}}$. Rates are usually written as *unit rates*. A **unit rate** is a rate with a second quantity of 1 unit, such as $\frac{17 \text{ mi}}{1 \text{ gal}}$, or 17 mi/gal. You can convert any rate to a unit rate.

 EXAMPLE
MCC9-12.N.Q.1

2 **Finding Unit Rates**

Takeru Kobayashi of Japan ate 53.5 hot dogs in 12 minutes to win a contest. Find the unit rate in hot dogs per minute. Round to the nearest hundredth.

$$\frac{53.5}{12} = \frac{x}{1}$$

Write a proportion to find an equivalent ratio with a second quantity of 1.

$$4.46 \approx x$$

Divide on the left side to find x.

The unit rate is approximately 4.46 hot dogs per minute.

 my.hrw.com

Online Video Tutor

 2. Cory earns $52.50 in 7 hours. Find the unit rate in dollars per hour.

Dimensional analysis is a process that uses rates to convert measurements from one unit to another. A rate such as $\frac{12 \text{ in.}}{1 \text{ ft}}$, in which the two quantities are equal but use different units, is called a **conversion factor**. To convert from one set of units to another, multiply by a conversion factor.

EXAMPLE **3** **Using Dimensional Analysis**

A **A large adult male human has about 12 pints of blood. Use dimensional analysis to convert this quantity to gallons.**

Step 1 Convert pints to quarts.

$12 \text{ pt} \cdot \dfrac{1 \text{ qt}}{2 \text{ pt}}$ *Multiply by a conversion factor whose first quantity is quarts and whose second quantity is pints.*

6 qt

12 pints is 6 quarts.

Step 2 Convert quarts to gallons.

$6 \text{ qt} \cdot \dfrac{1 \text{ gal}}{4 \text{ qt}}$ *Multiply by a conversion factor whose first quantity is gallons and whose second quantity is quarts.*

$\dfrac{6}{4} \text{ gal} = 1\dfrac{1}{2} \text{ gal}$

A large adult male human has about $1\frac{1}{2}$ gallons of blood.

B **The dwarf sea horse *Hippocampus zosterae* swims at a rate of 52.68 feet per hour. Use dimensional analysis to convert this speed to inches per minute.**

Use the conversion factor $\frac{12 \text{ in.}}{1 \text{ ft}}$ to convert feet to inches, and use the conversion factor $\frac{1 \text{ h}}{60 \text{ min}}$ to convert hours to minutes.

$\dfrac{52.68 \text{ ft}}{1 \text{ h}} \cdot \dfrac{12 \text{ in.}}{1 \text{ ft}} \cdot \dfrac{1 \text{ h}}{60 \text{ min}} = \dfrac{10.536 \text{ in.}}{1 \text{ min}}$

The speed is 10.536 inches per minute.

Check that the answer is reasonable. The answer is about 10 in./min.
- There are 60 min in 1 h, so 10 in./min is $60(10) = 600$ in./h.
- There are 12 in. in 1 ft, so 600 in./h is $\frac{600}{12} = 50$ ft/h. This is close to the rate given in the problem, 52.68 ft/h.

Hippocampus zosterae

3. A cyclist travels 56 miles in 4 hours. Use dimensional analysis to convert the cyclist's speed to feet per second. Round your answer to the nearest tenth, and show that your answer is reasonable.

In the proportion $\frac{a}{b} = \frac{c}{d}$, the products $a \cdot d$ and $b \cdot c$ are called **cross products**. You can solve a proportion for a missing value by using the Cross Products Property.

Know it! Note

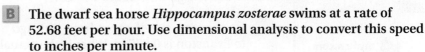

Cross Products Property		
WORDS	**NUMBERS**	**ALGEBRA**
In a proportion, cross products are equal.	$\dfrac{2}{3} \diagdown\!\!\!\!\diagup\, \dfrac{4}{6}$ $2 \cdot 6 = 3 \cdot 4$	If $\dfrac{a}{b} \diagdown\!\!\!\!\diagup\, \dfrac{c}{d}$ and $b \neq 0$ and $d \neq 0$, then $ad = bc$.

 EXAMPLE **4** Solving Proportions

MCC9-12.A.REI.2

Solve each proportion.

A $\dfrac{5}{9} = \dfrac{3}{w}$

$\dfrac{5}{9} \bowtie \dfrac{3}{w}$

$5(w) = 9(3)$ *Use cross products.*

$5w = 27$

$\dfrac{5w}{5} = \dfrac{27}{5}$ *Divide both sides by 5.*

$w = \dfrac{27}{5}$

B $\dfrac{8}{x + 10} = \dfrac{1}{12}$

$\dfrac{8}{x + 10} \bowtie \dfrac{1}{12}$

$8(12) = 1(x + 10)$ *Use cross products.*

$96 = x + 10$

$\underline{-10 \qquad -10}$ *Subtract 10 from both sides.*

$86 = x$

 Solve each proportion.

4a. $\dfrac{-5}{2} = \dfrac{y}{8}$ **4b.** $\dfrac{g + 3}{5} = \dfrac{7}{4}$

A **scale** is a ratio between two sets of measurements, such as 1 in : 5 mi. A **scale drawing** or **scale model** uses a scale to represent an object as smaller or larger than the actual object. A map is an example of a scale drawing.

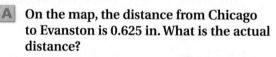 **EXAMPLE** **5** Scale Drawings and Scale Models

MCC9-12.A.CED.1

A On the map, the distance from Chicago to Evanston is 0.625 in. What is the actual distance?

$\dfrac{\text{map}}{\text{actual}} \rightarrow \dfrac{1 \text{ in.}}{18 \text{ mi}}$ *Write the scale as a fraction.*

$\dfrac{1}{18} \bowtie \dfrac{0.625}{x}$ *Let x be the actual distance.*

$x \cdot 1 = 18(0.625)$ *Use cross products to solve.*

$x = 11.25$

The actual distance is 11.25 mi.

B The actual distance between North Chicago and Waukegan is 4 mi. What is this distance on the map? Round to the nearest tenth.

$\dfrac{\text{map}}{\text{actual}} \rightarrow \dfrac{1 \text{ in.}}{18 \text{ mi}}$ *Write the scale as a fraction.*

$\dfrac{1}{18} \bowtie \dfrac{x}{4}$ *Let x be the distance on the map.*

$4 = 18x$ *Use cross products to solve the proportion.*

$\dfrac{4}{18} = \dfrac{18x}{18}$ *Since x is multiplied by 18, divide both sides by 18 to undo the multiplication.*

$0.2 \approx x$ *Round to the nearest tenth.*

The distance on the map is about 0.2 in.

Waukegan
North Chicago
Highland Park
Evanston
1 in : 18 mi
Chicago

Reading Math

A scale written without units, such as 32 : 1, means that 32 units of any measure correspond to 1 unit of that same measure.

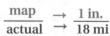 **5.** A scale model of a human heart is 16 ft long. The scale is 32 : 1. How many inches long is the actual heart it represents?

THINK AND DISCUSS

1. Explain two ways to solve the proportion $\frac{t}{4} = \frac{3}{5}$.

2. How could you show that the answer to Example 5A is reasonable?

3. GET ORGANIZED Copy and complete the graphic organizer. In each box, write an example of each use of ratios.

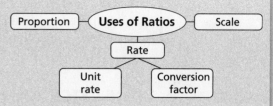

2-1 Exercises

my.hrw.com
Homework Help

GUIDED PRACTICE

1. Vocabulary What does it mean when two ratios form a *proportion*?

SEE EXAMPLE 1

2. The ratio of the sale price of a jacket to the original price is 3 : 4. The original price is $64. What is the sale price?

3. Chemistry The ratio of hydrogen atoms to oxygen atoms in water is 2 : 1. If an amount of water contains 341 trillion atoms of oxygen, how many hydrogen atoms are there?

SEE EXAMPLE 2

4. A computer's fan rotates 2000 times in 40 seconds. Find the unit rate in rotations per second.

5. Twelve cows produce 224,988 pounds of milk. Find the unit rate in pounds per cow.

6. A yellow jacket can fly 4.5 meters in 9 seconds. Find the unit rate in meters per second.

SEE EXAMPLE 3

7. Lydia wrote $4\frac{1}{2}$ pages of her science report in one hour. What was her writing rate in pages per minute?

8. A model airplane flies 18 feet in 2 seconds. What is the airplane's speed in miles per hour? Round your answer to the nearest hundredth.

9. A vehicle uses 1 tablespoon of gasoline to drive 125 yards. How many miles can the vehicle travel per gallon? Round your answer to the nearest mile. (*Hint:* There are 256 tablespoons in a gallon.)

SEE EXAMPLE 4   **Solve each proportion.**

10. $\dfrac{3}{z} = \dfrac{1}{8}$

11. $\dfrac{x}{3} = \dfrac{1}{5}$

12. $\dfrac{b}{4} = \dfrac{3}{2}$

13. $\dfrac{f+3}{12} = \dfrac{7}{2}$

14. $\dfrac{-1}{5} = \dfrac{3}{2d}$

15. $\dfrac{3}{14} = \dfrac{s-2}{21}$

16. $\dfrac{-4}{9} = \dfrac{7}{x}$

17. $\dfrac{3}{s-2} = \dfrac{1}{7}$

18. $\dfrac{10}{h} = \dfrac{52}{13}$

19. Archaeology Stonehenge II in Hunt, Texas, is a scale model of the ancient construction in Wiltshire, England. The scale of the model to the original is 3:5. The Altar Stone of the original construction is 4.9 meters tall. Write and solve a proportion to find the height of the model of the Altar Stone.

Alfred Sheppard, one of the builders of Stonehenge II.

PRACTICE AND PROBLEM SOLVING

Independent Practice	
For Exercises	See Example
20–21	1
22–23	2
24–25	3
26–37	4
38	5

my.hrw.com

Online Extra Practice

20. Gardening The ratio of the height of a bonsai ficus tree to the height of a full-size ficus tree is 1:9. The bonsai ficus is 6 inches tall. What is the height of a full-size ficus?

21. Manufacturing At one factory, the ratio of defective light bulbs produced to total light bulbs produced is about 3:500. How many light bulbs are expected to be defective when 12,000 are produced?

22. Four gallons of gasoline weigh 25 pounds. Find the unit rate in pounds per gallon.

23. Fifteen ounces of gold cost $6058.50. Find the unit rate in dollars per ounce.

24. Biology The tropical giant bamboo can grow 11.9 feet in 3 days. What is this rate of growth in inches per hour? Round your answer to the nearest hundredth, and show that your answer is reasonable.

25. Transportation The maximum speed of the Tupolev Tu-144 airliner is 694 m/s. What is this speed in kilometers per hour?

Solve each proportion.

26. $\dfrac{v}{6} = \dfrac{1}{2}$ **27.** $\dfrac{2}{5} = \dfrac{4}{y}$ **28.** $\dfrac{2}{h} = \dfrac{-5}{6}$ **29.** $\dfrac{3}{10} = \dfrac{b+7}{20}$

30. $\dfrac{5t}{9} = \dfrac{1}{2}$ **31.** $\dfrac{2}{3} = \dfrac{6}{q-4}$ **32.** $\dfrac{x}{8} = \dfrac{7.5}{20}$ **33.** $\dfrac{3}{k} = \dfrac{45}{18}$

34. $\dfrac{6}{a} = \dfrac{15}{17}$ **35.** $\dfrac{9}{2} = \dfrac{5}{x+1}$ **36.** $\dfrac{3}{5} = \dfrac{x}{100}$ **37.** $\dfrac{38}{19} = \dfrac{n-5}{20}$

38. Science The image shows a dust mite as seen under a microscope. The scale of the drawing to the dust mite is 100:1. Use a ruler to measure the length of the dust mite in the image in millimeters. What is the actual length of the dust mite?

39. Finance On a certain day, the exchange rate was 60 U.S. dollars for 50 euro. How many U.S. dollars were 70 euro worth that day? Show that your answer is reasonable.

40. Environmental Science An environmental scientist wants to estimate the number of carp in a pond. He captures 100 carp, tags all of them, and releases them. A week later, he captures 85 carp and records how many have tags. His results are shown in the table. Write and solve a proportion to estimate the number of carp in the pond.

Status	Number Captured
Tagged	20
Not tagged	65

© Linda Owen

41. **///ERROR ANALYSIS///** Below is a bonus question that appeared on an algebra test and a student's response.

> The ratio of junior varsity members to varsity members on the track team is 3:5. There are 24 members on the team. Write a proportion to find the number of junior varsity members.
>
> $\dfrac{3}{5} = \dfrac{x}{24}$

The student did not receive the bonus points. Why is this proportion incorrect?

42. **Sports** The table shows world record times for women's races of different distances.

World Records (Women)	
Distance (m)	Time (s)
100	10.5
200	21.3
800	113.3
5000	864.7

   a. Find the speed in meters per second for each race. Round your answers to the nearest hundredth.

   b. Which race has the fastest speed? the slowest?

   c. **Critical Thinking** Give a possible reason why the speeds are different.

43. **Entertainment** Lynn, Faith, and Jeremy are film animators. In one 8-hour day, Lynn rendered 203 frames, Faith rendered 216 frames, and Jeremy rendered 227 frames. How many more frames per hour did Faith render than Lynn did?

Solve each proportion.

44. $\dfrac{x-1}{3} = \dfrac{x+1}{5}$ 45. $\dfrac{m}{3} = \dfrac{m+4}{7}$ 46. $\dfrac{1}{x-3} = \dfrac{3}{x-5}$ 47. $\dfrac{a}{2} = \dfrac{a-4}{30}$

48. $\dfrac{3}{2y} = \dfrac{16}{y+2}$ 49. $\dfrac{n+3}{5} = \dfrac{n-1}{2}$ 50. $\dfrac{1}{y} = \dfrac{1}{6y-1}$ 51. $\dfrac{2}{n} = \dfrac{4}{n+3}$

52. $\dfrac{5t-3}{-2} = \dfrac{t+3}{2}$ 53. $\dfrac{3}{d+3} = \dfrac{4}{d+12}$ 54. $\dfrac{3x+5}{14} = \dfrac{x}{3}$ 55. $\dfrac{5}{2n} = \dfrac{8}{3n-24}$

56. **Decorating** A particular shade of paint is made by mixing 5 parts red paint with 7 parts blue paint. To make this shade, Shannon mixed 12 quarts of blue paint with 8 quarts of red paint. Did Shannon mix the correct shade? Explain.

H.O.T. 57. **Write About It** Give three examples of proportions. How do you know they are proportions? Then give three nonexamples of proportions. How do you know they are not proportions?

58. a. Marcus is shopping for a new jacket. He finds one with a price tag of $120. Above the rack is a sign that says that he can take off $\frac{1}{5}$. Find out how much Marcus can deduct from the price of the jacket.

   b. What price will Marcus pay for the jacket?

   c. Copy the model below. Complete it by placing numerical values on top and the corresponding fractional parts below.

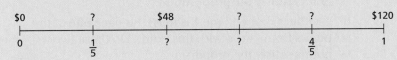

   d. Explain how this model shows proportional relationships.

59. One day the U.S. dollar was worth approximately 100 yen. An exchange of 2500 yen was made that day. What was the value of the exchange in dollars?

  Ⓐ $25   Ⓑ $400   Ⓒ $2500   Ⓓ $40,000

60. Brett walks at a speed of 4 miles per hour. He walks for 20 minutes in a straight line at this rate. Approximately what distance does Brett walk?

  Ⓕ 0.06 miles   Ⓖ 1.3 miles   Ⓗ 5 miles   Ⓙ 80 miles

61. A shampoo company conducted a survey and found that 3 out of 8 people use their brand of shampoo. Which proportion could be used to find the expected number of users n in a city of 75,000 people?

  Ⓐ $\dfrac{3}{8} = \dfrac{75{,}000}{n}$ Ⓑ $\dfrac{3}{75{,}000} = \dfrac{n}{8}$ Ⓒ $\dfrac{8}{3} = \dfrac{n}{75{,}000}$ Ⓓ $\dfrac{3}{8} = \dfrac{n}{75{,}000}$

62. A statue is 3 feet tall. The display case for a model of the statue can fit a model that is no more than 9 inches tall. Which of the scales below allows for the tallest model of the statue that will fit in the display case?

  Ⓕ 2:1   Ⓖ 1:1   Ⓗ 1:3   Ⓙ 1:4

CHALLENGE AND EXTEND

63. **Geometry** Complementary angles are two angles whose measures add up to 90°. The ratio of the measures of two complementary angles is 4:5. What are the measures of the angles?

64. A customer wanted 24 feet of rope. The clerk at the hardware store used what she thought was a yardstick to measure the rope, but the yardstick was actually 2 inches too short. How many inches were missing from the customer's piece of rope?

65. **Population** The population density of Jackson, Mississippi, is 672.2 people per square kilometer. What is the population density in people per square meter? Show that your answer is reasonable. (*Hint:* There are 1000 meters in 1 kilometer. How many square meters are in 1 square kilometer?)

FOCUS ON MATHEMATICAL PRACTICES

H.O.T. **66.** **Error Analysis** Sofia says that any real number is a solution to the equation $\dfrac{4}{2x-4} = \dfrac{2}{x-2}$. What mistake did she make?

H.O.T. **67.** **Make a Conjecture** Examine the graph.

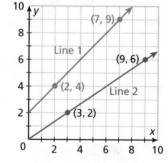

 a. Do the two points on Line 1 satisfy the proportion $\dfrac{y_1}{x_1} = \dfrac{y_2}{x_2}$? Explain.

 b. Do the two points on Line 2 satisfy the proportion $\dfrac{y_1}{x_1} = \dfrac{y_2}{x_2}$? Explain.

 c. Another point on Line 1 is (1, 3). Replace one of the points from part a with this point. Do these two points satisfy the proportion?

 d. Another point on Line 1 is (6, 4). Replace one of the points from part b with this point. Do these two points satisfy the proportion?

 e. Make a conjecture about whether the coordinates of any two points on each line will form a proportion.

H.O.T. **68.** **Problem Solving** Find a solution of $\dfrac{12}{x} = \dfrac{x}{3}$. Explain how you found it.

2-2

Applications of Proportions

 Essential Question: How can you create proportions and use them to solve problems?

Objectives

Use proportions to solve problems involving geometric figures.

Use proportions and similar figures to measure objects indirectly.

Vocabulary

similar
corresponding sides
corresponding angles
indirect measurement
scale factor

 **Animated Math**

 Reading Math

- $\overline{AB}$ means segment *AB*. *AB* means the length of $\overline{AB}$.
- $\angle A$ means angle *A*. $m\angle A$ means the measure of angle *A*.

Why learn this?

Proportions can be used to find the heights of tall objects, such as totem poles, that would otherwise be difficult to measure. (See Example 2.)

Similar figures have exactly the same shape but not necessarily the same size.

Corresponding sides of two figures are in the same relative position, and **corresponding angles** are in the same relative position. Two figures are similar if and only if the lengths of corresponding sides are proportional and all pairs of corresponding angles have equal measures.

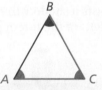
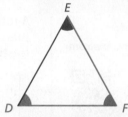

$$\frac{AB}{DE} = \frac{BC}{EF} = \frac{AC}{DF}$$

$m\angle A = m\angle D$
$m\angle B = m\angle E$
$m\angle C = m\angle F$

When stating that two figures are similar, use the symbol ~. For the triangles above, you can write $\triangle ABC \sim \triangle DEF$. Make sure corresponding vertices are in the same order. It would be incorrect to write $\triangle ABC \sim \triangle EFD$.

You can use proportions to find missing lengths in similar figures.

 COMMON CORE GPS **EXAMPLE** **1** MCC9-12.A.CED.1

Finding Missing Measures in Similar Figures

Find the value of *x* in each diagram.

A $\triangle RST \sim \triangle BCD$

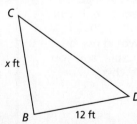

 my.hrw.com

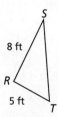

Online Video Tutor

R corresponds to *B*, *S* corresponds to *C*, and *T* corresponds to *D*.

$$\frac{5}{12} = \frac{8}{x}$$

$$5x = 96$$

$$\frac{5x}{5} = \frac{96}{5}$$

$$x = 19.2$$

$\dfrac{RT}{BD} = \dfrac{RS}{BC}$

Use cross products.

Since x is multiplied by 5, divide both sides by 5 to undo the multiplication.

The length of $\overline{BC}$ is 19.2 ft.

Find the value of x in each diagram.

B *FGHJKL ~ MNPQRS*

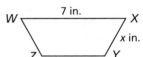

$$\frac{6}{4} = \frac{x}{2} \qquad \frac{NP}{GH} = \frac{RQ}{KJ}$$

$4x = 12$ *Use cross products.*

$$\frac{4x}{4} = \frac{12}{4} \qquad$$ *Since x is multiplied by 4,*

$x = 3$ *divide both sides by 4 to*

                  undo the multiplication.

The length of $\overline{QR}$ is 3 cm.

1. Find the value of x in the diagram if $ABCD \sim WXYZ$.

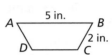

You can solve a proportion involving similar triangles to find a length that is not easily measured. This method of measurement is called **indirect measurement**. If two objects form right angles with the ground, you can apply indirect measurement using their shadows.

COMMON CORE GPS
MCC9-12.A.CED.1

EXAMPLE 2

Measurement Application

my.hrw.com

Online Video Tutor

A totem pole casts a shadow 45 feet long at the same time that a 6-foot-tall man casts a shadow that is 3 feet long. Write and solve a proportion to find the height of the totem pole.

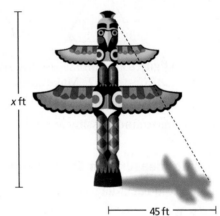

Both the man and the totem pole form right angles with the ground, and their shadows are cast at the same angle. You can form two similar right triangles.

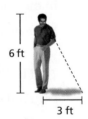

Helpful Hint

A height of 90 ft seems reasonable for a totem pole. If you got 900 or 9000 ft, that would not be reasonable, and you should check your work.

$$\frac{6}{x} = \frac{3}{45}$$

$3x = 270$

$$\frac{3x}{3} = \frac{270}{3}$$

$x = 90$

The totem pole is 90 feet tall.

$$\frac{man's\ height}{pole's\ height} = \frac{man's\ shadow}{pole's\ shadow}$$

Use cross products. Since x is multiplied by 3, divide both sides by 3 to undo the multiplication.

2a. A forest ranger who is 150 cm tall casts a shadow 45 cm long. At the same time, a nearby tree casts a shadow 195 cm long. Write and solve a proportion to find the height of the tree.

2b. A woman who is 5.5 feet tall casts a shadow 3.5 feet long. At the same time, a building casts a shadow 28 feet long. Write and solve a proportion to find the height of the building.

If every dimension of a figure is multiplied by the same number, the result is a similar figure. The multiplier is called a **scale factor** .

COMMON CORE GPS

EXAMPLE **3**
MCC9-12.N.Q.1

Changing Dimensions

my.hrw.com

Online Video Tutor

A Every dimension of a 2-by-4-inch rectangle is multiplied by 1.5 to form a similar rectangle. How is the ratio of the perimeters related to the ratio of corresponding sides? How is the ratio of the areas related to the ratio of corresponding sides?

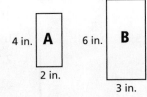
4 in. **A** 2 in.

6 in. **B** 3 in.

	Rectangle A	Rectangle B
$P = 2\ell + 2w$	$2(2) + 2(4) = 12$	$2(6) + 2(3) = 18$
$A = \ell w$	$4(2) = 8$	$6(3) = 18$

Sides: $\dfrac{4}{6} = \dfrac{2}{3}$ Perimeters: $\dfrac{12}{18} = \dfrac{2}{3}$ Areas: $\dfrac{8}{18} = \dfrac{4}{9} = \left(\dfrac{2}{3}\right)^2$

The ratio of the perimeters is equal to the ratio of corresponding sides. The ratio of the areas is the square of the ratio of corresponding sides.

Helpful Hint

A scale factor between 0 and 1 reduces a figure. A scale factor greater than 1 enlarges it.

B Every dimension of a cylinder with radius 4 cm and height 6 cm is multiplied by $\frac{1}{2}$ to form a similar cylinder. How is the ratio of the volumes related to the ratio of corresponding dimensions?

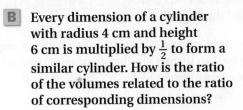
4 cm
A 6 cm

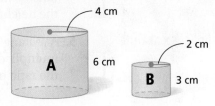
2 cm
B 3 cm

	Cylinder A	Cylinder B
$V = \pi r^2 h$	$\pi(4)^2(6) = 96\pi$	$\pi(2)^2(3) = 12\pi$

Radii: $\dfrac{4}{2} = \dfrac{2}{1} = 2$ Heights: $\dfrac{6}{3} = \dfrac{2}{1} = 2$ Volumes: $\dfrac{96\pi}{12\pi} = \dfrac{8}{1} = 8 = 2^3$

The ratio of the volumes is the cube of the ratio of corresponding dimensions.

CHECK IT OUT!

3. A rectangle has width 12 inches and length 3 inches. Every dimension of the rectangle is multiplied by $\frac{1}{3}$ to form a similar rectangle. How is the ratio of the perimeters related to the ratio of the corresponding sides?

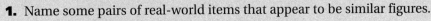
MCC.MP.4   MATHEMATICAL PRACTICES

THINK AND DISCUSS

1. Name some pairs of real-world items that appear to be similar figures.

Know it! Note

2. GET ORGANIZED Copy and complete the graphic organizer. In the top box, sketch and label two similar triangles. Then list the corresponding sides and angles in the bottom boxes.

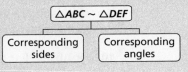
$\triangle ABC \sim \triangle DEF$

Corresponding sides

Corresponding angles

GUIDED PRACTICE

1. Vocabulary What does it mean for two figures to be *similar*?

SEE EXAMPLE 1 **Find the value of *x* in each diagram.**

2. △*ABC* ~ △*DEF*

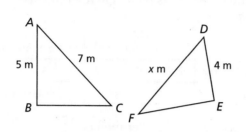

3. *RSTV* ~ *WXYZ*

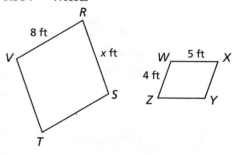

SEE EXAMPLE 2 **4.** Roger is 5 feet tall and casts a shadow 3.5 feet long. At the same time, the flagpole outside his school casts a shadow 14 feet long. Write and solve a proportion to find the height of the flagpole.

SEE EXAMPLE 3 **5.** A rectangle has length 12 feet and width 8 feet. Every dimension of the rectangle is multiplied by $\frac{3}{4}$ to form a similar rectangle. How is the ratio of the areas related to the ratio of corresponding sides?

PRACTICE AND PROBLEM SOLVING

Independent Practice

For Exercises	See Example
6–7	1
8	2
9	3

my.hrw.com

Online Extra Practice

Find the value of *x* in each diagram.

6. △*LMN* ~ △*RST*

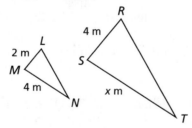

7. prism *A* ~ prism *B*

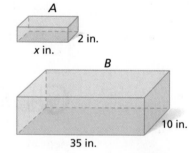

8. Write and solve a proportion to find the height of the taller tree in the diagram at right.

9. A triangle has side lengths of 5 inches, 12 inches, and 15 inches. Every dimension is multiplied by $\frac{1}{5}$ to form a new triangle. How is the ratio of the perimeters related to the ratio of corresponding sides?

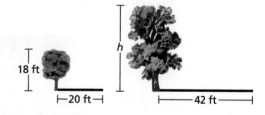

10. Hobbies For a baby shower gift, Heather crocheted a baby blanket whose length was $2\frac{1}{2}$ feet and whose width was 2 feet. She plans to crochet a proportionally larger similar blanket for the baby's mother. If she wants the length of the mother's blanket to be $6\frac{1}{4}$ feet, what should the width be? Show that your answer is reasonable.

11. **Real Estate** Refer to the home builder's advertisement. The family rooms in both models are rectangular. How much carpeting is needed to carpet the family room in the Weston model?

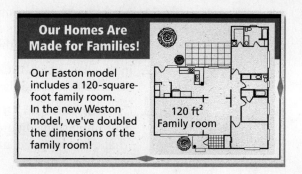

Our Homes Are Made for Families!

Our Easton model includes a 120-square-foot family room. In the new Weston model, we've doubled the dimensions of the family room!

120 ft² Family room

12. A rectangle has an area of 16 ft². Every dimension is multiplied by a scale factor, and the new rectangle has an area of 64 ft². What was the scale factor?

13. A cone has a volume of 98π cm³. Every dimension is multiplied by a scale factor, and the new cone has a volume of 6272π cm³. What was the scale factor?

Find the value of x in each diagram.

14. $FGHJK \sim MNPQR$

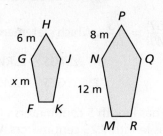

15. cylinder $A \sim$ cylinder B

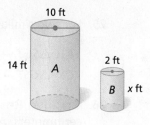

16. $\triangle BCD \sim \triangle FGD$

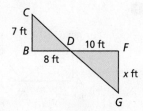

17. $\triangle RST \sim \triangle QSV$

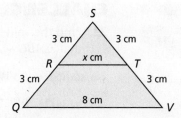

18. A tower casts a 450 ft shadow at the same time that a 4 ft child casts a 6 ft shadow. Write and solve a proportion to find the height of the tower.

H.O.T. 19. **Write About It** At Pizza Palace, a pizza with a diameter of 8 inches costs $6.00. The restaurant manager says that a 16-inch pizza should be priced at $12.00 because it is twice as large. Do you agree? Explain why or why not.

Real-World Connections

20. Another common application of proportion is *percents*. A percent is a ratio of a number to 100. For example, $80\% = \frac{80}{100}$.

   a. Write 12%, 18%, 25%, 67%, and 98% as ratios.

   b. Percents can also be written as decimals. Write each of your ratios from part **a** as a decimal.

   c. What do you notice about a percent and its decimal equivalent?

21. A lighthouse casts a shadow that is 36 meters long. At the same time, a person who is 1.5 meters tall casts a shadow that is 4.5 meters long. Write and solve a proportion to find the height of the lighthouse.

22. In the diagram, $\triangle ABC \sim \triangle DEC$. What is the distance across the river from A to B?

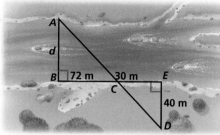

H.O.T. **23. Critical Thinking** If every dimension of a two-dimensional figure is multiplied by k, by what quantity is the area multiplied?

TEST PREP

24. A beach ball holds 800 cubic inches of air. Another beach ball has a radius that is half that of the larger ball. How much air does the smaller ball hold?

 Ⓐ 400 cubic inches   Ⓒ 100 cubic inches

 Ⓑ 200 cubic inches   Ⓓ 80 cubic inches

25. For two similar triangles, $\dfrac{SG}{MW} = \dfrac{GT}{WR} = \dfrac{TS}{RM}$. Which statement below is NOT correct?

 Ⓕ $\triangle SGT \sim \triangle MWR$ Ⓗ $\triangle TGS \sim \triangle RWM$

 Ⓖ $\triangle GST \sim \triangle MRW$ Ⓙ $\triangle GTS \sim \triangle WRM$

26. Gridded Response A rectangle has length 5 centimeters and width 3 centimeters. A similar rectangle has length 7.25 centimeters. What is the width in centimeters of this rectangle?

CHALLENGE AND EXTEND

27. Find the values of w, x, and y given that $\triangle ABC \sim \triangle DEF \sim \triangle GHJ$.

28. $\triangle RST \sim \triangle VWX$ and $\dfrac{RT}{VX} = b$.

 What is $\dfrac{\text{area of } \triangle RST}{\text{area of } \triangle VWX}$?

29. Multi-Step Rectangles A and B are similar. The area of A is 30.195 cm². The length of B is 6.1 cm. Each dimension of B is $\frac{2}{3}$ the corresponding dimension of A. What is the perimeter of B?

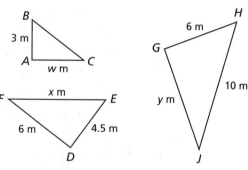

FOCUS ON MATHEMATICAL PRACTICES

H.O.T. **30. Modeling** It takes Padma 6 minutes to cut a length of timber into 3 pieces. How long would it take her to cut a length into 9 pieces? (*Hint:* Think about how many *cuts* it takes to cut the timber into 3 pieces or 9 pieces.)

H.O.T. **31. Problem Solving** You have a stack of $8\frac{1}{2}$ in. wide by 11 in. long sheets of paper, and start laying the sheets out as shown. The shape is the same number of sheets wide as it is long.

 a. When the shape is 68 in. wide, how long is it?

 b. When the area of the shape is 3366 in.², how many sheets are in it?

2-3 Precision and Accuracy

? Essential Question: How can you choose appropriate levels of precision and accuracy when solving problems?

Objectives
Analyze and compare measurements for precision and accuracy.

Choose an appropriate level of accuracy when reporting measurements.

Vocabulary
precision
accuracy
tolerance

Who uses this?
Chemists must understand precision and accuracy when weighing or mixing specific amounts of chemicals. (See Example 2.)

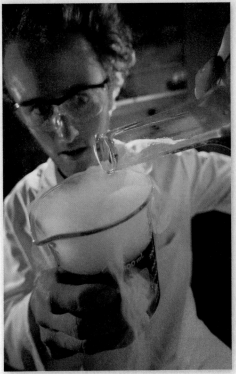

When you measure an object, you must use an instrument that will give an appropriate measurement. A scale to measure the mass of a person may show mass to the nearest kilogram. A scale to measure chemicals in a lab may show mass to the nearest milligram.

Precision is the level of detail in a measurement and is determined by the smallest unit or fraction of a unit that you can reasonably measure. Sometimes, the instrument determines the precision of a measurement. At other times, measurements are rounded to a specified precision.

A scale that shows the mass of an object to the nearest milligram is more precise than a scale that shows the mass of an object to the nearest kilogram, because a milligram is a smaller unit of measure than a kilogram. Likewise, a scale that shows the mass of an object as 24.23 grams is more precise than a scale that shows the mass of the same object as 24.2 grams.

COMMON CORE GPS MCC9-12.N.Q.3

EXAMPLE **1** **Comparing Precision of Measurements**

Choose the more precise measurement in each pair.

my.hrw.com

Online Video Tutor

A **3.4 kg; 3421 g**

3.4 kg   *Nearest tenth of a kilogram*

3421 g   *Nearest gram*

A gram is smaller than a tenth of a kilogram, so 3421 g is more precise.

B **3.4 cm; 3.43 cm**

3.4 cm   *Nearest tenth of a centimeter*

3.43 cm   *Nearest hundredth of a centimeter*

A hundredth of a centimeter is smaller than a tenth of a centimeter, so 3.43 cm is more precise.

C **3 ft; 36 in.**

3 ft   *Nearest foot*

36 in.   *Nearest inch*

An inch is smaller than a foot, so 36 in. is more precise.

© Kristy-Anne Glubish/Design Pics/Corbis

Choose the more precise measurement in each pair.

1a. 2 lb; 17 oz   **1b.** 7.85 m; 7.8 m   **1c.** 6 kg; 6000 g

A precise measurement is only useful if the measurement is also *accurate*. The **accuracy** of a measurement is the closeness of a measured value to the actual or true value. Two measurement tools may measure to the same precision, but not have the same accuracy. Similarly, using a more precise measuring instrument will not necessarily give a more accurate measurement.

EXAMPLE **2**

MCC9-12.N.Q.3

my.hrw.com

Online Video Tutor

Comparing Precision and Accuracy

Sam is a technician in a pharmaceutical lab. Each week, she must test the scales in the lab to make sure they are accurate. She uses a standard mass that is *exactly* 5.000 grams and gets the following results:

Scale 1   Scale 2   Scale 3

a. Which scale is the most precise?

Scales 1 and 3 measure to the nearest hundredth of a gram.

Scale 2 measures to the nearest thousandth of a gram.

Because a thousandth of a gram is smaller than a hundredth of a gram, Scale 2 is the most precise.

b. Which scale is the most accurate?

For each scale, find the absolute value of the difference of the standard mass and the scale reading.

Scale 1: $|5.000 - 5.01| = 0.01$
Scale 2: $|5.000 - 5.033| = 0.033$
Scale 3: $|5.000 - 4.98| = 0.02$

Because $0.01 < 0.02 < 0.033$, Scale 1 is the most accurate.

2. A standard mass of 16 ounces is used to test three postal scales. The results are shown below.

Scale A   Scale B   Scale C

a. Which scale is the most precise?

b. Which scale is the most accurate?

When you measure a group of objects that are expected to be similar, you may find that there are variations from the expected value. **Tolerance** describes the amount by which a measurement is permitted to vary from a specified value. Tolerance is often expressed as a range of values, such as 5 mm ± 0.3 mm, which is equivalent to 4.7 mm–5.3 mm.

EXAMPLE 3

Using a Specified Tolerance

Acme Nuts & Bolts is manufacturing a bolt to use in an airplane. The length of the bolt should be 50 mm, with a tolerance of 0.5 mm (50 mm ± 0.5 mm). A batch of bolts had the lengths shown in the table. Do all of the bolts measure within the specified tolerance? If not, which bolt(s) are not within the specified tolerance?

Bolt	Length (mm)
A	49.8
B	50.4
C	49.5
D	50.1
E	49.4
F	50.0

$50 - 0.5 = 49.5$ *50 mm ± 0.5 mm means that the*
$50 + 0.5 = 50.5$ *bolts must be between 49.5 and 50.5 mm.*

Bolt E measures 49.4 mm, so it is not within the specified tolerance.

 CHECK IT OUT!

3. A lacrosse ball must weigh 5.25 oz ± 0.25 oz. The weights of the lacrosse balls in one box are given in the table. Do all of the lacrosse balls weigh within the specified tolerance? If not, which lacrosse ball(s) are not within the specified tolerance?

Ball	Weight (oz)
A	5.41
B	5.23
C	5.54
D	5.33
E	5.21

Tolerance can also be expressed as a percent. A measurement written as 5 mm ± 5% means that the measurement can be greater or less than 5 mm by an amount equal to 5% of 5 mm, or 0.25 mm. Therefore, the measurement can have a range of 4.75 mm–5.25 mm.

EXAMPLE 4

Using Tolerance Expressed as a Percent

Write the possible range of each measurement. Round to the nearest hundredth if necessary.

A 50 kg ± 2%
$50(0.02) = 1$ *Find 2% of 50.*
50 kg ± 1 kg *Write the measurement and tolerance.*
49 kg–51 kg *Write the measurement as a range.*

B 125 lb ± 1.5%
$125(0.015) = 1.875$ *Find 1.5% of 125.*
125 lb ± 1.88 lb *Write the measurement and tolerance. Round to the nearest hundredth.*
123.12 lb–126.88 lb *Write the measurement as a range.*

C 45 mm ± 0.3%
$45(0.003) = 0.135$ *Find 0.3% of 45.*
45 mm ± 0.14 mm *Write the measurement and tolerance. Round to the nearest hundredth.*
44.86 mm–45.14 mm *Write the measurement as a range.*

 CHECK IT OUT! Write the possible range of each measurement. Round to the nearest hundredth if necessary.

4a. 4.1 in. ± 5%   **4b.** 475 m ± 2.5%   **4c.** 85 mg ± 0.5%

THINK AND DISCUSS

1. Explain the difference between precision and accuracy.

2. Describe a situation where the expected size of an object might be specified as 10 in. ± 0.5 in.

3. **GET ORGANIZED** Copy and complete the graphic organizer. In each box, write an example of when that characteristic of measurement would be important.

2-3 Exercises

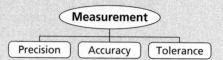

my.hrw.com
Homework Help

GUIDED PRACTICE

Vocabulary Apply the vocabulary from this lesson to answer each question.

1. A ruler that can measure length to a smaller unit than another ruler is said to be more _____?_____. (*precise* or *acurate*)

2. A scale that gives a mass closer to the true mass of an object than another scale of the exact same type is said to be more _____?_____. (*precise* or *accurate*)

SEE EXAMPLE 1

Choose the more precise measurement in each pair.

3. 4 mL; 4.3 mL   4. 7 m; 6.8 m   5. 2.4 mg; 2.37 mg
6. 7 lb; 6.5 lb   7. 47 ft; 47.3 ft   8. 14 oz; 13.9 oz

SEE EXAMPLE 2

9. Sarah is comparing five different scales using a standard mass that is exactly 10 grams. Her results are shown below.

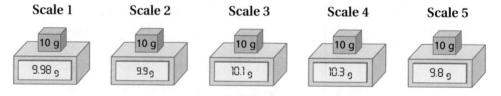

| Scale 1 | Scale 2 | Scale 3 | Scale 4 | Scale 5 |
| 9.98 g | 9.9 g | 10.1 g | 10.3 g | 9.8 g |

a. Which scale is the most precise?

b. Which scale is the most accurate?

10. A group of students compare the odometer readings on their bicycle computers after riding their bikes on a one-mile track. Their odometer readings are shown in the table. Whose odometer is the most precise? Whose is the most accurate?

Student	Distance (mi)
Jen	1.01
Bill	0.97
Rasheed	0.989
Sasha	1.02

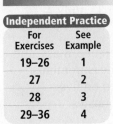

11. **Sports** A basketball for men's college games must have a mass of 595.5 ± 28.5 grams. Several basketballs are tested. Their masses are shown in the table. Do all of the basketballs fall within the specified tolerance? If not, which basketball(s) do not fall within the specified tolerance?

Basketball	1	2	3	4	5
Mass (g)	617.5	567.5	608	624.5	593.5

12. **Sports** A basketball for men's college games must bounce 51.5 ± 2.5 in. when dropped from a height of 6 feet. The bounce heights of several basketballs when dropped from a height of 6 feet are shown in the graph. Do all of the basketballs fall within the specified tolerance? If not, which basketball(s) do not have a bounce height within the specified tolerance?

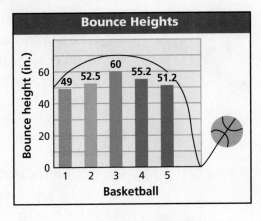

Bounce Heights

Write the possible range of each measurement. Round to the nearest hundredth if necessary.

13. 50 lb ± 2%

14. 100 yd ± 0.5%

15. 25 cm ± 4%

16. 400 L ± 6%

17. 250 mm ± 4%

18. 70 kg ± 3%

PRACTICE AND PROBLEM SOLVING

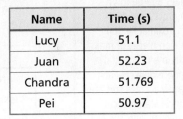

For Exercises	See Example
19–26	1
27	2
28	3
29–36	4

Choose the more precise measurement in each pair.

19. 4.33 g; 4337 mg

20. 11 ft; 122 in.

21. 6 tons; 11,000 lb

22. 3 c; 2 pt

23. 67 mm; 6.83 cm

24. 4.5 km; 3 mi

25. 12 cm; 0.0127 m

26. 7.23 lb; 115 oz

my.hrw.com

Online Extra Practice

27. Maria is trying to beat the school record for the 400-meter dash. Her friends timed her using the stopwatch functions in their cell phones. The official track timer, which is highly accurate, reported that she ran the race in 51.12 seconds. Her friends recorded the times shown in the table.

Name	Time (s)
Lucy	51.1
Juan	52.23
Chandra	51.769
Pei	50.97

a. Who recorded the most precise time?

b. Who recorded the most accurate time?

28. Anael cut several boards to build a deck. The boards must be 100 in. ± 0.25 in. Her measurements of the boards after cutting them are shown in the graph. Which boards, if any, can she not use?

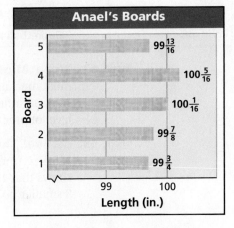

Anael's Boards

Write the possible range of each measurement. Round to the nearest hundredth if necessary.

29. 45 lb ± 2% **30.** 3 m ± 5% **31.** 37 °C ± 1.5% **32.** 750 kg ± 3%

33. 30 ft ± 4% **34.** 550 mL ± 8% **35.** 0.2 cm ± 5% **36.** 0.25 kg ± 10%

Round each measurement to the specified precision.

37. 5456.3 mi to the nearest mile

38. 3.627 m to the nearest hundredth of a meter

39. 119.8 ft to the nearest ten feet

40. 62.301 cg to the nearest tenth of a centigram

41. 5,721 mg to the nearest kilogram

42. 0.4586 km to the nearest meter

Choose the more precise measurement in each pair. If they are equally precise, write "neither."

43. 16.270 liters; 16,453.2 mL **44.** 437 cm; 437 mm **45.** 0.265 cm; 260 mm

46. 5.20 kg; 5200.0 mg **47.** 55 yd; 165 ft **48.** 67 min; 1.1 h

49. 33 mg; 0.033 g **50.** 42.7 cm; 427.0 mm **51.** 475.0 mL; 0.475 L

Rewrite each specified tolerance as a percent.

52. 100 m ± 2 m **53.** 50 g ± 2 g **54.** 240 ft ± 12 ft **55.** 750 kg ± 15 kg

56. 25 in. ± 0.25 in. **57.** 425 lb ± 8.5 lb **58.** 60 oz ± 1.5 oz **59.** 175 km ± 5.25 km

60. Technology Postcards that do not fit in the U.S. Postal Service's automatic sorting machines require additional postage for mailing. The machine will accept postcards whose length is between 5 and 6 inches and whose width is between $3\frac{1}{2}$ and $4\frac{1}{4}$ inches. Write these requirements as tolerances.

61. Sports For women's collegiate competition, a basketball's circumference, mass, and bounce height must fall within given tolerance levels of regulation measurements. The table shows these tolerance levels as well as measurements taken on five different basketballs. Which basketball meets all of the specified tolerances?

Technology

Automated equipment plays a large role in processing the approximately 584 million pieces of mail that the U.S. Postal Service delivers each day. Machines sort mail, cancel stamps, scan barcodes, and even "read" handwritten addresses.

Source: Postal Facts 2010, USPS

	Circumference (mm)	Mass (g)	Bounce Height (mm)
Tolerance	730.56 ± 6.5	538.5 ± 28.5	1358.5 ± 63.5
Basketball #1	729.8	509.3	1343.4
Basketball #2	723.5	529.8	1299.8
Basketball #3	734.2	542.6	1293.5
Basketball #4	725.5	528.0	1364.5
Basketball #5	740.0	555.9	1407.4

H.O.T. 62. Write About It Linda wants to purchase a new sofa. Before buying the sofa, Linda must measure her doorway to make sure that the sofa will fit through the door. The sofa manufacturer says that the sofa measures 39 inches from front to back. What level of precision would you recommend Linda measure to? Explain.

H.O.T. 63. Critical Thinking Yusuf measured a board and determined that it was 125.5 centimeters long. He then cut the board into eight equal pieces. His calculator shows that 125.5 ÷ 8 = 15.6875. Is it reasonable for Yusuf to record the length of the 8 smaller boards as 15.6875 centimeters? Explain why or why not.

64. The mass of a crystal is 0.9728 grams. What is the mass of the crystal to the nearest milligram?

- (A) 1 milligram
- (B) 9.73 milligrams
- (C) 973 milligrams
- (D) 972.8 milligrams

65. A piece used to assemble a computer must be 1.4 millimeters ± 0.02 millimeters in diameter. Which of the following measurements does NOT meet the specified tolerance?

- (F) 1.420 millimeters
- (G) 1.402 millimeters
- (H) 1.382 millimeters
- (J) 1.378 millimeters

66. Which measurement is most precise?

- (A) 475.3 milliliters
- (B) 475 milliliters
- (C) 0.475 liter
- (D) 0.5 liter

CHALLENGE AND EXTEND

Percent accuracy or *percent error* indicates how far a measurement is from the true value. An instrument that has 1.5% accuracy means that the measured value is within 1.5% of the true value.

67. A scale shows that a standard mass of exactly 5.000 grams has a mass of 5.002 grams. What is the percent accuracy of the scale?

68. A car odometer is accurate to within 0.5%. The odometer records the distance from Charlotte, North Carolina, to Orlando, Florida, as 525.3 miles. What is the range of possible values for the actual mileage?

69. Astronomy A scientist measures the distance to the moon using a method that has a percent error of 0.02%. He finds that the distance at a particular time is 384,403 kilometers. What is the range of possible values for the actual distance?

FOCUS ON MATHEMATICAL PRACTICES

H.O.T. **70. Problem Solving** An Internet sports site polled its readers with the question "Which team will win the division?" and posted the results. What is the smallest number of readers that could have picked Atlanta? Explain your answer.

Atlanta	33%
Tampa	29%
New Orleans	24%
Carolina	14%

3651 Responses

H.O.T. **71. Communication** Would you prefer to have an accurate room thermometer that is not very precise or a precise thermometer that is not very accurate? Explain.

H.O.T. **72. Error Analysis** Caleb uses the ruler shown to measure the length of a card. He says that the length is 3.1875 inches, so the measurement is precise to one ten-thousandth of an inch. Is he correct? Explain.

Ready to Go On?

my.hrw.com
Assessment and Intervention

2-1 Rates, Ratios, and Proportions

1. Last week, the ratio of laptops to desktops sold at a computer store was $2:3$. Eighteen desktop models were sold. How many laptop models were sold?

2. Anita read 150 pages in 5 hours. What is her reading rate in pages per minute?

3. Twenty-six crackers contain 156 Calories. Find the unit rate in Calories per cracker.

4. A store developed 1024 photographs in 8 hours. Find the unit rate in photographs per hour.

Solve each proportion.

5. $\dfrac{-18}{n} = \dfrac{9}{2}$

6. $\dfrac{d}{5} = \dfrac{2}{4}$

7. $\dfrac{4}{12} = \dfrac{r+2}{16}$

8. $\dfrac{-3}{7} = \dfrac{6}{x+6}$

2-2 Applications of Proportions

Find the value of n in each diagram.

9. $\triangle RST \sim \triangle XYZ$

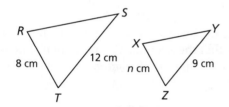

10. $ABCD \sim FGHJ$

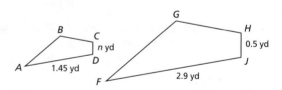

2-3 Precision and Accuracy

Choose the more precise measurement in each pair.

11. 2.5 ft; 2 ft

12. 1 yd; 3 ft

13. 5910 g; 5.9 kg

14. 16 oz; 16.0 oz

Write the possible range of each measurement. Round to the nearest hundredth if necessary.

15. $300 \text{ m} \pm 1\%$

16. $150 \text{ lb} \pm 6\%$

17. $60 \text{ L} \pm 0.5\%$

18. $220 \text{ kg} \pm 1.5\%$

PARCC Assessment Readiness

Selected Response

1. The fuel for a chain saw is a mix of oil and gasoline. The ratio of ounces of oil to gallons of gasoline is 7:19. There are 38 gallons of gasoline. How many ounces of oil are there?

- (A) 14 ounces
- (B) 20 ounces
- (C) 103.1 ounces
- (D) 3.5 ounces

2. A pipe is leaking at the rate of 8 fluid ounces per minute. Use dimensional analysis to find out how many gallons the pipe is leaking per hour.

- (F) 3,840 gal/h
- (G) 0.02 gal/h
- (H) 3.75 gal/h
- (J) 17.07 gal/h

3. Solve the proportion $\frac{5}{6} = \frac{x}{30}$.

- (A) $x = 0.03$
- (B) $x = 36$
- (C) $x = 26$
- (D) $x = 25$

4. Find the value of *MN* if *AB* = 21 cm, *BC* = 16.8 cm, and *LM* = 28 cm. *ABCD* ~ *LMNO*

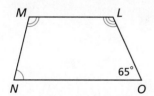
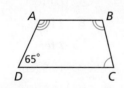

- (F) 23.8 cm
- (G) 22.4 cm
- (H) 12.6 cm
- (J) 22.8 cm

5. Complementary angles are two angles whose measures add to 90°. The ratio of the measures of two complementary angles is 4:11. What are the measures of the angles?

- (A) 24°, 66°
- (B) 26°, 64°
- (C) 51.4°, 38.6°
- (D) 24°, 114°

6. A weight that measures *exactly* 3.000 ounces is placed on three different balance scales. Scale 1 shows a weight of 3.03 ounces, scale 2 shows a weight of 2.99 ounces, and scale 3 shows a weight of 3.014 ounces. Which scale is the most precise? Which is the most accurate?

- (F) Scale 1 is the most precise.
  Scale 3 is the most accurate.
- (G) Scale 3 is the most precise.
  Scale 2 is the most accurate.
- (H) Scale 1 is the most precise.
  Scale 2 is the most accurate.
- (J) Scale 3 is the most precise.
  Scale 3 is the most accurate.

7. Round the measurement and underline the last significant digit.
254.8 liters to the nearest liter.

- (A) 25<u>4</u> liters
- (B) 2<u>6</u>0 liters
- (C) 25<u>5</u> liters
- (D) 2<u>5</u>0 liters

8. Write the possible range of the measurement to the nearest hundredth.
40 km ± 1%

- (F) 39.8 km—40.2 km
- (G) 39.99 km—40.01 km
- (H) 39 km—41 km
- (J) 39.6 km—40.4 km

Mini-Task

9. A recipe for a casserole calls for 2 cups of rice. The recipe makes 6 servings of casserole.

- **a.** How many cups of rice will you need to make 10 servings of casserole?

- **b.** If you have 5 cups of rice, how many servings can you make?

PARCC Assessment Readiness

COMMON CORE GPS

Selected Response

1. A clock loses 5 minutes every day. How much time will it lose in 2 hours?

   (A) 0.417 second

   (B) 25 seconds

   (C) 240 seconds

   (D) 600 seconds

2. A statue is 8 feet tall. The display case for a model of the statue is 18 inches tall. Which scale allows for the tallest model of the statue that will fit in the display case?

   (F) 1 inch : 2 inches

   (G) 1 inch : 7 inches

   (H) 1 inch : 5 inches

   (J) 1 inch : 10 inches

3. Mr. Phillips wants to install hardwood flooring in his den. The flooring costs \$25.86 per square yard. The blueprint below shows his house. What other information do you need in order to find the total cost of the flooring?

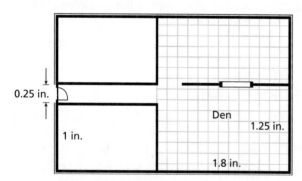

   (A) The lengths and widths of the adjoining rooms in the blueprint

   (B) The total area of the blueprint

   (C) The scale of inches in the blueprint to yards in the house

   (D) The width of the den

4. Which two phrases are equivalent to the expression $7t$?

   (F) the product of 7 and t; 7 multiplied by t

   (G) t subtracted from 7; t less than 7

   (H) t more than 7; t added to 7

   (J) the quotient of 7 and t; 7 divided by t

5. What is the solution of the equation $f - 10 = 10$?

   (A) $f = 20$

   (B) $f = -101$

   (C) $f = -20$

   (D) $f = 0$

6. On her math test, Suki was asked to round the measurement 718.4 meters to the nearest ten meters and underline the last significant digit. What should Suki write?

   (F) 72<u>9</u> meters

   (G) 7<u>2</u>0 meters

   (H) 7<u>1</u>0 meters

   (J) 72<u>8</u> meters

7. An architect built a scale model of a shopping mall. On the model, a circular fountain is 20 inches tall and 22.5 inches in diameter. The actual fountain is to be 8 feet tall. What will be the diameter of the fountain?

   (A) 7.1 feet

   (B) 9 feet

   (C) 7 feet

   (D) 10.5 feet

8. What is the solution of the equation $17a = 17$?

   (F) $a = 1$

   (G) $a = 17$

   (H) $a = -17$

   (J) $a = -1$

9. Ramon drives his car 150 miles in 3 hours. What is the unit rate?

Ⓐ 1 mile per 50 hours

Ⓑ 50 miles per hour

Ⓒ 30 miles per hour

Ⓓ 150 miles per 3 hours

10. Which is the most precise measurement?

Ⓕ $14\frac{3}{4}$ ft

Ⓖ 23 in.

Ⓗ 4 ft

Ⓙ $2\frac{11}{16}$ in.

11. What is the solution of $3n = 42$?

Ⓐ $n = 45$

Ⓑ $n = 39$

Ⓒ $n = 14$

Ⓓ $n = 15$

12. Which range of measurements is equivalent to 25 km ± 5%?

Ⓕ 24.95 km − 25.05 km

Ⓖ 23.75 km − 26.25 km

Ⓗ 24.38 km − 25.63 km

Ⓙ 20 km − 30 km

13. Isabel reads 15 books from the library each month for y months in a row. Which expression shows how many books Isabel read in all?

Ⓐ $15 + y$

Ⓑ $15 - y$

Ⓒ $15y$

Ⓓ $\frac{15}{y}$

14. If $8y = 32$, what is the value of $2y$?

Ⓕ 2

Ⓖ 8

Ⓗ 11

Ⓙ 24

15. What is the value of the expression $m + o$ when $m = 9$ and $o = 7$?

Ⓐ 15

Ⓑ 63

Ⓒ 2

Ⓓ 16

If you are stuck on a problem, skip it and come back later. Another problem might remind you of something that will help. If you feel yourself become tense, take a few deep breaths to relax.

16. Melissa invested her savings in a retirement account that pays simple interest. A portion of her account record is shown below. What is the interest rate on Melissa's account?

Date	Transaction	Amount	Balance
8/1	Beginning deposit	$6000.00	$6000.00
8/31	Interest payment	$192.00	$6192.00
9/1	Withdrawal	$1000.00	$5192.00
9/30	Interest payment	$166.14	$5358.14

Ⓕ 0.31%   Ⓗ 3.1%

Ⓖ 0.32%   Ⓙ 3.2%

17. At 2:45 P.M. you are 112 miles from Dallas. You want to be in Dallas at 4:30 P.M. What is the average speed you must travel to be on time?

Ⓐ 49.8 mi/h

Ⓑ 51 mi/h

Ⓒ 64 mi/h

Ⓓ 89.6 mi/h

18. A cyclist travels 45 miles in 4 hours. What is her speed in feet per second?

Ⓕ 16.5 ft/s

Ⓖ 31 ft/s

Ⓗ 66 ft/s

Ⓙ 59,400 ft/s

19. Julie's total cell phone bill consists of a monthly fee plus a charge per minute used. The expression that describes the total of Julie's cell phone bill is $0.07x + 29.99$. What does the variable x represent?

Ⓐ The number of months billed

Ⓑ The total amount of the bill

Ⓒ The number of minutes used

Ⓓ The monthly fee

20. In a test, a hybrid car drove 619 yards on 1 ounce of gasoline. To the nearest tenth, what is this rate in miles per gallon?

Ⓕ 7.5 miles/gallon

Ⓖ 15.0 miles/gallon

Ⓗ 22.5 miles/gallon

Ⓙ 45.0 miles/gallon

21. Which equation has the solution $x = -3$?

Ⓐ $2x = 6$

Ⓑ $-9 = -3x$

Ⓒ $-6 = 2x$

Ⓓ $-18x = 6$

22. In a scale model, a monument is 4.5 inches tall and 2.5 inches wide. The actual monument is 60 feet wide. How tall is the actual monument?

Ⓕ $33\frac{1}{3}$ feet

Ⓖ 90 feet

Ⓗ 108 feet

Ⓙ $112\frac{1}{2}$ feet

23. A consultant charges for her services based on the number of hours worked. The expression that gives the total cost for h hours is $125h + 150$. Which is the best interpretation of this expression?

Ⓐ The consultant charges $150 per hour plus a fee of $125.

Ⓑ The consultant charges $125 per hour plus a fee of $150.

Ⓒ The consultant charges $275 per hour.

Ⓓ The consultant's hourly charge varies from $125 to $150.

24. A rectangle has a length of 8 meters and a width of 3 meters. A larger, similar rectangle has a length of 22 meters. What is the width of the larger rectangle?

Ⓕ 58.67 meters   Ⓗ 8.25 meters

Ⓖ 17 meters   Ⓙ 9 meters

Mini-Tasks

25. Triangles C and D are similar. The area of triangle C is 47.6 in^2. The base of triangle D is 6.72 in. Each dimension of D is $\frac{6}{5}$ the corresponding dimension of C. What is the height of D?

26. A company sells furniture for home assembly. Their largest bookcase has shelves that should be 115 cm, with a tolerance of 0.6 cm. A set of six shelves had lengths of 115.2 cm, 114.9 cm, 115.0 cm, 114.3 cm, 114.7 cm, and 115.7 cm. Which, if any, of the shelves are not within the specified tolerance?

27. A toy company's total payment for salaries for the first two months of 2011 was $21,894.

  a. The total salaries for the first month of 2011 were $10,205. Write an equation to find the total salaries for the second month.

  b. What were the total salaries for the second month?

28. A plane is cruising at an altitude of 24,000 feet. It begins to descend at a constant rate of 20 feet per second.

  a. Write an expression for the altitude of the plane after t seconds.

  b. What is the altitude of the plane after 5 min?

29. Juan scored 26 points in the first half of the basketball game, and he scored n points in the second half of the game.

  a. Write an expression to determine the number of points he scored in all.

  b. Juan scored 44 points in all. Find the number of points he scored in the second half of the game.

30. On a sunny day, a 5-foot red kangaroo casts a shadow that is 7 feet long. The shadow of a nearby eucalyptus tree is 35 feet long.

  a. Write a proportion to determine the height of the tree.

  b. What is the height of the tree?

31. A right triangle has legs 15 inches and 12 inches. Every dimension is multiplied by $\frac{1}{3}$ to form a new right triangle with legs 5 inches and 4 inches. How is the ratio of the areas of the two triangles related to the ratio of corresponding sides?

32. Let *p* represent the price of a pair of jeans. Miles has a coupon for $10 off each pair of jeans that he buys.

  a. Use the variable *p* to write an expression for Miles's cost of a pair of a jeans with his coupon.

  b. Miles decides to buy 4 identical pairs of jeans. Write an expression for the total cost.

  c. Miles also buys a pair of socks for $5. Write an expression for Miles's total cost.

33. One day, the exchange rate was 60 U.S. dollars for 50 euro. At this rate, about how many U.S. dollars would be equivalent to 70 euro?

34. A map has the scale 1 inch:10 miles. On this map, the area of a national park is about 12.5 square inches. What is the approximate area of the park in acres? (1 square mile = 640 acres)

35. The table shows the typing rates of four applicants for a typing job.

Applicant	Words	Minute
Ann	112	6
Theo	206	8
June	195	7
Andy	120	5

  a. Based on typing rates, which applicant is the best choice to hire?

  b. What other information besides typing rate might you want to consider when choosing an applicant?

36. A polygon has an area of 3 square feet. What is the area of the polygon in square inches?

37. In the 2004 Olympics, the ratio of gold medals to silver medals won by the team from Hungary was 4:3. The ratio of silver medals to bronze medals won by the team was 2:1. The team won 3 bronze medals. How many gold medals did they win?

Performance Tasks

38. Luke is buying food for a neighborhood block party. He has $139 to spend, and he has already spent $121. He wants to buy some bags of hamburger buns that cost $4 each.

  a. How much money does Luke have left to spend?

  b. Define a variable or variables needed to model this situation.

  c. Using the number you found in part **a** and the variable(s) defined in part **b**, write an equation to find the number of bags of hamburger buns Luke can buy.

  d. Luke wants to buy 6 bags of hamburger buns. Does he have enough money? Explain how you found your answer.

39. Suppose a report indicates that the surveyed distance between two points is 1200 feet.

  a. If this is all of the information given about the surveyed distance, what might a reader think the measurement error is? Why?

  b. The error in the measurement is actually ± 0.1 feet. Explain how the distance might have been reported in a way that better indicates the true accuracy of the measurement.

40. To build an accurate scale model of the solar system, choose a diameter for the model of the Sun. Then other distances and sizes can be calculated proportionally.

	Sun	Mars	Pluto
Diameter (mi)	865,000	4,200	1,500
Distance from Sun (million mi)	—	141	3,670

  a. Sara wants to draw a scale model of the solar system in which the diameter of the Sun is 1 inch. What should the diameter of Pluto be?

  b. Do you think it is reasonable for Sara to draw this model? Why or why not?

my.hrw.com
Online Assessment
Go online for updated, PARCC-aligned assessment readiness.

Are You Ready?

my.hrw.com
Assessment and Intervention

 **Vocabulary**

Match each term on the left with a definition on the right.

1. equation
2. evaluate
3. inverse operations
4. like terms
5. solution of an equation

A. mathematical phrase that contains operations, numbers, and/or variables

B. mathematical statement that two expressions are equivalent

C. value of a variable that makes a statement true

D. terms that contain the same variables raised to the same powers

E. to find the value of an expression

F. operations that undo each other

 **Evaluate Expressions**

Evaluate each expression for $a = 2$ and $b = 6$.

6. $b - a$
7. ab
8. $b \div a$
9. $a + b$

 **Compare and Order Real Numbers**

Compare. Write $<$, $>$, or $=$.

10. $10 \;\rule{1em}{0.6em}\; 21$
11. $5.27 \;\rule{1em}{0.6em}\; 5.23$
12. $20\% \;\rule{1em}{0.6em}\; 0.2$
13. $\dfrac{1}{3} \;\rule{1em}{0.6em}\; \dfrac{2}{5}$

Combine Like Terms

Simplify each expression by combining like terms.

14. $6x + x$
15. $-8a + 3a$
16. $9x^2 - 15x^2$
17. $2.1x + 4.3x$

Distributive Property

Simplify each expression.

18. $2(x + 3)$
19. $(3 - d)5$
20. $4(r - 1)$
21. $3(4 + m)$

Career Readiness Small Business Owners

Owners of small businesses need to have knowledge of many aspects of business, including expenses, income, taxes, licenses, and fees. They must be able to predict how their business will perform. Small business owners can use systems of equations to predict sales necessary to break even or make a profit. Preparation for starting a small business should include a business math class and a study of laws governing hiring, record keeping, and accounting.

Reasoning with Equations and Inequalities

Online Edition

my.hrw.com

Access the complete online textbook, interactive features, and additional resources.

Online Video Tutor

Watch full explanations of every example in the textbook with these online videos.

Animated Math

Interactively explore key concepts with these online tutorials.

Portable Devices

eTextbook

Access your full textbook on your tablet or e-reader.

HMH Fuse

Make your learning experience completely portable and interactive with this app for iPad®.

Chapter Resources

Scan with your smart phone to jump directly to the online edition.

COMMON CORE GPS Unit Contents

Module 3 Solving Equations in One Variable

MCC9-12.A.CED.1, MCC9-12.A.CED.4, MCC9-12.A.REI.1, MCC9-12.A.REI.3

Module 4 Solving Inequalities in One Variable

MCC9-12.A.CED.1, MCC9-12.A.CED.3, MCC9-12.A.REI.3

Module 5 Solving Multi-Step Inequalities

MCC9-12.A.CED.1, MCC9-12.A.CED.3, MCC9-12.A.REI.3

Module 6 Solving Systems of Equations

MCC9-12.A.CED.1, MCC9-12.A.REI.5, MCC9-12.A.REI.6, MCC9-12.A.REI.11

Module 7 Special Systems and Systems of Inequalities

MCC9-12.A.CED.1, MCC9-12.A.CED.3, MCC9-12.A.REI.6, MCC9-12.A.REI.12

Homework Help provides video tutorials, step-by-step solutions, and additional practice for lesson exercises.

Solving Equations in One Variable

COMMON
CORE GPS

Contents

MATHEMATICAL
PRACTICES
The Common Core Georgia Performance Standards for Mathematical Practice describe varieties of expertise that all students should seek to develop. Opportunities to develop these practices are integrated throughout this program.

1 Make sense of problems and persevere in solving them.

2 Reason abstractly and quantitatively.

3 Construct viable arguments and critique the reasoning of others.

4 Model with mathematics.

5 Use appropriate tools strategically.

6 Attend to precision.

7 Look for and make use of structure.

8 Look for and express regularity in repeated reasoning.

Unpacking the Standards

Understanding the standards and the vocabulary terms in the standards will help you know exactly what you are expected to learn in this chapter.

 MCC9-12.A.CED.1

Create equations … in one variable and use them to solve problems.

Key Vocabulary

equation (ecuación)
A mathematical statement that two expressions are equivalent.
variable (variable)
A symbol used to represent a quantity that can change.

What It Means For You

You can write an equation to represent a real-world problem and then use algebra to solve the equation and find the answer.

EXAMPLE

Michael is saving money to buy a trumpet. The trumpet costs $670. He has $350 saved, and each week he adds $20 to his savings. How long will it take him to save enough money to buy the trumpet?

Let w represent the number of weeks.

cost of trumpet	=	current savings	+	additional savings
670	=	350	+	$20w$
320	=	$20w$		
16	=	w		

It will take Michael 16 weeks to save enough money.

 MCC9-12.A.REI.3

Solve linear equations … in one variable, including equations with coefficients represented by letters.

Key Vocabulary

linear equation in one variable
(ecuación lineal en una variable)
An equation that can be written in the form $ax = b$ where a and b are constants and $a \neq 0$.
coefficient (coeficiente) A number that is multiplied by a variable.
solution of an equation in one variable (solución de una ecuación en una variable) A value or values that make the equation true.

What It Means For You

You solve equations by finding the value of the variable that makes both sides equal.

EXAMPLE

The Fahrenheit temperature that corresponds to 35°C is the solution of the equation $35 = \frac{5}{9}(F - 32)$.

F	70	75	80	85	90	95
$\frac{5}{9}(F-32)$	21.1	23.9	26.7	29.4	32.2	35

When it is 35°C, it is 95°F.

Equation is true.

3-1 Solving Two-Step and Multi-Step Equations

Essential Question: How can you solve equations that involve more than one operation?

Objective
Solve equations in one variable that contain more than one operation.

Why learn this?
Equations containing more than one operation can model real-world situations, such as the cost of a music club membership.

Alex belongs to a music club. In this club, students can buy a student discount card for $19.95. This card allows them to buy CDs for $3.95 each. After one year, Alex has spent $63.40.

To find the number of CDs c that Alex bought, you can solve an equation.

Cost of discount card
↓
Cost per CD → $3.95c + 19.95 = 63.40$ ← Total cost

Notice that this equation contains multiplication and addition. Equations that contain more than one operation require more than one step to solve. Identify the operations in the equation and the order in which they are applied to the variable. Then use inverse operations and work backward to undo them one at a time.

$$3.95c + 19.95 = 63.40$$

Operations in the Equation	To Solve
❶ First c is multiplied by 3.95.	❶ Subtract 19.95 from both sides of the equation.
❷ Then 19.95 is added.	❷ Then divide both sides by 3.95.

Work Backward

COMMON CORE GPS MCC9-12.A.REI.3

EXAMPLE 1 Solving Two-Step Equations

my.hrw.com

Online Video Tutor

Solve $10 = 6 - 2x$. Check your answer.

$$\begin{array}{ll} 10 = 6 - 2x & \text{First x is multiplied by } -2. \text{ Then 6 is added.} \\ \underline{-6 \quad -6} & \text{Work backward: Subtract 6 from both sides.} \\ 4 = \quad -2x & \text{Since x is multiplied by } -2, \text{ divide both sides} \\ \dfrac{4}{-2} = \dfrac{-2x}{-2} & \quad \text{by } -2 \text{ to undo the multiplication.} \\ -2 = 1x \\ -2 = x \end{array}$$

Check
$$10 = 6 - 2x$$

10	$6 - 2(-2)$
10	$6 - (-4)$
10	$10 ✓$

 Solve each equation. Check your answer.

1a. $-4 + 7x = 3$ **1b.** $1.5 = 1.2y - 5.7$ **1c.** $\dfrac{n}{7} + 2 = 2$

EXAMPLE **2**

MCC9-12.A.REI.3

Solving Two-Step Equations That Contain Fractions

Solve $\dfrac{q}{15} - \dfrac{1}{5} = \dfrac{3}{5}$.

Method 1 Use fraction operations.

$$\dfrac{q}{15} - \dfrac{1}{5} = \dfrac{3}{5}$$

Since $\frac{1}{5}$ is subtracted from $\frac{q}{15}$, add $\frac{1}{5}$ to both sides to undo the subtraction.

$$\dfrac{+\dfrac{1}{5} \quad +\dfrac{1}{5}}{\dfrac{q}{15} \quad = \quad \dfrac{4}{5}}$$

Since q is divided by 15, multiply both sides by 15 to undo the division.

$$15\left(\dfrac{q}{15}\right) = 15\left(\dfrac{4}{5}\right)$$

$$q = \dfrac{15 \cdot 4}{5}$$ *Simplify.*

$$q = \dfrac{60}{5}$$

$$q = 12$$

Method 2 Multiply by the least common denominator (LCD) to clear the fractions.

$$\dfrac{q}{15} - \dfrac{1}{5} = \dfrac{3}{5}$$

$$15\left(\dfrac{q}{15} - \dfrac{1}{5}\right) = 15\left(\dfrac{3}{5}\right)$$

Multiply both sides by 15, the LCD of the fractions.

$$15\left(\dfrac{q}{15}\right) - 15\left(\dfrac{1}{5}\right) = 15\left(\dfrac{3}{5}\right)$$

Distribute 15 on the left side.

$$q - 3 = 9$$ *Simplify.*

$$\dfrac{+3 \quad +3}{q \quad = 12}$$

Since 3 is subtracted from q, add 3 to both sides to undo the subtraction.

 Solve each equation. Check your answer.

2a. $\dfrac{2x}{5} - \dfrac{1}{2} = 5$ **2b.** $\dfrac{3}{4}u + \dfrac{1}{2} = \dfrac{7}{8}$ **2c.** $\dfrac{1}{5}n - \dfrac{1}{3} = \dfrac{8}{3}$

Equations that are more complicated may have to be simplified before they can be solved. You may have to use the Distributive Property or combine like terms before you begin using inverse operations.

EXAMPLE **3**

MCC9-12.A.REI.3

Simplifying Before Solving Equations

Solve each equation.

A $6x + 3 - 8x = 13$

$$6x + 3 - 8x = 13$$

$$6x - 8x + 3 = 13$$ *Use the Commutative Property of Addition.*

$$-2x + 3 = 13$$ *Combine like terms.*

$$\dfrac{-3 \quad -3}{}$$ *Since 3 is added to $-2x$, subtract 3 from both sides to undo the addition.*

$$-2x = 10$$

$$\dfrac{-2x}{-2} = \dfrac{10}{-2}$$ *Since x is multiplied by -2, divide both sides by -2 to undo the multiplication.*

$$x = -5$$

Solve each equation.

B $9 = 6 - (x + 2)$

$9 = 6 + (-1)(x + 2)$ *Write subtraction as addition of the opposite.*

$9 = 6 + (-1)(x) + (-1)(2)$ *Distribute −1 on the right side.*

Simplify.

$9 = 6 - x - 2$

Use the Commutative Property of Addition.

$9 = 6 - 2 - x$ *Combine like terms.*

$9 = \quad 4 - x$

$\underline{-4 \quad -4}$ *Since 4 is added to −x, subtract 4 from both sides to undo the addition.*

$5 = \quad -x$

$\dfrac{5}{-1} = \dfrac{-x}{-1}$ *Since x is multiplied by −1, divide both sides by −1 to undo the multiplication.*

$-5 = x$

Solve each equation. Check your answer.

3a. $2a + 3 - 8a = 8$

3b. $-2(3 - d) = 4$

3c. $4(x - 2) + 2x = 40$

4 *Problem-Solving Application*

Alex belongs to a music club. In this club, students can buy a student discount card for $19.95. This card allows them to buy CDs for $3.95 each. After one year, Alex has spent $63.40. Write and solve an equation to find how many CDs Alex bought during the year.

1   **Understand the Problem**

The **answer** will be the number of CDs that Alex bought during the year.

List the important information:

- Alex paid $19.95 for a student discount card.
- Alex pays $3.95 for each CD purchased.
- After one year, Alex has spent $63.40.

2   **Make a Plan**

Let c represent the number of CDs that Alex purchased. That means Alex has spent $3.95c$. However, Alex must also add the amount spent on the card. Write an equation to represent this situation.

total cost	=	cost of compact discs	+	cost of discount card
63.40	=	3.95c	+	19.95

Helpful Hint

You can think of an opposite sign as a coefficient of −1.
$-(x + 2) = -1(x + 2)$ and $-x = -1x$.

Solve

$$63.40 = 3.95c + 19.95$$
$$\underline{-\,19.95 \qquad\quad -\,19.95}$$
$$43.45 = 3.95c$$
$$\frac{43.45}{3.95} = \frac{3.95c}{3.95}$$
$$11 = c$$

Since 19.95 is added to 3.95c, subtract 19.95 from both sides to undo the addition.

Since c is multiplied by 3.95, divide both sides by 3.95 to undo the multiplication.

Alex bought 11 CDs during the year.

 Look Back

Check that the answer is reasonable. The cost per CD is about $4, so if Alex bought 11 CDs, this amount is about $11(4) = \$44$.

Add the cost of the discount card, which is about $20: $44 + 20 = 64$. So the total cost was about $64, which is close to the amount given in the problem, $63.40.

 4. Sara paid $15.95 to become a member at a gym. She then paid a monthly membership fee. Her total cost for 12 months was $735.95. How much was the monthly fee?

EXAMPLE 5
MCC9-12.A.REI.3

Solving Equations to Find an Indicated Value

If $3a + 12 = 30$, find the value of $a + 4$.

Step 1 Find the value of a.

$$3a + 12 = 30$$
$$\underline{-\,12 \quad -\,12}$$
$$3a \quad\;\; = 18$$
$$\frac{3a}{3} = \frac{18}{3}$$
$$a = 6$$

Since 12 is added to 3a, subtract 12 from both sides to undo the addition.

Since a is multiplied by 3, divide both sides by 3 to undo the multiplication.

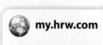 **my.hrw.com**

Online Video Tutor

Step 2 Find the value of $a + 4$.

$$a + 4$$
$$6 + 4$$
$$10$$

To find the value of a + 4, substitute 6 for a.
Simplify.

 5. If $2x + 4 = -24$, find the value of $3x$.

MCC.MP.3 | MATHEMATICAL PRACTICES

THINK AND DISCUSS

1. Explain the steps you would follow to solve $2x + 1 = 7$. How is this procedure different from the one you would follow to solve $2x - 1 = 7$?

2. GET ORGANIZED Copy and complete the graphic organizer. In each box, write and solve a multi-step equation. Use addition, subtraction, multiplication, and division at least one time each.

Solving Multi-Step Equations	

GUIDED PRACTICE

Solve each equation. Check your answer.

SEE EXAMPLE 1
1. $4a + 3 = 11$ **2.** $8 = 3r - 1$ **3.** $42 = -2d + 6$

4. $x + 0.3 = 3.3$ **5.** $15y + 31 = 61$ **6.** $9 - c = -13$

SEE EXAMPLE 2
7. $\frac{x}{6} + 4 = 15$ **8.** $\frac{1}{3}y + \frac{1}{4} = \frac{5}{12}$ **9.** $\frac{2}{7}j - \frac{1}{7} = \frac{3}{14}$

10. $15 = \frac{a}{3} - 2$ **11.** $4 - \frac{m}{2} = 10$ **12.** $\frac{x}{8} - \frac{1}{2} = 6$

SEE EXAMPLE 3
13. $28 = 8x + 12 - 7x$ **14.** $2y - 7 + 5y = 0$ **15.** $2.4 = 3(m + 4)$

16. $3(x - 4) = 48$ **17.** $4t + 7 - t = 19$ **18.** $5(1 - 2w) + 8w = 15$

SEE EXAMPLE 4
19. **Transportation** Paul bought a student discount card for the bus. The card cost $7 and allows him to buy daily bus passes for $1.50. After one month, Paul spent $29.50. How many daily bus passes did Paul buy?

SEE EXAMPLE 5
20. If $3x - 13 = 8$, find the value of $x - 4$.   **21.** If $3(x + 1) = 7$, find the value of $3x$.

22. If $-3(y - 1) = 9$, find the value of $\frac{1}{2}y$.   **23.** If $4 - 7x = 39$, find the value of $x + 1$.

PRACTICE AND PROBLEM SOLVING

Solve each equation. Check your answer.

For Exercises	See Example
24–29	1
30–35	2
36–41	3
42	4
43–46	5

Independent Practice

my.hrw.com

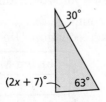

Online Extra Practice

24. $5 = 2g + 1$ **25.** $6h - 7 = 17$ **26.** $0.6v + 2.1 = 4.5$

27. $3x + 3 = 18$ **28.** $0.6g + 11 = 5$ **29.** $32 = 5 - 3t$

30. $2d + \frac{1}{5} = \frac{3}{5}$ **31.** $1 = 2x + \frac{1}{2}$ **32.** $\frac{z}{2} + 1 = \frac{3}{2}$

33. $\frac{2}{3} = \frac{4j}{6}$ **34.** $\frac{3}{4} = \frac{3}{8}x - \frac{3}{2}$ **35.** $\frac{1}{5} - \frac{x}{5} = -\frac{2}{5}$

36. $6 = -2(7 - c)$ **37.** $5(h - 4) = 8$ **38.** $-3x - 8 + 4x = 17$

39. $4x + 6x = 30$ **40.** $2(x + 3) = 10$ **41.** $17 = 3(p - 5) + 8$

42. **Consumer Economics** Jennifer is saving money to buy a bike. The bike costs $245. She has $125 saved, and each week she adds $15 to her savings. How long will it take her to save enough money to buy the bike?

43. If $2x + 13 = 17$, find the value of $3x + 1$. **44.** If $-(x - 1) = 5$, find the value of $-4x$.

45. If $5(y + 10) = 40$, find the value of $\frac{1}{4}y$.   **46.** If $9 - 6x = 45$, find the value of $x - 4$.

Geometry Write and solve an equation to find the value of x for each triangle.
(*Hint:* The sum of the angle measures in any triangle is 180°.)

47.   **48.**   **49.**

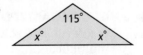

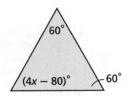

Write an equation to represent each relationship. Solve each equation.

50. Seven less than twice a number equals 19.

51. Eight decreased by 3 times a number equals 2.

52. The sum of two times a number and 5 is 11.

History

Martin Luther King Jr. entered college at age 15. During his life he earned 3 degrees and was awarded 20 honorary degrees.
Source: lib.lsu.edu

53. **History** In 1963, Dr. Martin Luther King Jr. began his famous "I have a dream" speech with the words "Five score years ago, a great American, in whose symbolic shadow we stand, signed the Emancipation Proclamation." The proclamation was signed by President Abraham Lincoln in 1863.

   a. Using the dates given, write and solve an equation that can be used to find the number of years in a score.

   b. How many score would represent 60?

Solve each equation. Check your answer.

54. $3t + 44 = 50$

55. $3(x - 2) = 18$

56. $15 = \dfrac{c}{3} - 2$

57. $2x + 6.5 = 15.5$

58. $3.9w - 17.9 = -2.3$

59. $17 = x - 3(x + 1)$

60. $5x + 9 = 39$

61. $15 + 5.5m = 70$

Biology Use the graph for Exercises 62 and 63.

62. The height of an ostrich is 20 inches more than 4 times the height of a kiwi. Write and solve an equation to find the height of a kiwi. Show that your answer is reasonable.

63. Five times the height of a kakapo minus 70 equals the height of an emu. Write and solve an equation to find the height of a kakapo. Show that your answer is reasonable.

64. The sum of two consecutive whole numbers is 57. What are the two numbers? (*Hint:* Let n represent the first number. Then $n + 1$ is the next consecutive whole number.)

65. Stan's, Mark's, and Wayne's ages are consecutive whole numbers. Stan is the youngest, and Wayne is the oldest. The sum of their ages is 111. Find their ages.

66. The sum of two consecutive even whole numbers is 206. What are the two numbers? (*Hint:* Let n represent the first number. What expression can you use to represent the second number?)

Largest Flightless Birds

Height (in.): Ostrich 108, Emu 60, Cassowary 60, Rhea 54, Emperor penguin 45

Source: The Top Ten of Everything

Real-World Connections

67. **a.** The cost of fighting a certain forest fire is $225 per acre. Complete the table.

   b. Write an equation for the relationship between the cost c of fighting the fire and the number of acres n.

Cost of Fighting Fire	
Acres	**Cost ($)**
100	22,500
200	▇
500	▇
1000	▇
1500	▇
n	▇

68. Critical Thinking The equation $2(m - 8) + 3 = 17$ has more than one solution method. Give at least two different "first steps" to solve this equation.

69. Write About It Write a series of steps that you can use to solve any multi-step equation.

TEST PREP

70. Lin sold 4 more shirts than Greg. Fran sold 3 times as many shirts as Lin. In total, the three sold 51 shirts. Which represents the number of shirts Greg sold?

    Ⓐ $3g = 51$ Ⓑ $3 + g = 51$ Ⓒ $8 + 5g = 51$ Ⓓ $16 + 5g = 51$

71. If $\frac{4m - 3}{7} = 3$, what is the value of $7m - 5$?

    Ⓕ 6   Ⓖ 10.5   Ⓗ 37   Ⓙ 68.5

72. The equation $c = 48 + 0.06m$ represents the cost c of renting a car and driving m miles. Which statement best describes this cost?

    Ⓐ The cost is a flat rate of $0.06 per mile.

    Ⓑ The cost is $0.48 for the first mile and $0.06 for each additional mile.

    Ⓒ The cost is a $48 fee plus $0.06 per mile.

    Ⓓ The cost is a $6 fee plus $0.48 per mile.

73. Gridded Response A telemarketer earns $150 a week plus $2 for each call that results in a sale. Last week she earned a total of $204. How many of her calls resulted in sales?

CHALLENGE AND EXTEND

Solve each equation. Check your answer.

74. $\frac{9}{2}x + 18 + 3x = \frac{11}{2}$ **75.** $\frac{15}{4}x - 15 = \frac{33}{4}$

76. $(x + 6) - (2x + 7) - 3x = -9$ **77.** $(4x + 2) - (12x + 8) + 2(5x - 3) = 6 + 11$

78. Find a value for b so that the solution of $4x + 3b = -1$ is $x = 2$.

79. Find a value for b so that the solution of $2x - 3b = 0$ is $x = -9$.

H.O.T. **80. Business** The formula $p = nc - e$ gives the profit p when a number of items n are each sold at a cost c and expenses e are subtracted.

    a. If $p = 2500$, $n = 2000$, and $e = 800$, what is the value of c?

    b. If $p = 2500$, $n = 1000$, and $e = 800$, what is the value of c?

    c. What if...? If n is divided in half while p and e remain the same, what is the effect on c?

FOCUS ON MATHEMATICAL PRACTICES

H.O.T. **81. Problem Solving** The temperature inside Earth increases as you get closer to its molten core. The temperature increases by about 25 °C for every kilometer you go below the surface. If the surface temperature is 19 °C and the temperature inside a mine is 64 °C, what is the depth of the mine?

H.O.T. **82. Analysis** Solve $2x + b = c$ and $2(x + b) = c$ for x. Explain why the solution to the first equation will be greater than the solution to the second equation when $b > 0$.

3-2

Algebra TASK

Model Equations with Variables on Both Sides

Algebra tile models can help you understand how to solve equations with variables on both sides.

Use with Solving Equations with Variables on Both Sides

 MATHEMATICAL PRACTICES

Use appropriate tools strategically.

MCC9-12.A.REI.1 Explain each step in solving a simple equation as following from the equality of numbers asserted at the previous step, starting from the assumption that the original equation has a solution. Construct a viable argument to justify a solution method. *Also* **MCC9-12.A.REI.3**

KEY

$\boxed{+} = 1$

$\boxed{-} = -1$

$\boxed{+} = x$ $\boxed{-} = -x$

REMEMBER

$\boxed{+} + \boxed{-} = 0$

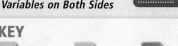

Use algebra tiles to model and solve $5x - 2 = 2x + 10$.

MODEL		ALGEBRA
	Model $5x - 2$ on the left side of the mat and $2x + 10$ on the right side. Remember that $5x - 2$ is the same as $5x + (-2)$.	$5x - 2 = 2x + 10$
	Remove 2 x-tiles from both sides. This represents subtracting $2x$ from both sides of the equation.	$5x - 2 - 2x = 2x - 2x + 10$ $3x - 2 = 10$
	Place 2 yellow tiles on both sides. This represents adding 2 to both sides of the equation. Remove zero pairs.	$3x - 2 + 2 = 10 + 2$ $3x = 12$
	Separate each side into 3 equal groups. Each group is $\frac{1}{3}$ of the side. One x-tile is equivalent to 4 yellow tiles.	$\frac{1}{3}(3x) = \frac{1}{3}(12)$ $x = 4$

Try This

Use algebra tiles to model and solve each equation.

1. $3x + 2 = 2x + 5$ **2.** $5x + 12 = 2x + 3$ **3.** $9x - 5 = 6x + 13$ **4.** $x = -2x + 9$

3-2

Solving Equations with Variables on Both Sides

? Essential Question: How can you solve equations that have the variable on both sides?

Objective
Solve equations in one variable that contain variable terms on both sides.

Vocabulary
identity

Why learn this?
You can compare prices and find the best value.

Many phone companies offer low rates for long-distance calls without requiring customers to sign up for their services. To compare rates, solve an equation with variables on both sides.

To solve an equation like this, use inverse operations to "collect" variable terms on one side of the equation.

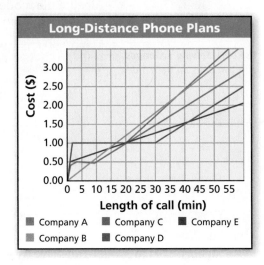

Long-Distance Phone Plans

- Company A
- Company B
- Company C
- Company D
- Company E

EXAMPLE MCC9-12.A.REI.3

my.hrw.com

Online Video Tutor

Solving Equations with Variables on Both Sides

Solve each equation.

A $7k = 4k + 15$

$$7k = 4k + 15$$
$$\underline{-4k \quad -4k}$$
$$3k = \quad\quad 15$$
$$\frac{3k}{3} = \frac{15}{3}$$
$$k = 5$$

To collect the variable terms on one side, subtract 4k from both sides.

Since k is multiplied by 3, divide both sides by 3 to undo the multiplication.

B $5x - 2 = 3x + 4$

$$5x - 2 = 3x + 4$$
$$\underline{-3x \quad\quad -3x}$$
$$2x - 2 = \quad\quad 4$$
$$\underline{+2 \quad\quad +2}$$
$$2x = \quad\quad 6$$
$$\frac{2x}{2} = \frac{6}{2}$$
$$x = 3$$

To collect the variable terms on one side, subtract 3x from both sides.

Since 2 is subtracted from 2x, add 2 to both sides to undo the subtraction.

Since x is multiplied by 2, divide both sides by 2 to undo the multiplication.

Check $5x - 2 = 3x + 4$

$5(3) - 2$	$3(3) + 4$
$15 - 2$	$9 + 4$
13	$13 \checkmark$

To check your solution, substitute 3 for x in the original equation.

Helpful Hint

Equations are often easier to solve when the variable has a positive coefficient. Keep this in mind when deciding on which side to "collect" variable terms.

 Solve each equation. Check your answer.

1a. $4b + 2 = 3b$

1b. $0.5 + 0.3y = 0.7y - 0.3$

To solve more complicated equations, you may need to first simplify by using the Distributive Property or combining like terms.

EXAMPLE **2** **Simplifying Each Side Before Solving Equations**

my.hrw.com

Online Video Tutor

Solve each equation.

A $2(y + 6) = 3y$

$$2(y + 6) = 3y$$ *Distribute 2 to the expression in*
$$2(y) + 2(6) = 3y$$ *parentheses.*
$$2y + 12 = 3y$$
$$\underline{-2y \qquad -2y}$$ *To collect the variable terms on one*
$$12 = y$$ *side, subtract 2y from both sides.*

Check $2(y + 6) = 3y$ *To check your solution, substitute*

$2(12 + 6)$	$3(12)$
$2(18)$	36
36	36 ✓

12 for y in the original equation.

B $2k - 5 = 3(1 - 2k)$

$$2k - 5 = 3(1 - 2k)$$ *Distribute 3 to the expression in*
$$2k - 5 = 3(1) - 3(2k)$$ *parentheses.*
$$2k - 5 = 3 - 6k$$
$$\underline{+6k \qquad\qquad +6k}$$ *To collect the variable terms on one*
$$8k - 5 = 3$$ *side, add 6k to both sides.*
$$\underline{+5 \qquad +5}$$ *Since 5 is subtracted from 8k, add 5*
$$8k = 8$$ *to both sides.*
$$\frac{8k}{8} = \frac{8}{8}$$ *Since k is multiplied by 8, divide both*
$$k = 1$$ *sides by 8.*

C $3 - 5b + 2b = -2 - 2(1 - b)$

$$3 - 5b + 2b = -2 - 2(1 - b)$$
$$3 - 5b + 2b = -2 - 2(1) - 2(-b)$$ *Distribute −2 to the expression in*
$$3 - 5b + 2b = -2 - 2 + 2b$$ *parentheses.*
$$3 - 3b = -4 + 2b$$ *Combine like terms.*
$$\underline{+3b \qquad\qquad +3b}$$ *Add 3b to both sides.*
$$3 = -4 + 5b$$
$$\underline{+4 \qquad\qquad +4}$$ *Since −4 is added to 5b, add 4 to*
$$7 = 5b$$ *both sides.*
$$\frac{7}{5} = \frac{5b}{5}$$ *Since b is multiplied by 5, divide*
$$1.4 = b$$ *both sides by 5.*

Solve each equation. Check your answer.

2a. $\frac{1}{2}(b + 6) = \frac{3}{2}b - 1$ **2b.** $3x + 15 - 9 = 2(x + 2)$

An **identity** is an equation that is always true, no matter what value is substituted for the variable. The solutions of an identity are all real numbers. Some equations are always false. These equations have no solutions.

EXAMPLE **3**
MCC9-12.A.REI.3

my.hrw.com

Online Video Tutor

Infinitely Many Solutions or No Solutions

Solve each equation.

A $x + 4 - 6x = 6 - 5x - 2$

$x + 4 - 6x = 6 - 5x - 2$	*Identify like terms.*
$4 - 5x = 4 - 5x$	*Combine like terms on the left and the right.*
$\underline{+5x \qquad +5x}$	*Add 5x to both sides.*
$4 \quad = 4 \checkmark$	*True statement*

The equation $x + 4 - 6x = 6 - 5x - 2$ is an identity. All values of x will make the equation true. All real numbers are solutions.

B $-8x + 6 + 9x = -17 + x$

$-8x + 6 + 9x = -17 + x$	*Identify like terms.*
$x + 6 = -17 + x$	*Combine like terms.*
$\underline{-x \qquad\qquad -x}$	*Subtract x from both sides.*
$6 = -17 \,✗$	*False statement*

The equation $-8x + 6 + 9x = -17 + x$ is always false. There is no value of x that will make the equation true. There are no solutions.

Writing Math

The solution set for Example 3B is an empty set—it contains no elements. The empty set can be written as $\varnothing$ or {}.

CHECK IT OUT!

Solve each equation.

3a. $4y + 7 - y = 10 + 3y$ **3b.** $2c + 7 + c = -14 + 3c + 21$

EXAMPLE **4**
MCC9-12.A.CED.1

my.hrw.com

Online Video Tutor

Consumer Application

The long-distance rates of two phone companies are shown in the table. How long is a call that costs the same amount no matter which company is used? What is the cost of that call?

Phone Company	Charges
Company A	36¢ plus 3¢ per minute
Company B	6¢ per minute

Let m represent minutes, and write expressions for each company's cost.

When is	36¢	plus	3¢ per minute	times number of minutes	the same as	6¢ per minute	times number of minutes	?
	36	+	3	(m)	=	6	(m)	

$36 + 3m =\quad 6m$	
$\underline{-3m \quad -3m}$	*To collect the variable terms on one side,*
$36 \quad = \quad 3m$	*subtract 3m from both sides.*
$\dfrac{36}{3} = \dfrac{3m}{3}$	*Since m is multiplied by 3, divide both sides by 3 to undo the multiplication.*
$12 = m$	

The charges will be the same for a 12-minute call using either phone service. To find the cost of this call, evaluate either expression for $m = 12$:

$$36 + 3m = 36 + 3(12) = 36 + 36 = 72 \qquad 6m = 6(12) = 72$$

The cost of a 12-minute call through either company is 72¢.

CHECK IT OUT!

4. Four times Greg's age, decreased by 3 is equal to 3 times Greg's age, increased by 7. How old is Greg?

THINK AND DISCUSS

1. Tell which of the following is an identity. Explain your answer.

   a. $4(a + 3) - 6 = 3(a + 3) - 6$ **b.** $8.3x - 9 + 0.7x = 2 + 9x - 11$

2. **GET ORGANIZED** Copy and complete the graphic organizer. In each box, write an example of an equation that has the indicated number of solutions.

An equation with variables on both sides can have...

| one solution: | many solutions: | no solution: |

3-2 Exercises

my.hrw.com
Homework Help

GUIDED PRACTICE

1. **Vocabulary** How can you recognize an identity?

Solve each equation. Check your answer.

SEE EXAMPLE **1**
   2. $2c - 5 = c + 4$ **3.** $8r + 4 = 10 + 2r$

   4. $2x - 1 = x + 11$ **5.** $28 - 0.3y = 0.7y - 12$

SEE EXAMPLE **2**
   6. $-2(x + 3) = 4x - 3$ **7.** $3c - 4c + 1 = 5c + 2 + 3$

   8. $5 + 3(q - 4) = 2(q + 1)$ **9.** $5 - (t + 3) = -1 + 2(t - 3)$

SEE EXAMPLE **3**
   10. $7x - 4 = -2x + 1 + 9x - 5$ **11.** $8x + 6 - 9x = 2 - x - 15$

   12. $6y = 8 - 9 + 6y$ **13.** $6 - 2x - 1 = 4x + 8 - 6x - 3$

SEE EXAMPLE **4**
   14. Consumer Economics A house-painting company charges $376 plus $12 per hour. Another painting company charges $280 plus $15 per hour.

     a. How long is a job for which both companies will charge the same amount?

     b. What will that cost be?

PRACTICE AND PROBLEM SOLVING

Solve each equation. Check your answer.

15. $7a - 17 = 4a + 1$ **16.** $2b - 5 = 8b + 1$ **17.** $4x - 2 = 3x + 4$

18. $2x - 5 = 4x - 1$ **19.** $8x - 2 = 3x + 12.25$ **20.** $5x + 2 = 3x$

21. $3c - 5 = 2c + 5$ **22.** $-17 - 2x = 6 - x$ **23.** $3(t - 1) = 9 + t$

24. $5 - x - 2 = 3 + 4x + 5$ **25.** $2(x + 4) = 3(x - 2)$ **26.** $3m - 10 = 2(4m - 5)$

27. $5 - (n - 4) = 3(n + 2)$ **28.** $6(x + 7) - 20 = 6x$ **29.** $8(x + 1) = 4x - 8$

30. $x - 4 - 3x = -2x - 3 - 1$ **31.** $-2(x + 2) = -2x + 1$ **32.** $2(x + 4) - 5 = 2x + 3$

Independent Practice

For Exercises	See Example
15–22	1
23–29	2
30–32	3
33	4

my.hrw.com

Online Extra Practice

33. Sports Justin and Tyson are beginning an exercise program to train for football season. Justin weighs 150 lb and hopes to gain 2 lb per week. Tyson weighs 195 lb and hopes to lose 1 lb per week.

   a. If the plan works, in how many weeks will the boys weigh the same amount?

   b. What will that weight be?

Write an equation to represent each relationship. Then solve the equation.

34. Three times the sum of a number and 4 is the same as 18 more than the number.

35. A number decreased by 30 is the same as 14 minus 3 times the number.

36. Two less than 2 times a number is the same as the number plus 64.

Solve each equation. Check your answer.

37. $2x - 2 = 4x + 6$ **38.** $3x + 5 = 2x + 2$ **39.** $4x + 3 = 5x - 4$

40. $-\frac{2}{5}p + 2 = \frac{1}{5}p + 11$ **41.** $5x + 24 = 2x + 15$ **42.** $5x - 10 = 14 - 3x$

43. $12 - 6x = 10 - 5x$ **44.** $5x - 7 = -6x - 29$ **45.** $1.8x + 2.8 = 2.5x + 2.1$

46. $2.6x + 18 = 2.4x + 22$ **47.** $1 - 3x = 2x + 8$ **48.** $\frac{1}{2}(8 - 6h) = h$

49. $3(x + 1) = 2x + 7$ **50.** $9x - 8 + 4x = 7x + 16$ **51.** $3(2x - 1) + 5 = 6(x + 1)$

52. Travel Rapid Rental Car company charges a $40 rental fee, $15 for gas, and $0.25 per mile driven. For the same car, Capital Cars charges $45 for rental and gas and $0.35 per mile.

   a. Find the number of miles for which the companies' charges will be the same. Then find that charge. Show that your answers are reasonable.

   b. The Barre family estimates that they will drive about 95 miles during their vacation to Hershey, Pennsylvania. Which company should they rent their car from? Explain.

   c. What if...? The Barres have extended their vacation and now estimate that they will drive about 120 miles. Should they still rent from the same company as in part **b**? Why or why not?

   d. Give a general rule for deciding which company to rent from.

53. Geometry The triangles shown have the same perimeter. What is the value of x?

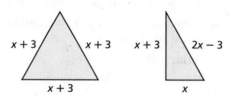

Real-World Connections

54. a. A fire currently covers 420 acres and continues to spread at a rate of 60 acres per day. How many total acres will be covered in the next 2 days? Show that your answer is reasonable.

   b. Write an expression for the total area covered by the fire in d days.

   c. The firefighters estimate that they can put out the fire at a rate of 80 acres per day. Write an expression for the total area that the firefighters can put out in d days.

   d. Set the expressions in parts **b** and **c** equal. Solve for d. What does d represent?

© Index Stock /Alamy

55. Critical Thinking Write an equation with variables on both sides that has no solution.

56. Biology The graph shows the maximum recorded speeds of the four fastest mammals.

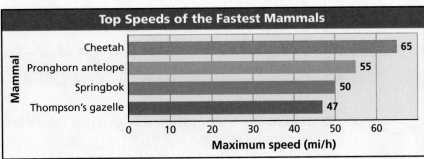

Source: The Top 10 of Everything

a. Write an expression for the distance in miles that a Thompson's gazelle can run at top speed in *x* hours.

b. Write an expression for the distance in miles that a cheetah can run at top speed in *x* hours.

c. A cheetah and a Thompson's gazelle are running at their top speeds. The cheetah is one mile behind the gazelle. Write an expression for the distance the cheetah must run to catch up with the gazelle.

d. Write and solve an equation that represents how long the cheetah will have to run at top speed to catch up with the gazelle.

e. A cheetah can maintain its top speed for only 300 yards. Will the cheetah be able to catch the gazelle? Explain.

H.O.T. 57. Write About It Write a series of steps that you can use to solve any equation with variables on both sides.

TEST PREP

58. Lindsey's monthly magazine subscription costs $1.25 per issue. Kenzie's monthly subscription costs $1.50 per issue, but she received her first 2 issues free. Which equation can be used to find the number of months after which the girls will have paid the same amount?

   Ⓐ $1.25m = 1.50m - 2$ Ⓒ $1.25m = 1.50(m - 2)$

   Ⓑ $1.25m = 1.50m - 2m$ Ⓓ $1.25m = 3m - 1.50$

59. What is the numerical solution of the equation *7 times a number equals 3 less than 5 times that number*?

   Ⓕ -1.5 Ⓖ 0.25 Ⓗ $\frac{2}{3}$ Ⓙ 4

60. Three packs of markers cost $9.00 less than 5 packs of markers. Which equation best represents this situation?

   Ⓐ $5x + 9 = 3x$ Ⓑ $3x + 9 = 5x$ Ⓒ $3x - 9 = 5x$ Ⓓ $9 - 3x = 5x$

61. Nicole has $120. If she saves $20 per week, in how many days will she have $500?

   Ⓕ 19 Ⓖ 25 Ⓗ 133 Ⓙ 175

62. Gridded Response Solve $-2(x - 1) + 5x = 2(2x - 1)$.

Solve each equation.

63. $4x + 2[4 - 2(x + 2)] = 2x - 4$

64. $\dfrac{x + 5}{2} + \dfrac{x - 1}{2} = \dfrac{x - 1}{3}$

65. $\dfrac{2}{3}w - \dfrac{1}{4} = \dfrac{2}{3}\left(w - \dfrac{1}{4}\right)$

66. $-5 - 7 - 3f = -f - 2(f + 6)$

67. $\dfrac{2}{3}x + \dfrac{1}{2} = \dfrac{3}{5}x - \dfrac{5}{6}$

68. $x - \dfrac{1}{4} = \dfrac{x}{3} + 7\dfrac{3}{4}$

69. Find three consecutive integers such that twice the greatest integer is 2 less than 3 times the least integer.

70. Find three consecutive integers such that twice the least integer is 12 more than the greatest integer.

71. Rob had twice as much money as Sam. Then Sam gave Rob 1 quarter, 2 nickels, and 3 pennies. Rob then gave Sam 8 dimes. If they now have the same amount of money, how much money did Rob originally have? Check your answer.

FOCUS ON MATHEMATICAL PRACTICES

H.O.T. **72. Comparison** One store charges $1.30 an ounce for a spice. Another store charges $1.20 an ounce but includes a half-ounce container when weighing. For what number of ounces is the cost at each store the same?

H.O.T. **73. Justify** Name the property that justifies each numbered step.

$$2x + 5 = 3(x - 3)$$
(1) $\qquad 2x + 5 = 3x - 9$
(2) $\qquad 2x + 5 + 9 = 3x - 9 + 9$
(3) $\quad 2x + 14 - 2x = 3x - 2x$
$$14 = x$$

H.O.T. **74. Modeling** Create an equation with variables on both sides of the equation and integer coefficients that has a solution of $n = -\dfrac{7}{12}$. Explain how you created the equation.

Career Path

Beth Simmons
Biology major

Q: What math classes did you take in high school?
A: Algebra 1 and 2, Geometry, and Precalculus

Q: What math classes have you taken in college?
A: Two calculus classes and a calculus-based physics class

Q: How do you use math?
A: I use math a lot in physics. Sometimes I would think a calculus topic was totally useless, and then we would use it in physics class! In biology, I use math to understand populations.

Q: What career options are you considering?
A: When I graduate, I could teach, or I could go to graduate school and do more research. I have a lot of options.

3-3 Solving for a Variable

Essential Question: How can you solve for a given variable in formulas or equations with more than one variable?

Objectives
Solve a formula for a given variable.

Solve an equation in two or more variables for one of the variables.

Vocabulary
formula
literal equation

Who uses this?
Athletes can "rearrange" the distance formula to calculate their average speed.

Many wheelchair athletes compete in marathons, which cover about 26.2 miles. Using the time t it took to complete the race, the distance d, and the *formula* $d = rt$, racers can find their average speed r.

A **formula** is an equation that states a rule for a relationship among quantities.

In the formula $d = rt$, d is isolated. You can "rearrange" a formula to isolate any variable by using inverse operations. This is called *solving for a variable*.

Solving for a Variable
Step 1 Locate the variable you are asked to solve for in the equation.
Step 2 Identify the operations on this variable and the order in which they are applied.
Step 3 Use inverse operations to undo operations and isolate the variable.

COMMON CORE GPS
EXAMPLE 1
MCC9-12.A.CED.4

Sports Application

In 2004, Ernst Van Dyk won the wheelchair race of the Boston Marathon with a time of about 1.3 hours. The race was about 26.2 miles. What was his average speed? Use the formula $d = rt$ and round your answer to the nearest tenth.

The question asks for speed, so first solve the formula $d = rt$ for r.

$d = \mathbf{r}t$ *Locate r in the equation.*

$\dfrac{d}{t} = \dfrac{rt}{t}$ *Since r is multiplied by t, divide both sides by t to undo the multiplication.*

$\dfrac{d}{t} = r$, or $r = \dfrac{d}{t}$

Now use this formula and the information given in the problem.

$r = \dfrac{d}{t} \approx \dfrac{26.2}{1.3}$

≈ 20.2

Van Dyk's average speed was about 20.2 miles per hour.

my.hrw.com

Online Video Tutor

Helpful Hint

A number divided by itself equals 1. For $t \neq 0$, $\dfrac{t}{t} = 1$.

CHECK IT OUT!

1. Solve the formula $d = rt$ for t. Find the time in hours that it would take Van Dyk to travel 26.2 miles if his average speed was 18 miles per hour. Round to the nearest hundredth.

© Ezra Shaw/Getty Images

Solving Formulas for a Variable

A The formula for a Fahrenheit temperature in terms of degrees Celsius is $F = \frac{9}{5}C + 32$. Solve for C.

$$F = \frac{9}{5}\boxed{C} + 32 \qquad \text{Locate } C \text{ in the equation.}$$

$$\frac{-32 \qquad\qquad -32}{F - 32 = \frac{9}{5}C} \qquad \begin{array}{l}\textit{Since 32 is added to } \frac{9}{5}C, \textit{ subtract 32 from both}\\ \textit{sides to undo the addition.}\end{array}$$

$$\left(\frac{5}{9}\right)(F - 32) = \left(\frac{5}{9}\right)\frac{9}{5}C \qquad \begin{array}{l}\textit{Since } C \textit{ is multiplied by } \frac{9}{5}, \textit{ divide both}\\ \textit{sides by } \frac{9}{5} \left(\textit{multiply by } \frac{5}{9}\right) \textit{ to undo the}\end{array}$$

$$\frac{5}{9}(F - 32) = C \qquad \textit{multiplication.}$$

Remember!

Dividing by a fraction is the same as multiplying by the reciprocal.

B The formula for a person's typing speed is $s = \frac{w - 10e}{m}$, where s is speed in words per minute, w is number of words typed, e is number of errors, and m is number of minutes typing. Solve for w.

$$s = \frac{\boxed{w} - 10e}{m} \qquad \textit{Locate } w \text{ in the equation.}$$

$$m(s) = m\left(\frac{w - 10e}{m}\right) \qquad \begin{array}{l}\textit{Since } w - 10e \textit{ is divided by } m, \textit{ multiply both}\\ \textit{sides by } m \textit{ to undo the division.}\end{array}$$

$$ms = w - 10e$$

$$\frac{+ 10e \qquad\qquad + 10e}{ms + 10e = w} \qquad \begin{array}{l}\textit{Since } 10e \textit{ is subtracted from } w, \textit{ add } 10e \textit{ to}\\ \textit{both sides to undo the subtraction.}\end{array}$$

 2. The formula for an object's final velocity f is $f = i - gt$, where i is the object's initial velocity, g is acceleration due to gravity, and t is time. Solve for i.

A formula is a type of *literal equation*. A **literal equation** is an equation with two or more variables. To solve for one of the variables, use inverse operations.

Solving Literal Equations for a Variable

A Solve $m - n = 5$ for m.

$$\boxed{m} - n = 5 \qquad \textit{Locate } m \text{ in the equation.}$$

$$\frac{+ n \quad + n}{m = 5 + n} \qquad \begin{array}{l}\textit{Since } n \textit{ is subtracted from } m, \textit{ add } n \textit{ to both sides to}\\ \textit{undo the subtraction.}\end{array}$$

B Solve $\frac{m}{k} = x$ for k.

$$\frac{m}{\boxed{k}} = x \qquad \textit{Locate } k \text{ in the equation.}$$

$$k\left(\frac{m}{k}\right) = kx \qquad \begin{array}{l}\textit{Since } k \textit{ appears in the denominator, multiply both}\\ \textit{sides by } k.\end{array}$$

$$m = kx$$

$$\frac{m}{x} = \frac{kx}{x} \qquad \begin{array}{l}\textit{Since } k \textit{ is multiplied by } x, \textit{ divide both sides by } x \textit{ to}\\ \textit{undo the multiplication.}\end{array}$$

$$\frac{m}{x} = k$$

 3a. Solve $5 - b = 2t$ for t.   **3b.** Solve $D = \frac{m}{V}$ for V.

THINK AND DISCUSS

1. Describe a situation in which a formula could be used more easily if it were "rearranged." Include the formula in your description.

2. Explain how to solve $P = 2\ell + 2w$ for w.

3. **GET ORGANIZED** Copy and complete the graphic organizer. Write a formula that is used in each subject. Then solve the formula for each of its variables.

Common Formulas	
Subject	**Formula**
Geometry	
Physical science	
Earth science	

3-3 Exercises

my.hrw.com
Homework Help

GUIDED PRACTICE

1. Vocabulary Explain why a *formula* is a type of *literal equation*.

SEE EXAMPLE 1

2. Construction The formula $a = 46c$ gives the floor area a in square meters that can be wired using c circuits.

    a. Solve $a = 46c$ for c.

    b. If a room is 322 square meters, how many circuits are required to wire this room?

SEE EXAMPLE 2

3. The formula for the volume of a rectangular prism with length ℓ, width w, and height h is $V = \ell wh$. Solve this formula for w.

SEE EXAMPLE 3

4. Solve $st + 3t = 6$ for s.

5. Solve $m - 4n = 8$ for m.

6. Solve $\dfrac{f+4}{g} = 6$ for f.

7. Solve $b + c = \dfrac{10}{a}$ for a.

PRACTICE AND PROBLEM SOLVING

Independent Practice	
For Exercises	See Example
8	1
9	2
10–13	3

my.hrw.com

Online Extra Practice

8. Geometry The formula $C = 2\pi r$ relates the circumference C of a circle to its radius r. (Recall that π is the constant ratio of circumference to diameter.)

    a. Solve $C = 2\pi r$ for r.

    b. If a circle's circumference is 15 inches, what is its radius? Leave the symbol π in your answer.

C is the distance around the circle.

r is the distance from the center of the circle to any point on the circle.

9. Finance The formula $A = P + I$ shows that the total amount of money A received from an investment equals the principal P (the original amount of money invested) plus the interest I. Solve this formula for I.

10. Solve $-2 = 4r + s$ for s.

11. Solve $xy - 5 = k$ for x.

12. Solve $\dfrac{m}{n} = p - 6$ for n.

13. Solve $\dfrac{x-2}{y} = z$ for y.

Solve for the indicated variable.

14. $S = 180n - 360$ for n
15. $\frac{x}{5} - g = a$ for x
16. $A = \frac{1}{2}bh$ for b

17. $y = mx + b$ for x
18. $a = 3n + 1$ for n
19. $PV = nRT$ for T

20. $T + M = R$ for T
21. $M = T - R$ for T
22. $PV = nRT$ for R

23. $2a + 2b = c$ for b
24. $5p + 9c = p$ for c
25. $ax + r = 7$ for r

26. $3x + 7y = 2$ for y
27. $4y + 3x = 5$ for x
28. $y = 3x + 3b$ for b

29. Estimation The table shows the flying time and distance traveled for five flights on a certain airplane.

   a. Use the data in the table to write a rule that *estimates* the relationship between flying time t and distance traveled d.

   b. Use your rule from part **a** to estimate the time that it takes the airplane to fly 1300 miles.

   c. Solve your rule for d.

   d. Use your rule from part **c** to estimate the distance the airplane can fly in 8 hours.

Flying Times		
Flight	**Time (h)**	**Distance (mi)**
A	2	1018
B	3	1485
C	4	2103
D	5	2516
E	6	2886

30. Sports To find a baseball pitcher's earned run average (ERA), you can use the formula $Ei = 9r$, where E represents ERA, i represents number of innings pitched, and r represents number of earned runs allowed. Solve the equation for E. What is a pitcher's ERA if he allows 5 earned runs in 18 innings pitched?

31. Meteorology For altitudes up to 36,000 feet, the relationship between temperature and altitude can be described by the formula $t = -0.0035a + g$, where t is the temperature in degrees Fahrenheit, a is the altitude in feet, and g is the ground temperature in degrees Fahrenheit. Solve this formula for a.

H.O.T. 32. Write About It In your own words, explain how to solve a literal equation for one of the variables.

33. Critical Thinking How is solving $a - ab = c$ for a different from the problems in this lesson? How might you solve this equation for a?

34. a. Suppose firefighters can extinguish a wildfire at a rate of 60 acres per day. Use this information to complete the table.

   b. Use the last row in the table to write an equation for acres A extinguished in terms of the number of days d.

   c. Graph the points in the table with *Days* on the horizontal axis and *Acres* on the vertical axis. Describe the graph.

Days	Acres
1	60
2	■
3	180
4	■
5	■
d	■

TEST PREP

35. Which equation is the result of solving $9 + 3x = 2y$ for x?

   (A) $\dfrac{9 + 3y}{2} = x$ (B) $\dfrac{2}{3}y - 9 = x$ (C) $x = \dfrac{2}{3}y - 3$ (D) $x = 2y - 3$

36. Which of the following is a correct method for solving $2a - 5b = 10$ for b?

   (F) Add $5b$ to both sides, then divide both sides by 2.

   (G) Subtract $5b$ from both sides, then divide both sides by 2.

   (H) Divide both sides by 5, then add $2a$ to both sides.

   (J) Subtract $2a$ from both sides, then divide both sides by -5.

37. The formula for the volume of a rectangular prism is $V = \ell wh$. Anna wants to make a cardboard box with a length of 7 inches, a width of 5 inches, and a volume of 210 cubic inches. Which variable does Anna need to solve for in order to build her box?

   (A) V (B) ℓ (C) w (D) h

CHALLENGE AND EXTEND

Solve for the indicated variable.

38. $3.3x + r = 23.1$ for x **39.** $\dfrac{2}{5}a - \dfrac{3}{4}b = c$ for a **40.** $\dfrac{3}{5}x + 1.4y = \dfrac{2}{5}$ for y

41. $t = \dfrac{d}{500} + \dfrac{1}{2}$ for d **42.** $s = \dfrac{1}{2}gt^2$ for g **43.** $v^2 = u^2 + 2as$ for s

44. Solve $y = mx + 6$ for m. What can you say about y if $m = 0$?

45. **Entertainment** The formula $S = \dfrac{h \cdot w \cdot f \cdot t}{35,000}$ gives the approximate size in kilobytes (Kb) of a compressed video. The variables h and w represent the height and width of the frame measured in pixels, f is the number of frames per second (fps) the video plays, and t is the time the video plays in seconds. Estimate the time a movie trailer will play if it has a frame height of 320 pixels, has a frame width of 144 pixels, plays at 15 fps, and has a size of 2370 Kb.

FOCUS ON MATHEMATICAL PRACTICES

H.O.T. **46.** **Analysis** Solve the equation $2x + 5y = 12 - y$ for y. Use the resulting equation to solve for x. Then, solve the original equation for x. Are both results for x the same? Why?

H.O.T. **47.** **Problem Solving** In ice hockey, the Goals Against Average (GAA) is calculated by multiplying the number of goals allowed by 60 and dividing by minutes played.

   a. How can you use the calculation to find the number of goals allowed by a goalie if the GAA and minutes played are known?

   b. Use the result of part a to find the number of goals allowed by a goalie who has a 2.80 GAA and has played 1050 minutes.

Ready to Go On?

my.hrw.com
Assessment and Intervention

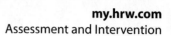

3-1 Solving Two-Step and Multi-Step Equations

Solve each equation.

1. $2r + 20 = 200$ **2.** $\frac{3}{5}k + 5 = 7$ **3.** $5n + 6 - 3n = -12$ **4.** $4(x - 7) = 2$

5. A taxicab company charges $2.10 plus $0.80 per mile. Carmen paid a fare of $11.70. Write and solve an equation to find the number of miles she traveled.

6. $4t - 13 = 57$ **7.** $5 - 2y = 15$ **8.** $\frac{k}{5} - 6 = 2$

9. $\frac{5}{6}f - \frac{3}{4}f + \frac{3}{4} = \frac{1}{2}$ **10.** $7x - 19x = 6$ **11.** $4 + 3a - 6 = 43$

12. If $8n + 22 = 70$, find the value of $3n$.

13. If $0 = 6n - 36$, find the value of $n - 5$.

14. The sum of the measures of two angles is 180°. One angle measures $3a$ and the other angle measures $2a - 25$ Find a. Then find the measure of each angle.

3-2 Solving Equations with Variables on Both Sides

Solve each equation.

15. $4x - 3 = 2x + 5$ **16.** $3(2x - 5) = 2(3x - 2)$ **17.** $2(2t - 3) = 6(t + 2)$

18. $7(x + 5) = -7(x + 5)$ **19.** $4x + 2 = 3x$ **20.** $-3r - 8 = -5r - 12$

21. $-a - 3 + 7 = 3a$ **22.** $-(x - 4) = 2x + 6$ **23.** $\frac{2}{3}n = 4n - \frac{10}{3}n - \frac{1}{2}$

24. $0.2(7 + 2t) = 0.4t + 1.4$

25. One photo shop charges $0.36 per print. Another photo shop charges $2.52 plus $0.08 per print. Juan finds that the cost of printing his photos is the same at either shop. How many photos does Juan have to print?

3-3 Solving for a Variable

26. Solve $2x + 3y = 12$ for x.   **27.** Solve $\frac{x}{r} = v$ for x.

28. Solve $5j + s = t - 2$ for t.   **29.** Solve $h + p = 3(k - 8)$ for k.

Solve for the indicated variable.

30. $C = \frac{360}{n}$ for n **31.** $S = \frac{n}{2}(a + \ell)$ for a

32. The formula $a = \frac{d}{g}$ gives the average gas mileage a of a vehicle that uses g gallons of gas to travel d miles. Use the formula to find how many gallons of gas a vehicle with an average gas mileage of 20.2 miles per gallon will use to travel 75 miles. Round your answer to the nearest tenth.

PARCC Assessment Readiness

Selected Response

1. Solve $\frac{h}{50} - \frac{1}{10} = \frac{1}{10}$.

(A) $h = -250$ (C) $h = -10$

(B) $h = 10$ (D) $h = 250$

2. Solve $30a + 23 - 25a = 28$.

(F) $a = 5$ (H) $a = 1$

(G) $a = -1$ (J) $a = -5$

3. Devon pays $49.95 for her roller skates. After that she pays $5.95 for each visit to the roller rink. What is the greatest number of visits she can afford if the total amount she spends cannot be more than $115.40?

(A) 2   (C) 65

(B) 11   (D) 19

4. If $3x - 8 = 31$, find the value of $4x$.

(F) 8   (H) 36

(G) 18   (J) 52

5. The formula $p = nc - e$ gives the profit p when a number of items n are each sold at a cost c and expenses e are subtracted. If $p = 4150$, $n = 3000$, and $e = 500$, what is the value of c?

(A) $1.38   (C) $0.72

(B) $1.55   (D) $1.22

6. Solve $50s - 13 = 55s - 93$.

(F) $s = 16$ (H) $s = 80$

(G) $s = -80$ (J) $s = -16$

7. Solve $4x - 3 - 2x = 9 + 2x - 12$. Tell whether the equation has infinitely many solutions or no solutions.

(A) Infinitely many solutions

(B) Only one solution

(C) Two solutions

(D) No solutions

8. An online video service charges a monthly membership fee of $7.50 and a charge of $1.00 per movie watched. Another service has no membership fee but charges $2.50 for each movie. How many movies need to be rented each month for the total fees to be the same from either company?

(F) 9 movies   (H) 3 movies

(G) 5 movies   (J) 7 movies

9. The formula for the resistance of a conductor with voltage V and current I is $r = \frac{V}{I}$. Solve for V.

(A) $I = Vr$ (C) $V = \frac{I}{r}$

(B) $V = \frac{r}{I}$ (D) $V = Ir$

10. A professional cyclist is training for the Tour de France. What was his average speed in kilometers per hour if he rode the 194 kilometers from Laval to Blois in 4.5 hours? Use the formula $d = rt$, and round your answer to the nearest tenth.

(F) 43.1 kph   (H) 189.5 kph

(G) 873.0 kph   (J) 116.3 kph

Mini-Task

11. Find three consecutive integers such that twice the greatest integer is 6 less than 3 times the least integer.

4

Solving Inequalities in One Variable

The Common Core Georgia Performance Standards for Mathematical Practice describe varieties of expertise that all students should seek to develop. Opportunities to develop these practices are integrated throughout this program.

1 Make sense of problems and persevere in solving them.

2 Reason abstractly and quantitatively.

3 Construct viable arguments and critique the reasoning of others.

4 Model with mathematics.

5 Use appropriate tools strategically.

6 Attend to precision.

7 Look for and make use of structure.

8 Look for and express regularity in repeated reasoning.

Unpacking the Standards

Understanding the standards and the vocabulary terms in the standards will help you know exactly what you are expected to learn in this chapter.

 MCC9-12.A.CED.3

Represent constraints by ... inequalities ... and interpret solutions as viable or nonviable options in a modeling context.

Key Vocabulary

inequality (desigualdad) A statement that compares two expressions by using one of the following signs: $<, >, \leq, \geq$, or $\neq$.

solution of an inequality in one variable (solución de una desigualdad en una variable) A value or values that make the inequality true.

What It Means For You

You can use inequalities to represent limits on the values in a situation so that the solutions make sense in a real-world context.

EXAMPLE

Anyone riding the large water slide at a park must be at least 40 inches tall.

Let h represent the heights that are allowed.

Height is at least 40 inches.

$$h \qquad \geq \qquad 40$$

 MCC9-12.A.REI.3

Solve linear ... inequalities in one variable, ...

Key Vocabulary

linear inequality in one variable (desigualdad lineal en una variable) An inequality that can be written in one of the following forms: $ax < b$, $ax > b$, $ax \leq b$, $ax \geq b$, or $ax \neq b$, where a and b are constants and $a \neq 0$.

What It Means For You

Solving inequalities lets you answer questions where a range of solutions is possible.

EXAMPLE

Solve the inequality for t to find what grades on the final exam will give Cleo a course grade of "A".

$705 + 2t \geq 895$ *Cleo has 705 points and needs at least 895.*

$2t \geq 190$ *Subtract 705 from both sides.*

$t \geq 95$ *Divide both sides by 2.*

Cleo needs to earn a 95 or above on the final exam.

Graphing and Writing Inequalities

 Essential Question: How can you graph and write inequalities?

Objectives
Identify solutions of inequalities in one variable.

Write and graph inequalities in one variable.

Vocabulary
inequality
solution of an inequality

Who uses this?
Members of a crew team can use inequalities to be sure they fall within a range of weights. (See Example 4.)

The athletes on a lightweight crew team must weigh 165 pounds or less. The acceptable weights for these athletes can be described using an *inequality*.

An **inequality** is a statement that two quantities are not equal. The quantities are compared by using one of the following signs:

 Animated Math

$<$	$>$	$\le$	$\ge$	$\ne$
$A < B$	$A > B$	$A \le B$	$A \ge B$	$A \ne B$
A is less than B.	A is greater than B.	A is less than or equal to B.	A is greater than or equal to B.	A is not equal to B.

A **solution of an inequality** is any value of the variable that makes the inequality true.

 COMMON CORE GPS
MCC9-12.A.REI.3

EXAMPLE 1 Identifying Solutions of Inequalities

Describe the solutions of $3 + x < 9$ in words.

Test values of x that are positive, negative, and 0.

 my.hrw.com

x	−2.75	0	5.99	6	6.01	6.1
3 + x	0.25	3	8.99	9	9.01	9.1
3 + x $\overset{?}{<}$ 9	0.25 $\overset{?}{<}$ 9	3 $\overset{?}{<}$ 9	8.99 $\overset{?}{<}$ 9	9 $\overset{?}{<}$ 9	9.01 $\overset{?}{<}$ 9	9.1 $\overset{?}{<}$ 9
Solution?	Yes	Yes	Yes	No	No	No

 Online Video Tutor

When the value of x is a number less than 6, the value of 3 + x is less than 9.
When the value of x is 6, the value of 3 + x is equal to 9.
When the value of x is a number greater than 6, the value of 3 + x is greater than 9.

Writing Math

The solutions in Example 1 can be written in *set-builder notation* as $\{x | x < 6\}$, read as "x such that x is less than 6."

The solutions of $3 + x < 9$ are numbers less than 6.

 CHECK IT OUT! **1.** Describe the solutions of $2p > 8$ in words.

© Charles Crust

An inequality like $3 + x < 9$ has too many solutions to list. You can use a graph on a number line to show all the solutions.

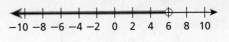

The solutions are shaded and an arrow shows that the solutions continue past those shown on the graph. To show that an endpoint is a solution, draw a solid circle at the number. To show that an endpoint is not a solution, draw an empty circle.

Graphing Inequalities

WORDS	ALGEBRA	GRAPH
All real numbers less than 5	$x < 5$	number line -4 to 6, open circle at 5
All real numbers greater than -1	$x > -1$	number line -4 to 6, open circle at -1
All real numbers less than or equal to $\frac{1}{2}$	$x \leq \frac{1}{2}$	number line -2 to 1, solid circle at $\frac{1}{2}$
All real numbers greater than or equal to 0	$x \geq 0$	number line -4 to 6, solid circle at 0

COMMON CORE GPS
EXAMPLE 2
Prep. for MCC9-12.A.REI.12

Graphing Inequalities

Graph each inequality.

A $b < -1.5$

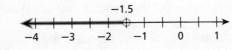

Draw an empty circle at -1.5.
Shade all the numbers less than -1.5 and draw an arrow pointing to the left.

B $r \geq 2$

Draw a solid circle at 2.
Shade all the numbers greater than 2 and draw an arrow pointing to the right.

my.hrw.com

Online Video Tutor

CHECK IT OUT!

Graph each inequality.

2a. $c > 2.5$ **2b.** $2^2 - 4 \geq w$ **2c.** $m \leq -3$

Student to Student

Graphing Inequalities

Victor Solomos
Palmer High School

To know which direction to shade a graph, I write inequalities with the variable on the left side of the inequality symbol. I know that the symbol has to point to the same number after I rewrite the inequality.

For example, I write $4 < y$ as $y > 4$.

Now the inequality symbol points in the direction that I should draw the shaded arrow on my graph.

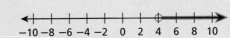

Digital Vision/gettyimages

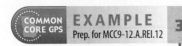
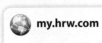

EXAMPLE **3**
Prep. for MCC9-12.A.REI.12

Writing an Inequality from a Graph

Write the inequality shown by each graph.

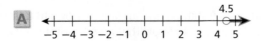
A
4.5
$\xleftarrow{\quad}$ | | | | | | | | | $\circ$ | $\rightarrow$
−5 −4 −3 −2 −1 0 1 2 3 4 5

Use any variable. The arrow points to the right, so use either > or ≥.
The empty circle at 4.5 means that 4.5 is not a solution, so use >.

$h > 4.5$

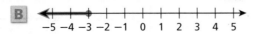
B
$\xleftarrow{\quad}$ | | $\bullet$ | | | | | | | | $\rightarrow$
−5 −4 −3 −2 −1 0 1 2 3 4 5

Use any variable. The arrow points to the left, so use either < or ≤.
The solid circle at −3 means that −3 is a solution, so use ≤.

$m \leq -3$

CHECK IT OUT!

3. Write the inequality shown by the graph.

2.5
$\xleftarrow{\quad}$ | | | | | | | $\circ$ | | | $\rightarrow$
−5 −4 −3 −2 −1 0 1 2 3 4 5

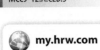

EXAMPLE **4**
MCC9-12.A.CED.3

Sports Application

The members of a lightweight crew team can weigh no more than 165 pounds each. Define a variable and write an inequality for the acceptable weights of the team members. Graph the solutions.

Let w represent the weights that are allowed.

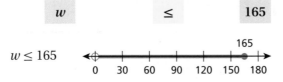

Athletes may weigh	no more than	165 pounds.
w	$\leq$	165

$w \leq 165$

165
$\xleftarrow{\quad} \circ$ | | | | | $\bullet$ | $\rightarrow$
0 30 60 90 120 150 180

Stop the graph at 0 because a person's weight must be a positive number.

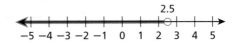

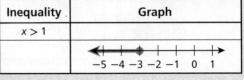

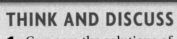
CHECK IT OUT!

4. A store's employees earn at least $8.25 per hour. Define a variable and write an inequality for the amount the employees may earn per hour. Graph the solutions.

MCC.MP.6   MATHEMATICAL PRACTICES

THINK AND DISCUSS

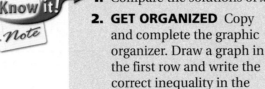
Know it! Note

1. Compare the solutions of $x > 2$ and $x \geq 2$.

2. GET ORGANIZED Copy and complete the graphic organizer. Draw a graph in the first row and write the correct inequality in the second row.

Inequality	Graph
$x > 1$	
	$\xleftarrow{\quad}$		$\bullet$				$\rightarrow$ −5 −4 −3 −2 −1 0 1

GUIDED PRACTICE

1. **Vocabulary** How is a *solution of an inequality* like a solution of an equation?

SEE EXAMPLE 1 Describe the solutions of each inequality in words.

2. $g - 5 \geq 6$ **3.** $-2 < h + 1$ **4.** $20 > 5t$ **5.** $5 - x \leq 2$

SEE EXAMPLE 2 Graph each inequality.

6. $x < -5$ **7.** $c \geq 3\frac{1}{2}$ **8.** $(4 - 2)^3 > m$ **9.** $p \geq \sqrt{17 + 8}$

SEE EXAMPLE 3 Write the inequality shown by each graph.

10.
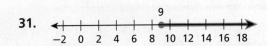

11. $-8\frac{1}{2}$

12. 5.5

13. -7

14.

15.

SEE EXAMPLE 4 Define a variable and write an inequality for each situation. Graph the solutions.

16. There must be at least 20 club members present in order to hold a meeting.

17. A trainer advises an athlete to keep his heart rate under 140 beats per minute.

PRACTICE AND PROBLEM SOLVING

Independent Practice	
For Exercises	See Example
18–21	1
22–25	2
26–31	3
32–33	4

Describe the solutions of each inequality in words.

18. $-2t > -8$ **19.** $0 > w - 2$ **20.** $3k > 9$ **21.** $\frac{1}{2}b \leq 6$

Graph each inequality.

22. $7 < x$ **23.** $t \leq -\frac{1}{2}$ **24.** $d > 4(5 - 8)$ **25.** $t \leq 3^2 - 2^2$

Write the inequality shown by each graph.

26.

27. -11

28. -3.5

29. -3.3

30.

31. 9

Define a variable and write an inequality for each situation. Graph the solutions.

32. The maximum speed allowed on Main Street is 25 miles per hour.

33. Applicants must have at least 5 years of experience.

Write each inequality in words.

34. $x > 7$ **35.** $h < -5$ **36.** $d \leq 23$ **37.** $r \geq -2$

Write each inequality with the variable on the left. Graph the solutions.

38. $19 < g$ **39.** $17 \geq p$ **40.** $10 < e$ **41.** $0 < f$

Define a variable and write an inequality for each situation. Graph the solutions.

42. The highest temperature ever recorded on Earth was 135.9 °F at Al Aziziyah, Libya, on September 13, 1922.

43. Businesses with profits less than $10,000 per year will be shut down.

44. You must be at least 46 inches tall to ride a roller coaster at an amusement park.

45. Due to a medical condition, a hiker can hike only in areas with an elevation no more than 5000 feet above sea level.

Write a real-world situation that could be described by each inequality.

46. $x \geq 0$ **47.** $x < 10$ **48.** $x \leq 12$ **49.** $x > 8.5$

Match each inequality with its graph.

50. $x \geq 5$

A.

51. $x < 5$

B.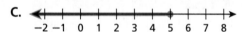

52. $x > 5$

C.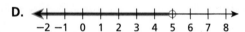

53. $x \leq 5$

D.

H.O.T. 54. ///ERROR ANALYSIS/// Two students graphed the inequality $4 > b$. Which graph is incorrect? Explain the error.

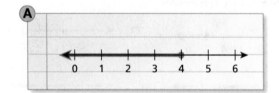 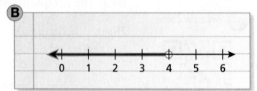

Real-World Connections

55. a. Mirna earned $125 baby-sitting during the spring break. She needs to save $90 for the German Club trip. She wants to spend the remainder of the money shopping. Write an inequality to show how much she can spend.

    b. Graph the inequality you wrote in part **a.**

    c. Mirna spends $15 on a bracelet. Write an inequality to show how much money she has left to spend.

© Creatas

56. Critical Thinking Graph all positive integer solutions of the inequality $x < 5$.

H.O.T. **57. Write About It** Explain how to write an inequality that is modeled by a graph. What characteristics do you look for in the graph?

58. Write About It You were told in the lesson that the phrase "no more than" means "less than or equal to" and the phrase "at least" means "greater than or equal to."

    a. What does the phrase "at most" mean?

    b. What does the phrase "no less than" mean?

TEST PREP

59. Which is NOT a solution of the inequality $5 - 2x \geq -3$?

    Ⓐ 0   Ⓑ 2   Ⓒ 4   Ⓓ 5

60. Which is NOT a solution of the inequality $3 - x < 2$?

    Ⓕ 1   Ⓖ 2   Ⓗ 3   Ⓙ 4

61. Which graph represents the solutions of $-2 \leq 1 - t$?

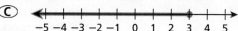
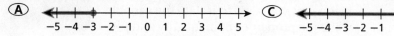
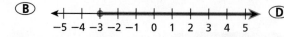
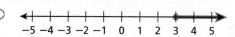

CHALLENGE AND EXTEND

Describe the values for x and y that make each inequality true.

62. $x + y \leq |x + y|$ **63.** $x^2 < xy$ **64.** $x - y \geq y - x$

Complete each statement. Write $<$ or $>$.

65. If $a > b$, then b ▮ a.   **66.** If $x > y$ and $y > z$, then x ▮ z.

67. Name a value of x that makes the statement $0.35 < x < 1.27$ true.

68. Is $\frac{5}{6}$ a solution of $x < 1$? How many solutions of $x < 1$ are between 0 and 1?

69. Write About It Explain how to graph all the solutions of $x \neq 5$.

FOCUS ON MATHEMATICAL PRACTICES

H.O.T. **70. Modeling** In order for Ramon to remain in his current weight class for a wrestling match on Saturday morning, he must weigh in at 152 pounds or more, but less than 160 pounds. Write a pair of inequalities that expresses the set of acceptable weights for Ramon. Define your variable.

H.O.T. **71. Problem Solving** Cary is making brownies using a recipe that calls for "at least 5 cups of flour but no more than 6 cups of flour." The only measuring cup he could find holds one quarter of a cup. Write a pair of inequalities to express how many *quarter cups* of flour Cary can use.

H.O.T. **72. Analysis** Imani and Trey are planning the seating at their wedding reception. They have 168 guests and each table can hold up to 16 guests, so they calculate that they need at least 10.5 tables to seat all of their guests. Graph their solution. In this context, how is the graph inaccurate? Make another graph that takes the context into account.

4-2

Solving Inequalities by Adding or Subtracting

? Essential Question: How can you use addition or subtraction to solve inequalities?

Objectives
Solve one-step inequalities by using addition.

Solve one-step inequalities by using subtraction.

Who uses this?

You can use inequalities to determine how many more photos you can take. (See Example 2.)

Tenea has a cell phone that also takes pictures. After taking some photos, Tenea can use a one-step inequality to determine how many more photos she can take.

Solving one-step inequalities is much like solving one-step equations. To solve an inequality, you need to isolate the variable using the properties of inequality and inverse operations.

Properties of Inequality

Addition and Subtraction

WORDS	NUMBERS	ALGEBRA
Addition You can add the same number to both sides of an inequality, and the statement will still be true.	$3 < 8$ $3 + 2 < 8 + 2$ $5 < 10$	$a < b$ $a + c < b + c$
Subtraction You can subtract the same number from both sides of an inequality, and the statement will still be true.	$9 < 12$ $9 - 5 < 12 - 5$ $4 < 7$	$a < b$ $a - c < b - c$

These properties are also true for inequalities that use the symbols $>$, $\geq$, and $\leq$.

COMMON CORE GPS
EXAMPLE 1
MCC9-12.A.REI.3

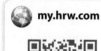

my.hrw.com

Online Video Tutor

Using Addition and Subtraction to Solve Inequalities

Solve each inequality and graph the solutions.

A $x + 9 < 15$

$$\begin{array}{r} x + 9 < 15 \\ \underline{-9 \quad -9} \\ x \quad < 6 \end{array}$$

Since 9 is added to x, subtract 9 from both sides to undo the addition.

B $d - 3 > -6$

$$\begin{array}{r} d - 3 > -6 \\ \underline{+3 \quad +3} \\ d \quad > -3 \end{array}$$

Since 3 is subtracted from d, add 3 to both sides to undo the subtraction.

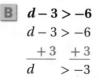

© Mingasson/Getty/HMH

Solve each inequality and graph the solutions.

C $0.7 \geq n - 0.4$

$$0.7 \geq n - 0.4$$
$$\underline{+\,0.4 \qquad +\,0.4}$$
$$1.1 \geq n$$
$$n \leq 1.1$$

Since 0.4 is subtracted from n, add 0.4 to both sides to undo the subtraction.

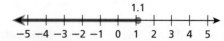

1.1

−5 −4 −3 −2 −1 0 1 2 3 4 5

 Solve each inequality and graph the solutions.

1a. $s + 1 \leq 10$ **1b.** $2\frac{1}{2} > -3 + t$ **1c.** $q - 3.5 < 7.5$

Since there can be an infinite number of solutions to an inequality, it is not possible to check all the solutions. You can check the endpoint and the direction of the inequality symbol.

The solutions of $x + 9 < 15$ are given by $x < 6$.

Step 1 Check the endpoint.

Substitute 6 for x in the related equation $x + 9 = 15$. The endpoint should be a solution of the equation.

$$x + 9 = 15$$
$$\begin{array}{c|c} 6 + 9 & 15 \\ \hline 15 & 15 \checkmark \end{array}$$

Step 2 Check the inequality symbol.

Substitute a number less than 6 for x in the original inequality. The number you choose should be a solution of the inequality.

$$x + 9 < 15$$
$$\begin{array}{c|c} 4 + 9 & < & 15 \\ 13 & < & 15 \checkmark \end{array}$$

my.hrw.com

Online Video Tutor

Make sence of problems and persevere in solving them.

Problem Solving Application

The memory in Tenea's camera phone allows her to take up to 20 pictures. Tenea has already taken 16 pictures. Write, solve, and graph an inequality to show how many more pictures Tenea could take.

1 **Understand the Problem**

The **answer** will be an inequality and a graph that show all the possible numbers of pictures that Tenea can take.

List the important information:
- Tenea can take up to, or *at most*, 20 pictures.
- Tenea has taken 16 pictures already.

2 **Make a Plan**

Write an inequality.

Let p represent the remaining number of pictures Tenea can take.

Number taken	plus	number remaining	is at most	20 pictures.
16	+	p	$\leq$	20

Solve

$$16 + p \leq 20$$
$$\underline{-16 \qquad -16}$$
$$p \leq 4$$

Since 16 is added to p, subtract 16 from both sides to undo the addition.

It is not reasonable for Tenea to take a negative or fractional number of pictures, so graph the nonnegative integers less than or equal to 4.

Tenea could take 0, 1, 2, 3, or 4 more pictures.

 Look Back

Check   Check the endpoint, 4.   Check a number less than 4.

$$16 + p = 20$$ $$16 + p \leq 20$$

$16 + 4$	20
20	20 ✓

$16 + 2$	$\leq$	20
18	$\leq$	20 ✓

Adding 0, 1, 2, 3, or 4 more pictures will not exceed 20.

2. The Recommended Dietary Allowance (RDA) of iron for a female in Sarah's age group (14–18 years) is 15 mg per day. Sarah has consumed 11 mg of iron today. Write and solve an inequality to show how many more milligrams of iron Sarah can consume without exceeding the RDA.

COMMON CORE GPS
EXAMPLE 3
MCC9-12.A.CED.1

my.hrw.com

Online Video Tutor

Sports Application

Josh can bench press 220 pounds. He wants to bench press at least 250 pounds. Write and solve an inequality to determine how many more pounds Josh must lift to reach his goal. Check your answer.

Let p represent the number of additional pounds Josh must lift.

220 pounds	plus	additional pounds	is at least	250 pounds.
220	+	p	$\geq$	250

$$220 + p \geq 250$$
$$\underline{-220 \qquad -220}$$
$$p \geq 30$$

Since 220 is added to p, subtract 220 from both sides to undo the addition.

Check   Check the endpoint, 30.   Check a number greater than 30.

$$220 + p = 250$$ $$220 + p \geq 250$$

$220 + 30$	250
250	250 ✓

$220 + 40$	$\geq$	250
260	$\geq$	250 ✓

Josh must lift at least 30 additional pounds to reach his goal.

3. What if...? Josh has reached his goal of 250 pounds and now wants to try to break the school record of 282 pounds. Write and solve an inequality to determine how many more pounds Josh needs to break the school record. Check your answer.

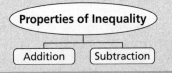

THINK AND DISCUSS

1. Show how to check your solution to Example 1B.

2. Explain how the Addition and Subtraction Properties of Inequality are like the Addition and Subtraction Properties of Equality.

3. **GET ORGANIZED** Copy and complete the graphic organizer. In each box, write an inequality that you must use the specified property to solve. Then solve and graph the inequality.

Properties of Inequality
├ Addition
└ Subtraction

4-2 Exercises

 my.hrw.com Homework Help

GUIDED PRACTICE

SEE EXAMPLE 1

Solve each inequality and graph the solutions.

1. $12 < p + 6$
2. $w + 3 \geq 4$
3. $-5 + x \leq -20$
4. $z - 2 > -11$

SEE EXAMPLE 2

5. **Health** For adults, the maximum safe water temperature in a spa is 104 °F. The water temperature in Bill's spa is 102 °F. The temperature is increased by t °F. Write, solve, and graph an inequality to show the values of t for which the water temperature is still safe.

SEE EXAMPLE 3

6. **Consumer Economics** A local restaurant will deliver food to your house if the purchase amount of your order is at least $25.00. The total for part of your order is $17.95. Write and solve an inequality to determine how much more you must spend for the restaurant to deliver your order.

PRACTICE AND PROBLEM SOLVING

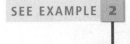

Independent Practice	
For Exercises	See Example
7–10	1
11	2
12	3

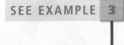

my.hrw.com

Online Extra Practice

Solve each inequality and graph the solutions.

7. $a - 3 \geq 2$
8. $2.5 > q - 0.8$
9. $-45 + x < -30$
10. $r + \frac{1}{4} \leq \frac{3}{4}$

11. **Engineering** The maximum load for a certain elevator is 2000 pounds. The total weight of the passengers on the elevator is 1400 pounds. A delivery man who weighs 243 pounds enters the elevator with a crate of weight w. Write, solve, and graph an inequality to show the values of w that will not exceed the weight limit of the elevator.

12. **Transportation** The gas tank in Mindy's car holds at most 15 gallons. She has already filled the tank with 7 gallons of gas. She will continue to fill the tank with g gallons more. Write and solve an inequality that shows all values of g that Mindy can add to the car's tank.

Write an inequality to represent each statement. Solve the inequality and graph the solutions.

13. Ten less than a number x is greater than 32.

14. A number n increased by 6 is less than or equal to 4.

15. A number r decreased by 13 is at most 15.

Solve each inequality and graph the solutions.

16. $x + 4 \leq 2$

17. $-12 + q > 39$

18. $x + \frac{3}{5} < 7$

19. $4.8 \geq p + 4$

20. $-12 \leq x - 12$

21. $4 < 206 + c$

22. $y - \frac{1}{3} > \frac{2}{3}$

23. $x + 1.4 \geq 1.4$

24. Use the inequality $s + 12 \geq 20$ to fill in the missing numbers.

    a. $s \geq$ ■

    b. $s + $ ■ ≥ 30

    c. $s - 8 \geq$ ■

25. **Health** A particular type of contact lens can be worn up to 30 days in a row. Alex has been wearing these contact lenses for 21 days. Write, solve, and graph an inequality to show how many more days Alex could wear his contact lenses.

Solve each inequality and match the solutions to the correct graph.

26. $1 \leq x - 2$

A.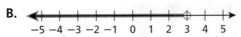

27. $8 > x - (-5)$

B.

28. $x + 6 > 9$

C.

29. $-4 \geq x - 7$

D.

H.O.T. 30. Estimation Is $x < 10$ a reasonable estimate for the solutions to the inequality $11.879 + x < 21.709$? Explain your answer.

31. **Sports** At the Seattle Mariners baseball team's home games, there are 45,611 seats in the four areas listed in the table. Suppose all the suite level and club level seats during a game are filled. Write and solve an inequality to determine how many people p could be sitting in the other types of seats.

Mariners Home Game Seating	
Type of Seat	**Number of Seats**
Main bowl	24,399
Upper bowl	16,022
Club level	4,254
Suite level	936

32. **Critical Thinking** Recall that a balance scale was used to model solving equations. Describe how a balance scale could model solving inequalities.

33. **Critical Thinking** Explain why $x + 4 \geq 6$ and $x - 4 \geq -2$ have the same solutions.

H.O.T. 34. Write About It How do the solutions of $x + 2 \geq 3$ differ from the solutions of $x + 2 > 3$? How do the graphs of the solutions differ?

35. **a.** Daryl finds that the distance from Columbus, Ohio, to Washington, D.C., is 411 miles. What is the round-trip distance?

    b. Daryl can afford to drive a total of 1000 miles. Write an inequality to show the number of miles m he can drive while in Washington, D.C.

    c. Solve the inequality and graph the solutions on a number line. Show that your answer is reasonable.

(tl), Buzz Orr/The Gazette/AP/Wide World Photos; (cr), PhotoDisc/getty/images; (bl), © Creatas

TEST PREP

36. Which is a reasonable solution of $4.7367 + p < 20.1784$?

  (A) 15 (B) 16 (C) 24 (D) 25

37. Which statement can be modeled by $x + 3 \leq 12$?

  (F) Sam has 3 bottles of water. Together, Sam and Dave have at most 12 bottles of water.

  (G) Jennie sold 3 cookbooks. To earn a prize, Jennie must sell at least 12 cookbooks.

  (H) Peter has 3 baseball hats. Peter and his brothers have fewer than 12 baseball hats.

  (J) Kathy swam 3 laps in the pool this week. She must swim more than 12 laps.

38. Which graph represents the solutions of $p + 3 < 1$?

  (A) 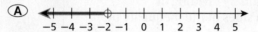 (C)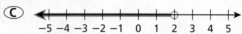

  (B) 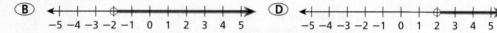 (D)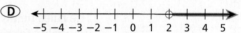

39. Which inequality does NOT have the same solutions as $n + 12 \leq 26$?

  (F) $n \leq 14$ (G) $n + 6 \leq 20$ (H) $10 \geq n - 4$ (J) $n - 12 \leq 14$

CHALLENGE AND EXTEND

Solve each inequality and graph the solutions.

40. $6\frac{9}{10} \geq 4\frac{4}{5} + x$

41. $r - 1\frac{2}{5} \leq 3\frac{7}{10}$

42. $6\frac{2}{3} + m > 7\frac{1}{6}$

Determine whether each statement is sometimes, always, or never true. Explain.

43. $a + b > a - b$

44. If $a > c$, then $a + b > c + b$.

45. If $a > b$ and $c > d$, then $a + c > b + d$.

46. If $x + b > c$ and $x > 0$ have the same solutions, what is the relationship between b and c?

FOCUS ON MATHEMATICAL PRACTICES

H.O.T. **47. Estimation** In 10 weeks, Yuri wants to have enough money to buy a racing bicycle that costs $1487.95. He currently has $292.50 in his savings account.

  a. Write an inequality that expresses how much Yuri still needs to save.

  b. Rewrite this inequality in a simpler form by rounding all numerical values to the nearest $100, and then solve it.

  c. Use the solution you just found to estimate how much money Yuri needs to save each week in order to purchase the bicycle.

H.O.T. **48. Modeling** A psychotherapist needs to complete a minimum number of internship hours before he or she can receive certification. Candace wrote the inequality $1840 + h \geq 3000$ to represent the hours she needs complete her certification. In total, how many hours does Candace need to serve as an intern? How many hours has Candace completed? How many hours does Candace still need to perform?

4-3 Solving Inequalities by Multiplying or Dividing

 Essential Question: How can you use multiplication or division to solve inequalities?

Objectives
Solve one-step inequalities by using multiplication.

Solve one-step inequalities by using division.

Who uses this?
You can solve an inequality to determine how much you can buy with a certain amount of money. (See Example 3.)

Remember, solving inequalities is similar to solving equations. To solve an inequality that contains multiplication or division, undo the operation by dividing or multiplying both sides of the inequality by the same number.

The rules below show the properties of inequality for multiplying or dividing by a positive number. The rules for multiplying or dividing by a negative number appear later in this lesson.

"This is all I have, so I'll take 3 pencils, 3 notebooks, a binder, and 0.9 calculators."

Properties of Inequality

Multiplication and Division by Positive Numbers

WORDS	NUMBERS	ALGEBRA
Multiplication You can multiply both sides of an inequality by the same *positive* number, and the statement will still be true.	$7 < 12$ $7(3) < 12(3)$ $21 < 36$	If $a < b$ and $c > 0$, then $ac < bc$.
Division You can divide both sides of an inequality by the same *positive* number, and the statement will still be true.	$15 < 35$ $\dfrac{15}{5} < \dfrac{35}{5}$ $3 < 7$	If $a < b$ and $c > 0$, then $\dfrac{a}{c} < \dfrac{b}{c}$.

These properties are also true for inequalities that use the symbols $>$, $\geq$, and $\leq$.

COMMON CORE GPS
MCC9-12.A.REI.3

EXAMPLE **1** Multiplying or Dividing by a Positive Number

Solve each inequality and graph the solutions.

my.hrw.com

Online Video Tutor

A $3x > -27$

$3x > -27$ *Since x is multiplied by 3, divide both sides by 3 to undo the multiplication.*

$\dfrac{3x}{3} > \dfrac{-27}{3}$

$x > -9$

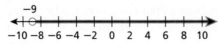

Solve each inequality and graph the solutions.

B $\frac{2}{3}r < 6$

$$\frac{2}{3}r < 6$$ *Since r is multiplied by $\frac{2}{3}$, multiply both sides by the reciprocal of $\frac{2}{3}$.*

$$\frac{3}{2}\left(\frac{2}{3}r\right) < \frac{3}{2}(6)$$

$$r < 9$$

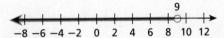

 CHECK IT OUT!

Solve each inequality and graph the solutions.

1a. $4k > 24$ **1b.** $-50 \geq 5q$ **1c.** $\frac{3}{4}g > 27$

What happens when you multiply or divide both sides of an inequality by a negative number?

Look at the number line below.

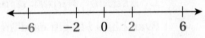

$2 < 6$		$6 > -2$	
-2 ▨ -6	*Multiply both sides by −1.*	-6 ▨ 2	*Multiply both sides by −1.*
$-2 > -6$	*Use the number line to determine the direction of the inequality.*	$-6 < 2$	*Use the number line to determine the direction of the inequality.*

Notice that when you multiply (or divide) both sides of an inequality by a negative number, you must reverse the inequality symbol. This means there is another set of properties of inequality for multiplying or dividing by a negative number.

 Know it! Note

Properties of Inequality

Multiplication and Division by Negative Numbers

WORDS	NUMBERS	ALGEBRA
Multiplication If you multiply both sides of an inequality by the same *negative* number, you must reverse the inequality symbol for the statement to still be true.	$8 > 4$ $8(-2) < 4(-2)$ $-16 < -8$	If $a > b$ and $c < 0$, then $ac < bc$.
Division If you divide both sides of an inequality by the same *negative* number, you must reverse the inequality symbol for the statement to still be true.	$12 > 4$ $\dfrac{12}{-4} < \dfrac{4}{-4}$ $-3 < -1$	If $a > b$ and $c < 0$, then $\dfrac{a}{c} < \dfrac{b}{c}$.

These properties are also true for inequalities that use the symbols <, ≥, and ≤.

EXAMPLE 2

MCC9-12.A.REI.3

Multiplying or Dividing by a Negative Number

Solve each inequality and graph the solutions.

my.hrw.com

Online Video Tutor

A $-8x > 72$

$$\frac{-8x}{-8} < \frac{72}{-8}$$

$$x < -9$$

Since x is multiplied by −8, divide both sides by −8. Change > to <.

B $-3 \le \dfrac{x}{-5}$

$$-5(-3) \ge -5\left(\frac{x}{-5}\right)$$

$$15 \ge x \ (\text{or } x \le 15)$$

Since x is divided by −5, multiply both sides by −5. Change ≤ to ≥.

CHECK IT OUT! Solve each inequality and graph the solutions.

2a. $10 \ge -x$ **2b.** $4.25 > -0.25h$

EXAMPLE 3

MCC9-12.A.CED.1

Consumer Application

my.hrw.com

Online Video Tutor

Ryan has a $16 gift card for a health store where a smoothie costs $2.50 with tax. What are the possible numbers of smoothies that Ryan can buy?

Let *s* represent the number of smoothies Ryan can buy.

$2.50	times	number of smoothies	is at most	$16.00.
2.50	•	s	≤	16.00

$2.50s \le 16.00$

$$\frac{2.50s}{2.50} \le \frac{16.00}{2.50}$$

Since s is multiplied by 2.50, divide both sides by 2.50. The symbol does not change.

$s \le 6.4$ *Ryan can buy only a whole number of smoothies.*

Ryan can buy 0, 1, 2, 3, 4, 5, or 6 smoothies.

CHECK IT OUT! **3.** A pitcher holds 128 ounces of juice. What are the possible numbers of 10-ounce servings that one pitcher can fill?

THINK AND DISCUSS

1. Compare the Multiplication and Division Properties of Inequality and the Multiplication and Division Properties of Equality.

2. GET ORGANIZED Copy and complete the graphic organizer. In each cell, write and solve an inequality.

Solving Inequalities by Using Multiplication and Division		
	By a Positive Number	**By a Negative Number**
Divide		
Multiply		

my.hrw.com
Homework Help

GUIDED PRACTICE

Solve each inequality and graph the solutions.

SEE EXAMPLE 1

1. $3b > 27$ **2.** $-40 \geq 8b$ **3.** $\dfrac{d}{3} > 6$ **4.** $24d \leq 6$

5. $1.1m \leq 1.21$ **6.** $\dfrac{2}{3}k > 6$ **7.** $9s > -18$ **8.** $\dfrac{4}{5} \geq \dfrac{r}{2}$

SEE EXAMPLE 2

9. $-2x < -10$ **10.** $\dfrac{b}{-2} \geq 8$ **11.** $-3.5n < 1.4$ **12.** $4 > -8g$

13. $\dfrac{d}{-6} < \dfrac{1}{2}$ **14.** $-10h \geq -6$ **15.** $12 > \dfrac{t}{-6}$ **16.** $-\dfrac{1}{2}m \geq -7$

SEE EXAMPLE 3

17. **Travel** Tom saved $550 to go on a school trip. The cost for a hotel room, including tax, is $80 per night. What are the possible numbers of nights Tom can stay at the hotel?

PRACTICE AND PROBLEM SOLVING

my.hrw.com

Online Extra Practice

Solve each inequality and graph the solutions.

18. $10 < 2t$ **19.** $\dfrac{1}{3}j \leq 4$ **20.** $-80 < 8c$ **21.** $21 > 3d$

22. $\dfrac{w}{4} \geq -2$ **23.** $\dfrac{h}{4} \leq \dfrac{2}{7}$ **24.** $6y < 4.2$ **25.** $12c \leq -144$

26. $\dfrac{4}{5}x \geq \dfrac{2}{5}$ **27.** $6b \geq \dfrac{3}{5}$ **28.** $-25 > 10p$ **29.** $\dfrac{b}{8} \leq -2$

30. $-9a > 81$ **31.** $\dfrac{1}{2} < \dfrac{r}{-3}$ **32.** $-6p > 0.6$ **33.** $\dfrac{y}{-4} > -\dfrac{1}{2}$

34. $-\dfrac{1}{6}f < 5$ **35.** $-2.25t < -9$ **36.** $24 \leq -10w$ **37.** $-11z > 121$

38. $\dfrac{3}{5} < \dfrac{f}{-5}$ **39.** $-k \geq 7$ **40.** $-2.2b < -7.7$ **41.** $16 \geq -\dfrac{4}{3}p$

42. **Camping** The rope Roz brought with her camping gear is 54 inches long. Roz needs to cut shorter pieces of rope that are each 18 inches long. What are the possible number of pieces Roz can cut?

Solve each inequality and graph the solutions.

43. $-8x < 24$ **44.** $3t \leq 24$ **45.** $\dfrac{1}{4}x < 5$ **46.** $\dfrac{4}{5}p \geq -24$

47. $54 \leq -9p$ **48.** $3t > -\dfrac{1}{2}$ **49.** $-\dfrac{3}{4}b > -\dfrac{3}{2}$ **50.** $216 > 3.6r$

Write an inequality for each statement. Solve the inequality and graph the solutions.

51. The product of a number and 7 is not less than 21.

52. The quotient of h and -6 is at least 5.

53. The product of $-\dfrac{4}{5}$ and b is at most -16.

54. Ten is no more than the quotient of t and 4.

H.O.T. **55.** **Write About It** Explain how you know whether to reverse the inequality symbol when solving an inequality.

56. **Geometry** The area of a rectangle is at most 21 square inches. The width of the rectangle is 3.5 inches. What are the possible measurements for the length of the rectangle?

Solve each inequality and match the solution to the correct graph.

57. $-0.5t \geq 1.5$

A.
$$-5\ -4\ -3\ -2\ -1\ \ 0\ \ 1\ \ 2\ \ 3\ \ 4\ \ 5$$

58. $\frac{1}{9}t \leq -3$

B.
$$-5\ -4\ -3\ -2\ -1\ \ 0\ \ 1\ \ 2\ \ 3\ \ 4\ \ 5$$

59. $-13.5 \leq -4.5t$

C.
$$-5\ -4\ -3\ -2\ -1\ \ 0\ \ 1\ \ 2\ \ 3\ \ 4\ \ 5$$

60. $\frac{t}{-6} \leq -\frac{1}{2}$

D.
$$-45\ -36\ -27\ -18\ -9\ \ 0\ \ 9$$

61. **Animals** A wildlife shelter is home to birds, mammals, and reptiles. If cat chow is sold in 20 lb bags, what is the least number of bags of cat chow needed for one year at this shelter?

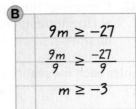

Food Consumed at a Wildlife Shelter per Week	
Type of Food	**Amount of Food (lb)**
Grapes	4
Mixed seed	10
Peanuts	5
Cat chow	10
Kitten chow	5

Orangutans weigh about 3.5 pounds at birth. As adults, female orangutans can weigh as much as 110 pounds, and male orangutans can weigh up to 300 pounds.

62. **Education** In order to earn an A in a college math class, a student must score no less than 90% of all possible points. One semester, a student with 567 points earned an A in the class. Write an inequality to show the numbers of points possible.

H.O.T. 63. **Critical Thinking** Explain why you cannot solve an inequality by multiplying both sides by zero.

H.O.T. 64. **/// ERROR ANALYSIS ///** Two students have different answers for a homework problem. Which answer is incorrect? Explain the error.

A
$$9m \geq -27$$
$$\frac{9m}{9} \geq \frac{-27}{9}$$
$$m \leq -3$$

B
$$9m \geq -27$$
$$\frac{9m}{9} \geq \frac{-27}{9}$$
$$m \geq -3$$

65. Jan has a budget of $800 for catering. The catering company charges $12.50 per guest. Write and solve an inequality to show the numbers of guests Jan can invite.

Real-World Connections

66. a. The Swimming Club can spend a total of $250 for hotel rooms for its spring trip. One hotel costs $75 per night. Write an inequality to find the number of rooms the club can reserve at this hotel. Let n be the number of rooms.

b. Solve the inequality you wrote in part **a.** Graph the solutions on a number line. Make sure your answer is reasonable.

c. Another hotel offers a rate of $65 per night. Does this allow the club to reserve more rooms? Explain your reasoning.

67. Which inequality does NOT have the same solutions as $-\frac{2}{3}y > 4$?

  Ⓐ $12 < -2y$

  Ⓑ $\frac{y}{2} < -12$

  Ⓒ $-\frac{3}{4}y > \frac{9}{2}$

  Ⓓ $-3y > 18$

68. The solutions of which inequality are NOT represented by the following graph?

  Ⓕ $\frac{x}{2} \geq -2$

  Ⓖ $-5x \geq 20$

  Ⓗ $3x \geq -12$

  Ⓙ $-7x \leq 28$

69. Which inequality can be used to find the number of 39-cent stamps you can purchase for $4.00?

  Ⓐ $0.39s \geq 4.00$

  Ⓑ $0.39s \leq 4.00$

  Ⓒ $\frac{s}{0.39} \leq 4.00$

  Ⓓ $\frac{4.00}{0.39} \leq s$

70. Short Response Write three different inequalities that have the same solutions as $x > 4$. Show your work and explain each step.

CHALLENGE AND EXTEND

Solve each inequality.

71. $2\frac{1}{3} \leq -\frac{5}{6}g$ **72.** $\frac{2x}{3} < 8.25$ **73.** $2\frac{5}{8}m > \frac{7}{10}$ **74.** $3\frac{3}{5}f \geq 14\frac{2}{5}$

75. Estimation What is the greatest possible integer solution of the inequality $3.806x < 19.902$?

76. Critical Thinking The Transitive Property of Equality states that if $a = b$ and $b = c$, then $a = c$. Is there a Transitive Property of Inequality using the symbol $<$? Give an example to support your answer.

77. Critical Thinking The Symmetric Property of Equality states that if $a = b$, then $b = a$. Is there a Symmetric Property of Inequality? Give an example to support your answer.

FOCUS ON MATHEMATICAL PRACTICES

H.O.T. **78. Error Analysis** Marigold solves an inequality as shown.

$$\frac{4}{5}x \geq -20$$
$$\frac{5}{4}\left(\frac{4}{5}x\right) \geq \frac{5}{4}(-20)$$
$$x \leq -\frac{100}{4}$$
$$x \leq -25$$

What mistake did Marigold make? What is the correct answer?

H.O.T. **79. Make a Conjecture** The solution to the inequality $kx < 6$ is $x > -2$.

  a. What can you say about the value of k just by looking at the inequality and its solution, without actually solving the problem?

  b. Find another solution for x by dividing both sides of $kx < 6$ by k.

  c. Use $x > -2$ and your solution from part b to make an equation, then solve for k. Does the solution support your conjecture from part a?

Ready to Go On?

my.hrw.com
Assessment and Intervention

4-1 Graphing and Writing Inequalities

Describe the solutions of each inequality in words.

1. $-2 < r$ **2.** $t - 1 \le 7$ **3.** $2s \ge 6$ **4.** $4 > 5 - x$

Graph each inequality.

5. $x > -2$ **6.** $m \le 1\frac{1}{2}$ **7.** $g < \sqrt{8+1}$ **8.** $h \ge 2^3$

Write the inequality shown by each graph.

9.
$$\xleftarrow{\quad} \; -5 \; -4 \; -3 \; -2 \; -1 \; 0 \; 1 \; 2 \; 3 \; 4 \; 5 \; \xrightarrow{\quad}$$

10.
$$\xleftarrow{\quad} \; -4 \; -3 \; -2 \; -1 \; 0 \; 1 \; 2 \; 3 \; 4 \; 5 \; 6 \; \xrightarrow{\quad}$$

11.
$$-1.5$$
$$\xleftarrow{\quad} \; -6 \; -5 \; -4 \; -3 \; -2 \; -1 \; 0 \; 1 \; 2 \; 3 \; 4 \; \xrightarrow{\quad}$$

Write an inequality for each situation and graph the solutions.

12. You must purchase at least 5 tickets to receive a discount.

13. Children under 13 are not admitted to certain movies without an adult.

14. A cell phone plan allows up to 250 free minutes per month.

4-2 Solving One-Step Inequalities by Adding or Subtracting

Solve each inequality and graph the solutions.

15. $k + 5 \le 7$ **16.** $4 > p - 3$ **17.** $r - 8 \ge -12$ **18.** $-3 + p < -6$

19. Allie must sell at least 50 gift baskets for the band fund-raiser. She already sold 36 baskets. Write and solve an inequality to determine how many more baskets Allie must sell for the fund-raiser.

20. Dante has at most $12 to spend on entertainment each week. So far this week, he spent $7.50. Write and solve an inequality to determine how much money Dante can spend on entertainment the rest of the week.

4-3 Solving One-Step Inequalities by Multiplying or Dividing

Solve each inequality and graph the solutions.

21. $-4x < 8$ **22.** $\frac{d}{3} \ge -3$ **23.** $\frac{3}{4}t \le 12$ **24.** $8 > -16c$

25. A spool of ribbon is 80 inches long. Riley needs to cut strips of ribbon that are 14 inches long. What are the possible numbers of strips that Riley can cut?

PARCC Assessment Readiness

Selected Response

1. Graph the inequality $m < -3.4$.

Ⓐ
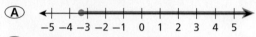

Ⓑ

Ⓒ

Ⓓ

2. Describe the solutions of $6 + y < 10$ in words.

Ⓕ The value of y is a number less than or equal to 3.

Ⓖ The value of y is a number less than 4.

Ⓗ The value of y is a number equal to 3.

Ⓙ The value of y is a number greater than 4.

3. To join the school swim team, swimmers must be able to swim at least 800 yards without stopping. Let n represent the number of yards a swimmer can swim without stopping. Write an inequality describing which values of n will result in a swimmer making the team.

Ⓐ $n \leq 800$ Ⓒ $n > 800$

Ⓑ $n \geq 800$ Ⓓ $n < 800$

4. Solve the inequality $n + 6 < -1.5$ and graph the solutions.

Ⓕ $n < 4.5$

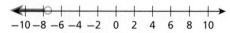

Ⓖ $n < -7.5$

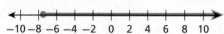

Ⓗ $n < -7.5$

Ⓙ $n < 4.5$

5. Solve the inequality $\frac{z}{-4} \leq 2$.

Ⓐ $z \geq -8$ Ⓒ $z \leq 8$

Ⓑ $z \leq -8$ Ⓓ $z \geq 8$

6. Carlotta subscribes to the HotBurn music service. She can download no more than 11 song files per week. Carlotta has already downloaded 8 song files this week. Write, solve, and graph an inequality to show how many more songs Carlotta can download.

Ⓕ $s \leq 3$

Ⓖ $s > 3$

Ⓗ $s \geq 3$

Ⓙ $s < 3$

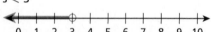

7. Marco's Drama class is performing a play. He wants to buy as many tickets as he can afford. If tickets cost $2.50 each and he has $14.75 to spend, how many tickets can he buy?

Ⓐ 4 tickets   Ⓒ 6 tickets

Ⓑ 0 tickets   Ⓓ 5 tickets

Mini-Task

8. Glen raised $275 for his softball team's fundraiser. He wants to raise at least $715.

a. Write and solve an inequality to determine how much more money Glen must raise to reach his goal. Let d represent the amount of money in dollars Glen must raise to reach his goal.

b. If Glen raises $50 per week, what is the minimum number of weeks it will take him to reach his goal?

5 Solving Multi-Step Inequalities

COMMON CORE GPS

Contents

The Common Core Georgia Performance Standards for Mathematical Practice describe varieties of expertise that all students should seek to develop. Opportunities to develop these practices are integrated throughout this program.

1 Make sense of problems and persevere in solving them.

2 Reason abstractly and quantitatively.

3 Construct viable arguments and critique the reasoning of others.

4 Model with mathematics.

5 Use appropriate tools strategically.

6 Attend to precision.

7 Look for and make use of structure.

8 Look for and express regularity in repeated reasoning.

Unpacking the Standards

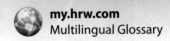

Understanding the standards and the vocabulary terms in the standards will help you know exactly what you are expected to learn in this chapter.

 MCC9-12.A.CED.1

Create ... inequalities ... in one variable and use them to solve problems.

What It Means For You

You can write an inequality to represent a real-world problem and then solve the inequality to find the possible answers.

EXAMPLE

Amy uses $\frac{3}{4}$ cup of vanilla yogurt to make a smoothie. What are the possible whole numbers of smoothies that Amy can make using 1 quart of vanilla yogurt?

Let s represent the number of smoothies Amy can make.

cups per smoothie		number of smoothies	$\leq$	cups per quart
$\frac{3}{4}$	$\cdot$	s	$\leq$	4
		$\frac{3}{4}s$	$\leq$	4
		s	$\leq$	$\frac{16}{3}$

Amy can make 0, 1, 2, 3, 4, or 5 smoothies.

 MCC9-12.A.REI.3

Solve linear ... inequalities in one variable, ...

Key Vocabulary

linear inequality in one variable
(desigualdad lineal en una variable)
An inequality that can be written in one of the following forms: $ax < b$, $ax > b$, $ax \leq b$, $ax \geq b$, or $ax \neq b$, where a and b are constants and $a \neq 0$.

What It Means For You

Solving inequalities lets you answer questions where a range of solutions is possible.

EXAMPLE

Solve the inequality for t to find what grades on the final exam will give Cleo a course grade of "A".

$705 + 2t \geq 895$ *Cleo has 705 points and needs at least 895.*

$2t \geq 190$ *Subtract 705 from both sides.*

$t \geq 95$ *Divide both sides by 2.*

Cleo needs to earn a 95 or above on the final exam.

Solving Two-Step and Multi-Step Inequalities

Essential Question: How can you solve inequalities that involve more than one operation?

Objective
Solve inequalities that contain more than one operation.

Who uses this?

Contestants at a county fair can solve an inequality to find how many pounds a prize-winning pumpkin must weigh. (See Example 3.)

At the county fair, contestants can enter contests that judge animals, recipes, crops, art projects, and more. Sometimes an average score or average weight is used to determine the winner of the blue ribbon. A contestant can use a multi-step inequality to determine what score or weight is needed in order to win.

Inequalities that contain more than one operation require more than one step to solve. Use inverse operations to undo the operations in the inequality one at a time.

COMMON CORE GPS

EXAMPLE 1

MCC9-12.A.REI.3

my.hrw.com

Online Video Tutor

Solving Multi-Step Inequalities

Solve each inequality and graph the solutions.

A $160 + 4f \le 500$

$$
\begin{aligned}
160 + 4f &\le 500 \\
-160 \quad\quad &-160 \\
\hline
4f &\le 340 \\
\frac{4f}{4} &\le \frac{340}{4} \\
f &\le 85
\end{aligned}
$$

Since 160 is added to 4f, subtract 160 from both sides to undo the addition.

Since f is multiplied by 4, divide both sides by 4 to undo the multiplication.

B $7 - 2t \le 21$

$$
\begin{aligned}
7 - 2t &\le 21 \\
-7 \quad\quad &-7 \\
\hline
-2t &\le 14 \\
\frac{-2t}{-2} &\ge \frac{14}{-2} \\
t &\ge -7
\end{aligned}
$$

Since 7 is added to −2t, subtract 7 from both sides to undo the addition.

Since t is multiplied by −2, divide both sides by −2 to undo the multiplication. Change ≤ to ≥.

 Solve each inequality and graph the solutions.

1a. $-12 \ge 3x + 6$ **1b.** $\dfrac{x+5}{-2} > 3$ **1c.** $\dfrac{1-2n}{3} \ge 7$

© Peter Beck/CORBIS

To solve more complicated inequalities, you may first need to simplify the expressions on one or both sides by using the order of operations, combining like terms, or using the Distributive Property.

Simplifying Before Solving Inequalities

Solve each inequality and graph the solutions.

A $-4 + (-8) < -5c - 2$

$\qquad -12 < -5c - 2$ *Combine like terms. Since 2 is subtracted from −5c,*

$\qquad \underline{\phantom{-12 <} +2 \qquad +2}$ *add 2 to both sides to undo the subtraction.*

$\qquad -10 < -5c$

$\qquad \dfrac{-10}{-5} > \dfrac{-5c}{-5}$ *Since c is multiplied by −5, divide both sides by −5*

$\qquad\qquad 2 > c \text{ (or } c < 2)$ *to undo the multiplication. Change < to >.*

A number line from −5 to 5 with an open circle at 2 and shading to the left.

B $-3(3 - x) < 4^2$

$\qquad -3(3 - x) < 4^2$ *Distribute −3 on the left side.*

$\qquad -3(3) - (-3)x < 4^2$

$\qquad -9 + 3x < 4^2$

$\qquad -9 + 3x < 16$ *Simplify the right side.*

$\qquad -9 + 3x < 16$ *Since −9 is added to 3x, add 9 to both sides*

$\qquad \underline{+9 \qquad\qquad +9}$ *to undo the addition.*

$\qquad\qquad\quad 3x < 25$ *Since x is multiplied by 3, divide both sides by*

$\qquad\qquad\quad \dfrac{3x}{3} < \dfrac{25}{3}$ *3 to undo the multiplication.*

$\qquad\qquad\quad x < 8\dfrac{1}{3}$

A number line from 0 to 10 with an open circle at $8\frac{1}{3}$ and shading to the left.

C $\dfrac{4}{5}x + \dfrac{1}{2} > \dfrac{3}{5}$

$\qquad 10\left(\dfrac{4}{5}x + \dfrac{1}{2}\right) > 10\left(\dfrac{3}{5}\right)$ *Multiply both sides by 10, the LCD of the fractions.*

$\qquad 10\left(\dfrac{4}{5}x\right) + 10\left(\dfrac{1}{2}\right) > 10\left(\dfrac{3}{5}\right)$ *Distribute 10 on the left side.*

$\qquad\qquad 8x + 5 > 6$ *Since 5 is added to 8x, subtract 5 from*

$\qquad\qquad \underline{ -5 \quad -5}$ *both sides to undo the addition.*

$\qquad\qquad 8x > 1$

$\qquad\qquad \dfrac{8x}{8} > \dfrac{1}{8}$ *Since x is multiplied by 8, divide both sides*

$\qquad\qquad\quad x > \dfrac{1}{8}$ *by 8 to undo the multiplication.*

A number line from $-\frac{1}{2}$ to $\frac{3}{4}$ with an open circle at $\frac{1}{8}$ and shading to the right.

Solve each inequality and graph the solutions.

2a. $2m + 5 > 5^2$ **2b.** $3 + 2(x + 4) > 3$ **2c.** $\dfrac{5}{8} < \dfrac{3}{8}x - \dfrac{1}{4}$

Gardening Application

To win the blue ribbon for the Heaviest Pumpkin Crop at the county fair, the average weight of John's two pumpkins must be greater than 819 lb. One of his pumpkins weighs 887 lb. What is the least number of pounds the second pumpkin could weigh in order for John to win the blue ribbon?

Let p represent the weight of the second pumpkin. The average weight of the pumpkins is the sum of each weight divided by 2.

(887	plus	p)	divided by	2	must be greater than	819.
(887	+	p)	÷	2	>	819

$$\frac{887 + p}{2} > 819$$
Since 887 + p is divided by 2, multiply both sides by 2 to undo the division.

$$2\left(\frac{887 + p}{2}\right) > 2(819)$$

$$887 + p > 1638$$
Since 887 is added to p, subtract 887 from both sides to undo the addition.

$$\frac{-887 \qquad -887}{p > \quad 751}$$

The second pumpkin must weigh more than 751 pounds.

Check   Check the endpoint, 751.   Check a number greater than 751.

$$\frac{887 + p}{2} = 819 \qquad\qquad \frac{887 + p}{2} > 819$$

$\frac{887 + 751}{2}$	819	$\frac{887 + 755}{2}$	>	819
$\frac{1638}{2}$	819	$\frac{1642}{2}$	>	819
819	819 ✓	821	>	819 ✓

 3. The average of Jim's two test scores must be at least 90 to make an A in the class. Jim got a 95 on his first test. What scores can Jim get on his second test to make an A in the class?

MCC.MP.1, MCC.MP.7   MATHEMATICAL PRACTICES

THINK AND DISCUSS

1. The inequality $v \geq 25$ states that 25 is the ___?___. (*value of v, minimum value of v*, or *maximum value of v*)

2. Describe two sets of steps for solving the inequality $\frac{x + 5}{3} > 7$.

 3. GET ORGANIZED Copy and complete the graphic organizer.

Solving Multi-Step Equations and Inequalities

How are they alike?   How are they different?

GUIDED PRACTICE

Solve each inequality and graph the solutions.

SEE EXAMPLE 1

1. $2m + 1 > 13$ **2.** $2d + 21 \leq 11$ **3.** $6 \leq -2x + 2$ **4.** $4c - 7 > 5$

5. $\dfrac{4 + x}{3} > -4$ **6.** $1 < 0.2x - 0.7$ **7.** $\dfrac{3 - 2x}{3} \leq 7$ **8.** $2x + 5 \geq 2$

SEE EXAMPLE 2

9. $4(x + 2) > 6$ **10.** $\dfrac{1}{4}x + \dfrac{2}{3} < \dfrac{3}{4}$ **11.** $4 - x + 6^2 \geq 21$

12. $4 - x > 3(4 - 2)$ **13.** $0.2(x - 10) > -1.8$ **14.** $3(j + 41) \leq 35$

SEE EXAMPLE 3

15. **Business** A sales representative is given a choice of two paycheck plans. One choice includes a monthly base pay of $300 plus 10% commission on his sales. The second choice is a monthly salary of $1200. For what amount of sales would the representative make more money with the first plan?

PRACTICE AND PROBLEM SOLVING

Solve each inequality and graph the solutions.

16. $4r - 9 > 7$ **17.** $3 \leq 5 - 2x$ **18.** $\dfrac{w + 3}{2} > 6$ **19.** $11w + 99 < 77$

20. $9 \geq \dfrac{1}{2}v + 3$ **21.** $-4x - 8 > 16$ **22.** $8 - \dfrac{2}{3}z \leq 2$ **23.** $f + 2\dfrac{1}{2} < -2$

24. $\dfrac{3n - 8}{5} \geq 2$ **25.** $-5 > -5 - 3w$ **26.** $10 > \dfrac{5 - 3p}{2}$ **27.** $2v + 1 > 2\dfrac{1}{3}$

28. $4(x + 3) > -24$ **29.** $4 > x - 3(x + 2)$ **30.** $-18 \geq 33 - 3h$

31. $-2 > 7x - 2(x - 4)$ **32.** $9 - (9)^2 > 10x - x$ **33.** $2a - (-3)^2 \geq 13$

34. $6 - \dfrac{x}{3} + 1 > \dfrac{2}{3}$ **35.** $12(x - 3) + 2x > 6$ **36.** $15 \geq 19 + 2(q - 18)$

37. **Communications** One cell phone company offers a plan that costs $29.99 and includes unlimited night and weekend minutes. Another company offers a plan that costs $19.99 and charges $0.35 per minute during nights and weekends. For what numbers of night and weekend minutes does the second company's plan cost more than the first company's plan?

Solve each inequality and graph the solutions.

38. $-12 > -4x - 8$ **39.** $5x + 4 \leq 14$ **40.** $\dfrac{2}{3}x - 5 > 7$

41. $x - 3x > 2 - 10$ **42.** $5 - x - 2 > 3$ **43.** $3 < 2x - 5(x + 3)$

44. $\dfrac{1}{6} - \dfrac{2}{3}m \geq \dfrac{1}{4}$ **45.** $4 - (r - 2) > 3 - 5$ **46.** $0.3 - 0.5n + 1 \geq 0.4$

47. $6^2 > 4(x + 2)$ **48.** $-4 - 2n + 4n > 7 - 2^2$ **49.** $\dfrac{1}{4}(p - 10) \geq 6 - 4$

50. Use the inequality $-4t - 8 \leq 12$ to fill in the missing numbers.

   a. $t \geq \blacksquare$ **b.** $t + 4 \geq \blacksquare$ **c.** $t - \blacksquare \geq 0$

   d. $t + 10 \geq \blacksquare$ **e.** $3t \geq \blacksquare$ **f.** $\dfrac{t}{\blacksquare} \geq -5$

Write an inequality for each statement. Solve the inequality and graph the solutions.

51. One-half of a number, increased by 9, is less than 33.

52. Six is less than or equal to the sum of 4 and $-2x$.

53. The product of 4 and the sum of a number and 12 is at most 16.

54. The sum of half a number and two-thirds of the number is less than 14.

Solve each inequality and match the solution to the correct graph.

55. $4x - 9 \geq 7$

A.

56. $-6 \geq 3(x - 2)$

B.

57. $-2x - 6 \geq -4 + 2$

C.

58. $\dfrac{1}{2} - \dfrac{1}{3}x \leq \left(\dfrac{2}{3} + \dfrac{1}{3}\right)^2$

D.

59. Entertainment A digital video recorder (DVR) records television shows on an internal hard drive. To use a DVR, you need a subscription with a DVR service company. Two companies advertise their charges for a DVR machine and subscription service.

EASY ELECTRONICS

$225 for DVR machine

$400 for lifetime subscription

CABLE SOLUTIONS

$275 for DVR machine

$15 per month for service

For what numbers of months will a consumer pay less for the machine and subscription at Easy Electronics than at Cable Solutions?

60. Geometry The area of the triangle shown is less than 55 square inches.

  a. Write an inequality that can be used to find x.

  b. Solve the inequality you wrote in part **a.**

  c. What is the maximum height of the triangle?

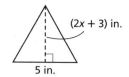

$(2x + 3)$ in.

5 in.

Real-World Connections

61. a. A band wants to create a CD of their last concert. They received a donation of $500 to cover the cost. The total cost is $350 plus $3 per CD. Complete the table to find a relationship between the number of CDs and the total cost.

  b. Write an equation for the cost c of the CDs based on the number of CDs n.

  c. Write an inequality that can be used to determine how many CDs can be made with the $500 donation. Solve the inequality and determine how many CDs the band can have made from the $500 donation.

Number	Process	Cost
1	350 + 3	353
2	■	■
3	■	■
10	■	■
n	■	

H.O.T. 62. Critical Thinking What is the least whole number that is a solution of $4r - 4.9 > 14.95$?

H.O.T. 63. Write About It Describe two sets of steps to solve $2(x + 3) > 10$.

TEST PREP

64. What are the solutions of $3y > 2x + 4$ when $y = 6$?

Ⓐ $7 > x$ Ⓑ $x > 7$ Ⓒ $x > 11$ Ⓓ $11 > x$

65. Cecilia has $30 to spend at a carnival. Admission costs $5.00, lunch will cost $6.00, and each ride ticket costs $1.25. Which inequality represents the number of ride tickets x that Cecilia can buy?

Ⓕ $30 - (5 - 6) + 1.25x \le 30$ Ⓗ $30 - (5 + 6) \le 1.25x$

Ⓖ $5 + 6 + 1.25x \le 30$ Ⓙ $30 + 1.25x \le 5 + 6$

66. Which statement is modeled by $2p + 5 < 11$?

Ⓐ The sum of 5 and 2 times p is at least 11.

Ⓑ Five added to the product of 2 and p is less than 11.

Ⓒ Two times p plus 5 is at most 11.

Ⓓ The product of 2 and p added to 5 is 11.

67. Gridded Response A basketball team scored 8 points more in its second game than in its first. In its third game, the team scored 42 points. The total number of points scored in the three games was more than 150. What is the least number of points the team might have scored in its *second* game?

CHALLENGE AND EXTEND

Solve each inequality and graph the solutions.

68. $3(x + 2) - 6x + 6 \le 0$ **69.** $-18 > -(2x + 9) - 4 + x$ **70.** $\dfrac{2 + x}{2} - (x - 1) > 1$

Write an inequality for each statement. Graph the solutions.

71. x is a positive number.   **72.** x is a negative number.

73. x is a nonnegative number.   **74.** x is not a positive number.

75. x times negative 3 is positive.   **76.** The opposite of x is greater than 2.

FOCUS ON MATHEMATICAL PRACTICES

H.O.T. 77. Modeling Mario wants to spend no more than $85 per month for texting. He is considering a plan that provides him with 200 free text messages for $40 per month, plus $0.10 for each additional text sent or received.

a. Complete the table to show how much Mario would pay for each number of text messages sent or received.

Number of messages	200	400	600	800	1000
Cost in dollars	▪	▪	▪	▪	▪

b. Based on the table, write and solve an inequality that represents the maximum number of texts that Mario can send or receive under this plan.

Solving Inequalities with Variables on Both Sides

 Essential Question: How can you solve inequalities that have the variable on both sides?

Objective
Solve inequalities that contain variable terms on both sides.

Who uses this?
Business owners can use inequalities to find the most cost-efficient services. (See Example 2.)

Some inequalities have variable terms on both sides of the inequality symbol. You can solve these inequalities like you solved equations with variables on both sides.

Use the properties of inequality to "collect" all the variable terms on one side and all the constant terms on the other side.

COMMON CORE GPS
MCC9-12.A.REI.3

EXAMPLE **1** Solving Inequalities with Variables on Both Sides

Solve each inequality and graph the solutions.

my.hrw.com

Online Video Tutor

A $x < 3x + 8$

$$x < 3x + 8$$
$$\underline{-x \quad -x}$$
$$0 < 2x + 8$$
$$\underline{-8 \quad\quad -8}$$
$$-8 < 2x$$

$$\frac{-8}{2} < \frac{2x}{2}$$

$$-4 < x \ (\text{or } x > -4)$$

To collect the variable terms on one side, subtract x from both sides.

Since 8 is added to 2x, subtract 8 from both sides to undo the addition.

Since x is multiplied by 2, divide both sides by 2 to undo the multiplication.

B $6x - 1 \le 3.5x + 4$

$$6x - 1 \le 3.5x + 4$$
$$\underline{-6x \quad\quad -6x}$$
$$-1 \le -2.5x + 4$$
$$\underline{-4 \quad\quad -4}$$
$$-5 \le -2.5x$$

$$\frac{-5}{-2.5} \ge \frac{-2.5x}{-2.5}$$

$$2 \ge x$$

Subtract 6x from both sides.

Since 4 is added to −2.5x, subtract 4 from both sides to undo the addition.

Since x is multiplied by −2.5, divide both sides by −2.5 to undo the multiplication. Reverse the inequality symbol.

Helpful Hint

When you divide by a negative number, remember to reverse the inequality symbol.

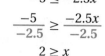
CHECK IT OUT! Solve each inequality and graph the solutions.

1a. $4x \ge 7x + 6$ **1b.** $5t + 1 < -2t - 6$

© Ariel Skelley/CORBIS

COMMON CORE GPS **EXAMPLE** **2**
MCC9-12.A.CED.1

Business Application

The *Daily Info* charges a fee of $650 plus $80 per week to run an ad. The *People's Paper* charges $145 per week. For how many weeks will the total cost at *Daily Info* be less expensive than the cost at *People's Paper*?

Let w be the number of weeks the ad runs in the paper.

Daily Info fee	plus	$80 per week	times	number of weeks	is less expensive than	*People's Paper* charge per week	times	number of weeks.
$650	+	$80	·	w	<	$145	·	w

$$650 + 80w < 145w$$

$\underline{ -80w \quad -80w}$ *Subtract 80w from both sides.*

$$650 \quad < \quad 65w$$ *Since w is multiplied by 65, divide both sides by 65 to undo the multiplication.*

$$\frac{650}{65} < \frac{65w}{65}$$

$$10 < w$$

The total cost at *Daily Info* is less than the cost at *People's Paper* if the ad runs for more than 10 weeks.

2. A-Plus Advertising charges a fee of $24 plus $0.10 per flyer to print and deliver flyers. Print and More charges $0.25 per flyer. For how many flyers is the cost at A-Plus Advertising less than the cost at Print and More?

You may need to simplify one or both sides of an inequality before solving it. Look for like terms to combine and places to use Distributive Property.

COMMON CORE GPS **EXAMPLE** **3**
MCC9-12.A.REI.3

Simplifying Each Side Before Solving

Solve each inequality and graph the solutions.

A $6(1 - x) < 3x$

$$6(1 - x) < 3x$$ *Distribute 6 on the left side of the inequality.*

$$6(1) - 6(x) < 3x$$

$$6 - 6x < 3x$$ *Add 6x to both sides so that the coefficient of x is positive.*

$\underline{ +6x \quad +6x}$

$$6 \quad < \quad 9x$$

$$\frac{6}{9} < \frac{9x}{9}$$ *Since x is multiplied by 9, divide both sides by 9 to undo the multiplication.*

$$\frac{2}{3} < x$$

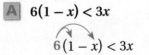

$-\frac{1}{3}$ 0 $\frac{1}{3}$ $\frac{2}{3}$ 1 $1\frac{1}{3}$ $1\frac{2}{3}$ 2 $2\frac{1}{3}$ $2\frac{2}{3}$ 3

Helpful Hint

In Example 3B, you can also multiply each term in the inequality by the same power of 10 to clear the decimals.
$$10(1.6x) \leq 10(-0.2x) + 10(0.9)$$
$$16x \leq -2x + 9$$

Solve each inequality and graph the solutions.

B $1.6x \leq -0.2x + 0.9$

$$
\begin{array}{rl}
1.6x \leq & -0.2x + 0.9 \\
\underline{+\,0.2x} & \underline{+\,0.2x} \\
1.8x \leq & 0.9
\end{array}
$$

Since −0.2x is added to 0.9, subtract −0.2x from both sides. Subtracting −0.2x is the same as adding 0.2x.

$$\frac{1.8x}{1.8} \leq \frac{0.9}{1.8}$$

Since x is multiplied by 1.8, divide both sides by 1.8 to undo the multiplication.

$$x \leq \frac{1}{2}$$

Number line graph with points labeled -2, $-1\frac{1}{2}$, -1, $-\frac{1}{2}$, 0, $\frac{1}{2}$, 1.

 CHECK IT OUT! Solve each inequality and graph the solutions. Check your answer.

3a. $5(2 - r) \geq 3(r - 2)$ **3b.** $0.5x - 0.3 + 1.9x < 0.3x + 6$

Some inequalities are true no matter what value is substituted for the variable. For these inequalities, all real numbers are solutions.

Some inequalities are false no matter what value is substituted for the variable. These inequalities have no solutions.

If both sides of an inequality are fully simplified and the same variable term appears on both sides, then the inequality has all real numbers as solutions or it has no solutions. Look at the other terms in the inequality to decide which is the case.

 EXAMPLE **4**
MCC9-12.A.REI.3

 my.hrw.com

Online Video Tutor

All Real Numbers as Solutions or No Solutions

Solve each inequality.

A $x + 5 \geq x + 3$

$x + 5 \geq x + 3$

The same variable term (x) appears on both sides. Look at the other terms.

For any number x, adding 5 will always result in a greater number than adding 3.

All values of x make the inequality true.
All real numbers are solutions.

B $2(x + 3) < 5 + 2x$

$2x + 6 < 5 + 2x$ *Distribute 2 on the left side.*

The same variable term $(2x)$ appears on both sides. Look at the other terms.

For any number $2x$, adding 6 will never result in a lesser number than adding 5.

No values of x make the inequality true.
There are no solutions.

 CHECK IT OUT! Solve each inequality.

4a. $4(y - 1) \geq 4y + 2$ **4b.** $x - 2 < x + 1$

THINK AND DISCUSS

1. Explain how you would collect the variable terms to solve the inequality $5c - 4 > 8c + 2$.

2. **GET ORGANIZED** Copy and complete the graphic organizer. In each box, give an example of an inequality of the indicated type.

Solutions of Inequalities with Variables on Both Sides

All real numbers   No solutions

5-2 Exercises

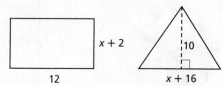

my.hrw.com
Homework Help

GUIDED PRACTICE

SEE EXAMPLE 1 Solve each inequality and graph the solutions.
1. $2x > 4x - 6$
2. $7y + 1 \leq y - 5$
3. $27x + 33 > 58x - 29$
4. $-3r < 10 - r$
5. $5c - 4 > 8c + 2$
6. $4.5x - 3.8 \geq 1.5x - 2.3$

SEE EXAMPLE 2 7. **School** The school band will sell pizzas to raise money for new uniforms. The supplier charges $100 plus $4 per pizza. If the band members sell the pizzas for $7 each, how many pizzas will they have to sell to make a profit?

SEE EXAMPLE 3 Solve each inequality and graph the solutions.
8. $5(4 + x) \leq 3(2 + x)$
9. $-4(3 - p) > 5(p + 1)$
10. $2(6 - x) < 4x$
11. $4x > 3(7 - x)$
12. $\frac{1}{2}f + \frac{3}{4} \geq \frac{1}{4}f$
13. $-36.72 + 5.65t < 0.25t$

SEE EXAMPLE 4 Solve each inequality.
14. $2(x - 2) \leq -2(1 - x)$
15. $4(y + 1) < 4y + 2$
16. $4v + 1 < 4v - 7$
17. $b - 4 \geq b - 6$
18. $3(x - 5) > 3x$
19. $2k + 7 \geq 2(k + 14)$

PRACTICE AND PROBLEM SOLVING

Solve each inequality and graph the solutions.
20. $3x \leq 5x + 8$
21. $9y + 3 > 4y - 7$
22. $1.5x - 1.2 < 3.1x - 2.8$
23. $7 + 4b \geq 3b$
24. $7 - 5t < 4t - 2$
25. $2.8m - 5.2 > 0.8m + 4.8$

26. **Geometry** For what values of x is the area of the rectangle greater than the area of the triangle?

$x + 2$

12

10

$x + 16$

Solve each inequality and graph the solutions.

27. $4(2 - x) \leq 5(x - 2)$ **28.** $-3(n + 4) < 6(1 - n)$ **29.** $9(w + 2) \leq 12w$

30. $4.5 + 1.3t > 3.8t - 3$ **31.** $\frac{1}{2}r + \frac{2}{3} \geq \frac{1}{3}r$ **32.** $2(4 - n) < 3n - 7$

Solve each inequality.

33. $3(2 - x) < -3(x - 1)$ **34.** $7 - y > 5 - y$ **35.** $3(10 + z) \leq 3z + 36$

36. $-5(k - 1) \geq 5(2 - k)$ **37.** $4(x - 1) \leq 4x$ **38.** $3(v - 9) \geq 15 + 3v$

Solve each inequality and graph the solutions.

39. $3t - 12 > 5t + 2$ **40.** $-5(y + 3) - 6 < y + 3$

41. $3x + 9 - 5x < x$ **42.** $18 + 9p > 12p - 31$

43. $2(x - 5) < -3x$ **44.** $-\frac{2}{5}x \leq \frac{4}{5} - \frac{3}{5}x$

45. $-2(x - 7) - 4 - x < 8x + 32$ **46.** $-3(2r - 4) \geq 2(5 - 3r)$

47. $-7x - 10 + 5x \geq 3(x + 4) + 8$ **48.** $-\frac{1}{3}(n + 8) + \frac{1}{3}n \leq 1 - n$

Recreation

49. **Recreation** A red kite is 100 feet off the ground and is rising at 8 feet per second. A blue kite is 180 feet off the ground and is rising at 5 feet per second. How long will it take for the red kite to be higher than the blue kite? Round your answer to the nearest second.

50. **Education** The table shows the enrollment in Howard High School and Phillips High School for three school years.

School Enrollment			
	Year 1	Year 2	Year 3
Howard High School	1192	1188	1184
Phillips High School	921	941	961

   a. How much did the enrollment change each year at Howard?

   b. Use the enrollment in year 1 and your answer from part **a** to write an expression for the enrollment at Howard in any year x.

   c. How much did the enrollment change each year at Phillips?

   d. Use the enrollment in year 1 and your answer from part **c** to write an expression for the enrollment at Phillips in any year x.

   e. Assume that the pattern in the table continues. Use your expressions from parts **b** and **d** to write an inequality that can be solved to find the year in which the enrollment at Phillips High School will be greater than the enrollment at Howard High School. Solve your inequality and graph the solutions.

The American Kitefliers Association has over 4000 members in 35 countries. Kitefliers participate in festivals, competitions, and kite-making workshops.

Real-World Connections

51. a. The school orchestra is creating a CD of their last concert. The total cost is $400 + 4.50 per CD. Write an expression for the cost of creating the CDs based on the number of CDs n.

   b. The orchestra plans to sell the CDs for $12. Write an expression for the amount the orchestra earns from the sale of n CDs.

   c. In order for the orchestra to make a profit, the amount they make selling the CDs must be greater than the cost of creating the CDs. Write an inequality that can be solved to find the number of CDs the orchestra must sell in order to make a profit. Solve your inequality.

(bl), © Brand X Pictures; (cl), HMH

Write an inequality to represent each relationship. Solve your inequality.

52. Four more than twice a number is greater than two-thirds of the number.

53. Ten less than five times a number is less than six times the number decreased by eight.

54. The sum of a number and twenty is less than four times the number decreased by one.

55. Three-fourths of a number is greater than or equal to five less than the number.

56. **Entertainment** Use the table to determine how many movies you would have to rent for Video View to be less expensive than Movie Place.

	Membership Fee ($)	Cost per Rental ($)
Movie Place	None	2.99
Video View	19.99	1.99

57. **Geometry** In an acute triangle, all angles measure less than 90°. Also, the sum of the measures of any two angles is greater than the measure of the third angle. Can the measures of an acute triangle be x, $x - 1$, and $2x$? Explain.

H.O.T. 58. **Write About It** Compare the steps you would follow to solve an inequality to the steps you would follow to solve an equation.

H.O.T. 59. **Critical Thinking** How can you tell just by looking at the inequality $x > x + 1$ that it has no solutions?

H.O.T. 60. /// **ERROR ANALYSIS** /// Two students solved the inequality $5x < 3 - 4x$. Which is incorrect? Explain the error.

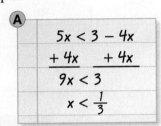

A
$$5x < 3 - 4x$$
$$\underline{+ 4x \qquad + 4x}$$
$$9x < 3$$
$$x < \frac{1}{3}$$

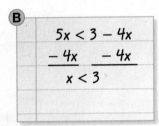

B
$$5x < 3 - 4x$$
$$\underline{- 4x \qquad - 4x}$$
$$x < 3$$

TEST PREP

61. If $a - b > a + b$, which statement is true?
    - Ⓐ The value of a is positive.
    - Ⓒ The value of a is negative.
    - Ⓑ The value of b is positive.
    - Ⓓ The value of b is negative.

62. If $-a < b$, which statement is always true?
    - Ⓕ $a < b$
    - Ⓖ $a > b$
    - Ⓗ $a < -b$
    - Ⓙ $a > -b$

63. Which is a solution of the inequality $7(2 - x) > 4(x - 2)$?
    - Ⓐ -2
    - Ⓑ 2
    - Ⓒ 4
    - Ⓓ 7

64. Which is the graph of $-5x < -2x - 6$?

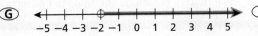

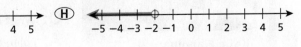

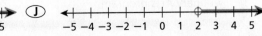

65. Short Response Write a real-world situation that could be modeled by the inequality $7x + 4 > 4x + 13$. Explain how the inequality relates to your situation.

CHALLENGE AND EXTEND

Solve each inequality.

66. $2\frac{1}{2} + 2x \geq 5\frac{1}{2} + 2\frac{1}{2}x$

67. $1.6x - 20.7 > 6.3x - (-2.2x)$

68. $1.3x - 7.5x < 8.5x - 29.4$

69. $-4w + \dfrac{-8 - 37}{9} \leq \dfrac{75 - 3}{9} + 3w$

70. Replace the square and circle with numbers so that the inequality has all real numbers as solutions. $\square - 2x < \bigcirc - 2x$

71. Replace the square and circle with numbers so that the inequality has no solutions. $\square - 2x < \bigcirc - 2x$

H.O.T. 72. Critical Thinking Explain whether there are any numbers that can replace the square and circle so that the inequality has all real numbers as solutions. $\square + 2x < \bigcirc + x$

FOCUS ON MATHEMATICAL PRACTICES

H.O.T. 73. Analysis The table below shows a step-by-step solution to the inequality $2x + 5 > 7x - 35$. Fill in the remaining inequality symbols and steps.

Left Side	Symbol	Right Side	Step
$2x + 5$	>	$7x - 35$	None
$2x$		$7x - 40$	Subtract 5
$-5x$		-40	
x		8	

Career Path

Q: What math classes did you take in high school?

A: Algebra 1, Geometry, and Algebra 2

Q: What math classes have you taken since high school?

A: I have taken a basic accounting class and a business math class.

Q: How do you use math?

A: I use math to estimate how much food I need to buy. I also use math when adjusting recipe amounts to feed large groups of people.

Q: What are your future plans?

A: I plan to start my own catering business. The math classes I took will help me manage the financial aspects of my business.

Katie Flannigan
Culinary Arts program

5-3 # Solving Compound Inequalities

Essential Question: How can you solve compound inequalities and graph their solutions?

Objectives
Solve compound inequalities in one variable.

Graph solution sets of compound inequalities in one variable.

Vocabulary
compound inequality
intersection
union

Who uses this?
A lifeguard can use compound inequalities to describe the safe pH levels in a swimming pool. (See Example 1.)

The inequalities you have seen so far are simple inequalities. When two simple inequalities are combined into one statement by the words AND or OR, the result is called a **compound inequality**.

 Compound Inequalities

WORDS	ALGEBRA	GRAPH
All real numbers greater than 2 AND less than 6	$x > 2$ AND $x < 6$ $2 < x < 6$	
All real numbers greater than or equal to 2 AND less than or equal to 6	$x \geq 2$ AND $x \leq 6$ $2 \leq x \leq 6$	
All real numbers less than 2 OR greater than 6	$x < 2$ OR $x > 6$	
All real numbers less than or equal to 2 OR greater than or equal to 6	$x \leq 2$ OR $x \geq 6$	

COMMON CORE GPS
MCC9-12.A.CED.1

EXAMPLE **1** *Chemistry Application*

A water analyst recommends that the pH level of swimming pool water be between 7.2 and 7.6 inclusive. Write a compound inequality to show the pH levels that are within the recommended range. Graph the solutions.

Let p be the pH level of swimming pool water.

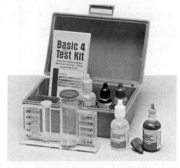

 my.hrw.com

Online Video Tutor

7.2	is less than or equal to	pH level	is less than or equal to	7.6
7.2	$\leq$	p	$\leq$	7.6

$7.2 \leq p \leq 7.6$

Helpful Hint

The phrase "between 7.2 and 7.6 *inclusive*" means 7.2 and 7.6 are solutions. Use a solid circle for endpoints that are solutions.

1. The free chlorine level in a pool should be between 1.0 and 3.0 parts per million inclusive. Write a compound inequality to show the levels that are within this range. Graph the solutions.

In this diagram, oval *A* represents some integer solutions of $x < 10$, and oval *B* represents some integer solutions of $x > 0$. The overlapping region represents numbers that belong in both ovals. Those numbers are solutions of *both $x < 10$ and $x > 0$*.

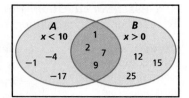

You can graph the solutions of a compound inequality involving AND by using the idea of an overlapping region. The overlapping region is called the **intersection** and shows the numbers that are solutions of both inequalities.

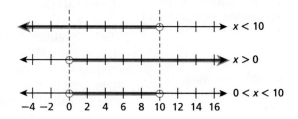

$x < 10$

$x > 0$

$0 < x < 10$

EXAMPLE 2
MCC9-12.A.REI.3

Solving Compound Inequalities Involving AND

Solve each compound inequality and graph the solutions.

A $4 \le x + 2 \le 8$

$$4 \le x + 2 \quad \text{AND} \quad x + 2 \le 8$$ *Write the compound inequality using AND.*
$$\underline{-2 \quad -2} \qquad \underline{-2 \quad -2}$$ *Solve each simple inequality.*
$$2 \le x \qquad \text{AND} \quad x \quad \le 6$$

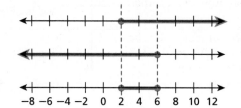

Graph $2 \le x$.

Graph $x \le 6$.

Graph the intersection by finding where the two graphs overlap.

B $-5 \le 2x + 3 < 9$

$$-5 \le 2x + 3 < 9$$ *Since 3 is added to 2x, subtract 3 from each part of the inequality.*
$$\underline{-3 \qquad -3 \quad -3}$$
$$-8 \le 2x \quad < 6$$

$$\frac{-8}{2} \le \frac{2x}{2} < \frac{6}{2}$$ *Since x is multiplied by 2, divide each part of the inequality by 2.*
$$-4 \le x < 3$$

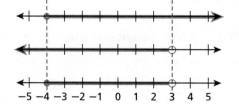

Graph $-4 \le x$.

Graph $x < 3$.

Graph the intersection by finding where the two graphs overlap.

my.hrw.com

Online Video Tutor

Remember!

The statement $-5 \le 2x + 3 \le 9$ consists of two inequalities connected by AND. Example 2B shows a "shorthand" method for solving this type of inequality.

CHECK IT OUT! Solve each compound inequality and graph the solutions.

2a. $-9 < x - 10 < -5$ **2b.** $-4 \le 3n + 5 < 11$

In this diagram, circle *A* represents some integer solutions of $x < 0$, and circle *B* represents some integer solutions of $x > 10$. The combined shaded regions represent numbers that are solutions of *either* $x < 0$ *or* $x > 10$.

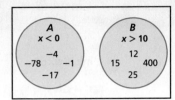

You can graph the solutions of a compound inequality involving OR by using the idea of combining regions. The combined regions are called the **union** and show the numbers that are solutions of either inequality.

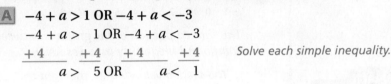

COMMON CORE GPS
MCC9-12.A.REI.3

EXAMPLE 3

my.hrw.com

Online Video Tutor

Solving Compound Inequalities Involving OR

Solve each compound inequality and graph the solutions.

A $-4 + a > 1$ OR $-4 + a < -3$

$$-4 + a > \quad 1 \text{ OR } -4 + a < -3$$
$$\underline{+4 \qquad +4 \qquad +4 \qquad +4}$$
$$a > \quad 5 \text{ OR} \qquad a < \quad 1$$

Solve each simple inequality.

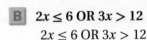

Graph a > 5.

Graph a < 1.

Graph the union by combining the regions.

B $2x \le 6$ OR $3x > 12$

$$2x \le 6 \text{ OR } 3x > 12$$
$$\frac{2x}{2} \le \frac{6}{2} \qquad \frac{3x}{3} > \frac{12}{3}$$
$$x \le 3 \text{ OR } \quad x > \quad 4$$

Solve each simple inequality.

Graph x ≤ 3.

Graph x > 4.

Graph the union by combining the regions.

CHECK IT OUT! Solve each compound inequality and graph the solutions.

3a. $2 + r < 12$ OR $r + 5 > 19$

3b. $7x \ge 21$ OR $2x < -2$

Every solution of a compound inequality involving AND must be a solution of both parts of the compound inequality. If no numbers are solutions of *both* simple inequalities, then the compound inequality has no solutions.

The solutions of a compound inequality involving OR are not always two separate sets of numbers. There may be numbers that are solutions of both parts of the compound inequality.

Writing a Compound Inequality from a Graph

Write the compound inequality shown by each graph.

A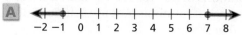

−2 −1 0 1 2 3 4 5 6 7 8

The shaded portion of the graph is not between two values, so the compound inequality involves OR.

> *On the left, the graph shows an arrow pointing left, so use either < or ≤. The solid circle at −1 means −1 is a solution, so use ≤.*

$x \leq -1$

> *On the right, the graph shows an arrow pointing right, so use either > or ≥. The solid circle at 7 means 7 is a solution, so use ≥.*

$x \geq 7$

The compound inequality is $x \leq -1$ OR $x \geq 7$.

B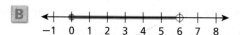

−1 0 1 2 3 4 5 6 7 8

The shaded portion of the graph is between the values 0 and 6, so the compound inequality involves AND.

> *The shaded values are to the right of 0, so use > or ≥. The solid circle at 0 means 0 is a solution, so use ≥.*

$x \geq 0$

> *The shaded values are to the left of 6, so use < or ≤. The empty circle at 6 means 6 is not a solution, so use <.*

$x < 6$

The compound inequality is $x \geq 0$ AND $x < 6$.

Writing Math

The compound inequality in Example 4B can also be written with the variable between the two endpoints.
$0 \leq x < 6$

 CHECK IT OUT! · Write the compound inequality shown by the graph.

4a.

−10 −9 −8 −7 −6 −5 −4 −3 −2 −1 0

4b.

−5 −4 −3 −2 −1 0 1 2 3 4 5

MCC.MP.2 · **MATHEMATICAL PRACTICES**

THINK AND DISCUSS

1. Describe how to write the compound inequality $y > 4$ AND $y \leq 12$ without using the joining word AND.

2. GET ORGANIZED Copy and complete the graphic organizers. Write three solutions in each of the three sections of the diagram. Then write each of your nine solutions in the appropriate column or columns of the table.

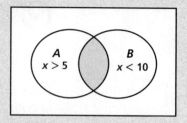

$x > 5$ AND $x < 10$	$x > 5$ OR $x < 10$

Know it! Note

GUIDED PRACTICE

1. **Vocabulary** The graph of a(n) ___?___ shows all values that are solutions to both simple inequalities that make a compound inequality. (*union* or *intersection*)

SEE EXAMPLE 1

2. **Biology** An iguana needs to live in a warm environment. The temperature in a pet iguana's cage should be between 70 °F and 95 °F inclusive. Write a compound inequality to show the temperatures that are within the recommended range. Graph the solutions.

Solve each compound inequality and graph the solutions.

SEE EXAMPLE 2

3. $-3 < x + 2 < 7$

4. $5 \le 4x + 1 \le 13$

5. $2 < x + 2 < 5$

6. $11 < 2x + 3 < 21$

SEE EXAMPLE 3

7. $x + 2 < -6$ OR $x + 2 > 6$

8. $r - 1 < 0$ OR $r - 1 > 4$

9. $n + 2 < 3$ OR $n + 3 > 7$

10. $x - 1 < -1$ OR $x - 5 > -1$

SEE EXAMPLE 4

Write the compound inequality shown by each graph.

11.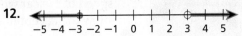

12.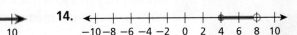

13.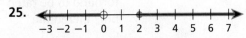

14.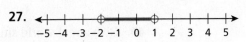

PRACTICE AND PROBLEM SOLVING

Independent Practice	
For Exercises	See Example
15	1
16–19	2
20–23	3
24–27	4

my.hrw.com

Online Extra Practice

15. **Meteorology** One layer of Earth's atmosphere is called the stratosphere. At one point above Earth's surface the stratosphere extends from an altitude of 16 km to an altitude of 50 km. Write a compound inequality to show the altitudes that are within the range of the stratosphere. Graph the solutions.

Solve each compound inequality and graph the solutions.

16. $-1 < x + 1 < 1$

17. $1 \le 2n - 5 \le 7$

18. $-2 < x - 2 < 2$

19. $5 < 3x - 1 < 17$

20. $x - 4 < -7$ OR $x + 3 > 4$

21. $2x + 1 < 1$ OR $x + 5 > 8$

22. $x + 1 < 2$ OR $x + 5 > 8$

23. $x + 3 < 0$ OR $x - 2 > 0$

Write the compound inequality shown by each graph.

24.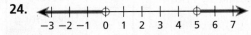

25.

26.

27.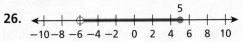

28. **Music** A typical acoustic guitar has a range of three octaves. When the guitar is tuned to "concert pitch," the range of frequencies for those three octaves is between 82.4 Hz and 659.2 Hz inclusive. Write a compound inequality to show the frequencies that are within the range of a typical acoustic guitar. Graph the solutions.

29. Jenna's band is going to record a CD at a recording studio. They will pay $225 to use the studio for one day and $80 per hour for sound technicians. Jenna has $200 and can reasonably expect to raise up to an additional $350 by taking pre-orders for the CDs.

    a. Explain how the inequality $200 \le 225 + 80n \le 550$ can be used to find the number of hours Jenna and her band can afford to use the studio and sound technicians.

    b. Solve the inequality. Are there any numbers in the solution set that are not reasonable in this situation?

    c. Suppose Jenna raises $350 in pre-orders. How much more money would she need to raise if she wanted to use the studio and sound technicians for 6 hours?

Write and graph a compound inequality for the numbers described.

30. all real numbers between -6 and 6

31. all real numbers less than or equal to 2 and greater than or equal to 1

32. all real numbers greater than 0 and less than 15

33. all real numbers between -10 and 10 inclusive

34. **Transportation** The cruise-control function on Georgina's car should keep the speed of the car within 3 mi/h of the set speed. Write a compound inequality to show the acceptable speeds s if the set speed is 55 mi/h. Graph the solutions.

35. **Chemistry** Water is not a liquid if its temperature is above 100 °C or below 0 °C. Write a compound inequality for the temperatures t when water is not a liquid.

Solve each compound inequality and graph the solutions.

36. $5 \le 4b - 3 \le 9$

37. $-3 < x - 1 < 4$

38. $r + 2 < -2$ OR $r - 2 > 2$

39. $2a - 5 < -5$ OR $3a - 2 > 1$

40. $x - 4 \ge 5$ AND $x - 4 \le 5$

41. $n - 4 < -2$ OR $n + 1 > 6$

42. **Sports** The ball used in a soccer game may not weigh more than 16 ounces or less than 14 ounces at the start of the match. After $1\frac{1}{2}$ ounces of air was added to a ball, the ball was approved for use in a game. Write and solve a compound inequality to show how much the ball might have weighed before the air was added.

43. **Meteorology** Tornado damage is rated using the Fujita scale shown in the table. A tornado has a wind speed of 200 miles per hour. Write and solve a compound inequality to show how many miles per hour the wind speed would need to increase for the tornado to be rated "devastating" but not "incredible."

Fujita Tornado Scale		
Category	Type	Wind Speed (mi/h)
F0	Weak	40 to 72
F1	Moderate	73 to 112
F2	Significant	113 to 157
F3	Severe	158 to 206
F4	Devastating	207 to 260
F5	Incredible	261 to 318

44. Give a real-world situation that can be described by a compound inequality. Write the inequality that describes your situation.

H.O.T. 45. **Write About It** How are the graphs of the compound inequality $x < 3$ AND $x < 7$ and the compound inequality $x < 3$ OR $x < 7$ different? How are the graphs alike? Explain.

H.O.T. **46. Critical Thinking** If there is no solution to a compound inequality, does the compound inequality involve OR or AND? Explain.

TEST PREP

47. Which of the following describes the solutions of $-x + 1 > 2$ OR $x - 1 > 2$?

Ⓐ all real numbers greater than 1 or less than 3

Ⓑ all real numbers greater than 3 or less than 1

Ⓒ all real numbers greater than -1 or less than 3

Ⓓ all real numbers greater than 3 or less than -1

48. Which of the following is a graph of the solutions of $x - 3 < 2$ AND $x + 3 > 2$?

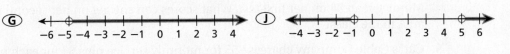

49. Which compound inequality is shown by the graph?

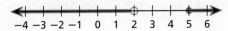

Ⓐ $x \leq 2$ OR $x > 5$

Ⓑ $x < 2$ OR $x \geq 5$

Ⓒ $x \leq 2$ OR $x \geq 5$

Ⓓ $x \geq 2$ OR $x > 5$

50. Which of the following is a solution of $x + 1 \geq 3$ AND $x + 1 \leq 3$?

Ⓕ 0   Ⓖ 1   Ⓗ 2   Ⓙ 3

CHALLENGE AND EXTEND

Solve and graph each compound inequality.

51. $2c - 10 < 5 - 3c < 7c$

52. $5p - 10 < p + 6 < 3p$

53. $2s \leq 18 - s$ OR $5s \geq s + 36$

54. $9 - x \geq 5x$ OR $20 - 3x \leq 17$

55. Write a compound inequality that represents all values of x that are NOT solutions to $x < -1$ OR $x > 3$.

56. For the compound inequality $x + 2 \geq a$ AND $x - 7 \leq b$, find values of a and b for which the only solution is $x = 1$.

FOCUS ON MATHEMATICAL PRACTICES

H.O.T. **57. Modeling** Ronaldo purchased a gym membership at a special rate that allows him at most 15 workouts per month. He has a trainer who requires him to work out at least 9 days per month. In the first half of April, Ronaldo completed d_1, workouts, with $d_1 \leq 9$. Using the variable d_2, write a compound inequality to describe how many times Ronaldo should work out in the second half of April.

H.O.T. **58. Counterexample** While working on a problem involving inequalities, Loretta noticed $12 \leq x \leq 16$ has 4 integer solutions, 12, 13, 14, and 15, but $12 < x < 16$ has only 2 integer solutions, 13 and 14. She proposed that $a \leq x \leq b$ always has 2 more integer solutions than $a < x < b$ whenever $a < b$. Can you think of a counterexample to disprove Loretta's conjecture?

Ready to Go On?

my.hrw.com
Assessment and Intervention

5-1 Solving Two-Step and Multi-Step Inequalities

Solve each inequality and graph the solutions.

1. $2x + 3 < 9$ **2.** $3t - 2 > 10$ **3.** $7 \geq 1 - 6r$

Solve each inequality.

4. $2(x - 3) > -1$ **5.** $\frac{1}{3}a + \frac{1}{2} > \frac{2}{3}$

6. $15 < 5(m - 7)$ **7.** $2 + (-6) > 0.8p$

8. The average of Mindy's two test scores must be at least 92 to make an A in the class. Mindy got an 88 on her first test. What scores can she get on her second test to make an A in the class?

9. Carl's Cable Company charges $55 for monthly service plus $4 for each pay-per-view movie. Teleview Cable Company charges $110 per month with no fee for movies. For what number of movies is the cost of Carl's Cable Company less than the cost of Teleview?

5-2 Solving Inequalities with Variables on Both Sides

Solve each inequality and graph the solutions.

10. $5x < 3x + 8$ **11.** $6p - 3 > 9p$ **12.** $r - 8 \geq 3r - 12$

Solve each inequality.

13. $3(y + 6) > 2(y + 4)$ **14.** $4(5 - g) \geq g$

15. $4x < 4(x - 1)$ **16.** $3(1 - x) \geq -3(x + 2)$

17. Phillip has $100 in the bank and deposits $18 per month. Gil has $145 in the bank and deposits $15 per month. For how many months will Gil have a larger bank balance than Phillip?

18. Hanna has a savings account with a balance of $210 and deposits $16 per month. Faith has a savings account with a balance of $175 and deposits $20 per month. Write and solve an inequality to determine the number of months Hanna's account balance will be greater than Faith's account balance.

5-3 Solving Compound Inequalities

Solve each compound inequality and graph the solutions.

19. $-2 \leq x + 3 < 9$ **20.** $m + 2 < -1$ OR $m - 2 > 6$

21. $-3 \geq x - 1 > 2$ **22.** $-2 > r + 2$ OR $r + 4 < 5$

23. It is recommended that a certain medicine be stored in temperatures above 32 °F and below 70 °F. Write a compound inequality to show the acceptable storage temperatures for this medicine.

PARCC Assessment Readiness

Selected Response

1. Solve the inequality $3n - 6 - n \le 4$ and graph the solutions.

Ⓐ $n \le -1$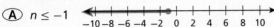

Ⓑ $n \ge -1$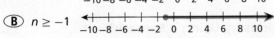

Ⓒ $n \ge 5$

Ⓓ $n \le 5$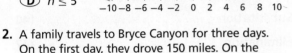

2. A family travels to Bryce Canyon for three days. On the first day, they drove 150 miles. On the second day, they drove 190 miles. What is the least number of miles they drove on the third day if their average number of miles per day was at least 185?

Ⓕ 200 mi   Ⓗ 555 mi

Ⓖ 175 mi   Ⓙ 215 mi

3. Solve the inequality $6x < 3x + 15$ and graph the solutions.

Ⓐ $x < 5$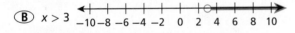

Ⓑ $x > 3$

Ⓒ $x < -5$

Ⓓ $x > 5$

4. Mrs. Williams is deciding between two field trips for her class. The Science Center charges $360 plus $5 per student. The Dino Discovery Museum simply charges $11 per student. For how many students will the Science Center charge less than the Dino Discovery Museum?

Ⓕ Fewer than 60 students

Ⓖ 354 or more students

Ⓗ More than 60 students

Ⓙ 354 or fewer students

5. Solve the inequality $3(y - 3) \le 3y + 2$.

Ⓐ $y \le -1\frac{1}{6}$ Ⓒ $y \le 1\frac{5}{6}$

Ⓑ no solutions   Ⓓ All real numbers are solutions.

6. Fly with Us owns an airplane that has seats for 240 people. The company flies this airplane only if there are at least 100 people on the plane. Write a compound inequality to show the possible number of people in a flight on this airplane. Let n represent the possible number of people in the flight.

Ⓕ $100 \ge n \ge 240$

Ⓖ $100 \le n \le 240$

Ⓗ $n \le 240$

Ⓙ $100 < n < 240$

7. Solve the compound inequality $1 < 3x - 2 \le 10$ and graph the solutions.

Ⓐ $1 < x$ AND $x \le 4$ Ⓒ $1 \le x$ AND $x \le 4$

Ⓑ $1 < x$ AND $x < 4$ Ⓓ $1 > x$ AND $x \ge 4$

8. Write the compound inequality shown by the graph.

Ⓕ $x < -5$ OR $x > 3$ Ⓗ $x \le -5$ OR $x > 3$

Ⓖ $x \le 3$ AND $x > -5$ Ⓙ $x \le -5$ AND $x > 3$

9. Which of the following is a solution of $x - 9 < 5$ AND $x + 5 \ge -1$?

Ⓐ 13   Ⓒ 14

Ⓑ 16   Ⓓ -7

Mini-Tasks

10. A volleyball team scored 6 more points in its first game than in its third game. In the second game, the team scored 23 points. The total number of points scored was less than 55.

a. Write and solve an inequality to find the number of points the team could have scored in its first game.

b. Janie scored 8 points in the first game. Is it possible that she scored exactly half the team's points in that game? Explain.

6 Solving Systems of Equations

COMMON
CORE GPS

Contents

MATHEMATICAL
PRACTICES
  The Common Core Georgia Performance Standards for Mathematical Practice describe varieties of expertise that all students should seek to develop. Opportunities to develop these practices are integrated throughout this program.

1 Make sense of problems and persevere in solving them.

2 Reason abstractly and quantitatively.

3 Construct viable arguments and critique the reasoning of others.

4 Model with mathematics.

5 Use appropriate tools strategically.

6 Attend to precision.

7 Look for and make use of structure.

8 Look for and express regularity in repeated reasoning.

Unpacking the Standards

Understanding the standards and the vocabulary terms in the standards will help you know exactly what you are expected to learn in this chapter.

 MCC9-12.A.CED.2

Create equations in two or more variables to represent relationships between quantities; graph equations on coordinate axes with labels and scales.

Key Vocabulary

equation (ecuación)
A mathematical statement that two expressions are equivalent.

What It Means For You

Creating equations in two variables to describe relationships gives you access to the tools of graphing and algebra to solve the equations.

EXAMPLE

A customer spent $29 on a bouquet of roses and daisies.

r = number of roses in bouquet
d = number of daises in bouquet

$2.5r + 1.75d = 29$

 MCC9-12.A.REI.6

Solve systems of linear equations exactly and approximately (e.g., with graphs), focusing on pairs of linear equations in two variables.

Key Vocabulary

system of linear equations (sistema de ecuaciones lineales) A system of equations in which all of the equations are linear.

What It Means For You

You can solve systems of equations to find out when two relationships involving the same variables are true at the same time.

EXAMPLE

The cost of bowling at bowling alley **A** or **B** is a function of the number of games g.

$$\text{Cost } A = 2.5g + 2$$
$$\text{Cost } B = 2g + 4$$

When are the costs the same?

$$\text{Cost } A = \text{Cost } B$$
$$2.5g + 2 = 2g + 4$$

The cost is $12 at both bowling alleys when g is 4.

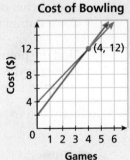

Cost of Bowling

6-1
Technology TASK

Solve Linear Equations by Using a Spreadsheet

You can use a spreadsheet to answer "What if…?" questions. By changing one or more values, you can quickly model different scenarios.

Use with Solving Systems by Graphing

Use appropriate tools strategically.

MCC9-12.A.REI.3 Solve linear equations and inequalities in one variable, including equations with coefficients represented by letters.

Activity

Company Z makes DVD players. The company's costs are $400 per week plus $20 per DVD player. Each DVD player sells for $45. How many DVD players must company Z sell in one week to make a profit?

Let n represent the number of DVD players company Z sells in one week.

$c = 400 + 20n$ *The total cost is $400 plus $20 times the number of DVD players made.*

$s = 45n$ *The total sales income is $45 times the number of DVD players sold.*

$p = s - c$ *The total profit is the sales income minus the total cost.*

1. Set up your spreadsheet with columns for number of DVD players, total cost, total income, and profit.

2. Under Number of DVD Players, enter 1 in cell A2.

3. Use the equations above to enter the formulas for total cost, total sales, and total profit in row 2.
   - In cell B2, enter the formula for total cost.
   - In cell C2, enter the formula for total sales income.
   - In cell D2, enter the formula for total profit.

Company Z Profit

	A	B	C	D
1	Number of DVD Players	Total Cost ($)	Total Income ($)	Profit ($)
2	1	420	45	-375

= 400 + 20*A2   = 45*A2   = C2 − B2

4. Fill columns A, B, C, and D by selecting cells A1 through D1, clicking the small box at the bottom right corner of cell D2, and dragging the box down through several rows.

5. Find the point where the profit is $0. This is known as the breakeven point, where total cost and total income are the same.

Company Z Profit

	A	B	C	D
1	Number of DVD Players	Total Cost ($)	Total Income ($)	Profit ($)
16	15	700	675	-25
17	16	720	720	0
18	17	740	765	25

Breakeven point

Profit begins.

Company Z must sell 17 DVD players to make a profit. The profit is $25.

Try This

For Exercises 1 and 2, use the spreadsheet from the activity.

1. If company Z sells 10 DVD players, will they make a profit? Explain. What if they sell 16?

2. Company Z makes a profit of $225 dollars. How many DVD players did they sell?

For Exercise 3, make a spreadsheet.

3. Company Y's costs are $400 per week plus $20 per DVD player. They want the breakeven point to occur with sales of 8 DVD players. What should the sales price be?

Solving Systems by Graphing

? **Essential Question:** How can you solve systems of linear equations by using graphs?

Objectives
Identify solutions of systems of linear equations in two variables.

Solve systems of linear equations in two variables by graphing.

Vocabulary
system of linear equations
solution of a system of linear equations

Why learn this?

You can compare costs by graphing a system of linear equations. (See Example 3.)

Sometimes there are different charges for the same service or product at different places. For example, Bowl-o-Rama charges $2.50 per game plus $2 for shoe rental while Bowling Pinz charges $2 per game plus $4 for shoe rental. A *system of linear equations* can be used to compare these charges.

A **system of linear equations** is a set of two or more linear equations containing two or more variables. A **solution of a system of linear equations** with two variables is an ordered pair that satisfies each equation in the system. So, if an ordered pair is a solution, it will make both equations true.

 EXAMPLE **1** **Identifying Solutions of Systems**

MCC9-12.A.REI.6

Tell whether the ordered pair is a solution of the given system.

A $(4, 1);$ $\begin{cases} x + 2y = 6 \\ x - y = 3 \end{cases}$

$x + 2y = 6$	
$4 + 2(1)$	6
$4 + 2$	6
6	$6 ✓$

$x - y = 3$	
$4 - 1$	3
3	$3 ✓$

Substitute 4 for x and 1 for y in each equation in the system.

The ordered pair $(4, 1)$ makes both equations true.

$(4, 1)$ is a solution of the system.

 Animated Math

B $(-1, 2);$ $\begin{cases} 2x + 5y = 8 \\ 3x - 2y = 5 \end{cases}$

$2x + 5y = 8$	
$2(-1) + 5(2)$	8
$-2 + 10$	8
8	$8 ✓$

$3x - 2y = 5$	
$3(-1) - 2(2)$	5
$-3 - 4$	5
-7	$5 ✗$

Substitute −1 for x and 2 for y in each equation in the system.

The ordered pair $(-1, 2)$ makes one equation true, but not the other.

$(-1, 2)$ is not a solution of the system.

my.hrw.com

Online Video Tutor

Helpful Hint

If an ordered pair does not satisfy the first equation in the system, there is no need to check the other equations.

 CHECK IT OUT! Tell whether the ordered pair is a solution of the given system.

1a. $(1, 3);$ $\begin{cases} 2x + y = 5 \\ -2x + y = 1 \end{cases}$

1b. $(2, -1);$ $\begin{cases} x - 2y = 4 \\ 3x + y = 6 \end{cases}$

All solutions of a linear equation are on its graph. To find a solution of a system of linear equations, you need a point that each line has in common. In other words, you need their point of intersection.

$$\begin{cases} y = 2x - 1 \\ y = -x + 5 \end{cases}$$

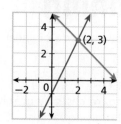

The point $(2, 3)$ is where the two lines intersect and is a solution of both equations, so $(2, 3)$ is the solution of the system.

EXAMPLE 2
MCC9-12.A.REI.6

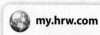
Solving a System of Linear Equations by Graphing

Solve each system by graphing. Check your answer.

A $\begin{cases} y = x - 3 \\ y = -x - 1 \end{cases}$

Graph the system.

The solution appears to be at $(1, -2)$.

Check
Substitute $(1, -2)$ into the system.

$y = x - 3$	
-2	$1 - 3$
-2	-2 ✓

$y = -x - 1$	
-2	$-1 - 1$
-2	-2 ✓

The solution is $(1, -2)$.

Sometimes it is difficult to tell exactly where the lines cross when you solve by graphing. It is good to confirm your answer by substituting it into both equations.

B $\begin{cases} x + y = 0 \\ y = -\dfrac{1}{2}x + 1 \end{cases}$

$$\begin{array}{r} x + y = \quad 0 \\ -x \qquad -x \\ \hline y = -x \end{array}$$

Rewrite the first equation in slope-intercept form.

Graph using a calculator and then use the intersection command.

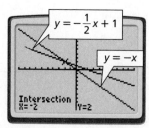

Check Substitute $(-2, 2)$ into the system.

$x + y = 0$	
$-2 + 2$	0
0	0 ✓

$y = -\dfrac{1}{2}x + 1$	
2	$-\dfrac{1}{2}(-2) + 1$
2	$1 + 1$
2	2 ✓

The solution is $(-2, 2)$.

 Solve each system by graphing. Check your answer.

2a. $\begin{cases} y = -2x - 1 \\ y = x + 5 \end{cases}$

2b. $\begin{cases} y = \dfrac{1}{3}x - 3 \\ 2x + y = 4 \end{cases}$

Problem-Solving Application

Bowl-o-Rama charges $2.50 per game plus $2 for shoe rental, and Bowling Pinz charges $2 per game plus $4 for shoe rental. For how many games will the cost to bowl be the same at both places? What is that cost?

1 Understand the Problem

The **answer** will be the number of games played for which the total cost is the same at both bowling alleys. **List the important information:**
- Game price: Bowl-o-Rama $2.50   Bowling Pinz: $2
- Shoe-rental fee: Bowl-o-Rama $2   Bowling Pinz: $4

2 Make a Plan

Write a system of equations, one equation to represent the price at each company. Let x be the number of games played and y be the total cost.

	Total cost	is	price per game	times	games	plus	shoe rental.
Bowl-o-Rama	y	=	2.5	•	x	+	2
Bowling Pinz	y	=	2	•	x	+	4

Make sense of problems and persevere in solving them.

3 Solve

Graph $y = 2.5x + 2$ and $y = 2x + 4$. The lines appear to intersect at $(4, 12)$. So, the cost at both places will be the same for 4 games bowled and that cost will be $12.

4 Look Back

Check $(4, 12)$ using both equations.
Cost of bowling 4 games at Bowl-o-Rama:
$2.5(4) + $2 = 10 + 2 = 12$ ✓
Cost of bowling 4 games at Bowling Pinz:
$2(4) + $4 = 8 + 4 = 12$ ✓

Cost of Bowling

3. Video club A charges $10 for membership and $3 per movie rental. Video club B charges $15 for membership and $2 per movie rental. For how many movie rentals will the cost be the same at both video clubs? What is that cost?

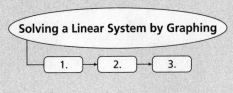
MCC.MP.6 | MATHEMATICAL PRACTICES

THINK AND DISCUSS

1. Explain how to use a graph to solve a system of linear equations.

2. Explain how to check a solution of a system of linear equations.

3. **GET ORGANIZED** Copy and complete the graphic organizer. In each box, write a step for solving a linear system by graphing. More boxes may be added.

Solving a Linear System by Graphing

1. → 2. → 3.

GUIDED PRACTICE

1. **Vocabulary** Describe a *solution of a system of linear equations.*

SEE EXAMPLE 1 · Tell whether the ordered pair is a solution of the given system.

2. $(2, -2)$; $\begin{cases} 3x + y = 4 \\ x - 3y = -4 \end{cases}$

3. $(3, -1)$; $\begin{cases} x - 2y = 5 \\ 2x - y = 7 \end{cases}$

4. $(-1, 5)$; $\begin{cases} -x + y = 6 \\ 2x + 3y = 13 \end{cases}$

SEE EXAMPLE 2 · Solve each system by graphing. Check your answer.

5. $\begin{cases} y = \dfrac{1}{2}x \\ y = -x + 3 \end{cases}$

6. $\begin{cases} y = x - 2 \\ 2x + y = 1 \end{cases}$

7. $\begin{cases} -2x - 1 = y \\ x + y = 3 \end{cases}$

SEE EXAMPLE 3 · 8. To deliver mulch, Lawn and Garden charges $30 per cubic yard of mulch plus a $30 delivery fee. Yard Depot charges $25 per cubic yard of mulch plus a $55 delivery fee. For how many cubic yards will the cost be the same? What will that cost be?

PRACTICE AND PROBLEM SOLVING

Independent Practice

For Exercises	See Example
9–11	1
12–15	2
16	3

Tell whether the ordered pair is a solution of the given system.

9. $(1, -4)$; $\begin{cases} x - 2y = 8 \\ 4x - y = 8 \end{cases}$

10. $(-2, 1)$; $\begin{cases} 2x - 3y = -7 \\ 3x + y = -5 \end{cases}$

11. $(5, 2)$; $\begin{cases} 2x + y = 12 \\ -3y - x = -11 \end{cases}$

Solve each system by graphing. Check your answer.

my.hrw.com

Online Extra Practice

12. $\begin{cases} y = \dfrac{1}{2}x + 2 \\ y = -x - 1 \end{cases}$

13. $\begin{cases} y = x \\ y = -x + 6 \end{cases}$

14. $\begin{cases} -2x - 1 = y \\ x = -y + 3 \end{cases}$

15. $\begin{cases} x + y = 2 \\ y = x - 4 \end{cases}$

16. **Multi-Step** Angelo runs 7 miles per week and increases his distance by 1 mile each week. Marc runs 4 miles per week and increases his distance by 2 miles each week. In how many weeks will Angelo and Marc be running the same distance? What will that distance be?

17. **School** The school band sells carnations on Valentine's Day for $2 each. They buy the carnations from a florist for $0.50 each, plus a $16 delivery charge.

   a. Write a system of equations to describe the situation.

   b. Graph the system. What does the solution represent?

   c. Explain whether the solution shown on the graph makes sense in this situation. If not, give a reasonable solution.

Real-World Connections

18. a. The Warrior baseball team is selling hats as a fund-raiser. They contacted two companies. Hats Off charges a $50 design fee and $5 per hat. Top Stuff charges a $25 design fee and $6 per hat. Write an equation for each company's pricing.

   b. Graph the system of equations from part **a.** For how many hats will the cost be the same? What is that cost?

   c. Explain when it is cheaper for the baseball team to use Top Stuff and when it is cheaper to use Hats Off.

Victoria Smith/HMH

Graphing Calculator Use a graphing calculator to graph and solve the systems of equations in Exercises 19–22. Round your answer to the nearest tenth.

19. $\begin{cases} y = 4.7x + 2.1 \\ y = 1.6x - 5.4 \end{cases}$

20. $\begin{cases} 4.8x + 0.6y = 4 \\ y = -3.2x + 2.7 \end{cases}$

21. $\begin{cases} y = \dfrac{5}{4}x - \dfrac{2}{3} \\ \dfrac{8}{3}x + y = \dfrac{5}{9} \end{cases}$

22. $\begin{cases} y = 6.9x + 12.4 \\ y = -4.1x - 5.3 \end{cases}$

23. Landscaping The gardeners at Middleton Place Gardens want to plant a total of 45 white and pink hydrangeas in one flower bed. In another flower bed, they want to plant 120 hydrangeas. In this bed, they want 2 times the number of white hydrangeas and 3 times the number of pink hydrangeas as in the first bed. Use a system of equations to find how many white and how many pink hydrangeas the gardeners should buy altogether.

Middleton Place Gardens, South Carolina, are the United States' oldest landscaped gardens. The gardens were established in 1741 and opened to the public in the 1920s.

24. Fitness Rusty burns 5 Calories per minute swimming and 11 Calories per minute jogging. In the morning, Rusty burns 200 Calories walking and swims for x minutes. In the afternoon, Rusty will jog for x minutes. How many minutes must he jog to burn at least as many Calories y in the afternoon as he did in the morning? Round your answer up to the next whole number of minutes.

25. A tree that is 2 feet tall is growing at a rate of 1 foot per year. A 6-foot tall tree is growing at a rate of 0.5 foot per year. In how many years will the trees be the same height?

26. Critical Thinking Write a real-world situation that could be represented by the system $\begin{cases} y = 3x + 10 \\ y = 5x + 20 \end{cases}$.

H.O.T. **27. Write About It** When you graph a system of linear equations, why does the intersection of the two lines represent the solution of the system?

TEST PREP

28. Taxi company A charges $4 plus $0.50 per mile. Taxi company B charges $5 plus $0.25 per mile. Which system best represents this problem?

Ⓐ $\begin{cases} y = 4x + 0.5 \\ y = 5x + 0.25 \end{cases}$

Ⓒ $\begin{cases} y = -4x + 0.5 \\ y = -5x + 0.25 \end{cases}$

Ⓑ $\begin{cases} y = 0.5x + 4 \\ y = 0.25x + 5 \end{cases}$

Ⓓ $\begin{cases} y = -0.5x + 4 \\ y = -0.25x + 5 \end{cases}$

29. Which system of equations represents the given graph?

Ⓕ $\begin{cases} y = 2x - 1 \\ y = \dfrac{1}{3}x + 3 \end{cases}$

Ⓗ $\begin{cases} y = 2x + 1 \\ y = \dfrac{1}{3}x - 3 \end{cases}$

Ⓖ $\begin{cases} y = -2x + 1 \\ y = 2x - 3 \end{cases}$

Ⓙ $\begin{cases} y = -2x - 1 \\ y = 3x - 3 \end{cases}$

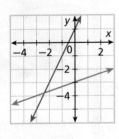

30. Gridded Response Which value of b will make the system $y = 2x + 2$ and $y = 2.5x + b$ intersect at the point $(2, 6)$?

CHALLENGE AND EXTEND

31. Entertainment If the pattern in the table continues, in what month will the number of sales of VCRs and DVD players be the same? What will that number be?

Total Number Sold				
Month	1	2	3	4
VCRs	500	490	480	470
DVD Players	250	265	280	295

32. Long Distance Inc. charges a $1.45 connection charge and $0.03 per minute. Far Away Calls charges a $1.52 connection charge and $0.02 per minute.

   a. For how many minutes will a call cost the same from both companies? What is that cost?

   b. When is it better to call using Long Distance Inc.? Far Away Calls? Explain.

   c. What if...? Long Distance Inc. raised its connection charge to $1.50 and Far Away Calls decreased its connection charge by 2 cents. How will this affect the graphs? Now which company is better to use for calling long distance? Why?

MATHEMATICAL PRACTICES

FOCUS ON MATHEMATICAL PRACTICES

H.O.T. 33. Error Analysis Mario says $(-1, 5)$ is a solution of the system of equations shown. Do you agree? Explain.

$$\begin{cases} x + y = 4 \\ x - y = 6 \end{cases}$$

H.O.T. 34. Problem Solving Amanda cut an 8-foot length of ribbon into two pieces. One piece is three times as long as the other.

   a. Write and graph a system of equations for the length of each piece of ribbon. Use x for the length of the shorter piece, and y for the longer.

   b. What does the point where the lines intersect represent?

   c. What is the system of equations if you define y as the length of the shorter piece and x as the longer piece? What is the solution?

Career Path

Ethan Reynolds
Applied Sciences major

Q: What math classes did you take in high school?

A: Career Math, Algebra, and Geometry

Q: What are you studying and what math classes have you taken?

A: I am really interested in aviation. I am taking Statistics and Trigonometry. Next year I will take Calculus.

Q: How is math used in aviation?

A: I use math to interpret aeronautical charts. I also perform calculations involving wind movements, aircraft weight and balance, and fuel consumption. These skills are necessary for planning and executing safe air flights.

Q: What are your future plans?

A: I could work as a commercial or corporate pilot or even as a flight instructor. I could also work toward a bachelor's degree in aviation management, air traffic control, aviation electronics, aviation maintenance, or aviation computer science.

6-2
Algebra TASK

Model Systems of Linear Equations

You can use algebra tiles to model and solve some systems of linear equations.

Use with Solving Systems by Substitution

MATHEMATICAL PRACTICES

Use appropriate tools strategically.

MCC9-12.A.REI.6 Solve systems of linear equations exactly ... , focusing on pairs of linear equations in two variables.

KEY	REMEMBER
$\boxed{+} = 1$ $\boxed{-} = -1$ $\boxed{+} = x$ $\boxed{-} = -x$	When two expressions are equal, you can substitute one for the other in any expression or equation.

Activity

Use algebra tiles to model and solve $\begin{cases} y = 2x - 3 \\ x + y = 9 \end{cases}$.

MODEL		ALGEBRA
	The first equation is solved for y. Model the second equation, $x + y = 9$, by substituting $2x - 3$ for y.	$x + y = 9$ $x + (2x - 3) = 9$ $3x - 3 = 9$
	Add 3 yellow tiles on both sides of the mat. This represents adding 3 to both sides of the equation. Remove zero pairs.	$3x - 3 = 9$ $\underline{+3 +3}$ $3x = 12$
	Divide each side into 3 equal groups. Align one x-tile with each group on the right side. One x-tile is equivalent to 4 yellow tiles. $x = 4$	$\dfrac{3x}{3} = \dfrac{12}{3}$ $x = 4$

To solve for y, substitute 4 for x in one of the equations:

$$y = 2x - 3$$
$$= 2(4) - 3$$
$$= 5$$

The solution is (4, 5).

Try This

Model and solve each system of equations.

1. $\begin{cases} y = x + 3 \\ 2x + y = 6 \end{cases}$
2. $\begin{cases} 2x + 3 = y \\ x + y = 6 \end{cases}$
3. $\begin{cases} 2x + 3y = 1 \\ x = -1 - y \end{cases}$
4. $\begin{cases} y = x + 1 \\ 2x - y = -5 \end{cases}$

Solving Systems by Substitution

CAMPING OUT FOR THE BEST TICKETS ISN'T WHAT IT USED TO BE...

Off the Mark by Mark Parisi. Cartoon copyrighted by Mark Parisi, printed with permission.

Essential Question: How can you solve systems of linear equations by using substitution?

Objective
Solve systems of linear equations in two variables by substitution.

Why learn this?

You can solve systems of equations to help select the best value among high-speed Internet providers. (See Example 3.)

Sometimes it is difficult to identify the exact solution to a system by graphing. In this case, you can use a method called *substitution*.

The goal when using substitution is to reduce the system to one equation that has only one variable. Then you can solve this equation, and substitute into an original equation to find the value of the other variable.

 Know it! Note

Solving Systems of Equations by Substitution
Step 1 Solve for one variable in at least one equation, if necessary.
Step 2 Substitute the resulting expression into the other equation.
Step 3 Solve that equation to get the value of the first variable.
Step 4 Substitute that value into one of the original equations and solve.
Step 5 Write the values from Steps 3 and 4 as an ordered pair, (x, y), and check.

COMMON CORE GPS
EXAMPLE **1**
MCC9-12.A.REI.6

 my.hrw.com

Online Video Tutor

Helpful Hint

You can substitute the value of one variable into *either* of the original equations to find the value of the other variable.

Solving a System of Linear Equations by Substitution

Solve each system by substitution.

A $\begin{cases} y = 2x \\ y = x + 5 \end{cases}$

Step 1 $y = 2x$ *Both equations are solved for y.*
$y = x + 5$

Step 2 $y = x + 5$ *Substitute 2x for y in the second equation.*
$2x = x + 5$

Step 3 $\dfrac{-x \qquad -x}{x = \qquad 5}$ *Solve for x.*

Step 4 $y = 2x$ *Write one of the original equations.*
$y = 2(5)$ *Substitute 5 for x.*
$y = 10$

Step 5 $(5, 10)$ *Write the solution as an ordered pair.*

Check   Substitute $(5, 10)$ into both equations in the system.

$$\begin{array}{c|c} \multicolumn{2}{c}{y = 2x} \\ \hline 10 & 2(5) \\ 10 & 10 \checkmark \end{array} \qquad \begin{array}{c|c} \multicolumn{2}{c}{y = x + 5} \\ \hline 10 & 5 + 5 \\ 10 & 10 \checkmark \end{array}$$

Solve each system by substitution.

B $\begin{cases} 2x + y = 5 \\ y = x - 4 \end{cases}$

Step 1 $y = x - 4$ *The second equation is solved for y.*

Step 2 $2x + y = 5$

$2x + (x - 4) = 5$ *Substitute x − 4 for y in the first equation.*

Step 3 $3x - 4 = 5$ *Simplify. Then solve for x.*

$\underline{\quad +4 \quad +4\quad}$ *Add 4 to both sides.*

$3x \quad = \quad 9$

$\dfrac{3x}{3} = \dfrac{9}{3}$ *Divide both sides by 3.*

$x = 3$

Step 4 $y = x - 4$ *Write one of the original equations.*

$y = 3 - 4$ *Substitute 3 for x.*

$y = -1$

Step 5 $(3, -1)$ *Write the solution as an ordered pair.*

C $\begin{cases} x + 4y = 6 \\ x + y = 3 \end{cases}$

Step 1 $x + 4y = 6$ *Solve the first equation for x by subtracting*

$\underline{\quad -4y \quad -4y\quad}$ *4y from both sides.*

$x \quad = \quad 6 - 4y$

Step 2 $x + y = 3$

$(6 - 4y) + y = 3$ *Substitute 6 − 4y for x in the second equation.*

Step 3 $6 - 3y = 3$ *Simplify. Then solve for y.*

$\underline{-6 \qquad\quad -6\quad}$ *Subtract 6 from both sides.*

$-3y = -3$

$\dfrac{-3y}{-3} = \dfrac{-3}{-3}$ *Divide both sides by −3.*

$y = 1$

Step 4 $x + y = 3$ *Write one of the original equations.*

$x + 1 = 3$ *Substitute 1 for y.*

$\underline{\quad -1 \quad -1\quad}$ *Subtract 1 from both sides.*

$x \quad = \quad 2$

Step 5 $(2, 1)$ *Write the solution as an ordered pair.*

Helpful Hint

Sometimes neither equation is solved for a variable. You can begin by solving either equation for either *x* or *y*.

Solve each system by substitution.

1a. $\begin{cases} y = x + 3 \\ y = 2x + 5 \end{cases}$ **1b.** $\begin{cases} x = 2y - 4 \\ x + 8y = 16 \end{cases}$ **1c.** $\begin{cases} 2x + y = -4 \\ x + y = -7 \end{cases}$

Sometimes you substitute an expression for a variable that has a coefficient. When solving for the second variable in this situation, you can use the Distributive Property.

EXAMPLE **2** **Using the Distributive Property**

my.hrw.com

Online Video Tutor

Solve $\begin{cases} 4y - 5x = 9 \\ x - 4y = 11 \end{cases}$ by substitution.

Step 1 $x - 4y = \quad 11$

$\underline{\quad + 4y \quad + 4y}$

$x \quad = \quad 4y + 11$

Solve the second equation for x by adding $4y$ to each side.

Step 2 $4y - 5x = 9$

$4y - 5(4y + 11) = 9$

Substitute $4y + 11$ for x in the first equation.

Step 3 $4y - 5(4y) - 5(11) = 9$

$4y - 20y - 55 = 9$

$-16y - 55 = \quad 9$

$\underline{\quad + 55 \quad + 55}$

$-16y \quad = \quad 64$

$\dfrac{-16y}{-16} = \dfrac{64}{-16}$

$y = -4$

Distribute -5 to the expression in parentheses. Simplify. Solve for y.

Add 55 to both sides.

Divide both sides by -16.

Step 4 $x - 4y = 11$

$x - 4(-4) = 11$

$x + 16 = \quad 11$

$\underline{\quad - 16 \quad - 16}$

$x \quad = \quad -5$

Write one of the original equations.

Substitute -4 for y.

Simplify.

Subtract 16 from both sides.

Step 5 $(-5, -4)$

Write the solution as an ordered pair.

> **Caution!**
>
> When you solve one equation for a variable, you must substitute the value or expression into the *other* original equation, not the one that has just been solved.

 2. Solve $\begin{cases} -2x + y = 8 \\ 3x + 2y = 9 \end{cases}$ by substitution.

Student to Student

Solving Systems by Substitution

Erika Chu
Terrell High School

I always look for a variable with a coefficient of 1 or −1 when deciding which equation to solve for x or y.

For the system

$$\begin{cases} 2x + y = 14 \\ -3x + 4y = -10 \end{cases}$$

I would solve the first equation for y because it has a coefficient of 1.

$2x + y = 14$

$\quad y = -2x + 14$

Then I use substitution to find the values of x and y.

$-3x + 4y = -10$

$-3x + 4(-2x + 14) = -10$

$-3x + (-8x) + 56 = -10$

$-11x + 56 = -10$

$-11x = -66$

$x = 6$

$y = -2x + 14$

$y = -2(6) + 14 = 2$

The solution is $(6, 2)$.

EXAMPLE 3

MCC9-12.A.CED.2

Consumer Economics Application

my.hrw.com

Online Video Tutor

One high-speed Internet provider has a $50 setup fee and costs $30 per month. Another provider has no setup fee and costs $40 per month.

a. In how many months will both providers cost the same? What will that cost be?

Write an equation for each option. Let t represent the total amount paid and m represent the number of months.

	Total paid	is	setup fee	plus	cost per month	times	months.
Option 1	t	$=$	50	$+$	30	$\cdot$	m
Option 2	t	$=$	0	$+$	40	$\cdot$	m

Step 1 $t = 50 + 30m$ *Both equations are solved for t.*
          $t = 40m$

Step 2 $50 + 30m = \quad 40m$ *Substitute 50 + 30m for t in the second equation.*

Step 3 $\dfrac{-30m \qquad -30m}{50 \quad = \quad 10m}$ *Solve for m. Subtract 30m from both sides.*

          $\dfrac{50}{10} = \dfrac{10m}{10}$ *Divide both sides by 10.*

          $5 = m$

Step 4 $t = 40m$ *Write one of the original equations.*
       $= 40(5)$ *Substitute 5 for m.*
       $= 200$

Step 5 $(5, 200)$ *Write the solution as an ordered pair.*

In 5 months, the total cost for each option will be the same—$200.

b. If you plan to cancel in 1 year, which is the cheaper provider? Explain.

Option 1: $t = 50 + 30(12) = 410$ Option 2: $t = 40(12) = 480$

Option 1 is cheaper.

CHECK IT OUT!

3. One cable television provider has a $60 setup fee and charges $80 per month, and another provider has a $160 equipment fee and charges $70 per month.

   a. In how many months will the cost be the same? What will that cost be?

   b. If you plan to move in 6 months, which is the cheaper option? Explain.

MCC.MP.1   MATHEMATICAL PRACTICES

THINK AND DISCUSS

1. If you graphed the equations in Example 1A, where would the lines intersect?

2. GET ORGANIZED Copy and complete the graphic organizer. In each box, solve the system by substitution using the first step given. Show that each method gives the same solution.

$\begin{cases} x + y = 8 \\ x - y = 2 \end{cases}$

Solve $x + y = 8$ for x.	Solve $x + y = 8$ for y.
Solve $x - y = 2$ for x.	**Solve** $x - y = 2$ for y.

Know it! Note

GUIDED PRACTICE

Solve each system by substitution.

SEE EXAMPLE 1

1. $\begin{cases} y = 5x - 10 \\ y = 3x + 8 \end{cases}$

2. $\begin{cases} 3x + y = 2 \\ 4x + y = 20 \end{cases}$

3. $\begin{cases} y = x + 5 \\ 4x + y = 20 \end{cases}$

SEE EXAMPLE 2

4. $\begin{cases} x - 2y = 10 \\ \frac{1}{2}x - 2y = 4 \end{cases}$

5. $\begin{cases} y - 4x = 3 \\ 2x - 3y = 21 \end{cases}$

6. $\begin{cases} x = y - 8 \\ -x - y = 0 \end{cases}$

SEE EXAMPLE 3

7. **Consumer Economics** The Strauss family is deciding between two lawn-care services. Green Lawn charges a $49 startup fee, plus $29 per month. Grass Team charges a $25 startup fee, plus $37 per month.

   a. In how many months will both lawn-care services cost the same? What will that cost be?

   b. If the family will use the service for only 6 months, which is the better option? Explain.

PRACTICE AND PROBLEM SOLVING

Independent Practice

For Exercises	See Example
8–10	1
11–16	2
17	3

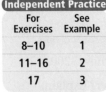

my.hrw.com

Online Extra Practice

Solve each system by substitution.

8. $\begin{cases} y = x + 3 \\ y = 2x + 4 \end{cases}$

9. $\begin{cases} y = 2x + 10 \\ y = -2x - 6 \end{cases}$

10. $\begin{cases} x + 2y = 8 \\ x + 3y = 12 \end{cases}$

11. $\begin{cases} 2x + 2y = 2 \\ -4x + 4y = 12 \end{cases}$

12. $\begin{cases} y = 0.5x + 2 \\ -y = -2x + 4 \end{cases}$

13. $\begin{cases} -x + y = 4 \\ 3x - 2y = -7 \end{cases}$

14. $\begin{cases} 3x + y = -8 \\ -2x - y = 6 \end{cases}$

15. $\begin{cases} x + 2y = -1 \\ 4x - 4y = 20 \end{cases}$

16. $\begin{cases} 4x = y - 1 \\ 6x - 2y = -3 \end{cases}$

17. **Recreation** Casey wants to buy a gym membership. One gym has a $150 joining fee and costs $35 per month. Another gym has no joining fee and costs $60 per month.

   a. In how many months will both gym memberships cost the same? What will that cost be?

   b. If Casey plans to cancel in 5 months, which is the better option for him? Explain.

Solve each system by substitution. Check your answer.

18. $\begin{cases} x = 5 \\ x + y = 8 \end{cases}$

19. $\begin{cases} y = -3x + 4 \\ x = 2y + 6 \end{cases}$

20. $\begin{cases} 3x - y = 11 \\ 5y - 7x = 1 \end{cases}$

21. $\begin{cases} \frac{1}{2}x + \frac{1}{3}y = 6 \\ x - y = 2 \end{cases}$

22. $\begin{cases} x = 7 - 2y \\ 2x + y = 5 \end{cases}$

23. $\begin{cases} y = 1.2x - 4 \\ 2.2x + 5 = y \end{cases}$

24. The sum of two numbers is 50. The first number is 43 less than twice the second number. Write and solve a system of equations to find the two numbers.

25. **Money** A jar contains n nickels and d dimes. There are 20 coins in the jar, and the total value of the coins is $1.40. How many nickels and how many dimes are in the jar? (*Hint:* Nickels are worth $0.05 and dimes are worth $0.10.)

26. Multi-Step Use the receipts below to write and solve a system of equations to find the cost of a large popcorn and the cost of a small drink.

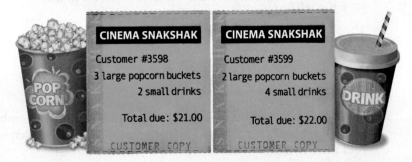

CINEMA SNAKSHAK

Customer #3598

3 large popcorn buckets
2 small drinks

Total due: $21.00

CUSTOMER COPY

CINEMA SNAKSHAK

Customer #3599

2 large popcorn buckets
4 small drinks

Total due: $22.00

CUSTOMER COPY

27. Finance Helene invested a total of $1000 in two simple-interest bank accounts. One account paid 5% annual interest; the other paid 6% annual interest. The total amount of interest she earned after one year was $58. Write and solve a system of equations to find the amount invested in each account. (*Hint:* Change the interest rates into decimals first.)

Geometry Two angles whose measures have a sum of 90° are called complementary angles. For Exercises 28–30, *x* and *y* represent the measures of complementary angles. Use this information and the equation given in each exercise to find the measure of each angle.

28. $y = 4x - 10$

29. $x = 2y$

30. $y = 2(x - 15)$

31. Aviation With a headwind, a small plane can fly 240 miles in 3 hours. With a tailwind, the plane can fly the same distance in 2 hours. Follow the steps below to find the rates of the plane and wind.

a. Copy and complete the table. Let *p* be the rate of the plane and *w* be the rate of the wind.

	Rate	•	Time	=	Distance
With Headwind	$p - w$	•		=	240
With Tailwind		•	2	=	

b. Use the information in each row to write a system of equations.

c. Solve the system of equations to find the rates of the plane and wind.

H.O.T. **32. Write About It** Explain how to solve a system of equations by substitution.

H.O.T. **33. Critical Thinking** Explain the connection between the solution of a system solved by graphing and the solution of the same system solved by substitution.

Real-World Connections

34. At the school store, Juanita bought 2 books and a backpack for a total of $26 before tax. Each book cost $8 less than the backpack.

a. Write a system of equations that can be used to find the price of each book and the price of the backpack.

b. Solve this system by substitution.

c. Solve this system by graphing. Discuss advantages and disadvantages of solving by substitution and solving by graphing.

35. Estimation Use the graph to estimate the solution to
$\begin{cases} 2x - y = 6 \\ x + y = -0.6 \end{cases}$. Round your answer to the nearest tenth.
Then solve the system by substitution.

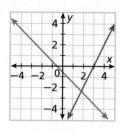

TEST PREP

36. Elizabeth met 24 of her cousins at a family reunion. The number of male cousins m was 6 less than twice the number of female cousins f. Which system can be used to find the number of male cousins and female cousins?

(A) $\begin{cases} m + f = 24 \\ f = 2m - 6 \end{cases}$ (B) $\begin{cases} m + f = 24 \\ f = 2m \end{cases}$ (C) $\begin{cases} m = 24 + f \\ m = f - 6 \end{cases}$ (D) $\begin{cases} f = 24 - m \\ m = 2f - 6 \end{cases}$

37. Which problem is best represented by the system $\begin{cases} d = n + 5 \\ d + n = 12 \end{cases}$?

(F) Roger has 12 coins in dimes and nickels. There are 5 more dimes than nickels.

(G) Roger has 5 coins in dimes and nickels. There are 12 more dimes than nickels.

(H) Roger has 12 coins in dimes and nickels. There are 5 more nickels than dimes.

(J) Roger has 5 coins in dimes and nickels. There are 12 more nickels than dimes.

CHALLENGE AND EXTEND

38. A car dealership has 378 cars on its lot. The ratio of new cars to used cars is 5:4. Write and solve a system of equations to find the number of new and used cars on the lot.

Solve each system by substitution.

39. $\begin{cases} 2r - 3s - t = 12 \\ s + 3t = 10 \\ t = 4 \end{cases}$ **40.** $\begin{cases} x + y + z = 7 \\ y + z = 5 \\ 2y - 4z = -14 \end{cases}$ **41.** $\begin{cases} a + 2b + c = 19 \\ -b + c = -5 \\ 3b + 2c = 15 \end{cases}$

FOCUS ON MATHEMATICAL PRACTICES

H.O.T. **42. Reasoning** Examine the system. $\begin{cases} 2m + 3n = 31 \\ n - m = 7 \end{cases}$

   a. Solve the system by substitution.

   b. Would you get the same answer whether you solved for m or n first? Explain.

   c. Why does it make sense to solve for n in the second equation first?

H.O.T. **43. Error Analysis** Marjorie attempted to solve the system of equations shown, but ran into trouble. What mistake did she make? $\begin{cases} 3x + y = 3 \\ 14x + 4y = 2 \end{cases}$

   Step 1: $3x + y = 3 \rightarrow y = 3 - 3x$

   Step 2: $3x + y = 3 \rightarrow 3x + (3 - 3x) = 3$

   Step 3: $3x + (3 - 3x) = 3$

            $3 = 3$

H.O.T. **44. Precision** Explain why it is not always possible to solve a system of linear equations by graphing, but it is always possible to solve a system using substitution.

Solving Systems by Elimination

 Essential Question: How can you solve systems of linear equations by using elimination?

Objectives

Solve systems of linear equations in two variables by elimination.

Compare and choose an appropriate method for solving systems of linear equations.

Why learn this?

You can solve a system of linear equations to determine how many flowers of each type you can buy to make a bouquet. (See Example 4.)

Another method for solving systems of equations is *elimination*. Like substitution, the goal of elimination is to get one equation that has only one variable.

Remember that an equation stays balanced if you add equal amounts to both sides. Consider the system $\begin{cases} x - 2y = -19 \\ 5x + 2y = 1 \end{cases}$. Since $5x + 2y = 1$, you can add $5x + 2y$ to one side of the first equation and 1 to the other side and the balance is maintained.

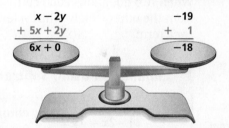

Since $-2y$ and $2y$ have **opposite coefficients**, you can eliminate the y by adding the two equations. The result is one equation that has only one variable: $6x = -18$.

When you use the elimination method to solve a system of linear equations, align all like terms in the equations. Then determine whether any like terms can be eliminated because they have opposite coefficients.

Solving Systems of Equations by Elimination
Step 1 Write the system so that like terms are aligned.
Step 2 Eliminate one of the variables and solve for the other variable.
Step 3 Substitute the value of the variable into one of the original equations and solve for the other variable.
Step 4 Write the answers from Steps 2 and 3 as an ordered pair, (x, y), and check.

Later in this lesson you will learn how to multiply one or more equations by a number in order to produce opposites that can be eliminated.

Photofusion Picture Library/Alamy

 **EXAMPLE** 1
MCC9-12.A.REI.6

Elimination Using Addition

Solve $\begin{cases} x - 2y = -19 \\ 5x + 2y = 1 \end{cases}$ by elimination.

Step 1	$x - 2y = -19$	Write the system so that like terms are aligned.
	$\underline{+\ 5x + 2y =\qquad 1}$	Notice that $-2y$ and $2y$ are opposites.
Step 2	$6x\ + 0 = -18$	Add the equations to eliminate y.
	$6x = -18$	Simplify and solve for x.
	$\dfrac{6x}{6} = \dfrac{-18}{6}$	Divide both sides by 6.
	$x = -3$	

Step 3	$x - 2y = -19$	Write one of the original equations.
	$-3 - 2y = -19$	Substitute -3 for x.
	$\underline{+3\qquad\quad +3}$	Add 3 to both sides.
	$-2y = -16$	
	$\dfrac{-2y}{-2} = \dfrac{-16}{-2}$	Divide both sides by -2.
	$y = 8$	

Step 4 $(-3, 8)$ Write the solution as an ordered pair.

 1. Solve $\begin{cases} y + 3x = -2 \\ 2y - 3x = 14 \end{cases}$ by elimination. Check your answer.

When two equations each contain the same term, you can subtract one equation from the other to solve the system. To subtract an equation, add the opposite of *each* term.

Elimination Using Subtraction

Solve $\begin{cases} 3x + 4y = 18 \\ -2x + 4y = 8 \end{cases}$ by elimination.

Step 1	$3x + 4y = 18$	
	$-\ (-2x + 4y =\ \ 8)$	Notice that both equations contain $4y$.
	$3x + 4y =\ \ 18$	Add the opposite of each term
	$\underline{+\ 2x - 4y = -8}$	in the second equation.
Step 2	$5x\ +\ \ 0 = 10$	Eliminate y.
	$5x = 10$	Simplify and solve for x.
	$x = 2$	

Step 3	$-2x + 4y =\ \ 8$	Write one of the original equations.
	$-2(2) + 4y =\ \ 8$	Substitute 2 for x.
	$-4 + 4y =\ \ 8$	
	$\underline{+\ 4\qquad\quad +4}$	Add 4 to both sides.
	$4y = 12$	Simplify and solve for y.
	$y = 3$	

Step 4 $(2, 3)$ Write the solution as an ordered pair.

2. Solve $\begin{cases} 3x + 3y = 15 \\ -2x + 3y = -5 \end{cases}$ by elimination. Check your answer.

In some cases, you will first need to multiply one or both of the equations by a number so that one variable has opposite coefficients.

COMMON CORE GPS **EXAMPLE 3** MCC9-12.A.REI.6

my.hrw.com

Online Video Tutor

Elimination Using Multiplication First

Solve each system by elimination.

A $\begin{cases} 2x + y = 3 \\ -x + 3y = -12 \end{cases}$

Step 1

$2x + y = 3$

$+ 2(-x + 3y = -12)$ *Multiply each term in the second equation by 2 to get opposite x-coefficients.*

$2x + y = 3$

$+ (-2x + 6y = -24)$ *Add the new equation to the first equation to eliminate x.*

Step 2 $7y = -21$

$y = -3$ *Solve for y.*

Step 3 $2x + y = 3$ *Write one of the original equations.*

$2x + (-3) = 3$ *Substitute −3 for y.*

$\underline{+\ 3 \quad +3}$ *Add 3 to both sides.*

$2x = 6$ *Solve for x.*

$x = 3$

Step 4 $(3, -3)$ *Write the solution as an ordered pair.*

> **Helpful Hint**
>
> In Example 3A, you could have also multiplied the first equation by −3 to eliminate y.

B $\begin{cases} 7x - 12y = -22 \\ 5x - 8y = -14 \end{cases}$

Step 1

$2(7x - 12y = -22)$

$+ (-3)(5x - 8y = -14)$ *Multiply the first equation by 2 and the second equation by −3 to get opposite y-coefficients.*

$14x - 24y = -44$

$+ (-15x + 24y = 42)$ *Add the new equations to eliminate y.*

Step 2 $-x = -2$

$x = 2$ *Solve for x.*

Step 3 $7x - 12y = -22$ *Write one of the original equations.*

$7(2) - 12y = -22$ *Substitute 2 for x.*

$14 - 12y = -22$

$\underline{-14 \qquad -14}$ *Subtract 14 from both sides.*

$-12y = -36$ *Solve for y.*

$y = 3$

Step 4 $(2, 3)$ *Write the solution as an ordered pair.*

Solve each system by elimination. Check your answer.

3a. $\begin{cases} 3x + 2y = 6 \\ -x + y = -2 \end{cases}$ **3b.** $\begin{cases} 2x + 5y = 26 \\ -3x - 4y = -25 \end{cases}$

EXAMPLE **4**

COMMON CORE GPS
MCC9-12.A.CED.2

Consumer Economics Application

my.hrw.com

Online Video Tutor

Sam spent $24.75 to buy 12 flowers for his mother. The bouquet contained roses and daisies. How many of each type of flower did Sam buy?

Write a system. Use r for the number of roses and d for the number of daisies.

$$2.50r + 1.75d = 24.75 \qquad \textit{The cost of roses and daisies totals \$24.75.}$$

$$r + d = 12 \qquad \textit{The total number of roses and daisies is 12.}$$

Step 1
$$2.50r + 1.75d = 24.75$$
$$+ (-2.50)(r + d = 12)$$

Multiply the second equation by −2.50 to get opposite r-coefficients.

$$2.50r + 1.75d = 24.75$$
$$+ (-2.50r - 2.50d = -30.00)$$

Add this equation to the first equation to eliminate r.

Step 2
$$-0.75d = -5.25$$
$$d = 7 \qquad \textit{Solve for d.}$$

Step 3
$$r + d = 12 \qquad \textit{Write one of the original equations.}$$
$$r + 7 = 12 \qquad \textit{Substitute 7 for d.}$$
$$\underline{-7 \quad -7} \qquad \textit{Subtract 7 from both sides.}$$
$$r = 5$$

Step 4
$$(5, 7) \qquad \textit{Write the solution as an ordered pair.}$$

Sam can buy 5 roses and 7 daisies.

ROSES
$2.50 each

DAISIES
$1.75 each

CHECK IT OUT!

4. What if...? Sally spent $14.85 to buy 13 flowers. She bought lilies, which cost $1.25 each, and tulips, which cost $0.90 each. How many of each flower did Sally buy?

All systems can be solved in more than one way. For some systems, some methods may be better than others.

Know it! Note

Systems of Linear Equations

METHOD	USE WHEN...	EXAMPLE
Graphing	• Both equations are solved for y. • You want to estimate a solution.	$\begin{cases} y = 3x + 2 \\ y = -2x + 6 \end{cases}$
Substitution	• A variable in either equation has a coefficient of 1 or −1. • Both equations are solved for the same variable. • Either equation is solved for a variable.	$\begin{cases} x + 2y = 7 \\ x = 10 - 5y \end{cases}$ or $\begin{cases} x = 2y + 10 \\ x = 3y + 5 \end{cases}$
Elimination	• Both equations have the same variable with the same or opposite coefficients. • A variable term in one equation is a multiple of the corresponding variable term in the other equation.	$\begin{cases} 3x + 2y = 8 \\ 5x + 2y = 12 \end{cases}$ or $\begin{cases} 6x + 5y = 10 \\ 3x + 2y = 15 \end{cases}$

THINK AND DISCUSS

1. Explain how multiplying the second equation in a system by -1 and eliminating by adding is the same as elimination by subtraction. Give an example of a system for which this applies.

2. Explain why it does not matter which variable you solve for first when solving a system by elimination.

3. GET ORGANIZED Copy and complete the graphic organizer. In each box, write an example of a system of equations that you could solve using the given method.

Solving Systems of Linear Equations

| Substitution | Elimination using addition or subtraction | Elimination using multiplication |

6-3 Exercises

my.hrw.com
Homework Help

GUIDED PRACTICE

Solve each system by elimination. Check your answer.

SEE EXAMPLE 1

1. $\begin{cases} -x + y = 5 \\ x - 5y = -9 \end{cases}$

2. $\begin{cases} x + y = 12 \\ x - y = 2 \end{cases}$

3. $\begin{cases} 2x + 5y = -24 \\ 3x - 5y = 14 \end{cases}$

SEE EXAMPLE 2

4. $\begin{cases} x - 10y = 60 \\ x + 14y = 12 \end{cases}$

5. $\begin{cases} 5x + y = 0 \\ 5x + 2y = 30 \end{cases}$

6. $\begin{cases} -5x + 7y = 11 \\ -5x + 3y = 19 \end{cases}$

SEE EXAMPLE 3

7. $\begin{cases} 2x + 3y = 12 \\ 5x - y = 13 \end{cases}$

8. $\begin{cases} -3x + 4y = 12 \\ 2x + y = -8 \end{cases}$

9. $\begin{cases} 2x + 4y = -4 \\ 3x + 5y = -3 \end{cases}$

SEE EXAMPLE 4

10. Consumer Economics Each family in a neighborhood is contributing $20 worth of food to the neighborhood picnic. The Harlin family is bringing 12 packages of buns. The hamburger buns cost $2.00 per package. The hot-dog buns cost $1.50 per package. How many packages of each type of bun did they buy?

PRACTICE AND PROBLEM SOLVING

Solve each system by elimination. Check your answer.

Independent Practice	
For Exercises	See Example
11–13	1
14–16	2
17–19	3
20	4

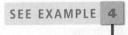

my.hrw.com

Online Extra Practice

11. $\begin{cases} -x + y = -1 \\ 2x - y = 0 \end{cases}$

12. $\begin{cases} -2x + y = -20 \\ 2x + y = 48 \end{cases}$

13. $\begin{cases} 3x - y = -2 \\ -2x + y = 3 \end{cases}$

14. $\begin{cases} x - y = 4 \\ x - 2y = 10 \end{cases}$

15. $\begin{cases} x + 2y = 5 \\ 3x + 2y = 17 \end{cases}$

16. $\begin{cases} 3x - 2y = -1 \\ 3x - 4y = 9 \end{cases}$

17. $\begin{cases} x - y = -3 \\ 5x + 3y = 1 \end{cases}$

18. $\begin{cases} 9x - 3y = 3 \\ 3x + 8y = -17 \end{cases}$

19. $\begin{cases} 5x + 2y = -1 \\ 3x + 7y = 11 \end{cases}$

20. Multi-Step Mrs. Gonzalez bought centerpieces to put on each table at a graduation party. She spent $31.50. There are 8 tables each requiring either a candle or vase. Candles cost $3 and vases cost $4.25. How many of each type did she buy?

21. **Geometry** The difference between the length and width of a rectangle is 2 units. The perimeter is 40 units. Write and solve a system of equations to determine the length and width of the rectangle. (*Hint:* The perimeter of a rectangle is $2\ell + 2w$.)

22. **///ERROR ANALYSIS///** Which is incorrect? Explain the error.

(A)
$$\begin{cases} x + y = -3 & x + y = -3 \\ 3x + y = 3 & -(3x + y = 3) \end{cases}$$
$$\overline{\;-2x = 0}$$
$$x = 0$$

(B)
$$\begin{cases} x + y = -3 & x + y = -3 \\ 3x + y = 3 & -(3x + y = 3) \end{cases}$$
$$\overline{\;-2x = -6}$$
$$x = 3$$

23. **Chemistry** A chemist has a bottle of a 1% acid solution and a bottle of a 5% acid solution. She wants to mix the two solutions to get 100 mL of a 4% acid solution. Follow the steps below to find how much of each solution she should use.

	1% Solution	+	5% Solution	=	4% Solution
Amount of Solution (mL)	x	+	y	=	▪
Amount of Acid (mL)	$0.01x$	+	▪	=	$0.04(100)$

a. Copy and complete the table.

b. Use the information in the table to write a system of equations.

c. Solve the system of equations to find how much she will use from each bottle to get 100 mL of a 4% acid solution.

Math History

In 1247, Qin Jiushao wrote *Mathematical Treatise in Nine Sections*. Its contents included solving systems of equations and the Chinese Remainder Theorem.

Critical Thinking Which method would you use to solve each system? Explain.

24. $\begin{cases} \dfrac{1}{2}x - 5y = 30 \\ \dfrac{1}{2}x + 7y = 6 \end{cases}$

25. $\begin{cases} -x + 2y = 3 \\ 4x - 5y = -3 \end{cases}$

26. $\begin{cases} 3x - y = 10 \\ 2x - y = 7 \end{cases}$

27. $\begin{cases} 3y + x = 10 \\ x = 4y + 2 \end{cases}$

28. $\begin{cases} y = -4x \\ y = 2x + 3 \end{cases}$

29. $\begin{cases} 2x + 6y = 12 \\ 4x + 5y = 15 \end{cases}$

30. **Business** A local boys club sold 176 bags of mulch and made a total of $520. They did not sell any of the expensive cocoa mulch. Use the table to determine how many bags of each type of mulch they sold.

Mulch Prices ($)	
Cocoa	4.75
Hardwood	3.50
Pine Bark	2.75

Real-World Connections

31. a. The school store is running a promotion on school supplies. Different supplies are placed on two shelves. You can purchase 3 items from shelf A and 2 from shelf B for $16. Or you can purchase 2 items from shelf A and 3 from shelf B for $14. Write a system of equations that can be used to find the individual prices for the supplies on shelf A and on shelf B.

b. Solve the system of equations by elimination.

c. If the supplies on shelf A are normally $6 each and the supplies on shelf B are normally $3 each, how much will you save on each package plan from part a?

H.O.T. **32. Write About It** Solve the system $\begin{cases} 3x + y = 1 \\ 2x + 4y = -6 \end{cases}$. Explain how you can check your solution algebraically and graphically.

TEST PREP

33. A math test has 25 problems. Some are worth 2 points, and some are worth 3 points. The test is worth 60 points total. Which system can be used to determine the number of 2-point problems and the number of 3-point problems on the test?

Ⓐ $\begin{cases} x + y = 25 \\ 2x + 3y = 60 \end{cases}$ Ⓑ $\begin{cases} x + y = 60 \\ 2x + 3y = 25 \end{cases}$ Ⓒ $\begin{cases} x - y = 25 \\ 2x + 3y = 60 \end{cases}$ Ⓓ $\begin{cases} x - y = 60 \\ 2x - 3y = 25 \end{cases}$

34. An electrician charges $15 plus $11 per hour. Another electrician charges $10 plus $15 per hour. For what amount of time will the cost be the same? What is that cost?

Ⓕ 1 hour; $25

Ⓗ $1\frac{1}{2}$ hours; $30

Ⓖ $1\frac{1}{4}$ hours; $28.75

Ⓙ $1\frac{3}{4}$ hours; $32.50

35. Short Response Three hundred fifty-eight tickets to the school basketball game on Friday were sold. Student tickets were $1.50, and nonstudent tickets were $3.25. The school made $752.25.

a. Write a system of linear equations that could be used to determine how many student and how many nonstudent tickets were sold. Define the variables you use.

b. Solve the system you wrote in part **a.** How many student and how many nonstudent tickets were sold?

CHALLENGE AND EXTEND

H.O.T. **36.** If two equations in a system are represented by $Ax + By = C$ and $Dx + Ey = F$, where A, B, C, D, E, and F are constants, you can write a third equation by doing the following:

Multiply the second equation by a nonzero constant k to get $kDx + kEy = kF$.

Add this new equation to the first equation $Ax + By = C$ to get $(A + kD)x + (B + kE)y = C + kF$.

Prove that if (x_1, y_1) is a solution of the original system, then it is a solution of the system represented by $Ax + By = C$ and $(A + kD)x + (B + kE)y = C + kF$.

FOCUS ON MATHEMATICAL PRACTICES

H.O.T. **37. Reasoning** To solve the system of linear equations shown by elimination, which variable would you eliminate first? Explain your thinking, then find the solution of the system.

$\begin{cases} 3x - 2y = 1 \\ 2x + 2y = 4 \end{cases}$

H.O.T. **38. Comparison** To solve the system of linear equations shown by elimination, Mateo began by multiplying the first equation by 3. Mariana began by multiplying the second equation by -2. What will each student find as the sum of the equations? Which sum will be easier to solve?

$\begin{cases} \frac{2}{3}x + 12y = 14 \\ -2x + 6y = 0 \end{cases}$

Ready to Go On?

my.hrw.com
Assessment and Intervention

6-1 Solving Systems by Graphing

Tell whether the ordered pair is a solution of the given system.

1. $(-2, 1)$; $\begin{cases} y = -2x - 3 \\ y = x + 3 \end{cases}$

2. $(9, 2)$; $\begin{cases} x - 4y = 1 \\ 2x - 3y = 3 \end{cases}$

3. $(3, -1)$; $\begin{cases} y = -\dfrac{1}{3}x \\ y + 2x = 5 \end{cases}$

Solve each system by graphing.

4. $\begin{cases} y = x + 5 \\ y = \dfrac{1}{2}x + 4 \end{cases}$

5. $\begin{cases} y = -x - 2 \\ 2x - y = 2 \end{cases}$

6. $\begin{cases} \dfrac{2x + y}{3} = -3 \\ 4x + y = 7 \end{cases}$

7. Banking Christiana and Marlena opened their first savings accounts on the same day. Christiana opened her account with $50 and plans to deposit $10 every month. Marlena opened her account with $30 and plans to deposit $15 every month. After how many months will their two accounts have the same amount of money? What will that amount be?

6-2 Solving Systems by Substitution

Solve each system by substitution.

8. $\begin{cases} y = -x + 5 \\ 2x + y = 11 \end{cases}$

9. $\begin{cases} 4x - 3y = -1 \\ 3x - y = -2 \end{cases}$

10. $\begin{cases} y = -x \\ y = -2x - 5 \end{cases}$

11. $\begin{cases} x + y = -1 \\ y = -2x + 3 \end{cases}$

12. $\begin{cases} x = y - 7 \\ -y - 2x = 8 \end{cases}$

13. $\begin{cases} \dfrac{1}{2}x + y = 9 \\ 3x - 4y = -6 \end{cases}$

14. The Nash family's car needs repairs. Estimates for parts and labor from two garages are shown.

Garage	Parts ($)	Labor ($ per hour)
Motor Works	650	70
Jim's Car Care	800	55

For how many hours of labor will the total cost of fixing the car be the same at both garages? What will that cost be? Which garage will be cheaper if the repairs require 8 hours of labor? Explain.

6-3 Solving Systems by Elimination

Solve each system by elimination.

15. $\begin{cases} x + 3y = 15 \\ 2x - 3y = -6 \end{cases}$

16. $\begin{cases} x + y = 2 \\ 2x + y = -1 \end{cases}$

17. $\begin{cases} -2x + 5y = -1 \\ 3x + 2y = 11 \end{cases}$

18. It takes Akira 10 minutes to make a black and white drawing and 25 minutes for a color drawing. On Saturday he made a total of 9 drawings in 2 hours. Write and solve a system of equations to determine how many drawings of each type Akira made.

1. The Fun Guys game rental store charges an annual fee of $5 plus $5.50 per game rented. The Game Bank charges an annual fee of $17 plus $2.50 per game. For how many game rentals will the cost be the same at both stores? What is that cost?

Ⓐ 4 games; $27 Ⓒ 3 games; $22

Ⓑ 6 games; $38 Ⓓ 2 games; $16

2. If the pattern in the table continues, in what month will the number of sales of CDs and movie tickets be the same? What number will that be?

Total Number Sold				
Month	1	2	3	4
CDs	700	685	670	655
Movie tickets	100	145	190	235

Ⓕ Month 10; 550 Ⓗ Month 8; 580

Ⓖ Month 9; 580 Ⓙ Month 11; 550

3. Solve $\begin{cases} 4x - 4y = -16 \\ x - 2y = -12 \end{cases}$ by substitution. Express your answer as an ordered pair.

Ⓐ (8, −4) Ⓒ (−2, 4)

Ⓑ (4, 8) Ⓓ (4, −8)

4. Solve $\begin{cases} 2x - 5y = -7 \\ 5x - 3y = 11 \end{cases}$ by elimination.

Express your answer as an ordered pair.

Ⓕ (3, 4) Ⓗ $\left(\dfrac{4}{7}, \dfrac{8}{5}\right)$

Ⓖ (3, 2) Ⓙ (4, 3)

5. At the local pet store, zebra fish cost $2.10 each and neon tetras cost $1.85 each. If Marsha bought 13 fish for a total cost of $25.80, not including tax, how many of each type of fish did she buy?

Ⓐ 5 zebra fish, 8 neon tetras

Ⓑ 7 zebra fish, 6 neon tetras

Ⓒ 8 zebra fish, 5 neon tetras

Ⓓ 6 zebra fish, 7 neon tetras

6. Which system of equations is shown on the graph?

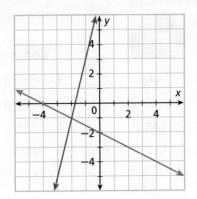

Ⓕ $\begin{cases} x + 2y = -4 \\ y = 4x + 7 \end{cases}$ Ⓗ $\begin{cases} x = \frac{1}{2}x - 2 \\ y = 4x + 7 \end{cases}$

Ⓖ $\begin{cases} y = -\frac{1}{2}x - 2 \\ y = -4x + 7 \end{cases}$ Ⓙ $\begin{cases} x + 2y = 4 \\ 4x - y = -7 \end{cases}$

7. The sum of the digits of a two-digit number is 8. If the number is multiplied by 4, the result is 104. Write and solve a system of equations. Find the number.

Ⓐ $\begin{cases} x + y = 8 \\ 4(x + y) = 104 \end{cases}$

The number is 35.

Ⓒ $\begin{cases} x + y = 8 \\ 4(2x + y) = 104 \end{cases}$

The number is 18.

Ⓑ $\begin{cases} x + y = 8 \\ 4(10x + y) = 104 \end{cases}$

The number is 17.

Ⓓ $\begin{cases} x + y = 8 \\ 4(10x + y) = 104 \end{cases}$

The number is 26.

Mini-Task

8. Gracey's little sister Eliza was born when Gracey was 7 years old. Now, Eliza is half as old as Gracey. Write and solve an equation to find the age of each sister.

7 Special Systems and Systems of Inequalities

COMMON
CORE GPS

Contents

MATHEMATICAL
PRACTICES
The Common Core Georgia Performance Standards for Mathematical Practice describe varieties of expertise that all students should seek to develop. Opportunities to develop these practices are integrated throughout this program.

1 Make sense of problems and persevere in solving them.

2 Reason abstractly and quantitatively.

3 Construct viable arguments and critique the reasoning of others.

4 Model with mathematics.

5 Use appropriate tools strategically.

6 Attend to precision.

7 Look for and make use of structure.

8 Look for and express regularity in repeated reasoning.

Unpacking the Standards

my.hrw.com
Multilingual Glossary

Understanding the standards and the vocabulary terms in the standards will help you know exactly what you are expected to learn in this chapter.

 MCC9-12.A.REI.12

Graph the solutions to a linear inequality in two variables as a half-plane (excluding the boundary in the case of a strict inequality), and graph the solution set to a system of linear inequalities in two variables as the intersection of the corresponding half-planes.

Key Vocabulary

half-plane (semiplano) The part of the coordinate plane on one side of a line, which may include the line.

solution of a linear inequality in two variables (solución de una desigualdad lineal en dos variables) An ordered pair or ordered pairs that make the inequality true.

system of linear inequalities (sistema de desigualdades lineales) A system of inequalities in which all of the inequalities are linear.

What It Means For You

Systems of linear inequalities model many real-life situations where you want to know when one or more conditions are met, but where there are many possible solutions.

EXAMPLE   **Linear Inequality**

$$y > \frac{2}{3}x - 1$$

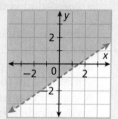

EXAMPLE   **System of Two Linear Inequalities**

$$\begin{cases} y > \dfrac{2}{3}x - 1 \\ y \le -2x - 2 \end{cases}$$

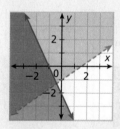

EXAMPLE   **System of Three Linear Inequalities**

Tracy works at least 5 hours per week as a cashier: $c \ge 5$

Tracy works at least 10 hours per week at a library: $p \ge 10$

Tracy works at most 24 hours per week: $c + p \le 24$

How can Tracy divide her time between the two jobs?

Sample Solutions	
Cashier (hours)	Page (hours)
5	10
5	16
8	12
8	16
10	12
12	12

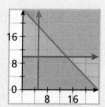

Solving Special Systems

Essential Question: How can you solve consistent and inconsistent systems of linear equations?

Objectives
Solve special systems of linear equations in two variables.

Classify systems of linear equations and determine the number of solutions.

Vocabulary
consistent system
inconsistent system
independent system
dependent system

Why learn this?

Linear systems can be used to analyze business growth, such as comic book sales. (See Example 4.)

When two lines intersect at a point, there is exactly one solution to the system. A system with at least one solution is a **consistent system**.

When the two lines in a system do not intersect, they are parallel lines. There are no ordered pairs that satisfy both equations, so there is no solution. A system that has no solution is an **inconsistent system**.

COMMON CORE GPS
EXAMPLE 1
MCC9-12.A.REI.6

my.hrw.com

Online Video Tutor

Systems with No Solution

Show that $\begin{cases} y = x - 1 \\ -x + y = 2 \end{cases}$ has no solution.

Method 1 Compare slopes and y-intercepts.

$y = x - 1 \rightarrow y = 1x - 1$ *Write both equations in slope-intercept form.*
$-x + y = 2 \rightarrow y = 1x + 2$ *The lines are parallel because they have the same slope and different y-intercepts.*

This system has no solution.

Method 2 Graph the system.
The lines are parallel.

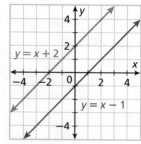

This system has no solution.

Method 3 Solve the system algebraically. Use the substitution method.

$-x + (x - 1) = 2$ *Substitute x − 1 for y in the second equation, and solve.*
$-1 = 2$ ✗   *False*

This system has no solution.

 1. Show that $\begin{cases} y = -2x + 5 \\ 2x + y = 1 \end{cases}$ has no solution.

If two linear equations in a system have the same graph, the graphs are coincident lines, or the same line. There are infinitely many solutions of the system because every point on the line represents a solution of both equations.

COMMON CORE GPS   EXAMPLE   2
MCC9-12.A.REI.6

my.hrw.com
Online Video Tutor

Systems with Infinitely Many Solutions

Show that $\begin{cases} y = 2x + 1 \\ 2x - y + 1 = 0 \end{cases}$ has infinitely many solutions.

Method 1 Compare slopes and y-intercepts.

$$y = 2x + 1 \rightarrow y = 2x + 1$$
$$2x - y + 1 = 0 \rightarrow y = 2x + 1$$

Write both equations in slope-intercept form. The lines have the same slope and the same y-intercept.

If this system were graphed, the graphs would be the same line. There are infinitely many solutions.

Method 2 Solve the system algebraically. Use the elimination method.

$$y = 2x + 1 \rightarrow -2x + y = 1$$
$$2x - y + 1 = 0 \rightarrow \underline{+2x - y = -1}$$
$$0 = 0 \checkmark$$

Write equations to line up like terms.
Add the equations.
True. The equation is an identity.

There are infinitely many solutions.

Caution!

0 = 0 is a true statement. It does not mean the system has zero solutions or no solution.

 2. Show that $\begin{cases} y = x - 3 \\ x - y - 3 = 0 \end{cases}$ has infinitely many solutions.

Consistent systems can either be independent or dependent.

- An **independent system** has exactly one solution. The graph of an independent system consists of two intersecting lines.
- A **dependent system** has infinitely many solutions. The graph of a dependent system consists of two coincident lines.

Classification of Systems of Linear Equations

CLASSIFICATION	CONSISTENT AND INDEPENDENT	CONSISTENT AND DEPENDENT	INCONSISTENT
Number of Solutions	Exactly one	Infinitely many	None
Description	Different slopes	Same slope, same y-intercept	Same slope, different y-intercepts
Graph	Intersecting lines	Coincident lines	Parallel lines

 EXAMPLE 3
MCC9-12.A.REI.6

Classifying Systems of Linear Equations

Classify each system. Give the number of solutions.

Online Video Tutor

A $\begin{cases} 2y = x + 2 \\ -\dfrac{1}{2}x + y = 1 \end{cases}$

$2y = x + 2 \rightarrow y = \dfrac{1}{2}x + 1$ *Write both equations in slope-intercept form.*

$-\dfrac{1}{2}x + y = 1 \rightarrow y = \dfrac{1}{2}x + 1$ *The lines have the same slope and the same y-intercepts. They are the same.*

The system is consistent and dependent. It has infinitely many solutions.

B $\begin{cases} y = 2(x - 1) \\ y = x + 1 \end{cases}$

$y = 2(x - 1) \rightarrow y = 2x - 2$ *Write both equations in slope-intercept form.*

$y = x + 1 \rightarrow y = 1x + 1$ *The lines have different slopes. They intersect.*

The system is consistent and independent. It has one solution.

 Classify each system. Give the number of solutions.

3a. $\begin{cases} x + 2y = -4 \\ -2(y + 2) = x \end{cases}$ **3b.** $\begin{cases} y = -2(x - 1) \\ y = -x + 3 \end{cases}$ **3c.** $\begin{cases} 2x - 3y = 6 \\ y = \dfrac{2}{3}x \end{cases}$

EXAMPLE 4
MCC9-12.A.CED.2

Business Application

Online Video Tutor

The sales manager at Comics Now is comparing its sales with the sales of its competitor, Dynamo Comics. If the sales patterns continue, will the sales for Comics Now ever equal the sales for Dynamo Comics? Explain.

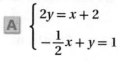

Comic Books Sold per Year (thousands)	2005	2006	2007	2008
Comics Now	130	170	210	250
Dynamo Comics	180	220	260	300

Use the table to write a system of linear equations. Let y represent the sales total and x represent the number of years since 2005.

	Sales total	equals	increase in sales per year	times	years	plus	beginning sales.
Comics Now	y	=	40	•	x	+	130
Dynamo Comics	y	=	40	•	x	+	180

Helpful Hint

The increase in sales is the difference between sales each year.

$\begin{cases} y = 40x + 130 \\ y = 40x + 180 \end{cases}$

$y = 40x + 130$ *Both equations are in slope-intercept form.*

$y = 40x + 180$ *The lines have the same slope, but different y-intercepts.*

The graphs of the two equations are parallel lines, so there is no solution. If the patterns continue, sales for the two companies will never be equal.

 4. Matt has $100 in a checking account and deposits $20 per month. Ben has $80 in a checking account and deposits $30 per month. Will the accounts ever have the same balance? Explain.

THINK AND DISCUSS

1. What methods can be used to determine the number of solutions of a system of linear equations?

2. GET ORGANIZED Copy and complete the graphic organizer. In each box, write the word or words that describes a system with that number of solutions and sketch a graph.

Linear System of Equations

No solution

Exactly one

Infinitely many

7-1 Exercises

my.hrw.com
Homework Help

GUIDED PRACTICE

1. Vocabulary A _____?_____ system can be independent or dependent. (*consistent* or *inconsistent*)

SEE EXAMPLE 1 Show that each system has no solution.

2. $\begin{cases} y = x + 1 \\ -x + y = 3 \end{cases}$

3. $\begin{cases} 3x + y = 6 \\ y = -3x + 2 \end{cases}$

4. $\begin{cases} -y = 4x + 1 \\ 4x + y = 2 \end{cases}$

SEE EXAMPLE 2 Show that each system has infinitely many solutions.

5. $\begin{cases} y = -x + 3 \\ x + y - 3 = 0 \end{cases}$

6. $\begin{cases} y = 2x - 4 \\ 2x - y - 4 = 0 \end{cases}$

7. $\begin{cases} -7x + y = -2 \\ 7x - y = 2 \end{cases}$

SEE EXAMPLE 3 Classify each system. Give the number of solutions.

8. $\begin{cases} y = 2x + 3 \\ -2y = 2x + 6 \end{cases}$

9. $\begin{cases} y = -3x - 1 \\ 3x + y = 1 \end{cases}$

10. $\begin{cases} 9y = 3x + 18 \\ \frac{1}{3}x - y = -2 \end{cases}$

SEE EXAMPLE 4 **11. Athletics** Micah walks on a treadmill at 4 miles per hour. He has walked 2 miles when Luke starts running at 6 miles per hour on the treadmill next to him. If their rates continue, will Luke's distance ever equal Micah's distance? Explain.

PRACTICE AND PROBLEM SOLVING

Show that each system has no solution.

12. $\begin{cases} y = 2x - 2 \\ -2x + y = 1 \end{cases}$

13. $\begin{cases} x + y = 3 \\ y = -x - 1 \end{cases}$

14. $\begin{cases} x + 2y = -4 \\ y = -\frac{1}{2}x - 4 \end{cases}$

15. $\begin{cases} -6 + y = 2x \\ y = 2x - 36 \end{cases}$

Show that each system has infinitely many solutions.

16. $\begin{cases} y = -2x + 3 \\ 2x + y - 3 = 0 \end{cases}$

17. $\begin{cases} y = x - 2 \\ x - y - 2 = 0 \end{cases}$

18. $\begin{cases} x + y = -4 \\ y = -x - 4 \end{cases}$

19. $\begin{cases} -9x - 3y = -18 \\ 3x + y = 6 \end{cases}$

Classify each system. Give the number of solutions.

20. $\begin{cases} y = -x + 5 \\ x + y = 5 \end{cases}$

21. $\begin{cases} y = -3x + 2 \\ y = 3x \end{cases}$

22. $\begin{cases} y - 1 = 2x \\ y = 2x - 1 \end{cases}$

23. **Sports** Mandy is skating at 5 miles per hour. Nikki is skating at 6 miles per hour and started 1 mile behind Mandy. If their rates stay the same, will Mandy catch up with Nikki? Explain.

24. **Multi-Step** Photocopier A can print 35 copies per minute. Photocopier B can print 35 copies per minute. Copier B is started and makes 10 copies. Copier A is then started. If the copiers continue, will the number of copies from machine A ever equal the number of copies from machine B? Explain.

25. **Entertainment** One week Trey rented 4 DVDs and 2 video games for $18. The next week he rented 2 DVDs and 1 video game for $9. Find the rental costs for each video game and DVD. Explain your answer.

26. Rosa bought 1 pound of cashews and 2 pounds of peanuts for $10. At the same store, Sabrina bought 2 pounds of cashews and 1 pound of peanuts for $11. Find the cost per pound for cashews and peanuts.

27. **Geology** Pam and Tommy collect geodes. Pam's parents gave her 2 geodes to start her collection, and she buys 4 every year. Tommy has 2 geodes that were given to him for his birthday. He buys 4 every year. If Pam and Tommy continue to buy the same amount of geodes per year, when will Tommy have as many geodes as Pam? Explain your answer.

28. Use the data given in the tables.

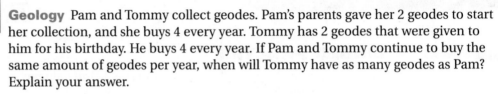

x	3	4	5	6
y	6	8	10	12

x	12	13	14	15
y	24	26	28	30

   a. Write an equation to describe the data in each table.

   b. Graph the system of equations from part **a**. Describe the graph.

   c. How could you have predicted the graph by looking at the equations?

   d. **What if...?** Each *y*-value in the second table increases by 1. How does this affect the graphs of the two equations? How can you tell how the graphs would be affected without actually graphing?

29. **Critical Thinking** Describe the graphs of two equations if the result of solving the system by substitution or elimination is the statement $1 = 3$.

Geology

Geodes are rounded, hollow rock formations. Most are partially or completely filled with layers of colored quartz crystals. The world's largest geode was discovered in Spain in 2000. It is 26 feet long and 5.6 feet high.

Real-World Connections

30. The Crusader pep club is selling team buttons that support the sports teams. They contacted Buttons, Etc. which charges $50 plus $1.10 per button, and Logos, which charges $40 plus $1.10 per button.

   a. Write an equation for each company's cost.

   b. Use the system from part **a** to find when the price for both companies is the same. Explain.

   c. What part of the equation should the pep club negotiate to change so that the cost of Buttons, Etc. is the same as Logos? What part of the equation should change in order to get a better price?

H.O.T. 31. ///ERROR ANALYSIS/// Student A says there is no solution to the graphed system of equations. Student B says there is one solution. Which student is incorrect? Explain the error.

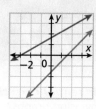

H.O.T. 32. Write About It Compare the graph of a system that is consistent and independent with the graph of a system that is consistent and dependent.

TEST PREP

33. Which of the following classifications fit the following system?

$$\begin{cases} 2x - y = 3 \\ 6x - 3y = 9 \end{cases}$$

    Ⓐ Inconsistent and independent   Ⓒ Inconsistent and dependent

    Ⓑ Consistent and independent   Ⓓ Consistent and dependent

34. Which of the following would be enough information to classify a system of two linear equations?

    Ⓕ The graphs have the same slope.

    Ⓖ The y-intercepts are the same.

    Ⓗ The graphs have different slopes.

    Ⓙ The y-intercepts are different.

CHALLENGE AND EXTEND

H.O.T. 35. What conditions are necessary for the system $\begin{cases} y = 2x + p \\ y = 2x + q \end{cases}$ to have infinitely many solutions? no solution?

H.O.T. 36. Solve the systems in parts **a** and **b.** Use this information to make a conjecture about all solutions that exist for the system in part **c.**

    a. $\begin{cases} 3x + 4y = 0 \\ 4x + 3y = 0 \end{cases}$ **b.** $\begin{cases} 2x + 5y = 0 \\ 5x + 2y = 0 \end{cases}$ **c.** $\begin{cases} ax + by = 0 \\ bx + ay = 0 \end{cases}$, for $a > 0, b > 0, a \neq b$

FOCUS ON MATHEMATICAL PRACTICES

H.O.T. 37. Reasoning In the graph of a linear system of equations, the lines have different slopes and the same y-intercept.

    a. Write and solve a system of equations whose graph fits this description.

    b. In general, what is the solution to a system like this? Explain.

H.O.T. 38. Analysis Chris manages a video rental store and an online video rental service. He found equations for how the number of rentals for each service changed over time and graphed them as shown. Explain what the graph means in this context.

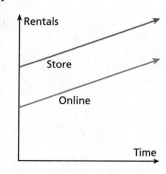

Solving Linear Inequalities

Essential Question: How can you solve linear inequalities by using graphs?

Objective
Graph and solve linear inequalities in two variables.

Vocabulary
linear inequality
solution of a linear inequality

Animated Math

Who uses this?

Consumers can use linear inequalities to determine how much food they can buy for an event. (See Example 3.)

A **linear inequality** is similar to a linear equation, but the equal sign is replaced with an inequality symbol. A **solution of a linear inequality** is any ordered pair that makes the inequality true.

 EXAMPLE 1
Prep. for MCC9-12.A.REI.12

 my.hrw.com

Online Video Tutor

Identifying Solutions of Inequalities

Tell whether the ordered pair is a solution of the inequality.

A $(7, 3); y < x - 1$

$$\begin{array}{c|c} y & < \ x - 1 \\ \hline 3 & 7 - 1 \\ 3 & < \ 6 \ \checkmark \end{array}$$

Substitute (7, 3) for (x, y).

$(7, 3)$ is a solution.

B $(4, 5); y > 3x + 2$

$$\begin{array}{c|c} y & > \ 3x + 2 \\ \hline 5 & 3(4) + 2 \\ 5 & 12 + 2 \\ 5 & > \ 14 \ \cancel{X} \end{array}$$

Substitute (4, 5) for (x, y).

$(4, 5)$ is not a solution.

CHECK IT OUT!
Tell whether the ordered pair is a solution of the inequality.
1a. $(4, 5); y < x + 1$ **1b.** $(1, 1); y > x - 7$

A linear inequality describes a region of a coordinate plane called a *half-plane*. All points in the region are solutions of the linear inequality. The boundary line of the region is the graph of the related equation.

When the inequality is written as $y \le$ or $y \ge$, the points on the boundary line are solutions of the inequality, and the line is **solid**.

When the inequality is written as $y <$ or $y >$, the points on the boundary line are not solutions of the inequality, and the line is **dashed**.

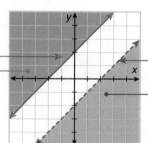

When the inequality is written as $y >$ or $y \ge$, the points **above** the boundary line are solutions of the inequality.

When the inequality is written as $y <$ or $y \le$, the points **below** the boundary line are solutions of the inequality.

	Graphing Linear Inequalities	
Step 1	Solve the inequality for y.	
Step 2	Graph the boundary line. Use a solid line for $\leq$ or $\geq$. Use a dashed line for $<$ or $>$.	
Step 3	Shade the half-plane above the line for $y >$ or $y \geq$. Shade the half-plane below the line for $y <$ or $y \leq$. Check your answer.	

 COMMON CORE GPS **EXAMPLE** **2**
MCC9-12.A.REI.12

Graphing Linear Inequalities in Two Variables

Graph the solutions of each linear inequality.

my.hrw.com

Online Video Tutor

A $y < 3x + 4$

Step 1 The inequality is already solved for y.

Step 2 Graph the boundary line $y = 3x + 4$. Use a dashed line for $<$.

Step 3 The inequality is $<$, so shade below the line.

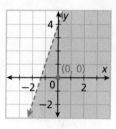

Helpful Hint

The point $(0, 0)$ is a good test point to use if it does not lie on the boundary line.

Check

$$\begin{array}{c|c} y & < 3x + 4 \\ \hline 0 & 3(0) + 4 \\ 0 & 0 + 4 \\ 0 & < 4 \checkmark \end{array}$$

Substitute (0, 0) for (x, y) because it is not on the boundary line.

The point (0, 0) satisfies the inequality, so the graph is shaded correctly.

B $3x + 2y \geq 6$

Step 1 Solve the inequality for y.

$$\begin{array}{r} 3x + 2y \geq 6 \\ \underline{-3x \qquad -3x} \\ 2y \geq -3x + 6 \\ y \geq -\frac{3}{2}x + 3 \end{array}$$

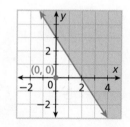

Step 2 Graph the boundary line $y = -\frac{3}{2}x + 3$. Use a solid line for $\geq$.

Step 3 The inequality is $\geq$, so shade above the line.

Check

$$\begin{array}{c|c} y & \geq \frac{3}{2}x + 3 \\ \hline 0 & \frac{3}{2}(0) + 3 \\ 0 & 0 + 3 \\ 0 & \geq 3 ✗ \end{array}$$

A false statement means that the half-plane containing (0, 0) should NOT be shaded. (0, 0) is not one of the solutions, so the graph is shaded correctly.

 Graph the solutions of each linear inequality.

2a. $4x - 3y > 12$ **2b.** $2x - y - 4 > 0$ **2c.** $y \geq -\frac{2}{3}x + 1$

EXAMPLE 3
MCC9-12.A.CED.3

Consumer Economics Application

my.hrw.com

Online Video Tutor

Sarah can spend at most $7.50 on vegetables for a party. Broccoli costs $1.25 per bunch and carrots cost $0.75 per package.

a. Write a linear inequality to describe the situation.

Let x represent the number of bunches of broccoli and let y represent the number of packages of carrots.

Write an inequality. Use $\leq$ for "at most."

Cost of broccoli	plus	cost of carrots	is at most	$7.50.
$1.25x$	$+$	$0.75y$	$\leq$	7.50

Solve the inequality for y.

$$1.25x + 0.75y \leq 7.50$$

$$100(1.25x + 0.75y) \leq 100(7.50)$$

$$125x + 75y \leq 750$$

$$\underline{-125x \qquad\qquad -125x}$$

$$75y \leq 750 - 125x$$

$$\frac{75y}{75} \leq \frac{750 - 125x}{75}$$

$$y \leq 10 - \frac{5}{3}x$$

You can multiply both sides of the inequality by 100 to eliminate the decimals.

Subtraction Property of Inequality

Division Property of Inequality

b. Graph the solutions.

Step 1 Since Sarah cannot buy a negative amount of vegetables, the system is graphed only in Quadrant I. Graph the boundary line $y = -\frac{5}{3}x + 10$. Use a solid line for $\leq$.

Step 2 Shade below the line. Sarah must buy whole numbers of bunches or packages. All points on or below the line with whole-number coordinates represent combinations of broccoli and carrots that Sarah can buy.

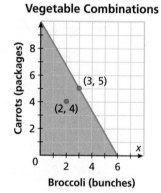

Vegetable Combinations

Carrots (packages)

(3, 5)

(2, 4)

Broccoli (bunches)

c. Give two combinations of vegetables that Sarah can buy.

Two different combinations that Sarah could buy for $7.50 or less are 2 bunches of broccoli and 4 packages of carrots, or 3 bunches of broccoli and 5 packages of carrots.

CHECK IT OUT!

3. Dirk is going to bring two types of olives to the Honor Society induction and can spend no more than $6. Green olives cost $2 per pound and black olives cost $2.50 per pound.

    a. Write a linear inequality to describe the situation.

    b. Graph the solutions.

    c. Give two combinations of olives that Dirk could buy.

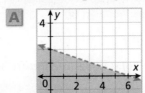

Writing an Inequality from a Graph

Write an inequality to represent each graph.

A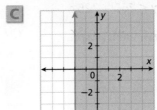

y-intercept: 2; slope: $-\dfrac{1}{3}$

Write an equation in slope-intercept form.

$$y = mx + b \longrightarrow y = -\dfrac{1}{3}x + 2$$

The graph is shaded *below* a *dashed* boundary line.

Replace = with < to write the inequality $y < -\dfrac{1}{3}x + 2$.

B

y-intercept: −2; slope: 5

Write an equation in slope-intercept form.

$$y = mx + b \longrightarrow y = 5x + (-2)$$

The graph is shaded *above* a *solid* boundary line.

Replace = with ≥ to write the inequality $y \ge 5x - 2$.

C

y-intercept: none; slope: undefined

The graph is a vertical line at $x = -2$.

The graph is shaded on the *right* side of a *solid* boundary line.

Replace = with ≥ to write the inequality $x \ge -2$.

CHECK IT OUT!

Write an inequality to represent each graph.

4a.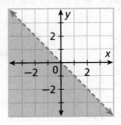

4b.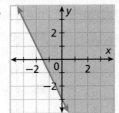

MCC.MP.6   **MATHEMATICAL PRACTICES**

THINK AND DISCUSS

1. Tell how graphing a linear inequality is the same as graphing a linear equation. Tell how it is different.

2. Explain how you would write a linear inequality from a graph.

3. **GET ORGANIZED** Copy and complete the graphic organizer.

Inequality	$y < 5x + 2$	$y > 7x - 3$	$y \le 9x + 1$	$y \ge -3x - 2$
Symbol	<			
Boundary Line	Dashed			
Shading	Below			

GUIDED PRACTICE

1. **Vocabulary** Can a *solution of a linear inequality* lie on a dashed boundary line? Explain.

SEE EXAMPLE 1

Tell whether the ordered pair is a solution of the given inequality.

2. $(0, 3); y \leq -x + 3$ 3. $(2, 0); y > -2x - 2$ 4. $(-2, 1); y < 2x + 4$

SEE EXAMPLE 2

Graph the solutions of each linear inequality.

5. $y \leq -x$ 6. $y > 3x + 1$ 7. $-y < -x + 4$ 8. $-y \geq x + 1$

SEE EXAMPLE 3

9. **Multi-Step** Jack is making punch with orange juice and pineapple juice. He can make at most 16 cups of punch.

   a. Write an inequality to describe the situation.

   b. Graph the solutions.

   c. Give two combinations of cups of orange juice and pineapple juice that Jack can use in his punch.

SEE EXAMPLE 4

Write an inequality to represent each graph.

10.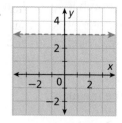

11.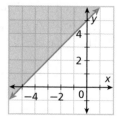

PRACTICE AND PROBLEM SOLVING

Independent Practice	
For Exercises	See Example
12–14	1
15–18	2
19	3
20–21	4

my.hrw.com

Online Extra Practice

Tell whether the ordered pair is a solution of the given inequality.

12. $(2, 3); y \geq 2x + 3$ 13. $(1, -1); y < 3x - 3$ 14. $(0, 7); y > 4x + 7$

Graph the solutions of each linear inequality.

15. $y > -2x + 6$ 16. $-y \geq 2x$ 17. $x + y \leq 2$ 18. $x - y \geq 0$

19. **Multi-Step** Beverly is serving hamburgers and hot dogs at her cookout. Hamburger meat costs $3 per pound, and hot dogs cost $2 per pound. She wants to spend no more than $30.

   a. Write an inequality to describe the situation.

   b. Graph the solutions.

   c. Give two combinations of pounds of hamburger and hot dogs that Beverly can buy.

Write an inequality to represent each graph.

20.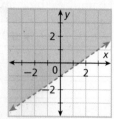

21.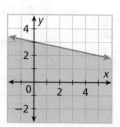

22. **Business** An electronics store makes $125 profit on every DVD player it sells and $100 on every CD player it sells. The store owner wants to make a profit of at least $500 a day selling DVD players and CD players.

    a. Write a linear inequality to determine the number of DVD players x and the number of CD players y that the owner needs to sell to meet his goal.

    b. Graph the linear inequality.

    c. Describe the possible values of x. Describe the possible values of y.

    d. List three combinations of DVD players and CD players that the owner could sell to meet his goal.

Graph the solutions of each linear inequality.

23. $y \le 2 - 3x$ **24.** $-y < 7 + x$ **25.** $2x - y \le 4$ **26.** $3x - 2y > 6$

27. **Geometry** Marvin has 18 yards of fencing that he can use to put around a rectangular garden.

    a. Write an inequality to describe the possible lengths and widths of the garden.

    b. Graph the inequality and list three possible solutions to the problem.

    c. What are the dimensions of the largest *square* garden that can be fenced in with whole-number dimensions?

28. **Hobbies** Stephen wants to buy yellow tangs and clown fish for his saltwater aquarium. He wants to spend no more than $77 on fish. At the store, yellow tangs cost $15 each and clown fish cost $11 each. Write and graph a linear inequality to find the number of yellow tangs x and the number of clown fish y that Stephen could purchase. Name a solution of your inequality that is not reasonable for the situation. Explain.

Graph each inequality on a coordinate plane.

29. $y > 1$ **30.** $-2 < x$ **31.** $x \ge -3$ **32.** $y \le 0$

33. $0 \ge x$ **34.** $-12 + y > 0$ **35.** $x + 7 < 7$ **36.** $-4 \ge x - y$

37. **School** At a high school football game, tickets at the gate cost $7 per adult and $4 per student. Write a linear inequality to determine the number of adult and student tickets that need to be sold so that the amount of money taken in at the gate is at least $280. Graph the inequality and list three possible solutions.

H.O.T. 38. **Critical Thinking** Why must a region of a coordinate plane be shaded to show all solutions of a linear inequality?

39. **Write About It** Give a real-world situation that can be described by a linear inequality. Then graph the inequality and give two solutions.

Real-World Connections

40. Gloria is making teddy bears. She is making boy and girl bears. She has enough stuffing to create 50 bears. Let x represent the number of girl bears and y represent the number of boy bears.

    a. Write an inequality that shows the possible number of boy and girl bears Gloria can make.

    b. Graph the inequality.

    c. Give three possible solutions for the numbers of boy and girl bears that can be made.

H.O.T. 41. /// ERROR ANALYSIS /// Student A wrote $y < 2x - 1$ as the inequality represented by the graph. Student B wrote $y \le 2x - 1$ as the inequality represented by the graph. Which student is incorrect? Explain the error.

H.O.T. 42. Write About It How do you decide to shade above or below a boundary line? What does this shading represent?

TEST PREP

43. Which point is a solution of the inequality $y > -x + 3$?

   Ⓐ $(0, 3)$ Ⓑ $(1, 4)$ Ⓒ $(-1, 4)$ Ⓓ $(0, -3)$

44. Which inequality is represented by the graph at right?

   Ⓕ $2x + y \ge 3$ Ⓗ $2x + y \le 3$

   Ⓖ $2x + y > 3$ Ⓙ $2x + y < 3$

45. Which of the following describes the graph of $3 \le x$?

   Ⓐ The boundary line is dashed, and the shading is to the right.

   Ⓑ The boundary line is dashed, and the shading is to the left.

   Ⓒ The boundary line is solid, and the shading is to the right.

   Ⓓ The boundary line is solid, and the shading is to the left.

CHALLENGE AND EXTEND

Graph each inequality.

46. $0 \ge -6 - 2x - 5y$ **47.** $y > |x|$ **48.** $y \ge |x - 3|$

49. A linear inequality has the points $(0, 3)$ and $(-3, 1.5)$ as solutions on the boundary line. Also, the point $(1, 1)$ is not a solution. Write the linear inequality.

50. Two linear inequalities are graphed on the same coordinate plane. The point $(0, 0)$ is a solution of both inequalities. The entire coordinate plane is shaded except for Quadrant I. What are the two inequalities?

FOCUS ON MATHEMATICAL PRACTICES

H.O.T. 51. Analysis Equivalent inequalities have the same boundaries and contain the same points in their solutions. Is the inequality $x - y < 12$ equivalent to $y < x - 12$? Explain why or why not.

H.O.T. 52. Modeling Angie volunteers at the local animal sanctuary. They are fencing a space that will house no more than 10 dogs. They want to house some adult dogs x and some puppies y.

   a. Write an inequality that describes the situation.

   b. Graph the inequality. How is your graphed inequality different than the actual situation?

H.O.T. 53. Make a Conjecture The solutions to an inequality of the form $y > ax + b$ are always found above the boundary line. Where do you think the solutions to an inequality of the form $x > ay + b$ can be found? Explain your reasoning.

Solving Systems of Linear Inequalities

? Essential Question: How can you solve systems of linear inequalities by using graphs?

Objective
Graph and solve systems of linear inequalities in two variables.

Vocabulary
system of linear inequalities
solutions of a system of linear inequalities

Who uses this?
The owner of a surf shop can use systems of linear inequalities to determine how many surfboards and wakeboards need to be sold to make a certain profit. (See Example 4.)

A **system of linear inequalities** is a set of two or more linear inequalities containing two or more variables. The **solutions of a system of linear inequalities** are all of the ordered pairs that satisfy all the linear inequalities in the system.

COMMON CORE GPS **EXAMPLE** **1**
Prep. for MCC9-12.A.REI.12

my.hrw.com

Online Video Tutor

Identifying Solutions of Systems of Linear Inequalities

Tell whether the ordered pair is a solution of the given system.

A $(2, 1)$; $\begin{cases} y < -x + 4 \\ y \le x + 1 \end{cases}$

$(2, 1)$

$$\begin{array}{c|c} y < -x + 4 \\ \hline 1 & -2 + 4 \\ 1 < 2 ✓ \end{array}$$

$(2, 1)$

$$\begin{array}{c|c} y \le x + 1 \\ \hline 1 & 2 + 1 \\ 1 \le 3 ✓ \end{array}$$

$(2, 1)$ is a solution to the system because it satisfies both inequalities.

B $(2, 0)$; $\begin{cases} y \ge 2x \\ y < x + 1 \end{cases}$

$(2, 0)$

$$\begin{array}{c|c} y \ge 2x \\ \hline 0 & 2(2) \\ 0 \ge 4 ✗ \end{array}$$

$(2, 0)$

$$\begin{array}{c|c} y < x + 1 \\ \hline 0 & 2 + 1 \\ 0 < 3 ✓ \end{array}$$

$(2, 0)$ is not a solution to the system because it does not satisfy both inequalities.

Remember!

An ordered pair must be a solution of all inequalities to be a solution of the system.

CHECK IT OUT!
Tell whether the ordered pair is a solution of the given system.

1a. $(0, 1)$; $\begin{cases} y < -3x + 2 \\ y \ge x - 1 \end{cases}$

1b. $(0, 0)$; $\begin{cases} y > -x + 1 \\ y > x - 1 \end{cases}$

To show all the solutions of a system of linear inequalities, graph the solutions of each inequality. The solutions of the system are represented by the overlapping shaded regions. Below are graphs of Examples 1A and 1B.

Example 1A

(2, 1) is in the overlapping shaded regions, so it is a solution.

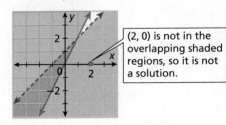

Example 1B

(2, 0) is not in the overlapping shaded regions, so it is not a solution.

EXAMPLE 2

Solving a System of Linear Inequalities by Graphing

Graph the system of linear inequalities. Give two ordered pairs that are solutions and two that are not solutions.

$$\begin{cases} 8x + 4y \le 12 \\ y > \dfrac{1}{2}x - 2 \end{cases}$$

$8x + 4y \le 12$ *Solve the first inequality for y.*
$\qquad 4y \le -8x + 12$
$\qquad\quad y \le -2x + 3$

Graph the system.

$$\begin{cases} y \le -2x + 3 \\ y > \dfrac{1}{2}x - 2 \end{cases}$$

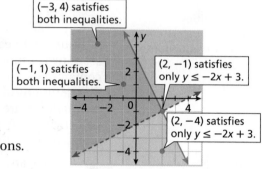

(−3, 4) satisfies both inequalities.

(−1, 1) satisfies both inequalities.

(2, −1) satisfies only $y \le -2x + 3$.

(2, −4) satisfies only $y \le -2x + 3$.

$(-1, 1)$ and $(-3, 4)$ are solutions.
$(2, -1)$ and $(2, -4)$ are not solutions.

CHECK IT OUT! Graph each system of linear inequalities. Give two ordered pairs that are solutions and two that are not solutions.

2a. $\begin{cases} y \le x + 1 \\ y > 2 \end{cases}$ **2b.** $\begin{cases} y > x - 7 \\ 3x + 6y \le 12 \end{cases}$

Previously, you saw that in systems of linear equations, if the lines are parallel, there are no solutions. With systems of linear inequalities, that is not always true.

EXAMPLE 3

Graphing Systems with Parallel Boundary Lines

Graph each system of linear inequalities. Describe the solutions.

A $\begin{cases} y < 2x - 3 \\ y > 2x + 2 \end{cases}$ **B** $\begin{cases} y > x - 3 \\ y \le x + 1 \end{cases}$ **C** $\begin{cases} y \le -3x - 2 \\ y \le -3x + 4 \end{cases}$

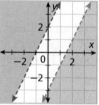   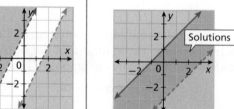   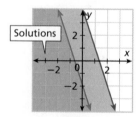

This system has no solution.

The solutions are all points between the parallel lines and on the solid line.

The solutions are the same as the solutions of $y \le -3x - 2$.

Graph each system of linear inequalities. Describe the solutions.

3a. $\begin{cases} y > x + 1 \\ y \le x - 3 \end{cases}$ **3b.** $\begin{cases} y \ge 4x - 2 \\ y \le 4x + 2 \end{cases}$ **3c.** $\begin{cases} y > -2x + 3 \\ y > -2x \end{cases}$

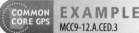 EXAMPLE **4**
MCC9-12.A.CED.3

Business Application

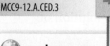 **my.hrw.com**

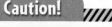

Online Video Tutor

A surf shop makes the profits given in the table. The shop owner sells at least 10 surfboards and at least 20 wakeboards per month. He wants to earn at least $2000 a month. Show and describe all possible combinations of surfboards and wakeboards that the store owner needs to sell to meet his goals. List two possible combinations.

Profit per Board Sold ($)	
Surfboard	150
Wakeboard	100

Step 1 Write a system of inequalities.
Let x represent the number of surfboards and y represent the number of wakeboards.

$x \ge 10$ *He sells at least 10 surfboards.*

$y \ge 20$ *He sells at least 20 wakeboards.*

$150x + 100y \ge 2000$ *He wants to earn a total of at least $2000.*

Step 2 Graph the system.
The graph should be in only the first quadrant because sales are not negative.

Caution!
//////

An ordered pair solution of the system need not have whole numbers, but answers to many application problems may be restricted to whole numbers.

Step 3 Describe all possible combinations.
To meet the sales goals, the shop could sell any combination represented by an ordered pair of whole numbers in the solution region. Answers must be whole numbers because the shop cannot sell part of a surfboard or wakeboard.

Sales Goals

Step 4 List two possible combinations.
Two possible combinations are:
15 surfboards and 25 wakeboards
25 surfboards and 20 wakeboards

 4. At her party, Alice is serving pepper jack cheese and cheddar cheese. She wants to have at least 2 pounds of each. Alice wants to spend at most $20 on cheese. Show and describe all possible combinations of the two cheeses Alice could buy. List two possible combinations.

Price per Pound ($)	
Pepper Jack	4
Cheddar	2

MCC.MP.1   **MATHEMATICAL PRACTICES**

THINK AND DISCUSS

1. How would you write a system of linear inequalities from a graph?

2. GET ORGANIZED Copy and complete each part of the graphic organizer. In each box, draw a graph and list one solution.

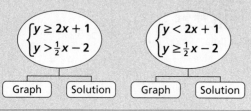

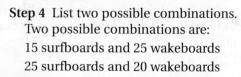

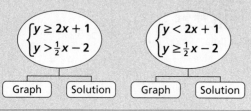

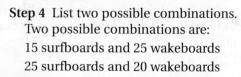

$\begin{cases} y \ge 2x + 1 \\ y > \frac{1}{2}x - 2 \end{cases}$ $\begin{cases} y < 2x + 1 \\ y \ge \frac{1}{2}x - 2 \end{cases}$

Graph   Solution   Graph   Solution

GUIDED PRACTICE

1. **Vocabulary** A solution of a system of inequalities is a solution of _____?_____ of the inequalities in the system. (*at least one* or *all*)

SEE EXAMPLE 1   Tell whether the ordered pair is a solution of the given system.

2. $(0, 0)$; $\begin{cases} y < -x + 3 \\ y < x + 2 \end{cases}$ 3. $(0, 0)$; $\begin{cases} y < 3 \\ y > x - 2 \end{cases}$ 4. $(1, 0)$; $\begin{cases} y > 3x \\ y \le x + 1 \end{cases}$

SEE EXAMPLE 2   Graph each system of linear inequalities. Give two ordered pairs that are solutions and two that are not solutions.

5. $\begin{cases} y < 2x - 1 \\ y > 2 \end{cases}$ 6. $\begin{cases} x < 3 \\ y > x - 2 \end{cases}$ 7. $\begin{cases} y \ge 3x \\ 3x + y \ge 3 \end{cases}$ 8. $\begin{cases} 2x - 4y \le 8 \\ y > x - 2 \end{cases}$

SEE EXAMPLE 3   Graph each system of linear inequalities. Describe the solutions.

9. $\begin{cases} y > 2x + 3 \\ y < 2x \end{cases}$ 10. $\begin{cases} y \le -3x - 1 \\ y \ge -3x + 1 \end{cases}$ 11. $\begin{cases} y > 4x - 1 \\ y \le 4x + 1 \end{cases}$

12. $\begin{cases} y < -x + 3 \\ y > -x + 2 \end{cases}$ 13. $\begin{cases} y > 2x - 1 \\ y > 2x - 4 \end{cases}$ 14. $\begin{cases} y \le -3x + 4 \\ y \le -3x - 3 \end{cases}$

SEE EXAMPLE 4   15. **Business** Sandy makes $2 profit on every cup of lemonade that she sells and $1 on every cupcake that she sells. Sandy wants to sell at least 5 cups of lemonade and at least 5 cupcakes per day. She wants to earn at least $25 per day. Show and describe all the possible combinations of lemonade and cupcakes that Sandy needs to sell to meet her goals. List two possible combinations.

PRACTICE AND PROBLEM SOLVING

Independent Practice	
For Exercises	See Example
16–18	1
19–22	2
23–28	3
29	4

my.hrw.com

Online Extra Practice

Tell whether the ordered pair is a solution of the given system.

16. $(0, 0)$; $\begin{cases} y > -x - 1 \\ y < 2x + 4 \end{cases}$ 17. $(0, 0)$; $\begin{cases} x + y < 3 \\ y > 3x - 4 \end{cases}$ 18. $(1, 0)$; $\begin{cases} y > 3x \\ y > 3x + 1 \end{cases}$

Graph each system of linear inequalities. Give two ordered pairs that are solutions and two that are not solutions.

19. $\begin{cases} y < -3x - 3 \\ y \ge 0 \end{cases}$ 20. $\begin{cases} y < -1 \\ y > 2x - 1 \end{cases}$ 21. $\begin{cases} y > 2x + 4 \\ 6x + 2y \ge -2 \end{cases}$ 22. $\begin{cases} 9x + 3y \le 6 \\ y > x \end{cases}$

Graph each system of linear inequalities. Describe the solutions.

23. $\begin{cases} y < 3 \\ y > 5 \end{cases}$ 24. $\begin{cases} y < x - 1 \\ y > x - 2 \end{cases}$ 25. $\begin{cases} x \ge 2 \\ x \le 2 \end{cases}$

26. $\begin{cases} y > -4x - 3 \\ y < -4x + 2 \end{cases}$ 27. $\begin{cases} y > -1 \\ y > 2 \end{cases}$ 28. $\begin{cases} y \le 2x + 1 \\ y \le 2x - 4 \end{cases}$

29. Multi-Step Linda works at a pharmacy for $15 an hour. She also baby-sits for $10 an hour. Linda needs to earn at least $90 per week, but she does not want to work more than 20 hours per week. Show and describe the number of hours Linda could work at each job to meet her goals. List two possible solutions.

30. Farming Tony wants to plant at least 40 acres of corn and at least 50 acres of soybeans. He wants no more than 200 acres of corn and soybeans. Show and describe all the possible combinations of the number of acres of corn and of soybeans Tony could plant. List two possible combinations.

Graph each system of linear inequalities.

31. $\begin{cases} y \geq -3 \\ y \geq 2 \end{cases}$ **32.** $\begin{cases} y > -2x - 1 \\ y > -2x - 3 \end{cases}$ **33.** $\begin{cases} x \leq -3 \\ x \geq 1 \end{cases}$ **34.** $\begin{cases} y < 4 \\ y > 0 \end{cases}$

Write a system of linear inequalities to represent each graph.

35. 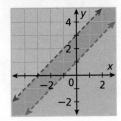   **36.** 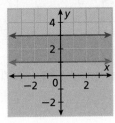   **37.**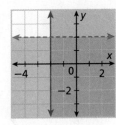

38. Military For males to enter the United States Air Force Academy, located in Colorado Springs, CO, they must be at least 17 but less than 23 years of age. Their standing height must be not less than 60 inches and not greater than 80 inches. Graph all possible heights and ages for eligible male candidates. Give three possible combinations.

39. ///ERROR ANALYSIS/// Two students wrote a system of linear inequalities to describe the graph. Which student is incorrect? Explain the error.

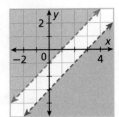

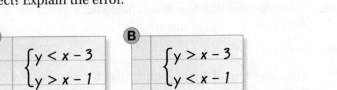

A $\begin{cases} y < x - 3 \\ y > x - 1 \end{cases}$ **B** $\begin{cases} y > x - 3 \\ y < x - 1 \end{cases}$

40. Recreation Vance wants to fence in a rectangular area for his dog. He wants the length of the rectangle to be at least 30 feet and the perimeter to be no more than 150 feet. Graph all possible dimensions of the rectangle.

H.O.T. 41. Critical Thinking Can the solutions of a system of linear inequalities be the points on a line? Explain.

Real-World Connections

42. Gloria is starting her own company making teddy bears. She has enough bear bodies to create 40 bears. She will make girl bears and boy bears.

  a. Write an inequality to show this situation.

  b. Gloria will charge $15 for girl bears and $12 for boy bears. She wants to earn at least $540 a week. Write an inequality to describe this situation.

  c. Graph this situation and locate the solution region.

H.O.T. **43. Write About It** What must be true of the boundary lines in a system of two linear inequalities if there is no solution of the system? Explain.

TEST PREP

44. Which point is a solution of $\begin{cases} 2x + y \geq 3 \\ y \geq -2x + 1 \end{cases}$?

    Ⓐ $(0, 0)$ Ⓑ $(0, 1)$ Ⓒ $(1, 0)$ Ⓓ $(1, 1)$

45. Which system of inequalities best describes the graph?

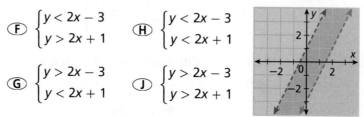

  Ⓕ $\begin{cases} y < 2x - 3 \\ y > 2x + 1 \end{cases}$ Ⓗ $\begin{cases} y < 2x - 3 \\ y < 2x + 1 \end{cases}$

  Ⓖ $\begin{cases} y > 2x - 3 \\ y < 2x + 1 \end{cases}$ Ⓙ $\begin{cases} y > 2x - 3 \\ y > 2x + 1 \end{cases}$

46. Short Response Graph and describe $\begin{cases} y + x > 2 \\ y \leq -3x + 4 \end{cases}$. Give two possible solutions of the system.

CHALLENGE AND EXTEND

47. Estimation Graph the given system of inequalities. Estimate the area of the overlapping solution regions.

$$\begin{cases} y \geq 0 \\ y \leq x + 3.5 \\ y \leq -x + 3.5 \end{cases}$$

48. Write a system of linear inequalities for which $(-1, 1)$ and $(1, 4)$ are solutions and $(0, 0)$ and $(2, -1)$ are not solutions.

49. Graph $|y| < 1$.

50. Write a system of linear inequalities for which the solutions are all the points in the third quadrant.

FOCUS ON MATHEMATICAL PRACTICES

H.O.T. **51. Problem Solving** Without graphing, describe the solution or solutions to the system of inequalities shown. How did you find your answer? $\begin{cases} x - y < 3 \\ x - y > 3 \end{cases}$

H.O.T. **52. Analysis** Is it possible for a system of two linear inequalities to have a single point as a solution? What about a system of more than two inequalities? If either case is possible, write such a system and name the solution.

H.O.T. **53. Reasoning** Use a graph to find three solutions to the system of inequalities shown. What approach did you use to graph the system? $\begin{cases} y < x^2 + 5 \\ y > x^2 \end{cases}$

Technology TASK

Solve Systems of Linear Inequalities

A graphing calculator gives a visual solution to a system of linear inequalities.

Use with Solving Systems of Linear Inequalities

MATHEMATICAL PRACTICES

Use appropriate tools strategically.

MCC9-12.A.REI.12 Graph the ... solution set to a system of linear inequalities in two variables as the intersection of the corresponding half-planes.

Activity

Graph the system $\begin{cases} y > 2x - 4 \\ 2.75y - x < 6 \end{cases}$. **Give two ordered pairs that are solutions.**

1 The first inequality is solved for y.

2 Graph the first inequality. First graph the boundary line $y = 2x - 4$. Press **Y=** and enter $2x - 4$ for **Y1**.

The inequality contains the symbol $>$. The solution region is above the boundary line. Press ◀ to move the cursor to the left of **Y1**. Press **ENTER** until the icon that looks like a region above a line appears. Press **GRAPH**.

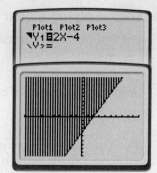

3 Solve the second inequality for y.

$2.75y - x < 6$

$\qquad 2.75y < x + 6$

$\qquad\quad y < \dfrac{x + 6}{2.75}$

4 Graph the second inequality. First graph the boundary line $y = \dfrac{x + 6}{2.75}$. Press **Y=** and enter $(x + 6)/2.75$ for **Y2**.

The inequality contains the symbol $<$. The solution region is below the boundary line. Press ◀ to move the cursor to the left of **Y2**. Press **ENTER** until the icon that looks like a region below a line appears. Press **GRAPH**.

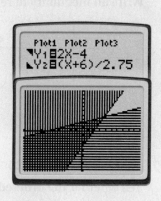

5 The solutions of the system are represented by the overlapping shaded regions. The points $(0, 0)$ and $(-1, 0)$ are in the shaded region.

Check   Test $(0, 0)$ in both inequalities.

$y > 2x - 4$		$2.75y - x < 6$	
0	$2(0) - 4$	$2.75(0) - 0$	6
0	> -4 ✓	0	< 6 ✓

Test $(-1, 0)$ in both inequalities.

$y > 2x - 4$		$2.75y - x < 6$	
0	$2(-1) - 4$	$2.75(0) - (-1)$	6
0	> -6 ✓	1	< 6 ✓

Try This

Graph each system. Give two ordered pairs that are solutions.

1. $\begin{cases} x + 5y > -10 \\ x - y < 4 \end{cases}$

2. $\begin{cases} y > x - 2 \\ y \leq x + 2 \end{cases}$

3. $\begin{cases} y > x - 2 \\ y \leq 3 \end{cases}$

4. $\begin{cases} y < x - 3 \\ y - 3 > x \end{cases}$

Ready to Go On?

my.hrw.com
Assessment and Intervention
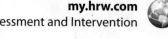

7-1 Solving Special Systems

Solve each system of linear equations.

1. $\begin{cases} y = -2x - 6 \\ 2x + y = 5 \end{cases}$

2. $\begin{cases} x + y = 2 \\ 2x + 2y = -6 \end{cases}$

3. $\begin{cases} y = -2x + 4 \\ 2x + y = 4 \end{cases}$

Classify each system. Give the number of solutions.

4. $\begin{cases} 3x = -6y + 3 \\ 2y = -x + 1 \end{cases}$

5. $\begin{cases} y = -4x + 2 \\ 4x + y = -2 \end{cases}$

6. $\begin{cases} 4x - 3y = 8 \\ y = 4(x + 2) \end{cases}$

7-2 Solving Linear Inequalities

Tell whether the ordered pair is a solution of the inequality.

7. $(3, -2); y < -2x + 1$

8. $(2, 1); y \geq 3x - 5$

9. $(1, -6); y \leq 4x - 10$

Graph the solutions of each linear inequality.

10. $y \geq 4x - 3$

11. $3x - y < 5$

12. $2x + 3y < 9$

13. $y \leq -\frac{1}{2}x$

14. Theo's mother has given him at most $150 to buy clothes for school. The pants cost $30 each and the shirts cost $15 each. Write a linear inequality to describe the situation. Graph the solutions and give three combinations of pants and shirts that Theo could buy.

Write an inequality to represent each graph.

15.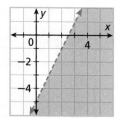

16.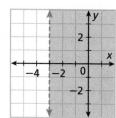

17.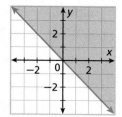

7-3 Solving Systems of Linear Inequalities

Tell whether the ordered pair is a solution of the given system.

18. $(-3, -1); \begin{cases} y > -2 \\ y < x + 4 \end{cases}$

19. $(-3, 0); \begin{cases} y \leq x + 4 \\ y \geq -2x - 6 \end{cases}$

20. $(0, 0); \begin{cases} y \geq 3x \\ 2x + y < -1 \end{cases}$

Graph each system of linear inequalities. Give two ordered pairs that are solutions and two that are not solutions.

21. $\begin{cases} y > -2 \\ y < x + 3 \end{cases}$

22. $\begin{cases} x + y \leq 2 \\ 2x + y \geq -1 \end{cases}$

23. $\begin{cases} 2x - 5y \leq -5 \\ 3x + 2y < 10 \end{cases}$

Graph each system of linear inequalities. Describe the solutions.

24. $\begin{cases} y \ge x + 1 \\ y \ge x - 4 \end{cases}$
    25. $\begin{cases} y \ge 2x - 1 \\ y < 2x - 3 \end{cases}$
    26. $\begin{cases} y < -3x + 5 \\ y > -3x - 2 \end{cases}$

27. A grocer sells mangos for \$4/lb and apples for \$3/lb. The grocer starts with 45 lb of mangos and 50 lb of apples each day. The grocer's goal is to make at least \$300 by selling mangos and apples each day. Show and describe all possible combinations of mangos and apples that could be sold to meet the goal. List two possible combinations.

PARCC Assessment Readiness

Selected Response

1. Elena and her husband Marc both drive to work. Elena's car has a current mileage (total distance driven) of 5,000 and she drives 15,000 miles more each year. Marc's car has a current mileage of 32,000 and he drives 15,000 miles more each year. Will the mileages for the two cars ever be equal? Explain.

(A) No; The equations have different slopes, so the lines do not intersect.

(B) Yes; The equations have different y-intercepts, so the lines intersect.

(C) No; the equations have equal slopes but different y-intercepts, so the lines do not intersect.

(D) Yes; The equations have different slopes, so the lines intersect.

2. Classify $\begin{cases} x - 8y = 6 \\ 2x - 16y = 12 \end{cases}$. Give the number of solutions.

(F) This system is consistent. It has infinitely many solutions.

(G) This system is inconsistent. It has infinitely many solutions.

(H) This system is inconsistent. It has no solutions.

(J) This system is consistent. It has one solution.

3. Solve $\begin{cases} y = -x + 8 \\ x + y = 7 \end{cases}$

(A) This system has infinitely many solutions.

(B) This system has no solutions.

(C) $\left(\dfrac{1}{2}, \dfrac{15}{2} \right)$

(D) $\left(-\dfrac{1}{2}, \dfrac{17}{2} \right)$

4. Write an inequality to represent the graph.

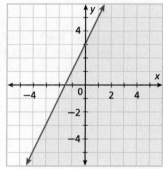

(F) $y > 2x + 3$ **(H)** $y < 3x + 2$

(G) $y \le 2x + 3$ **(J)** $y < 2x + 3$

Mini-Task

5. Graph the system of linear inequalities $\begin{cases} y < -3x + 2 \\ y \ge 4x - 1 \end{cases}$.

Give two ordered pairs that are solutions and two that are not solutions.

PARCC Assessment Readiness

Selected Response

1. What value of n makes the equation below have no solution?

$$2x + 2 = nx - 3$$

- **A** -2
- **B** 0
- **C** 2
- **D** 3

2. Which of the equations below represents the second step of the solution process?

Step 1: $3(5x - 2) + 27 = -24$
Step 2:
Step 3: $\qquad 15x + 21 = -24$
Step 4: $\qquad\qquad 15x = -45$
Step 5: $\qquad\qquad\quad x = -3$

- **F** $3(5x + 27) - 2 = -24$
- **G** $3(5x + 25) = -24$
- **H** $15x - 2 + 27 = -24$
- **J** $15x - 6 + 27 = -24$

3. Cass drove 3 miles to school, and then she drove m miles to a friend's house. The total mileage for these two trips was 8 miles. Which equation CANNOT be used to determine the number of miles Cass drove?

- **A** $3 + m = 8$
- **B** $3 - m = 8$
- **C** $8 - 3 = m$
- **D** $8 - m = 3$

4. If $\dfrac{20}{x} = \dfrac{4}{x - 5}$, which of the following is a true statement?

- **F** $x(x - 5) = 80$
- **G** $20x = 4(x - 5)$
- **H** $20(x - 5) = 4x$
- **J** $24 = 2x - 5$

5. A bike rental shop charges a one-time charge of $8 plus an hourly fee to rent a bike. Dan paid $24.50 to rent a bike for $5\frac{1}{2}$ hours. What is the bike shop's hourly fee in dollars?

- **A** $3.00
- **C** $5.50
- **B** $4.45
- **D** $8

6. Which algebraic expression means "5 less than y"?

- **F** $5 - y$
- **G** $y - 5$
- **H** $5 < y$
- **J** $5 \div y$

7. If $t + 8 = 2$, find the value of $2t$.

- **A** -12
- **B** -6
- **C** 12
- **D** 20

8. The length of the rectangle is $2(x + 1)$ meters and the perimeter is 60 meters. What is the length of the rectangle?

- **F** 12 meters
- **G** 26 meters
- **H** 28 meters
- **J** 56 meters

9. Samantha opened a bank account in June and deposited some money. She deposited twice that amount in August. At the end of August, Samantha had less than $600 in her account. If she made no other withdrawals or deposits, which inequality could be used to determine the maximum amount Samantha could have deposited in June?

- **A** $2x < 600$
- **B** $2x > 600$
- **C** $3x < 600$
- **D** $3x > 600$

10. For which inequality is -2 a solution?

- **F** $2x < -4$
- **G** $-2x < 4$
- **H** $-2x > -4$
- **J** $-2x < -4$

11. Which graph shows the solutions of
$-2(1 - x) < 3(x - 2)$?

(A)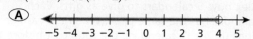
  $-5\ -4\ -3\ -2\ -1\ \ 0\ \ 1\ \ 2\ \ 3\ \ 4\ \ 5$

(B)
  $-5\ -4\ -3\ -2\ -1\ \ 0\ \ 1\ \ 2\ \ 3\ \ 4\ \ 5$

(C)
  $-5\ -4\ -3\ -2\ -1\ \ 0\ \ 1\ \ 2\ \ 3\ \ 4\ \ 5$

(D)
  $-5\ -4\ -3\ -2\ -1\ \ 0\ \ 1\ \ 2\ \ 3\ \ 4\ \ 5$

12. Which compound inequality has no solution?

(F) $x > 1$ OR $x < -2$

(G) $x < 1$ AND $x > -2$

(H) $x < 1$ OR $x < -2$

(J) $x > 1$ AND $x < -2$

13. Which inequality has the same solutions as $p < -2$?

(A) $p + 1 < -2$

(B) $p + 4 < 2$

(C) $2p + 1 < -4$

(D) $3p < -12$

14. What is the greatest integer solution of $5 - 3m > 11$?

(F) 0

(G) -1

(H) -2

(J) -3

15. The sum of the measures of any two sides of a triangle must be greater than the measure of the third side. What is the greatest possible integer value for x?

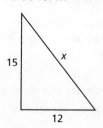

(A) 27

(B) 3

(C) 26

(D) 180

16. For which inequality is 3 a solution?

(F) $x - 5 > -2$

(H) $2x + 1 \leq 4$

(G) $x + 4 \leq 7$

(J) $2x - 1 \geq 7$

17. Which of the problems below could be solved by finding the solution of this system?

$$\begin{cases} 2x + 2y = 56 \\ y = \dfrac{1}{3}x \end{cases}$$

(A) The area of a rectangle is 56 square units. The width is one-third the length. Find the length of the rectangle.

(B) The area of a rectangle is 56 square units. The length is one-third the perimeter. Find the length of the rectangle.

(C) The perimeter of a rectangle is 56 units. The length is one-third more than the width. Find the length of the rectangle.

(D) The perimeter of a rectangle is 56 units. The width is one-third the length. Find the length of the rectangle.

18. What is the slope of a line perpendicular to a line that passes through $(3, 8)$ and $(1, -4)$?

(F) $-\dfrac{1}{6}$

(H) 2

(G) $-\dfrac{1}{2}$

(J) 6

19. Which inequality is graphed below?

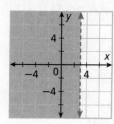

(A) $-x > -3$

(C) $2x < -6$

(B) $-y > -3$

(D) $3y < 9$

20. A chemist has a bottle of a 10% acid solution and a bottle of a 30% acid solution. He mixes the solutions together to get 500 mL of a 25% acid solution. How much of the 30% solution did he use?

(F) 125 mL

(H) 375 mL

(G) 150 mL

(J) 450 mL

21. Which ordered pair is NOT a solution of the system graphed below?

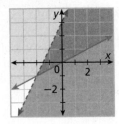

Ⓐ (0, 0)

Ⓑ (0, 3)

Ⓒ (1, 1)

Ⓓ (2, 1)

22. The fare for a cab is $3.50 per trip plus $1.25 per mile. Which describes the cab fare in dollars as a function of miles traveled?

Ⓕ $f(x) = 3.5x + 1.25$

Ⓖ $f(x) = 3.5x + 0.125$

Ⓗ $f(x) = 1.25x + 3.5$

Ⓙ $f(x) = 1.25x + 0.35$

23. Hillary needs markers and poster board for a project. The markers are $0.79 each and the poster board is $1.89 per sheet. She needs at least 4 sheets of poster board. Hillary has $15 to spend on project materials. Which system models this information?

Ⓐ $\begin{cases} p \geq 4 \\ 0.79m + 1.89p \leq 15 \end{cases}$

Ⓑ $\begin{cases} 0.79m \geq 1.89p \\ 4p \leq 15 \end{cases}$

Ⓒ $\begin{cases} 4p \geq 1.89 \\ m + 4p \leq 15 \end{cases}$

Ⓓ $\begin{cases} p + m \leq 15 \\ 0.79m + 1.89p \geq 4 \end{cases}$

Mini-Tasks

24. Alex buys 5 calendars to give as gifts. Each calendar has the same price. When the cashier rings up Alex's calendars, the total cost before tax is $58.75.

  a. Write and solve an equation to find the cost of each calendar.

  b. The total cost of Alex's calendars after tax is $63.45. Find the percent sales tax. Show your work and explain in words how you found your answer.

25. Write 2 different inequalities that have the same solution as $n > 3$ such that

  a. the first inequality uses the symbol $>$ and requires addition or subtraction to solve.

  b. the second inequality uses the symbol $<$ and requires multiplication or division to solve.

26. Alison has twice as many video games as Kyle. Maurice has 5 more video games than Alison. The total number of video games is less than 40.

  a. Write an inequality to represent this situation.

  b. Solve the inequality to determine the greatest number of video games Maurice could have. Justify each step in your solution.

27. Donna's Deli delivers lunches for $7 per person plus a $35 delivery fee. Larry's Lunches delivers lunches for $11 per person.

  a. Write an expression to represent the cost of x lunches from Donna's Deli. Write an expression to represent the cost of ordering x lunches from Larry's Lunches.

  b. Write an inequality to determine the number of lunches for which the cost of Larry's Lunches is less than the cost of Donna's Deli.

  c. Solve the inequality and explain what the answer means. Which restaurant charges less for an order of 10 lunches?

28. Graph $y > \dfrac{-x}{3} - 1$ on a coordinate plane. Name one point that is a solution of the inequality.

29. Marc and his brother Ty start saving money at the same time. Marc has $145 and will add $10 to his savings every week. Ty has $20 and will add $15 to his savings every week. After how many weeks will Marc and Ty have the same amount saved? What is that amount? Show your work.

30. A movie producer is looking for extras to act as office employees in his next movie. The producer needs extras that are at least 40 years old but less than 70 years old. They should be at least 60 inches tall but less than 75 inches tall. Graph all the possible combinations of ages and heights for extras that match the producer's needs. Let *x* represent age and *y* represent height. Show your work.

Performance Tasks

31. Korena is laying out a flower garden in her front yard. The garden will be 6 feet wide, and one side will be flush against her house. She wants to add a decorative border around the other three sides, and she has 22 feet of decorative border. She also needs the garden to have an area of at least 50 square feet to fit all of her plants.

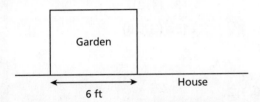

a. Write formulas for the area of the garden and for the length of the decorative border. Write both formulas in terms of length ℓ and width *w*.

b. Solve both formulas from part **a** for ℓ.

c. Use your formulas to find out if there is a length ℓ that satisfies Korena's requirement for the area and fits the amount of border she has. Explain your reasoning.

d. Describe one way Korena could change her plans so that she has the materials she needs to make her garden. Explain your reasoning and detail your changes.

32. Serena wants to use the interest earned for one year from her college savings to update the software on her computer. She can invest up to $10,000, and she needs at least $300 for the software. She wants to put part of this amount into a money market account that earns 2.5% simple interest per year. She puts the other part in a certificate of deposit (CD), which earns 4% simple interest per year.

a. Use x to represent the money invested in the CD and y to represent the money invested in the money market account. Write an inequality to represent the amount of money she can invest.

b. Using the same variables as in part **a**, write an inequality to represent the amount of interest she needs to earn in one year.

c. Graph the system of inequalities. Identify a solution that meets Serena's requirements, and calculate how much money she will earn on interest with that solution.

d. Serena wants to put as little money in the CD as possible, because unlike the money market account, she can't withdraw any money from the CD until the end of the year. What is the least amount of money Serena can put in the CD and still earn enough interest? Round to the nearest whole dollar, and explain how you found your answer.

  my.hrw.com
Online Assessment
Go online for updated, PARCC-aligned assessment readiness.

Are You Ready?

my.hrw.com
Assessment and Intervention

✓ Vocabulary

Match each term on the left with a definition on the right.

1. absolute value
2. algebraic expression
3. input
4. output
5. x-axis

A. a letter used to represent a value that can change

B. the value generated for y

C. a group of numbers, symbols, and variables with one or more operations

D. the distance of a number from zero on the number line

E. the horizontal number line in the coordinate plane

F. a value substituted for x

✓ Ordered Pairs

Graph each point on the same coordinate plane.

6. $(-2, 4)$ 7. $(0, -5)$ 8. $(1, -3)$ 9. $(4, 2)$

10. $(3, -2)$ 11. $(-1, -2)$ 12. $(-1, 3)$ 13. $(-4, 0)$

✓ Function Tables

Generate ordered pairs for each function for $x = -2, -1, 0, 1, 2$.

14. $y = -2x - 1$ 15. $y = x + 1$ 16. $y = -x^2$

17. $y = \frac{1}{2}x + 2$ 18. $y = (x + 1)^2$ 19. $y = (x - 1)^2$

✓ Solve Multi-Step Equations

Solve each equation. Check your answer.

20. $17x - 15 = 12$ 21. $-7 + 2t = 7$ 22. $-6 = \frac{p}{3} + 9$

23. $5n - 10 = 35$ 24. $3r - 14 = 7$ 25. $9 = \frac{x}{2} + 1$

26. $-2.4 + 1.6g = 5.6$ 27. $34 - 2x = 12$ 28. $2(x + 5) = -8$

Career Readiness Market Researchers

Market researchers gather information and statistical data. They use graphs, including trend lines, to analyze the data. They determine what kinds of products people want to buy, and how much they are willing to pay. Market researchers advise companies about the types of people who are likely to buy their products. They usually need a college degree, with a strong background in math, especially statistics. They work in all areas of industry and as self-employed consultants.

COMMON CORE GPS

UNIT 3

Linear and Exponential Functions

Online Edition

my.hrw.com
Access the complete online textbook, interactive features, and additional resources.

Animated Math
Interactively explore key concepts with these online tutorials.

Multilingual Glossary
Enhance your math vocabulary with this illustrated online glossary in 13 languages.

Portable Devices

On the Spot
Watch video tutorials anywhere, anytime with this app for iPhone® and iPad®.

HMH Fuse
Make your learning experience completely portable and interactive with this app for iPad®.

Chapter Resources
Scan with your smart phone to jump directly to the online edition.

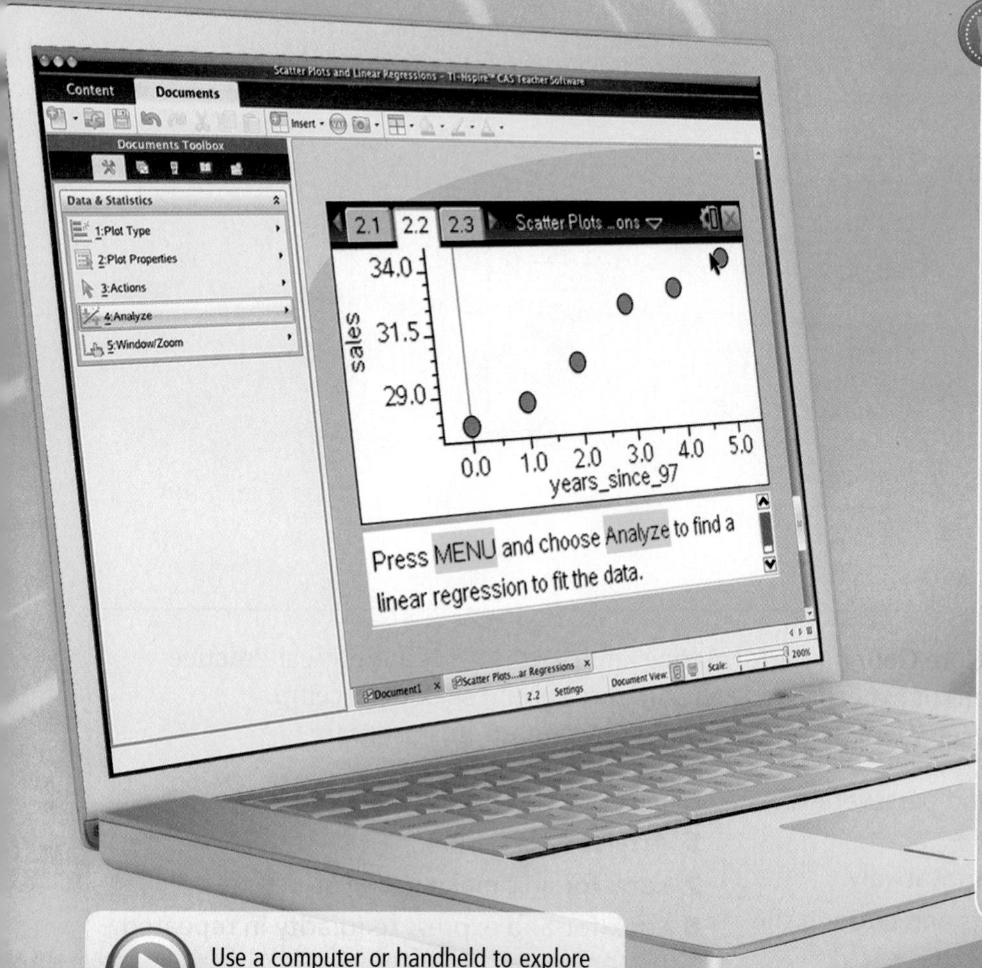

Use a computer or handheld to explore scatter plots with TI-Nspire™ activities.

COMMON CORE GPS

Unit Contents

Module 8 **Functional Relationships**
MCC9-12.A.REI.10, MCC9-12.F.BF.1, MCC9-12.F.IF.4, MCC9-12.F.IF.5

Module 9 **Graphs and Transformations**
MCC9-12.A.REI.10, MCC9-12.F.BF.2, MCC9-12.F.BF.3, MCC9-12.F.IF.3

Module 10 **Linear Functions and Slope**
MCC9-12.F.IF.5, MCC9-12.F.IF.6, MCC9-12.F.LE.1, MCC9-12.F.LE.5

Module 11 **Graphs and Equations of Linear Functions**
MCC9-12.F.BF.1, MCC9-12.F.BF.3, MCC9-12.F.IF.7, MCC9-12.F.LE.1b

Module 12 **Exponential Functions**
MCC9-12.F.BF.2, MCC9-12.F.IF.3, MCC9-12.F.IF.7e, MCC9-12.F.LE.2

Module 13 **Comparing and Modeling with Functions**
MCC9-12.F.BF.3, MCC9-12.F.IF.9, MCC9-12.F.LE.2, MCC9-12.F.LE.3

Functional Relationships

COMMON
CORE GPS

Contents

MATHEMATICAL
PRACTICES

The Common Core Georgia Performance Standards for Mathematical Practice
describe varieties of expertise that all students should seek to develop.
Opportunities to develop these practices are integrated throughout this program.

1 Make sense of problems and persevere in
solving them.

2 Reason abstractly and quantitatively.

3 Construct viable arguments and critique the
reasoning of others.

4 Model with mathematics.

5 Use appropriate tools strategically.

6 Attend to precision.

7 Look for and make use of structure.

8 Look for and express regularity in repeated
reasoning.

Unpacking the Standards

Understanding the standards and the vocabulary terms in the standards will help you know exactly what you are expected to learn in this chapter.

 MCC9-12.F.IF.1

Understand that a function from one set (called the domain) to another set (called the range) assigns to each element of the domain exactly one element of the range. …

Key Vocabulary

function (función)
  A relation in which every domain value is paired with exactly one range value.
domain (dominio)
  The set of all first coordinates (or x-values) of a relation or function.
range of a function or relation (rango de una función o relación)
  The set of all second coordinates (or y-values) of a function or relation.
element (elemento)
  Each member in a set.

What It Means For You

A function model guarantees you that for any input value, you will get a unique output value.

EXAMPLE   **Relationship is a function**

$$y = x^2$$

One output for every input: When -2 is input, the output is always 4.

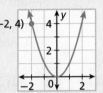

NON-EXAMPLE   **Relationship is NOT a function**

$$y^2 = x$$

Two outputs for every input but 0: When 4 is input, the output can be -2 or 2.

 MCC9-12.F.IF.4

For a function that models a relationship between two quantities, interpret key features of graphs and tables in terms of the quantities, and sketch graphs showing key features given a verbal description of the relationship.

What It Means For You

Learning to interpret a graph enables a deep visual understanding of all sorts of relationships.

EXAMPLE

A group of friends walked to the town market, did some shopping there, then returned home.

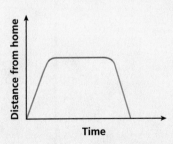

8-1

Graphing Relationships

? **Essential Question:** How can you use key features to sketch a graph of a real-world situation?

Objectives
Match simple graphs with situations.

Graph a relationship.

Vocabulary
continuous graph
discrete graph

Who uses this?

Cardiologists can use graphs to analyze their patients' heartbeats. (See Example 2.)

Graphs can be used to illustrate many different situations. For example, trends shown on a cardiograph can help a doctor see how the patient's heart is functioning.

To relate a graph to a given situation, use key words in the description.

 EXAMPLE **1**
MCC9-12.F.IF.4

Relating Graphs to Situations

The air temperature was constant for several hours at the beginning of the day and then rose steadily for several hours. It stayed the same temperature for most of the day before dropping sharply at sundown. Choose the graph that best represents this situation.

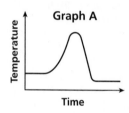 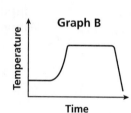 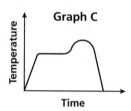

Step 1 Read the graphs from left to right to show time passing.

Step 2 List key words in order and decide which graph shows them.

Key Words	Segment Description	Graphs
Was constant	Horizontal	Graphs A and B
Rose steadily	Slanting upward	Graphs A and B
Stayed the same	Horizontal	Graph B
Dropped sharply	Slanting downward	Graph B

Step 3 Pick the graph that shows all the key phrases in order.

horizontal, **slanting upward,**
horizontal, **slanting downward**

The correct graph is B.

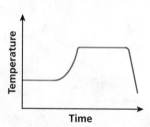

 **my.hrw.com**

Online Video Tutor

---

 1. The air temperature increased steadily for several hours and then remained constant. At the end of the day, the temperature increased slightly again before dropping sharply. Choose the graph above that best represents this situation.

As seen in Example 1, some graphs are connected lines or curves called **continuous graphs**. Some graphs are only distinct points. These are called **discrete graphs**.

The graph on theme-park attendance is an example of a discrete graph. It consists of distinct points because each year is distinct and people are counted in whole numbers only. The values between the whole numbers are not included, since they have no meaning for the situation.

Theme Park Attendance

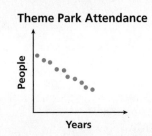

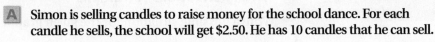

Sketching Graphs for Situations

Sketch a graph for each situation. Tell whether the graph is continuous or discrete.

A Simon is selling candles to raise money for the school dance. For each candle he sells, the school will get $2.50. He has 10 candles that he can sell.

Simon's Earnings

The amount earned (y-axis) increases by $2.50 for each candle Simon sells (x-axis).

Since Simon can only sell whole numbers of candles, the graph is 11 distinct points.

The graph is discrete.

B Angelique's heart rate is being monitored while she exercises on a treadmill. While walking, her heart rate remains the same. As she increases her pace, her heart rate rises at a steady rate. When she begins to run, her heart rate increases more rapidly and then remains high while she runs. As she decreases her pace, her heart rate slows down and returns to her normal rate.

As time passes during her workout (moving left to right along the *x*-axis), her heart rate (*y*-axis) does the following:

- remains the same,
- rises at a steady rate,
- increases more rapidly (steeper than previous segment),
- remains high,
- slows down,
- and then returns to her normal rate.

Angelique's Heart Rate

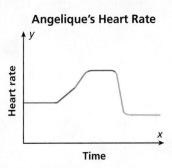

The graph is continuous.

 Sketch a graph for each situation. Tell whether the graph is continuous or discrete.

2a. Jamie is taking an 8-week keyboarding class. At the end of each week, she takes a test to find the number of words she can type per minute. She improves each week.

2b. Henry begins to drain a water tank by opening a valve. Then he opens another valve. Then he closes the first valve. He leaves the second valve open until the tank is empty.

When sketching or interpreting a graph, pay close attention to the labels on each axis. Both graphs below show a relationship about a child going down a slide. **Graph A** represents the child's *distance from the ground* over time. **Graph B** represents the child's *speed* over time.

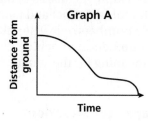

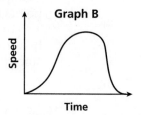

Writing Situations for Graphs

Write a possible situation for the given graph.

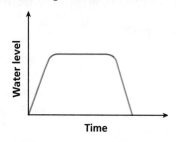

Step 1 Identify labels.
x-axis: time y-axis: water level

Step 2 Analyze sections.
Over time, the water level
- increases steadily,
- remains unchanged,
- and then decreases steadily.

Possible Situation: A watering can is filled with water. It sits for a while until some flowers are planted. The water is then emptied on top of the planted flowers.

3. Write a possible situation for the given graph.

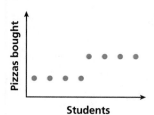

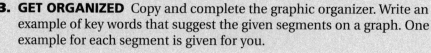

MCC.MP.2, MCC.MP.4   MATHEMATICAL PRACTICES

THINK AND DISCUSS

1. Should a graph of age related to height be a continuous graph or a discrete graph? Explain.

2. Give an example of a situation that, when graphed, would include a horizontal segment.

3. GET ORGANIZED Copy and complete the graphic organizer. Write an example of key words that suggest the given segments on a graph. One example for each segment is given for you.

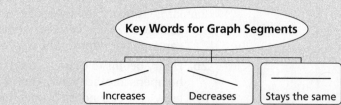

Know it! Note

GUIDED PRACTICE

Vocabulary Apply the vocabulary from this lesson to answer each question.

1. A ___?___ graph is made of connected lines or curves. (*continuous* or *discrete*)

2. A ___?___ graph is made of only distinct points. (*continuous* or *discrete*)

SEE EXAMPLE 1

Choose the graph that best represents each situation.

3. A person alternates between running and walking.

4. A person gradually speeds up to a constant running pace.

5. A person walks, gradually speeds up to a run, and then slows back down to a walk.

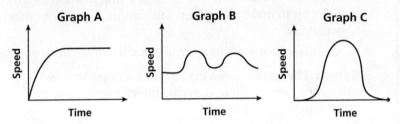

SEE EXAMPLE 2

6. Maxine is buying extra pages for her photo album. Each page holds exactly 8 photos. Sketch a graph to show the maximum number of photos she can add to her album if she buys 1, 2, 3, or 4 extra pages. Tell whether the graph is continuous or discrete.

SEE EXAMPLE 3

Write a possible situation for each graph.

7. 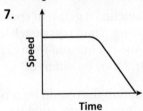   8. 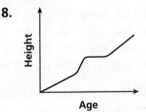   9.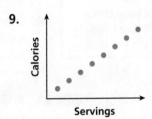

PRACTICE AND PROBLEM SOLVING

Independent Practice

For Exercises	See Example
10–12	1
13	2
14–16	3

Choose the graph that best represents each situation.

10. A flag is raised up a flagpole quickly at the beginning and then more slowly near the top.

11. A flag is raised up a flagpole in a jerky motion, using a hand-over-hand method.

12. A flag is raised up a flagpole at a constant rate of speed.

my.hrw.com

Online Extra Practice

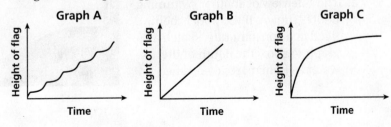

13. For six months, a puppy gained weight at a steady rate. Sketch a graph to illustrate the weight of the puppy during that time period. Tell whether the graph is continuous or discrete.

Write a possible situation for each graph.

14.

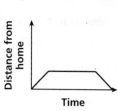

15.

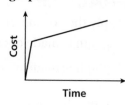

16.

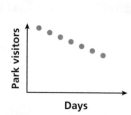

17. Data Collection Use a graphing calculator and motion detector for the following.

   a. On a coordinate plane, draw a graph relating distance from a starting point walking at various speeds and time.

   b. Using the motion detector as the starting point, walk away from the motion detector to make a graph on the graphing calculator that matches the one you drew.

   c. Compare your walking speeds to each change in steepness on the graph.

18. Sports The graph shows the speed of a horse during and after a race. Use it to describe the changing pace of the horse during the race.

Horse Race

19. Recreation You hike up a mountain path starting at 10 A.M. You camp overnight and then walk back down the same path at the same pace at 10 A.M. the next morning. On the same set of axes, graph the relationship between distance from the top of the mountain and the time of day for both the hike up and the hike down. What does the point of intersection of the graphs represent?

20. Critical Thinking Suppose that you sketched a graph of speed related to time for a brick that fell from the top of a building. Then you sketched a graph for speed related to time for a ball that was rolled down a hill and then came to rest. How would the graphs be the same? How would they be different?

H.O.T 21. Write About It Describe a real-life situation that could be represented by a distinct graph. Then describe a real-life situation that could be represented by a continuous graph.

Real-World Connections

22. A rectangular pool that is 4 feet deep at all places is being filled at a constant rate.

   a. Sketch a graph to show the depth of the water as it increases over time.

   b. The side view of another swimming pool is shown. If the pool is being filled at a constant rate, sketch a graph to show the depth of the water as it increases over time.

TEST PREP

23. Which situation would NOT be represented by a discrete graph?

   Ⓐ Amount of money earned based on the number of cereal bars sold

   Ⓑ Number of visitors to a grocery store per day for one week

   Ⓒ The amount of iced tea in a pitcher at a restaurant during the lunch hour

   Ⓓ The total cost of buying 1, 2, or 3 CDs at the music store

24. Which situation is best represented by the graph?

   Ⓕ A snowboarder starts at the bottom of the hill and takes a ski lift to the top.

   Ⓖ A cruise boat travels at a steady pace from the port to its destination.

   Ⓗ An object falls from the top of a building and gains speed at a rapid pace before hitting the ground.

   Ⓙ A marathon runner starts at a steady pace and then runs faster at the end of the race before stopping at the finish line.

H.O.T. 25. **Short Response** Marla participates in a triathlon consisting of swimming, biking, and running. Would a graph of Marla's speed during the triathlon be a continuous graph or a distinct graph? Explain.

CHALLENGE AND EXTEND

Pictured are three vases and graphs representing the height of water as it is poured into each of the vases at a constant rate. Match each vase with the correct graph.

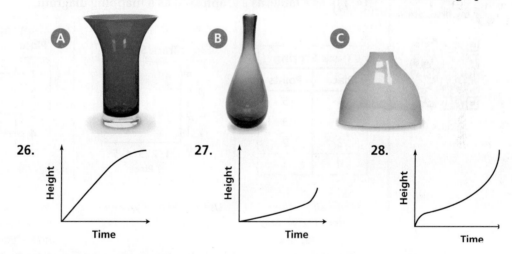

26.

27.

28.

MATHEMATICAL PRACTICES

FOCUS ON MATHEMATICAL PRACTICES

H.O.T. 29. **Modeling** As Kayla burns a candle, she records the amount of time that passes and the height of the burning candle. Which graph could reasonably represent her data? Explain your choice.

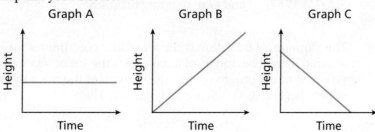

Graph A   Graph B   Graph C

8-2 Relations and Functions

 Essential Question: How can you identify the domain and range of a relation and tell whether a relation is a function?

Objectives
Identify functions.

Find the domain and range of relations and functions.

Vocabulary
relation
domain
range
function

Why learn this?
You can use a relation to show finishing positions and scores in a track meet.

Previously, you saw relationships represented by graphs. Relationships can also be represented by a set of ordered pairs, called a **relation**.

In the scoring system of some track meets, **first place** is worth 5 points, **second place** is worth 3 points, **third place** is worth 2 points, and **fourth place** is worth 1 point. This scoring system is a relation, so it can be shown as ordered pairs, $\{(1, 5), (2, 3), (3, 2), (4, 1)\}$. You can also show relations in other ways, such as tables, graphs, or *mapping diagrams*.

COMMON CORE GPS
Prep. for MCC9-12.F.IF.1

EXAMPLE 1

my.hrw.com

Online Video Tutor

Showing Multiple Representations of Relations

Express the relation for the track meet scoring system, $\{(1, 5), (2, 3), (3, 2), (4, 1)\}$, as a table, as a graph, and as a mapping diagram.

Table

Track Scoring	
Place	**Points**
1	5
2	3
3	2
4	1

Write all *x*-values under "Place" and all *y*-values under "Points."

Graph

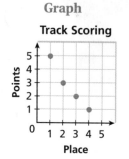

Track Scoring

Use the *x*- and *y*-values to plot the ordered pairs.

Mapping Diagram

Place		Points
1	→	5
2	→	3
3	→	2
4	→	1

Write all *x*-values under "Place" and all *y*-values under "Points." Draw an arrow from each *x*-value to its corresponding *y*-value.

 1. Express the relation $\{(1, 3) (2, 4), (3, 5)\}$ as a table, as a graph, and as a mapping diagram.

The **domain** of a relation is the set of first coordinates (or *x*-values) of the ordered pairs. The **range** of a relation is the set of second coordinates (or *y*-values) of the ordered pairs. The domain of the track meet scoring system is {1, 2, 3, 4}. The range is {5, 3, 2, 1}.

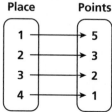

Alfo Foto Agency

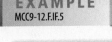

EXAMPLE 2
MCC9-12.F.IF.5

Finding the Domain and Range of a Relation

Give the domain and range of the relation.

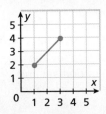

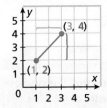

The domain is all *x*-values from 1 through 3, inclusive.

The range is all *y*-values from 2 through 4, inclusive.

D: $1 \le x \le 3$ R: $2 \le y \le 4$

my.hrw.com

Online Video Tutor

Give the domain and range of each relation.

2a.

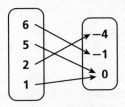

2b.

x	y
1	1
4	4
8	1

A **function** is a special type of relation that pairs each domain value with exactly one range value.

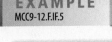

EXAMPLE 3
MCC.9-12.F.IF.1

Identifying Functions

Give the domain and range of each relation. Tell whether the relation is a function. Explain.

Ⓐ

Field Trip	
Students x	**Buses y**
75	2
68	2
125	3

my.hrw.com

Online Video Tutor

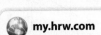

Writing Math

When there is a finite number of values in a domain or range, list the values inside braces.

D: $\{75, 68, 125\}$
R: $\{2, 3\}$

Even though 2 appears twice in the table, it is written only once when writing the range.

This relation is a function. Each domain value is paired with exactly one range value.

Ⓑ

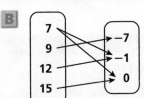

Use the arrows to determine which domain values correspond to each range value.

D: $\{7, 9, 12, 15\}$
R: $\{-7, -1, 0\}$

This relation is not a function. Each domain value does not have exactly one range value. The domain value 7 is paired with the range values −1 and 0.

Give the domain and range of each relation. Tell whether the relation is a function. Explain.

C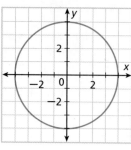

Draw lines to see the domain and range values.

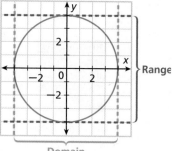

D: $-4 \le x \le 4$ R: $-4 \le y \le 4$

x	4	0	0	−4
y	0	4	−4	0

To compare domain and range values, make a table using points from the graph.

This relation is not a function because there are several domain values that have more than one range value. For example, the domain value 0 is paired with both 4 and −4.

CHECK IT OUT!

Give the domain and range of each relation. Tell whether the relation is a function. Explain.

3a. $\{(8, 2), (-4, 1), (-6, 2), (1, 9)\}$ **3b.**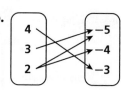

MCC.MP.3   MATHEMATICAL PRACTICES

THINK AND DISCUSS

1. Describe how to tell whether a set of ordered pairs is a function.

2. Can the graph of a vertical line segment represent a function? Explain.

3. GET ORGANIZED Copy and complete the graphic organizer by explaining when a relation is a function and when it is not a function.

A relation is...	
A function if...	Not a function if...

Helpful Hint

To find the domain and range of a graph, it may help to draw lines to see the x- and y-values.

GUIDED PRACTICE

Vocabulary Apply the vocabulary from this lesson to answer each question.

1. Use a mapping diagram to show a relation that is not a *function*.

2. The set of *x*-values for a relation is also called the __?__. (*domain* or *range*)

SEE EXAMPLE 1

Express each relation as a table, as a graph, and as a mapping diagram.

3. $\{(1, 1), (1, 2)\}$

4. $\left\{(-1, 1), \left(-2, \frac{1}{2}\right), \left(-3, \frac{1}{3}\right), \left(-4, \frac{1}{4}\right)\right\}$

5. $\{(-1, 1), (-3, 3), (5, -5), (-7, 7)\}$

6. $\{(0, 0), (2, -4), (2, -2)\}$

SEE EXAMPLE 2

Give the domain and range of each relation.

7. $\{(-5, 7), (0, 0), (2, -8), (5, -20)\}$

8. $\{(1, 2), (2, 4), (3, 6), (4, 8), (5, 10)\}$

9.

x	3	5	2	8	6
y	9	25	4	81	36

10.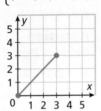

SEE EXAMPLE 3

Multi-Step Give the domain and range of each relation. Tell whether the relation is a function. Explain.

11. $\{(1, 3), (1, 0), (1, -2), (1, 8)\}$

12. $\{(-2, 1), (-1, 2), (0, 3), (1, 4)\}$

13.

x	−2	−1	0	1	2
y	1	1	1	1	1

14.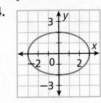

PRACTICE AND PROBLEM SOLVING

Express each relation as a table, as a graph, and as a mapping diagram.

15. $\{(-2, -4), (-1, -1), (0, 0), (1, -1), (2, -4)\}$

16. $\left\{(2, 1), \left(2, \frac{1}{2}\right), (2, 2), \left(2, 2\frac{1}{2}\right)\right\}$

Independent Practice	
For Exercises	See Example
15–16	1
17–18	2
19–20	3

Give the domain and range of each relation.

17.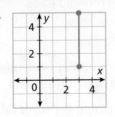

18.

x	y
4	4
5	5
6	6
7	7
8	8

Multi-Step Give the domain and range of each relation. Tell whether the relation is a function. Explain.

19.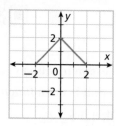

20.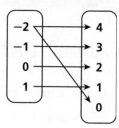

21. **Consumer Application** An electrician charges a base fee of $75 plus $50 for each hour of work. Create a table that shows the amount the electrician charges for 1, 2, 3, and 4 hours of work. Let *x* represent the number of hours and *y* represent the amount charged for *x* hours. Is this relation a function? Explain.

22. **Geometry** Write a relation as a set of ordered pairs in which the *x*-value represents the side length of a square and the *y*-value represents the area of that square. Use a domain of 2, 4, 6, 9, and 11.

23. **Multi-Step** Create a mapping diagram to display the numbers of days in 1, 2, 3, and 4 weeks. Is this relation a function? Explain.

24. **Nutrition** The illustrations list the number of grams of fat and the number of Calories from fat for selected foods.

   a. Create a graph for the relation between grams of fat and Calories from fat.

   b. Is this relation a function? Explain.

Hamburger
Fat (g):   14
Fat (Cal): 126

Cheeseburger
Fat (g):   18
Fat (Cal): 162

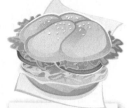

Grilled chicken filet
Fat (g):   3.5
Fat (Cal): 31.5

Breaded chicken filet
Fat (g):   11
Fat (Cal): 99

Taco salad
Fat (g):   19
Fat (Cal): 171

25. **Recreation** A shop rents canoes for a $7 equipment fee plus $2 per hour, with a maximum cost of $15 per day. Express the number of hours *x* and the cost *y* as a relation in table form, and find the cost to rent a canoe for 1, 2, 3, 4, and 5 hours. Is this relation a function? Explain.

26. **Health** You can burn about 6 Calories per minute bicycling. Let *x* represent the number of minutes bicycled, and let *y* represent the number of Calories burned.

   a. Write ordered pairs to show the number of Calories burned by bicycling for 60, 120, 180, 240, or 300 minutes. Graph the ordered pairs.

   b. Find the domain and range of the relation.

   c. Does this graph represent a function? Explain.

27. **Critical Thinking** For a function, can the number of elements in the range be greater than the number of elements in the domain? Explain.

28. **Critical Thinking** Tell whether each statement is true or false. If false, explain why.

   a. All relations are functions.   b. All functions are relations.

Real-World Connections

29. **a.** The graph shows the amount of water being pumped into a pool over a 5-hour time period. Find the domain and range.

   b. Does the graph represent a function? Explain.

   c. Give the time and volume as ordered pairs at 2 hours and at 3 hours 30 minutes.

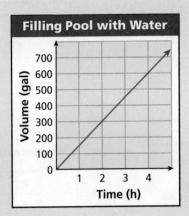

Filling Pool with Water

30. H.O.T. **///ERROR ANALYSIS///** When asked whether the relation $\{(-4, 16), (-2, 4), (0, 0), (2, 4)\}$ is a function, a student stated that the relation is not a function because 4 appears twice. What error did the student make? How would you explain to the student why this relation is a function?

31. H.O.T. **Write About It** Describe a real-world situation for a relation that is NOT a function. Create a mapping diagram to show why the relation is not a function.

TEST PREP

32. Which of the following relations is NOT a function?

   Ⓐ $\{(6, 2), (-1, 2), (-3, 2), (-5, 2)\}$

   Ⓑ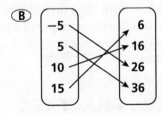

   Ⓒ

x	3	5	7
y	1	15	30

   Ⓓ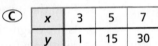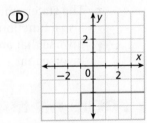

33. Which is NOT a correct way to describe the function $\{(-3, 2), (1, 8), (-1, 5), (3, 11)\}$?

   Ⓕ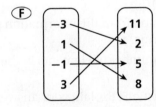

   Ⓖ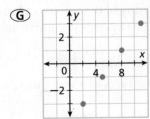

   Ⓗ Domain: $\{-3, 1, -1, 3\}$

   Range: $\{2, 8, 5, 11\}$

   Ⓙ

x	y
-3	2
-1	5
1	8
3	11

34. Which graph represents a function?

Ⓐ

Ⓑ

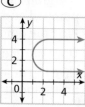
Ⓒ

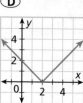
Ⓓ

35. Extended Response Use the table for the following.

x	−3	−1	0	1	3
y	5	7	9	11	13

   a. Express the relation as ordered pairs.

   b. Give the domain and range of the relation.

   c. Does the relation represent a function? Explain your answer.

CHALLENGE AND EXTEND

36. What values of a make the relation $\{(a, 1), (2, 3), (4, 5)\}$ a function? Explain.

37. What values of b make the relation $\{(5, 6), (7, 8), (9, b)\}$ a function? Explain.

38. The *inverse* of a relation is created by interchanging the x- and y- coordinates of each ordered pair in the relation.

   a. Find the inverse of the following relation: $\{(-2, 5), (0, 4), (3, -8), (7, 5)\}$.

   b. Is the original relation a function? Why or why not? Is the inverse of the relation a function? Why or why not?

   c. The statement "If a relation is a function, then the inverse of the relation is also a function" is sometimes true. Give an example of a relation and its inverse that are both functions. Then give an example of a relation and its inverse that are both not functions.

FOCUS ON MATHEMATICAL PRACTICES

H.O.T. **39. Analysis** Gina surveys 15 high school students, asking them what grade they're in and how much they spent that day on lunch. She makes a table of the data, and then draws a graph. She labels her x-axis *Grade Level* and her y-axis *Cost of Lunch*.

   a. What is the domain of her graph?

   b. Can you find the range of the graph from the information given? If not, describe the range in general terms.

   c. What is the maximum possible number of elements in the range? What is the minimum?

   d. Is it likely that the graph is a function? Explain your answer.

H.O.T. **40. Error Analysis** Nick matches each day of the week to anyone in his class of 20 students that was born on that day. He says this is a function. Oscar says this relation is not a function.

   a. Who do you think is correct? Explain why.

   b. How could Nick relate the same two sets in a way that creates a function?

8-2

Algebra TASK

Use with Relations and Functions

The Vertical-Line Test

The *vertical-line test* can be used to visually determine whether a graphed relation is a function.

MATHEMATICAL PRACTICES

Look for and express regularity in repeated reasoning.

MCC9-12.F.IF.1 Understand that a function from one set (called the domain) to another set (called the range) assigns to each element of the domain exactly one element of the range. . . .

Activity

1 Look at the values in Table 1. Is every *x*-value paired with exactly one *y*-value? If not, what *x*-value(s) are paired with more than one *y*-value?

2 Is the relation a function? Explain.

3 Graph the points from the Table 1. Draw a vertical line through each point of the graph. Does any vertical line touch more than one point?

Table 1	
x	**y**
−2	−5
−1	−3
0	−1
1	1
2	3
3	5

4 Look at the values in Table 2. Is every *x*-value paired with exactly one *y*-value? If not, what *x*-value(s) are paired with more than one *y*-value?

5 Is the relation a function? Explain.

6 Graph the points from the Table 2. Draw a vertical line through each point of the graph. Does any vertical line touch more than one point?

7 What is the *x*-value of the two points that are on the same vertical line? Is that *x*-value paired with more than one *y*-value?

Table 2	
x	**y**
−2	−3
1	4
0	5
1	2
2	3
3	5

8 Write a statement describing how to use a vertical line to tell if a relation is a function. This is called the vertical-line test.

9 Why does the vertical-line test work?

Try This

Use the vertical-line test to determine whether each relation is a function. If a relation is not a function, list two ordered pairs that show the same *x*-value with two different *y*-values.

1.

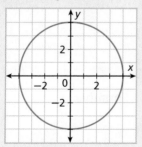

2.

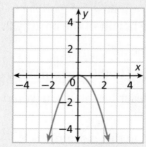

3.

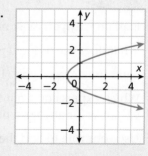

8-3 Algebra TASK

Model Variable Relationships

You can use models to represent an algebraic relationship. Using these models, you can write an algebraic expression to help describe and extend patterns.

Use with Writing Functions

MATHEMATICAL PRACTICES Look for and express regularity in repeated reasoning.

The diagrams below represent the side views of tables. Each has a tabletop and a base. Copy and complete the chart using the pattern shown in the diagrams.

Tabletop →
Base →

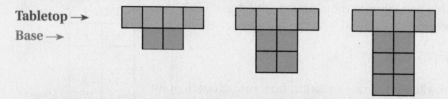

TERM NUMBER	FIGURE	DESCRIPTION OF FIGURE	EXPRESSION FOR NUMBER OF BLOCKS	VALUE OF TERM (NUMBER OF BLOCKS)	ORDERED PAIR
1		length of tabletop = 4 height of base = 1	$4 + (2)1$	6	$(1, 6)$
2		length of tabletop = 4 height of base = 2	■	8	■
3		length of tabletop = 4 height of base = 3	■	10	■
4	■	■	■	■	■
5	■	■	■	■	■
n	✕	■	■	✕	■

Try This

1. Explain why you must multiply the height of the base by 2.

2. What does the ordered pair (1, 6) mean?

3. Does the ordered pair (10, 24) belong in this pattern? Why or why not?

4. Which expression from the table describes how you would find the total number of blocks for any term number n?

5. Use your rule to find the 25th term in this pattern.

8-3

Writing Functions

? Essential Question: How can you use function notation to write and evaluate functions?

Objectives
Identify independent and dependent variables.

Write an equation in function notation and evaluate a function for given input values.

Vocabulary
independent variable
dependent variable
function rule
function notation

Why learn this?
You can use a function rule to calculate how much money you will earn for working specific amounts of time.

Suppose Tasha baby-sits and charges $5 per hour.

Time Worked (h) x	1	2	3	4
Amount Earned ($) y	5	10	15	20

The amount of money Tasha earns is $5 times the number of hours she works. Write an equation using two different variables to show this relationship.

Amount earned is $5 times the number of hours worked.

$$y = 5 \cdot x$$

Tasha can use this equation to find how much money she will earn for any number of hours she works.

 **EXAMPLE 1**

MCC9-12.A.CED.2

 my.hrw.com

Online Video Tutor

Using a Table to Write an Equation

Determine a relationship between the x- and y-values. Write an equation.

x	1	2	3	4
y	−2	−1	0	1

Step 1 List possible relationships between the first x- and y-values.

$1 - 3 = -2$ or $1(-2) = -2$

Step 2 Determine if one relationship works for the remaining values.

$2 - 3 = -1$ ✓ $\qquad$ $2(-2) \neq -1$ ✗

$3 - 3 = 0$ ✓ $\qquad$ $3(-2) \neq 0$ ✗

$4 - 3 = 1$ ✓ $\qquad$ $4(-2) \neq 1$ ✗

The first relationship works. The value of y is 3 less than x.

Step 3 Write an equation.

$y = x - 3$ $\qquad$ *The value of y is 3 less than x.*

 1. Determine a relationship between the x- and y-values in the relation $\{(1, 3), (2, 6), (3, 9), (4, 12)\}$. Write an equation.

The equation in Example 1 describes a function because for each x-value (input), there is only one y-value (output).

RubberBall/Alamy

The **input** of a function is the **independent variable**. The **output** of a function is the **dependent variable**. The value of the dependent variable *depends* on, or is a function of, the value of the independent variable. For Tasha, the amount she earns depends on, or is a function of, the amount of time she works.

 EXAMPLE 2
MCC9-12.F.IF.1

Identifying Independent and Dependent Variables

Identify the independent and dependent variables in each situation.

A In the winter, more electricity is used when the temperature goes down, and less is used when the temperature rises.

The amount of electricity used *depends on* the temperature.
Dependent: **amount of electricity**   Independent: temperature

B The cost of shipping a package is based on its weight.

The cost of shipping a package *depends on* its weight.
Dependent: **cost**   Independent: weight

C The faster Ron walks, the quicker he gets home.

The time it takes Ron to get home *depends on* the speed he walks.
Dependent: **time**   Independent: speed

CHECK IT OUT! Identify the independent and dependent variables in each situation.

2a. A company charges $10 per hour to rent a jackhammer.

2b. Apples cost $0.99 per pound.

Helpful Hint

There are several different ways to describe the variables of a function.

Independent Variable	Dependent Variable
x-values	*y*-values
Domain	Range
Input	Output
x	$f(x)$

An algebraic expression that defines a function is a **function rule**. $5 \cdot x$ in the equation about Tasha's earnings is a function rule.

If x is the independent variable and y is the dependent variable, then **function notation** for y is $f(x)$, read "f of x," where f names the function. When an equation in two variables describes a function, you can use function notation to write it.

The dependent variable	is	a function of	the independent variable.
y	is	a function of	x.
y	$=$	f	(x)

Since $y = f(x)$, Tasha's earnings, $y = 5x$, can be rewritten in function notation by substituting $f(x)$ for y: $f(x) = 5x$. Sometimes functions are written using y, and sometimes functions are written using $f(x)$.

 EXAMPLE 3
MCC9-12.F.IF.2

Writing Functions

Identify the independent and dependent variables. Write an equation in function notation for each situation.

A A lawyer's fee is $200 per hour for her services.

The fee for the lawyer depends on how many hours she works.
Dependent: **fee**   Independent: hours
Let h represent the number of hours the lawyer works.
The function for the lawyer's fee is $f(h) = 200h$.

Identify the independent and dependent variables. Write an equation in function notation for each situation.

B The admission fee to a local carnival is $8. Each ride costs $1.50.

The **total cost** depends on the number of rides ridden, plus $8.

Dependent: **total cost**   Independent: number of rides

Let r represent the number of rides ridden.

The function for the total cost of the carnival is $f(r) = 1.50r + 8$.

 Identify the independent and dependent variables. Write an equation in function notation for each situation.

3a. Steven buys lettuce that costs $1.69/lb.

3b. An amusement park charges a $6.00 parking fee plus $29.99 per person.

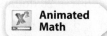 **Animated Math**

You can think of a function as an **input-output** machine. For Tasha's earnings, $f(x) = 5x$, if you input a value x, the output is $5x$.

If Tasha wanted to know how much money she would earn by working 6 hours, she could input 6 for x and find the output. This is called *evaluating the function*.

Input
x 6 2

Function
$f(x) = 5x$

30 5x 10
Output

COMMON CORE GPS MCC9-12.F.IF.2

my.hrw.com

Online Video Tutor

4 **Evaluating Functions**

Evaluate each function for the given input values.

A For $f(x) = 5x$, find $f(x)$ when $x = 6$ and when $x = 7.5$.

$$f(x) = 5x \qquad\qquad f(x) = 5x$$
$$f(6) = 5(6) \quad \text{Substitute 6 for x.} \qquad f(7.5) = 5(7.5) \quad \text{Substitute 7.5 for x.}$$
$$= 30 \quad \text{Simplify.} \qquad\qquad\qquad = 37.5 \quad \text{Simplify.}$$

B For $g(t) = 2.30t + 10$, find $g(t)$ when $t = 2$ and when $t = -5$.

$$g(t) = 2.30t + 10 \qquad\qquad g(t) = 2.30t + 10$$
$$g(2) = 2.30(2) + 10 \qquad\qquad g(-5) = 2.30(-5) + 10$$
$$= 4.6 + 10 \qquad\qquad\qquad = -11.5 + 10$$
$$= 14.6 \qquad\qquad\qquad\qquad = -1.5$$

C For $h(x) = \frac{1}{2}x - 3$, find $h(x)$ when $x = 12$ and when $x = -8$.

$$h(x) = \frac{1}{2}x - 3 \qquad\qquad h(x) = \frac{1}{2}x - 3$$
$$h(12) = \frac{1}{2}(12) - 3 \qquad\qquad h(-8) = \frac{1}{2}(-8) - 3$$
$$= 6 - 3 \qquad\qquad\qquad = -4 - 3$$
$$= 3 \qquad\qquad\qquad\qquad = -7$$

Reading Math

Functions can be named with any letter; f, g, and h are the most common. You read $f(6)$ as "f of 6," and $g(2)$ as "g of 2."

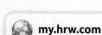 **Evaluate each function for the given input values.**

4a. For $h(c) = 2c - 1$, find $h(c)$ when $c = 1$ and $c = -3$.

4b. For $g(t) = \frac{1}{4}t + 1$, find $g(t)$ when $t = -24$ and $t = 400$.

When a function describes a real-world situation, every real number is not always reasonable for the domain and range. For example, a number representing the length of an object cannot be negative, and only whole numbers can represent a number of people.

EXAMPLE 5

Finding the Reasonable Domain and Range of a Function

my.hrw.com

Online Video Tutor

Manuel has already sold $20 worth of tickets to the school play. He has 4 tickets left to sell at $2.50 per ticket. Write a function to describe how much money Manuel can collect from selling tickets. Find the reasonable domain and range for the function.

Money collected from ticket sales	is	$2.50	per	ticket	plus	the $20 already sold.
$f(x)$	=	$2.50	·	x	+	20

If he sells x more tickets, he will have collected $f(x) = 2.50x + 20$ dollars.

Manuel has only 4 tickets left to sell, so he could sell 0, 1, 2, 3, or 4 tickets. A reasonable domain is {0, 1, 2, 3, 4}.

Substitute these values into the function rule to find the range values.

x	0	1	2	3	4
f(x)	2.50(0) + 20 = 20	2.50(1) + 20 = 22.50	2.50(2) + 20 = 25	2.50(3) + 20 = 27.50	2.50(4) + 20 = 30

The reasonable range for this situation is {$20, $22.50, $25, $27.50, $30}.

CHECK IT OUT!

5. The settings on a space heater are the whole numbers from 0 to 3. The total number of watts used for each setting is 500 times the setting number. Write a function to describe the number of watts used for each setting. Find the reasonable domain and range for the function.

MCC.MP.4, MCC.MP.6   MATHEMATICAL PRACTICES

THINK AND DISCUSS

1. When you input water into an ice machine, the output is ice cubes. Name another real-world object that has an input and an output.

2. How do you identify the independent and dependent variables in a situation?

3. Explain how to find reasonable domain values for a function.

4. GET ORGANIZED Copy and complete the graphic organizer. Use the function $y = x + 3$ and the domain {−2, −1, 0, 1, 2}.

Know it!
Note

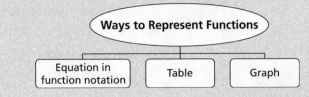

Ways to Represent Functions

| Equation in function notation | Table | Graph |

Exercises

GUIDED PRACTICE

Vocabulary Apply the vocabulary from this lesson to answer each question.

1. The output of a function is the ___?___ variable. (*independent* or *dependent*)

2. An algebraic expression that defines a function is a ___?___. (*function rule* or *function notation*)

SEE EXAMPLE 1 Determine a relationship between the *x*- and *y*-values. Write an equation.

3.

x	1	2	3	4
y	−1	0	1	2

4. $\{(1, 4), (2, 7), (3, 10), (4, 13)\}$

SEE EXAMPLE 2 Identify the independent and dependent variables in each situation.

5. A small-size bottle of water costs $1.99 and a large-size bottle of water costs $3.49.

6. An employee receives 2 vacation days for every month worked.

SEE EXAMPLE 3 Identify the independent and dependent variables. Write an equation in function notation for each situation.

7. An air-conditioning technician charges customers $75 per hour.

8. An ice rink charges $3.50 for skates and $1.25 per hour.

SEE EXAMPLE 4 Evaluate each function for the given input values.

9. For $f(x) = 7x + 2$, find $f(x)$ when $x = 0$ and when $x = 1$.

10. For $g(x) = 4x - 9$, find $g(x)$ when $x = 3$ and when $x = 5$.

11. For $h(t) = \frac{1}{3}t - 10$, find $h(t)$ when $t = 27$ and when $t = -15$.

SEE EXAMPLE 5 12. A construction company uses beams that are 2, 3, or 4 meters long. The measure of each beam must be converted to centimeters. Write a function to describe the situation. Find the reasonable domain and range for the function. (*Hint*: 1 m = 100 cm)

PRACTICE AND PROBLEM SOLVING

Independent Practice

For Exercises	See Example
13–14	1
15–16	2
17–19	3
20–22	4
23	5

Determine a relationship between the *x*- and *y*-values. Write an equation.

13.

x	1	2	3	4
y	−2	−4	−6	−8

14. $\{(1, -1), (2, -2), (3, -3), (4, -4)\}$

Identify the independent and dependent variables in each situation.

15. Gardeners buy fertilizer according to the size of a lawn.

16. The cost to gift wrap an order is $3 plus $1 per item wrapped.

Identify the independent and dependent variables. Write an equation in function notation for each situation.

17. To rent a DVD, a customer must pay $3.99 plus $0.99 for every day that it is late.

18. Stephen charges $25 for each lawn he mows.

19. A car can travel 28 miles per gallon of gas.

Evaluate each function for the given input values.

20. For $f(x) = x^2 - 5$, find $f(x)$ when $x = 0$ and when $x = 3$.

21. For $g(x) = x^2 + 6$, find $g(x)$ when $x = 1$ and when $x = 2$.

22. For $f(x) = \frac{2}{3}x + 3$, find $f(x)$ when $x = 9$ and when $x = -3$.

23. A mail-order company charges \$5 per order plus \$2 per item in the order, up to a maximum of 4 items. Write a function to describe the situation. Find the reasonable domain and range for the function.

24. **Transportation** Air Force One can travel 630 miles per hour. Let h be the number of hours traveled. The function $d = 630h$ gives the distance d in miles that Air Force One travels in h hours.

   a. Identify the independent and dependent variables. Write $d = 630h$ using function notation.

   b. What are reasonable values for the domain and range in the situation described?

   c. How far can Air Force One travel in 12 hours?

25. Complete the table for $g(z) = 2z - 5$.

z	1	2	3	4
g(z)				

26. Complete the table for $h(x) = x^2 + x$.

x	0	1	2	3
h(x)				

27. **Estimation** For $f(x) = 3x + 5$, estimate the output when $x = -6.89$, $x = 1.01$, and $x = 4.67$.

28. **Transportation** A car can travel 30 miles on a gallon of gas and has a 20-gallon gas tank. Let g be the number of gallons of gas the car has in its tank. The function $d = 30g$ gives the distance d in miles that the car travels on g gallons.

   a. What are reasonable values for the domain and range in the situation described?

   b. How far can the car travel on 12 gallons of gas?

H.O.T. 29. **Critical Thinking** Give an example of a real-life situation for which the reasonable domain consists of 1, 2, 3, and 4 and the reasonable range consists of 2, 4, 6, and 8.

H.O.T. 30. ///**ERROR ANALYSIS**/// Rashid saves \$150 each month. He wants to know how much he will have saved in 2 years. He writes the rule $s = m + 150$ to help him figure out how much he will save, where s is the amount saved and m is the number of months he saves. Explain why his rule is incorrect.

31. **Write About It** Give a real-life situation that can be described by a function. Identify the independent variable and the dependent variable.

Real-World Connections

32. The table shows the volume v of water pumped into a pool after t hours.

   a. Determine a relationship between the time and the volume of water and write an equation.

   b. Identify the independent and dependent variables.

   c. If the pool holds 10,000 gallons, how long will it take to fill?

Amount of Water in Pool	
Time (h)	Volume (gal)
0	0
1	1250
2	2500
3	3750
4	5000

TEST PREP

33. Marsha buys x pens at \$0.70 per pen and one pencil for \$0.10. Which function gives the total amount Marsha spends?

    (A) $c(x) = 0.70x + 0.10x$ (C) $c(x) = (0.70 + 0.10)x$

    (B) $c(x) = 0.70x + 1$ (D) $c(x) = 0.70x + 0.10$

34. Belle is buying pizzas for her daughter's birthday party, using the prices in the table. Which equation best describes the relationship between the total cost c and the number of pizzas p?

Pizzas	Total Cost ($)
5	26.25
10	52.50
15	78.75

    (F) $c = 26.25p$ (H) $c = p + 26.25$

    (G) $c = 5.25p$ (J) $c = 6p - 3.75$

35. **Gridded Response** What is the value of $f(x) = 5 - \frac{1}{2}x$ when $x = 3$?

CHALLENGE AND EXTEND

36. The formula to convert a temperature that is in degrees Celsius x to degrees Fahrenheit $f(x)$ is $f(x) = \frac{9}{5}x + 32$. What are reasonable values for the domain and range when you convert to Fahrenheit the temperature of water as it rises from 0° to 100° Celsius?

37. **Math History** In his studies of the motion of free-falling objects, Galileo Galilei found that regardless of its mass, an object will fall a distance d that is related to the square of its travel time t in seconds. The modern formula that describes free-fall motion is $d = \frac{1}{2}gt^2$, where g is the acceleration due to gravity and t is the length of time in seconds the object falls. Find the distance an object falls in 3 seconds. (*Hint*: Research to find acceleration due to gravity in meters per second squared.)

FOCUS ON MATHEMATICAL PRACTICES

H.O.T. 38. **Problem Solving** Alejandro's grandmother gives him \$25 dollars to start his savings account. For every dollar d he adds to this account, his grandmother puts in an additional \$5.

    a. Write an equation that describes t, the total in his savings account, after he has added d dollars.

    b. What is the independent variable for this equation? What is the dependent variable? Explain how you know.

    c. Write the equation from part a in function notation.

H.O.T. 39. **Modeling** Jasmine's monthly cell phone bill varies according to the number of minutes she uses. The table shows the relationship.

Minutes	0	100	200	300	400
Monthly Cost	\$15	\$25	\$35	\$45	\$55

Write a function in the form $f(x) = mx + b$ that relates the number of minutes Jasmine uses to her monthly cost. What does the value of m mean in the context of Jasmine's bill? What about the value of b?

H.O.T. 40. **Analysis** You can perform basic operations, such as addition, subtraction, multiplication, and division, with functions. For example, when $f(x) = 4x$ and $g(x) = 2x - 1$, $f(x) + g(x) = 4x + (2x - 1) = 6x - 1$. Find $f(x) - g(x)$.

Ready to Go On?

my.hrw.com
Assessment and Intervention

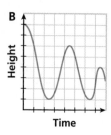
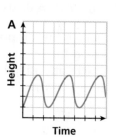

8-1 Graphing Relationships

Choose the graph that best represents each situation.

1. A person bungee jumps from a high platform.

2. A person jumps on a trampoline in a steady motion.

3. Xander takes a quiz worth 100 points. Each question is worth 20 points. Sketch a graph to show his score if he misses 1, 2, 3, 4, or 5 questions.

8-2 Relations and Functions

Give the domain and range of each relation. Tell whether the relation is a function. Explain.

4.

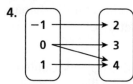

5.

x	−2	−2	0	2	2
y	3	3	3	3	3

6.

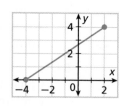

7. A local parking garage charges $5.00 for the first hour plus $1.50 for each additional hour or part of an hour. Write a relation as a set of ordered pairs in which the x-value represents the number of hours and the y-value represents the cost for x hours. Use a domain of 1, 2, 3, 4, 5. Is this relation a function? Explain.

8. A baseball coach is taking the team for ice cream. Four students can ride in each car. Create a mapping diagram to show the number of cars needed to transport 8, 10, 14, and 16 students. Is this relation a function? Explain.

8-3 Writing Functions

Determine a relationship between the x- and y-values. Write an equation.

9.

x	1	2	3	4
y	−6	−5	−4	−3

10.

x	1	2	3	4
y	−3	−6	−9	−12

11. A printer can print 8 pages per minute. Identify the dependent and independent variables for the situation. Write an equation in function notation.

Evaluate each function for the given input values.

12. For $f(x) = 3x - 1$, find $f(x)$ when $x = 2$.

13. For $g(x) = x^2 - x$, find $g(x)$ when $x = -2$.

14. A photographer charges a sitting fee of $15 plus $3 for each pose. Write a function to describe the situation. Find a reasonable domain and range for up to 5 poses.

Selected Response

1. Give the domain and range of the relation.

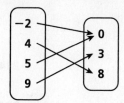

(A) D: {−2, 4, 5, 9}; R: {0, 3, 8}

(B) D: {0, 3, 8}; R: {−2, 4, 5, 9}

(C) D: −2 < x < 9; R: 0 < x < 8

(D) D: −2 ≤ x ≤ 9; R: 0 ≤ x ≤ 8

2. Which graph represents a function?

(F)

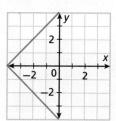

(G)

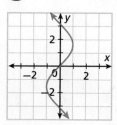

(H)

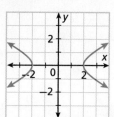

(J)

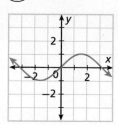

3. Write a possible situation for the graph.

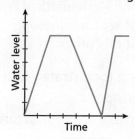

(A) A pool is filled with water, and people are having fun swimming and jumping in and out of the pool.

(B) A pool is filled with water using one valve. Shortly after it is full, the pool needs to be emptied. Then it is refilled immediately, using two valves this time.

(C) A pool is filled with water using one valve. Immediately after it is full, the pool needs to be emptied. It is refilled immediately after it is completely empty, using two valves this time.

(D) A pool is filled with water. Shortly after it is full, the pool needs to be emptied. It is refilled immediately after it is completely empty, using one valve.

4. Determine a relationship between the *x*- and *y*-values. Write an equation.

x	1	2	3	4
y	4	5	6	7

(F) $y = -x + 3$ (H) $y = x + 3$

(G) $y = x + 4$ (J) $y = 3x + 1$

Mini-Task

5. A function is graphed below.

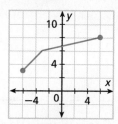

What are the domain and range of the function?

Graphs and Transformations

Contents

MATHEMATICAL PRACTICES The Common Core Georgia Performance Standards for Mathematical Practice describe varieties of expertise that all students should seek to develop. Opportunities to develop these practices are integrated throughout this program.

1 Make sense of problems and persevere in solving them.

2 Reason abstractly and quantitatively.

3 Construct viable arguments and critique the reasoning of others.

4 Model with mathematics.

5 Use appropriate tools strategically.

6 Attend to precision.

7 Look for and make use of structure.

8 Look for and express regularity in repeated reasoning.

Unpacking the Standards

my.hrw.com
Multilingual Glossary

Understanding the standards and the vocabulary terms in the standards will help you know exactly what you are expected to learn in this chapter.

 MCC9-12.F.IF.1

Understand that a function from one set (called the domain) to another set (called the range) assigns to each element of the domain exactly one element of the range. …

Key Vocabulary

function (función)
A relation in which every domain value is paired with exactly one range value.

domain (dominio)
The set of all first coordinates (or x-values) of a relation or function.

range of a function or relation (rango de una función o relación)
The set of all second coordinates (or y-values) of a function or relation.

element (elemento)
Each member in a set.

What It Means For You

A function model guarantees you that for any input value, you will get a unique output value.

EXAMPLE   **Relationship is a function**

$$y = x^2$$

One output for every input: When -2 is input, the output is always 4.

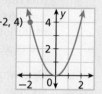

NON-EXAMPLE   **Relationship is NOT a function**

$$y^2 = x$$

Two outputs for every input but 0: When 4 is input, the output can be -2 or 2.

Graphing Functions

Essential Question: How can you graph functions over a given domain?

Objectives

Graph functions given a limited domain.

Graph functions given a domain of all real numbers.

Who uses this?

Scientists can use a function to make conclusions about rising sea level.

Sea level is rising at an approximate rate of 2.5 millimeters per year. If this rate continues, the function $y = 2.5x$ can describe how many millimeters y sea level will rise in the next x years.

One way to understand functions such as the one above is to graph them. You can graph a function by finding ordered pairs that satisfy the function.

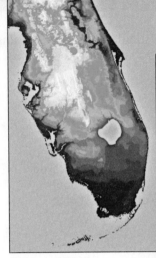

Current Florida coastline.

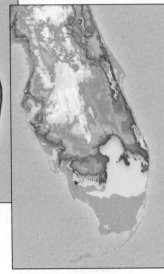

Possible Florida coastline in 2400 years.

COMMON CORE GPS

EXAMPLE **1**
MCC9-12.F.IF.5

my.hrw.com

Online Video Tutor

Graphing Solutions Given a Domain

Graph each function for the given domain.

A $-x + 2y = 6$; D: $\{-4, -2, 0, 2\}$

Step 1 Solve for y since you are given values of the domain, or x.

$$-x + 2y = 6$$
$$\underline{+x \qquad\quad +x} \qquad \textit{Add x to both sides.}$$
$$2y = x + 6$$

$$\frac{2y}{2} = \frac{x + 6}{2} \qquad \textit{Since y is multiplied by 2, divide both sides by 2.}$$

$$y = \frac{x}{2} + \frac{6}{2} \qquad \textit{Rewrite } \tfrac{x + 6}{2} \textit{ as two separate fractions.}$$

$$y = \frac{1}{2}x + 3 \qquad \textit{Simplify.}$$

Helpful Hint

Sometimes solving for y first makes it easier to substitute values of x and find an ordered pair.

Step 2 Substitute the given values of the domain for x and find values of y.

x	$y = \frac{1}{2}x + 3$	(x, y)
-4	$y = \frac{1}{2}(-4) + 3 = 1$	$(-4, 1)$
-2	$y = \frac{1}{2}(-2) + 3 = 2$	$(-2, 2)$
0	$y = \frac{1}{2}(0) + 3 = 3$	$(0, 3)$
2	$y = \frac{1}{2}(2) + 3 = 4$	$(2, 4)$

Step 3 Graph the ordered pairs.

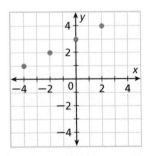

Graph each function for the given domain.

B $f(x) = |x|$; D: $\{-2, -1, 0, 1, 2\}$

Step 1 Use the given values of the domain to find values of $f(x)$.

x	f(x) = |x|	(x, f(x))
−2	$f(x) = \lvert -2 \rvert = 2$	(−2, 2)
−1	$f(x) = \lvert -1 \rvert = 1$	(−1, 1)
0	$f(x) = \lvert 0 \rvert = 0$	(0, 0)
1	$f(x) = \lvert 1 \rvert = 1$	(1, 1)
2	$f(x) = \lvert 2 \rvert = 2$	(2, 2)

Step 2 Graph the ordered pairs.

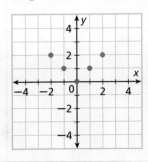

Graph each function for the given domain.

1a. $-2x + y = 3$; D: $\{-5, -3, 1, 4\}$

1b. $f(x) = x^2 + 2$; D: $\{-3, -1, 0, 1, 3\}$

If the domain of a function is all real numbers, any number can be used as an input value. This process will produce an infinite number of ordered pairs that satisfy the function. Therefore, arrowheads are drawn at both "ends" of a smooth line or curve to represent the infinite number of ordered pairs. If a domain is not given, assume that the domain is all real numbers.

	Graphing Functions Using a Domain of All Real Numbers
Step 1	Use the function to generate ordered pairs by choosing several values for x.
Step 2	Plot enough points to see a pattern for the graph.
Step 3	Connect the points with a line or smooth curve.

EXAMPLE 2 Graphing Functions

Graph each function.

A $2x + 1 = y$

Step 1 Choose several values of x and generate ordered pairs.

x	2x + 1 = y	(x, y)
−3	$2(-3) + 1 = -5$	(−3, −5)
−2	$2(-2) + 1 = -3$	(−2, −3)
−1	$2(-1) + 1 = -1$	(−1, −1)
0	$2(0) + 1 = 1$	(0, 1)
1	$2(1) + 1 = 3$	(1, 3)
2	$2(2) + 1 = 5$	(2, 5)
3	$2(3) + 1 = 7$	(3, 7)

Step 2 Plot enough points to see a pattern.

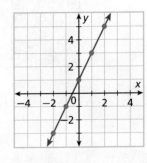

Step 3 The ordered pairs appear to form a line. Draw a line through all the points to show all the ordered pairs that satisfy the function. Draw arrowheads on both "ends" of the line.

my.hrw.com

Online Video Tutor

Helpful Hint

When choosing values of x, be sure to choose both positive and negative values. You may not need to graph all the points to see the pattern.

Graph each function.

B $y = x^2$

Step 1 Choose several values of x and generate ordered pairs.

x	y = x²	(x, y)
−3	$y = (-3)^2 = 9$	(−3, 9)
−2	$y = (-2)^2 = 4$	(−2, 4)
−1	$y = (-1)^2 = 1$	(−1, 1)
0	$y = (0)^2 = 0$	(0, 0)
1	$y = (1)^2 = 1$	(1, 1)
2	$y = (2)^2 = 4$	(2, 4)

Step 2 Plot enough points to see a pattern.

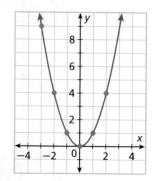

Step 3 The ordered pairs appear to form an almost U-shaped graph. **Draw a smooth curve** through the points to show all the ordered pairs that satisfy the function. Draw arrowheads on the "ends" of the curve.

Check If the graph is correct, any point on it will satisfy the function. Choose an ordered pair on the graph that was not in your table, such as (3, 9). Check whether it satisfies $y = x^2$.

$$y = x^2$$

9	3^2
9	9 ✓

Substitute the values for x and y into the function. Simplify.

The ordered pair (3, 9) satisfies the function.

 **Graph each function.**

2a. $f(x) = 3x - 2$ **2b.** $y = |x - 1|$

EXAMPLE **3**
MCC9-12.F.IF.2

 my.hrw.com

Online Video Tutor

Finding Values Using Graphs

Use a graph of the function $f(x) = \frac{1}{3}x + 2$ to find the value of $f(x)$ when $x = 6$. Check your answer.

Locate 6 on the x-axis. Move **up** to the graph of the function. Then move **left** to the y-axis to find the corresponding value of y.

$f(x) = 4$

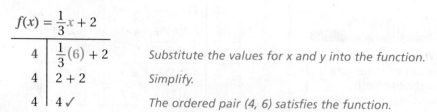

Check Use substitution.

$$f(x) = \frac{1}{3}x + 2$$

4	$\frac{1}{3}(6) + 2$
4	$2 + 2$
4	4 ✓

Substitute the values for x and y into the function.

Simplify.

The ordered pair (4, 6) satisfies the function.

Writing Math

"The value of y is 4 when $x = 6$" can also be written as $f(6) = 4$.

 3. Use the graph above to find the value of x when $f(x) = 3$. Check your answer.

Recall that in real-world situations you may have to limit the domain to make answers reasonable. For example, quantities such as time, distance, and number of people can be represented using only nonnegative values. When both the domain and the range are limited to nonnegative values, the function is graphed only in Quadrant I.

COMMON CORE GPS
EXAMPLE 4
MCC9-12.F.IF.7a

my.hrw.com

Online Video Tutor

MATHEMATICAL PRACTICES

Make sense of problems and persevere in solving them.

Problem-Solving Application

The function $y = 2.5x$ describes how many millimeters sea level y rises in x years. Graph the function. Use the graph to estimate how many millimeters sea level will rise in 3.5 years.

1 Understand the Problem

The **answer** is a graph that can be used to find the value of y when x is 3.5.

List the important information:
• The function $y = 2.5x$ describes how many millimeters sea level rises.

2 Make a Plan

Think: What values should I use to graph this function? Both, the number of years sea level has risen and the distance sea level rises, cannot be negative. Use only nonnegative values for both the domain and the range. The function will be graphed in Quadrant I.

3 Solve

Choose several nonnegative values of x to find values of y. Then graph the ordered pairs.

x	$y = 2.5x$	(x, y)
0	$y = 2.5(0) = 0$	$(0, 0)$
1	$y = 2.5(1) = 2.5$	$(1, 2.5)$
2	$y = 2.5(2) = 5$	$(2, 5)$
3	$y = 2.5(3) = 7.5$	$(3, 7.5)$
4	$y = 2.5(4) = 10$	$(4, 10)$

Draw a line through the points to show all the ordered pairs that satisfy this function.

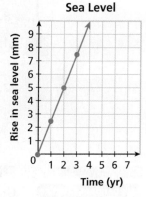

Sea Level

Rise in sea level (mm) vs. Time (yr)

Use the graph to estimate the y-value when x is 3.5. Sea level will rise about 8.75 millimeters in 3.5 years.

4 Look Back

As the number of years increases, sea level also increases, so the graph is reasonable. When x is between 3 and 4, y is between 7.5 and 10. Since 3.5 is between 3 and 4, it is reasonable to estimate y to be 8.75 when x is 3.5.

 CHECK IT OUT!

4. The fastest recorded Hawaiian lava flow moved at an average speed of 6 miles per hour. The function $y = 6x$ describes the distance y the lava moved on average in x hours. Graph the function. Use the graph to estimate how many miles the lava moved after 5.5 hours.

THINK AND DISCUSS

1. How do you find the range of a function if the domain is all real numbers?

2. Explain how to use a graph to find the value of a function for a given value of x.

3. **GET ORGANIZED** Copy and complete the graphic organizer. Explain how to graph a function for each situation.

Graphing a Function
- Not a real-world situation
- Real-world situation

9-1 Exercises

GUIDED PRACTICE

SEE EXAMPLE 1 — **Graph each function for the given domain.**

1. $3x - y = 1$; D: $\{-3, -1, 0, 4\}$

2. $f(x) = -|x|$; D: $\{-5, -3, 0, 3, 5\}$

3. $f(x) = x + 4$; D: $\{-5, -3, 0, 4\}$

4. $y = x^2 - 1$; D: $\{-3, -1, 0, 1, 3\}$

SEE EXAMPLE 2 — **Graph each function.**

5. $f(x) = 6x + 4$

6. $y = \frac{1}{2}x + 4$

7. $x + y = 0$

8. $y = |x| - 4$

9. $f(x) = 2x^2 - 7$

10. $y = -x^2 + 5$

SEE EXAMPLE 3 — 11. Use a graph of the function $f(x) = \frac{1}{2}x - 2$ to find the value of y when $x = 2$. Check your answer.

SEE EXAMPLE 4 — 12. **Oceanography** The floor of the Atlantic Ocean is spreading at an average rate of 1 inch per year. The function $y = x$ describes the number of inches y the ocean floor spreads in x years. Graph the function. Use the graph to estimate the number of inches the ocean floor will spread in $10\frac{1}{2}$ years.

PRACTICE AND PROBLEM SOLVING

For Exercises	See Example
13–16	1
17–24	2
25–26	3
27	4

Graph each function for the given domain.

13. $2x + y = 4$; D: $\{-3, -1, 4, 7\}$

14. $y = |x| - 1$; D: $\{-4, -2, 0, 2, 4\}$

15. $f(x) = -7x$; D: $\{-2, -1, 0, 1\}$

16. $y = (x + 1)^2$; D: $\{-2, -1, 0, 1, 2\}$

Graph each function.

17. $y = -3x + 5$

18. $f(x) = 3x$

19. $x + y = 8$

20. $f(x) = 2x + 2$

21. $y = -|x| + 10$

22. $f(x) = -5 + x^2$

23. $y = |x + 1| + 1$

24. $y = (x - 2)^2 - 1$

25. Use a graph of the function $f(x) = -2x - 3$ to find the value of y when $x = -4$. Check your answer.

26. Use a graph of the function $f(x) = \frac{1}{3}x + 1$ to find the value of y when $x = 6$. Check your answer.

27. Transportation An electric motor scooter can travel at 0.25 miles per minute. The function $y = 0.25x$ describes the number of miles y the scooter can travel in x minutes. Graph the function. Use the graph to estimate the number of miles an electric motor scooter travels in 15 minutes.

Graph each function.

28. $f(x) = x - 1$

29. $12 - x - 2y = 0$

30. $3x - y = 13$

31. $y = x^2 - 2$

32. $x^2 - y = -4$

33. $2x^2 = f(x)$

34. $f(x) = |2x| - 2$

35. $y = |-x|$

36. $-|2x + 1| = y$

37. Find the value of x so that $(x, 12)$ satisfies $y = 4x + 8$.

38. Find the value of x so that $(x, 6)$ satisfies $y = -x - 4$.

39. Find the value of y so that $(-2, y)$ satisfies $y = -2x^2$.

For each function, determine whether the given points are on the graph.

40. $y = 7x - 2$; $(1, 5)$ and $(2, 10)$

41. $y = |x| + 2$; $(3, 5)$ and $(-1, 3)$

42. $y = x^2$; $(1, 1)$ and $(-3, -9)$

43. $y = \frac{1}{4}x - 2$; $\left(1, -\frac{3}{4}\right)$ and $(4, -1)$

H.O.T. 44. ///**ERROR ANALYSIS**/// Student A says that $(3, 2)$ is on the graph of $y = 4x - 5$, but student B says that it is not. Who is incorrect? Explain the error.

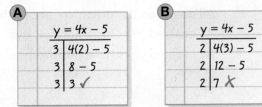

A		B	
$y = 4x - 5$		$y = 4x - 5$	
3	4(2) − 5	2	4(3) − 5
3	8 − 5	2	12 − 5
3	3 ✓	2	7 ✗

Determine whether $(0, -7)$, $\left(-6, -\frac{5}{3}\right)$, **and** $(-2, -3)$ **lie on the graph of each function.**

45. $x + 3y = -11$

46. $y + |x| = -1$

47. $x^2 - y = 7$

For each function, find three ordered pairs that lie on the graph of the function.

48. $-6 = 3x + 2y$

49. $y = 1.1x + 2$

50. $y = \frac{4}{5}x$

51. $y = 3x - 1$

52. $y = |x| + 6$

53. $y = x^2 - 5$

54. Critical Thinking Graph the functions $y = |x|$ and $y = -|x|$. Describe how they are alike. How are they different?

55. A pool containing 10,000 gallons of water is being drained. Every hour, the volume of the water in the pool decreases by 1500 gallons.

  a. Write an equation to describe the volume v of water in the pool after h hours.

  b. How much water is in the pool after 1 hour?

  c. Create a table of values showing the volume of the water in gallons in the pool as a function of the time in hours and graph the function.

56. Estimation Use the graph to estimate the value of y when $x = 2.117$.

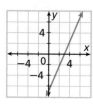

H.O.T. 57. Write About It Why is a graph a convenient way to show the ordered pairs that satisfy a function?

TEST PREP

58. Which function is graphed?

(A) $2y - 3x = 2$ (C) $y = 2x - 1$

(B) $5x + y = 1$ (D) $y = 5x + 8$

59. Which ordered pair is NOT on the graph of $y = 4 - |x|$?

(F) $(0, 4)$ (H) $(-1, 3)$

(G) $(4, 0)$ (J) $(3, -1)$

60. Which function has $(3, 2)$ on its graph?

(A) $2x - 3y = 12$ (C) $y = -\dfrac{2}{3}x + 4$

(B) $-2x - 3y = 12$ (D) $y = -\dfrac{3}{2}x + 4$

61. Which statement(s) is true about the function $y = x^2 + 1$?

I.   All points on the graph are above the origin.

II. All ordered pairs have positive x-values.

III. All ordered pairs have positive y-values.

(F) I Only   (G) II Only   (H) I and II   (J) I and III

CHALLENGE AND EXTEND

62. Graph the function $y = x^3$. Make sure you have enough ordered pairs to see the shape of the graph.

63. The temperature of a liquid that started at 64 °F is increasing by 4 °F per hour. Write a function that describes the temperature of the liquid over time. Graph the function to show the temperatures over the first 10 hours.

FOCUS ON MATHEMATICAL PRACTICES

H.O.T. 64. Modeling Does the ordered pair $\left(\dfrac{1}{2}, 1\right)$ name a point on the graph of $f(x) = 2x$?

Can you find an ordered pair on the graph where *both* coordinates are non-integers? If the function is graphed on a coordinate plane where every integer has a grid line, where can you find points with two non-integer coordinates?

H.O.T. 65. Analysis When you graph a function by making a table of values and plotting the points, and then draw a line through the points, you draw arrowheads on both ends of the graphed line. What do these arrowheads tell you about the line? Is it possible to draw a coordinate plane large enough that the arrowheads are no longer necessary? Explain.

9-1
Technology TASK

Connect Function Rules, Tables, and Graphs

You can use a graphing calculator to understand the connections among function rules, tables, and graphs.

Use with Graphing Functions

 Use appropriate tools strategically.

MCC9-12.F.IF.1 Understand that a function . . . assigns to each element of the domain exactly one element of the range. . . . The graph of *f* is the graph of the equation $y = f(x)$.

Activity

Make a table of values for the function $f(x) = 4x + 3$.
Then graph the function.

① Press **Y=** and enter the function rule **4x + 3**.

② Press **2nd** **WINDOW** (TBLSET). Make sure **Indpnt: Auto** and **Depend: Auto** are selected.

③ To view the table, press **2nd** **GRAPH** (TABLE). The *x*-values and the corresponding *y*-values appear in table form. Use the up and down arrow keys to scroll through the table.

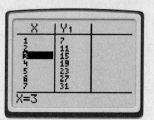

④ To view the table with the graph, press **MODE** and select **G-T** view. Press **ENTER**. Be sure to use the standard window.

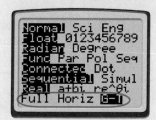

⑤ Press **TRACE** to see both the graph and a table of values.

⑥ Press the left arrow key several times to move the cursor. Notice that the point on the graph and the values in the table correspond.

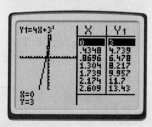

Try This

Make a table of values for each function. Then graph the function.

1. $f(x) = 2x - 1$ **2.** $f(x) = 1.5x$ **3.** $f(x) = \frac{1}{2}x + 2$

4. Explain the relationship between a function, its table of values, and the graph of the function.

9-2 Exploring Transformations

Essential Question: How can you identify the effect of a given transformation on a graph?

Objectives

Apply transformations to points and sets of points.

Interpret transformations of real-world data.

Vocabulary
transformation
translation
reflection
stretch
compression

Why learn this?

Changes in recording studio fees can be modeled by transformations. (See Example 4.)

A **transformation** is a change in the position, size, or shape of a figure. A **translation**, or slide, is a transformation that moves each point in a figure the same distance in the same direction.

Translating Points

Perform the given translation on the point $(2, -1)$. Give the coordinates of the translated point.

A 4 units left

Translating $(2, -1)$ 4 units left results in the point $(-2, -1)$.

B 2 units right and 3 units up

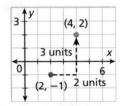

Translating $(2, -1)$ 2 units right and 3 units up results in the point $(4, 2)$.

CHECK IT OUT! Perform the given translation on the point $(-1, 3)$. Give the coordinates of the translated point.

1a. 4 units right

1b. 1 unit left and 2 units down

Notice that when you translate **left or right,** the *x*-coordinate changes, and when you translate **up or down,** the *y*-coordinate changes.

Translations	
Horizontal Translation	**Vertical Translation**
Each point shifts *right* or *left* by a number of units.	Each point shifts *up* or *down* by a number of units.
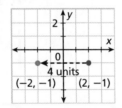 The *x*-coordinate changes. $(1, 2) \rightarrow (1 + 3, 2)$ $(x, y) \rightarrow (x + h, y)$	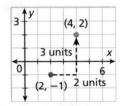 The *y*-coordinate changes. $(1, 2) \rightarrow (1, 2 + 2)$ $(x, y) \rightarrow (x, y + k)$
left if $h < 0$ right if $h > 0$	down if $k < 0$ up if $k > 0$

© PunchStock

A **reflection** is a transformation that flips a figure across a line called the line of reflection. Each reflected point is the same distance from the line of reflection, but on the opposite side of the line.

Reflections	
Reflection Across *y*-axis	**Reflection Across *x*-axis**
Each point flips across the *y*-axis.	Each point flips across the *x*-axis.
The *x*-coordinate changes. $(1, 2) \rightarrow (-1, 2)$ $(x, y) \rightarrow (-x, y)$	The *y*-coordinate changes. $(1, 2) \rightarrow (1, -2)$ $(x, y) \rightarrow (x, -y)$

You can transform a function by transforming its ordered pairs. When a function is translated or reflected, the original graph and the graph of the transformation are *congruent* because the size and shape of the graphs are the same.

COMMON CORE GPS
MCC9-12.F.BF.3

EXAMPLE 2

Translating and Reflecting Functions

Use a table to perform each transformation of $y = f(x)$. Use the same coordinate plane as the original function.

A translation 2 units down

Identify important points from the graph and make a table.

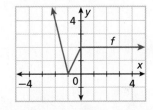

x	y	y − 2
−2	4	4 − 2 = 2
−1	0	0 − 2 = −2
0	2	2 − 2 = 0
2	2	2 − 2 = 0

The entire graph shifts 2 units down. Subtract 2 from each y-coordinate.

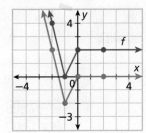

B reflection across *y*-axis

Identify important points from the graph and make a table.

−x	x	y
−1(−2) = 2	−2	4
−1(−1) = 1	−1	0
−1(0) = 0	0	2
−1(2) = −2	2	2

Multiply each x-coordinate by −1. The entire graph flips across the y-axis.

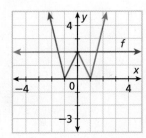

my.hrw.com

Online Video Tutor

Helpful Hint

Transform *x* by adding a table column on the left side; transform *y* by adding a column on the right side.

CHECK IT OUT! For the function from Example 2, use a table to perform each transformation of $y = f(x)$. Use the same coordinate plane as the original function.

2a. translation 3 units right   **2b.** reflection across *x*-axis

Imagine grasping two points on the graph of a function that lie on opposite sides of the *y*-axis. If you pull the points away from the *y*-axis, you would create a horizontal **stretch** of the graph. If you push the points towards the *y*-axis, you would create a horizontal **compression**.

Stretches and compressions are not congruent to the original graph.

Stretches and Compressions		
	Horizontal	**Vertical**
Stretch	Each point is *pulled away* from the *y*-axis.  The *x*-coordinate changes. $(4, 0) \rightarrow (2(4), 0)$ $(x, y) \rightarrow (bx, y)$ $\lvert b \rvert > 1$	Each point is *pulled away* from the *x*-axis. The *y*-coordinate changes. $(0, 4) \rightarrow (0, 2(4))$ $(x, y) \rightarrow (x, ay)$ $\lvert a \rvert > 1$
Compression	Each point is *pushed toward* the *y*-axis. The *x*-coordinate changes. $(4, 0) \rightarrow \left(\frac{1}{2}(4), 0\right)$ $(x, y) \rightarrow (bx, y)$ $0 < \lvert b \rvert < 1$	Each point is *pushed toward* the *x*-axis. The *y*-coordinate changes. $(0, 4) \rightarrow \left(0, \frac{1}{2}(4)\right)$ $(x, y) \rightarrow (x, ay)$ $0 < \lvert a \rvert < 1$

COMMON CORE GPS

EXAMPLE **3**

MCC9-12.F.BF.3

my.hrw.com

Online Video Tutor

Stretching and Compressing Functions

Use a table to perform a horizontal compression of $y = f(x)$ by a factor of $\frac{1}{2}$. Use the same coordinate plane as the original function.

Identify important points from the graph and make a table.

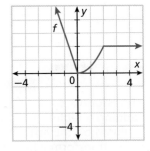

$\frac{1}{2}x$	*x*	*y*
$\frac{1}{2}(-1) = -\frac{1}{2}$	−1	3
$\frac{1}{2}(0) = 0$	0	0
$\frac{1}{2}(2) = 1$	2	2
$\frac{1}{2}(4) = 2$	4	2

Multiply each x-coordinate by $\frac{1}{2}$.

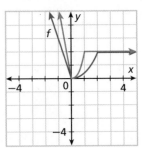

3. For the function from Example 3, use a table to perform a vertical stretch of $y = f(x)$ by a factor of 2. Graph the transformed function on the same coordinate plane as the original function.

EXAMPLE **4** *Business Application*

MCC9-12.F.BF.3

my.hrw.com

Online Video Tutor

Recording studio fees are usually based on an hourly rate, but the rate can be modified due to various options. The graph shows a basic hourly studio rate. Sketch a graph to represent each situation below and identify the transformation of the original graph that it represents.

Recording Studio Fees

A The engineer's time is needed, so the hourly rate is 1.5 times the original rate.

If the fees are 1.5 times the basic hourly rate, the value of each *y*-coordinate would be multiplied by 1.5. This represents a vertical stretch by a factor of 1.5.

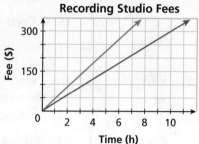

Recording Studio Fees

B A $20 setup fee is added to the basic hourly rate.

If the prices are $20 more than the original estimate, the value of each *y*-coordinate would increase by 20. This represents a vertical translation up 20 units.

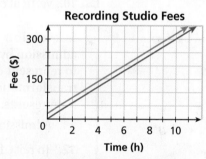

Recording Studio Fees

4. What if...? Suppose that a discounted rate is $\frac{3}{4}$ of the original rate. Sketch a graph to represent the situation and identify the transformation of the original graph that it represents.

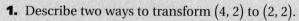

MCC.MP.1, MCC.MP.7

MATHEMATICAL PRACTICES

THINK AND DISCUSS

1. Describe two ways to transform $(4, 2)$ to $(2, 2)$.

2. Compare a vertical stretch with a horizontal compression.

3. GET ORGANIZED Copy and complete the graphic organizer. In each box, describe the transformations indicated by the given rule.

$(x, y) \longrightarrow (bx, y)$	$(x, y) \longrightarrow (-x, y)$
Transformations	
$(x, y) \longrightarrow (x + h, y)$	$(x, y) \longrightarrow (x, ay)$

GUIDED PRACTICE

1. **Vocabulary** A transformation that pushes a graph toward the *x*-axis is a ___?___ .
   (*reflection* or *compression*)

SEE EXAMPLE 1 **Perform the given translation on the point** $(4, 2)$ **and give the coordinates of the translated point.**

2. 5 units left   3. 3 units down   4. 1 unit right, 6 units up

SEE EXAMPLE 2 **Use a table to perform each transformation of** $y = f(x)$. **Use the same coordinate plane as the original function.**

5. translation 2 units up

6. reflection across the *y*-axis

7. reflection across the *x*-axis

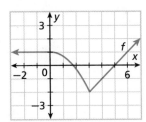

SEE EXAMPLE 3 **Use a table to perform each transformation of** $y = f(x)$. **Use the same coordinate plane as the original function.**

8. horizontal stretch by a factor of 3

9. vertical stretch by a factor of 3

10. vertical compression by a factor of $\frac{1}{3}$

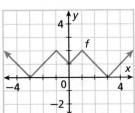

SEE EXAMPLE 4 **Recreation** The graph shows the price for admission by age at a local zoo. Sketch a graph to represent each situation and identify the transformation of the original graph that it represents.

11. Admission is half price on Wednesdays.

12. To raise funds for endangered species, the zoo charges $1.50 extra per ticket.

13. The maximum age for each ticket price is increased by 5 years.

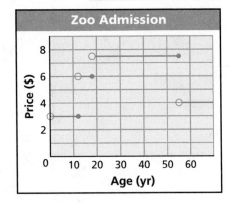

Zoo Admission

PRACTICE AND PROBLEM SOLVING

Independent Practice

For Exercises	See Example
14–16	1
17–20	2
21–24	3
25–27	4

Perform the given translation on $(3, 1)$. **Give the coordinates of the translated point.**

14. 2 units right   15. 4 units up   16. 5 units left, 4 units down

Use a table to perform each transformation of $y = f(x)$. **Use the same coordinate plane as the original function.**

17. translation 2 units down   18. reflection across the *x*-axis

19. translation 3 units right   20. reflection across the *y*-axis

21. vertical compression by a factor of $\frac{2}{3}$ 22. horizontal compression by a factor of $\frac{1}{2}$

23. horizontal stretch by a factor of $\frac{3}{2}$ 24. vertical stretch by a factor of 2

Technology The graph shows the cost of Web page hosting depending on the Web space used. Sketch a graph to represent each situation and identify the transformation of the original graph that it represents.

25. The prices are reduced by $5.

26. The prices are discounted by 25%.

27. A special is offered for double the amount of Web space for the same price.

Web Page Hosting

Price ($)	

Web space (MB)

Estimation The table gives the coordinates for the vertices of a triangle. Estimate the area of each transformed triangle by graphing it and counting the number of squares it covers on the coordinate plane. How does the area of each transformed triangle compare with the area of the original triangle?

x	y
−2	2
2	−4
4	−2

28. reflection across the *y*-axis

29. 5 units left, 3 units up

30. horizontal stretch by a factor of 2

31. horizontal compression by a factor of $\frac{2}{3}$

32. vertical compression by a factor of $\frac{2}{3}$

33. reflection across the *x*-axis

34. 1 unit left, 6 units down

35. vertical stretch by a factor of 3

Entertainment

The amusement park industry in the United States includes about 700 parks and accounted for over $8.5 billion in revenues in 2001.
Source: Statistical Abstract of the United States

36. **Entertainment** The revenue from an amusement park ride is given by the admission price of $3 times the number of riders. As part of a promotion, the first 10 riders ride for free.

   a. What kind of transformation describes the change in the revenue based on the promotion?

   b. Write a function rule for this transformation.

37. **Business** An automotive mechanic charges $50 to diagnose the problem in a vehicle and $65 per hour for labor to fix it.

   a. If the mechanic increases his diagnostic fee to $60, what kind of transformation is this to the graph of the total repair bill?

   b. If the mechanic increases his labor rate to $75 per hour, what kind of transformation is this to the graph of the total repair bill?

   c. If it took 3 hours to repair your car, which of the two rate increases would have a greater effect on your total bill?

38. The student council wants to buy vases for the flowers for the school prom. A florist charges a $20 delivery fee plus $1.25 per vase. A home-decorating store charges a $10 delivery fee plus $1.25 per vase.

   a. The function $f(x) = 20 + 1.25x$ models the cost of ordering x vases from the florist, and the function $g(x) = 10 + 1.25x$ models the cost of ordering x vases from the home-decorating store. What do the graphs of these functions look like?

   b. How are the graphs related to each other?

   c. How could you modify these functions so that their graphs are identical?

   d. If the florist decided to waive the $20 delivery fee as long as the number of vases ordered was more than 150, how would the graph of f change? How would it compare with the graph of the other function?

Transportation Use the graph and the following information for Exercises 39–43.

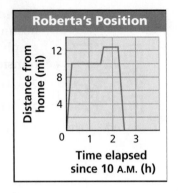

Roberta's Position

Roberta left her house at 10:00 A.M. and drove to the library. She was at the library studying until 11:30 A.M. Then she drove to the grocery store. At 12:15 P.M. Roberta left the grocery store and drove home. The graph shows Roberta's position with respect to time.

Sketch a graph to reflect each change to the original story. Assume the time Roberta spends inside each building remains the same.

39. Roberta drove at half the speed from her house to the library.

40. The grocery store she went to is twice as far from the library.

41. The grocery store is 2.5 miles closer to the house than the library is.

Change the original story about Roberta to match each graph.

42.
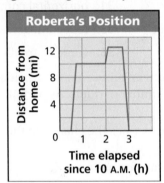

43.
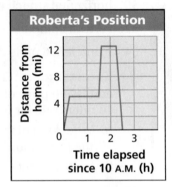

H.O.T. 44. Critical Thinking Suppose two transformations are performed on a single point: a translation and a reflection. Does the order in which the transformations are performed make a difference? Does the type of translation or reflection matter? Explain your reasoning.

H.O.T. 45. Write About It Describe how transformations might make graphing easier.

TEST PREP

46. The function $c(p) = 0.99p$ represents the cost in dollars of p pounds of peaches. If the cost per pound increases by 10%, how will the graph of the function change?

  Ⓐ Translation 0.1 unit up   Ⓒ Horizontal stretch by a factor of 1.1

  Ⓑ Translation 0.1 unit right   Ⓓ Vertical stretch by a factor of 1.1

47. Which transformation would change the point $(5, 3)$ into $(-5, 3)$?

  Ⓕ Reflection across the x-axis   Ⓗ Reflection across the y-axis

  Ⓖ Translation 5 units down   Ⓙ Translation 5 units left

48. The graph of the function f is a line that intersects the y-axis at the point $(0, 3)$ and the x-axis at the point $(3, 0)$. Which transformation of f does NOT intersect the y-axis at the point $(0, 6)$?

  Ⓐ Translation 3 units up   Ⓒ Vertical stretch by a factor of 2

  Ⓑ Translation 3 units right   Ⓓ Horizontal compression by a factor of $\frac{1}{2}$

49. Which transformation is displayed in the graph?

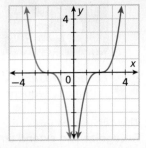

(F) Reflection across the *x*-axis

(G) Translation 5 units down

(H) Reflection across the *y*-axis

(J) Translation 5 units left

50. Which represents a translation 4 units right and 2 units down?

(A) From $(4, 2)$ to $(0, 0)$ (C) From $(-4, -2)$ to $(0, 0)$

(B) From $(4, -2)$ to $(0, 0)$ (D) From $(-4, 2)$ to $(0, 0)$

51. Short Response Graph the points $(-1, 3)$ and $(-1, -3)$. Describe two different transformations that would transform $(-1, 3)$ to $(-1, -3)$.

CHALLENGE AND EXTEND

52. Suppose the rule $(x, y) \rightarrow (2x, y - 3)$ is used to translate a point. If the coordinates of the translated point are $(22, 7)$, what was the original point?

53. History From 1999 to 2001 the cost for mailing *n* first class letters through the United States Postal Service was $c(n) = 0.33n$. In 2001 the rate was increased by $0.01 per letter. In 2002 the rate was increased an additional $0.03 per letter.

a. Write an equation that represents the cost of mailing *n* first class letters in 2002.

b. What transformation describes the total change in price?

c. Graph both functions and estimate the maximum number of first class letters you could mail for $5.00 in both 1999 and 2002.

d. Explain the effect of the reasonable domain and range for these functions on your answer for part **c**.

54. Name a point that when reflected across the *x*-axis has the same coordinates as if it were reflected across the *y*-axis. How many points are there that satisfy this condition?

FOCUS ON MATHEMATICAL PRACTICES

[H.O.T.] **55. Communication** Germaine says, "I'm a little confused by the difference between translations and transformations. Is a translation a transformation or is a transformation a translation?" Answer her question and explain.

[H.O.T.] **56. Properties** Rudy reflects a rectangle across the *y*-axis and then translates it 3 units right and 4 units down. Is the new rectangle congruent to the old? Justify your answer.

[H.O.T.] **57. Analysis** The function $y = x$ is transformed into a new function $y = 3x$. How does this transformation affect the graph of the function?

[H.O.T.] **58. Make a Conjecture** A point undergoes a reflection across the *x*-axis, but stays in the same location.

a. Find two different sets of coordinates that the point might have.

b. Make a conjecture about which points stay in the same place when reflected across the *x*-axis.

c. Use the coordinate definition of a reflection across the *x*-axis to justify your conjecture in part b.

Arithmetic Sequences

Essential Question: How can you recognize and extend an arithmetic sequence and find a given term of the sequence?

Objectives
Recognize and extend an arithmetic sequence.

Find a given term of an arithmetic sequence.

Vocabulary
sequence
term
arithmetic sequence
common difference

Why learn this?
The distance between you and a lightning strike can be approximated by using an arithmetic sequence.

During a thunderstorm, you can estimate your distance from a lightning strike by counting the number of seconds from the time you see the lightning until the time you hear the thunder.

Time (s)	Distance (mi)
1	0.2
2	0.4
3	0.6
4	0.8
5	1.0
6	1.2
7	1.4
8	1.6

$+ 0.2$
$+ 0.2$
$+ 0.2$
$+ 0.2$
$+ 0.2$
$+ 0.2$
$+ 0.2$

When you list the times and distances in order, each list forms a *sequence*. A **sequence** is a list of numbers that may form a pattern. Each number in a sequence is a **term**.

In the distance sequence, each distance is 0.2 mi greater than the previous distance. When the terms of a sequence differ by the same nonzero number d, the sequence is an **arithmetic sequence** and d is the **common difference**. The distances in the table form an arithmetic sequence with $d = 0.2$.

The variable a is often used to represent terms in a sequence. The variable a_9, read "a sub 9," is the ninth term in a sequence. To designate any term, or the nth term, in a sequence, you write a_n, where n can be any number.

To find a term in an arithmetic sequence, add d to the previous term.

Finding a Term of an Arithmetic Sequence

The nth term of an arithmetic sequence with common difference d is
$$a_n = a_{n-1} + d.$$

COMMON CORE GPS
MCC9-12.F.BF.2

EXAMPLE 1 Identifying Arithmetic Sequences

my.hrw.com

Online Video Tutor

Determine whether each sequence appears to be an arithmetic sequence. If so, find the common difference and the next three terms in the sequence.

A 12, 8, 4, 0, ...

Step 1 Find the difference between successive terms.

12, 8, 4, 0, ...
$-4\ -4\ -4$

Add −4 to each term to find the next term. The common difference is −4.

Step 2 Use the common difference to find the next 3 terms.

12, 8, 4, 0, −4, −8, −12
$-4\ -4\ -4$

$a_n = a_{n-1} + d$

The sequence appears to be an arithmetic sequence with a common difference of −4. The next 3 terms are −4, −8, −12.

B **1, 4, 9, 16, …**

Find the difference between successive terms.

1,　4,　9,　16, …

+3 +5 +7

The difference between successive terms is not the same.

This sequence is not an arithmetic sequence.

 CHECK IT OUT! **Determine whether each sequence appears to be an arithmetic sequence. If so, find the common difference and the next three terms.**

1a. $-\dfrac{3}{4}, -\dfrac{1}{4}, \dfrac{1}{4}, \dfrac{3}{4}, \ldots$　　　　　**1b.** $-4, -2, 1, 5, \ldots$

To find the nth term of an arithmetic sequence when n is a large number, you need an equation or rule. Look for a pattern to find a rule for the sequence below.

1	2	3	4…	n	← Position
↓	↓	↓	↓		
3,	5,	7,	9…		← Term
a_1	a_2	a_3	a_4	a_n	

The sequence starts with 3. The common difference d is 2. You can use the first term and the common difference to write a rule for finding a_n.

Words	Numbers	Algebra
1st term	3	a_1
2nd term = 1st term plus common difference	$3 + (1)2 = 5$	$a_1 + 1d$
3nd term = 1st term plus 2 common differences	$3 + (2)2 = 7$	$a_1 + 2d$
4th term = 1st term plus 3 common differences	$3 + (3)2 = 9$	$a_1 + 3d$
⋮	⋮	⋮
nth term = 1st term plus $(n-1)$ common differences	$3 + (n-1)2$	$a_1 + (n-1)d$

The pattern in the table shows that to find the nth term, add the **first term** to the product of $(n-1)$ and the **common difference**.

 Finding the nth Term of an Arithmetic Sequence

The nth term of an arithmetic sequence with **common difference** d and **first term** a_1 is

$$a_n = a_1 + (n-1)d.$$

 **COMMON CORE GPS**
EXAMPLE **2**
MCC9-12.F.BF.2

Finding the nth Term of an Arithmetic Sequence

Find the indicated term of each arithmetic sequence.

A **22nd term: 5, 2, −1, −4, …**

Step 1 Find the common difference.

5,　2,　−1,　−4, …

−3 −3 −3

The common difference is −3.

 my.hrw.com

Online Video Tutor

Step 2 Find the 22nd term.

$$a_n = a_1 + (n-1)d \qquad \textit{Write the rule to find the nth term.}$$
$$a_{22} = 5 + (22-1)(-3) \qquad \textit{Substitute 5 for a}_1\textit{, 22 for n, and −3 for d.}$$
$$= 5 + (21)(-3) \qquad \textit{Simplify the expression in parentheses.}$$
$$= 5 - 63 \qquad \textit{Multiply.}$$
$$= -58 \qquad \textit{Subtract.}$$

B 15th term: $a_1 = 7; d = 3$

$$a_n = a_1 + (n-1)d \qquad \textit{Write the rule to find the nth term.}$$
$$a_{15} = 7 + (15-1)3 \qquad \textit{Substitute 7 for a}_1\textit{, 15 for n, and 3 for d.}$$
$$= 7 + (14)3 \qquad \textit{Simplify the expression in parentheses.}$$
$$= 7 + 42 \qquad \textit{Multiply.}$$
$$= 49 \qquad \textit{Add.}$$

 **Find the indicated term of each arithmetic sequence.**
2a. 60th term: $11, 5, -1, -7, \ldots$ **2b.** 12th term: $a_1 = 4.2; d = 1.4$

 EXAMPLE 3
MCC9-12.F.LE.2

Travel Application

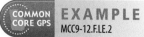 my.hrw.com

Online Video Tutor

The odometer on a car reads 60,473 on day 1. Every day, the car is driven 54 miles. If this pattern continues, what is the odometer reading on day 20?

Notice that the sequence for the situation is arithmetic with $d = 54$ because the odometer reading will increase by 54 miles per day.

Since the odometer reading on day 1 is 60,473 miles, $a_1 = 60{,}473$.

Since you want to find the odometer reading on day 20, you will need to find the **20th term** of the sequence, so $n = 20$.

$$a_n = a_1 + (n-1)d \qquad \textit{Write the rule to find the nth term.}$$
$$a_{20} = 60{,}473 + (20-1)54 \qquad \textit{Substitute 60,473 for a}_1\textit{, 54 for d, and 21 for n.}$$
$$= 60{,}473 + (19)54 \qquad \textit{Simplify the expression in parentheses.}$$
$$= 60{,}473 + 1026 \qquad \textit{Multiply.}$$
$$= 61{,}499 \qquad \textit{Add.}$$

The odometer will read 61,499 miles on day 20.

 3. Each time a truck stops, it drops off 250 pounds of cargo. After stop 1, its cargo weighed 2000 pounds. How much does the load weigh after stop 6?

 MCC.MP.3 / MATHEMATICAL PRACTICES

THINK AND DISCUSS

1. Explain how to determine if a sequence appears to be arithmetic.

 **2. GET ORGANIZED** Copy and complete the graphic organizer with steps for finding the *n*th term of an arithmetic sequence.

Finding the *n*th Term of an Arithmetic Sequence → 1. → 2.

my.hrw.com
Homework Help

GUIDED PRACTICE

1. **Vocabulary** When trying to find the *n*th term of an arithmetic sequence you must first know the _____?_____. (*common difference* or *sequence*)

SEE EXAMPLE 1

Multi-Step Determine whether each sequence appears to be an arithmetic sequence. If so, find the common difference and the next three terms.

2. 2, 8, 14, 20, …

3. 2.1, 1.4, 0.7, 0, …

4. 1, 1, 2, 3, …

5. 0.1, 0.3, 0.9, 2.7, …

SEE EXAMPLE 2

Find the indicated term of each arithmetic sequence.

6. 21st term: 3, 8, 13, 18, …

7. 18th term: $a_1 = -2$; $d = -3$

SEE EXAMPLE 3

8. **Shipping** To package and ship an item, it costs $5.75 for the first pound and $0.75 for each additional pound. What is the cost of shipping a 12-pound package?

PRACTICE AND PROBLEM SOLVING

Independent Practice

For Exercises	See Example
9–12	1
13–14	2
15	3

my.hrw.com

Online Extra Practice

Multi-Step Determine whether each sequence appears to be an arithmetic sequence. If so, find the common difference and the next three terms.

9. −1, 10, −100, 1,100, …

10. 0, −2, −4, −6, …

11. −22, −31, −40, −49, …

12. 0.2, 0.5, 0.9, 1.1, …

Find the indicated term of each arithmetic sequence.

13. 31st term: 1.40, 1.55, 1.70, …

14. 50th term: $a_1 = 2.2$; $d = 1.1$

15. **Travel** Rachel signed up for a frequent-flier program. She receives 4300 frequent-flier miles for her first round trip and 1300 frequent-flier miles for each additional round-trip. How many frequent-flier miles will she have after 5 round-trips?

Find the common difference for each arithmetic sequence.

16. 0, 6, 12, 18, …

17. $\frac{1}{2}, \frac{3}{4}, 1, \frac{5}{4}, \ldots$

18. 107, 105, 103, 101, …

19. 7.9, 5.7, 3.5, 1.3, …

20. $\frac{1}{5}, \frac{2}{5}, \frac{3}{5}, \frac{4}{5}, \ldots$

21. 4.25, 4.32, 4.39, 4.46, …

Find the next four terms in each arithmetic sequence.

22. −4, −7, −10, −13, …

23. $\frac{1}{8}, 0, -\frac{1}{8}, -\frac{1}{4}, \ldots$

24. 505, 512, 519, 526, …

25. 1.8, 1.3, 0.8, 0.3, …

26. $\frac{2}{3}, \frac{4}{3}, 2, \frac{8}{3}, \ldots$

27. −1.1, −0.9, −0.7, −0.5

Find the given term of each arithmetic sequence.

28. 5, 10, 15, 20, …; 17th term

29. 121, 110, 99, 88, …; 10th term

30. −2, −5, −8, −11, …; 41st term

31. −30, −22, −14, −6, …; 20th term

32. **Critical Thinking** Is the sequence $5a - 1, 3a - 1, a - 1, -a - 1, \ldots$ arithmetic? If not, explain why not. If so, find the common difference and the next three terms.

33. Recreation The rates for a go-cart course are shown.

a. Explain why the relationship described on the flyer could be represented by an arithmetic sequence.

b. Find the cost for 1, 2, 3, and 4 laps. Write a rule to find the nth term of the sequence.

c. How much would 15 laps cost?

d. **What if...?** After 9 laps, you get the 10th one free. Will the sequence still be arithmetic? Explain.

JESSIKA'S SPEEDWAY
License: **$7**
Per Lap: **$2**

Find the given term of each arithmetic sequence.

34. 2.5, 8.5, 14.5, 20.5, …; 30th term

35. 189.6, 172.3, 155, 137.7, …; 18th term

36. $\frac{1}{4}, \frac{3}{4}, \frac{5}{4}, \frac{7}{4}$, …; 15th term

37. $\frac{2}{3}, \frac{11}{12}, \frac{7}{6}, \frac{17}{12}$, …; 25th term

38. Number Theory The sequence 1, 1, 2, 3, 5, 8, 13, … is a famous sequence called the Fibonacci sequence. After the first two terms, each term is the sum of the previous two terms.

a. Write the first 10 terms of the Fibonacci sequence. Is the Fibonacci sequence arithmetic? Explain.

b. Notice that the third term is divisible by 2. Are the 6th and 9th terms also divisible by 2? What conclusion can you draw about every third term? Why is this true?

c. Can you find any other patterns? (*Hint:* Look at every 4th and 5th term.)

39. Entertainment Seats in a concert hall are arranged in the pattern shown.

a. The numbers of seats in the rows form an arithmetic sequence. Write a rule for the arithmetic sequence.

b. How many seats are in the 15th row?

c. A ticket costs $40. Suppose every seat in the first 10 rows is filled. What is the total revenue from those seats?

d. **What if...?** An extra chair is added to each row. Write the new rule for the arithmetic sequence and find the new total revenue from the first 10 rows.

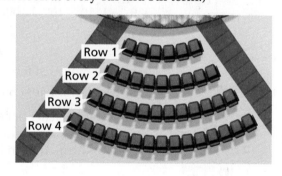

Row 1
Row 2
Row 3
Row 4

H.O.T. 40. Write About It Explain how to find the common difference of an arithmetic sequence. How can you determine whether the arithmetic sequence has a positive common difference or a negative common difference?

41. Juan is traveling to visit universities. He notices mile markers along the road. He records the mile marker every 10 minutes. His father is driving at a constant speed.

a. Copy and complete the table.

b. Write the rule for the sequence.

c. What does the common difference represent?

d. If this sequence continues, find the mile marker for time interval 10.

Time Interval	Mile Marker
1	520
2	509
3	498
4	▉
5	▉
6	▉

TEST PREP

42. What are the next three terms in the arithmetic sequence −21, −12, −3, 6, … ?

   Ⓐ 9, 12, 15   Ⓑ 15, 24, 33   Ⓒ 12, 21, 27   Ⓓ 13, 20, 27

43. What is the common difference for the data listed in the second column?

   Ⓕ −1.8   Ⓗ 2.8

   Ⓖ 1.8   Ⓙ −3.6

Altitude (ft)	Boiling Point of Water (°F)
1000	210.2
2000	208.4
3000	206.6

44. Which of the following sequences is NOT arithmetic?

   Ⓐ −4, 2, 8, 14, …   Ⓑ 9, 4, −1, −6, …   Ⓒ 2, 4, 8, 16, …   Ⓓ $\frac{1}{3}$, $1\frac{1}{3}$, $2\frac{1}{3}$, $3\frac{1}{3}$, …

CHALLENGE AND EXTEND

45. The first term of an arithmetic sequence is 2, and the common difference is 9. Find two consecutive terms of the sequence that have a sum of 355. What positions in the sequence are the terms?

46. The 60th term of an arithmetic sequence is 106.5, and the common difference is 1.5. What is the first term of the sequence?

47. **Athletics** Verona is training for a marathon. The first part of her training schedule is shown below.

Session	1	2	3	4	5	6
Distance Run (mi)	3.5	5	6.5	8	9.5	11

  a. If Verona continues this pattern, during which training session will she run 26 miles? Is her training schedule an arithmetic sequence? Explain.

  b. If Verona's training schedule starts on a Monday and she runs every third day, on which day will she run 26 miles?

FOCUS ON MATHEMATICAL PRACTICES

H.O.T. **48.** **Communication** As part of a game, Darryl says "I wrote an arithmetic sequence that has a common difference of +5. What is my sequence?" Pat says, "I can't tell. You haven't given me enough information." Is Pat correct? If so, what other information does Darryl have to provide? If not, what is Darryl's sequence?

H.O.T. **49.** **Problem Solving** Gena starts an exercise program by running half a mile on Saturday morning. Each week, she increases the distance she runs by a quarter mile. Is this pattern an arithmetic sequence? Explain. If it is, find the common difference and write the first 6 terms of the sequence.

H.O.T. **50.** **Patterns** Many sequences are not arithmetic but still form a clear pattern. Predict the next three terms of each sequence. Are any of them arithmetic sequences?

  a. 1, 2, 4, 8, 16, …   b. 9, 6, 3, 0, …   c. 2, −2, 3, −3, 4, −4, …

H.O.T. **51.** **Modeling** Arithmetic sequences can be written as functions, in which the input is the position of the term and the output is the value of the term. Write a function that models the sequence 4, 7, 10, 13,…. (*Hint:* Remember that the position of the first term of a sequence is 1, not 0.)

Ready to Go On?

my.hrw.com
Assessment and Intervention

9-1 Graphing Functions

Graph each function for the given domain.

1. $2x - y = 3$; D: $\left\{-2, 0, 1, 3\right\}$ **2.** $y = 4 - x^2$; D: $\left\{-1, 0, 1, 2\right\}$ **3.** $y = 3 - 2x$; D: $\left\{-1, 0, 1, 3\right\}$

Graph each function.

4. $x + y = 6$ **5.** $y = |x| - 3$ **6.** $y = x^2 + 1$

7. The function $y = 8x$ represents how many miles y a certain storm travels in x hours. Graph the function and estimate the number of miles the storm travels in 10.5 h.

9-2 Exploring Transformations

The graph shows some credit card fees for cash advances. Sketch a graph to represent each situation and identify the transformation of the original graph that it represents.

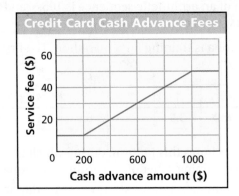

8. Each fee is increased by $15.

9. Each fee is decreased by 40%.

9-3 Arithmetic Sequences

Determine whether each sequence appears to be an arithmetic sequence. If so, find the common difference and the next three terms.

10. 7, 3, −1, −5, …   **11.** 3, 6, 12, 24, …   **12.** −3.5, −2, −0.5, 1, …

Find the indicated term of the arithmetic sequence.

13. 31st term: 12, 7, 2, −3, …   **14.** 22nd term: $a_1 = 6$; $d = 4$

15. With no air resistance, an object would fall 16 feet during the first second, 48 feet during the second second, 80 feet during the third second, 112 feet during the fourth second, and so on. How many feet will the object fall during the ninth second?

PARCC Assessment Readiness

Selected Response

1. Find the 20th term in the arithmetic sequence −4, 1, 6, 11, 16,…

   Ⓐ 96   Ⓒ 95

   Ⓑ 72   Ⓓ 91

2. Which situation is best represented by the graph?

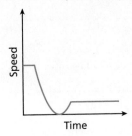

   Ⓕ An airplane starts slowly on the runway, and then quickly takes off before finding a nice cruising speed.

   Ⓖ A swimmer starts at a steady pace, slows down to a stop, and then starts swimming again, but at a slower pace than when she first started.

   Ⓗ After a ball is thrown into the air, it falls back to the ground and bounces.

   Ⓙ The driver of a car starts on flat ground and drives quickly up a hill, then keeps driving.

3. Use the graph of the function $f(x) = 2x + 2$ to find the value of y when $x = 2$.

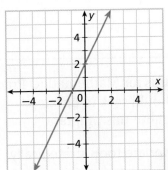

   Ⓐ −2   Ⓒ 6

   Ⓑ 7   Ⓓ 0

4. Determine whether the sequence appears to be an arithmetic sequence. If so, find the common difference and the next three terms in the sequence. −5, −11, −17, −23, −29, . . .

   Ⓕ Not an arithmetic sequence

   Ⓖ Yes; common difference −7; next three terms are −36, −43, −50

   Ⓗ Yes; common difference −6; next 3 terms are −35, −41, −47

   Ⓙ Yes; common difference 6; next three terms are −23, −17, −11

5. Sylvie is going on vacation. She has already driven 60 miles in one hour. Her average speed for the rest of the trip is 57 miles per hour. How far will Sylvie have driven 7 hours later?

   Ⓐ 399 miles   Ⓒ 459 miles

   Ⓑ 402 miles   Ⓓ 420 miles

6. Graph the function $y = -x^2 - 2$.

   Ⓕ   Ⓖ

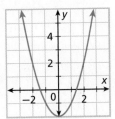 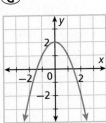

   Ⓗ   Ⓙ

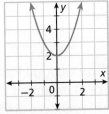 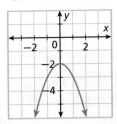

Mini-Task

7. A motorist is driving across the country at a steady speed at 54.5 miles per hour. At the end of the 17th hour, the odometer reads 62,416. What was the odometer reading when she started her trip?

COMMON CORE GPS

Contents

MATHEMATICAL PRACTICES

The Common Core Georgia Performance Standards for Mathematical Practice describe varieties of expertise that all students should seek to develop. Opportunities to develop these practices are integrated throughout this program.

1 Make sense of problems and persevere in solving them.

2 Reason abstractly and quantitatively.

3 Construct viable arguments and critique the reasoning of others.

4 Model with mathematics.

5 Use appropriate tools strategically.

6 Attend to precision.

7 Look for and make use of structure.

8 Look for and express regularity in repeated reasoning.

Unpacking the Standards

Understanding the standards and the vocabulary terms in the standards will help you know exactly what you are expected to learn in this chapter.

COMMON CORE GPS
MCC9-12.F.IF.6

Calculate and interpret the average rate of change of a function (presented symbolically or as a table) over a specified interval. Estimate the rate of change from a graph.

Key Vocabulary

rate of change (tasa de cambio)
A ratio that compares the amount of change in a dependent variable to the amount of change in an independent variable.

What It Means For You

Average rate of change measures the change in the dependent variable against the change in the independent variable over a specific interval. This helps you understand how quickly the values in a function change.

EXAMPLE

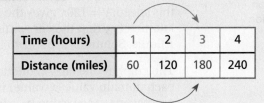

Time (hours)	1	2	3	4
Distance (miles)	60	120	180	240

$$\text{Average rate of change} = \frac{180 - 60}{3 - 1} = 60 \text{ mi/h}$$

10-1 Identifying Linear Functions

 Essential Question: How can you identify and graph linear functions?

Objectives
Identify linear functions and linear equations.

Graph linear functions that represent real-world situations and give their domain and range.

Vocabulary
linear function
linear equation

Why learn this?
Linear functions can describe many real-world situations, such as distances traveled at a constant speed.

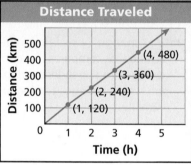

Most people believe that there is no speed limit on the German autobahn. However, many stretches have a speed limit of 120 km/h. If a car travels continuously at this speed, $y = 120x$ gives the number of kilometers y that the car would travel in x hours. Solutions are shown in the graph.

The graph represents a function because each domain value (x-value) is paired with exactly one range value (y-value). Notice that the graph is a straight line. A function whose graph forms a straight line is called a **linear function**.

Distance Traveled

COMMON CORE GPS
EXAMPLE MCC9-12.F.LE.1b **1**

Identifying a Linear Function by Its Graph

my.hrw.com

Online Video Tutor

Identify whether each graph represents a function. Explain. If the graph does represent a function, is the function linear?

A
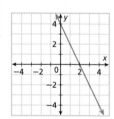

Each domain value is paired with exactly one range value. The graph forms a line.

linear function

B
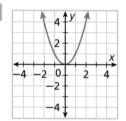

Each domain value is paired with exactly one range value. The graph is not a line.

not a linear function

C
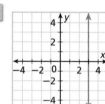

The only domain value, 3, is paired with many different range values.

not a function

 CHECK IT OUT! Identify whether each graph represents a function. Explain. If the graph does represent a function, is the function linear?

1a. 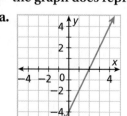   1b. 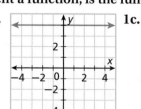   1c.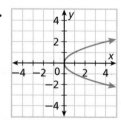

You can sometimes identify a linear function by looking at a table or a list of ordered pairs. In a linear function, a constant change in x corresponds to a constant change in y.

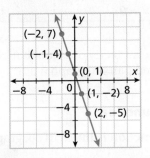

In this table, a constant change of $+1$ in x corresponds to a constant change of -3 in y. These points satisfy a linear function.

The points from this table lie on a line.

In this table, a constant change of $+1$ in x does *not* correspond to a constant change in y. These points do *not* satisfy a linear function.

The points from this table do not lie on a line.

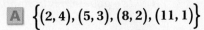

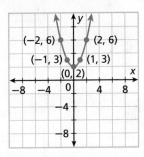

EXAMPLE 2

Identifying a Linear Function by Using Ordered Pairs

my.hrw.com

Online Video Tutor

Tell whether each set of ordered pairs satisfies a linear function. Explain.

A $\{(2, 4), (5, 3), (8, 2), (11, 1)\}$

x	y
2	4
5	3
8	2
11	1

+3 ... −1

Write the ordered pairs in a table. Look for a pattern.

A constant change of $+3$ in x corresponds to a constant change of -1 in y.

These points satisfy a linear function.

B $\{(-10, 10), (-5, 4), (0, 2), (5, 0)\}$

x	y
−10	10
−5	4
0	2
5	0

+5 ... −6, −2, −2

Write the ordered pairs in a table. Look for a pattern.

A constant change of $+5$ in x corresponds to different changes in y.

These points do not satisfy a linear function.

CHECK IT OUT!

2. Tell whether the set of ordered pairs $\{(3, 5), (5, 4), (7, 3), (9, 2), (11, 1)\}$ satisfies a linear function. Explain.

Another way to determine whether a function is linear is to look at its equation. A function is linear if it is described by a *linear equation*. A **linear equation** is any equation that can be written in the *standard form* shown below.

Standard Form of a Linear Equation

$Ax + By = C$ where A, B, and C are real numbers and A and B are not both 0

Notice that when a linear equation is written in standard form
- x and y both have exponents of 1.
- x and y are not multiplied together.
- x and y do not appear in denominators, exponents, or radical signs.

Linear		Not Linear	
$3x + 2y = 10$	Standard form	$3xy + x = 1$	x and y are multiplied.
$y - 2 = 3x$	Can be written as $3x - y = -2$	$x^3 + y = -1$	x has an exponent other than 1.
$-y = 5x$	Can be written as $5x + y = 0$	$x + \dfrac{6}{y} = 12$	y is in a denominator.

For any two points, there is exactly one line that contains them both. This means you need only two ordered pairs to graph a line.

COMMON CORE GPS
EXAMPLE **3**
MCC9-12.F.IF.7a

my.hrw.com

Online Video Tutor

Graphing Linear Functions

Tell whether each function is linear. If so, graph the function.

A $y = x + 3$

$$y = \quad x + 3 \qquad \text{Write the equation in standard form.}$$
$$\underline{-x \quad -x} \qquad \text{Subtraction Property of Equality}$$
$$y - x = \qquad 3$$
$$-x + y = \qquad 3 \qquad \text{The equation is in standard form } (A = -1, B = 1, C = 3).$$

The equation can be written in standard form, so the function is linear.

To graph, choose three values of x, and use them to generate ordered pairs. (You only need two, but graphing three points is a good check.)

Plot the points and connect them with a straight line.

Remember!

- $y - x = y + (-x)$
- $y + (-x) = -x + y$
- $-x = -1x$
- $y = 1y$

x	$y = x + 3$	(x, y)
0	$y = 0 + 3 = 3$	$(0, 3)$
1	$y = 1 + 3 = 4$	$(1, 4)$
2	$y = 2 + 3 = 5$	$(2, 5)$

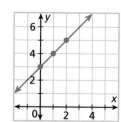

B $y = x^2$

This is not linear, because x has an exponent other than 1.

 CHECK IT OUT! **Tell whether each function is linear. If so, graph the function.**
3a. $y = 5x - 9$ **3b.** $y = 12$ **3c.** $y = 2^x$

For linear functions whose graphs are not horizontal, the domain and range are all real numbers. However, in many real-world situations, the domain and range must be restricted. For example, some quantities cannot be negative, such as time.

Sometimes domain and range are restricted even further to a set of points. For example, a quantity such as number of people can only be whole numbers. When this happens, the graph is not actually connected because every point on the line is not a solution. However, you may see these graphs shown connected to indicate that the linear pattern, or trend, continues.

COMMON
CORE GPS
EXAMPLE **4**
MCC9-12.F.IF.7a

my.hrw.com

Online Video Tutor

Remember!

$f(x) = y$, so in Example 4, graph the function values (dependent variable) on the *y*-axis.

Career Application

Sue rents a manicure station in a salon and pays the salon owner $5.50 for each manicure she gives. The amount Sue pays each day is given by $f(x) = 5.50x$, where *x* is the number of manicures. Graph this function and give its domain and range.

Choose several values of x and make a table of ordered pairs.

Graph the ordered pairs.

x	$f(x) = 5.50x$
0	$f(0) = 5.50(0) = 0$
1	$f(1) = 5.50(1) = 5.50$
2	$f(2) = 5.50(2) = 11.00$
3	$f(3) = 5.50(3) = 16.50$
4	$f(4) = 5.50(4) = 22.00$
5	$f(5) = 5.50(5) = 27.50$

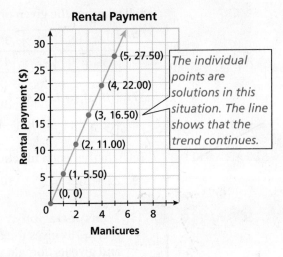

The individual points are solutions in this situation. The line shows that the trend continues.

The number of manicures must be a whole number, so the domain is $\{0, 1, 2, 3, \ldots\}$. The range is $\{0, 5.50, 11.00, 16.50, \ldots\}$.

4. **What if...?** At another salon, Sue can rent a station for $10.00 per day plus $3.00 per manicure. The amount she would pay each day is given by $f(x) = 3x + 10$, where *x* is the number of manicures. Graph this function and give its domain and range.

MCC.MP.3
MATHEMATICAL
PRACTICES

THINK AND DISCUSS

1. Suppose you are given five ordered pairs that satisfy a function. When you graph them, four lie on a straight line, but the fifth does not. Is the function linear? Why or why not?

2. In Example 4, why is every point on the line not a solution?

3. **GET ORGANIZED** Copy and complete the graphic organizer. In each box, describe how to use the information to identify a linear function. Include an example.

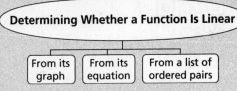

Determining Whether a Function Is Linear

From its graph | From its equation | From a list of ordered pairs

my.hrw.com
Homework Help

GUIDED PRACTICE

1. **Vocabulary** Is the *linear equation* $3x - 2 = y$ in standard form? Explain.

SEE EXAMPLE 1

Identify whether each graph represents a function. Explain. If the graph does represent a function, is the function linear?

2.
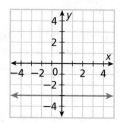

3.
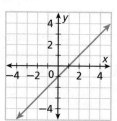

4.
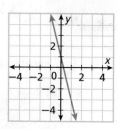

SEE EXAMPLE 2

Tell whether the given ordered pairs satisfy a linear function. Explain.

5.
x	5	4	3	2	1
y	0	2	4	6	8

6.
x	1	4	9	16	25
y	1	2	3	4	5

7. $\left\{(0, 5), (-2, 3), (-4, 1), (-6, -1), (-8, -3)\right\}$

8. $\left\{(2, -2), (-1, 0), (-4, 1), (-7, 3), (-10, 6)\right\}$

SEE EXAMPLE 3

Tell whether each function is linear. If so, graph the function.

9. $2x + 3y = 5$

10. $2y = 8$

11. $\dfrac{x^2 + 3}{5} = y$

12. $\dfrac{x}{5} = \dfrac{y}{3}$

SEE EXAMPLE 4

13. **Transportation** A train travels at a constant speed of 75 mi/h. The function $f(x) = 75x$ gives the distance that the train travels in x hours. Graph this function and give its domain and range.

14. **Entertainment** A movie rental store charges a $6.00 membership fee plus $2.50 for each movie rented. The function $f(x) = 2.50x + 6$ gives the cost of renting x movies. Graph this function and give its domain and range.

PRACTICE AND PROBLEM SOLVING

Independent Practice

For Exercises	See Example
15–17	1
18–20	2
21–24	3
25	4

my.hrw.com

Online Extra Practice

Identify whether each graph represents a function. Explain. If the graph does represent a function, is the function linear?

15.
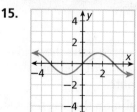

16.
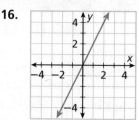

17.
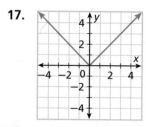

Tell whether the given ordered pairs satisfy a linear function. Explain.

18.
x	−3	0	3	6	9
y	−2	−1	0	2	4

19.
x	−1	0	1	2	3
y	−3	−2	−1	0	1

20. $\left\{(3, 4), (0, 2), (-3, 0), (-6, -2), (-9, -4)\right\}$

Tell whether each function is linear. If so, graph the function.

21. $y = 5$
22. $4y - 2x = 0$
23. $\frac{3}{x} + 4y = 10$
24. $5 + 3y = 8$

25. **Transportation** The gas tank in Tony's car holds 15 gallons, and the car can travel 25 miles for each gallon of gas. When Tony begins with a full tank of gas, the function $f(x) = -\frac{1}{25}x + 15$ gives the amount of gas $f(x)$ that will be left in the tank after traveling x miles (if he does not buy more gas). Graph this function and give its domain and range.

Tell whether the given ordered pairs satisfy a function. If so, is it a linear function?

26. $\{(2, 5), (2, 4), (2, 3), (2, 2), (2, 1)\}$

27. $\{(-8, 2), (-6, 0), (-4, -2), (-2, -4), (0, -6)\}$

28.

x	−10	−6	−2	2	4
y	0	0.25	0.50	0.75	1

29.

x	−5	−1	3	7	11
y	1	1	1	1	1

Tell whether each equation is linear. If so, write the equation in standard form and give the values of A, B, and C.

30. $2x - 8y = 16$
31. $y = 4x + 2$
32. $2x = \frac{y}{3} - 4$
33. $\frac{4}{x} = y$

34. $\frac{x + 4}{2} = \frac{y - 4}{3}$
35. $x = 7$
36. $xy = 6$
37. $3x - 5 + y = 2y - 4$

38. $y = -x + 2$
39. $5x = 2y - 3$
40. $2y = -6$
41. $y = \sqrt{x}$

Graph each linear function.

42. $y = 3x + 7$
43. $y = x + 25$
44. $y = 8 - x$
45. $y = 2x$

46. $-2y = -3x + 6$
47. $y - x = 4$
48. $y - 2x = -3$
49. $x = 5 + y$

50. **Measurement** One inch is equal to approximately 2.5 centimeters. Let x represent inches and y represent centimeters. Write an equation in standard form relating x and y. Give the values of A, B, and C.

51. **Wages** Molly earns $8.00 an hour at her job.
   a. Let x represent the number of hours that Molly works. Write a function using x and $f(x)$ that describes Molly's pay for working x hours.
   b. Graph this function and give its domain and range.

H.O.T. 52. **Write About It** For $y = 2x - 1$, make a table of ordered pairs and a graph. Describe the relationships between the equation, the table, and the graph.

H.O.T. 53. **Critical Thinking** Describe a real-world situation that can be represented by a linear function whose domain and range must be limited. Give your function and its domain and range.

Real-World Connections

54. **a.** Juan is running on a treadmill. The table shows the number of Calories Juan burns as a function of time. Explain how you can tell that this relationship is linear by using the table.
   b. Create a graph of the data.
   c. How can you tell from the graph that the relationship is linear?

Time (min)	Calories
3	27
6	54
9	81
12	108
15	135
18	162
21	189

55. Physical Science A ball was dropped from a height of 100 meters. Its height above the ground in meters at different times after its release is given in the table. Do these ordered pairs satisfy a linear function? Explain.

Time (s)	0	1	2	3
Height (m)	100	90.2	60.8	11.8

H.O.T. 56. Critical Thinking Is the equation $x = 9$ a linear equation? Does it describe a linear function? Explain.

TEST PREP

57. Which is NOT a linear function?

(A) $y = 8x$ (B) $y = x + 8$ (C) $y = \dfrac{8}{x}$ (D) $y = 8 - x$

58. The speed of sound in 0 °C air is about 331 feet per second. Which function could be used to describe the distance in feet d that sound will travel in air in s seconds?

(F) $d = s + 331$ (G) $d = 331s$ (H) $s = 331d$ (J) $s = 331 - d$

H.O.T. 59. Extended Response Write your own linear function. Show that it is a linear function in at least three different ways. Explain any connections you see between your three methods.

CHALLENGE AND EXTEND

60. What equation describes the x-axis? the y-axis? Do these equations represent linear functions?

Geometry Copy and complete each table below. Then tell whether the table shows a linear relationship.

61.

Perimeter of a Square	
Side Length	Perimeter
1	
2	
3	
4	

62.

Area of a Square	
Side Length	Area
1	
2	
3	
4	

63.

Volume of a Cube	
Side Length	Volume
1	
2	
3	
4	

FOCUS ON MATHEMATICAL PRACTICES

H.O.T. 64. Reasoning A function crosses the x-axis at the points (0,0) and (4,0) and nowhere else. Could the function be a linear function? Explain your answer.

H.O.T. 65. Analysis Fill each of the three areas of the Venn diagram with two different equations.

H.O.T. 66. Modeling Describe a problem situation that can be modeled by a linear function with a domain of D: $0 < x \le 10$, where 0 is not part of the range. Give the function and its range.

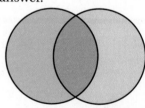

Linear   Function

10-2 Using Intercepts

? Essential Question: How can you find *x*- and *y*-intercepts and use them to graph linear functions?

Objectives
Find *x*- and *y*-intercepts and interpret their meanings in real-world situations.

Use *x*- and *y*-intercepts to graph lines.

Vocabulary
y-intercept
x-intercept

Who uses this?
Divers can use intercepts to determine the time a safe ascent will take.

A diver explored the ocean floor 120 feet below the surface and then ascended at a rate of 30 feet per minute. The graph shows the diver's elevation below sea level during the ascent.

The **y-intercept** is the *y*-coordinate of the point where the graph intersects the *y*-axis. The *x*-coordinate of this point is always 0.

The **x-intercept** is the *x*-coordinate of the point where the graph intersects the *x*-axis. The *y*-coordinate of this point is always 0.

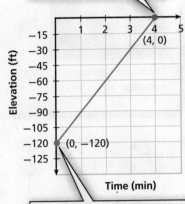

The x-intercept is 4. It represents the time that the diver reaches the surface, or when depth = 0.

The y-intercept is −120. It represents the diver's elevation at the start of the ascent, when time = 0.

COMMON CORE GPS MCC9-12.F.IF.4

EXAMPLE 1 Finding Intercepts

my.hrw.com

Online Video Tutor

Find the *x*- and *y*-intercepts.

A

The graph intersects the x-axis at (−4, 0).
The *x*-intercept is −4.

The graph intersects the y-axis at (0, −3).
The *y*-intercept is −3.

B $3x - 2y = 12$

To find the *x*-intercept, replace *y* with 0 and solve for *x*.

$$3x - 2y = 12$$
$$3x - 2(0) = 12$$
$$3x - 0 = 12$$
$$3x = 12$$
$$\frac{3x}{3} = \frac{12}{3}$$
$$x = 4$$

The *x*-intercept is 4.

To find the *y*-intercept, replace *x* with 0 and solve for *y*.

$$3x - 2y = 12$$
$$3(0) - 2y = 12$$
$$0 - 2y = 12$$
$$-2y = 12$$
$$\frac{-2y}{-2} = \frac{12}{-2}$$
$$y = -6$$

The *y*-intercept is −6.

 CHECK IT OUT! Find the *x*- and *y*-intercepts.

1a.

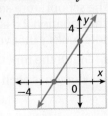

1b. $-3x + 5y = 30$

1c. $4x + 2y = 16$

Madison Stewart
Jefferson High School

Finding Intercepts

I use the "cover-up" method to find intercepts. To use this method, make sure the equation is in standard form first.

If I have $4x - 3y = 12$:

First, I cover $4x$ with my finger and solve the equation I can still see.

 $- 3y = 12$
$y = -4$

The y-intercept is −4.

Then I cover $-3y$ with my finger and do the same thing.

$4x$ $= 12$
$x = 3$

The x-intercept is 3.

COMMON CORE GPS

EXAMPLE 2
MCC9-12.F.IF.7a

my.hrw.com

Online Video Tutor

Travel Application

The Sandia Peak Tramway in Albuquerque, New Mexico, travels a distance of about 4500 meters to the top of Sandia Peak. Its speed is 300 meters per minute. The function $f(x) = 4500 - 300x$ gives the tram's distance in meters from the top of the peak after x minutes. Graph this function and find the intercepts. What does each intercept represent?

Neither time nor distance can be negative, so choose several nonnegative values for x. Use the function to generate ordered pairs.

x	0	2	5	10	15
$f(x) = 4500 - 300x$	4500	3900	3000	1500	0

Graph the ordered pairs. Connect the points with a line.

Caution!

The graph is not the path of the tram. Even though the line is descending, the graph describes the distance from the peak as the tram goes *up* the mountain.

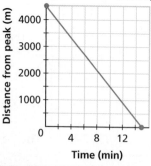

Sandia Peak Tramway

- *y*-intercept: 4500. This is the starting distance from the top (time = 0).

- *x*-intercept: 15. This the time when the tram reaches the peak (distance = 0).

2. The school store sells pens for $2.00 and notebooks for $3.00. The equation $2x + 3y = 60$ describes the number of pens x and notebooks y that you can buy for $60.

   a. Graph the function and find its intercepts.

   b. What does each intercept represent?

(t),©LWA–Dann Tardif/CORBIS; (cr),© Buddy Mays/CORBIS

Remember, to graph a linear function, you need to plot only two ordered pairs. It is often simplest to find the ordered pairs that contain the intercepts.

Graphing Linear Equations by Using Intercepts

Use intercepts to graph the line described by each equation.

my.hrw.com

Online Video Tutor

A $2x - 4y = 8$

Step 1 Find the intercepts.

x-intercept:

$2x - 4y = 8$
$2x - 4(0) = 8$
$2x = 8$
$\dfrac{2x}{2} = \dfrac{8}{2}$
$x = 4$

y-intercept:

$2x - 4y = 8$
$2(0) - 4y = 8$
$-4y = 8$
$\dfrac{-4y}{-4} = \dfrac{8}{-4}$
$y = -2$

Step 2 Graph the line.

Plot (4, 0) and (0, −2).
Connect with a straight line.

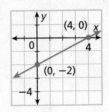

Helpful Hint

You can use a third point to check your line. Either choose a point from your graph and check it in the equation, or use the equation to generate a point and check that it is on your graph.

B $\dfrac{2}{3}y = 4 - \dfrac{1}{2}x$

Step 1 Write the equation in standard form.

$6\left(\dfrac{2}{3}y\right) = 6\left(4 - \dfrac{1}{2}x\right)$ *Multiply both sides by 6, the LCD of the fractions, to clear the fractions.*

$4y = 24 - 3x$

$3x + 4y = 24$ *Write the equation in standard form.*

Step 2 Find the intercepts.

x-intercept:

$3x + 4y = 24$
$3x + 4(0) = 24$
$3x = 24$
$\dfrac{3x}{3} = \dfrac{24}{3}$
$x = 8$

y-intercept:

$3x + 4y = 24$
$3(0) + 4y = 24$
$4y = 24$
$\dfrac{4y}{4} = \dfrac{24}{4}$
$y = 6$

Step 3 Graph the line.

Plot (8, 0) and (0, 6).
Connect with a straight line.

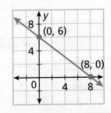

CHECK IT OUT!

Use intercepts to graph the line described by each equation.

3a. $-3x + 4y = -12$ **3b.** $y = \dfrac{1}{3}x - 2$

MCC.MP.1   MATHEMATICAL PRACTICES

THINK AND DISCUSS

1. A function has x-intercept 4 and y-intercept 2. Name two points on the graph of this function.

2. What is the y-intercept of $2.304x + y = 4.318$? What is the x-intercept of $x - 92.4920y = -21.5489$?

3. GET ORGANIZED Copy and complete the graphic organizer.

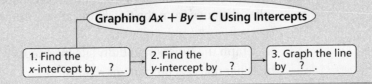

Graphing $Ax + By = C$ Using Intercepts

| 1. Find the x-intercept by ___?___. | 2. Find the y-intercept by ___?___. | 3. Graph the line by ___?___. |

10-2 Exercises

my.hrw.com
Homework Help

GUIDED PRACTICE

1. **Vocabulary** The ____?____ is the y-coordinate of the point where a graph crosses the y-axis. (*x-intercept* or *y-intercept*)

SEE EXAMPLE **1**

Find the x- and y-intercepts.

2.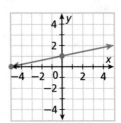

3.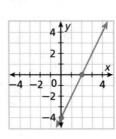

4.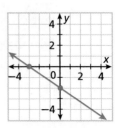

5. $2x - 4y = 4$

6. $-2y = 3x - 6$

7. $4y + 5x = 2y - 3x + 16$

SEE EXAMPLE **2**

8. **Biology** To thaw a specimen stored at $-25\,°C$, the temperature of a refrigeration tank is raised $5\,°C$ every hour. The temperature in the tank after x hours can be described by the function $f(x) = -25 + 5x$.

a. Graph the function and find its intercepts.

b. What does each intercept represent?

SEE EXAMPLE **3**

Use intercepts to graph the line described by each equation.

9. $4x - 5y = 20$

10. $y = 2x + 4$

11. $\frac{1}{3}x - \frac{1}{4}y = 2$

12. $-5y + 2x = -10$

PRACTICE AND PROBLEM SOLVING

Independent Practice

For Exercises	See Example
13–21	1
22–23	2
24–29	3

my.hrw.com

Online Extra Practice

Find the x- and y-intercepts.

13.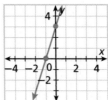

14.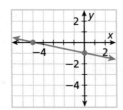

15.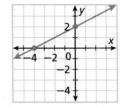

16. $6x + 3y = 12$

17. $4y - 8 = 2x$

18. $-2y + x = 2y - 8$

19. $4x + y = 8$

20. $y - 3x = -15$

21. $2x + y = 10x - 1$

22. **Environmental Science** A fishing lake was stocked with 300 bass. Each year, the population decreases by 25. The population of bass in the lake after x years is represented by the function $f(x) = 300 - 25x$.

a. Graph the function and find its intercepts.

b. What does each intercept represent?

23. **Sports** Julie is running a 5-kilometer race. She runs 1 kilometer every 5 minutes. Julie's distance from the finish line after x minutes is represented by the function $f(x) = 5 - \frac{1}{5}x$.

a. Graph the function and find its intercepts.

b. What does each intercept represent?

Use intercepts to graph the line described by each equation.

24. $4x - 6y = 12$

25. $2x + 3y = 18$

26. $\frac{1}{2}x - 4y = 4$

27. $y - x = -1$

28. $5x + 3y = 15$

29. $x - 3y = -1$

Bamboo is the world's fastest-growing woody plant. Some varieties can grow more than 30 centimeters a day and up to 40 meters tall.

30. Biology A bamboo plant is growing 1 foot per day. When you first measure it, it is 4 feet tall.

 a. Write an equation to describe the height y, in feet, of the bamboo plant x days after you measure it.

 b. What is the y-intercept?

 c. What is the meaning of the y-intercept in this problem?

31. Estimation Look at the scatter plot and trend line.

 a. Estimate the x- and y-intercepts.

 b. What is the real-world meaning of each intercept?

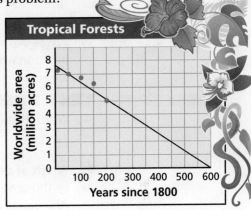

Tropical Forests

32. Personal Finance A bank employee notices an abandoned checking account with a balance of $412. If the bank charges a $4 monthly fee for the account, the function $b = 412 - 4m$ shows the balance b in the account after m months.

 a. Graph the function and give its domain and range. (*Hint:* The bank will keep charging the monthly fee even after the account is empty.)

 b. Find the intercepts. What does each intercept represent?

 c. When will the bank account balance be 0?

H.O.T. 33. Critical Thinking Complete the following to learn about intercepts and horizontal and vertical lines.

 a. Graph $x = -6$, $x = 1$, and $x = 5$. Find the intercepts.

 b. Graph $y = -3$, $y = 2$, and $y = 7$. Find the intercepts.

 c. Write a rule describing the intercepts of linear equations whose graphs are horizontal and vertical lines.

Match each equation with a graph.

34. $-2x - y = 4$

35. $y = 4 - 2x$

36. $2y + 4x = 8$

37. $4x - 2y = 8$

A.

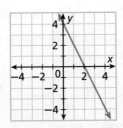

B.

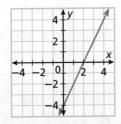

C.

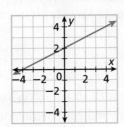

D.

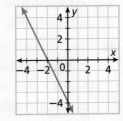

Real-World Connections

38. Kristyn rode a stationary bike at the gym. She programmed the timer for 20 minutes. The display counted backward to show how much time remained in her workout. It also showed her mileage.

   a. What are the intercepts?

   b. What do the intercepts represent?

Time Remaining (min)	Distance Covered (mi)
20	0
16	0.35
12	0.70
8	1.05
4	1.40
0	1.75

H.O.T. 39. Write About It Write a real-world problem that could be modeled by a linear function whose x-intercept is 5 and whose y-intercept is 60.

TEST PREP

40. Which is the x-intercept of $-2x = 9y - 18$?

   Ⓐ -9 Ⓑ -2 Ⓒ 2 Ⓓ 9

41. Which of the following situations could be represented by the graph?

   Ⓕ Jamie owed her uncle $200. Each week for 40 weeks she paid him $5.

   Ⓖ Jamie owed her uncle $200. Each week for 5 weeks she paid him $40.

   Ⓗ Jamie owed her uncle $40. Each week for 5 weeks she paid him $200.

   Ⓙ Jamie owed her uncle $40. Each week for 200 weeks she paid him $5.

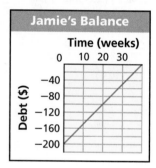

42. Gridded Response What is the y-intercept of $60x + 55y = 660$?

CHALLENGE AND EXTEND

Use intercepts to graph the line described by each equation.

43. $\frac{1}{2}x + \frac{1}{5}y = 1$ **44.** $0.5x - 0.2y = 0.75$ **45.** $y = \frac{3}{8}x + 6$

46. For any linear equation $Ax + By = C$, what are the intercepts?

47. Find the intercepts of $22x - 380y = 20{,}900$. Explain how to use the intercepts to determine appropriate scales for the graph.

FOCUS ON MATHEMATICAL PRACTICES

H.O.T. 48. Reasonableness Teresa wants to graph the equation $\frac{x}{4.8} - \frac{y}{8.8} = 5$. What is a reasonable scale for each axis that would show both intercepts near the edge of the graph?

H.O.T. 49. Analysis Consider the equation $\frac{x}{a} + \frac{y}{b} = 1$.

   a. What are the intercepts?

   b. Write a linear equation in this form with an x-intercept of 15 and a y-intercept of 60.

   c. Rewrite your answer to part b using integer coefficients.

Victoria Smith/HMH

Mastering the Standards

for Mathematical Practice

The topics described in the Standards for Mathematical Content will vary from year to year. However, the *way* in which you learn, study, and think about mathematics will not. The Standards for Mathematical Practice describe skills that you will use in all of your math courses.

Mathematical Practices

1. *Make sense of problems and persevere in solving them.*
2. *Reason abstractly and quantitatively.*
3. *Construct viable arguments and critique the reasoning of others.*
4. *Model with mathematics.*
5. *Use appropriate tools strategically.*
6. *Attend to precision.*
7. *Look for and make use of structure.*
8. *Look for and express regularity in repeated reasoning.*

1 Make sense of problems and persevere in solving them.

Mathematically proficient students start by explaining to themselves the meaning of a problem... They analyze givens, constraints, relationships, and goals. They make conjectures about the form... of the solution and plan a solution pathway...

In your book

Focus on Problem Solving describes a four-step plan for problem solving. The plan is introduced at the beginning of your book, and practice with the plan appears throughout the book.

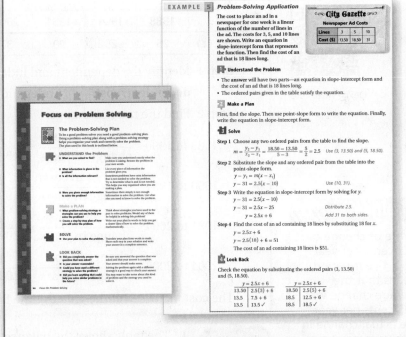

10-3 # Rate of Change and Slope

 **Essential Question:** How can you calculate and interpret the rate of change of a linear function?

Objectives
Find rates of change and slopes.

Relate a constant rate of change to the slope of a line.

Vocabulary
rate of change
rise
run
slope

 Animated Math

Why learn this?
Rates of change can be used to find how quickly costs have increased.

In 1985, the cost of sending a 1-ounce letter was 22 cents. In 1988, the cost was 25 cents. How fast did the cost change from 1985 to 1988? In other words, at what *rate* did the cost change?

A **rate of change** is a ratio that compares the amount of change in a dependent variable to the amount of change in an independent variable.

$$\text{rate of change} = \frac{\text{change in dependent variable}}{\text{change in independent variable}}$$

COMMON CORE GPS
EXAMPLE 1
MCC9-12.F.IF.6

 my.hrw.com

Online Video Tutor

Consumer Application

The table shows the cost of mailing a 1-ounce letter in different years. Find the rate of change in cost for each time interval. During which time interval did the cost increase at the greatest rate?

Year	1988	1990	1991	2004	2008
Cost (¢)	25	25	29	37	42

Step 1 Identify the dependent and independent variables.

dependent: cost   independent: year

Step 2 Find the rates of change.

1988 to 1990 $\dfrac{\text{change in cost}}{\text{change in years}} = \dfrac{25 - 25}{1990 - 1988} = \dfrac{0}{2} = 0$ *0 cents / year*

1990 to 1991 $\dfrac{\text{change in cost}}{\text{change in years}} = \dfrac{29 - 25}{1991 - 1990} = \dfrac{4}{1} = 4$ *4 cents / year*

1991 to 2004 $\dfrac{\text{change in cost}}{\text{change in years}} = \dfrac{37 - 29}{2004 - 1991} = \dfrac{8}{13} \approx 0.62 \approx$ *0.62 cents / year*

2004 to 2008 $\dfrac{\text{change in cost}}{\text{change in years}} = \dfrac{42 - 37}{2008 - 2004} = \dfrac{5}{4} = 1.25$ *1.25 cents / year*

The cost increased at the greatest rate from 1990 to 1991.

 Caution!

A rate of change of 1.25 cents per year for a 4-year period means that the *average* change was 1.25 cents per year. The *actual* change in each year may have been different.

 CHECK IT OUT!

1. The table shows the balance of a bank account on different days of the month. Find the rate of change for each time interval. During which time interval did the balance decrease at the greatest rate?

Day	1	6	16	22	30
Balance ($)	550	285	210	210	175

EXAMPLE 2

Finding Rates of Change from a Graph

Graph the data from Example 1 and show the rates of change.

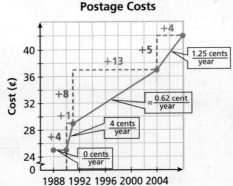

Postage Costs

Graph the ordered pairs. The vertical blue segments show the changes in the dependent variable, and the horizontal green segments show the changes in the independent variable.

Notice that the greatest rate of change is represented by the steepest of the red line segments.

Also notice that between 1988 and 1990, when the cost did not change, the red line segment is horizontal.

CHECK IT OUT!

2. Graph the data from Check It Out Problem 1 and show the rates of change.

If all of the connected segments have the same rate of change, then they all have the same steepness and together form a straight line. The constant rate of change of a nonvertical line is called the *slope* of the line.

Slope of a Line

The **rise** is the difference in the *y*-values of two points on a line.

The **run** is the difference in the *x*-values of two points on a line.

The **slope** of a line is the ratio of rise to run for any two points on the line.

$$\text{slope} = \frac{\text{rise}}{\text{run}} = \frac{\text{change in } y}{\text{change in } x}$$

(Remember that *y* is the **dependent variable** and *x* is the **independent variable**.)

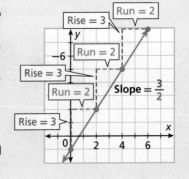

EXAMPLE 3

Finding Slope

Find the slope of the line.

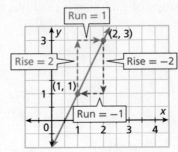

Begin at one point and count vertically to find the rise.

Then count horizontally to the second point to find the run.

It does not matter which point you start with. The slope is the same.

$$\text{slope} = \frac{2}{1} = 2$$

$$\text{slope} = \frac{-2}{-1} = 2$$

CHECK IT OUT!

3. Find the slope of the line that contains $(0, -3)$ and $(5, -5)$.

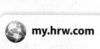

EXAMPLE 4
MCC9-12.F.IF.6

Finding Slopes of Horizontal and Vertical Lines

Find the slope of each line.

A

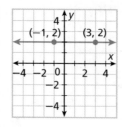

$$\frac{\text{rise}}{\text{run}} = \frac{0}{4} = 0$$

The slope is 0.

B

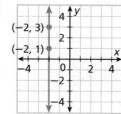

$$\frac{\text{rise}}{\text{run}} = \frac{2}{0}$$ *You cannot divide by 0.*

The slope is undefined.

CHECK IT OUT!   Find the slope of each line.

4a.

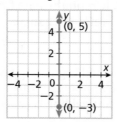

4b.

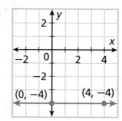

As shown in the previous examples, slope can be positive, negative, zero, or undefined. You can tell which of these is the case by looking at the graph of a line—you do not need to calculate the slope.

Positive Slope	Negative Slope	Zero Slope	Undefined Slope

Line rises from left to right.	Line falls from left to right.	Horizontal line	Vertical line

EXAMPLE 5
MCC9-12.F.IF.4

Describing Slope

Tell whether the slope of each line is positive, negative, zero, or undefined.

A

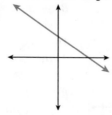

The line falls from left to right.

The slope is negative.

B

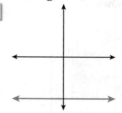

The line is horizontal.

The slope is 0.

Tell whether the slope of each line is positive, negative, zero, or undefined.

5a.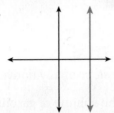

5b.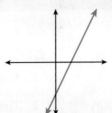

A line's slope is a measure of its steepness. Some lines are steeper than others. As the absolute value of the slope increases, the line becomes steeper.
As the absolute value of the slope decreases, the line becomes less steep.

Comparing Slopes		
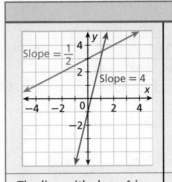	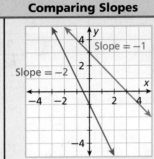	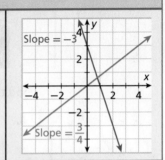
The line with slope 4 is steeper than the line with slope $\frac{1}{2}$. $$\|4\| > \left\|\frac{1}{2}\right\|$$	The line with slope -2 is steeper than the line with slope -1. $$\|-2\| > \|-1\|$$	The line with slope -3 is steeper than the line with slope $\frac{3}{4}$. $$\|-3\| > \left\|\frac{3}{4}\right\|$$

MATHEMATICAL PRACTICES

THINK AND DISCUSS

1. What is the rise shown in the graph? What is the run? What is the slope?

2. The rate of change of the profits of a company over one year is negative. How have the profits of the company changed over that year?

3. Would you rather climb a hill with a slope of 4 or a hill with a slope of $\frac{5}{2}$? Explain your answer.

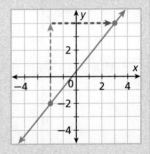

4. **GET ORGANIZED** Copy and complete the graphic organizer. In each box, sketch a line whose slope matches the given description.

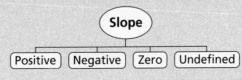

GUIDED PRACTICE

1. **Vocabulary** The *slope* of any nonvertical line is ___?___. (*positive* or *constant*)

SEE EXAMPLE 1

2. The table shows the volume of gasoline in a gas tank at different times. Find the rate of change for each time interval. During which time interval did the volume decrease at the greatest rate?

Time (h)	0	1	3	6	7
Volume (gal)	12	9	5	1	1

SEE EXAMPLE 2

3. The table shows a person's heart rate over time. Graph the data and show the rates of change.

Time (min)	0	2	5	7	10
Heart Rate (beats/min)	64	92	146	84	64

Find the slope of each line.

SEE EXAMPLE 3

4.

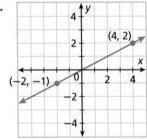

5.

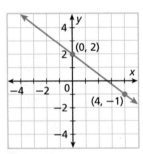

SEE EXAMPLE 4

6.

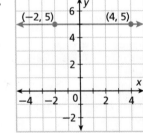

7.

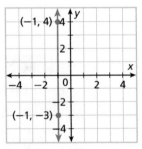

SEE EXAMPLE 5

Tell whether the slope of each line is positive, negative, zero, or undefined.

8.

9.

10.

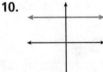

11.

PRACTICE AND PROBLEM SOLVING

Independent Practice

For Exercises	See Example
12	1
13	2
14–15	3
16–17	4
18–19	5

my.hrw.com

Online Extra Practice

12. The table shows the length of a baby at different ages. Find the rate of change for each time interval. Round your answers to the nearest tenth. During which time interval did the baby have the greatest growth rate?

Age (mo)	3	9	18	26	33
Length (in.)	23.5	27.5	31.6	34.5	36.7

13. The table shows the distance of an elevator from the ground floor at different times. Graph the data and show the rates of change.

Time (s)	0	15	23	30	35
Distance (m)	30	70	0	45	60

Find the slope of each line.

14.

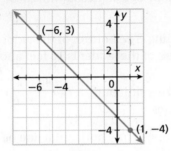

15.

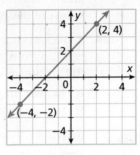

16.

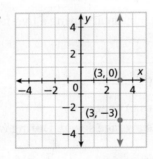

17.

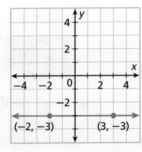

Tell whether the slope of each line is positive, negative, zero, or undefined.

18.

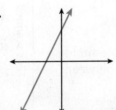

19.

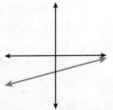

Travel

The Incline Railway's climb up Lookout Mountain has been called "America's Most Amazing Mile." A round-trip on the railway lasts about 1.5 hours.

20. Travel The Lookout Mountain Incline Railway in Chattanooga, Tennessee, is the steepest passenger railway in the world. A section of the railway has a slope of about 0.73. In this section, a vertical change of 1 unit corresponds to a horizontal change of what length? Round your answer to the nearest hundredth.

21. Critical Thinking Previously you learned that in a linear function, a constant change in x corresponds to a constant change in y. How is this related to slope?

22. **a.** The graph shows a relationship between a person's age and his or her estimated maximum heart rate in beats per minute. Find the slope.

    b. Describe the rate of change in this situation.

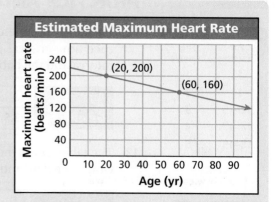

Estimated Maximum Heart Rate

(20, 200)

(60, 160)

Maximum heart rate (beats/min)

Age (yr)

23. **Construction** Most staircases in use today have 9-inch treads and $8\frac{1}{2}$-inch risers. What is the slope of a staircase with these measurements?

24. A ladder is leaned against a building. The bottom of the ladder is 9 feet from the building. The top of the ladder is 16 feet above the ground.

    a. Draw a diagram to represent this situation.

    b. What is the slope of the ladder?

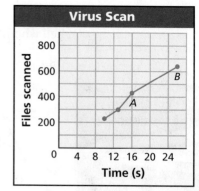

Tread

Riser

H.O.T. 25. Write About It Why will the slope of any horizontal line be 0? Why will the slope of any vertical line be undefined?

26. The table shows the distance traveled by a car during a five-hour road trip.

Time (h)	0	1	2	3	4	5
Distance (mi)	0	40	80	80	110	160

    a. Graph the data and show the rates of change.

    b. The rate of change represents the average speed. During which hour was the car's average speed the greatest?

27. **Estimation** The graph shows the number of files scanned by a computer virus detection program over time.

    a. Estimate the coordinates of point A.

    b. Estimate the coordinates of point B.

    c. Use your answers from parts **a** and **b** to estimate the rate of change (in files per second) between points A and B.

Virus Scan

Files scanned

B

A

Time (s)

H.O.T. 28. Data Collection Use a graphing calculator and a motion detector for the following. Set the equipment so that the graph shows distance on the y-axis and time on the x-axis.

    a. Experiment with walking in front of the motion detector. How must you walk to graph a straight line? Explain.

    b. Describe what you must do differently to graph a line with a positive slope vs. a line with a negative slope.

    c. How can you graph a line with slope 0? Explain.

TEST PREP

29. The slope of which line has the greatest absolute value?

Ⓐ line *A* Ⓒ line *C*

Ⓑ line *B* Ⓓ line *D*

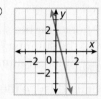

30. For which line is the run equal to 0?

Ⓐ line *A* Ⓒ line *C*

Ⓑ line *B* Ⓓ line *D*

31. Which line has a slope of 4?

Ⓕ   Ⓗ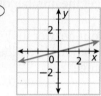

Ⓖ 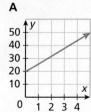   Ⓙ

CHALLENGE AND EXTEND

32. **Recreation** Tara and Jade are hiking up a hill. Each has a different stride. The run for Tara's stride is 32 inches, and the rise is 8 inches. The run for Jade's stride is 36 inches. What is the rise of Jade's stride?

H.O.T. 33. **Economics** The table shows cost in dollars charged by an electric company for various amounts of energy in kilowatt-hours.

Energy (kWh)	0	200	400	600	1000	2000
Cost ($)	3	3	31	59	115	150

   a. Graph the data and show the rates of change.

   b. Compare the rates of change for each interval. Are they all the same? Explain.

   c. What do the rates of change represent?

   d. Describe in words the electric company's billing plan.

FOCUS ON MATHEMATICAL PRACTICES

H.O.T. 34. **Estimation** Estimate each slope, then order them from least to greatest.

A   B   C   D

Explore Constant Changes

There are many real-life situations in which the amount of change is constant. In these activities, you will explore what happens when

• a quantity increases by a constant amount.

• a quantity decreases by a constant amount.

Use with Rate of Change and Slope

 Reason abstractly and quantitatively.

MCC9-12.F.IF.6 Calculate and interpret the average rate of change of a function (presented symbolically or as a table) over a specified interval. Estimate the rate of change from a graph.

Activity 1

Janice has read 7 books for her summer reading club. She plans to read 2 books each week for the rest of the summer. The table shows the total number of books that Janice will have read after different numbers of weeks have passed.

1 What number is added to the number of books in each row to get the number of books in the next row?

2 What does your answer to Problem 1 represent in Janice's situation? Describe the meaning of the constant change.

3 Graph the ordered pairs from the table. Describe how the points are related.

4 Look again at your answer to Problem 1. Explain how this number affects your graph.

Janice's Summer Reading	
Week	Total Books Read
0	7
1	9
2	11
3	13
4	15
5	17

Try This

At a particular college, a full-time student must take at least 12 credit hours per semester and may take up to 18 credit hours per semester. Tuition costs $200 per credit hour.

1. Copy and complete the table by using the information above.

2. What number is added to the cost in each row to get the cost in the next row?

3. What does your answer to Problem 2 above represent in the situation? Describe the meaning of the constant change.

4. Graph the ordered pairs from the table. Describe how the points are related.

5. Look again at your answer to Problem 2. Explain how this number affects your graph.

6. Compare your graphs from Activity 1 and Problem 4. How are they alike? How are they different?

7. **Make a Conjecture** Describe the graph of any situation that involves repeated addition of a positive number. Why do you think your description is correct?

Tuition Costs	
Credit Hours	Cost ($)
12	
13	
14	
15	
16	
17	
18	

Activity 2

An airplane is 3000 miles from its destination. The plane is traveling at a rate of 540 miles per hour. The table shows how far the plane is from its destination after various amounts of time have passed.

1 What number is subtracted from the distance in each row to get the distance in the next row?

2 What does your answer to Problem 1 represent in the situation? Describe the meaning of the constant change.

3 Graph the ordered pairs from the table. Describe how the points are related.

4 Look again at your answer to Problem 1. Explain how this number affects your graph.

Airplane's Distance	
Time (h)	Distance to Destination (mi)
0	3000
1	2460
2	1920
3	1380
4	840

Try This

A television game show begins with 20 contestants. Each week, the players vote 2 contestants off the show.

8. Copy and complete the table by using the information above.

9. What number is subtracted from the number of contestants in each row to get the number of contestants in the next row?

10. What does your answer to Problem 9 represent in the situation? Describe the meaning of the constant change.

11. Graph the ordered pairs from the table. Describe how the points are related.

12. Look again at your answer to Problem 9. Explain how this number affects your graph.

13. Compare your graphs from Activity 2 and Problem 11. How are they alike? How are they different?

14. Make a Conjecture Describe the graph of any situation that involves repeated subtraction of a positive number. Why do you think your description is correct?

15. Compare your two graphs from Activity 1 with your two graphs from Activity 2. How are they alike? How are they different?

16. Make a Conjecture How are graphs of situations involving repeated subtraction different from graphs of situations involving repeated addition? Explain your answer.

Game Show	
Week	Contestants Remaining
0	20
1	▦
2	▦
3	▦
4	▦
5	▦
6	▦

The Slope Formula

Essential Question: How can you calculate and interpret the slope of a linear function?

Objective
Find slope by using the slope formula.

Why learn this?
You can use the slope formula to find how quickly a quantity, such as the amount of water in a reservoir, is changing. (See Example 3.)

In a previous lesson, slope was described as the constant rate of change of a line. You saw how to find the slope of a line by using its graph.

There is also a formula you can use to find the slope of a line, which is usually represented by the letter m. To use this formula, you need the coordinates of two different points on the line.

Slope Formula		
WORDS	**FORMULA**	**EXAMPLE**
The slope of a line is the ratio of the difference in y-values to the difference in x-values between any two different points on the line.	If (x_1, y_1) and (x_2, y_2) are any two different points on a line, the slope of the line is $m = \frac{y_2 - y_1}{x_2 - x_1}$.	If $(2, -3)$ and $(1, 4)$ are two points on a line, the slope of the line is $m = \frac{4 - (-3)}{1 - 2} = \frac{7}{-1} = -7$.

COMMON CORE GPS
MCC9-12.F.IF.6

EXAMPLE 1 **Finding Slope by Using the Slope Formula**

Find the slope of the line that contains $(4, -2)$ and $(-1, 2)$.

my.hrw.com

Online Video Tutor

$m = \dfrac{y_2 - y_1}{x_2 - x_1}$ *Use the slope formula.*

$= \dfrac{2 - (-2)}{-1 - 4}$ *Substitute $(4, -2)$ for (x_1, y_1) and $(-1, 2)$ for (x_2, y_2).*

$= \dfrac{4}{-5}$ *Simplify.*

$= -\dfrac{4}{5}$

The slope of the line that contains $(4, -2)$ and $(-1, 2)$ is $-\dfrac{4}{5}$.

 1a. Find the slope of the line that contains $(-2, -2)$ and $(7, -2)$.

1b. Find the slope of the line that contains $(5, -7)$ and $(6, -4)$.

1c. Find the slope of the line that contains $\left(\dfrac{3}{4}, \dfrac{7}{5}\right)$ and $\left(\dfrac{1}{4}, \dfrac{2}{5}\right)$.

Sometimes you are not given two points to use in the formula. You might have to choose two points from a graph or a table.

EXAMPLE 2

Finding Slope from Graphs and Tables

Each graph or table shows a linear relationship. Find the slope.

A

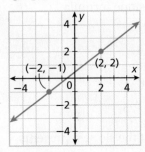

Let $(2, 2)$ be (x_1, y_1) and $(-2, -1)$ be (x_2, y_2).

$m = \dfrac{y_2 - y_1}{x_2 - x_1}$ *Use the slope formula.*

$= \dfrac{-1 - 2}{-2 - 2}$ *Substitute $(2, 2)$ for (x_1, y_1) and $(-2, -1)$ for (x_2, y_2).*

$= \dfrac{-3}{-4}$ *Simplify.*

$= \dfrac{3}{4}$

B

x	2	2	2	2
y	0	1	3	5

Step 1 Choose any two points from the table. Let $(2, 0)$ be (x_1, y_1) and $(2, 3)$ be (x_2, y_2).

Step 2 Use the slope formula.

$m = \dfrac{y_2 - y_1}{x_2 - x_1}$ *Use the slope formula.*

$= \dfrac{3 - 0}{2 - 2}$ *Substitute $(2, 0)$ for (x_1, y_1) and $(2, 3)$ for (x_2, y_2).*

$= \dfrac{3}{0}$ *Simplify.*

The slope is undefined.

 CHECK IT OUT!

Each graph or table shows a linear relationship. Find the slope.

2a.

2b.

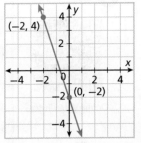

2c.

x	0	2	5	6
y	1	5	11	13

2d.

x	-2	0	2	4
y	3	0	-3	-6

Remember that slope is a rate of change. In real-world problems, finding the slope can give you information about how a quantity is changing.

EXAMPLE 3 MCC9-12.F.IF.4

Environmental Science Application

The graph shows how much water is in a reservoir at different times. Find the slope of the line. Then tell what the slope represents.

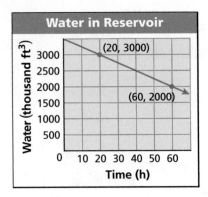

Water in Reservoir

Step 1 Use the slope formula.

$$m = \frac{y_2 - y_1}{x_2 - x_1}$$

$$= \frac{2000 - 3000}{60 - 20}$$

$$= \frac{-1000}{40} = -25$$

Step 2 Tell what the slope represents.

In this situation, y represents volume of water and x represents time.

So slope represents $\frac{\text{change in volume}}{\text{change in time}}$ in units of $\frac{\text{thousands of cubic feet}}{\text{hours}}$.

A slope of -25 means the amount of water in the reservoir is decreasing (negative change) at a rate of 25 thousand cubic feet each hour.

3. The graph shows the height of a plant over a period of days. Find the slope of the line. Then tell what the slope represents.

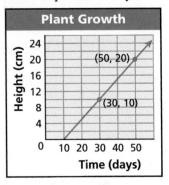

Plant Growth

If you know the equation that describes a line, you can find its slope by using any two ordered-pair solutions. It is often easiest to use the ordered pairs that contain the intercepts.

EXAMPLE 4 MCC9-12.F.IF.6

Finding Slope from an Equation

Find the slope of the line described by $6x - 5y = 30$.

Step 1 Find the x-intercept.

$6x - 5y = 30$

$6x - 5(0) = 30$ *Let y = 0.*

$6x = 30$

$\frac{6x}{6} = \frac{30}{6}$

$x = 5$

Step 2 Find the y-intercept.

$6x - 5y = 30$

$6(0) - 5y = 30$ *Let x = 0.*

$-5y = 30$

$\frac{-5y}{-5} = \frac{30}{-5}$

$y = -6$

Step 3 The line contains $(5, 0)$ and $(0, -6)$. Use the slope formula.

$$m = \frac{y_2 - y_1}{x_2 - x_1} = \frac{-6 - 0}{0 - 5} = \frac{-6}{-5} = \frac{6}{5}$$

4. Find the slope of the line described by $2x + 3y = 12$.

THINK AND DISCUSS

1. The slope of a line is the difference of the ____?____ divided by the difference of the ____?____ for any two points on the line.

2. Two points lie on a line. When you substitute their coordinates into the slope formula, the value of the denominator is 0. Describe this line.

3. **GET ORGANIZED** Copy and complete the graphic organizer. In each box, describe how to find slope using the given method.

Finding Slope
From a graph | From a table | From an equation

10-4 Exercises

my.hrw.com
Homework Help

GUIDED PRACTICE

SEE EXAMPLE 1
Find the slope of the line that contains each pair of points.

1. $(3, 6)$ and $(6, 9)$

2. $(2, 7)$ and $(4, 4)$

3. $(-1, -5)$ and $(-9, -1)$

SEE EXAMPLE 2
Each graph or table shows a linear relationship. Find the slope.

4.
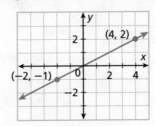

5.

x	y
0	25
2	45
4	65
6	85

SEE EXAMPLE 3
Find the slope of each line. Then tell what the slope represents.

6.
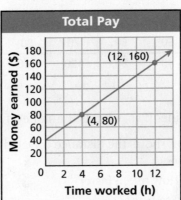

7.
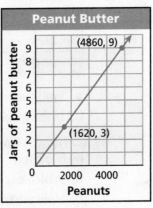

SEE EXAMPLE 4
Find the slope of the line described by each equation.

8. $8x + 2y = 96$

9. $5x = 90 - 9y$

10. $5y = 160 + 9x$

PRACTICE AND PROBLEM SOLVING

Independent Practice

For Exercises	See Example
11–13	1
14–15	2
16–17	3
18–20	4

my.hrw.com

Online Extra Practice

Find the slope of the line that contains each pair of points.

11. $(2, 5)$ and $(3, 1)$ **12.** $(-9, -5)$ and $(6, -5)$ **13.** $(3, 4)$ and $(3, -1)$

Each graph or table shows a linear relationship. Find the slope.

14.

x	y
1	18.5
2	22
3	25.5
4	29

15.

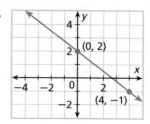

Find the slope of each line. Then tell what the slope represents.

16.

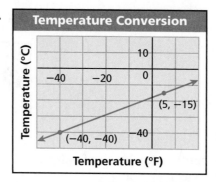

17.

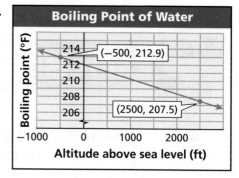

Find the slope of the line described by each equation.

18. $7x + 13y = 91$ **19.** $5y = 130 - 13x$ **20.** $7 - 3y = 9x$

H.O.T. **21.** ⫻ **ERROR ANALYSIS** ⫻ Two students found the slope of the line that contains $(-6, 3)$ and $(2, -1)$. Who is incorrect? Explain the error.

A
$$m = \frac{-1 - 3}{2 - (-6)} = \frac{-4}{8} = -\frac{1}{2}$$

B
$$m = \frac{-1 - 3}{-6 - 2} = \frac{-4}{-8} = \frac{1}{2}$$

H.O.T. **22.** **Environmental Science** The table shows how the number of cricket chirps per minute changes with the air temperature.

Temperature (°F)	40	50	60	70	80	90
Chirps per minute	0	40	80	120	160	200

   a. Find the rates of change.

   b. Is the graph of the data a line? If so, what is the slope? If not, explain why not.

23. **Critical Thinking** The graph shows the distance traveled by two cars.

   a. Which car is going faster? How much faster?

   b. How are the speeds related to slope?

   c. At what rate is the distance between the cars changing?

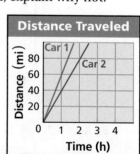

H.O.T. **24.** **Write About It** You are given the coordinates of two points on a line. Describe two different ways to find the slope of that line.

Real-World Connections

25. **a.** One way to estimate your maximum heart rate is to subtract your age from 220. Write a function to describe the relationship between maximum heart rate y and age x.

b. The graph of this function is a line. Find its slope. Then tell what the slope represents.

TEST PREP

26. The equation $2y + 3x = -6$ describes a line with what slope?

(A) $\frac{3}{2}$ (B) 0 (C) $\frac{1}{2}$ (D) $-\frac{3}{2}$

27. A line with slope $-\frac{1}{3}$ could pass through which of the following pairs of points?

(F) $\left(0, -\frac{1}{3}\right)$ and $(1, 1)$ (H) $(0, 0)$ and $\left(-\frac{1}{3}, -\frac{1}{3}\right)$

(G) $(-6, 5)$ and $(-3, 4)$ (J) $(5, -6)$ and $(4, 3)$

28. **Gridded Response** Find the slope of the line that contains $(-1, 2)$ and $(5, 5)$.

CHALLENGE AND EXTEND

Find the slope of the line that contains each pair of points.

29. $(a, 0)$ and $(0, b)$ 30. $(2x, y)$ and $(x, 3y)$ 31. (x, y) and $(x + 2, 3 - y)$

Find the value of x so that the points lie on a line with the given slope.

32. $(x, 2)$ and $(-5, 8)$, $m = -1$ 33. $(4, x)$ and $(6, 3x)$, $m = \frac{1}{2}$

34. $(1, -3)$ and $(3, x)$, $m = -1$ 35. $(-10, -4)$ and (x, x), $m = \frac{1}{7}$

36. A line contains the point $(1, 2)$ and has a slope of $\frac{1}{2}$. Use the slope formula to find another point on this line.

37. The points $(-2, 4)$, $(0, 2)$, and $(3, x - 1)$ all lie on the same line. What is the value of x? (*Hint:* Remember that the slope of a line is constant for any two points on the line.)

MATHEMATICAL PRACTICES

FOCUS ON MATHEMATICAL PRACTICES

H.O.T. 38. **Error Analysis** Kayla incorrectly estimated that the slope of a line segment connecting the points $(3, 21)$ and $(45, 61)$ is slightly greater than 1. Name one way that she could have made this mistake.

H.O.T. 39. **Problem Solving** A bicyclist starts traveling back to town at a speed of 16 miles per hour from a rest stop 56 miles away. Write ordered pairs that relate her hours traveled to her distance from town after 1 hour of biking and after 3 hours of biking. Then, find the slope between the two points. What does the sign of the slope mean in this context?

Ready to Go On?

my.hrw.com
Assessment and Intervention

10-1 Identifying Linear Functions

Tell whether the given ordered pairs satisfy a linear function. Explain.

1.

x	−2	−1	0	1	2
y	1	0	1	4	9

2. $\{(-3, 8), (-2, 6), (-1, 4), (0, 2), (1, 0)\}$

10-2 Using Intercepts

Use intercepts to graph the line described by each equation.

3. $2x - 4y = 16$ **4.** $-3y + 6x = -18$ **5.** $y = -3x + 3$

10-3 Rate of Change and Slope

6. The chart gives the amount of water in a rain gauge in inches at various times. Graph the data and show the rates of change.

Time (h)	1	2	3	4	5
Rain (in.)	0.2	0.4	0.7	0.8	1.0

7. Find the slope of the line graphed below.

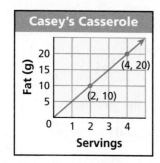

Casey's Casserole

10-4 The Slope Formula

Find the slope of each line. Then tell what the slope represents.

8.

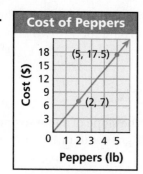

Cost of Peppers

9.

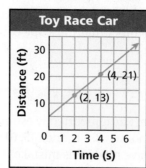

Toy Race Car

10.

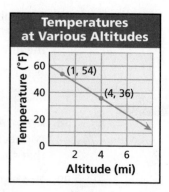

Temperatures at Various Altitudes

Selected Response

1. Tell whether the set of ordered pairs {(1, 1),(3, 5), (5, 9), (7, 13)} is a linear function. Explain.

   Ⓐ No; there is a constant change in x that corresponds to a constant change in y.

   Ⓑ Yes; there is no constant change in x that corresponds to a constant change in y.

   Ⓒ No; there is no constant change in x that corresponds to a constant change in y.

   Ⓓ Yes; there is a constant change in x that corresponds to a constant change in y.

2. This table shows the number of swimmers in the ocean at a given time. Find the rate of change for each time period. During which period did the number of swimmers increase at the fastest rate?

Time	10:30 am	12:30 pm	1:30 pm	3:30 pm	5:30 pm
Number of swimmers	41	55	64	70	80

   Ⓕ Between 10:30 and 12:30: 7 $\frac{\text{swimmers}}{\text{hour}}$

   Ⓖ Between 3:30 and 5:30: 5 $\frac{\text{swimmers}}{\text{hour}}$

   Ⓗ Between 12:30 and 1:30: 9 $\frac{\text{swimmers}}{\text{hour}}$

   Ⓙ Between 1:30 and 3:30: 3 $\frac{\text{swimmers}}{\text{hour}}$

3. Identify whether each graph represents a function. If the graph does represent a function, is the function linear?

Graph A

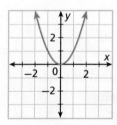

Graph B

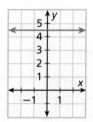

Graph C

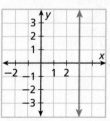

   Ⓐ Graph A: not a linear function
       Graph B: not a function
       Graph C: not a function

   Ⓑ Graph A: not a function
       Graph B: not a function
       Graph C: linear function

   Ⓒ Graph A: not a linear function
       Graph B: linear function
       Graph C: linear function

   Ⓓ Graph A: not a linear function
       Graph B: linear function
       Graph C: not a function

4. Find the x- and y-intercepts of $-x + 2y = 8$.

   Ⓕ x-intercept: -8, y-intercept: 4

   Ⓖ x-intercept: -8, y-intercept: 3

   Ⓗ x-intercept: -11, y-intercept: 4

   Ⓙ x-intercept: -11, y-intercept: 3

5. Find the slope of the line that contains (1, 6) and (10, −9).

   Ⓐ $-\frac{3}{11}$ Ⓒ $-\frac{5}{3}$

   Ⓑ $-\frac{3}{5}$ Ⓓ $-\frac{11}{3}$

6. Find the x- and y-intercepts.

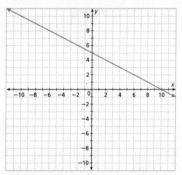

   Ⓕ x-intercept: 10, y-intercept: 5

   Ⓖ x-intercept: 5, y-intercept: 10

   Ⓗ x-intercept: -10, y-intercept: 5

   Ⓙ x-intercept: 10, y-intercept: -5

Mini-Task

7. Find the value of a such that the points $(4, a)$ and $(8, 3a)$ lie on a line with slope $m = \frac{1}{3}$.

UNIT 3

Module

11 Graphs and Equations of Linear Functions

COMMON CORE GPS

Contents

MATHEMATICAL PRACTICES

The Common Core Georgia Performance Standards for Mathematical Practice describe varieties of expertise that all students should seek to develop. Opportunities to develop these practices are integrated throughout this program.

1 Make sense of problems and persevere in solving them.
2 Reason abstractly and quantitatively.
3 Construct viable arguments and critique the reasoning of others.
4 Model with mathematics.
5 Use appropriate tools strategically.
6 Attend to precision.
7 Look for and make use of structure.
8 Look for and express regularity in repeated reasoning.

Unpacking the Standards

Understanding the standards and the vocabulary terms in the standards will help you
know exactly what you are expected to learn in this chapter.

 MCC9-12.A.CED.2

Create equations in two … variables
to represent relationships between
quantities; graph equations on
coordinate axes with labels and scales.

Key Vocabulary

equation (ecuación)
A mathematical statement that two
expressions are equivalent.

What It Means For You

You can represent mathematical relationships with words,
equations, tables, and graphs.

EXAMPLE

Membership costs $150 plus $75 per month.

$$y = 75x + 150$$

Months	0	1	2	3	4
Cost ($)	150	225	300	375	450

Gym Membership

 MCC9-12.F.BF.3

Identify the effect on the graph of
replacing $f(x)$ by $f(x) + k$, $k\,f(x)$, $f(kx)$, and
$f(x + k)$ for specific values of k (both
positive and negative); …

Key Vocabulary

function notation (notación de función)
If x is the independent variable and
y is the dependent variable, then the
function notation for y is $f(x)$, read
"f of x," where f names the function.

What It Means For You

You can change a function by adding or multiplying by a constant.
The result will be a new function that is a transformation of the
original function.

EXAMPLE   Vertical translations of the function $f(x) = x$

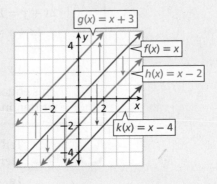

Direct Variation

? **Essential Question:** How can you identify, write, and graph direct variation equations?

Objective
Identify, write, and graph direct variation.

Vocabulary
direct variation
constant of variation

Who uses this?
Chefs can use direct variation to determine ingredients needed for a certain number of servings.

A recipe for paella calls for 1 cup of rice to make 5 servings. In other words, a chef needs 1 cup of rice for every 5 servings.

Paella is a rice dish that originated in Valencia, Spain.

Rice (c) *x*	1	2	3	4
Servings *y*	5	10	15	20

The equation $y = 5x$ describes this relationship. In this relationship, the number of servings *varies directly* with the number of cups of rice.

A **direct variation** is a special type of linear relationship that can be written in the form $y = kx$, where k is a nonzero constant called the **constant of variation**.

EXAMPLE 1 MCC9-12.F.LE.1b

my.hrw.com

Online Video Tutor

Identifying Direct Variations from Equations

Tell whether each equation represents a direct variation. If so, identify the constant of variation.

A $y = 4x$

This equation represents a direct variation because it is in the form $y = kx$. The constant of variation is 4.

B $-3x + 5y = 0$

$$-3x + 5y = 0 \qquad \text{Solve the equation for } y.$$
$$\underline{+3x \qquad\quad +3x} \qquad \text{Since } -3x \text{ is added to } 5y, \text{ add } 3x \text{ to both sides.}$$
$$5y = 3x$$
$$\frac{5y}{5} = \frac{3x}{5} \qquad \text{Since } y \text{ is multiplied by 5, divide both sides by 5.}$$
$$y = \frac{3}{5}x$$

This equation represents a direct variation because it can be written in the form $y = kx$. The constant of variation is $\frac{3}{5}$.

C $2x + y = 10$

$$2x + y = 10 \qquad \text{Solve the equation for } y.$$
$$\underline{-2x \qquad\quad -2x} \qquad \text{Since } 2x \text{ is added to } y, \text{ subtract } 2x \text{ from both sides.}$$
$$y = -2x + 10$$

This equation does not represent a direct variation because it cannot be written in the form $y = kx$.

 CHECK IT OUT! Tell whether each equation represents a direct variation. If so, identify the constant of variation.

1a. $3y = 4x + 1$ **1b.** $3x = -4y$ **1c.** $y + 3x = 0$

What happens if you solve $y = kx$ for k?

$$y = kx$$

$$\frac{y}{x} = \frac{kx}{x} \qquad \textit{Divide both sides by x (x \neq 0).}$$

$$\frac{y}{x} = k$$

So, in a direct variation, the ratio $\frac{y}{x}$ is equal to the constant of variation. Another way to identify a direct variation is to check whether $\frac{y}{x}$ is the same for each ordered pair (except where $x = 0$).

 **EXAMPLE** MCC9-12.F.LE.1b **2**

Identifying Direct Variations from Ordered Pairs

Tell whether each relationship is a direct variation. Explain.

my.hrw.com

Online Video Tutor

A

x	1	3	5
y	6	18	30

Method 1 Write an equation.

$y = 6x$ *Each y-value is 6 times the corresponding x-value.*

This is a direct variation because it can be written as $y = kx$, where $k = 6$.

Method 2 Find $\frac{y}{x}$ for each ordered pair.

$$\frac{6}{1} = 6 \qquad\qquad \frac{18}{3} = 6 \qquad\qquad \frac{30}{5} = 6$$

This is a direct variation because $\frac{y}{x}$ is the same for each ordered pair.

B

x	2	4	8
y	−2	0	4

Method 1 Write an equation.

$y = x - 4$ *Each y-value is 4 less than the corresponding x-value.*

This is not a direct variation because it cannot be written as $y = kx$.

Method 2 Find $\frac{y}{x}$ for each ordered pair.

$$\frac{-2}{2} = -1 \qquad\qquad \frac{0}{4} = 0 \qquad\qquad \frac{4}{8} = \frac{1}{2}$$

This is not a direct variation because $\frac{y}{x}$ is not the same for all ordered pairs.

 Tell whether each relationship is a direct variation. Explain.

2a.

x	y
−3	0
1	3
3	6

2b.

x	y
2.5	−10
5	−20
7.5	−30

2c.

x	y
−2	5
1	3
4	1

If you know one ordered pair that satisfies a direct variation, you can write the equation. You can also find other ordered pairs that satisfy the direct variation.

EXAMPLE 3 MCC9-12.A.CED.2

Writing and Solving Direct Variation Equations

The value of y varies directly with x, and $y = 6$ when $x = 12$. Find y when $x = 27$.

Method 1 Find the value of k and then write the equation.

$y = kx$ *Write the equation for a direct variation.*

$6 = k(12)$ *Substitute 6 for y and 12 for x. Solve for k.*

$\dfrac{1}{2} = k$ *Since k is multiplied by 12, divide both sides by 12.*

The equation is $y = \dfrac{1}{2}x$. When $x = 27$, $y = \dfrac{1}{2}(27) = 13.5$.

Method 2 Use a proportion.

$\dfrac{6}{12} \diagdown \dfrac{y}{27}$ *In a direct variation, $\dfrac{y}{x}$ is the same for all values of x and y.*

$12y = 162$ *Use cross products.*

$y = 13.5$ *Since y is multiplied by 12, divide both sides by 12.*

 CHECK IT OUT!

3. The value of y varies directly with x, and $y = 4.5$ when $x = 0.5$. Find y when $x = 10$.

EXAMPLE 4 MCC9-12.A.CED.2

Graphing Direct Variations

The three-toed sloth is an extremely slow animal. On the ground, it travels at a speed of about 6 feet per minute. Write a direct variation equation for the distance y a sloth will travel in x minutes. Then graph.

Step 1 Write a direct variation equation.

distance	=	6 feet per minute	times	number of minutes
y	$=$	6	$\cdot$	x

Step 2 Choose values of x and generate ordered pairs.

x	$y = 6x$	(x, y)
0	$y = 6(0) = 0$	$(0, 0)$
1	$y = 6(1) = 6$	$(1, 6)$
2	$y = 6(2) = 12$	$(2, 12)$

Step 3 Graph the points and connect.

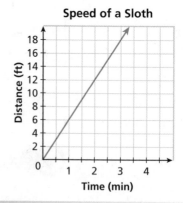

Speed of a Sloth

 CHECK IT OUT!

4. The perimeter y of a square varies directly with its side length x. Write a direct variation equation for this relationship. Then graph.

Look at the graph in Example 4. It passes through $(0, 0)$ and has a slope of 6. The graph of any direct variation $y = kx$

- is a line through $(0, 0)$.
- has a slope of k.

THINK AND DISCUSS

1. How do you know that a direct variation is linear?

2. How does the graph of a direct variation differ from the graphs of other types of linear relationships?

3. **GET ORGANIZED** Copy and complete the graphic organizer. In each box, describe how you can use the given information to identify a direct variation.

Recognizing a Direct Variation		
From an Equation	From Ordered Pairs	From a Graph

11-1 Exercises

my.hrw.com
Homework Help

GUIDED PRACTICE

1. **Vocabulary** If x varies directly with y, then the relationship between the two variables is said to be a ____?____. (*direct variation* or *constant of variation*)

SEE EXAMPLE 1 Tell whether each equation represents a direct variation. If so, identify the constant of variation.

2. $y = 4x + 9$

3. $2y = -8x$

4. $x + y = 0$

SEE EXAMPLE 2 Tell whether each relationship is a direct variation. Explain.

5.
x	10	5	2
y	12	7	4

6.
x	3	-1	-4
y	-6	2	8

SEE EXAMPLE 3

7. The value of y varies directly with x, and $y = -3$ when $x = 1$. Find y when $x = -6$.

8. The value of y varies directly with x, and $y = 6$ when $x = 18$. Find y when $x = 12$.

SEE EXAMPLE 4

9. **Wages** Cameron earns $7 per hour at her after-school job. The total amount of her paycheck varies directly with the amount of time she works. Write a direct variation equation for the amount of money y that she earns for working x hours. Then graph.

PRACTICE AND PROBLEM SOLVING

Tell whether each equation represents a direct variation. If so, identify the constant of variation.

10. $y = \frac{1}{6}x$

11. $4y = x$

12. $x = 2y - 12$

Tell whether each relationship is a direct variation. Explain.

13.
x	6	9	17
y	13.2	19.8	37.4

14.
x	-6	3	12
y	4	-2	-8

Independent Practice

For Exercises	See Example
10–12	1
13–14	2
15–16	3
17	4

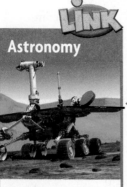

my.hrw.com

Online Extra Practice

15. The value of y varies directly with x, and $y = 8$ when $x = -32$. Find y when $x = 64$.

16. The value of y varies directly with x, and $y = \frac{1}{2}$ when $x = 3$. Find y when $x = 1$.

17. While on his way to school, Norman saw that the cost of gasoline was $2.50 per gallon. Write a direct variation equation to describe the cost y of x gallons of gas. Then graph.

Tell whether each relationship is a direct variation. Explain your answer.

18. The equation $-15x + 4y = 0$ relates the length of a videotape in inches x to its approximate playing time in seconds y.

19. The equation $y - 2.00x = 2.50$ relates the cost y of a taxicab ride to distance x of the cab ride in miles.

Each ordered pair is a solution of a direct variation. Write the equation of direct variation. Then graph your equation and show that the slope of the line is equal to the constant of variation.

20. $(2, 10)$ **21.** $(-3, 9)$ **22.** $(8, 2)$ **23.** $(1.5, 6)$

24. $(7, 21)$ **25.** $(1, 2)$ **26.** $(2, -16)$ **27.** $\left(\frac{1}{7}, 1\right)$

28. $(-2, 9)$ **29.** $(9, -2)$ **30.** $(4, 6)$ **31.** $(3, 4)$

32. $(5, 1)$ **33.** $(1, -6)$ **34.** $\left(-1, \frac{1}{2}\right)$ **35.** $(7, 2)$

Astronomy

36. **Astronomy** Weight varies directly with gravity. A Mars lander weighed 767 pounds on Earth but only 291 pounds on Mars. Its accompanying Mars rover weighed 155 pounds on Mars. How much did it weigh on Earth? Round your answer to the nearest pound.

The Mars rover *Spirit* landed on Mars in January 2004 and immediately began sending photos of the planet's surface back to Earth.

37. **Environment** Mischa bought an energy-efficient washing machine. She will save about 15 gallons of water per wash load.

  a. Write an equation of direct variation to describe how many gallons of water y Mischa saves for x loads of laundry she washes.

  b. Graph your direct variation from part **a.** Is every point on the graph a solution in this situation? Why or why not?

  c. If Mischa does 2 loads of laundry per week, how many gallons of water will she have saved at the end of a year?

H.O.T. 38. **Critical Thinking** If you double an x-value in a direct variation, will the corresponding y-value double? Explain.

H.O.T. 39. **Write About It** In a direct variation $y = kx$, k is sometimes called the "constant of proportionality." How are proportions related to direct variations?

Real-World Connections

40. Rhea exercised on a treadmill at the gym. When she was finished, the display showed that she had walked at an average speed of 3 miles per hour.

  a. Write an equation that gives the number of miles y that Rhea would cover in x hours if she walked at this speed.

  b. Explain why this is a direct variation and find the value of k. What does this value represent in Rhea's situation?

TEST PREP

41. Which equation does NOT represent a direct variation?

(A) $y = \frac{1}{3}x$ (B) $y = -2x$ (C) $y = 4x + 1$ (D) $6x - y = 0$

42. Identify which set of data represents a direct variation.

(F)

x	1	2	3
y	1	2	3

(H)

x	1	2	3
y	3	5	7

(G)

x	1	2	3
y	0	1	2

(J)

x	1	2	3
y	3	4	5

43. Two yards of fabric cost $13, and 5 yards of fabric cost $32.50. Which equation relates the cost of the fabric c to its length ℓ?

(A) $c = 2.6\ell$ (B) $c = 6.5\ell$ (C) $c = 13\ell$ (D) $c = 32.5\ell$

44. Gridded Response A car is traveling at a constant speed. After 3 hours, the car has traveled 180 miles. If the car continues to travel at the same constant speed, how many hours will it take to travel a total of 270 miles?

CHALLENGE AND EXTEND

45. Transportation The function $y = 20x$ gives the number of miles y that a sport-utility vehicle (SUV) can travel on x gallons of gas. The function $y = 60x$ gives the number of miles y that a hybrid car can travel on x gallons of gas.

  a. If you drive 120 miles, how much gas will you save by driving the hybrid instead of the SUV?

  b. Graph both functions on the same coordinate plane. Will the lines ever meet other than at the origin? Explain.

  c. What if...? Shannon drives 15,000 miles in one year. How many gallons of gas will she use if she drives the SUV? the hybrid?

46. Suppose the equation $ax + by = c$, where a, b, and c are real numbers, describes a direct variation. What do you know about the value of c?

FOCUS ON MATHEMATICAL PRACTICES

MATHEMATICAL
PRACTICES

H.O.T. 47. Error Analysis Jon is on the 30th floor of a building where each floor is 10 feet high. The building next door has floors that are 12 feet high. Jon sets up the direct variation equation $30 = 10k$, solves for k, and calculates that the floor across from him in the other building is the 36th floor. What error did Jon make? What is the correct answer?

H.O.T. 48. Communication Write three different direct variation equations that have 0.75 as the constant of variation. Use different coefficients and variables in each equation and identify each independent variable.

H.O.T. 49. Problem Solving The function $p = 10 + 12t$ gives the cost of renting a kayak at Boatwerks for t hours, and $p = 10 + 7t$ gives the cost of renting a paddleboard. Subtract $10 + 7t$ from $10 + 12t$ to create a new function.

  a. What does the new function represent?

  b. Which, if any, of the three functions represents direct variation?

11-2 Slope-Intercept Form

Essential Question: How can you write a linear equation in slope-intercept form and use that form to draw its graph?

Objectives
Write a linear equation in slope-intercept form.

Graph a line using slope-intercept form.

Who uses this?
Consumers can use slope-intercept form to model and calculate costs, such as the cost of renting a moving van. (See Example 4.)

You have seen that you can graph a line if you know two points on the line. Another way is to use the slope of the line and the point that contains the y-intercept.

 COMMON CORE GPS
MCC9-12.F.IF.7a

EXAMPLE 1 Graphing by Using Slope and y-intercept

Graph the line with slope -2 and y-intercept 4.

my.hrw.com

Online Video Tutor

Step 1 The y-intercept is 4, so the line contains $(0, 4)$. Plot $(0, 4)$.

Step 2 Slope $= \dfrac{\text{change in } y}{\text{change in } x} = \dfrac{-2}{1}$

Count 2 units down and 1 unit right from $(0, 4)$ and plot another point.

Step 3 Draw the line through the two points.

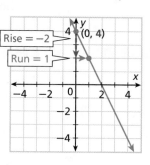

Writing Math

Any integer can be written as a fraction with 1 in the denominator.

$-2 = \dfrac{-2}{1}$

CHECK IT OUT!

Graph each line given the slope and y-intercept.

1a. slope $= 2$, y-intercept $= -3$　**1b.** slope $= -\dfrac{2}{3}$, y-intercept $= 1$

If you know the slope of a line and the y-intercept, you can write an equation that describes the line.

Step 1 If a line has slope 2 and the y-intercept is 3, then $m = 2$ and $(0, 3)$ is on the line. Substitute these values into the slope formula.

Slope formula $\rightarrow m = \dfrac{y_2 - y_1}{x_2 - x_1}$　　$2 = \dfrac{y - 3}{x - 0}$ ←Since you don't know (x_2, y_2), use (x, y).

Step 2 Solve for y: $2 = \dfrac{y - 3}{x - 0}$

$2 = \dfrac{y - 3}{x}$　　　*Simplify the denominator.*

$2 \cdot x = \left(\dfrac{y - 3}{x}\right) \cdot x$　　*Multiply both sides by x.*

$2x = y - 3$

$\underline{+3 \qquad +3}$　　　*Add 3 to both sides.*

$2x + 3 = y$, or $y = 2x + 3$

280 *Module 11 Graphs and Equations of Linear Functions*

Slope-Intercept Form of a Linear Equation

If a line has **slope m** and the **y-intercept** is b, then the line is described by the equation $y = mx + b$.

Any linear equation can be written in slope-intercept form by solving for y and simplifying. In this form, you can immediately see the slope and y-intercept. Also, you can quickly graph a line when the equation is written in slope-intercept form.

COMMON CORE GPS

EXAMPLE **2**
MCC9-12.A.CED.2

 my.hrw.com

Online Video Tutor

Animated Math

Writing Linear Equations in Slope-Intercept Form

Write the equation that describes each line in slope-intercept form.

A slope $= \dfrac{1}{3}$, y-intercept $= 6$

$y = mx + b$ *Substitute the given*
$y = \dfrac{1}{3}x + 6$ *values for m and b.*
               Simplify if necessary.

B slope $= 0$, y-intercept $= -5$

$y = mx + b$
$y = 0x + (-5)$
$y = -5$

C

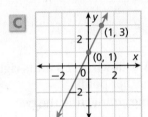

Step 1 Find the y-intercept. The graph crosses the y-axis at $(0, 1)$, so $b = 1$.

Step 2 Find the slope. The line contains the points $(0, 1)$ and $(1, 3)$.

$m = \dfrac{y_2 - y_1}{x_2 - x_1}$ *Use the slope formula.*

$m = \dfrac{3 - 1}{1 - 0} = \dfrac{2}{1} = 2$ *Substitute (0, 1) for (x_1, y_1) and (1, 3) for (x_2, y_2).*

Step 3 Write the equation.

$y = mx + b$ *Write the slope-intercept form.*
$y = 2x + 1$ *Substitute 2 for m and 1 for b.*

D slope $= 4$, $(2, 5)$ is on the line

Step 1 Find the y-intercept.

$y = mx + b$ *Write the slope-intercept form.*
$5 = 4(2) + b$ *Substitute 4 for m, 2 for x, and 5 for y.*
$5 = 8 + b$ *Solve for b. Since 8 is added to b, subtract 8 from both*
$\underline{-8 \quad -8}$ *sides to undo the addition.*
$-3 = b$

Step 2 Write the equation.

$y = mx + b$ *Write the slope-intercept form.*
$y = 4x + (-3)$ *Substitute 4 for m and −3 for b.*
$y = 4x - 3$

Write the equation that describes each line in slope-intercept form.

2a. slope $= -12$, y-intercept $= -\dfrac{1}{2}$

2b. slope $= 1$, y-intercept $= 0$

2c. slope $= 8$, $(-3, 1)$ is on the line.

my.hrw.com

Online Video Tutor

EXAMPLE 3 Using Slope-Intercept Form to Graph
MCC9-12.F.IF.7a

Write each equation in slope-intercept form. Then graph the line described by the equation.

A $y = 4x - 3$

$y = 4x - 3$ is in the form $y = mx + b$.

slope: $m = 4 = \frac{4}{1}$

y-intercept: $b = -3$

Step 1 Plot $(0, -3)$.

Step 2 Count 4 units up and 1 unit right and plot another point.

Step 3 Draw the line connecting the two points.

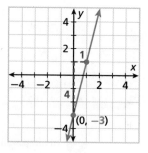

B $y = -\frac{2}{3}x + 2$

$y = -\frac{2}{3}x + 2$ is in the form $y = mx + b$.

slope: $m = -\frac{2}{3} = \frac{-2}{3}$

y-intercept: $b = 2$

Step 1 Plot $(0, 2)$

Step 2 Count 2 units down and 3 units right and plot another point.

Step 3 Draw the line connecting the two points.

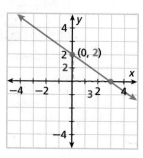

C $3x + 2y = 8$

Step 1 Write the equation in slope-intercept form by solving for y.

$$3x + 2y = 8$$
$$\underline{-3x \qquad -3x} \qquad \text{Subtract } 3x \text{ from both sides.}$$
$$2y = 8 - 3x$$
$$\frac{2y}{2} = \frac{8 - 3x}{2} \qquad \text{Since } y \text{ is multiplied by 2, divide both sides by 2.}$$
$$y = 4 - \frac{3}{2}x \qquad \frac{3x}{2} = \frac{3}{2}x$$
$$y = -\frac{3}{2}x + 4 \qquad \text{Write the equation in the form } y = mx + b.$$

Step 2 Graph the line.

$y = -\frac{3}{2}x + 4$ is in the form $y = mx + b$.

slope: $m = -\frac{3}{2} = \frac{-3}{2}$

y-intercept: $b = 4$

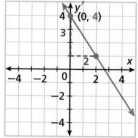

- Plot $(0, 4)$.
- Then count 3 units down and 2 units right and plot another point.
- Draw the line connecting the two points.

Helpful Hint

To divide $(8 - 3x)$ by 2, you can multiply by $\frac{1}{2}$ and use the Distributive Property.

$$\frac{8 - 3x}{2} = \frac{1}{2}(8 - 3x)$$
$$= \frac{1}{2}(8) + \frac{1}{2}(-3x)$$
$$= 4 - \frac{3}{2}x$$

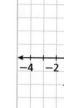 **CHECK IT OUT!** Write each equation in slope-intercept form. Then graph the line described by the equation.

3a. $y = \frac{2}{3}x$ **3b.** $6x + 2y = 10$ **3c.** $y = -4$

EXAMPLE **4** | MCC9-12.F.BF.1

Consumer Application

my.hrw.com

Online Video Tutor

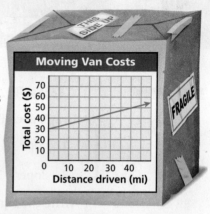

Moving Van Costs

To rent a van, a moving company charges $30.00 plus $0.50 per mile. The cost as a function of the number of miles driven is shown in the graph.

a. Write an equation that represents the cost as a function of the number of miles.

Cost	is	$0.50 per mile	times	miles	plus	$30.00
y	=	0.5	•	x	+	30

An equation is $y = 0.5x + 30$.

b. Identify the slope and *y*-intercept and describe their meanings.

The *y*-intercept is 30. This is the cost for 0 miles, or the initial fee of $30.00.

The slope is 0.5. This is the rate of change of the cost: $0.50 per mile.

c. Find the cost of the van for 150 miles.

$y = 0.5x + 30$

$= 0.5(150) + 30 = 105$ *Substitute 150 for x in the equation.*

The cost of the van for 150 miles is $105.

CHECK IT OUT!

4. A caterer charges a $200 fee plus $18 per person served. The cost as a function of the number of guests is shown in the graph.

  a. Write an equation that represents the cost as a function of the number of guests.

  b. Identify the slope and *y*-intercept and describe their meanings.

  c. Find the cost of catering an event for 200 guests.

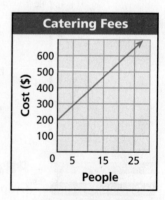

Catering Fees

MCC.MP.7, MCC.MP.8   **MATHEMATICAL PRACTICES**

THINK AND DISCUSS

1. If a linear function has a *y*-intercept of *b*, at what point does its graph cross the *y*-axis?

2. Where does the line described by $y = 4.395x - 23.75$ cross the *y*-axis?

3. GET ORGANIZED Copy and complete the graphic organizer.

Know it! Note

(Graphing the Line Described by $y = mx + b$)

| 1. Plot the point ___?___ . | 2. Find a second point on the line by ___?___ . | 3. Draw ___?___ . |

GUIDED PRACTICE

SEE EXAMPLE 1 Graph each line given the slope and y-intercept.

1. slope $= \frac{1}{3}$, y-intercept $= -3$

2. slope $= 0.5$, y-intercept $= 3.5$

3. slope $= 5$, y-intercept $= -1$

4. slope $= -2$, y-intercept $= 2$

SEE EXAMPLE 2 Write the equation that describes each line in slope-intercept form.

5.

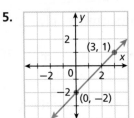

6. slope $= 8$, y-intercept $= 2$

7. slope $= 0$, y-intercept $= -3$

8. slope $= 5$, $(2, 7)$ is on the line.

9. slope $= -2$, $(1, -3)$ is on the line.

SEE EXAMPLE 3 Write each equation in slope-intercept form. Then graph the line described by the equation.

10. $y = \frac{2}{5}x - 6$

11. $3x - y = 1$

12. $2x + y = 4$

SEE EXAMPLE 4 **13.** Helen is in a bicycle race. She has already biked 10 miles and is now biking at a rate of 18 miles per hour. Her distance as a function of time is shown in the graph.

    a. Write an equation that represents the distance Helen has biked as a function of time.

    b. Identify the slope and y-intercept and describe their meanings.

    c. How far will Helen have biked after 2 hours?

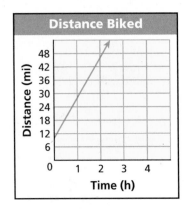

PRACTICE AND PROBLEM SOLVING

Graph each line given the slope and y-intercept.

Independent Practice	
For Exercises	See Example
14–17	1
19–22	2
23–25	3
26	4

my.hrw.com

Online Extra Practice

14. slope $= \frac{1}{4}$, y-intercept $= 7$

15. slope $= -6$, y-intercept $= -3$

16. slope $= 1$, y-intercept $= -4$

17. slope $= -\frac{4}{5}$, y-intercept $= 6$

Write the equation that describes each line in slope-intercept form.

18.

19. slope $= 5$, y-intercept $= -9$

20. slope $= -\frac{2}{3}$, y-intercept $= 2$

21. slope $= -\frac{1}{2}$, $(6, 4)$ is on the line.

22. slope $= 0$, $(6, -8)$ is on the line.

Write each equation in slope-intercept form. Then graph the line described by the equation.

23. $-\dfrac{1}{2}x + y = 4$ **24.** $\dfrac{2}{3}x + y = 2$ **25.** $2x + y = 8$

26. **Fitness** Pauline's health club has an enrollment fee of $175 and costs $35 per month. Total cost as a function of number of membership months is shown in the graph.

    a. Write an equation that represents the total cost as a function of months.

    b. Identify the slope and y-intercept and describe their meanings.

    c. Find the cost of one year of membership.

Health Club Membership Costs

27. A company rents video games. The table shows the linear relationship between the number of games a customer can rent at one time and the monthly cost of the service.

    a. Graph the relationship.

    b. Write an equation that represents the monthly cost as a function of games rented at one time.

Games Rented at One Time	1	2	3
Monthly Cost ($)	14	18	22

H.O.T. Critical Thinking Tell whether each situation is possible or impossible. If possible, draw a sketch of the graphs. If impossible, explain.

28. Two different lines have the same slope.

29. Two different linear functions have the same y-intercept.

30. Two intersecting lines have the same slope.

31. A linear function does not have a y-intercept.

Match each equation with its corresponding graph.

32.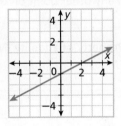

33.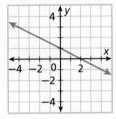

34.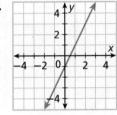

A. $y = 2x - 1$ **B.** $y = \dfrac{1}{2}x - 1$ **C.** $y = -\dfrac{1}{2}x + 1$

H.O.T. 35. Write About It Write an equation that describes a vertical line. Can you write this equation in slope-intercept form? Why or why not?

Real-World Connections

36. a. Ricardo and Sam walk from Sam's house to school. Sam lives 3 blocks from Ricardo's house. The graph shows their distance from Ricardo's house as they walk to school. Create a table of these values.

    b. Find an equation for the distance as a function of time.

    c. What are the slope and y-intercept? What do they represent in this situation?

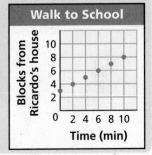

Walk to School

37. Which function has the same y-intercept as $y = \frac{1}{2}x - 2$?

    (A) $2x + 3y = 6$ (B) $x + 4y = -8$ (C) $-\frac{1}{2}x + y = 4$ (D) $\frac{1}{2}x - 2y = -2$

38. What is the slope-intercept form of $x - y = -8$?

    (F) $y = -x - 8$ (G) $y = x - 8$ (H) $y = -x + 8$ (J) $y = x + 8$

39. Which function has a y-intercept of 3?

    (A) $2x - y = 3$ (B) $2x + y = 3$ (C) $2x + y = 6$ (D) $y = 3x$

40. Gridded Response What is the slope of the line described by $-6x = -2y + 5$?

41. Short Response Write a function whose graph has the same slope as the line described by $3x - 9y = 9$ and the same y-intercept as $8x - 2y = 6$. Show your work.

CHALLENGE AND EXTEND

42. The standard form of a linear equation is $Ax + By = C$. Rewrite this equation in slope-intercept form. What is the slope? What is the y-intercept?

43. What value of n in the equation $nx + 5 = 3y$ would give a line with slope -2?

44. If b is the y-intercept of a linear function whose graph has slope m, then $y = mx + b$ describes the line. Below is an incomplete justification of this statement. Fill in the missing information.

Statements	Reasons
1. $m = \dfrac{y_2 - y_1}{x_2 - x_1}$	1. Slope formula
2. $m = \dfrac{y - b}{x - 0}$	2. By definition, if b is the y-intercept, then $\left(\blacksquare, b\right)$ is a point on the line. (x, y) is any other point on the line.
3. $m = \dfrac{y - b}{x}$	3. _____?
4. $m\,\blacksquare = y - b$	4. Multiplication Property of Equality (Multiply both sides of the equation by x.)
5. $mx + b = y$, or $y = mx + b$	5. _____?

FOCUS ON MATHEMATICAL PRACTICES

H.O.T. 45. Modeling Create a real-world situation that could be modeled by a linear function with a slope of 2 and a y-intercept of -30. Explain the meaning of the slope and the y-intercept in your context.

H.O.T. 46. Proof The graph of $y = 2x + 1$ is shown. Suppose n is any value of x. Prove that, as n increases by any positive number k, the linear function $y = 2x + 1$ grows by an amount related only to k and not to n. (*Hint:* Evaluate y for the two values of x shown on the graph and subtract.)

11-3 Point-Slope Form

 Essential Question: How can you write a linear equation in point-slope form and use two points to draw its graph?

Objectives
Graph a line and write a linear equation using point-slope form.

Write a linear equation given two points.

Why learn this?
You can use point-slope form to represent a cost function, such as the cost of placing a newspaper ad. (See Example 5.)

> PIES
> old,
> ded.
> yful!
> teer.

> **KITTENS AVAILABLE**
> to good home. 2 mo. old, litter trained. Very cute and playful! $10 adoption fee.

> DO
> 8 n
> sho
> Ve
> ha

If you know the slope and any point on the line, you can write an equation of the line by using the slope formula. For example, suppose a line has a slope of 3 and contains $(2, 1)$. Let (x, y) be any other point on the line.

$$m = \frac{y_2 - y_1}{x_2 - x_1} \longrightarrow 3 = \frac{y - 1}{x - 2} \qquad \text{Substitute into the slope formula.}$$

 Slope formula

$$3(x - 2) = \left(\frac{y - 1}{x - 2}\right)(x - 2) \qquad \text{Multiplication Property of Equality}$$

$$3(x - 2) = y - 1 \qquad \text{Simplify.}$$

$$y - 1 = 3(x - 2)$$

Point-Slope Form of a Linear Equation

The line with slope m that contains the point (x_1, y_1) can be described by the equation $y - y_1 = m(x - x_1)$.

 COMMON CORE GPS **EXAMPLE** **1**
MCC9-12.A.CED.2

Writing Linear Equations in Point-Slope Form

Write an equation in point-slope form for the line with the given slope that contains the given point.

 my.hrw.com

Online Video Tutor

A slope $= \frac{5}{2}$; $(-3, 0)$

$y - y_1 = m(x - x_1)$ *Write the point-slope form.*

$y - 0 = \frac{5}{2}[x - (-3)]$ *Substitute $\frac{5}{2}$ for m, -3 for x_1, and 0 for y_1.*

$y - 0 = \frac{5}{2}(x + 3)$ *Rewrite subtraction of negative numbers as addition.*

B slope $= -7$; $(4, 2)$

$y - y_1 = m(x - x_1)$

$y - 2 = -7(x - 4)$

C slope $= 0$; $(-2, -3)$

$y - y_1 = m(x - x_1)$

$y - (-3) = 0[x - (-2)]$

$y + 3 = 0(x + 2)$

 CHECK IT OUT! Write an equation in point-slope form for the line with the given slope that contains the given point.

1a. slope $= 2$; $\left(\frac{1}{2}, 1\right)$ **1b.** slope $= 0$; $(3, -4)$

Previously, you graphed a line given its equation in slope-intercept form. You can also graph a line when given its equation in point-slope form. Start by using the equation to identify a point on the line. Then use the slope of the line to identify a second point.

COMMON CORE GPS
MCC9-12.A.CED.2

EXAMPLE 2

Using Point-Slope Form to Graph

Graph the line described by each equation.

A $y - 1 = 3(x - 1)$

$y - 1 = 3(x - 1)$ is in the form $y - y_1 = m(x - x_1)$.

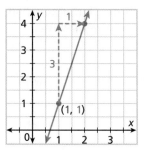

The line contains the point $(1, 1)$.

slope: $m = 3 = \dfrac{3}{1}$

Step 1 Plot $(1, 1)$.

Step 2 Count **3 units up** and **1 unit right** and plot another point.

Step 3 Draw the line connecting the two points.

B $y + 2 = -\dfrac{1}{2}(x - 3)$

Step 1 Write the equation in point-slope form: $y - y_1 = m(x - x_1)$.

$y - (-2) = -\dfrac{1}{2}(x - 3)$ *Rewrite addition of 2 as subtraction of −2.*

Step 2 Graph the line.

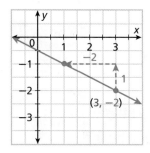

The line contains the point $(3, -2)$.

slope: $m = -\dfrac{1}{2} = \dfrac{1}{-2}$

- Plot $(3, -2)$.

- Count 1 unit up and 2 units left and plot another point.

- Draw the line connecting the two points.

Helpful Hint

For a negative fraction, you can write the negative sign in one of three places.

$$-\dfrac{1}{2} = \dfrac{-1}{2} = \dfrac{1}{-2}$$

Graph the line described by each equation.

2a. $y + 2 = -(x - 2)$ **2b.** $y + 3 = -2(x - 1)$

COMMON CORE GPS
MCC9-12.A.CED.2

EXAMPLE 3

Writing Linear Equations in Slope-Intercept Form

Write the equation that describes each line in slope-intercept form.

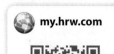

A slope $= -4$, $(-1, -2)$ is on the line.

Step 1 Write the equation in point-slope form: $y - y_1 = m(x - x_1)$.

$y - (-2) = -4[x - (-1)]$

Step 2 Write the equation in slope-intercept form by solving for y.

$y - (-2) = -4[x - (-1)]$

$y + 2 = -4(x + 1)$ *Rewrite subtraction of negative numbers as*

$y + 2 = -4x - 4$ *addition. Distribute −4 on the right side.*

$\underline{ -2 \qquad\quad -2}$ *Subtract 2 from both sides.*

$y = -4x - 6$

B $(1, -4)$ **and** $(3, 2)$ **are on the line.**

Step 1 Find the slope.

$$m = \frac{y_2 - y_1}{x_2 - x_1} = \frac{2 - (-4)}{3 - 1} = \frac{6}{2} = 3$$

Step 2 Substitute the slope and one of the points into the point-slope form. Then write the equation in slope-intercept form.

$y - y_1 = m(x - x_1)$

$y - 2 = 3(x - 3)$ *Use (3, 2).*

$y - 2 = 3x - 9$ *Distribute 3 on the right side.*

$y = 3x - 7$ *Add 2 to both sides.*

C *x*-intercept = –2, *y*-intercept = 4

Step 1 Use the intercepts to find two points: $(-2, 0)$ and $(0, 4)$.

Step 2 Find the slope.

$$m = \frac{y_2 - y_1}{x_2 - x_1} = \frac{4 - 0}{0 - (-2)} = \frac{4}{2} = 2$$

Step 3 Write the equation in slope-intercept form.

$y = mx + b$ *Write the slope-intercept form.*

$y = 2x + 4$ *Substitute 2 for m and 4 for b.*

 Write the equation that describes each line in slope-intercept form.

3a. slope = $\frac{1}{3}$, $(-3, 1)$ is on the line.

3b. $(1, -2)$ and $(3, 10)$ are on the line.

 **EXAMPLE 4**

MCC9-12.F.IF.8

my.hrw.com

Online Video Tutor

Using Two Points to Find Intercepts

The points $(4, 8)$ and $(-1, -12)$ are on a line. Find the intercepts.

Step 1 Find the slope.
$$m = \frac{y_2 - y_1}{x_2 - x_1} = \frac{-12 - 8}{-1 - 4} = \frac{-20}{-5} = 4$$

Step 2 Write the equation in slope-intercept form.

$y - y_1 = m(x - x_1)$ *Write the point-slope form.*

$y - 8 = 4(x - 4)$ *Substitute (4, 8) for (x_1, y_1) and 4 for m.*

$y - 8 = 4x - 16$ *Distribute 4 on the right side.*

$y = 4x - 8$ *Add 8 to both sides.*

Step 3 Find the intercepts.

x-intercept:		*y*-intercept:	
$y = 4x - 8$	*Replace y with*	$y = 4x - 8$	*Use the slope-*
$0 = 4x - 8$	*0 and solve*	$b = -8$	*intercept form*
$8 = 4x$	*for x.*		*to identify the*
$2 = x$			*y-intercept.*

The *x*-intercept is 2, and the *y*-intercept is –8.

 4. The points $(2, 15)$ and $(-4, -3)$ are on a line. Find the intercepts.

MATHEMATICAL
PRACTICES

**Make sense of problems
and persevere in solving
them.**

Problem-Solving Application

The cost to place an ad in a
newspaper for one week is a linear
function of the number of lines in
the ad. The costs for 3, 5, and 10 lines
are shown. Write an equation in
slope-intercept form that represents
the function. Then find the cost of an
ad that is 18 lines long.

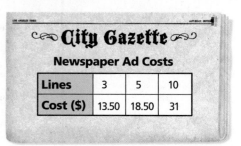

⤳ City Gazette ⤳

Newspaper Ad Costs

Lines	3	5	10
Cost ($)	13.50	18.50	31

1 **Understand the Problem**

• The **answer** will have two parts—an equation in slope-intercept form and
the cost of an ad that is 18 lines long.
• The ordered pairs given in the table satisfy the equation.

2 **Make a Plan**

First, find the slope. Then use point-slope form to write the equation. Finally,
write the equation in slope-intercept form.

3 **Solve**

Step 1 Choose any two ordered pairs from the table to find the slope.

$$m = \frac{y_2 - y_1}{x_2 - x_1} = \frac{18.50 - 13.50}{5 - 3} = \frac{5}{2} = 2.5 \quad \text{Use (3, 13.50) and (5, 18.50).}$$

Step 2 Substitute the slope and any ordered pair from the table into the
point-slope form.

$$y - y_1 = m(x - x_1)$$
$$y - 31 = 2.5(x - 10) \qquad \text{Use (10, 31).}$$

Step 3 Write the equation in slope-intercept form by solving for y.

$$y - 31 = 2.5(x - 10)$$
$$y - 31 = 2.5x - 25 \qquad \text{Distribute 2.5.}$$
$$y = 2.5x + 6 \qquad \text{Add 31 to both sides.}$$

Step 4 Find the cost of an ad containing 18 lines by substituting 18 for x.

$$y = 2.5x + 6$$
$$y = 2.5(18) + 6 = 51$$

The cost of an ad containing 18 lines is $51.

4 **Look Back**

Check the equation by substituting the ordered pairs (3, 13.50)
and (5, 18.50).

$y = 2.5x + 6$	
13.50	$2.5(3) + 6$
13.5	$7.5 + 6$
13.5	13.5 ✓

$y = 2.5x + 6$	
18.50	$2.5(5) + 6$
18.5	$12.5 + 6$
18.5	18.5 ✓

CHECK IT OUT!

5. **What if...?** At a different newspaper,
the costs to place an ad for one week
are shown. Write an equation in slope-
intercept form that represents this
linear function. Then find the cost of
an ad that is 21 lines long.

Lines	Cost ($)
3	12.75
5	17.25
10	28.50

THINK AND DISCUSS

1. How are point-slope form and slope-intercept form alike? different?

2. When is point-slope form useful? When is slope-intercept form useful?

3. **GET ORGANIZED** Copy and complete the graphic organizer. In each box, describe how to find the equation of a line by using the given method.

Writing the Equation of a Line

| If you know two points on the line | If you know the slope and *y*-intercept | If you know the slope and a point on the line |

11-3 Exercises

my.hrw.com
Homework Help

GUIDED PRACTICE

SEE EXAMPLE **1** Write an equation in point-slope form for the line with the given slope that contains the given point.

1. slope = $\frac{1}{5}$; $(2, -6)$ **2.** slope = -4; $(1, 5)$ **3.** slope = 0; $(3, -7)$

SEE EXAMPLE **2** Graph the line described by each equation.

4. $y - 1 = -(x - 3)$ **5.** $y + 2 = -2(x + 4)$ **6.** $y + 1 = -\frac{1}{2}(x + 4)$

SEE EXAMPLE **3** Write the equation that describes each line in slope-intercept form.

7. slope = $-\frac{1}{3}$, $(-3, 8)$ is on the line. **8.** slope = 2; $(1, 1)$ is on the line.

9. $(-2, 2)$ and $(2, -2)$ are on the line. **10.** $(1, 1)$ and $(-5, 3)$ are on the line.

11. *x*-intercept = 8, *y*-intercept = 4 **12.** *x*-intercept = -2, *y*-intercept = 3

SEE EXAMPLE **4** Each pair of points is on a line. Find the intercepts.

13. $(5, 2)$ and $(7, 4)$ **14.** $(-1, 5)$ and $(-3, -5)$ **15.** $(2, 9)$ and $(-4, -9)$

SEE EXAMPLE **5** **16.** **Measurement** An oil tank is being filled at a constant rate. The depth of the oil is a function of the number of minutes the tank has been filling, as shown in the table. Write an equation in slope-intercept form that represents this linear function. Then find the depth of the oil after one-half hour.

Time (min)	Depth (ft)
0	3
10	5
15	6

PRACTICE AND PROBLEM SOLVING

Write an equation in point-slope form for the line with the given slope that contains the given point.

17. slope = $\frac{2}{9}$; $(-1, 5)$ **18.** slope = 0; $(4, -2)$ **19.** slope = 8; $(1, 8)$

Independent Practice

For Exercises	See Example
17–19	1
20–22	2
23–30	3
31–33	4
34	5

my.hrw.com

Online Extra Practice

Graph the line described by each equation.

20. $y - 4 = -\frac{1}{2}(x + 3)$ **21.** $y + 2 = \frac{3}{5}(x - 1)$ **22.** $y - 0 = 4(x - 1)$

Write the equation that describes each line in slope-intercept form.

23. slope $= -\frac{2}{7}$, $(14, -3)$ is on the line.   **24.** slope $= \frac{4}{5}$, $(-15, 1)$ is on the line.

25. slope $= -6$, $(9, 3)$ is on the line.   **26.** $(7, 8)$ and $(-7, 6)$ are on the line.

27. $(2, 7)$ and $(4, -4)$ are on the line.   **28.** $(-1, 2)$ and $(4, -23)$ are on the line.

29. x-intercept $= 3$, y-intercept $= -6$ **30.** x-intercept $= 4$, y-intercept $= -1$

Each pair of points is on a line. Find the intercepts.

31. $(-1, -4)$ and $(6, 10)$ **32.** $(3, 4)$ and $(-6, 16)$ **33.** $(4, 15)$ and $(-2, 6)$

34. **History** The amount of fresh water left in the tanks of a 19th-century clipper ship is a linear function of the time since the ship left port, as shown in the table. Write an equation in slope-intercept form that represents the function. Then find the amount of water that will be left in the ship's tanks 50 days after leaving port.

Fresh Water Aboard Ship	
Time (days)	Amount (gal)
1	3555
8	3240
15	2925

Science

As altitude increases, the amount of breathable oxygen decreases. At elevations above 8000 feet, this can cause altitude sickness. To prevent this, mountain climbers often use tanks containing a mixture of air and pure oxygen.

35. **Science** At higher altitudes, water boils at lower temperatures. This relationship between altitude and boiling point is linear. At an altitude of 1000 feet, water boils at 210 °F. At an altitude of 3000 feet, water boils at 206 °F. Write an equation in slope-intercept form that represents this linear function. Then find the boiling point at 6000 feet.

36. **Consumer Economics** Lora has a gift card from an online music store where all downloads cost the same amount. After downloading 2 songs, the balance on her card was $18.10. After downloading a total of 5 songs, the balance was $15.25.

  a. Write an equation in slope-intercept form that represents the amount in dollars remaining on the card as a function of songs downloaded.

  b. Identify the slope of the line and tell what the slope represents.

  c. Identify the y-intercept of the line and tell what it represents.

  d. How many additional songs can Lora download when there is $15.25 left on the card?

Graph the line with the given slope that contains the given point.

37. slope $= -3$; $(2, 4)$ **38.** slope $= -\frac{1}{4}$; $(0, 0)$ **39.** slope $= \frac{1}{2}$; $(-2, -1)$

Tell whether each statement is sometimes, always, or never true.

40. A line described by the equation $y = mx + b$ contains the point $(0, b)$.

41. The slope of the line that contains the points $(0, 0)$ and (c, d) is negative if both c and d are negative.

42. The y-intercept of the graph of $y - y_1 = m(x - x_1)$ is negative if y_1 is negative.

43. **Meteorology** Snowfall accumulates at an average rate of 2.5 inches per hour during a snowstorm. Two hours after the snowstorm begins, the average depth of snow on the ground is 11 inches.

  a. Write an equation in point-slope form that represents the depth of the snow in inches as a function of hours since the snowstorm began.

  b. How much snow is on the ground when the snowstorm starts?

  c. The snowstorm begins at 2:15 P.M. and continues until 6:30 P.M. How much snow is on the ground at the end of the storm?

Write an equation in point-slope form that describes each graph.

44.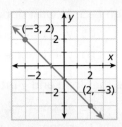

45.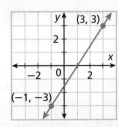

46.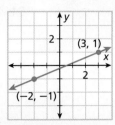

The tables show linear relationships between *x* and *y*. Copy and complete the tables.

47.

x	−2	0	▧	7
y	−18	▧	12	27

48.

x	−4	1	0	▧
y	14	4	▧	−6

49. **ERROR ANALYSIS** Two students used point-slope form to find an equation that describes the line with slope −3 through $(-5, 2)$. Who is incorrect? Explain the error.

A

$$y - y_1 = m(x - x_1)$$
$$y - 2 = -3(x - 5)$$

B

$$y - y_1 = m(x - x_1)$$
$$y - 2 = -3[x - (-5)]$$
$$y - 2 = -3(x + 5)$$

50. Critical Thinking Compare the methods for finding the equation that describes a line when you know

- a point on the line and the slope of the line.
- two points on the line.

How are the methods alike? How are they different?

51. Write About It Explain why the first statement is false but the second is true.

- All linear equations can be written in point-slope form.
- All linear equations that describe functions can be written in point-slope form.

52. Multi-Step The table shows the mean scores on a standardized test for several different years.

Years Since 1985	0	5	10	17	21
Mean Combined Score	994	1009	1001	1016	1020

a. Make a scatter plot of the data and add a trend line to your graph.

b. Use your trend line to estimate the slope and *y*-intercept, and write an equation in slope-intercept form.

c. What do the slope and *y*-intercept represent in this situation?

53. a. Stephen is walking from his house to his friend Sharon's house. When he is 12 blocks away, he looks at his watch. He looks again when he is 8 blocks away and finds that 6 minutes have passed. Write two ordered pairs for these data in the form (time, blocks).

b. Write a linear equation for these two points.

c. What is the total amount of time it takes Stephen to reach Sharon's house? Explain how you found your answer.

TEST PREP

54. Which equation describes the line through $(-5, 1)$ with slope of 1?

     Ⓐ $y + 1 = x - 5$ Ⓒ $y - 1 = -5(x - 1)$

     Ⓑ $y + 5 = x - 1$ Ⓓ $y - 1 = x + 5$

55. A line contains $(4, 4)$ and $(5, 2)$. What are the slope and y-intercept?

     Ⓕ slope = -2; y-intercept = 2   Ⓗ slope = -2; y-intercept = 12

     Ⓖ slope = 1.2; y-intercept = -2 Ⓙ slope = 12; y-intercept = 1.2

CHALLENGE AND EXTEND

56. A linear function has the same y-intercept as $x + 4y = 8$ and its graph contains the point $(2, 7)$. Find the slope and y-intercept.

57. Write the equation of a line in slope-intercept form that contains $\left(\frac{3}{4}, \frac{1}{2}\right)$ and has the same slope as the line described by $y + 3x = 6$.

58. Write the equation of a line in slope-intercept form that contains $\left(-\frac{1}{2}, -\frac{1}{3}\right)$ and $\left(1\frac{1}{2}, 1\right)$.

FOCUS ON MATHEMATICAL PRACTICES

H.O.T. 59. Analysis A line contains $(8, 16)$ and has a negative y-intercept. Write a possible point-slope equation of the line.

H.O.T. 60. Comparison The slope-intercept and point-slope forms are related.

    a. A line has a slope of 3 and y-intercept of -4. Write equations of the line in slope-intercept form and point-slope form. What do you notice?

    b. For any slope m and y-intercept $(0, b)$, show that the point-slope and slope-intercept form of the line are equivalent.

Career Path

Michael Raynor
Data mining major

Q: What math classes did you take in high school?

A: Algebra 1 and 2, Geometry, and Statistics

Q: What math classes have you taken in college?

A: Applied Statistics, Data Mining Methods, Web Mining, and Artificial Intelligence

Q: How do you use math?

A: Once for a class, I used software to analyze basketball statistics. What I learned helped me develop strategies for our school team.

Q: What are your future plans?

A: There are many options for people with data mining skills. I could work in banking, pharmaceuticals, or even the military. But my dream job is to develop game strategies for an NBA team.

11-3 Technology TASK

Use with Point-Slope Form

Graph Linear Functions

You can use a graphing calculator to quickly graph lines whose equations are in point-slope form. To enter an equation into your calculator, it must be solved for y, but it does not necessarily have to be in slope-intercept form.

 MATHEMATICAL PRACTICES

Use appropriate tools strategically.

MCC9-12.F.IF.7 Graph functions expressed symbolically and show key features of the graph, by hand in simple cases and using technology for more complicated cases.

Activity

Graph the line with slope 2 that contains the point $(2, 6.09)$.

1 Use point-slope form.

$$y - y_1 = m(x - x_1)$$
$$y - 6.09 = 2(x - 2)$$

2 Solve for y by adding 6.09 to both sides of the equation.

$$y - 6.09 = 2(x - 2)$$
$$\underline{+ 6.09 \qquad + 6.09}$$
$$y \qquad = 2(x - 2) + 6.09$$

3 Enter this equation into your calculator.

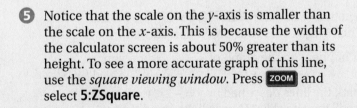

4 Graph in the *standard viewing window* by pressing **ZOOM** and selecting **6:ZStandard**. In this window, both the x- and y-axes go from -10 to 10.

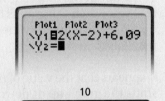

5 Notice that the scale on the y-axis is smaller than the scale on the x-axis. This is because the width of the calculator screen is about 50% greater than its height. To see a more accurate graph of this line, use the *square viewing window*. Press **ZOOM** and select **5:ZSquare**.

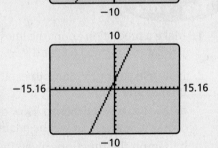

Try This

1. Graph the function represented by the line with slope -1.5 that contains the point $(2.25, -3)$. View the graph in the standard viewing window.

2. Now view the graph in the square viewing window. Press **WINDOW** and write down the minimum and maximum values on the x- and y-axes.

3. In which graph does the line appear steeper? Why?

4. Explain why it might sometimes be useful to look at a graph in a square window.

11-4 Technology TASK

The Family of Linear Functions

Use with Transforming Linear Functions

A *family of functions* is a set of functions whose graphs have basic characteristics in common. For example, all linear functions form a family. You can use a graphing calculator to explore families of functions.

 **Use appropriate tools strategically.**

MCC9-12.F.BF.3 Identify the effect on the graph of replacing $f(x)$ by $f(x) + k$, $kf(x)$, $f(kx)$, and $f(x + k)$ for specific values of k (both positive and negative); ... . Experiment with cases and illustrate an explanation of the effects on the graph using technology.

Activity

Graph the lines described by $y = x - 2$, $y = x - 1$, $y = x$, $y = x + 1$, $y = x + 2$, $y = x + 3$, and $y = x + 4$. How does the value of b affect the graph described by $y = x + b$?

1 All of the functions are in the form $y = x + b$. Enter them into the **Y=** editor.

[Y=] [X,T,θ,n] [–] 2 [ENTER]

[X,T,θ,n] [–] 1 [ENTER]

and so on.

2 Press [ZOOM] and select **6:Zstandard**. Think about the different values of b as you watch the graphs being drawn. Notice that the lines are all parallel.

3 It appears that the value of b in $y = x + b$ shifts the graph up or down—up if b is positive and down if b is negative.

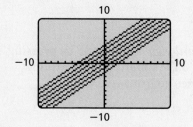

Try This

1. Make a prediction about the lines described by $y = 2x - 3$, $y = 2x - 2$, $y = 2x - 1$, $y = 2x$, $y = 2x + 1$, $y = 2x + 2$, and $y = 2x + 3$. Then graph. Was your prediction correct?

2. Now use your calculator to explore what happens to the graph of $y = mx$ when you change the value of m.

   a. Make a Prediction How do you think the lines described by $y = -2x$, $y = -x$, $y = x$, and $y = 2x$ will be related? How will they be alike? How will they be different?

   b. Graph the functions given in part **a**. Was your prediction correct?

   c. How is the effect of m different when m is positive from when m is negative?

11-4 Transforming Linear Functions

? **Essential Question:** How can you identify the effect of a given transformation on the graph of a linear function?

Objectives
Transform linear functions.

Solve problems involving linear transformations.

Why learn this?
Transformations allow you to visualize and compare many different functions at once.

You have learned to transform functions by transforming each point. Transformations can also be expressed by using function notation.

Helpful Hint

To remember the difference between vertical and horizontal translations, think: "Add to *y*, go high." "Add to *x*, go left."

Translations and Reflections	
Translations	
Horizontal Shift of $|h|$ Units 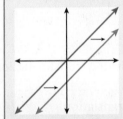 Input value changes. $f(x) \rightarrow f(x - h)$ $h > 0$ moves right $h < 0$ moves left	**Vertical Shift of $|k|$ Units** Output value changes. $f(x) \rightarrow f(x) + k$ $k > 0$ moves up $k < 0$ moves down
Reflections	
Reflection Across y-axis Input value changes. $f(x) \rightarrow f(-x)$ The lines are symmetric about the y-axis.	**Reflection Across x-axis** Output value changes. $f(x) \rightarrow -f(x)$ The lines are symmetric about the x-axis.

COMMON CORE GPS **EXAMPLE** **1** MCC9-12.F.BF.3

my.hrw.com

Online Video Tutor

Translating and Reflecting Linear Functions

Let $g(x)$ be the indicated transformation of $f(x)$. Write the rule for $g(x)$.

A $f(x) = 2x + 3$; vertical translation 4 units up

Translating $f(x)$ 4 units up adds 4 to each output value.

$g(x) = f(x) + 4$ *Add 4 to $f(x)$.*

$g(x) = (2x + 3) + 4$ *Substitute $2x + 3$ for $f(x)$.*

$g(x) = 2x + 7$ *Simplify.*

Check Graph $f(x)$ and $g(x)$ on a graphing calculator. The slopes are the same, but the y-intercept has moved 4 units up from 3 to 7. ✔

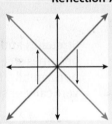

Let $g(x)$ be the indicated transformation of $f(x)$. Write the rule for $g(x)$.

B linear function defined in the table; reflection across y-axis

x	$f(x)$
-1	0
0	2
1	4

Step 1 Write the rule for $f(x)$ in slope-intercept form.

The y-intercept is 2. *The table contains $(0, 2)$.*

Find the slope:

$$m = \frac{2 - 0}{0 - (-1)} = \frac{2}{1} = 2 \quad \text{Use } (-1, 0) \text{ and } (0, 2).$$

$$y = mx + b \qquad\qquad \text{Slope-intercept form}$$

$$y = 2x + 2 \qquad\qquad \text{Substitute 2 for m and 2 for b.}$$

$$f(x) = 2x + 2 \qquad\quad \text{Replace y with } f(x).$$

Step 2 Write the rule for $g(x)$. Reflecting $f(x)$ across the y-axis replaces each x with $-x$.

$$g(x) = 2(-x) + 2 \qquad\qquad g(x) = f(-x)$$

$$g(x) = -2x + 2$$

Check Graph $f(x)$ and $g(x)$ on a graphing calculator. The graphs are symmetric about the y-axis. ✔

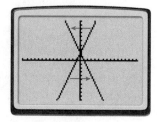

 CHECK IT OUT! Let $g(x)$ be the indicated transformation of $f(x)$. Write the rule for $g(x)$.

1a. $f(x) = 3x + 1$; translation 2 units right

1b. linear function defined in the table; a reflection across the x-axis

x	-1	0	1
y	1	2	3

Stretches and compressions change the slope of a linear function. If the line becomes steeper, the function has been stretched vertically or compressed horizontally. If the line becomes flatter, the function has been compressed vertically or stretched horizontally.

 Know it! *Note*

Stretches and Compressions	
Horizontal	**Vertical**
Horizontal Stretch/Compression by a Factor of b	**Vertical Stretch/Compression by a Factor of a**
Input value changes. $f(x) \to f\left(\frac{1}{b}x\right)$	Output value changes. $f(x) \to a \cdot f(x)$
$b > 1$ stretches away from the y-axis. $0 < \lvert b \rvert < 1$ compresses toward the y-axis.	$a > 1$ stretches away from the x-axis. $0 < \lvert a \rvert < 1$ compresses toward the x-axis.

Stretching and Compressing Linear Functions

Let $g(x)$ be a horizontal compression of $f(x) = 2x - 1$ by a factor of $\frac{1}{3}$. Write the rule for $g(x)$, and graph the function.

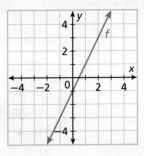

Horizontally compressing $f(x)$ by a factor of $\frac{1}{3}$ replaces each x with $\frac{1}{b}x$ where $b = \frac{1}{3}$.

$g(x) = 2\left(\frac{1}{b}\right)x - 1$ *For horizontal compression, use $\frac{1}{b}$.*

$\quad\quad = 2\left(\dfrac{1}{\frac{1}{3}}\right)x - 1$ *Substitute $\frac{1}{3}$ for b.*

$\quad\quad = 2(3x) - 1$ *Replace x with 3x.*

$g(x) = 6x - 1$ *Simplify.*

Check Graph both functions on the same coordinate plane. The graph of $g(x)$ is steeper than $f(x)$, which indicates that $g(x)$ has been horizontally compressed from $f(x)$, or pushed toward the y-axis.

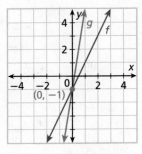

 2. Let $g(x)$ be a vertical compression of $f(x) = 3x + 2$ by a factor of $\frac{1}{4}$. Write the rule for $g(x)$.

Some linear functions involve more than one transformation. Combine transformations by applying individual transformations one at a time in the order in which they are given.

For multiple transformations, create a temporary function—such as $h(x)$ in Example 3 below—to represent the first transformation, and then transform it to find the combined transformation.

Combining Transformations of Linear Functions

Let $g(x)$ be a vertical shift of $f(x) = x$ down 2 units followed by a vertical stretch by a factor of 5. Write the rule for $g(x)$.

Step 1 First perform the translation.

Translating $f(x) = x$ down 2 units subtracts 2 from the function. You can use $h(x)$ to represent the translated function.

$h(x) = f(x) - 2$ *Subtract 2 from the function.*

$h(x) = x - 2$ *Substitute x for f(x).*

Step 2 Then perform the stretch.

Stretching $h(x)$ vertically by a factor of 5 multiplies the function by 5.

$g(x) = 5 \cdot h(x)$ *Multiply the function by 5.*

$g(x) = 5(x - 2)$ *Because h(x) = x − 2, substitute x − 2 for h(x).*

$g(x) = 5x - 10$ *Simplify.*

 3. Let $g(x)$ be a vertical compression of $f(x) = x$ by a factor of $\frac{1}{2}$ followed by a horizontal shift 8 units left. Write the rule for $g(x)$.

EXAMPLE **4**

Fund-raising Application

The Dance Club is selling beaded purses as a fund-raiser. The function $R(n) = 12.5n$ represents the club's revenue in dollars where n is the number of purses sold.

a. The club paid $75 for the materials needed to make the purses. Write a new function $P(n)$ for the club's profit.

The initial costs must be subtracted from the revenue.

$R(n) = 12.5n$ *Original function*

$P(n) = 12.5n - 75$ *Subtract the expenses.*

b. **Graph $P(n)$ and $R(n)$ on the same coordinate plane.**

Graph both functions. The lines have the same slope but different y-intercepts.

Note that the profit can be negative but the number of purses sold cannot be less than 0.

c. **Describe the transformation(s) that have been applied.**

The graphs indicate that $P(n)$ is a translation of $R(n)$. Because 75 was subtracted, $P(n) = R(n) - 75$. This indicates a vertical shift 75 units down.

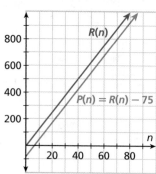

 CHECK IT OUT!

4. **What if...?** The club members decided to double the price of each purse.

a. Write a new profit function $S(n)$ for the club.

b. Graph $S(n)$ and $P(n)$ on the same coordinate plane.

c. Describe the transformation(s) that have been applied.

MCC.MP.1, MCC.MP.6   MATHEMATICAL PRACTICES

THINK AND DISCUSS

1. Identify the horizontal translation that would have the same effect on the graph of $f(x) = x$ as a vertical translation of 6 units.

2. Give an example of two different transformations of $f(x) = 2x$ that would result in $g(x) = 2x - 6$.

3. Describe the transformation that would cause all of the function values to double.

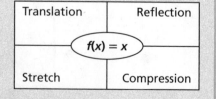

4. **GET ORGANIZED** Copy and complete the graphic organizer. In each box, give an example of the indicated transformation of the parent function $f(x) = x$. Include an equation and a graph.

Translation	Reflection
$f(x) = x$	
Stretch	Compression

GUIDED PRACTICE

SEE EXAMPLE **1** Let $g(x)$ be the indicated transformation of $f(x)$.
Write the rule for $g(x)$.

1. linear function defined by the table; vertical
translation 1.5 units up

x	−2	−1	0
$f(x)$	3.5	2	0.5

SEE EXAMPLE **2** 2. $f(x) = -x + 5$; horizontal translation 2 units left

3. $f(x) = \frac{1}{3}x - 2$; vertical stretch by a factor of 3

4. $f(x) = -2x + 0.5$; horizontal stretch by a factor of $\frac{4}{3}$.

SEE EXAMPLE **3** Let $g(x)$ be the indicated combined transformation of $f(x) = x$. Write the rule for $g(x)$.

5. vertical compression by a factor of $\frac{2}{3}$ followed by a vertical shift 6 units down

6. horizontal shift right 4 units followed by a horizontal stretch by a factor of $\frac{3}{2}$

SEE EXAMPLE **4** 7. **Advertising** An electronics company is changing its Internet ad from a banner
ad to a pop-up ad. The cost of the banner ad in dollars is represented by
$C(n) = 0.30n + 5.00$ where n is the average number of hits per hour. The cost
of the pop-up ad will double the cost per hit.

   a. Write a new cost function $D(n)$ for the ads.

   b. Graph $C(n)$ and $D(n)$ on the same coordinate plane.

   c. Describe the transformation(s) that have been applied.

PRACTICE AND PROBLEM SOLVING

my.hrw.com

Online Extra Practice

Let $g(x)$ be the indicated transformation of $f(x)$. Write the rule for $g(x)$.

8.

Reflection across
the x-axis

9.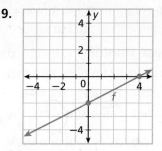

Vertical translation
2 units down

10.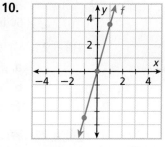

Horizontal compression
by a factor of 0.5

11. linear function defined by
the table; vertical stretch
by a factor of 1.2 units

x	1	5	9
$f(x)$	0	−2	−4

12. $f(x) = -3x + 7$; vertical compression by a factor of $\frac{3}{4}$

Let $g(x)$ be the indicated combined transformation of $f(x) = x$. Write the rule for $g(x)$.

13. horizontal stretch by a factor of 2.75 followed by a horizontal shift 1 unit left

14. vertical shift 6 units down followed by a vertical compression by a factor of $\frac{2}{3}$

15. Consumer Economics In 1997, Southwestern Bell increased the price for local pay-phone calls. Before then, the price of a call could be determined by $f(x) = 0.15x + 0.25$, where x was the number of minutes after the *first* minute. The company increased the cost of the first minute by 10 cents.

  a. Write a new price function $g(x)$ for a phone call.

  b. Graph $f(x)$ and $g(x)$ on the same coordinate plane.

  c. Describe the transformation(s) that have been applied.

Write the rule for the transformed function $g(x)$ and graph.

16.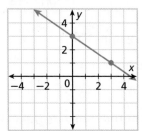

Reflection across the y-axis

17.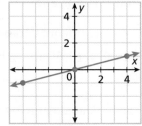

Vertical stretch by a factor of 8

18.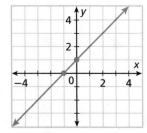

Horizontal stretch by a factor of 3

History Historic tolls for traveling on the Cumberland Road in Pennsylvania are shown on the sign. Toll was paid every 15 miles.

19. Write a function to represent the cost for 1 horse and rider to travel n miles with a score of sheep. What transformation describes the change in cost if the sheep were replaced by cattle?

20. Write a function to represent the cost for a carriage with 2 horses and 4 wheels to travel n miles. Name two different transformations that would represent a 6¢ increase in the toll rate.

Cumberland Road Rates of Toll

Every Score of Sheep . . . . 6¢
Every Score of Hogs . . . . 6¢
Every Score of Cattle . . . . . . 12¢
Every Horse and Rider. . . . . 4¢
Every Pair of Oxen . . . . 3¢

Every Carriage with 2 Horses and
   4 Wheels . . . . 12¢

Any person refusing or neglecting
   to pay toll . . . a fine of $3.00

H.O.T. 21. Critical Thinking Consider the linear function $f(x) = x$.

  a. Shift $f(x)$ 2 units up and then reflect it over the x-axis.

  b. Perform the same transformations on $f(x)$ again but in reverse order.

  c. Make a conjecture about the order in which transformations are performed.

H.O.T. 22. Write About It Which transformations affect the slope of a linear function, and which transformations affect the y-intercept? Support your answers.

23. Use the data set $\{1, 5, 10, 17, 23, 23, 38, 60\}$.

  a. Find the mean, median, mode, and range.

  b. How does adding 7 to each number affect the mean, median, mode, and range?

  c. How does multiplying each number by 4 affect the mean, median, mode, and range?

  d. How does multiplying each number by 2 and then adding 5 affect the mean, median, mode, and range?

TEST PREP

24. The cost function C of rent at an apartment complex increased $50 last year and another $60 this year. Which function accurately reflects these changes?

    (A) $60(C + 50)$ (B) $60(50C)$ (C) $(C + 50) + 60$ (D) $50C + 60$

25. Given $f(x) = 28.5x + 45.6$, which function decreases the y-intercept by 20.3?

    (F) $g(x) = 8.2x + 45.6$ (H) $g(x) = 28.5x + 25.3$

    (G) $g(x) = 8.2x + 66.1$ (J) $g(x) = 28.5x + 66.1$

26. Which transformation describes a line that is parallel to $f(x)$?

    (A) $f(3x)$ (B) $f\left(\dfrac{x}{2}\right)$ (C) $f(x - 4)$ (D) $f(-2x)$

27. Which transformation of $f(x) = \dfrac{1}{2}x - 1$ could result in the graph shown?

    (F) vertical shift 2 units down and reflection across x-axis

    (G) horizontal shift 2 units left and reflection across x-axis

    (H) vertical shift 2 units up and reflection across x-axis

    (J) horizontal shift 2 units right and reflection across x-axis

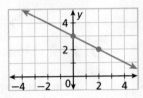

CHALLENGE AND EXTEND

28. Give two different combinations of transformations that would transform $f(x) = 3x + 4$ into $g(x) = 15x - 10$.

29. Give an example of two transformations of $f(x) = x$ that can be performed in any order and result in the same transformed function.

30. **Education** The graph shows the tuition at a university based on the number of credit hours taken. The rate per credit hour varies according to the number of hours taken: less than 12 hours, 12 to 18 hours, and greater than 18 hours.

    a. Write the linear function that represents each segment of the graph.

    b. Write the linear functions that would reflect a 12% increase in all tuition costs.

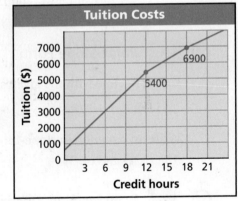

FOCUS ON MATHEMATICAL PRACTICES

H.O.T. 31. **Modeling** What transformation would you use to triple the slope of a line while leaving its x-intercept constant?

H.O.T. 32. **Reasoning** Explain why reflecting the function $f(x) = 0$ across either axis does not change the graph.

H.O.T. 33. **Analysis** Let $f(x) = 2x + 1$.

    a. $f(x)$ is reflected across the x-axis to obtain $g(x)$. Write the equation of $g(x)$.

    b. $g(x)$ is reflected across the y-axis to obtain $h(x)$. Write the equation of $h(x)$. How is the slope of $h(x)$ related to the slope of $f(x)$?

    c. What single transformation of $f(x)$ could you use to get $h(x)$?

Ready to Go On?

11-1 Direct Variation

Tell whether each relationship is a direct variation. If so, identify the constant of variation.

1.

x	1	4	8	12
y	3	6	10	14

2.

x	−6	−2	0	3
y	−3	−1	0	1.5

11-2 Slope-Intercept Form

Write each equation in slope-intercept form. Then graph the line described by the equation.

3. $2x + y = 5$

4. $2x - 6y = 6$

5. $3x + y = 3x - 4$

6. Entertainment At a chili cook-off, people pay a $3.00 entrance fee and $0.50 for each bowl of chili they taste. The graph shows the total cost per person as a function of the number of bowls of chili tasted.

   a. Write an equation that represents the total cost per person as a function of the number of bowls of chili tasted.

   b. Identify the slope and y-intercept and describe their meanings.

11-3 Point-Slope Form

Graph the line with the given slope that contains the given point.

7. slope $= -3$; $(0, 3)$

8. slope $= -\dfrac{2}{3}$; $(-3, 5)$

9. slope $= 2$; $(-3, -1)$

Write an equation in slope-intercept form for the line through the two points.

10. $(3, 1)$ and $(4, 3)$

11. $(-1, -1)$ and $(1, 7)$

12. $(1, -4)$ and $(-2, 5)$

11-4 Transforming Linear Functions

Graph $f(x)$ and $g(x)$. Then describe the transformation(s) from the graph of $f(x)$ to the graph of $g(x)$.

13. $f(x) = 5x$, $g(x) = -5x$

14. $f(x) = \dfrac{1}{2}x - 1$, $g(x) = \dfrac{1}{2}x + 4$

PARCC Assessment Readiness

Selected Response

1. Write a function to describe the following:

The graph of $f(x) = |x|$ is made narrower, reflected across the x-axis, and translated 8 units up.

Ⓐ $g(x) = -\left|\frac{1}{5}x + 8\right|$

Ⓑ $g(x) = \left|-\frac{1}{5}x + 8\right|$

Ⓒ $g(x) = -|5x| + 8$

Ⓓ $g(x) = |-5x + 8|$

2. The points $(-4, -3)$ and $(-1, -8)$ are on a line. Find the intercepts to the nearest tenth.

Ⓕ $x = 5.8; y = -9.7$

Ⓖ $x = 3; y = -5$

Ⓗ $x = -5.8; y = -9.7$

Ⓙ $x = -5; y = -11$

3. The cost $f(x)$ in dollars to fill a car's tank with gas and get a car wash is a linear function of the capacity in gallons x of gas of the tank. The costs of a fill-up and a car wash for three different customers are shown in the table. Write an equation for the function in slope-intercept form. Then, find the cost of a fill-up and a car wash for a customer with a truck whose tank size is 22 gallons.

Tank size (gal) (x)	Total cost ($) f(x)
11	21.45
15	28.25
17	31.65

Ⓐ $f(x) = 1.50x + 3.00$; Cost for truck = $36.00

Ⓑ $f(x) = 1.70x + 2.75$; Cost for truck = $40.15

Ⓒ $f(x) = 0.59x + 1.62$; Cost for truck = $14.60

Ⓓ $f(x) = 1.60x + 2.25$; Cost for truck = $37.45

4. The value of y varies directly with x, and $y = 27$ when $x = 18$. Find y when $x = 36$.

Ⓕ $y = 36$

Ⓖ $y = 24$

Ⓗ $y = 1.5$

Ⓙ $y = 54$

5. Identify the vertex and give the minimum or maximum value of the function. Explain.
$y = |x - 3| + 1$

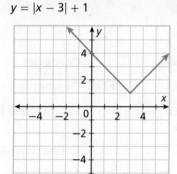

Ⓐ The vertex is $(3, 1)$. The graph opens upward, so the function has a minimum. The minimum is 1.

Ⓑ The vertex is $(3, 1)$. The graph does not intersect the x-axis, so the function has no minimum.

Ⓒ The vertex is $(3, 1)$. The graph opens upward, so the function has a maximum. The maximum is 6.

Ⓓ The vertex is $(1, 3)$. The graph opens upward, so the function has a minimum. The minimum is 1.

6. Write the equation that describes the line in slope-intercept form.
slope = 4, point $(3, -2)$ is on the line

Ⓕ $y = 4x + 14$ Ⓗ $y = 4x + 10$

Ⓖ $y = 4x - 14$ Ⓙ $y = 4x - 2$

Mini-Task

7. The water level of a river is 34 feet and it is receding at a rate of 0.5 foot per day.

a. Write an equation that represents the water level, w, after d days.

b. Identify the slope and y-intercept and describe their meanings.

c. In how many days will the water level be 26 feet?

12

Exponential Functions

COMMON CORE GPS

Contents

MATHEMATICAL PRACTICES

The Common Core Georgia Performance Standards for Mathematical Practice describe varieties of expertise that all students should seek to develop. Opportunities to develop these practices are integrated throughout this program.

1 Make sense of problems and persevere in solving them.

2 Reason abstractly and quantitatively.

3 Construct viable arguments and critique the reasoning of others.

4 Model with mathematics.

5 Use appropriate tools strategically.

6 Attend to precision.

7 Look for and make use of structure.

8 Look for and express regularity in repeated reasoning.

Unpacking the Standards

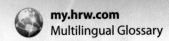

my.hrw.com
Multilingual Glossary

Understanding the standards and the vocabulary terms in the standards will help you know exactly what you are expected to learn in this chapter.

 MCC9-12.F.BF.2

Write arithmetic and geometric sequences both recursively and with an explicit formula, use them to model situations, and translate between the two forms.

Key Vocabulary

arithmetic sequence (sucesión aritmética) A sequence whose successive terms differ by the same nonzero number d, called the *common difference*.

geometric sequence (sucesión geométrica) A sequence in which the ratio of successive terms is a constant r, called the *common ratio*, where $r \neq 0$ and $r \neq 1$.

recursive formula (fórmula recurrente) A formula for a sequence in which one or more previous terms are used to generate the next term.

What It Means For You

You can write rules for arithmetic and geometric sequences as a function of the term number or with respect to the previous term. You can use the form that is more useful for a particular situation.

EXAMPLE   **Explicit and Recursive Formulas**

In the geometric sequence below, each term is twice the previous term. So, the common ratio is $r = 2$.

1	2	3	4	← Position, n
↓	↓	↓	↓	
3	6	12	24	← Term, a_n
a_1	a_2	a_3	a_4	

Explicit formula: $a_n = a_1 r^{n-1}$, so $a_n = 3 \cdot 2^{n-1}$

Recursive formula: The recursive formula gives the first term and for finding successive terms:
$a_n = a_{n-1} r$, so $a_1 = 3$, $a_n = 2a_{n-1}$

 MCC9-12.F.IF.7e

Graph exponential … functions, showing intercepts and end behavior, …

Key Vocabulary

exponential function (función exponencial) A function of the form $f(x) = ab^x$, where a and b are real numbers with $a \neq 0$, $b > 0$, and $b \neq 1$.

What It Means For You

The graph of an exponential function $f(x) = ab^x$ has y-intercept a. If $a > 0$, the function may model growth or decay.

EXAMPLE

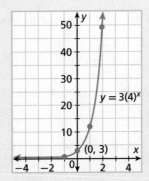

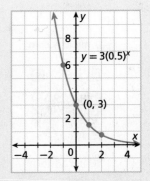

The graph nears the x-axis as x decreases and rises faster and faster as x increases.

The graph nears the x-axis as x increases and rises faster and faster as x decreases.

Unpacking the Standards   **307**

12-1 # Geometric Sequences

Essential Question: How can you recognize, extend, and find a given term of a geometric sequence?

Objectives
Recognize and extend geometric sequences.

Find the *n*th term of a geometric sequence.

Vocabulary
geometric sequence
common ratio

Who uses this?

Bungee jumpers can use geometric sequences to calculate how high they will bounce.

The table shows the heights of a bungee jumper's bounces.

The height of the bounces shown in the table form a *geometric sequence*. In a **geometric sequence**, the ratio of successive terms is the same number *r*, called the **common ratio**.

Bounce	1	2	3
Height (ft)	200	80	32

The variable *a* is often used to represent terms in a sequence. The variable a_4 (read "*a* sub 4") is the fourth term in a sequence.

Geometric sequences can be thought of as functions. The term number, or position in the sequence, is the input, and the term itself is the output.

$$1 \quad 2 \quad 3 \quad 4 \quad \longleftarrow \text{Position}$$

$$3 \quad 6 \quad 12 \quad 24 \quad \longleftarrow \text{Term}$$
$$a_1 \quad a_2 \quad a_3 \quad a_4$$

To find a term in a geometric sequence, multiply the previous term by *r*.

Finding a Term of a Geometric Sequence

The *n*th term of a geometric sequence with **common ratio** *r* is

$$a_n = a_{n-1}r$$

COMMON CORE GPS **EXAMPLE** 1
MCC9-12.F.BF.2

 **my.hrw.com**

Online Video Tutor

Extending Geometric Sequences

Find the next three terms in each geometric sequence.

A 1, 3, 9, 27, …

Step 1 Find the value of *r* by dividing each term by the one before it.

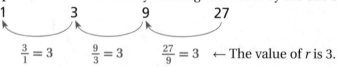

$$\frac{3}{1} = 3 \qquad \frac{9}{3} = 3 \qquad \frac{27}{9} = 3 \quad \longleftarrow \text{The value of } r \text{ is 3.}$$

Step 2 Multiply each term by 3 to find the next three terms.

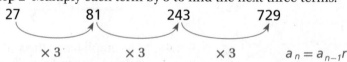

$$\times 3 \qquad \times 3 \qquad \times 3 \qquad a_n = a_{n-1}r$$

The next three terms are 81, 243, and 729.

Mark A. Johnson/photolibrary

Helpful Hint

When the terms in a geometric sequence alternate between positive and negative, the value of r is negative.

B $-16, 4, -1, \frac{1}{4}, \ldots$

Step 1 Find the value of r by dividing each term by the one before it.

$$-16 \qquad 4 \qquad -1 \qquad \frac{1}{4}$$

$$\frac{4}{-16} = -\frac{1}{4} \qquad \frac{-1}{4} = -\frac{1}{4} \qquad \frac{\frac{1}{4}}{-1} = -\frac{1}{4} \quad \leftarrow \text{The value of } r \text{ is } -\frac{1}{4}.$$

Step 2 Multiply each term by $-\frac{1}{4}$ to find the next three terms.

$$\frac{1}{4} \qquad -\frac{1}{16} \qquad \frac{1}{64} \qquad -\frac{1}{256}$$

$$\times \left(-\frac{1}{4}\right) \qquad \times \left(-\frac{1}{4}\right) \qquad \times \left(-\frac{1}{4}\right) \qquad a_n = a_{n-1}r$$

The next three terms are $-\frac{1}{16}, \frac{1}{64},$ and $-\frac{1}{256}.$

 CHECK IT OUT! Find the next three terms in each geometric sequence.

1a. $5, -10, 20, -40, \ldots$ **1b.** $512, 384, 288, \ldots$

To find the output a_n of a geometric sequence when n is a large number, you need an equation, or function rule.

The pattern in the table shows that to get the nth term, multiply the first term by the common ratio raised to the power $n - 1$.

Words	Numbers	Algebra
1st term	3	a_1
2nd term	$3 \cdot 2^1 = 6$	$a_1 \cdot r^1$
3rd term	$3 \cdot 2^2 = 12$	$a_1 \cdot r^2$
4th term	$3 \cdot 2^3 = 24$	$a_1 \cdot r^3$
nth term	$3 \cdot 2^{n-1}$	$a_1 \cdot r^{n-1}$

If the first term of a geometric sequence is a_1, the nth term is a_n, and the common ratio is r, then

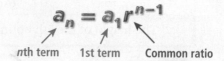

$$a_n = a_1 r^{n-1}$$

nth term   1st term   Common ratio

COMMON CORE GPS

EXAMPLE 2

MCC9-12.F.BF.2

my.hrw.com

Online Video Tutor

Finding the nth Term of a Geometric Sequence

A The first term of a geometric sequence is 128, and the common ratio is 0.5. What is the 10th term of the sequence?

$a_n = a_1 r^{n-1}$ *Write the formula.*

$a_{10} = 128(0.5)^{10-1}$ *Substitute 128 for a_1, 10 for n, and 0.5 for r.*

$= 128(0.5)^9$ *Simplify the exponent.*

$= 0.25$ *Use a calculator.*

B For a geometric sequence, $a_1 = 8$ and $r = 3$. Find the 5th term of this sequence.

$a_n = a_1 r^{n-1}$ *Write the formula.*

$a_5 = 8(3)^{5-1}$ *Substitute 8 for a_1, 5 for n, and 3 for r.*

$= 8(3)^4$ *Simplify the exponent.*

$= 648$ *Use a calculator.*

C What is the 13th term of the geometric sequence $8, -16, 32, -64, \dots$?

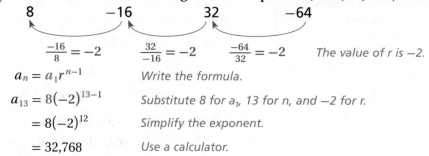

$8 \qquad -16 \qquad 32 \qquad -64$

$\dfrac{-16}{8} = -2 \qquad \dfrac{32}{-16} = -2 \qquad \dfrac{-64}{32} = -2 \qquad$ *The value of r is -2.*

$a_n = a_1 r^{n-1}$ *Write the formula.*

$a_{13} = 8(-2)^{13-1}$ *Substitute 8 for a_1, 13 for n, and -2 for r.*

$\quad = 8(-2)^{12}$ *Simplify the exponent.*

$\quad = 32{,}768$ *Use a calculator.*

CHECK IT OUT!   **2.** What is the 8th term of the sequence $1000, 500, 250, 125, \dots$?

COMMON CORE GPS   **EXAMPLE**   **3**   MCC9-12.F.BF.2

Sports Application

my.hrw.com

Online Video Tutor

A bungee jumper jumps from a bridge. The diagram shows the bungee jumper's height above the ground at the top of each bounce. The heights form a geometric sequence. What is the bungee jumper's height at the top of the 5th bounce?

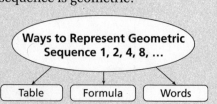

First bounce 200 ft

Second bounce 80 ft

Third bounce 32 ft

$200 \qquad 80 \qquad 32$

$\dfrac{80}{200} = 0.4 \qquad \dfrac{32}{80} = 0.4$

$a_n = a_1 r^{n-1}$ *Write the formula.*

$a_5 = 200(0.4)^{5-1}$ *Substitute 200 for a_1, 5 for n, and 0.4 for r.*

$\quad = 200(0.4)^4$ *Simplify the exponent.*

$\quad = 5.12$ *Use a calculator.*

The height of the 5th bounce is 5.12 feet.

CHECK IT OUT!   **3.** The table shows a car's value for 3 years after it is purchased. The values form a geometric sequence. How much will the car be worth in the 10th year?

Year	Value ($)
1	10,000
2	8,000
3	6,400

MCC.MP.3   MATHEMATICAL PRACTICES

THINK AND DISCUSS

1. How do you determine whether a sequence is geometric?

Know it! Note

2. GET ORGANIZED Copy and complete the graphic organizer. In each box, write a way to represent the geometric sequence.

Ways to Represent Geometric Sequence 1, 2, 4, 8, ...

Table   Formula   Words

12-1 Exercises

GUIDED PRACTICE

1. Vocabulary What is the *common ratio* of a geometric sequence?

SEE EXAMPLE **1**   **Find the next three terms in each geometric sequence.**

   2. 2, 4, 8, 16, …   **3.** 400, 200, 100, 50, …   **4.** 4, −12, 36, −108, …

SEE EXAMPLE **2**   **5.** The first term of a geometric sequence is 1, and the common ratio is 10. What is the 10th term of the sequence?

   6. What is the 11th term of the geometric sequence 3, 6, 12, 24, … ?

SEE EXAMPLE **3**   **7. Sports** In the NCAA men's basketball tournament, 64 teams compete in round 1. Fewer teams remain in each following round, as shown in the graph, until all but one team have been eliminated. The numbers of teams in each round form a geometric sequence. How many teams compete in round 5?

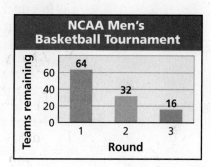

PRACTICE AND PROBLEM SOLVING

my.hrw.com

Online Extra Practice

Find the next three terms in each geometric sequence.

8. −2, 10, −50, 250, …   **9.** 32, 48, 72, 108, …   **10.** 625, 500, 400, 320, …

11. 6, 42, 294, …   **12.** 6, −12, 24, −48, …   **13.** 40, 10, $\frac{5}{2}$, $\frac{5}{8}$, …

14. The first term of a geometric sequence is 18 and the common ratio is 3.5. What is the 5th term of the sequence?

15. What is the 14th term of the geometric sequence 1000, 100, 10, 1, … ?

16. Physical Science A ball is dropped from a height of 500 meters. The table shows the height of each bounce, and the heights form a geometric sequence. How high does the ball bounce on the 8th bounce? Round your answer to the nearest tenth of a meter.

Bounce	Height (m)
1	400
2	320
3	256

Find the missing term(s) in each geometric sequence.

17. 20, 40, ▮, ▮, …   **18.** ▮, 6, 18, ▮, …   **19.** 9, 3, 1, ▮, …

20. 3, 12, ▮, 192, ▮, …   **21.** 7, 1, ▮, ▮, $\frac{1}{343}$, …   **22.** ▮, 100, 25, ▮, $\frac{25}{16}$, …

23. −3, ▮, −12, 24, ▮, …   **24.** ▮, ▮, 1, −3, 9, …   **25.** 1, 17, 289, ▮, …

Determine whether each sequence could be geometric. If so, give the common ratio.

26. 2, 10, 50, 250, …   **27.** 15, 5, $\frac{5}{3}$, $\frac{5}{9}$, …   **28.** 6, 18, 24, 38, …

29. 9, 3, −1, −5, …   **30.** 7, 21, 63, 189, …   **31.** 4, 1, −2, −4, …

H.O.T. 32. Multi-Step Billy earns money by mowing lawns for the summer. He offers two payment plans, as shown at right.

    a. Do the payments for plan 2 form a geometric sequence? Explain.

    b. If you were one of Billy's customers, which plan would you choose? (Assume that the summer is 10 weeks long.) Explain your choice.

33. Measurement When you fold a piece of paper in half, the thickness of the folded piece is twice the thickness of the original piece. A piece of copy paper is about 0.1 mm thick.

    a. How thick is a piece of copy paper that has been folded in half 7 times?

    b. Suppose that you could fold a piece of copy paper in half 12 times. How thick would it be? Write your answer in centimeters.

List the first four terms of each geometric sequence.

34. $a_1 = 3, a_n = 3(2)^{n-1}$ **35.** $a_1 = -2, a_n = -2(4)^{n-1}$ **36.** $a_1 = 5, a_n = 5(-2)^{n-1}$

37. $a_1 = 2, a_n = 2(2)^{n-1}$ **38.** $a_1 = 2, a_n = 2(5)^{n-1}$ **39.** $a_1 = 12, a_n = 12\left(\dfrac{1}{4}\right)^{n-1}$

H.O.T. 40. Critical Thinking What happens to the terms of a geometric sequence when r is doubled? Use an example to support your answer.

41. Geometry The steps below describe how to make a geometric figure by repeating the same process over and over on a smaller and smaller scale.

    Step 1 (stage 0) Draw a large square.

    Step 2 (stage 1) Divide the square into four equal squares.

    Step 3 (stage 2) Divide each small square into four equal squares.

    Step 4 Repeat Step 3 indefinitely.

    a. Draw stages 0, 1, 2, and 3.

    b. How many small squares are in each stage? Organize your data relating stage and number of small squares in a table.

    c. Does the data in part **b** form a geometric sequence? Explain.

    d. Write a rule to find the number of small squares in stage n.

H.O.T. 42. Write About It Write a series of steps for finding the nth term of a geometric sequence when you are given the first several terms.

Real-World Connections

43. a. Three years ago, the annual tuition at a university was $3000. The following year, the tuition was $3300, and last year, the tuition was $3630. If the tuition has continued to grow in the same manner, what is the tuition this year? What do you expect it to be next year?

    b. What is the common ratio?

    c. What would you predict the tuition was 4 years ago? How did you find that value?

TEST PREP

44. Which of the following is a geometric sequence?

(A) $\frac{1}{2}, 1, \frac{3}{2}, 2, \ldots$

(C) 3, 8, 13, 18, …

(B) −2, −6, −10, −14, …

(D) 5, 10, 20, 40, …

45. Which equation represents the nth term in the geometric sequence 2, −8, 32, −128, …?

(F) $a_n = (-4)^n$

(G) $a_n = (-4)^{n-1}$

(H) $a_n = 2(-4)^n$

(J) $a_n = 2(-4)^{n-1}$

46. The frequency of a musical note, measured in hertz (Hz), is called its pitch. The pitches of the A keys on a piano form a geometric sequence, as shown.

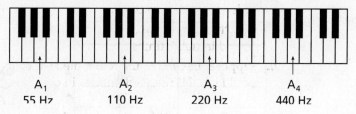

A_1	A_2	A_3	A_4
55 Hz	110 Hz	220 Hz	440 Hz

What is the frequency of A_7?

(A) 880 Hz

(B) 1760 Hz

(C) 3520 Hz

(D) 7040 Hz

CHALLENGE AND EXTEND

Find the next three terms in each geometric sequence.

47. $x, x^2, x^3, \ldots$

48. $2x^2, 6x^3, 18x^4, \ldots$

49. $\frac{1}{y^3}, \frac{1}{y^2}, \frac{1}{y}, \ldots$

50. $\frac{1}{(x+1)^2}, \frac{1}{x+1}, 1, \ldots$

51. The 10th term of a geometric sequence is 0.78125. The common ratio is −0.5. Find the first term of the sequence.

52. The first term of a geometric sequence is 12 and the common ratio is $\frac{1}{2}$. Is 0 a term in this sequence? Explain.

53. A geometric sequence starts with 14 and has a common ration of 0.4. Colin finds that another number in the sequence is 0.057344. Which term in the sequence did Colin find?

H.O.T. 54. The first three terms of a sequence are 1, 2, and 4. Susanna said the 8th term of this sequence is 128. Paul said the 8th term is 29. Explain how the students found their answers. Why could these both be considered correct answers?

FOCUS ON MATHEMATICAL PRACTICES

H.O.T. 55. Reasoning A geometric sequence can be written as a function, in which the input p is the position of the term and the output is the term's value. Write the first 4 terms of each sequence.

a. $f(p) = 2(1.5)^{p-1}$

b. $f(p) = 256\left(\frac{1}{4}\right)^{p-1}$

c. $f(p) = 3(-3)^p$

H.O.T. 56. Reasonableness A company promises that its Superbounce Ball will reach at least 50% of its drop height after the third bounce. The heights of successive bounces form a geometric sequence. Jay drops the ball and measures its first bounce at 80% of the drop height. Is the company's claim reasonable? Explain.

Exponential Functions

Essential Question: How can you identify, evaluate, and graph exponential functions?

Objectives
Evaluate exponential functions.

Identify and graph exponential functions.

Vocabulary
exponential function

Who uses this?
Scientists model populations with exponential functions.

The table and the graph show an insect population that increases over time.

Time (days)	Population
0	2
1	6
2	18
3	54

⟩× 3
⟩× 3
⟩× 3

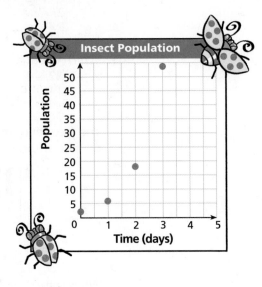

Insect Population

A function rule that describes the pattern above is $f(x) = 2(3)^x$. This type of function, in which the independent variable appears in an exponent, is an **exponential function**. Notice that 2 is the starting population and 3 is the amount by which the population is multiplied each day.

Exponential Functions

An exponential function has the form $f(x) = ab^x$, where $a \neq 0$, $b \neq 1$, and $b > 0$.

COMMON CORE GPS
MCC9-12.F.BF.1a

EXAMPLE 1 Evaluating an Exponential Function

my.hrw.com

Online Video Tutor

A The function $f(x) = 2(3)^x$ models an insect population after x days. What will the population be on the 5th day?

$f(x) = 2(3)^x$ *Write the function.*
$f(5) = 2(3)^5$ *Substitute 5 for x.*
$= 2(243)$ *Evaluate 3^5.*
$= 486$ *Multiply.*

There will be 486 insects on the 5th day.

B The function $f(x) = 1500(0.995)^x$, where x is the time in years, models a prairie dog population. How many prairie dogs will there be in 8 years?

$f(x) = 1500(0.995)^x$
$f(8) = 1500(0.995)^8$ *Substitute 8 for x.*
≈ 1441 *Use a calculator. Round to the nearest whole number.*

There will be about 1441 prairie dogs in 8 years.

Helpful Hint

In Example 1B, round your answer to the nearest whole number because there can only be a whole number of prairie dogs.

 CHECK IT OUT!

1. The function $f(x) = 8(0.75)^x$ models the width of a photograph in inches after it has been reduced by 25% x times. What is the width of the photograph after it has been reduced 3 times?

Remember that linear functions have constant first differences and quadratic functions have constant second differences. Exponential functions do not have constant differences, but they do have *constant ratios*.

As the *x*-values increase by a constant amount, the *y*-values are multiplied by a constant amount. This amount is the constant ratio and is the value of *b* in $f(x) = ab^x$.

x	$f(x) = 2(3)^x$
1	6
2	18
3	54
4	162

+1 ×3
+1 ×3
+1 ×3

COMMON CORE GPS
EXAMPLE 2
MCC9-12.F.LE.1c

my.hrw.com

Online Video Tutor

Identifying an Exponential Function

Tell whether each set of ordered pairs satisfies an exponential function. Explain your answer.

A $\{(-1, 1.5), (0, 3), (1, 6), (2, 12)\}$

x	y
−1	1.5
0	3
1	6
2	12

+1 ×2
+1 ×2
+1 ×2

This is an exponential function. As the *x*-values increase by a constant amount, the *y*-values are multiplied by a constant amount.

B $\{(-1, -9), (1, 9), (3, 27), (5, 45)\}$

x	y
−1	−9
1	9
3	27
5	45

+2 ×(−1)
+2 ×3
+2 ×$\frac{5}{3}$

This is *not* an exponential function. As the *x*-values increase by a constant amount, the *y*-values are *not* multiplied by a constant amount.

 CHECK IT OUT! Tell whether each set of ordered pairs satisfies an exponential function. Explain your answer.

2a. $\{(-1, 1), (0, 0), (1, 1), (2, 4)\}$ **2b.** $\{(-2, 4), (-1, 2), (0, 1), (1, 0.5)\}$

To graph an exponential function, choose several values of *x* (positive, negative, and 0) and generate ordered pairs. Plot the points and connect them with a smooth curve.

COMMON CORE GPS
EXAMPLE 3
MCC9-12.F.IF.7e

my.hrw.com

Online Video Tutor

Graphing $y = ab^x$ with $a > 0$ and $b > 1$

Graph $y = 3(4)^x$.

Choose several values of x and generate ordered pairs.

x	$y = 3(4)^x$
−1	0.75
0	3
1	12
2	48

Graph the ordered pairs and connect with a smooth curve.

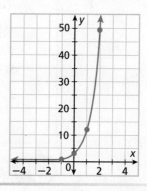

 CHECK IT OUT! **3a.** Graph $y = 2^x$. **3b.** Graph $y = 0.2(5)^x$.

EXAMPLE **4**

COMMON CORE GPS
MCC9-12.F.IF.7e

Graphing $y = ab^x$ with $a < 0$ and $b > 1$

Graph $y = -5(2)^x$.

Choose several values of x and generate ordered pairs.

x	$y = -5(2)^x$
-1	-2.5
0	-5
1	-10
2	-20

Graph the ordered pairs and connect with a smooth curve.

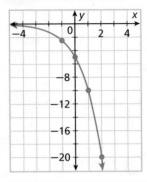

my.hrw.com

Online Video Tutor

CHECK IT OUT! **4a.** Graph $y = -6^x$.   **4b.** Graph $y = -3(3)^x$.

EXAMPLE **5**

COMMON CORE GPS
MCC9-12.F.IF.7e

Graphing $y = ab^x$ with $0 < b < 1$

Graph each exponential function.

 **my.hrw.com**

Online Video Tutor

A $y = 3\left(\dfrac{1}{2}\right)^x$

Choose several values of x and generate ordered pairs.

x	$y = 3\left(\dfrac{1}{2}\right)^x$
-1	6
0	3
1	1.5
2	0.75

Graph the ordered pairs and connect with a smooth curve.

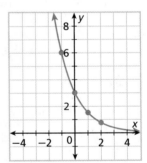

B $y = -2(0.4)^x$

Choose several values of x and generate ordered pairs.

x	$y = -2(0.4)^x$
-2	-12.5
-1	-5
0	-2
1	-0.8

Graph the ordered pairs and connect with a smooth curve.

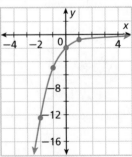

CHECK IT OUT! **Graph each exponential function.**

5a. $y = 4\left(\dfrac{1}{4}\right)^x$ **5b.** $y = -2(0.1)^x$

The box summarizes the general shapes of exponential function graphs.

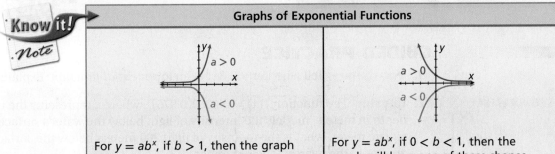

| Graphs of Exponential Functions |

For $y = ab^x$, if $b > 1$, then the graph will have one of these shapes.

For $y = ab^x$, if $0 < b < 1$, then the graph will have one of these shapes.

COMMON CORE GPS **EXAMPLE** MCC9-12.F.BF.1a **6**

Statistics Application

In the year 2000, the world population was about 6 billion, and it was growing by 1.21% each year. At this growth rate, the function $f(x) = 6(1.0121)^x$ gives the population, in billions, x years after 2000. Using this model, in about what year does the population reach 7 billion?

my.hrw.com

Online Video Tutor

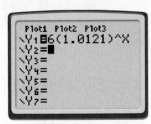

Enter the function into the Y= editor of a graphing calculator.

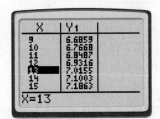

TABLE

Press **2nd** **GRAPH**. *Use the arrow keys to find a y-value as close to 7 as possible. The corresponding x-value is 13.*

Caution! //////

The function values give the population *in billions*, so a *y*-value of 7 means 7 billion.

The world population reaches 7 billion in about 2013.

6. An accountant uses $f(x) = 12{,}330(0.869)^x$, where x is the time in years since the purchase, to model the value of a car. When will the car be worth $2000?

MCC.MP.7 MATHEMATICAL PRACTICES

THINK AND DISCUSS

1. How can you find the constant ratio of a set of exponential data?

2. GET ORGANIZED Copy and complete the graphic organizer. In each box, give an example of an appropriate exponential function and sketch its graph.

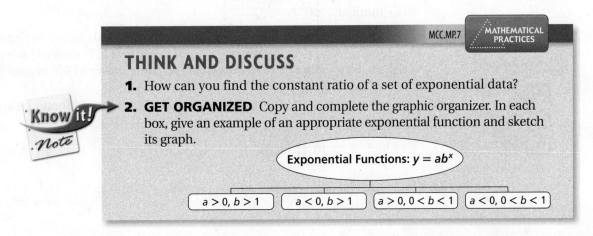

Exponential Functions: $y = ab^x$

| $a > 0, b > 1$ | $a < 0, b > 1$ | $a > 0, 0 < b < 1$ | $a < 0, 0 < b < 1$ |

GUIDED PRACTICE

1. **Vocabulary** Tell whether $y = 3x^4$ is an *exponential function*. Explain your answer.

SEE EXAMPLE 1

2. **Physics** The function $f(x) = 50,000(0.975)^x$, where x represents the underwater depth in meters, models the intensity of light below the water's surface in lumens per square meter. What is the intensity of light 200 meters below the surface? Round your answer to the nearest whole number.

SEE EXAMPLE 2

Tell whether each set of ordered pairs satisfies an exponential function. Explain your answer.

3. $\{(-1, -1), (0, 0), (1, -1), (2, -4)\}$

4. $\{(0, 1), (1, 4), (2, 16), (3, 64)\}$

Graph each exponential function.

SEE EXAMPLE 3

5. $y = 3^x$

6. $y = 5^x$

7. $y = 10(3)^x$

8. $y = 5(2)^x$

SEE EXAMPLE 4

9. $y = -2(3)^x$

10. $y = -4(2)^x$

11. $y = -3(2)^x$

12. $y = 2(3)^x$

SEE EXAMPLE 5

13. $y = -\left(\frac{1}{4}\right)^x$

14. $y = \left(\frac{1}{3}\right)^x$

15. $y = 2\left(\frac{1}{4}\right)^x$

16. $y = -2(0.25)^x$

SEE EXAMPLE 6

17. The function $f(x) = 57.8(1.02)^x$ gives the number of passenger cars, in millions, in the United States x years after 1960. Using this model, in about what year does the number of passenger cars reach 200 million?

PRACTICE AND PROBLEM SOLVING

Independent Practice	
For Exercises	See Example
18–20	1
21–24	2
25–27	3
28–30	4
31–33	5
34	6

my.hrw.com

Online Extra Practice

18. **Sports** If a golf ball is dropped from a height of 27 feet, the function $f(x) = 27\left(\frac{2}{3}\right)^x$ gives the height in feet of each bounce, where x is the bounce number. What will be the height of the 4th bounce?

19. Suppose the depth of a lake can be described by the function $y = 334(0.976)^x$, where x represents the number of weeks from today. Today, the depth of the lake is 334 ft. What will the depth be in 6 weeks? Round your answer to the nearest whole number.

20. **Physics** A ball rolling down a slope travels continuously faster. Suppose the function $y = 1.3(1.41)^x$ describes the speed of the ball in inches per minute. How fast will the ball be rolling in 15 minutes? Round your answer to the nearest hundredth.

Tell whether each set of ordered pairs satisfies an exponential function. Explain your answer.

21. $\left\{(-2, 9), (-1, 3), (0, 1), \left(1, \frac{1}{3}\right)\right\}$

22. $\{(-1, 0), (0, 1), (1, 4), (2, 9)\}$

23. $\{(-1, -5), (0, -3), (1, -1), (2, 1)\}$

24. $\{(-3, 6.25), (-2, 12.5), (-1, 25), (0, 50)\}$

Graph each exponential function.

25. $y = 1.5^x$

26. $y = \frac{1}{3}(3)^x$

27. $y = 100(0.7)^x$

28. $y = -2(4)^x$

29. $y = -1(5)^x$

30. $y = -\frac{1}{2}(4)^x$

31. $y = 4\left(\frac{1}{2}\right)^x$

32. $y = -2\left(\frac{1}{3}\right)^x$

33. $y = 0.5(0.25)^x$

34. Technology Moore's law states that the maximum number of transistors that can fit on a silicon chip doubles every two years. The function $f(x) = 42(1.41)^x$ models the number of transistors, in millions, that can fit on a chip, where x is the number of years since 2000. Using this model, in what year can a chip hold 1 billion transistors?

35. Multi-Step A computer randomly creates three different functions. The functions are $y = (3.1x + 7)^2$, $y = 4.8(2)^x$, and $y = \frac{1}{5}(6)^x$. The computer then generates the y value 38.4. Given the three different functions, determine which one is exponential *and* produces the generated number.

Early silicon chips were about the size of your pinky finger and held one transistor. Today, chips the size of a baby's fingernail hold over 100 million transistors.

36. Contests As a promotion, a clothing store draws the name of one of its customers each week. The prize is a coupon for the store. If the winner is not present at the drawing, he or she cannot claim the prize, and the amount of the coupon increases for the following week's drawing. The function $f(x) = 20(1.2)^x$ gives the amount of the coupon in dollars after x weeks of the prize going unclaimed.

Clothes for everyone!
Math Apparel
Win Valuable Store Coupon
Must be present to win!

  a. What is the amount of the coupon after 2 weeks of the prize going unclaimed?

  b. After how many weeks of the prize going unclaimed will the amount of the coupon be greater than $100?

  c. What is the original amount of the coupon?

  d. Find the percent increase each week.

H.O.T. 37. Critical Thinking In the definition of exponential function, the value of b cannot be 1, and the value of a cannot be 0. Why?

Graphing Calculator Graph each group of functions on the same screen. How are their graphs alike? How are they different?

38. $y = 2^x, y = 3^x, y = 4^x$

39. $y = \left(\frac{1}{2}\right)^x, y = \left(\frac{1}{3}\right)^x, y = \left(\frac{1}{4}\right)^x$

Evaluate each of the following for the given value of x.

40. $f(x) = 4^x; x = 3$

41. $f(x) = -(0.25)^x; x = 1.5$

42. $f(x) = 0.4(10)^x; x = -3$

Real-World Connections

43. a. The annual tuition at a community college since 2001 is modeled by the equation $C = 2000(1.08)^n$, where C is the tuition cost and n is the number of years since 2001. What was the tuition cost in 2001?

  b. What is the annual percentage of tuition increase?

  c. Find the tuition cost in 2006.

H.O.T. 44. Write About It Your employer offers two salary plans. With plan A, your salary is $f(x) = 10,000(2x)$, where x is the number of years you have worked for the company. With plan B, your salary is $g(x) = 10,000(2)^x$. Which plan would you choose? Why?

TEST PREP

45. Which graph shows an exponential function?

Ⓐ

Ⓒ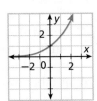

Ⓑ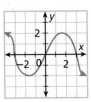

Ⓓ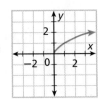

46. The function $f(x) = 15(1.4)^x$ represents the area in square inches of a photograph after it has been enlarged x times by a factor of 140%. What is the area of the photograph after it has been enlarged 4 times?

Ⓕ 5.6 square inches

Ⓖ 57.624 square inches

Ⓗ 41.16 square inches

Ⓙ 560 square inches

47. Look at the pattern. How many squares will there be in the nth stage?

Stage 0

Stage 1   Stage 2

Ⓐ $5n$ Ⓑ $2.5 \cdot 2^n$ Ⓒ 25^{n-1} Ⓓ 5^n

CHALLENGE AND EXTEND

Solve each equation.

48. $4^x = 64$

49. $\left(\dfrac{1}{3}\right)^x = \dfrac{1}{27}$

50. $2^x = \dfrac{1}{16}$

H.O.T. 51. Graph the following functions: $y = 2(2)^x$, $y = 3(2)^x$, $y = -2(2)^x$. Then make a conjecture about the relationship between the value of a and the y-intercept of $y = ab^x$.

FOCUS ON MATHEMATICAL PRACTICES

H.O.T. 52. Problem Solving $p = 0.915^d$ approximates the probability that a professional golfer will sink a putt from a distance of d feet. At what whole number of feet does the probability first drop below 0.5?

H.O.T. 53. Communication The population of a bacteria colony after t hours can be modeled by the function $f(x) = 32(1.25)^t$. What do the numbers 32 and 1.25 represent in the context of the situation?

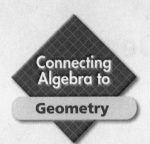

Changing Dimensions

Connecting Algebra to Geometry

What happens to the volume of a three-dimensional figure when you repeatedly double the dimensions?

Recall these formulas for the volumes of common three-dimensional figures.

Cube $V = s^3$ **Rectangular Prism** $V = \ell w h$ **Pyramid** $V = \frac{1}{3}(\text{area of base}) \cdot h$

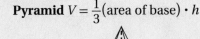

Base

Changing the dimensions of three-dimensional figures results in geometric sequences.

Example

Find the volume of a cube with a side length of 3 cm. Double the side length and find the new volume. Repeat two more times. Show the patterns for the side lengths and volumes as geometric sequences. Identify the common ratios.

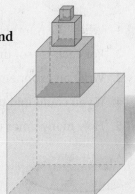

Cube	Side Length (cm)	Volume (cm³)
1	3	27
2	6	216
3	12	1,728
4	24	13,824

($\times 2$ between side lengths; $\times 8$ between volumes)

The side lengths and the volumes form geometric sequences. The sequence of the side lengths has a common ratio of 2. The sequence of the volumes has a common ratio of 2^3, or 8.

The patterns in the example above are a specific instance of a general rule.

> When the dimensions of a solid figure are multiplied by x, the volume of the figure is multiplied by x^3.

Try This

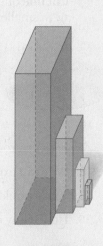

1. The large rectangular prism at right is 8 in. wide, 16 in. long, and 32 in. tall. The dimensions are multiplied by $\frac{1}{2}$ to create each next smaller prism. Show the patterns for the dimensions and the volumes as geometric sequences. Identify the common ratios.

2. A pyramid has a height of 8 cm and a square base of 3 cm on each edge. Triple the dimensions two times. Show the patterns for the dimensions and the volumes as geometric sequences. Identify the common ratios.

Model Growth and Decay

You can fold and cut paper to model quantities that increase or decrease exponentially.

Use with Exponential Growth and Decay

Look for and express regularity in repeated reasoning.

MCC.9-12.F.IE.2 Construct … exponential functions … given … a description of a relationship …. *Also* **MCC.9-12.F.IE.1**

Activity 1

① Copy the table at right.

② Fold a piece of notebook paper in half. Then open it back up. Count the number of regions created by the fold. Record your answer in the table.

③ Now fold the paper in half twice. Record the number of regions created by the folds in the table.

④ Repeat this process for 3, 4, and 5 folds.

Folds	Regions
0	1
1	
2	
3	
4	
5	

Try This

1. When the number of folds increases by 1, the number of regions ___?___ .

2. For each row of the table, write the number of regions as a power of 2.

3. Write an exponential expression for the number of regions formed by n folds.

4. If you could fold the paper 8 times, how many regions would be formed?

5. How many times would you have to fold the paper to make 512 regions?

Activity 2

① Copy the table at right.

② Begin with a square piece of paper. The area of the paper is 1 square unit. Cut the paper in half. Each piece has an area of $\frac{1}{2}$ square unit. Record the result in the table.

③ Cut one of those pieces in half again, and record the area of one of the new, smaller pieces in the table.

④ Repeat this process for 3, 4, and 5 cuts.

Cuts	Area
0	1
1	
2	
3	
4	
5	

Try This

6. When the number of cuts increases by 1, the area ___?___ .

7. For each row of the table, write the area as a power of 2.

8. Write an exponential expression for the area after n cuts.

9. What would be the area after 7 cuts?

10. How many cuts would you have to make to get an area of $\frac{1}{256}$ square unit?

12-3 Exponential Growth and Decay

Essential Question: How can you use exponential growth and decay functions to solve problems?

Objective
Solve problems involving exponential growth and decay.

Vocabulary
exponential growth
compound interest
exponential decay
half-life

Animated Math

Why learn this?
Exponential growth and decay describe many real-world situations, such as the value of artwork. (See Example 1.)

Exponential growth occurs when a quantity increases by the same rate *r* in each time period *t*. When this happens, the value of the quantity at any given time can be calculated as a function of the rate and the original amount.

Exponential Growth

An exponential growth function has the form $y = a(1 + r)^t$, where $a > 0$.

y represents the final amount.

a represents the original amount.

r represents the rate of growth expressed as a decimal.

t represents time.

COMMON CORE GPS MCC9-12.F.LE.2

EXAMPLE 1

my.hrw.com

Online Video Tutor

Exponential Growth

The original value of a painting is $1400, and the value increases by 9% each year. Write an exponential growth function to model this situation. Then find the value of the painting in 25 years.

Step 1 Write the exponential growth function for this situation.

$$y = a(1 + r)^t \qquad \textit{Write the formula.}$$
$$= 1400(1 + 0.09)^t \qquad \textit{Substitute 1400 for a and 0.09 for r.}$$
$$= 1400(1.09)^t \qquad \textit{Simplify.}$$

Step 2 Find the value in 25 years.

$$y = 1400(1.09)^t$$
$$= 1400(1.09)^{25} \qquad \textit{Substitute 25 for t.}$$
$$\approx 12{,}072.31 \qquad \textit{Use a calculator and round to the nearest hundredth.}$$

The value of the painting in 25 years is $12,072.31.

Helpful Hint

In Example 1, round to the nearest hundredth because the problem deals with money. This means you are rounding to the nearest cent.

CHECK IT OUT!

1. A sculpture is increasing in value at a rate of 8% per year, and its value in 2000 was $1200. Write an exponential growth function to model this situation. Then find the sculpture's value in 2006.

A common application of exponential growth is *compound interest*. Recall that simple interest is earned or paid only on the principal. **Compound interest** is interest earned or paid on *both* the principal and previously earned interest.

 Know it! Note

Compound Interest

$$A = P\left(1 + \frac{r}{n}\right)^{nt}$$

A represents the balance after *t* years.

P represents the principal, or original amount.

r represents the annual interest rate expressed as a decimal.

n represents the number of times interest is compounded per year.

t represents time in years.

COMMON CORE GPS **EXAMPLE** 2 MCC9-12.F.LE.2

 my.hrw.com

Online Video Tutor

Finance Application

Write a compound interest function to model each situation. Then find the balance after the given number of years.

A **$1000 invested at a rate of 3% compounded quarterly; 5 years**

Step 1 Write the compound interest function for this situation.

$A = P\left(1 + \frac{r}{n}\right)^{nt}$ *Write the formula.*

$= 1000\left(1 + \frac{0.03}{4}\right)^{4t}$ *Substitute 1000 for P, 0.03 for r, and 4 for n.*

$= 1000(1.0075)^{4t}$ *Simplify.*

Step 2 Find the balance after 5 years.

$A = 1000(1.0075)^{4(5)}$ *Substitute 5 for t.*

$= 1000(1.0075)^{20}$

≈ 1161.18 *Use a calculator and round to the nearest hundredth.*

The balance after 5 years is $1161.18.

B **$18,000 invested at a rate of 4.5% compounded annually; 6 years**

Step 1 Write the compound interest function for this situation.

$A = P\left(1 + \frac{r}{n}\right)^{nt}$ *Write the formula.*

$= 18,000\left(1 + \frac{0.045}{1}\right)^{t}$ *Substitute 18,000 for P, 0.045 for r, and 1 for n.*

$= 18,000(1.045)^{t}$ *Simplify.*

Step 2 Find the balance after 6 years.

$A = 18,000(1.045)^{6}$ *Substitute 6 for t.*

$\approx 23,440.68$ *Use a calculator and round to the nearest hundredth.*

The balance after 6 years is $23,440.68.

 **Reading Math**

For compound interest,
• *annually* means "once per year" ($n = 1$).
• *quarterly* means "4 times per year" ($n = 4$).
• *monthly* means "12 times per year" ($n = 12$).

 CHECK IT OUT! Write a compound interest function to model each situation. Then find the balance after the given number of years.

2a. $1200 invested at a rate of 3.5% compounded quarterly; 4 years

2b. $4000 invested at a rate of 3% compounded monthly; 8 years

Exponential decay occurs when a quantity decreases by the same rate r in each time period t. Just like exponential growth, the value of the quantity at any given time can be calculated by using the rate and the original amount.

Exponential Decay

An exponential decay function has the form $y = a(1 - r)^t$, where $a > 0$.

y represents the final amount.

a represents the original amount.

r represents the rate of decay as a decimal.

t represents time.

Notice an important difference between exponential growth functions and exponential decay functions. For exponential growth, the value inside the parentheses will be greater than 1 because r is added to 1. For exponential decay, the value inside the parentheses will be less than 1 because r is subtracted from 1.

 EXAMPLE MCC9-12.F.LE.2 **3**

Exponential Decay

The population of a town is decreasing at a rate of 1% per year. In 2000 there were 1300 people. Write an exponential decay function to model this situation. Then find the population in 2008.

Step 1 Write the exponential decay function for this situation.

$y = a(1 - r)^t$ *Write the formula.*

$= 1300(1 - 0.01)^t$ *Substitute 1300 for a and 0.01 for r.*

$= 1300(0.99)^t$ *Simplify.*

Step 2 Find the population in 2008.

$y = 1300(0.99)^8$ *Substitute 8 for t.*

≈ 1200 *Use a calculator and round to the nearest whole number.*

The population in 2008 is approximately 1200 people.

 my.hrw.com

Online Video Tutor

Helpful Hint

In Example 3, round your answer to the nearest whole number because there can only be a whole number of people.

 CHECK IT OUT!

3. The fish population in a local stream is decreasing at a rate of 3% per year. The original population was 48,000. Write an exponential decay function to model this situation. Then find the population after 7 years.

A common application of exponential decay is *half-life*. The **half-life** of a substance is the time it takes for one-half of the substance to decay into another substance.

Half-life

$A = P(0.5)^t$

A represents the final amount.

P represents the original amount.

t represents the number of half-lives in a given time period.

 EXAMPLE *Science Application*

MCC9-12.F.LE.2

Fluorine-20 has a half-life of 11 seconds.

A **Find the amount of fluorine-20 left from a 40-gram sample after 44 seconds.**

Step 1 Find *t*, the number of half-lives in the given time period.

$$\frac{44 \text{ s}}{11 \text{ s}} = 4$$

Divide the time period by the half-life. The value of t is 4.

Step 2 $A = P(0.5)^t$ *Write the formula.*

$= 40(0.5)^4$ *Substitute 40 for P and 4 for t.*

$= 2.5$ *Use a calculator.*

There are 2.5 grams of fluorine-20 remaining after 44 seconds.

B **Find the amount of fluorine-20 left from a 40-gram sample after 2.2 minutes. Round your answer to the nearest hundredth.**

Step 1 Find *t*, the number of half-lives in the given time period.

$2.2(60) = 132$ *Find the number of seconds in 2.2 minutes.*

$\frac{132 \text{ s}}{11 \text{ s}} = 12$ *Divide the time period by the half-life. The value of t is $\frac{132}{11} = 12$.*

Step 2 $A = P(0.5)^t$ *Write the formula.*

$= 40(0.5)^{12}$ *Substitute 40 for P and 12 for t.*

≈ 0.01 *Use a calculator. Round to the nearest hundredth.*

There is about 0.01 gram of fluorine-20 remaining after 2.2 minutes.

 4a. Cesium-137 has a half-life of 30 years. Find the amount of cesium-137 left from a 100-milligram sample after 180 years.

4b. Bismuth-210 has a half-life of 5 days. Find the amount of bismuth-210 left from a 100-gram sample after 5 weeks. (*Hint:* Change 5 weeks to days.)

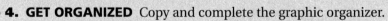

MCC.MP.6 MATHEMATICAL PRACTICES

THINK AND DISCUSS

1. Describe three real-world situations that can be described by exponential growth or exponential decay functions.

2. The population of a town after *t* years can be modeled by $P = 1000(1.02)^t$. Is the population increasing or decreasing? By what percentage rate?

3. An exponential function is a function of the form $y = ab^x$. Explain why both exponential growth functions and exponential decay functions are exponential functions.

 4. GET ORGANIZED Copy and complete the graphic organizer.

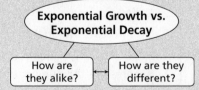

GUIDED PRACTICE

1. **Vocabulary** The function $y = 0.68(2)^x$ is an example of _____?_____.
   (*exponential growth* or *exponential decay*)

SEE EXAMPLE **1** Write an exponential growth function to model each situation. Then find the value of the function after the given amount of time.

2. The cost of tuition at a college is $12,000 and is increasing at a rate of 6% per year; 4 years.

3. The number of student-athletes at a local high school is 300 and is increasing at a rate of 8% per year; 5 years.

SEE EXAMPLE **2** Write a compound interest function to model each situation. Then find the balance after the given number of years.

4. $1500 invested at a rate of 3.5% compounded annually; 4 years

5. $4200 invested at a rate of 2.8% compounded quarterly; 6 years

SEE EXAMPLE **3** Write an exponential decay function to model each situation. Then find the value of the function after the given amount of time.

6. The value of a car is $18,000 and is depreciating at a rate of 12% per year; 10 years.

7. The amount (to the nearest hundredth) of a 10-mg dose of a certain antibiotic decreases in your bloodstream at a rate of 16% per hour; 4 hours.

SEE EXAMPLE **4** 8. Bismuth-214 has a half-life of approximately 20 minutes. Find the amount of bismuth-214 left from a 30-gram sample after 1 hour.

9. Mendelevium-258 has a half-life of approximately 52 days. Find the amount of mendelevium-258 left from a 44-gram sample after 156 days.

PRACTICE AND PROBLEM SOLVING

Independent Practice	
For Exercises	See Example
10–13	1
14–17	2
18–19	3
20	4

my.hrw.com

Online Extra Practice

Write an exponential growth function to model each situation. Then find the value of the function after the given amount of time.

10. Annual sales for a company are $149,000 and are increasing at a rate of 6% per year; 7 years.

11. The population of a small town is 1600 and is increasing at a rate of 3% per year; 10 years.

12. A new savings account starts at $700 and increases at 1.2% yearly; 8 years.

13. Membership of a local club grows at a rate of 7.8% yearly and currently has 30 members; 6 years.

Write a compound interest function to model each situation. Then find the balance after the given number of years.

14. $28,000 invested at a rate of 4% compounded annually; 5 years

15. $7000 invested at a rate of 3% compounded quarterly; 10 years

16. $3500 invested at a rate of 1.8% compounded monthly; 4 years

17. $12,000 invested at a rate of 2.6% compounded annually; 15 years

Write an exponential decay function to model each situation. Then find the value of the function after the given amount of time.

18. The population of a town is 18,000 and is decreasing at a rate of 2% per year; 6 years.

19. The value of a book is $58 and decreases at a rate of 10% per year; 8 years.

20. The half-life of bromine-82 is approximately 36 hours. Find the amount of bromine-82 left from an 80-gram sample after 6 days.

Identify each of the following functions as exponential growth or decay. Then give the rate of growth or decay as a percent.

21. $y = 3(1.61)^t$ **22.** $y = 39(0.098)^t$ **23.** $y = a\left(\dfrac{2}{3}\right)^t$ **24.** $y = a\left(\dfrac{3}{2}\right)^t$

25. $y = a(1.1)^t$ **26.** $y = a(0.8)^t$ **27.** $y = a\left(\dfrac{5}{4}\right)^t$ **28.** $y = a\left(\dfrac{1}{2}\right)^t$

Write an exponential growth or decay function to model each situation. Then find the value of the function after the given amount of time.

29. The population of a country is 58,000,000 and grows by 0.1% per year; 3 years.

30. An antique car is worth $32,000, and its value grows by 7% per year; 5 years.

31. An investment of $8200 loses value at a rate of 2% per year; 7 years.

32. A new car is worth $25,000, and its value decreases by 15% each year; 6 years.

33. The student enrollment in a local high school is 970 students and increases by 1.2% per year; 5 years.

34. **Archaeology** Carbon-14 dating is a way to determine the age of very old organic objects. Carbon-14 has a half-life of about 5700 years. An organic object with $\frac{1}{2}$ as much carbon-14 as its living counterpart died 5700 years ago. In 1999, archaeologists discovered the oldest bridge in England near Testwood, Hampshire. Carbon dating of the wood revealed that the bridge was 3500 years old. Suppose that when the bridge was built, the wood contained 15 grams of carbon-14. How much carbon-14 would it have contained when it was found by the archaeologists? Round to the nearest hundredth.

A computer-generated image of what the bridge at Testwood might have looked like

H.O.T. **35.** **/// ERROR ANALYSIS ///** Two students were asked to find the value of a $1000-item after 3 years. The item was depreciating (losing value) at a rate of 40% per year. Which is incorrect? Explain the error.

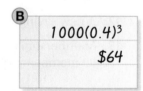

A $1000(0.6)^3$ $216

B $1000(0.4)^3$ $64

H.O.T. **36.** **Critical Thinking** The value of a certain car can be modeled by the function $y = 20{,}000(0.84)^t$, where t is time in years. Will the value ever be zero? Explain.

37. The value of a rare baseball card increases every year at a rate of 4%. Today, the card is worth $300. The owner expects to sell the card as soon as the value is over $600. How many years will the owner wait before selling the card? Round your answer to the nearest whole number.

Tom Goskar/Wessex Archaeology Ltd.

Atlantic Ocean

North Sea

England

Testwood•

Real-World Connections

38. a. The annual tuition at a prestigious university was $20,000 in 2002. It generally increases at a rate of 9% each year. Write a function to describe the cost as a function of the number of years since 2002. Use 2002 as year zero when writing the function rule.

b. What do you predict the cost of tuition will be in 2008?

c. Use a table of values to find the first year that the cost of the tuition is more than twice the cost in 2002.

39. Multi-Step At bank A, $600 is invested with an interest rate of 5% compounded annually. At bank B, $500 is invested with an interest rate of 6% compounded quarterly. Which account will have a larger balance after 10 years? 20 years?

40. Estimation The graph shows the decay of 100 grams of sodium-24. Use the graph to estimate the number of hours it will take the sample to decay to 10 grams. Then estimate the half-life of sodium-24.

H.O.T. 41. Graphing Calculator Use a graphing calculator to graph $y = 10(1 + r)^x$ for $r = 10\%$ and $r = 20\%$. Compare the two graphs. How does the value of r affect the graphs?

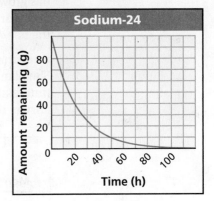

42. Write About It Write a real-world situation that could be modeled by $y = 400(1.08)^t$.

43. Write About It Write a real-world situation that could be modeled by $y = 800(0.96)^t$.

H.O.T. 44. Critical Thinking The amount of water in a container doubles every minute. After 6 minutes, the container is full. Your friend says it was half full after 3 minutes. Do you agree? Why or why not?

TEST PREP

45. A population of 500 is decreasing by 1% per year. Which function models this situation?

Ⓐ $y = 500(0.01)^t$ Ⓑ $y = 500(0.1)^t$ Ⓒ $y = 500(0.9)^t$ Ⓓ $y = 500(0.99)^t$

46. Which function is NOT an exponential decay model?

Ⓕ $y = 5\left(\dfrac{1}{3}\right)^x$ Ⓖ $y = -5\left(\dfrac{1}{3}\right)^x$ Ⓗ $y = 5(3)^{-x}$ Ⓙ $y = 5(3^{-1})^x$

47. Stephanie wants to save $1000 for a down payment on a car that she wants to buy in 3 years. She opens a savings account that pays 5% interest compounded annually. About how much should Stephanie deposit now to have enough money for the down payment in 3 years?

Ⓐ $295   Ⓑ $333   Ⓒ $500   Ⓓ $865

48. Short Response In 2000, the population of a town was 1000 and was growing at a rate of 5% per year.

a. Write an exponential growth function to model this situation.

b. In what year is the population 1300? Show how you found your answer.

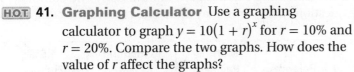
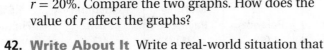

49. You invest $700 at a rate of 6% compounded quarterly. Use a graph to estimate the number of years it will take for your investment to increase to $2300.

50. Omar invested $500 at a rate of 4% compounded annually. How long will it take for Omar's money to double? How long would it take if the interest were 8% compounded annually?

51. An 80-gram sample of a radioactive substance decayed to 10 grams after 300 minutes. Find the half-life of the substance.

52. Praseodymium-143 has a half-life of 2 weeks. The original measurement for the mass of a sample was lost. After 6 weeks, 15 grams of praseodymium-143 remain. How many grams was the original sample?

53. Phillip invested some money in a business 8 years ago. Since then, his investment has grown at an average rate of 1.3% compounded quarterly. Phillip's investment is now worth $250,000. How much was his original investment? Round your answer to the nearest dollar.

54. **Personal Finance** Anna has a balance of $200 that she owes on her credit card. She plans to make a $30 payment each month. There is also a 1.5% finance charge (interest) on the remaining balance each month. Copy and complete the table to answer the questions below. You may add more rows to the table as necessary.

Month	Balance ($)	Monthly Payment ($)	Remaining Balance ($)	1.5% Finance Charge ($)	New Balance ($)
1	200	30	170	2.55	172.55
2	172.55	30	▩	▩	▩
3	▩	30	▩	▩	▩
4	▩	30	▩	▩	▩

   a. How many months will it take Anna to pay the entire balance?

   b. By the time Anna pays the entire balance, how much total interest will she have paid?

FOCUS ON MATHEMATICAL PRACTICES

H.O.T. 55. Counterexamples Show that $y = (1 + 0.2)^x$ and $y = 1^x + 0.2^x$ are not equivalent.

H.O.T. 56. Modeling Ricardo is researching a groundhog population.

   a. Ricardo finds that the population increases by 4% every 6 months. Write an exponential function with t in *years* that models the size of the population in terms of percent of the original population.

   b. Ricardo wonders when the population will reach 180% of its initial value. He finds that $(1.04)^{15} \approx 1.8$. Use this and your function from part **a** to find the number of years needed. Show your work.

H.O.T. 57. Estimation Phosphorus-32 has a half-life of 14.29 days. Consider what percent of a sample remains after each of the first three periods of 14.29 days. Then estimate how long it would take for 11.5% of a sample of phosphorus-32 to remain. Explain your reasoning.

Mastering the Standards

for Mathematical Practice

The topics described in the Standards for Mathematical Content will vary from year to year. However, the *way* in which you learn, study, and think about mathematics will not. The Standards for Mathematical Practice describe skills that you will use in all of your math courses.

Mathematical Practices

1. *Make sense of problems and persevere in solving them.*
2. *Reason abstractly and quantitatively.*
3. *Construct viable arguments and critique the reasoning of others.*
4. *Model with mathematics.*
5. *Use appropriate tools strategically.*
6. *Attend to precision.*
7. *Look for and make use of structure.*
8. *Look for and express regularity in repeated reasoning.*

---

④ Model with mathematics.

Mathematically proficient students can apply... mathematics... to... problems... in everyday life, society, and the workplace...

In your book

Real-World Connections and **Focus on Mathematical Practices** exercises apply mathematics to other disciplines and in real-world scenarios.

Real-World Connections

61. a. A band wants to create a CD of their last concert. They received a donation of $500 to cover the cost. The total cost is $350 plus $3 per CD. Complete the table to find a relationship between the number of CDs and the total cost.

 b. Write an equation for the cost *c* of the CDs based on the number of CDs *n*.

 c. Write an inequality that can be used to determine how many CDs can be made with the $500 donation. Solve the inequality and determine how many CDs the band can have made from the $500 donation.

Number	Process	Cost
1	350 + 3	353
2		
3		
10		
n		

124 Chapter 2 Inequalities

MATHEMATICAL PRACTICES

FOCUS ON MATHEMATICAL PRACTICES

HOT **70. Modeling** In order for Ramon to remain in his current weight class for a wrestling match on Saturday morning, he must weigh in at 152 pounds or more, but less than 160 pounds. Write a pair of inequalities that expresses the set of acceptable weights for Ramon. Define your variable.

HOT **71. Problem Solving** Cary is making brownies using a recipe that calls for "at least 5 cups of flour but no more than 6 cups of flour." The only measuring cup he could find holds one quarter of a cup. Write a pair of inequalities to express how many *quarter cups* of flour Cary can use.

HOT **72. Analysis** Imani and Trey are planning the seating at their wedding reception. They have 168 guests and each table can hold up to 16 guests, so they calculate that they need at least 10.5 tables to seat all of their guests. Graph their solution. In this context, how is the graph inaccurate? Make another graph that takes the context into account.

2-1 Graphing and Writing Inequalities **105**

Patterns and Recursion

Essential Question: How can you use recursion to identify and extend a sequence or function?

Objective
Identify and extend patterns using recursion.

In a **recursive pattern** or *recursive sequence*, each term is defined using one or more previous terms. For example, the sequence 1, 4, 7, 10, 13, ... can be defined recursively as follows: The first term is 1 and each term after the first is equal to the preceding term plus 3.

Vocabulary
recursive pattern

You can use recursive techniques to identify patterns. The table summarizes the characteristics of four types of patterns.

Using Recursive Techniques to Identify Patterns	
Type of Pattern	**Characteristics**
Linear	First differences are constant.
Quadratic	Second differences are constant.
Cubic	Third differences are constant.
Exponential	Ratios between successive terms are constant.

COMMON CORE GPS Prep. for MCC9-12.F.IF.3

EXAMPLE 1

Identifying and Extending a Pattern

Identify the type of pattern. Then find the next three numbers in the pattern.

You may need to use trial and error when identifying a pattern. If first, second, and third differences are not constant, check for constant ratios.

A 4, 6, 10, 16, 24, ...

Find first, second, and, if necessary, third differences.

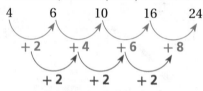

Second differences are constant, so the pattern is quadratic.

Extend the pattern by continuing the sequence of first and second differences.

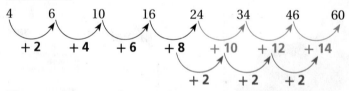

The next three numbers in the pattern are 34, 46, and 60.

B $\frac{1}{8}, \frac{1}{2}, 2, 8, 32$

Find the ratio between successive terms.

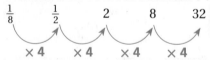

Ratios between terms are constant, so the pattern is exponential.

Extend the pattern by continuing the sequence of ratios.

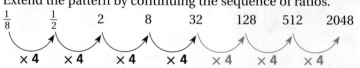

The next three numbers in the pattern are 128, 512, and 2048.

Identify the type of pattern. Then find the next three numbers in the pattern.

1a. 56, 47, 38, 29, 20, ...   **1b.** 1, 8, 27, 64, 125, ...

You can use a similar process to determine whether a function is linear, quadratic, cubic, or exponential. Note that before comparing y-values, you must first make sure there is a constant change in the corresponding x-values.

Using Recursive Techniques to Identify Functions	
Type of Function	**Characteristics (Given a Constant Change in x-values)**
Linear	First differences of y-values are constant.
Quadratic	Second differences of y-values are constant.
Cubic	Third differences of y-values are constant.
Exponential	Ratios between successive y-values are constant.

COMMON CORE GPS   **EXAMPLE** 2
Prep. for MCC9-12.F.IF.3

Identifying a Function

The ordered pairs {(−4, −4), (0, 0), (4, 4), (8, 32), (12, 108)} satisfy a function. Determine whether the function is linear, quadratic, cubic, or exponential. Then find three additional ordered pairs that satisfy the function.

Make a table. Check for a constant change in the x-values. Then find first, second, and third differences of y-values.

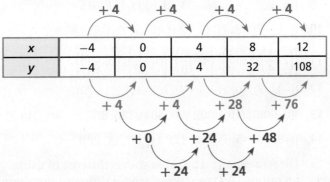

There is a constant change in the x-values. Third differences are constant. The function is a cubic function.

To find additional ordered pairs, extend the pattern by working backward from the constant third differences.

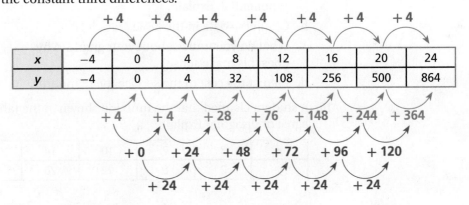

 **Helpful Hint**

In Example 2, the constant third differences are 24. To extend the pattern, first find each second difference by adding 24 to the previous second difference. Then find each first difference by adding the second difference below to the previous first difference.

Three additional ordered pairs that satisfy this function are (16, 256), (20, 500), and (24, 864).

Several ordered pairs that satisfy a function are given. Determine whether the function is linear, quadratic, cubic, or exponential. Then find three additional ordered pairs that satisfy the function.

2a. {(0, 1), (1, 3), (2, 9), (3, 19), (4, 33)}

2b. $\left\{\left(1, \frac{1}{2}\right), \left(3, \frac{1}{6}\right), \left(5, \frac{1}{18}\right), \left(7, \frac{1}{54}\right), \left(9, \frac{1}{162}\right)\right\}$

EXTENSION

Exercises

my.hrw.com
Homework Help

Identify the type of pattern. Then find the next three numbers in the pattern.

1. 25, 28, 31, 34, 37, ...

2. 20, 45, 80, 125, 180, ...

3. 128, 64, 32, 16, 8, ...

4. 4, 32, 108, 256, 500, ...

5. $\frac{1}{2}, \frac{3}{4}, 1, 1\frac{1}{4}, 1\frac{1}{2}, ...$

6. 0.3, 0.03, 0.003, 0.0003, 0.00003, ...

7. 127, 66, 29, 10, 3, ...

8. 2, 8, 18, 32, 50, ...

Several ordered pairs that satisfy a function are given. Determine whether the function is linear, quadratic, cubic, or exponential. Then find three additional ordered pairs that satisfy the function.

9. {(3, 1), (5, −3), (7, −7), (9, −11), (11, −15)}

10. {(−1, −2), (2, 7), (5, 124), (8, 511), (11, 1330)}

11. $\left\{\left(2, \frac{1}{4}\right), \left(3, \frac{1}{8}\right), \left(4, \frac{1}{16}\right), \left(5, \frac{1}{32}\right), \left(6, \frac{1}{64}\right)\right\}$

12. {(−3, −7), (0, 2), (3, −7), (6, −34), (9, −79)}

13. {(0, 600), (10, 480), (20, 384), (30, 307.2), (40, 245.76)}

14. {(−8, 2), (−5, 7), (−2, 12), (1, 17), (4, 22)}

15. Entertainment The table shows the cost of using an online DVD rental service for different numbers of months.

Online DVD Rentals	
Months	**Cost ($)**
3	50
6	92
9	134
12	176
15	218

  a. Determine whether the function that models the data is linear, quadratic, cubic, or exponential. Explain.

  b. Graph the data in the table.

  c. What do you notice about your graph? Why does this make sense?

  d. Predict the cost of the service for 18 months.

16. A student claimed that the function shown in the table is a quadratic function. Do you agree or disagree? Explain.

x	3	7	10	14	17
y	2	6	12	20	30

+4   +6   +8   +10

+2   +2   +2

17. **Business** The table shows the annual sales for a small company.

Annual Sales	
Year	Sales ($)
2006	513,000
2007	516,000
2008	521,000
2009	528,000
2010	537,000

   a. Determine whether the function that models the data is linear, quadratic, cubic, or exponential. Explain.

   b. Suppose sales continue to grow according to the pattern in the table. Predict the annual sales for 2011, 2012, and 2013.

   c. If the pattern continues, in what year will annual sales be $17,000 greater than the previous year's sales?

18. **Critical Thinking** Use the table for the following problems.

x	0	1	2	3	4
y	3	6	▨	▨	▨

   a. Copy and complete the table so that the function is a linear function.

   b. Copy and complete the table so that the function is a quadratic function.

   c. Copy and complete the table so that the function is an exponential function.

   d. For which of these three types of functions is there more than one correct way to complete the table? Explain.

Use the description to write the first five terms in each numerical pattern.

19. The first term is 8. Each following term is 11 less than the term before it.

20. The first term is 1000. Each following term is 40% of the term before it.

21. The first two terms are 1 and 2. Each following term is the sum of the two terms before it.

Make a table for a function that has the given characteristics. Include at least five ordered pairs.

22. The function is linear. The first differences are −3.

23. The function is quadratic. The second differences are 6.

24. The function is cubic. The third differences are 1.

A *recursive formula* for a sequence shows how to find the value of a term from one or more terms that come before it. For example, the recursive formula $a_n = a_{n-1} + 3$ tells you that each term is equal to the preceding term plus 3. Given that $a_1 = 5$, you can use the formula to generate the sequence 5, 8, 11, 14, ...

Write the first four terms of each sequence.

25. $a_n = a_{n-1} + 2; a_1 = 12$

26. $a_n = a_{n-1} - 7; a_1 = 16$

27. $a_n = 2a_{n-1}; a_1 = 4$

28. $a_n = 0.6a_{n-1}; a_1 = 100$

29. $a_n = 5a_{n-1} - 2; a_1 = 0$

30. $a_n = (a_{n-1})^2; a_1 = -2$

31. A *recursive function* defines a function for whole numbers by referring to the value of the function at previous whole numbers. Consider the recursive function $f(n) = f(n-1) + 5$ with $f(0) = 1$.

   a. According to the formula, $f(1) = f(0) + 5$. What is the value of $f(1)$?

   b. Use the formula to find $f(2), f(3), f(4),$ and $f(5)$.

   c. Graph $f(n)$ by plotting points at $x = 0, x = 1, x = 2, x = 3, x = 4,$ and $x = 5$.

   d. What do you notice about your graph? What does this tell you about $f(n)$?

Ready to Go On?

my.hrw.com
Assessment and Intervention

✓ 12-1 Geometric Sequences

Find the next three terms in each geometric sequence.

1. 3, 6, 12, 24, …

2. −1, 2, −4, 8, …

3. −2400, −1200, −600, −300, …

4. The first term of a geometric sequence is 2 and the common ratio is 3. What is the 8th term of the sequence?

5. What is the 15th term of the geometric sequence 4, 12, 36, 108, …?

✓ 12-2 Exponential Functions

6. The function $f(x) = 3(1.1)^x$ gives the length (in inches) of an image after being enlarged by 10% x times. What is the length of the image after it has been enlarged 4 times? Round your answer to the nearest hundredth.

Graph each exponential function.

7. $y = 3^x$

8. $y = 2(2)^x$

9. $y = -2(4)^x$

10. $y = -(0.5)^x$

11. The function $f(x) = 40(0.8)^x$ gives the amount of a medication in milligrams present in a patient's system x hours after taking a 40-mg dose. In how many hours will there be less than 2 mg of the drug in a patient's system?

Tell whether each set of ordered pairs satisfies an exponential function. Explain.

12. $\{(0, 1), (2, 9), (4, 81), (6, 729)\}$

13. $\{(-2, -8), (-1, -4), (0, 0), (1, 4)\}$

✓ 12-3 Exponential Growth and Decay

Write a function to model each situation. Then find the value of the function after the given amount of time.

14. Fiona's salary is $30,000, and she expects to receive a 3% raise each year; 10 years.

15. $2000 is invested at a rate of 4.5% compounded monthly; 3 years.

16. A $1200 computer is losing value at a rate of 20% per year; 4 years.

17. Strontium-90 has a half-life of 29 years. About how much strontium-90 will be left from a 100-mg sample after 290 years? Round your answer to the nearest thousandth.

PARCC Assessment Readiness

Selected Response

1. The function $f(x) = 5,000(0.972)^x$, where x is the time in years, models a declining lemming population. How many lemmings will there be in 6 years?

　Ⓐ About 30,006 lemmings

　Ⓑ About 29,160 lemmings

　Ⓒ About 5,001 lemmings

　Ⓓ About 4,217 lemmings

2. Find the next three terms in the geometric sequence $-36, 6, -1, \frac{1}{6}, \dots$

　Ⓕ $-\frac{1}{1296}, \frac{1}{216}, -\frac{1}{36}$

　Ⓖ $\frac{1}{36}, -\frac{1}{216}, \frac{1}{1296}$

　Ⓗ $-1, 6, -36$

　Ⓙ $-\frac{1}{36}, \frac{1}{216}, -\frac{1}{1296}$

3. The value of a gold coin picturing the head of the Roman Emperor Vespasian is $105. This value is increasing at a rate of 10% per year. Write an exponential growth function to model this situation. Then find the value of the coin in 11 years.

　Ⓐ $f(t) = 1.1(105)^t$; about $1270.

　Ⓑ $f(t) = 105(1.1)^t$; about $300.

　Ⓒ $f(t) = 105 + 1.1t$; about $117.

　Ⓓ $f(t) = 105(1.1t)$; about $1271.

4. Write a compound interest function to model the following situation. Then, find the balance after the given number of years.

$17,400 invested at a rate of 2.5% compounded annually; 8 years

　Ⓕ $17,400 (1.025)^{8t}$; $84,504

　Ⓖ $17,400 (0.025)^t$; $26,550,293

　Ⓗ $17,400 (1.025)^t$; $21,200

　Ⓙ $17,400 (3.5)^t$; $391,826,318

5. Graph $y = 3(2)^x$.

　Ⓐ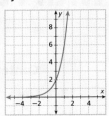

　Ⓑ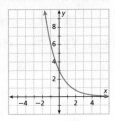

　Ⓒ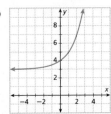

　Ⓓ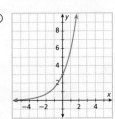

6. The first term of a geometric sequence is 512, and the common ratio is 0.5. What is the 8th term of the sequence?.

　Ⓕ 4　　　　　　Ⓗ 22.63

　Ⓖ 8　　　　　　Ⓙ 2

Mini-Task

7. Tell whether the set of ordered pairs satisfies an exponential function. Explain your answer.
$\{(1, -6), (2, -18), (3, -54), (4, -162)\}$

COMMON
CORE GPS

Contents

MATHEMATICAL
PRACTICES   The Common Core Georgia Performance Standards for Mathematical Practice describe varieties of expertise that all students should seek to develop. Opportunities to develop these practices are integrated throughout this program.

1 Make sense of problems and persevere in solving them.

2 Reason abstractly and quantitatively.

3 Construct viable arguments and critique the reasoning of others.

4 Model with mathematics.

5 Use appropriate tools strategically.

6 Attend to precision.

7 Look for and make use of structure.

8 Look for and express regularity in repeated reasoning.

Unpacking the Standards

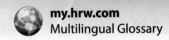

Understanding the standards and the vocabulary terms in the standards will help you know exactly what you are expected to learn in this chapter.

 COMMON CORE GPS **MCC9-12.F.LE.2**

Construct linear and exponential functions, including arithmetic and geometric sequences, given a graph, a description of a relationship, or two input-output pairs (include reading these from a table).

What It Means For You

You can construct a model of a linear or exponential function from different descriptions or displays of the same situation.

EXAMPLE   **Geometric Sequence**

A ball is dropped 81 inches onto a hard surface. The table shows the ball's height on successive bounces. Write a model for the height reached as a function of the number of bounces.

Bounce	1	2	3	4
Height (in.)	54	36	24	16

Consecutive terms have a common ratio of $\frac{2}{3}$. You can write a model as an exponential function or as a geometric sequence:

Exponential function: $f(x) = 81\left(\frac{2}{3}\right)^x$, where x is the bounce number

Geometric sequence: $a_1 = 54$, $a_n = \frac{2}{3}a_{n-1}$, where n is the bounce number

Mastering the Standards

for Mathematical Practice

The topics described in the Standards for Mathematical Content will vary from year to year. However, the *way* in which you learn, study, and think about mathematics will not. The Standards for Mathematical Practice describe skills that you will use in all of your math courses.

Mathematical Practices

1. *Make sense of problems and persevere in solving them.*
2. *Reason abstractly and quantitatively.*
3. *Construct viable arguments and critique the reasoning of others.*
4. *Model with mathematics.*
5. *Use appropriate tools strategically.*
6. *Attend to precision.*
7. *Look for and make use of structure.*
8. *Look for and express regularity in repeated reasoning.*

⑤ Use appropriate tools strategically.

Mathematically proficient students consider the available tools when solving a... problem... [and] are... able to use technological tools to explore and deepen their understanding...

In your book

Algebra Tasks and **Technology Tasks** use concrete and technological tools to explore mathematical concepts.

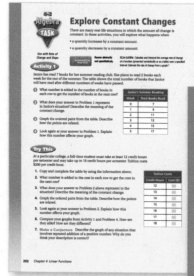

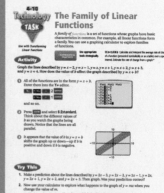

Linear, Quadratic, and Exponential Models

Essential Question: How can you distinguish between situations that can be modeled by linear and exponential functions?

Objectives

Compare linear, quadratic, and exponential models.

Given a set of data, decide which type of function models the data and write an equation to describe the function.

Why learn this?

Different situations in sports can be described by linear, quadratic, or exponential models.

Look at the tables and graphs below. The data show three ways you have learned that variable quantities can be related. The relationships shown are linear, quadratic, and exponential.

Remember!

A linear function is a function whose rule is a first-degree polynomial and whose graph is a line. A quadratic function is a function whose rule is a second-degree polynomial and whose graph is a U-shaped curve called a parabola.

Linear		Quadratic		Exponential	
Training Heart Rate		**Volleyball Height**		**Volleyball Tournament**	
Age (yr)	Beats/min	Time (s)	Height (ft)	Round	Teams Left
20	170	0.4	10.44	1	16
30	161.5	0.8	12.76	2	8
40	153	1	12	3	4
50	144.5	1.2	9.96	4	2

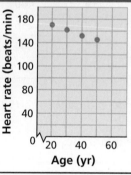

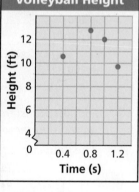

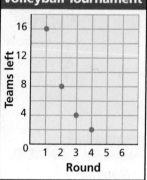

In the real world, people often gather data and then must decide what kind of relationship (if any) they think best describes their data.

COMMON CORE GPS
MCC9-12.F.LE.1

EXAMPLE **1**

Graphing Data to Choose a Model

Graph each data set. Which kind of model best describes the data?

A

Time (h)	0	1	2	3
Bacteria	10	20	40	80

Plot the data points and connect them.

The data appear to be exponential.

Bacteria Population

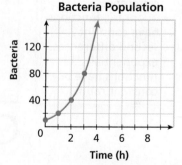

Online Video Tutor

my.hrw.com

Graph each data set. Which kind of model best describes the data?

°C	0	5	10	15	20
°F	32	41	50	59	68

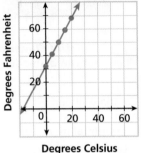

Celsius to Fahrenheit

Plot the data points and connect them.
The data appear to be linear.

CHECK IT OUT! Graph each data set. Which kind of model best describes the data?

1a. $\{(-3, 0.30), (-2, 0.44), (0, 1), (1, 1.5), (2, 2.25), (3, 3.38)\}$

1b. $\{(-3, -14), (-2, -9), (-1, -6), (0, -5), (1, -6), (2, -9), (3, -14)\}$

Another way to decide which kind of relationship (if any) best describes a data set is to use patterns.

COMMON CORE GPS MCC9-12.F.LE.1

EXAMPLE 2

Using Patterns to Choose a Model

Look for a pattern in each data set to determine which kind of model best describes the data.

 my.hrw.com

Online Video Tutor

A

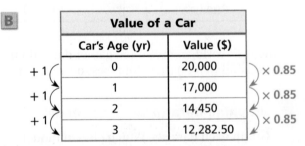

Height of Bridge Suspension Cables	
Cable's Distance from Tower (ft)	Cable's Height (ft)
0	400
100	256
200	144
300	64

For every constant change in distance of +100 feet, there is a constant second difference of +32.
The data appear to be quadratic.

Remember!

When the independent variable changes by a constant amount,
- linear functions have constant first differences.
- quadratic functions have constant second differences.
- exponential functions have a constant ratio.

B

Value of a Car	
Car's Age (yr)	Value ($)
0	20,000
1	17,000
2	14,450
3	12,282.50

For every constant change in age of +1 year, there is a constant ratio of 0.85.
The data appear to be exponential.

CHECK IT OUT! **2.** Look for a pattern in the data set $\{(-2, 10), (-1, 1), (0, -2), (1, 1), (2, 10)\}$ to determine which kind of model best describes the data.

After deciding which model best fits the data, you can write a function. The general forms of linear, quadratic, and exponential functions are shown below.

General Forms of Functions

LINEAR	QUADRATIC	EXPONENTIAL
$y = mx + b$	$y = ax^2 + bx + c$	$y = ab^x$

MCC9-12.F.LE.2

EXAMPLE 3

Problem-Solving Application

Use the data in the table to describe how the ladybug population is changing. Then write a function that models the data. Use your function to predict the ladybug population after one year.

my.hrw.com

Online Video Tutor

Ladybug Population	
Time (mo)	Ladybugs
0	10
1	30
2	90
3	270

MATHEMATICAL PRACTICES

Make sense of problems and persevere in solving them.

1 Understand the Problem

The **answer** will have three parts—a description, a function, and a prediction.

2 Make a Plan

Determine whether the data is linear, quadratic, or exponential. Use the general form to write a function. Then use the function to find the population after one year.

3 Solve

Step 1 Describe the situation in words.

Ladybug Population	
Time (mo)	Ladybugs
0	10
1	30
2	90
3	270

+1, +1, +1 on the left; ×3, ×3, ×3 on the right.

Each month, the ladybug population is multiplied by 3. In other words, the population triples each month.

Step 2 Write the function.

There is a constant ratio of 3. The data appear to be exponential.

$y = ab^x$	*Write the general form of an exponential function.*
$y = a(3)^x$	*Substitute the constant ratio, 3, for b.*
$10 = a(3)^0$	*Choose an ordered pair from the table, such as (0, 10). Substitute for x and y.*
$10 = a(1)$	*Simplify. $3^0 = 1$*
$10 = a$	*The value of a is 10.*
$y = 10(3)^x$	*Substitute 10 for a in $y = a(3)^x$.*

Helpful Hint

You can choose any given ordered pair to substitute for x and y. However, it is often easiest to choose an ordered pair that contains 0.

13-1 Linear, Quadratic, and Exponential Models **343**

Christine Lee Zilka/Getty Images

Step 3 Predict the ladybug population after one year.

$$y = 10(3)^x \quad \textit{Write the function.}$$
$$= 10(3)^{12} \quad \textit{Substitute 12 for x (1 year = 12 mo).}$$
$$= 5{,}314{,}410 \quad \textit{Use a calculator.}$$

There will be 5,314,410 ladybugs after one year.

 Look Back

You chose the ordered pair $(0, 10)$ to write the function. Check that every other ordered pair in the table satisfies your function.

$y = 10(3)^x$	
30	$10(3)^1$
30	$10(3)$
30	$30 \checkmark$

$y = 10(3)^x$	
90	$10(3)^2$
90	$10(9)$
90	$90 \checkmark$

$y = 10(3)^x$	
270	$10(3)^3$
270	$10(27)$
270	$270 \checkmark$

CHECK IT OUT! **3.** Use the data in the table to describe how the oven temperature is changing. Then write a function that models the data. Use your function to predict the temperature after 1 hour.

Oven Temperature				
Time (min)	0	10	20	30
Temperature (°F)	375	325	275	225

Student to Student / *Checking Units*

I used to get a lot of answers wrong because of the units. If a question asked for the value of something after 1 year, I would always just substitute 1 into the function.

I finally figured out that you have to check what x is. If x represents months and you're trying to find the value after 1 year, then you have to substitute 12, not 1, because there are 12 months in a year.

Michael Gambhir
Warren High School

MCC.MP.3

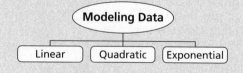

THINK AND DISCUSS

1. Do you think that every data set will be able to be modeled by a linear, quadratic, or exponential function? Why or why not?

2. In Example 3, is it certain that there will be 5,314,410 ladybugs after one year? Explain.

 3. GET ORGANIZED Copy and complete the graphic organizer. In each box, list some characteristics and sketch a graph of each type of model.

Modeling Data — Linear — Quadratic — Exponential

GUIDED PRACTICE

SEE EXAMPLE 1   Graph each data set. Which kind of model best describes the data?

1. $\{(-1, 4), (-2, 0.8), (0, 20), (1, 100), (-3, 0.16)\}$

2. $\{(0, 3), (1, 9), (2, 11), (3, 9), (4, 3)\}$

3. $\{(2, -7), (-2, -9), (0, -8), (4, -6), (6, -5)\}$

SEE EXAMPLE 2   Look for a pattern in each data set to determine which kind of model best describes the data.

4. $\{(-2, 1), (-1, 2.5), (0, 3), (1, 2.5), (2, 1)\}$

5. $\{(-2, 0.75), (-1, 1.5), (0, 3), (1, 6), (2, 12)\}$

6. $\{(-2, 2), (-1, 4), (0, 6), (1, 8), (2, 10)\}$

SEE EXAMPLE 3   7. **Consumer Economics** Use the data in the table to describe the cost of grapes. Then write a function that models the data. Use your function to predict the cost of 6 pounds of grapes.

Total Cost of Grapes				
Amount (lb)	1	2	3	4
Cost ($)	1.79	3.58	5.37	7.16

PRACTICE AND PROBLEM SOLVING

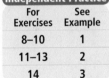

Independent Practice	
For Exercises	See Example
8–10	1
11–13	2
14	3

my.hrw.com

Online Extra Practice

Graph each data set. Which kind of model best describes the data?

8. $\{(-3, -5), (-2, -8), (-1, -9), (0, -8), (1, -5), (2, 0), (3, 7)\}$

9. $\{(-3, -1), (-2, 0), (-1, 1), (0, 2), (1, 3), (2, 4), (3, 5)\}$

10. $\{(0, 0.1), (2, 0.9), (3, 2.7), (4, 8.1)\}$

Look for a pattern in each data set to determine which kind of model best describes the data.

11. $\{(-2, 5), (-1, 4), (0, 3), (1, 2), (2, 1)\}$

12. $\{(-2, 12), (-1, 15), (0, 16), (1, 15), (2, 12)\}$

13. $\{(-2, 8), (-1, 4), (0, 2), (1, 1), (2, 0.5)\}$

14. **Business** Use the data in the table to describe how the company's sales are changing. Then write a function that models the data. Use your function to predict the amount of sales after 10 years.

Company Sales				
Year	0	1	2	3
Sales ($)	25,000	30,000	36,000	43,200

15. **Multi-Step** Jay's hair grows about 6 inches each year. Write a function that describes the length ℓ in inches that Jay's hair will grow for each year k. Which kind of model best describes the function?

Tell which kind of model best describes each situation.

16. The height of a plant at weekly intervals over the last 6 weeks was 1 inches, 1.5 inches, 2 inches, 2.5 inches, 3 inches., and 3.5 inches.

17. The number of games a baseball player played in the last four years was 162, 162, 162, and 162.

18. The height of a ball in a certain time interval was recorded as 30.64 feet, 30.96 feet, 31 feet, 30.96 feet, and 30.64 feet.

Write a function to model each set of data.

19.

x	−1	0	1	2	4
y	0.05	0.2	0.8	3.2	51.2

20.

x	−2	0	2	4	8
y	5	4	3	2	0

Tell which kind of model best describes each graph.

21.

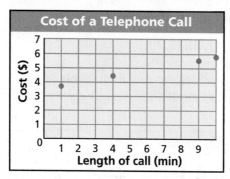

Cost of a Telephone Call

22.

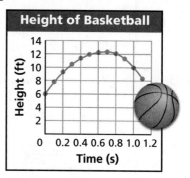

Height of Basketball

H.O.T. 23. Write About It Write a set of data that you could model with an exponential function. Explain why the exponential model would work.

24. ///**ERROR ANALYSIS**/// A student concluded that the data set would best be modeled by a quadratic function. Explain the student's error.

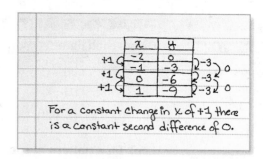

H.O.T. 25. Critical Thinking Sometimes the graphs of quadratic data and exponential data can look very similar. Describe how you can tell them apart.

Real-World Connections

26. a. Examine the two models that represent annual tuition for two colleges. Describe each model as linear, quadratic, or exponential.

b. Write a function rule for each model.

c. Both models have the same values for 2004. What does this mean?

d. Why do both models have the same value for year 1?

Years After 2004	Tuition at College 1 ($)	Tuition at College 2 ($)
0	2000.00	2000.00
1	2200.00	2200.00
2	2400.00	2420.00
3	2600.00	2662.00
4	2800.00	2928.20

TEST PREP

27. Which function best models the data: $\{(-4, -2), (-2, -1), (0, 0), (2, 1), (4, 2)\}$?

(A) $y = \left(\dfrac{1}{2}\right)^x$ (B) $y = \dfrac{1}{2}x^2$ (C) $y = \dfrac{1}{2}x$ (D) $y = \left(\dfrac{1}{2}x\right)^2$

28. A city's population is increasing at a rate of 2% per year. Which type of model describes this situation?

(F) Exponential   (G) Quadratic   (H) Linear   (J) None of these

29. Which data set is best modeled by a linear function?

(A) $\{(-2, 0), (-1, 2), (0, -4), (1, -1), (2, 2)\}$

(B) $\{(-2, 2), (-1, 4), (0, 6), (1, 16), (2, 32)\}$

(C) $\{(-2, 2), (-1, 4), (0, 6), (1, 8), (2, 10)\}$

(D) $\{(-2, 0), (-1, 5), (0, 7), (1, 5), (2, 0)\}$

CHALLENGE AND EXTEND

30. **Finance** An accountant estimates that a certain new automobile worth $18,000 will lose value at a rate of 16% per year.

   a. Make a table that shows the worth of the car for years 0, 1, 2, 3, and 4. What is the real-world meaning of year 0?

   b. Which type of model best represents the data in your table? Explain.

   c. Write a function for your data.

   d. What is the value of the car after $5\frac{1}{2}$ years?

   e. What is the value of the car after 8 years?

31. **Pet Care** The table shows general guidelines for the weight of a Great Dane at various ages.

   a. None of the three models in this lesson—linear, quadratic, or exponential—fits this data exactly. Which of these is the *best* model for the data? Explain your choice.

   b. What would you predict for the weight of a Great Dane who is 1 year old?

   c. Do you think you could use your model to find the weight of a Great Dane at any age? Why or why not?

Great Dane	
Age (mo)	Weight (kg)
2	12
4	23
6	33
8	40
10	45

FOCUS ON MATHEMATICAL PRACTICES

H.O.T. 32. **Reasoning** For $f(x) = 5^x$ and $g(x) = 2^x$, $h(x) = f(x) - g(x)$. Evaluate $h(x)$ for $x = 3, 4, 5, 6, 7$. Which type of function best models $h(x)$? Explain.

H.O.T. 33. **Properties** You know that a function is linear, quadratic, or exponential. You find that the average rate of change between two values of x is positive, but between two other values of x, the rate of change is negative. What type of function is it? How do you know?

H.O.T. 34. **Modeling** Yvonne knows that a home was valued at $150,000 initially and $180,000 one year later. Find a linear function that describes the data, and then find an exponential function. Finally, find the value of the house after 5 years using each function.

Linear and Nonlinear Rates of Change

Essential Question: How can you identify linear and nonlinear rates of change and the functions they are associated with?

Objectives

Identify linear and nonlinear rates of change.

Compare rates of change.

Recall that a *rate of change* is a ratio that compares the amount of change in a dependent variable to the amount of change in an independent variable.

$$\text{rate of change} = \frac{\text{change in dependent variable}}{\text{change in independent variable}}$$

The table shows the price of one ounce of gold in 2005 and 2008. The year is the independent variable and the price is the dependent variable. The rate of change is $\frac{870-513}{2008-2005} = \frac{357}{3} = 119$, or \$119 per year.

Price of Gold	
Year	**Price (\$/oz)**
2005	513
2008	870

COMMON CORE GPS MCC9-12.F.IF.6

EXAMPLE 1 Identifying Constant and Variable Rates of Change

Determine whether each function has a constant or variable rate of change.

A {(0, 0), (1, 4), (3, 8), (6, 8), (8, 6)}

Find the ratio of the amount of change in the dependent variable y to the corresponding amount of change in the independent variable x.

x	y
0	0
1	4
3	8
6	8
8	6

+1)+4
+2)+4
+3)+0
+2)−2

The rates of change are
$\frac{4}{1} = 4$, $\frac{4}{2} = 2$, $\frac{0}{3} = 0$, and $\frac{-2}{2} = -1$.
The function has a variable rate of change.

B {(0, 1), (1, 2), (4, 5), (6, 7), (7, 8)}

Find the ratio of the amount of change in the dependent variable y to the corresponding amount of change in the independent variable x.

x	y
0	1
1	2
4	5
6	7
7	8

+1)+1
+3)+3
+2)+2
+1)+1

The rates of change are
$\frac{1}{1} = 1$, $\frac{3}{3} = 1$, $\frac{2}{2} = 1$, and $\frac{1}{1} = 1$.
The function has a constant rate of change.

 CHECK IT OUT! Determine whether each function has a constant or variable rate of change.

1a. {(−3, 10), (0, 7), (1, 6), (4, 3), (7, 0)}

1b. {(−2, −3), (2, 5), (3, 7), (5, 9), (8, 12)}

The functions in Examples 1A and 1B are graphed below.

Example 1A (variable rate of change)

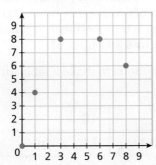

Example 1B (constant rate of change)

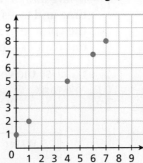

A function is a *linear function* if and only if the function has a constant rate of change. The graph of such a function is a straight line and the rate of change is the slope of the line, as in Example 1B.

A function with a variable rate of change, as in Example 1A, is a *nonlinear function*. Examples of nonlinear functions include quadratic functions and exponential functions.

EXAMPLE 2

Identifying Linear and Nonlinear Functions

Use rates of change to determine whether each function is linear or nonlinear.

A

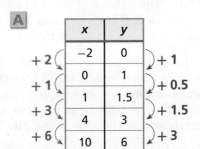

x	y
−2	0
0	1
1	1.5
4	3
10	6

+2, +1   +1, +0.5
+1, +3   +1.5, +3
+6

Find the rates of change.

$\frac{1}{2}$ $\frac{0.5}{1} = \frac{1}{2}$ $\frac{1.5}{3} = \frac{1}{2}$ $\frac{3}{6} = \frac{1}{2}$

There is a constant rate of change, $\frac{1}{2}$, so this function is linear.

B

x	y
−6	18
−2	2
2	2
0	0
4	8

+4, −16   +4, +0
−2, −2   +4, +8

Find the rates of change.

$\frac{-16}{4} = -4$ $\frac{0}{4} = 0$ $\frac{-2}{-2} = 1$ $\frac{8}{4} = \frac{1}{2}$

The rates of change are not constant, so this function is nonlinear.

CHECK IT OUT!

Use rates of change to determine whether each function is linear or nonlinear.

2a.

x	y
−2	$\frac{1}{4}$
−1	$\frac{1}{2}$
0	1
3	8
4	16

2b.

x	y
−5	3
−1	3
1	3
3	3
7	3

When you are given a verbal description of a function, you can determine whether the function is linear or nonlinear by making a table of values and examining the rates of change. You can compare two functions by comparing their rates of change.

EXAMPLE 3

COMMON CORE GPS MCC9-12.F.IF.6

Physical Science Application

Two water tanks contain 512 gallons of water each. Tank A begins to drain, losing half of its volume of water every hour. Tank B begins to drain at the same time and loses 40 gallons of water every hour. Identify the function that gives the volume of water in each tank as linear or nonlinear. Which tank loses water more quickly between hour 4 and hour 5?

Use the verbal descriptions to make a table for the volume of water in each tank.

Time (h)	0	1	2	3	4	5
Water in Tank A (gal)	512	256	128	64	32	16

Time (h)	0	1	2	3	4	5
Water in Tank B (gal)	512	472	432	392	352	312

For tank A, the rates of change are −256, −128, −64, −32, and −16, so the rate of change is variable and the function is nonlinear.

For tank B, the rates of change are all −40, so the rate of change is constant and the function is linear.

Between hours 4 and 5, the volume of water in tank A decreases at a rate of 16 gallons per hour. The volume of water in tank B decreases at a rate of 40 gallons per hour. Tank B loses water more quickly.

 CHECK IT OUT!

3. Reka and Charlotte each invest $500. Each month, Charlotte's investment grows by $25, while Reka's investment grows by 5% of the previous month's amount. Identify the function that gives the value of each investment as linear or nonlinear. Who is earning money more quickly between month 3 and month 4?

EXTENSION

Exercises

my.hrw.com
Homework Help

Use rates of change to determine whether each function is linear or nonlinear.

1.

x	4	5	7	10	12
y	−2	−1	1	4	6

2.

x	−2	3	4	6	8
y	−4	6	8	14	20

3.

x	0	3	9	12	18
y	14	12	8	6	2

4.

x	−8	−6	−4	−2	0
y	−3	1	3	5	9

5. Hobbies Caitlin and Greg collect stamps. Each starts with a collection of 50 stamps. Caitlin adds 15 stamps to her collection each week. Greg adds 1 stamp to his collection the first week, 3 stamps the second week, 5 stamps the third week, and so on. Identify the function that gives the number of stamps in each collection as linear or nonlinear. Which collection is growing more quickly between week 5 and week 6?

Determine whether each function has a constant or variable rate of change.

6. 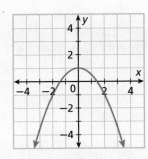 **7.** 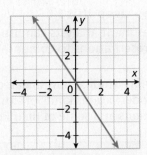 **8.**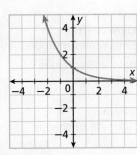

9. $y = 2x^2$ **10.** $y + 1 = 3x$ **11.** $y = -7$

12. $y = \frac{1}{5}x$ **13.** $y = 5^x$ **14.** $y = x^2 + 1$

15. $y = 3\sqrt{x}$ **16.** $y = \frac{x - 3}{2x}$ **17.** $x + y = 6.25$

Determine whether each statement is sometimes, always, or never true.

18. A function whose graph is a straight line has a variable rate of change.

19. A quadratic function has a constant rate of change.

20. The rate of change of a linear function is negative.

21. The rate of change between two points on the graph of a nonlinear function is 0.

22. Critical Thinking The figure shows the graph of the exponential function $y = \left(\frac{1}{2}\right)^x$.

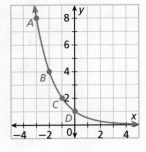

  a. Find the rates of change between points A and B, between points B and C, and between points A and D.

  b. What do you notice about the rates of change you found in part **a**? Do you think this would be true for the rate of change between any two points on the graph?

  c. How do your findings about the rates of change relate to the shape of the graph?

23. A model rocket is launched from the ground. The graph shows the height of the rocket at various times.

  a. Find the rates of change between points A and B and between points B and C.

  b. Which rate of change is greater? What does this tell you about the motion of the rocket?

  c. Find the rates of change between points C and D and between points D and E.

  d. What does the sign of the rates of change you found in part **c** tell you about the motion of the rocket? Explain.

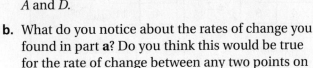
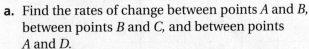

Model Rocket

Comparing Functions

Essential Question: How can you compare properties of two functions each represented in a different way?

Objectives
Compare functions in different representations.

Estimate and compare rates of change.

Vocabulary
average rate of change

Who uses this?

Investment analysts can use different function representations to compare investments. (See Example 2.)

You have studied how linear, quadratic, and exponential functions can be used to model various kinds of situations. The table below shows the three types of functions and some of their key properties.

	Linear	Quadratic	Exponential
Equation	$y = mx + b$ Example: $y = 2x + 1$	$y = ax^2 + bx + c,$ $a \neq 0$ Example: $y = x^2 - 2x + 3$	$y = ab^x,\ a \neq 0,\ b \neq 1,$ $b > 0$ Example: $y = 0.5(2)^x$
Graph			
Table			

Linear table:

x	y	
0	1	+2
1	3	+2
2	5	+2
3	7	+2
4	9	+2

Constant first differences

Quadratic table:

x	y
0	3
1	2
2	3
3	6
4	11

−1, +1, +3, +5; +2, +2, +2

Constant second differences

Exponential table:

x	y	
0	0.5	×2
1	1	×2
2	2	×2
3	4	×2
4	8	×2

Constant ratios

COMMON CORE GPS MCC9-12.F.IF.9

EXAMPLE 1

Comparing Linear Functions

Deirdre and Beth each deposit money into their checking accounts weekly. Their account information for the past several weeks is shown below.

my.hrw.com

Online Video Tutor

Deirdre's Account

Weeks	Account Balance ($)
0	60
1	75
2	90
3	105
4	120

Beth's Account

Compare the accounts by finding slopes and *y*-intercepts and interpreting those values in the context of the situation.

	Deirdre	Beth	Interpret and Compare.
Slope	Slope	Slope	The slope is the rate of change. Beth is saving at a higher rate.
	Use (1, 75) and (2, 90).	Use (1, 60) and (2, 80).	
	$\frac{90-75}{2-1}=15$	$\frac{80-60}{2-1}=20$	
y-intercept	*y*-intercept	*y*-intercept	The *y*-intercept is the beginning account balance. Deirdre started with more money.
	(0, 60)	(0, 40)	
	y-intercept = 60	*y*-intercept = 40	

1. Dave and Arturo each deposit money into their checking accounts weekly. Their account information for the past several weeks is shown. Compare the accounts by finding and interpreting slopes and *y*-intercepts.

Dave's Account

Weeks	0	1	2	3
Account Balance ($)	30	42	54	66

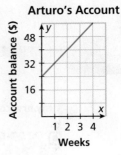

Arturo's Account

Remember that nonlinear functions do not have a constant rate of change. One way to compare two nonlinear functions is to calculate their *average rates of change* over a certain interval. For a function $f(x)$ whose graph contains the points (x_1, y_1) and (x_2, y_2), the **average rate of change** over the interval $[x_1, x_2]$ is the slope of the line through (x_1, y_1) and (x_2, y_2).

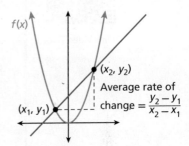

Average rate of change $= \frac{y_2 - y_1}{x_2 - x_1}$

Reading Math

The notation [0, 20] means all *x*-values from 0 to 20, including 0 and 20.

COMMON CORE GPS
EXAMPLE 2
MCC9-12.F.IF.9

my.hrw.com

Online Video Tutor

Comparing Exponential Functions

An investment analyst offers two different investment options for her customers. Compare the investments by finding and interpreting the average rates of change from year 0 to year 20.

Investment A

Years	Value ($)
0	10.00
5	13.38
10	17.91
15	23.97
20	32.07
25	42.92

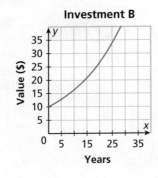

Investment B

Calculate the average rates of change over [0, 20] by using the points whose x-coordinates are 0 and 20.

Investment A

$$\frac{32.07 - 10.00}{20-0} = \frac{22.07}{20} \approx 1.10 \quad \textit{Use (0, 10.00) and (20, 32.07).}$$

Investment B

$$\frac{27 - 10}{20-0} = \frac{17}{20} = 0.85 \qquad \textit{Use the graph to estimate. When x = 20,}$$
$$\textit{y} \approx \textit{27. Use (0, 10) and (20, 27).}$$

From year 0 to year 20, investment A increased at an average rate of $1.10 per year, while investment B increased at an average rate of $0.85 per year.

 **2.** Compare the same investments' average rates of change from year 10 to year 25.

 EXAMPLE 3
MCC9-12.F.LE.3

my.hrw.com

Online Video Tutor

Comparing Different Types of Functions

A town has approximately 1000 homes. The town council is considering plans for future development. Plan A calls for an increase of 200 homes per year. Plan B calls for a 10% increase each year. Compare the plans.

Let x be the number of years. Let y be the number of homes. Write functions to model each plan.

Plan A: $y = 200x + 1000$

Plan B: $y = 1000(1.10)^x$

Use your calculator to graph both functions.

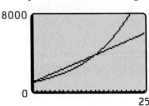

The graphs show that under plan A, there will be more homes built than under plan B in early years.

But by the end of the 15th year, the number of homes built under plan B exceeds the number of homes built under plan A. From that point on, plan B results in more homes than plan A by ever-increasing amounts every year.

 3. Two neighboring schools use different models for anticipated growth in enrollment: School A has 850 students and predicts an increase of 100 students per year. School B also has 850 students, but predicts an increase of 8% per year. Compare the models.

THINK AND DISCUSS

1. Explain why you need to use the word *average* when comparing rates of change for quadratic or exponential functions, but not for linear functions.

2. A function can be represented by an equation or a graph. Describe a possible advantage of each representation.

3. GET ORGANIZED Copy and complete the graphic organizer. Complete the sentence in each column by writing important values to compare.

Comparing Functions			
Linear to Linear	**Exponential to Exponential**	**Quadratic to Quadratic**	**Linear to Quadratic**
Compare…	Compare…	Compare…	Compare…

13-2 Exercises

my.hrw.com
Homework Help

GUIDED PRACTICE

SEE EXAMPLE 1

1. Personal Finance Fay and Kara each withdraw money from their savings accounts weekly, as shown. Compare the accounts by finding and interpreting slopes and *y*-intercepts.

Fay's Account

Weeks	0	1	2	3
Account Balance ($)	425	375	325	255

Kara's Account

SEE EXAMPLE 2

2. Biology A biologist tracked the hourly growth of two different strains of bacteria in the lab. Her data are shown below. Compare the number of bacteria by finding and interpreting the average rates of change from hour 0 to hour 4.

Bacteria A

Hours	Number of Bacteria
0	5
1	15
2	45
3	135
4	405

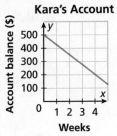

Bacteria B

3. **Business** A bicycle store has approximately 200 bicycles in stock. The store owner is considering plans for expanding his inventory. Plan A calls for an increase of 30 bicycles per year. Plan B calls for a 10% increase each year. Compare the plans.

PRACTICE AND PROBLEM SOLVING

H.O.T. 4. **Recreation** Kevin and Darius each hiked a mountain trail at different rates, as shown below. Compare the hikes by finding and interpreting slopes and *y*-intercepts.

Kevin's Hike

Time (h)	0	1	2	3
Distance from Camp (mi)	1.5	3.5	5.5	7.5

Darius's Hike

$y = 2.2x + 1$

5. **Anthropology** An archeologist used these functions to model the changing populations of two ancient cities as they grew in size. Compare the populations by finding and interpreting the average rates of change over the interval [0, 40].

City A

Area (mi²)	Population
0	0
10	31
20	89
30	164
40	252
50	353

City B

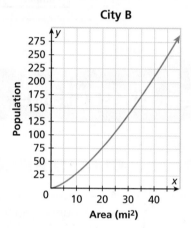

H.O.T. 6. **Recreation** A summer boating camp has 75 boats. The camp director is considering two proposals for increasing the number of boats to match the increase in the number of campers. Proposal A recommends increasing the number of boats by 5 boats per year. Proposal B recommends a 5% increase each year. Compare the proposals.

7. **Business** The revenue of a company based on the price of its product is modeled by the function below.
   a. Estimate the average rate of change over [0, 4].
   b. What price that will yield the maximum revenue?

Product Price and Revenue

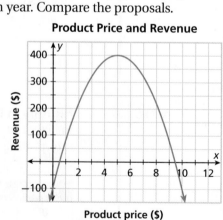

8. **Critical Thinking** A karate center has 120 students. The director wants to set a goal to motivate her instructors to increase student enrollment. Under plan A, the goal is to increase the number of students by 12% each year. Under plan B, the goal is to increase the number of students by 20 each year.
   a. Compare the plans.
   b. Which plan should the director choose to double the enrollment in the shortest amount of time? Explain.
   c. Which plan should she use to triple the enrollment in the shortest amount of time? Explain.

9. **Write About It** Compare the characteristics of linear, quadratic, and exponential functions. Explain how to decide which type of function is being shown on a graph and in a table.

TEST PREP

10. Tanya has $2000 in savings. She wants to save more money. She is considering two plans. Under plan A, she will increase her balance by $1000 per year. Under plan B, she will increase her balance by 20% each year. How much more will she save with plan B after 10 years? Round your answer to the nearest dollar.

  (A) $383   (B) $9,562   (C) $12,000   (D) $12,383

CHALLENGE AND EXTEND

H.O.T. 11. Prove that linear functions grow by equal differences over equal intervals.

Given: $x_2 - x_1 = x_4 - x_3$;

f is a linear function of the form $f(x) = mx + b$.

Prove: $f(x_2) - f(x_1) = f(x_4) - f(x_3)$

H.O.T. 12. Prove that exponential functions grow by equal factors over equal intervals.

Given: $x_2 - x_1 = x_4 - x_3$;

g is an exponential function of the form $g(x) = ab^x$.

Prove: $\dfrac{g(x_2)}{g(x_1)} = \dfrac{g(x_4)}{g(x_3)}$

FOCUS ON MATHEMATICAL PRACTICES

H.O.T. 13. Comparison For a math project, two groups of students wrote functions to describe a six-month repayment plan for a loan. Group A set up the function $f(t) = 100 + 100(1.2)^t$, where $t = 0$ for the first month, $t = 1$ for the second, and so on. Group B described their function using a table. The first three months' payments are shown.

Month	1	2	3
Payment	$150	$187.50	$234.38

Compare the total amounts repaid in 6 months using the two plans.

H.O.T. 14. Analysis For each function pair, use your knowledge of transformations to explain how the graph of $g(x)$ differs from the graph of $f(x)$.

  a. $f(x) = 500(1.45)^x$; $g(x) = 500(1.45)^x + 50$
  b. $f(x) = 5(0.85)^x$; $g(x) = 5(0.85)^{x-3}$
  c. $f(x) = 2(5)^x$; $g(x) = 6(5)^x$

Transforming Exponential Functions

? **Essential Question:** How can you identify the effect of a given transformation on the graph of an exponential function?

Objectives
Transform exponential functions by changing parameters.

Describe the effects of changes in the coefficients of exponential functions.

You can perform the same transformations on exponential functions that you performed on polynomial, quadratic, and linear functions.

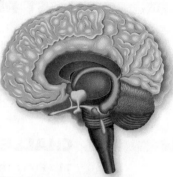

The hippocampus, in orange, directs the storage of memory in the brain.

Helpful Hint

It may help you remember the direction of the shift if you think of "*h* is for **h**orizontal."

Transformations of Exponential Functions		
Transformation	**$f(x)$ Notation**	**Examples**
Vertical translation	$f(x) + k$	$y = 2^x + 3$ 3 units up $y = 2^x - 6$ 6 units down
Horizontal translation	$f(x - h)$	$y = 2^{x-2}$ 2 units right $y = 2^{x+1}$ 1 unit left
Vertical stretch or compression	$af(x)$	$y = 6(2^x)$ stretch by 6 $y = \frac{1}{2}(2^x)$ compression by $\frac{1}{2}$
Horizontal stretch or compression	$f\left(\frac{1}{b}x\right)$	$y = 2^{\left(\frac{1}{5}x\right)}$ stretch by 5 $y = 2^{3x}$ compression by $\frac{1}{3}$
Reflection	$-f(x)$ $f(-x)$	$y = -2^x$ across x-axis $y = 2^{-x}$ across y-axis

COMMON CORE GPS MCC9-12.F.BF.3

EXAMPLE **1** **Translating Exponential Functions**

Make a table of values, and graph the function $g(x) = 2^x - 4$. Describe the asymptote. Tell how the graph is transformed from the graph of $f(x) = 2^x$.

x	-2	-1	0	1	2	3
$g(x)$	-3.75	-3.5	-3	-2	0	4

The asymptote is $y = -4$, and the graph approaches this line as the value of x decreases. The transformation moves the graph of $f(x) = 2^x$ down 4 units. The range changes to $\{y \mid y > -4\}$.

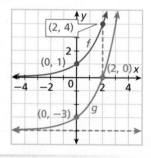

CHECK IT OUT!

1. Make a table of values, and graph $j(x) = 2^{x-2}$. Describe the asymptote. Tell how the graph is transformed from the graph of $f(x) = 2^x$.

doc-stock/Alamy

EXAMPLE 2 **Stretching, Compressing, and Reflecting Exponential Functions**

Graph the exponential function. Find the y-intercept and the asymptote. Describe how the graph is transformed from the graph of its parent function.

A $g(x) = 2(3^x)$

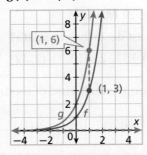

parent function: $f(x) = 3^x$

y-intercept: 2, asymptote: $y = 0$

The graph of $g(x)$ is a vertical stretch of the parent function $f(x) = 3^x$ by a factor of 2.

B $h(x) = -\frac{1}{4}(2^x)$

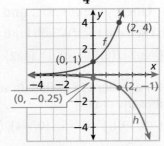

parent function: $f(x) = 2^x$

y-intercept: $-\frac{1}{4}$, asymptote: $y = 0$

The graph of $h(x)$ is a reflection of the parent function $f(x) = 2^x$ across the x-axis and a vertical compression by a factor of $\frac{1}{4}$. The range is $\{y \mid y < 0\}$.

CHECK IT OUT! Graph the exponential function. Find the y-intercept and the asymptote. Describe how the graph is transformed from the graph of its parent function.

2a. $h(x) = \frac{1}{3}(5^x)$

2b. $g(x) = 2(2^{-x})$

 EXTENSION

Exercises

my.hrw.com
Homework Help

Make a table of values, and graph each function. Describe the asymptote. Tell how the graph is transformed from the graph of $f(x) = 3^x$.

1. $g(x) = 3^x + 2$

2. $h(x) = 3^x - 2$

3. $j(x) = 3^{x+1}$

Graph each exponential function. Find the y-intercept and the asymptote. Describe how the graph is transformed from the graph of its parent function.

4. $g(x) = 3(4^x)$

5. $h(x) = \frac{1}{3}(4^x)$

6. $j(x) = -\frac{1}{3}(4^x)$

7. $k(x) = -2(4^x)$

8. $m(x) = -(4^{-x})$

9. $n(x) = e^{2x}$

Make a table of values, and graph each function. Describe the asymptote. Tell how the graph is transformed from the graph of $f(x) = 5^x$.

10. $g(x) = 5^x - 1$

11. $h(x) = 5^{x+2}$

12. $j(x) = 5^{x-1} - 1$

Graph each exponential function. Find the y-intercept and the asymptote. Describe how the graph is transformed from the graph of its parent function.

13. $g(x) = 4\left(\frac{1}{2}\right)^x$

14. $h(x) = 0.25\left(\frac{1}{2}\right)^x$

15. $j(x) = -0.25\left(\frac{1}{2}\right)^x$

16. $k(x) = -\left(\frac{1}{2}\right)^{\frac{x}{2}}$

17. $m(x) = 4\left(\frac{1}{2}\right)^{-x}$

18. $n(x) = -4\left(\frac{1}{2}\right)^{-x}$

Ready to Go On?

my.hrw.com
Assessment and Intervention

13-1 **Linear, Quadratic, and Exponential Models**

Graph each data set. Which kind of model best describes the data?

1. $\{(-2, 5), (3, 10), (0, 1), (1, 2), (0.5, 1.25)\}$ 2. $\{(0, 3), (2, 12), (-1, 1.5), (-3, 0.375), (4, 48)\}$

Look for a pattern in each data set to determine which kind of model best describes the data.

3. $\{(-2, -6), (-1, -5), (0, -4), (1, -3), (2, -2)\}$ 4. $\{(-2, -24), (-1, -12), (0, -6), (1, -3)\}$

5. Write a function that models the data. Then use your function to predict how long the humidifier will produce steam with 10 quarts of water.

Input and Output of a Humidifier	
Water Volume (qt)	**Steam Time (h)**
3	4.5
4	6
5	7.5
6	9

13-2 **Comparing Functions**

6. Sam has $5000 in a savings account. He is considering two plans to save more money. Under plan A, Sam will increase his account balance by $500 per year. Under plan B, he will increase his account balance by 10% per year. How much money will Sam have in his account with each plan after 5 years? Which is the better plan to save more money? Explain.

7. Decide which linear function is increasing at a greater rate.

- Function 1 has x-intercept −7 and y-intercept 4.

- Function 2 includes the points in the table.

x	0	2	4	6
y	−8	−3	2	7

8. Michael is studying population changes in two types of birds living on an island. Compare the populations by finding and interpreting the average rates of change over the interval [0, 18]

Bird A

Time (months)	0	6	12	18
Population (thousands)	8.3	8.6	8.8	9.1

Bird B

$y = 3.6(1.06)^x$

Selected Response

1. Look for a pattern in the data set. Which kind of model best describes the data?

Population Growth of Bacteria	
Time (hours)	Number of Bacteria
0	2,000
1	5,000
2	12,500
3	31,250
4	78,125

(A) cubic   (C) quadratic

(B) exponential   (D) linear

2. Two insect colonies start out with the same populations but have different growth rates. Compare the colonies by finding and interpreting the average rates of change from week 0 to week 15.

Colony A

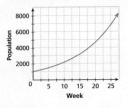

Colony B

Week	0	5	10	15	20	25
Population	1000	1539	2367	3642	5604	8623

(F) Colony A: about 150 per week,
Colony B: about 176 per week.

(G) Colony A: about 150 per week,
Colony B: about 243 per week.

(H) Colony A: about 2200 per week,
Colony B: about 2642 per week.

(J) Colony A: about 2200 per week,
Colony B: about 176 per week.

3. Use the information in the table to predict the number of termites in the termite colony after one year.

Termite Colony Population	
Time (months)	Number of Termites
0	20
1	80
2	320
3	1,280

(A) 16,777,216 termites

(B) 9,920 termites

(C) 5,120 termites

(D) 335,544,320 termites

Mini-Tasks

4. Suppose you have $10,000 to invest and a choice between two investment plans. In each plan, the interest you earn each year is added to the value of the investment.
In Plan A, you earn $500 in interest every year.
In Plan B, you earn 4% of your current investment value every year.

  a. Write a function for each of the plans.

  b. Which plan has a greater value in year 10?

  c. Which plan has a greater value in year 20?

5. A realtor estimates that a certain new house worth $500,000 will gain value at a rate of 6% per year.

  a. Make a table that shows the worth of the house for years 0, 1, 2, 3, and 4.

  b. What is the real-world meaning of year 0?

  c. Which type of model best represents the data in your table? Explain.

  d. Write a function for the data.

Selected Response

1. Benito has x apples. He cuts each apple in half and gives each half to a different horse. Which expression represents the number of horses Benito feeds?

   (A) $x \cdot \frac{1}{2}$ (C) $x \cdot 1\frac{1}{2}$

   (B) $x \div \frac{1}{2}$ (D) $x \div 1\frac{1}{2}$

2. What is the value of $\frac{2a}{a^3}$ if $4 - a = -6$?

   (F) $\frac{1}{50}$ (H) $\frac{1}{2}$

   (G) 8   (J) 10

3. Which equation describes the relationship between x and y in the table below?

x	−8	−4	0	4	8
y	2	1	0	−1	−2

   (A) $y = -4x$ (C) $y = 4x$

   (B) $y = -\frac{1}{4}x$ (D) $y = \frac{1}{4}x$

4. Which graph is described by $x - 3y = -3$?

   (F)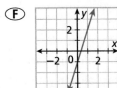

   (G)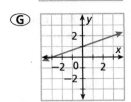

   (H)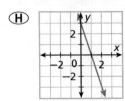

   (J)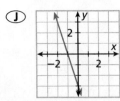

5. Which steps could you use to graph the line that has slope 2 and contains the point $(-1, 3)$?

   (A) Plot $(-1, 3)$. Move 1 unit up and 2 units right and plot another point.

   (B) Plot $(-1, 3)$. Move 2 units up and 1 unit right and plot another point.

   (C) Plot $(-1, 3)$. Move 1 unit up and 2 units left and plot another point.

   (D) Plot $(-1, 3)$. Move 2 units up and 1 unit left and plot another point.

6. Which relation is NOT a function?

   (F) $\{(1, -5), (3, 1), (-5, 4), (4, -2)\}$

   (G) $\{(2, 7), (3, 7), (4, 7), (5, 8)\}$

   (H) $\{(1, -5), (-1, 6), (1, 5), (6, -3)\}$

   (J) $\{(3, -2), (5, -6), (7, 7), (8, 8)\}$

7. A bird flies from the ground to the top of a tree, sits there and sings for a while, flies down to the top of a picnic table to eat crumbs, and then flies back to the top of the tree to sing some more. Which graph best represents this situation?

   (A)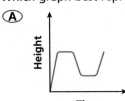

   (B)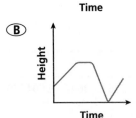

   (C)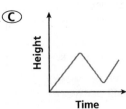

   (D)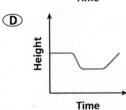

If possible, use the same calculator you usually use in math class. A timed test is not the right place to figure out where buttons are and how they work. Also, replace your batteries the night before the test. If your batteries run out, you may be given a replacement calculator you are not familiar with.

8. The graph below shows a function.

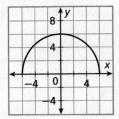

What is the domain of the function?

Ⓕ $x \geq 0$

Ⓖ $x \geq -6$

Ⓗ $0 \leq x \leq 6$

Ⓙ $-6 \leq x \leq 6$

9. Frank borrowed $5000 with an annual simple interest rate. The amount of interest he owed after 6 months was $300. What is the interest rate of the loan?

Ⓐ 1%

Ⓑ 6%

Ⓒ 10%

Ⓓ 12%

10. What is the value of $f(x) = -3 - x$ when $x = -7$?

Ⓕ −10

Ⓖ −4

Ⓗ 4

Ⓙ 10

11. Which relationship is a direct variation?

Ⓐ
x	1	2	3	4
y	−1	0	1	2

Ⓑ
x	1	2	3	4
y	0	−1	−2	−3

Ⓒ
x	1	2	3	4
y	3	5	7	9

Ⓓ
x	1	2	3	4
y	3	6	9	12

12. Which shows the slope-intercept form of $2x + 3y = 6$?

Ⓕ $y = \frac{2}{3}x + 2$ Ⓗ $y = -\frac{2}{3}x + 2$

Ⓖ $y = \frac{2}{3}x + 6$ Ⓙ $y = -\frac{2}{3}x + 6$

13. Company A charges $30 plus $0.40 per mile for a car rental. The total charge for m miles is given by $f(m) = 30 + 0.4m$. For a similar car, company B charges $30 plus $0.30 per mile. The total charge for m miles is given by $g(m) = 30 + 0.3m$. Which best describes the transformation from the graph of $f(m)$ to the graph of $g(m)$?

Ⓐ Translation up

Ⓑ Translation down

Ⓒ Rotation

Ⓓ Reflection

14. For $h(x) = x^3 + 2x$, what is $h(4)$?

Ⓕ 20   Ⓗ 48

Ⓖ 24   Ⓙ 72

15. A sequence is defined by the rule $a_n = -3(2)^{n-1}$. What is the 5th term of the sequence?

Ⓐ 5

Ⓑ −30

Ⓒ −48

Ⓓ −216

16. Which could be the graph of $y = -2^x$?

Ⓕ
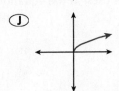

Ⓖ
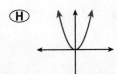

Ⓗ
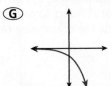

Ⓙ
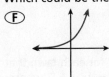

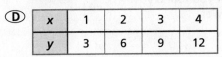

17. Which equation models exponential decay?

Ⓐ $y = -0.12(1.05)^t$

Ⓑ $y = 0.12(1.05)^t$

Ⓒ $y = 1.05(0.12)^t$

Ⓓ $y = 0.12(1 + 0.5)^t$

18. Which ordered pair lies on the graph of $y = 3(2)^{x+1}$?

Ⓕ $(-1, 0)$

Ⓖ $(0, 9)$

Ⓗ $(1, 12)$

Ⓙ $(3, 24)$

19. Which rule defines the sequence –3, 15, –75, 375...?

Ⓐ $a_n = -5(3)^{n-1}$

Ⓑ $a_n = -3(-5)^{n-1}$

Ⓒ $a_n = 3(-5)^{n-1}$

Ⓓ $a_n = 5(-3)^{n-1}$

20. The function $f(t) = 30,000(0.8)^t$ gives the value of a vehicle where t is the number of years after purchase. According to the function, what will be the value of the car 8 years after purchase, rounded to the nearest dollar?

Ⓕ $5,033

Ⓖ $19,200

Ⓗ $24,000

Ⓙ $192,000

21. Brian calculates the charge for each lawn that he mows using the function $y = 4x + 5.5$, where x is the number of hours spent mowing the lawn. Brian never takes more than 2 hours to mow a lawn. Which best represents the reasonable range for the function?

Ⓐ $0 < y \leq 2$

Ⓑ $0 < y \leq 13.5$

Ⓒ $5.5 < y \leq 13.5$

Ⓓ $y > 13.5$

22. A line passes through the point $(5, -1)$. The slope of the line is $-\frac{1}{2}$. Which of these is the equation of the line?

Ⓕ $2x - y = 11$

Ⓖ $x - 2y = 3$

Ⓗ $2x + y = 9$

Ⓙ $x + 2y = 3$

23. A gym membership costs $25 a month plus $3 per visit. This is modeled by the function $c = 3v + 25$, where c is the cost per month and v is the number of visits. If the slope of this function's graph were to increase, what does that mean about the prices that the gym charges?

Ⓐ The gym raised its monthly fee.

Ⓑ The gym lowered the cost per visit.

Ⓒ The gym raised the cost per visit.

Ⓓ The gym lowered its monthly fee.

24. A video club costs $25 to join and it costs $2.50 to rent a video. Which gives the independent and dependent variables and a function that describes this situation?

Ⓕ Independent: number of videos rented; dependent: total cost; $f(x) = 2.5x - 25$

Ⓖ Independent: number of videos rented; dependent: total cost; $f(x) = 2.5x + 25$

Ⓗ Independent: number of videos rented; dependent: total cost; $f(x) = 25x + 2.5$

Ⓙ Independent: total cost; dependent: number of videos rented; $f(x) = 25x - 2.5$

Mini-Tasks

25. A video store charges a $10 membership fee plus $2 for each movie rental. The total cost for x movie rentals is given by $f(x) = 2x + 10$.

a. Graph this function.

b. Give a reasonable domain and range.

26. The table below shows the federal minimum wage in different years.

Year	1960	1970	1980	1990	2000
Minimum Wage ($)	1.00	1.60	3.10	3.80	5.15

a. Find the rate of change for each ten-year time period. Show your work.

b. During which time period did the minimum wage increase the fastest? Explain what the rate of change for this time period means.

27. a. Find the slope of the line below. Explain how you found your answer.

b. Write an equation in slope-intercept form for the line. Explain how you found your answer.

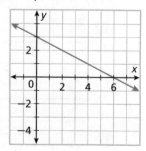

28. The table shows the number of people newly infected by a certain virus with one person as the original source.

Week	1	2	3	4	5	6	7
Newly Infected People	1	3	9	27	81	243	729

  a. Is the data set best described by a linear function or an exponential function? Write a function to model the data.

  b. Use the function to predict the number of people that will become infected in the 10th week. Show your work.

29. Ella and Mia went on a camping trip. The total cost for their trip was $124, which the girls divided evenly. Ella paid for 4 nights at the campsite and $30 for supplies. Mia paid for 2 nights at the campsite and $46 for supplies.

  a. Write an equation that could be used to find the cost of one night's stay at the campsite. Explain what the variable in your equation represents.

  b. Solve your equation from part **a** to find the cost of one night's stay at the campsite. Show your work.

30. Study the sequence below.

  18, 24.5, 31, 37.5, 44,…

  a. Could this sequence be arithmetic? Explain.

  b. Find the 100th term of the sequence. Show your work.

31. The fare for a taxi ride depends on the distance traveled. It costs $9.50 to go 3 miles and $17 to go 6 miles.

  a. Assume that taxi fare is a linear function of distance. Write an equation that gives the fare y for a trip of x miles.

  b. How much do you pay for each additional mile that you ride in the taxi?

Performance Tasks

32. Connie is interested in yoga classes. Yoga Studio charges a one-time fee of $75 for a medical examination and $20 for each class. Stretch Classic charges $25 for each class. Both companies only allow full-hour sessions.

  a. Sketch a graph of the cost associated with each facility on the same coordinate grid. Tell whether each graph is continuous or discrete.

  b. Write functions for the cost associated with each facility.

  c. Connie wants to do yoga at home, but she read an article that recommended at least 28 sessions with a trainer before starting a home yoga practice. Assuming the quality of the classes is the same, which company should Connie choose? Explain your reasoning.

33. A loan's interest rate for an entire year is called its annual percentage rate, or APR, but APR can have two meanings. When the compounding of the interest is not taken into account, it is called the *nominal* APR, and when the compounding is taken into account, it is called the *effective* APR. To convert from nominal APR to effective APR, you can use the formula

$$\text{effective APR} = \left(1 + \frac{\text{nominal APR}}{n}\right)^n - 1,$$

where n is the number of times the interest is compounded per year. You can use this formula to compare the loans offered by two used car dealerships for different compounding periods.

  a. Secondhand Cars is offering a loan with a nominal APR of 13.2%, compounded monthly. Convert this nominal APR to an effective APR, and round to the nearest tenth of a percent.

  b. Gently Used Motors is offering a loan with a nominal APR of 13.4%, compounded semi-annually. Convert this nominal APR to an effective APR and round to the nearest tenth of a percent. Which dealership offers the better interest rate? Explain.

  c. Suppose both Secondhand Cars and Gently Used Motors are offering you a loan of $5000. For both, your first payment is not due for one year, but you have to pay interest for that year. What is the difference in the amounts owed after one year?

  d. Why would a used car dealership offering a loan be more likely to advertise the nominal APR instead of the effective APR?

my.hrw.com
Online Assessment

Go online for updated, PARCC-aligned assessment readiness.

Are You Ready?

my.hrw.com
Assessment and Intervention

 Vocabulary

Match each term on the left with a definition on the right.

1. difference
2. factor
3. natural numbers
4. ratio
5. sum

A. the result of an addition

B. a whole number that is multiplied by another whole number to get a product

C. numbers that can be expressed in the form $\frac{a}{b}$, where a and b are both integers and $b \neq 0$

D. the result of a subtraction

E. a comparison of two quantities by division

F. the counting numbers: 1, 2, 3, …

 Solve Proportions

Solve each proportion.

6. $\frac{3}{4} = \frac{x}{12}$

7. $\frac{15}{9} = \frac{3}{x}$

8. $\frac{10}{20} = \frac{x}{100}$

9. $\frac{250}{1500} = \frac{x}{100}$

✓ Compare and Order Real Numbers

Compare. Write <, >, or =.

10. $20 \;\blacksquare\; 13$

11. $\frac{2}{3} \;\blacksquare\; \frac{1}{2}$

12. $\frac{3}{4} \;\blacksquare\; \frac{7}{9}$

13. $0.75 \;\blacksquare\; \frac{9}{12}$

Order the numbers from least to greatest.

14. $\frac{1}{2}, \frac{4}{5}, \frac{1}{8}, \frac{3}{4}, \frac{2}{3}$

15. $0.12, \frac{2}{5}, \frac{3}{4}, 0.3, \frac{1}{3}$

✓ Multiply Decimals

Multiply.

16. 0.25×300

17. 0.5×4000

18. 0.05×200

19. 0.125×9600

✓ Divide Decimals

Divide.

20. $435 \div 10$

21. $32 \div 100$

22. $777 \div 1000$

23. $295 \div 10,000$

Career Readiness Statisticians

Statisticians apply mathematical principles to collect, analyze, and present numerical data. They design surveys and experiments, and interpret the results. Statisticians work in many different fields, such as government, economics, scientific research, software engineering, education, and sports. Most statisticians have a college degree in statistics or mathematics. However, sports statisticians require less academic training.

Describing Data

Online Edition

my.hrw.com

Access the complete online textbook, interactive features, and additional resources.

Online Video Tutor

Watch full explanations of every example in the textbook with these online videos.

TI-Nspire™ Activities

Enhance your learning with cutting edge technology from Texas Instruments.

Portable Devices

eTextbook

Access your full textbook on your tablet or e-reader.

On the Spot

Watch video tutorials anywhere, anytime with this app for iPhone® and iPad®.

Chapter Resources

Scan with your smart phone to jump directly to the online edition.

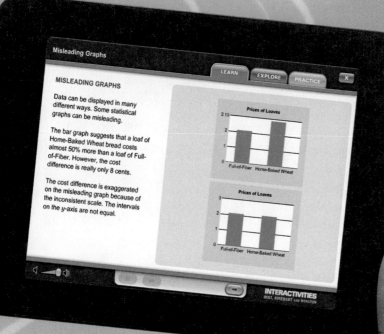

COMMON CORE GPS | **Unit Contents**

Use this **Animated Math** activity to explore misleading graphs.

COMMON
CORE GPS

Contents

MATHEMATICAL
PRACTICES
The Common Core Georgia Performance Standards for Mathematical Practice
describe varieties of expertise that all students should seek to develop.
Opportunities to develop these practices are integrated throughout this program.

1 Make sense of problems and persevere in
solving them.

2 Reason abstractly and quantitatively.

3 Construct viable arguments and critique the
reasoning of others.

4 Model with mathematics.

5 Use appropriate tools strategically.

6 Attend to precision.

7 Look for and make use of structure.

8 Look for and express regularity in repeated
reasoning.

Unpacking the Standards

my.hrw.com
Multilingual Glossary

Understanding the standards and the vocabulary terms in the standards will help you know exactly what you are expected to learn in this chapter.

 MCC9-12.S.ID.1

Represent data with plots on the real number line (dot plots, histograms, and box plots).

Key Vocabulary

histogram (histograma) A bar graph used to display data grouped in intervals

box-and-whisker plot (gráfica de mediana y rango) A method of showing how data are distributed by using the median, quartiles, and minimum and maximum values; also called a box plot.

What It Means For You

Displaying numerical data on the real number line gives you an instant visual image of how the data are distributed, and helps you draw conclusions about the center and spread of the data.

EXAMPLE **Histogram**

A histogram gives you an overall picture of how data are distributed, but does not indicate any particular values or statistics.

Golf Tournament Scores

EXAMPLE **Box-and-whisker plot**

A box-and-whisker plot includes five statistical values.

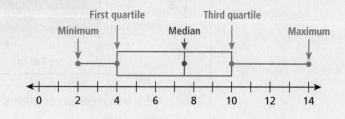

 MCC9-12.S.ID.3

Interpret differences in shape, center, and spread in the context of the data sets, accounting for possible effects of extreme data points (outliers).

Key Vocabulary

outlier (valor extremo) A data value that is far removed from the rest of the data.

What It Means For You

Always examine the displays and statistics for a data set in its own particular context so that you can draw valid conclusions.

EXAMPLE **Outliers**

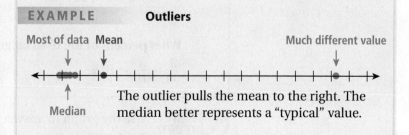

The outlier pulls the mean to the right. The median better represents a "typical" value.

14-1 Organizing and Displaying Data

Essential Question: How can you use various types of graphs to organize and display data?

Objectives
Organize data in tables and graphs.

Choose a table or graph to display data.

Vocabulary
bar graph
line graph
circle graph

Who uses this?
Nutritionists can display health information about food in bar graphs.

Bar graphs, line graphs, and *circle graphs* can be used to present data in a visual way.

A **bar graph** displays data with vertical or horizontal bars. Bar graphs are a good way to display data that can be organized into categories. Using a bar graph, you can quickly compare the categories.

COMMON CORE GPS
EXAMPLE 1 MCC9-12.S.ID.1

my.hrw.com

Online Video Tutor

Reading and Interpreting Bar Graphs

Use the graph to answer each question.

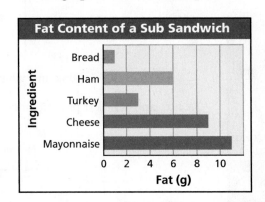

Fat Content of a Sub Sandwich

A Which ingredient contains the most fat?

mayonnaise   *The bar for mayonnaise is the longest.*

B How many more grams of fat are in ham than in turkey?

$6 - 3 = 3$ *There are 6 grams of fat in ham and 3 grams of fat in turkey.*

C How many total fat grams are in this sandwich?

$1 + 6 + 3 + 9 + 11 = 30$ *Add the number of fat grams for each ingredient.*

D What percent of the total fat grams in this sandwich are from turkey?

$\frac{3}{30} = \frac{1}{10} = 10\%$ *Out of 30 total fat grams, 3 fat grams are from turkey.*

Use the graph to answer each question.

1a. Which ingredient contains the least amount of fat?

1b. Which ingredients contain at least 8 grams of fat?

Victoria Smith/HMH

A double-bar graph can be used to compare two data sets. A double-bar graph has a key to distinguish between the two sets of data.

COMMON CORE GPS
MCC9-12.S.ID.1

EXAMPLE 2

my.hrw.com

Online Video Tutor

Reading and Interpreting Double Bar Graphs

Use the graph to answer each question.

A **In which year did State College have the greatest average attendance for basketball?**

2003

Find the tallest orange bar.

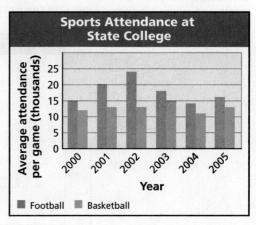

B **On average, how many more people attended a football game than a basketball game in 2001?**

20,000 − 13,000 = 7000

Find the height of each bar for 2001 and subtract.

2. Use the graph to determine which years had the same average basketball attendance. What was the average attendance for those years?

A **line graph** displays data using line segments. Line graphs are a good way to display data that changes over a period of time.

COMMON CORE GPS
MCC9-12.S.ID.1

EXAMPLE 3

my.hrw.com

Online Video Tutor

Reading and Interpreting Line Graphs

Use the graph to answer each question.

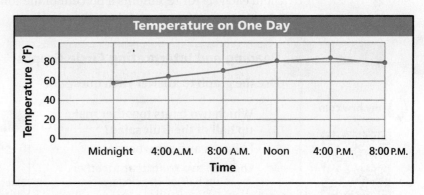

A **At what time was the temperature the warmest?**

4:00 P.M.   *Identify the highest point.*

B **During which 4-hour time period did the temperature increase the most?**

From 8:00 A.M. to noon   *Look for the segment with the greatest positive slope.*

3. Use the graph to estimate the difference in temperature between 4:00 A.M. and noon.

A double-line graph can be used to compare how two related data sets change over time. A double-line graph has a key to distinguish between the two sets of data.

COMMON CORE GPS
MCC9-12.S.ID.1

EXAMPLE 4

Reading and Interpreting Double-Line Graphs

my.hrw.com

Online Video Tutor

Use the graph to answer each question.

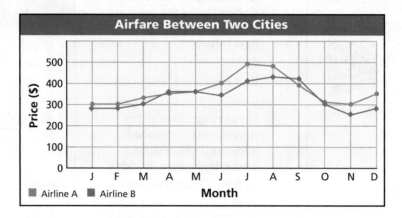

Airfare Between Two Cities

■ Airline A   ■ Airline B

A In which month(s) did airline B charge more than airline A?

April and September   *Identify the points when the purple line is higher than the blue line.*

B During which month(s) did the airlines charge the same airfare?

May   *Look for the point where the data points overlap.*

 4. Use the graph to describe the general trend of the data.

A **circle graph** shows parts of a whole. The entire circle represents 100% of the data and each sector represents a percent of the total. Circle graphs are good for comparing each category of data to the whole set.

COMMON CORE GPS
MCC9-12.S.ID.1

EXAMPLE 5

Reading and Interpreting Circle Graphs

my.hrw.com

Online Video Tutor

Use the graph to answer each question.

A Which two fruits together make up half of the fruit salad?

bananas and strawberries

Look for two fruits that together make up half of the circle.

B Which fruit is used more than any other?

cantaloupe

Look for the largest sector of the graph.

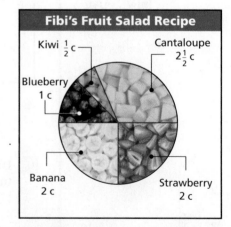

Fibi's Fruit Salad Recipe

Kiwi $\frac{1}{2}$ c   Cantaloupe $2\frac{1}{2}$ c

Blueberry 1 c

Banana 2 c   Strawberry 2 c

Reading Math

The sections of a circle graph are called *sectors*.

 5. Use the graph to determine what percent of the fruit salad is cantaloupe.

Sam Dudgeon/HMH

Choosing and Creating an Appropriate Display

Use the given data to make a graph. Explain why you chose that type of graph.

my.hrw.com

Online Video Tutor

A

Livestock Show Entries	
Animal	**Number**
Chicken	38
Goat	10
Horse	32
Pig	12
Sheep	25

A bar graph is appropriate for this data because it will be a good way to compare categories.

Step 1 Determine an appropriate scale and interval. The scale must include all of the data values. The scale is separated into equal parts, called intervals.

Step 2 Use the data to determine the lengths of the bars. Draw bars of equal width. The bars should not touch.

Step 3 Title the graph and label the horizontal and vertical scales.

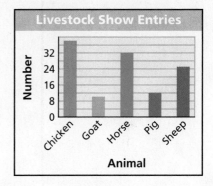

B

Division of Crops	
Crop	**Area (acres)**
Corn	70
Fallow	50
Mixed vegetables	10
Soybeans	40
Wheat	30

A circle graph is appropriate for this data because it shows categories as parts of a whole.

Step 1 Calculate the percent of the total represented by each category.

Corn: $\frac{70}{200} = 0.35 = 35\%$

Soybeans: $\frac{40}{200} = 0.2 = 20\%$

Fallow: $\frac{50}{200} = 0.25 = 25\%$

Wheat: $\frac{30}{200} = 0.15 = 15\%$

Mixed vegetables: $\frac{10}{200} = 0.05 = 5\%$

Step 2 Find the angle measure for each sector of the graph. Since there are 360° in a circle, multiply each percent by 360°.

Corn: $0.35 \times 360° = 126°$
Fallow: $0.25 \times 360° = 90°$
Mixed vegetables: $0.05 \times 360° = 18°$
Soybeans: $0.2 \times 360° = 72°$
Wheat: $0.15 \times 360° = 54°$

Step 3 Use a compass to draw a circle. Mark the center and use a straightedge to draw one radius. Then use a protractor to draw each central angle.

Step 4 Title the graph and label each sector.

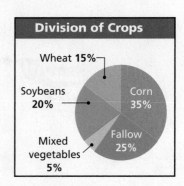

Use the given data to make a graph. Explain why you chose that type of graph.

 C

Chinnick College Enrollment	
Year	Students
1930	586
1955	2,361
1980	15,897
2005	21,650

A line graph is appropriate for this data because it will show the change in enrollment over a period of time.

Step 1 Determine the scale and interval for each set of data. Time should be plotted on the horizontal axis because it is independent.

Step 2 Plot a point for each pair of values. Connect the points using line segments.

Step 3 Title the graph and label the horizontal and vertical scales.

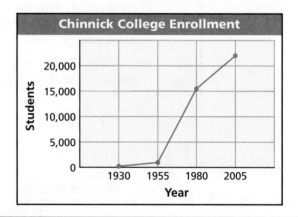

 CHECK IT OUT!

6. **Use the given data to make a graph. Explain why you chose that type of graph.**

The data below shows how Vera spends her time during a typical 5-day week during the school year.

Vera's Schedule						
Activity	Sleeping	Eating	School	Sports	Homework	Other
Time (h)	45	8	30	10	10	17

 MCC.MP.7 · MATHEMATICAL PRACTICES

THINK AND DISCUSS

1. What are some comparisons you can make by looking at a bar graph?

2. Name some key components of a good line graph.

3. **GET ORGANIZED** Copy and complete the graphic organizer. In each box, tell which kind of graph is described.

Know it! Note

Graph Type
- Compares categories
- Shows change over time
- Shows how a whole is divided in parts

GUIDED PRACTICE

Vocabulary Use the vocabulary from this lesson to answer the following questions.

1. In a *circle graph*, what does each sector represent?

2. In a *line graph*, how does the slope of a line segment relate to the rate of change?

SEE EXAMPLE 1 Use the bar graph for Exercises 3 and 4.

3. Estimate the total number of animals at the shelter.

4. There are 3 times as many ___?___ as ___?___ at the animal shelter.

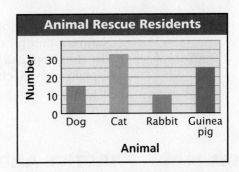

SEE EXAMPLE 2 Use the double-bar graph for Exercises 5–7.

5. About how much more is a club level seat at stadium A than at stadium B?

6. Which type of seat is the closest in price at the two stadiums?

7. Describe one relationship between the ticket prices at stadium A and stadium B.

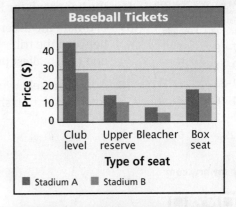

SEE EXAMPLE 3 Use the line graph for Exercises 8 and 9.

8. Estimate the number of tickets sold during the week of the greatest sales.

9. Which one-week period of time saw the greatest change in sales?

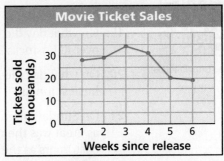

SEE EXAMPLE 4 Use the double-line graph for Exercises 10–12.

10. When was the support for the two candidates closest?

11. Estimate the difference in voter support for the two candidates five weeks before the election.

12. Describe the general trend(s) of voter support for the two candidates.

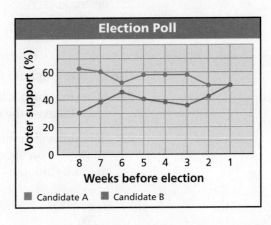

Use the circle graph for Exercises 13–15.

13. Which color is least represented in the ball playpen?

14. There are 500 balls in the playpen. How many are yellow?

15. Which two colors are approximately equally represented in the ball playpen?

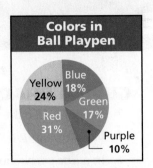

Colors in Ball Playpen

Yellow 24% | Blue 18% | Green 17% | Red 31% | Purple 10%

16. The table shows the breakdown of Karim's monthly budget of $100. Use the given data to make a graph. Explain why you chose that type of graph.

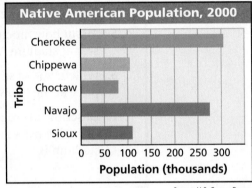

Item/Activity	Spending ($)
Clothing	35
Food	25
Entertainment	25
Other	15

PRACTICE AND PROBLEM SOLVING

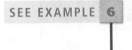

Independent Practice

For Exercises	See Example
17–18	1
19–21	2
22–23	3
24–26	4
27–28	5
29	6

my.hrw.com

Online Extra Practice

Use the bar graph for Exercises 17 and 18.

17. Estimate the difference in population between the tribes with the largest and the smallest population.

18. Approximately what percent of the total population shown in the table is Cherokee?

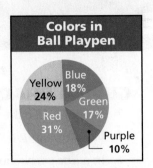

Native American Population, 2000

Tribe: Cherokee, Chippewa, Choctaw, Navajo, Sioux

Population (thousands): 0 50 100 150 200 250 300

Source: U.S. Census Bureau

Use the double bar graph for Exercises 19–21.

19. On what day did Ray do the most overall business?

20. On what day did Ray have the busiest lunch?

21. On Sunday, about how many times as great was the number of dinner customers as the number of lunch customers?

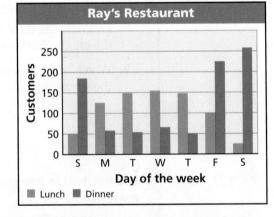

Ray's Restaurant

Customers: 0 50 100 150 200 250

Day of the week: S M T W T F S

■ Lunch ■ Dinner

Use the line graph for Exercises 22 and 23.

22. Between which two games did Marlon's score increase the most?

23. Between which three games did Marlon's score increase by about the same amount?

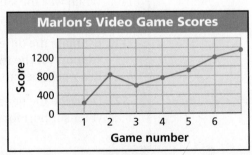

Marlon's Video Game Scores

Score: 0 400 800 1200

Game number: 1 2 3 4 5 6

Use the double-line graph for Exercises 24–26.

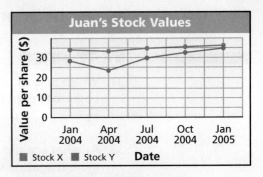

24. What was the average value per share of Juan's two stocks in July 2004?

25. Which stock's value changed the most over any time period?

26. Describe the trend of the values of both stocks.

Use the circle graph for Exercises 27 and 28.

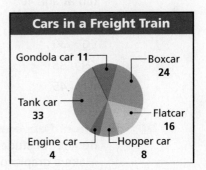

27. About what percent of the total number of cars are hopper cars?

28. About what percent of the total number of cars are gondola or tank cars?

29. The table shows the weight of twin babies at various times from birth to four weeks old. Use the given data to make a graph. Explain why you chose that type of graph.

Age (days)	Boy's Weight (lb)	Girl's Weight (lb)
1	5.3	5.7
3	5.0	5.2
7	5.5	5.9
14	6.2	6.8
28	7.9	7.5

Write *bar, double-bar, line, double-line,* or *circle* to indicate the type of graph that would best display the data described.

30. attendance at a carnival each year over a ten-year period

31. attendance at two different carnivals each year over a ten-year period

32. attendance at five different carnivals during the same year

33. attendance at a carnival by age group as it relates to total attendance

34. **Critical Thinking** Give an example of real-world data that would best be displayed by each type of graph: line graph, circle graph, double-bar graph.

Real-World Connections

35. The first modern Olympic Games took place in 1896 in Athens, Greece. The circle graph shows the total number of medals won by several countries at the Olympic Games of 1896.

    a. Which country won the most medals? Estimate the percent of the medals won by this country.

    b. Which country won the second most medals? Estimate the percent of the medals won by this country.

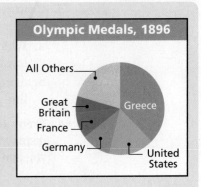

36. Write About It Explain how you could use a line graph to make predictions.

TEST PREP

37. Which type of graph would best display the contribution of each high school basketball player to the team, in terms of points scored?

Ⓐ Bar graph   Ⓑ Line graph   Ⓒ Double-line graph   Ⓓ Circle graph

38. At what age did Marianna have 75% more magazine subscriptions than she did at age 40?

Ⓕ 25

Ⓖ 30

Ⓗ 35

Ⓙ 45

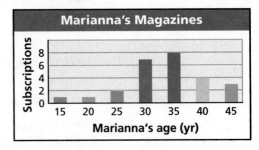

HOT **39. Short Response** The table shows the number of students in each algebra class. Make a graph to display the data. Explain why you chose that type of graph.

Teacher	Students
Mr. Abrams	34
Ms. Belle	29
Mr. Marvin	25
Ms. Swanson	27

CHALLENGE AND EXTEND

Students and teachers at Lauren's school went on one of three field trips.

40. On which trip were there more boys than girls?

HOT **41.** A total of 60 people went to the museum. Estimate the number of girls who went to the museum.

HOT **42.** Explain why it is not possible to determine whether fewer teachers went to the museum than to the zoo or the opera.

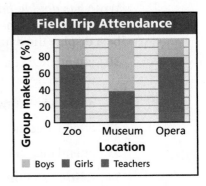

FOCUS ON MATHEMATICAL PRACTICES

HOT **43. Communication** A double–line graph displays the high temperatures and the low temperatures for each day of a week.

a. What does a temperature that lies between the high temperature line and the low temperature line represent?

b. Armin says a double-bar graph would better represent the data than a double-line graph. How might Armin support his choice?

HOT **44. Error Analysis** Darnell says the best graphical display for the data in the table is a circle graph. Do you agree? If not, what display would you chose?

Favorite Lunch	Male	Female
Pizza	23	17
Turkey Burger	14	9
Veggie Lasagna	3	21

Frequency and Histograms

Essential Question: How can you organize and display data using stem-and-leaf plots and histograms?

Objectives
Create stem-and-leaf plots.

Create frequency tables and histograms.

Vocabulary
stem-and-leaf plot
frequency
frequency table
histogram
cumulative frequency

Why learn this?
Stem-and-leaf plots can be used to organize data, like the number of students in elective classes. (See Example 1.)

A **stem-and-leaf plot** arranges data by dividing each data value into two parts. This allows you to see each data value.

The digits other than the last digit of each value are called a stem. → **2|3** ← The last digit of a value is called a leaf.

Key: 2|3 means 23 ← The key tells you how to read each value.

COMMON CORE GPS
MCC9-12.S.ID.1

EXAMPLE 1

Making a Stem-and-Leaf Plot

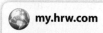
my.hrw.com

Online Video Tutor

A The numbers of students in each of the elective classes at a school are given below. Use the data to make a stem-and-leaf plot.

24, 14, 12, 25, 32, 18, 23, 24, 9, 18, 34, 28, 24, 27

Number of Students in Elective Classes

Stem	Leaves
0	9
1	2 4 8 8
2	3 4 4 4 5 7 8
3	2 4

Key: 2|3 means 23

The tens digits are the stems.

The ones digits are the leaves. List the leaves from least to greatest within each row.

Title the graph and add a key.

Writing Math

Stems are always consecutive numbers. In Example 1B, neither player has scores that start with 15, so there are no leaves in that row.

B Marty's and Bill's scores for ten games of bowling are given below. Use the data to make a back-to-back stem-and-leaf plot.

Marty: 137, 149, 167, 134, 121, 127, 143, 123, 168, 162
Bill: 129, 138, 141, 124, 139, 160, 149, 145, 128, 130

Bowling Scores

Marty		Bill
7 3 1	12	4 8 9
7 4	13	0 8 9
9 3	14	1 5 9
	15	
8 7 2	16	0

Key: |14|1 means 141
3|14| means 143

The first two digits are the stems.

The ones digits are the leaves.

Put Marty's scores on the left side and Bill's scores on the right.

Title the graph and add a key.

The graph shows that three of Marty's scores were higher than Bill's highest score.

CHECK IT OUT!

1. The temperatures in degrees Celsius for two weeks are given below. Use the data to make a stem-and-leaf plot.

7, 32, 34, 31, 26, 27, 23, 19, 22, 29, 30, 36, 35, 31

The **frequency** of a data value is the number of times it occurs. A **frequency table** shows the frequency of each data value. If the data is divided into intervals, the table shows the frequency of each interval.

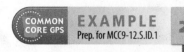

EXAMPLE 2
Prep. for MCC9-12.S.ID.1

my.hrw.com

Online Video Tutor

Making a Frequency Table

The final scores for each golfer in a tournament are given below. Use the data to make a frequency table with intervals.

77, 71, 70, 82, 75, 76, 72, 70, 77, 74, 71, 75, 68, 72, 75, 74

Step 1 Identify the least and greatest values.

The least value is 68. The greatest value is 82.

Step 2 Divide the data into equal intervals.

For this data set, use an interval of 3.

Step 3 List the intervals in the first column of the table. Count the number of data values in each interval and list the count in the last column. Give the table a title.

Golf Tournament Scores	
Scores	Frequency
68–70	3
71–73	4
74–76	6
77–79	2
80–82	1

2. The numbers of days of Maria's last 15 vacations are listed below. Use the data to make a frequency table with intervals.

4, 8, 6, 7, 5, 4, 10, 6, 7, 14, 12, 8, 10, 15, 12

A **histogram** is a bar graph used to display the frequency of data divided into equal intervals. The bars must be of equal width and should touch, but not overlap.

EXAMPLE 3
MCC9-12.S.ID.1

my.hrw.com

Online Video Tutor

Making a Histogram

Use the frequency table in Example 2 to make a histogram.

Step 1 Use the scale and interval from the frequency table.

Step 2 Draw a bar for the number of scores in each interval.

All bars should be the same width. The bars should touch, but not overlap.

Step 3 Title the graph and label the horizontal and vertical scales.

Helpful Hint

The intervals in a histogram must be of equal size.

3. Make a histogram for the number of days of Maria's last 15 vacations.

4, 8, 6, 7, 5, 4, 10, 6, 7, 14, 12, 8, 10, 15, 12

Cumulative frequency shows the frequency of all data values less than or equal to a given value. You could just count the number of values, but if the data set has many values, you might lose track. Recording the data in a cumulative frequency table can help you keep track of the data values as you count.

Making a Cumulative Frequency Table

The heights in inches of the players on a school basketball team are given below.

72, 68, 71, 70, 73, 69, 79, 76, 72, 75, 72, 74, 68, 70, 69, 75, 72, 71, 73, 76

  a. **Use the data to make a cumulative frequency table.**

   Step 1 Choose intervals for the first column of the table.

   Step 2 Record the frequency of values in each interval for the second column.

   Step 3 Add the frequency of each interval to the frequencies of all the intervals before it. Put that number in the third column of the table.

   Step 4 Title the table.

Basketball Players' Heights		
Height (in.)	Frequency	Cumulative Frequency
68–70	6	6
71–73	8	14
74–76	5	19
77–79	1	20

  b. **How many players have heights under 74 in?**

   All heights under 74 in. are displayed in the first two rows of the table, so look at the cumulative frequency shown in the second row.

   There are 14 players with heights under 74 in.

CHECK IT OUT!

4. The numbers of vowels in each sentence of a short essay are listed below.

   33, 36, 39, 37, 34, 35, 43, 35, 28, 32, 36, 35, 29, 40, 33, 41, 37

   a. Use the data to make a cumulative frequency table.

   b. How many sentences contain 35 vowels or fewer?

THINK AND DISCUSS

1. In a stem-and-leaf plot, the number of _____?_____ is always the same as the number of data values. (*stems* or *leaves*)

2. Explain how to make a histogram from a stem-and-leaf plot.

3. GET ORGANIZED Copy and complete the graphic organizer.

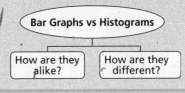

Bar Graphs vs Histograms

How are they alike?   How are they different?

GUIDED PRACTICE

1. **Vocabulary** A(n) _____?_____ is a data display that shows individual data values. (*stem-and-leaf plot* or *histogram*)

SEE EXAMPLE 1

2. **Sports** The ages of professional basketball players at the time the players were recruited are given. Use the data to make a stem-and-leaf plot.

Ages When Recruited
21 23 21 18 22 19 24 22 21 22 20 21

3. **Weather** The average monthly rainfall for two cities (in inches) is given below. Use the data to make a back-to-back stem-and-leaf plot.

Average Monthly Rainfall (in.)											
Austin, TX	1.9	2.4	1.9	3.0	3.6	3.3	1.9	2.1	3.2	3.5	2.2	2.3
New York, NY	3.3	3.1	3.9	3.7	4.2	3.3	4.1	4.1	3.6	3.3	4.2	3.6

SEE EXAMPLE 2

4. **Sports** The finishing times of runners in a 5K race, to the nearest minute, are given. Use the data to make a frequency table with intervals.

Finishing Times in 5K Race (to the nearest minute)
19 25 23 29 32 30 21 22 24
19 28 26 31 34 30 28 25 24

SEE EXAMPLE 3

5. **Biology** The breathing intervals of gray whales are given. Use the frequency table to make a histogram for the data.

Breathing Intervals (min)	
Interval	**Frequency**
5–7	4
8–10	7
11–13	7
14–16	8

SEE EXAMPLE 4

6. The scores made by a group of eleventh-grade students on the mathematics portion of the SAT are given.

Scores on Mathematics Portion of SAT
520 560 720 690 540 630 790 540
600 580 710 500 540 660 630

   a. Use the data to make a cumulative frequency table.

   b. How many students scored 650 or higher on the mathematics portion of the SAT?

PRACTICE AND PROBLEM SOLVING

7. The numbers of people who visited a park each day over two weeks during different seasons are given below. Use the data to make a back-to-back stem-and-leaf plot.

Visitors to a Park													
Summer	25	25	26	27	27	57	59	22	23	29	22	23	54	53
Winter	11	12	13	9	30	27	4	19	14	19	21	33	35	9

8. **Weather** The daily high temperatures in degrees Fahrenheit in a town during one month are given. Use the data to make a stem-and-leaf plot.

Daily High Temperatures (°F)
68 72 79 77 70 72 75 71 64 64
68 62 70 71 78 83 83 87 91 89
87 75 73 70 69 69 62 58 71 76

9. The overall GPAs of several high school seniors are given. Use the data to make a frequency table with intervals.

Overall GPAs
3.6 2.9 3.1 3.0 2.5 2.6 3.8 2.9
2.2 2.9 3.1 3.3 3.6 3.0 2.3 2.8 2.9

10. **Chemistry** The atomic masses of the nonmetal elements are given in the table. Use the frequency table to make a histogram for the data.

Atomic Masses of Nonmetal Elements					
Interval	0–49.9	50–99.9	100–149.9	150–199.9	200–249.9
Frequency	11	3	2	0	2

11. The numbers of pretzels found in several samples of snack mix are given in the table.

   a. Use the data to make a cumulative frequency table.

   b. How many samples of snack mix had fewer than 42 pretzels?

Numbers of Pretzels
42 39 39 38 40
41 44 42 38 44
47 36 40 40 43 38

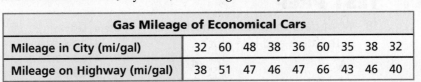

12. **Automobiles** The table shows gas mileage for the most economical cars in July 2004, including three hybrids.

Gas Mileage of Economical Cars	
Mileage in City (mi/gal)	32 60 48 38 36 60 35 38 32
Mileage on Highway (mi/gal)	38 51 47 46 47 66 43 46 40

Make a back-to-back stem-and-leaf plot for the data.

13. Damien's math test scores are given in the table:

   a. Make a stem-and-leaf plot of Damien's test scores.

   b. Make a histogram of the test scores using intervals of 5.

   c. Make a histogram of the test scores using intervals of 10.

   d. Make a histogram of the test scores using intervals of 20.

   e. How does the size of the interval affect the appearance of the histogram?

   f. **Write About It** Which histogram makes Damien's grades look highest? Explain.

Damien's Math Test Scores
75 84 68
72 59 88
72 77 81
84 60 70

14. **ERROR ANALYSIS** Two students made stem-and-leaf plots for the following data: 530, 545, 550, 555, 570. Which is incorrect? Explain the error.

A

Stem	Leaves
53	0
54	5
55	0 5
57	0

Key: 52|5 means 525

B

Stem	Leaves
53	0
54	5
55	0 5
56	
57	0

Key: 52|5 means 525

15. The 2004 Olympic results for women's weightlifting in the 48 kg weight class are 210, 205, 200, 190, 187.5, 182.5, 180, 177.5, 175, 172.5, 170, 167.5, and 165, measured in kilograms. Medals are awarded to the athletes who can lift the most weight.

    a. Create a frequency table beginning at 160 and using intervals of 10 kg.

    b. Create a histogram of the data.

    c. Tara Cunningham from the United States lifted 172.5 kg. Did she win a medal? How do you know?

16. Entertainment The top ten movies in United States theaters for the weekend of June 25–27, 2004, grossed the following amounts (in millions of dollars). Create a histogram for the data. Make the first interval 5–9.9.

Ticket Sales (million $)				
23.9	19.7	18.8	13.5	13.1
11.2	10.2	7.5	6.1	5.1

H.O.T. 17. Critical Thinking Margo's homework assignment is to make a data display of some data she finds in a newspaper. She found a frequency table with the given intervals.

Explain why Margo must be careful when drawing the bars of the histogram.

Age
Under 18
18–30
31–54
55 and older

TEST PREP

18. What data value occurs most often in the stem-and-leaf plot?

    Ⓐ 7   Ⓒ 47

    Ⓑ 4.7   Ⓓ 777

Stem	Leaves
3	2 3 4 4 7 9
4	0 1 5 7 7 7 8
5	1 2 2 3

Key: 3|2 means 3.2

19. The table shows the results of a survey about time spent on the Internet each month. Which statement is NOT supported by the data in the table?

Time Spent on the Internet per Month		
Time (h)	Frequency	Cumulative Frequency
0–4	4	4
5–9	6	10
10–14	3	13
15–19	16	29
20–24	12	41
25–29	7	48
30–34	2	50

    Ⓕ The interval of 30 to 34 h/mo has the lowest frequency.

    Ⓖ More than half of those who responded spend more than 20 h/mo on the Internet.

    Ⓗ Only four people responded that they spend less than 5 h/mo on the Internet.

    Ⓙ Sixteen people responded that they spend less than 20 h/mo on the Internet.

20. The frequencies of starting salary ranges for college graduates are noted in the table. Which histogram best reflects the data?

Starting Salaries	
Salary Range ($)	Frequency
20,000–29,000	JHT JHT JHT JHT II
30,000–39,000	JHT JHT JHT JHT JHT JHT
40,000–49,000	JHT JHT JHT I
50,000–59,000	I

Ⓐ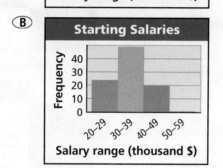

Ⓒ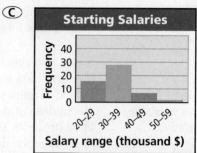

Ⓑ

Ⓓ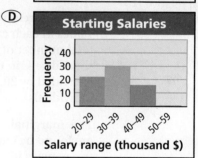

CHALLENGE AND EXTEND

21. The cumulative frequencies of each interval have been given. Use this information to complete the frequency column.

Interval	Frequency	Cumulative Frequency
13–16	▦	8
17–20	▦	16
21–24	▦	57
25–28	▦	123

FOCUS ON MATHEMATICAL PRACTICES

H.O.T. 22. Error Analysis Rajiv says that a stem-and-leaf plot with 12 stems definitely represents a data set of 12 values. Do you agree? Explain.

H.O.T. 23. Reasoning The table shows the lengths of students' right feet.

a. Find the cumulative frequencies for the intervals in the table.

b. How many students have a right foot length greater than 19 cm but less than 26 cm?

c. How many students have a right foot length of 21 cm? Explain.

d. Which type of graphical display would you use for the data in the table? Justify your choice.

Students' Right Foot Lengths	
Length (cm)	Frequency
14–16	2
17–19	19
20–22	13
23–25	6
26–28	1

Two-Way Tables

 Essential Question: How can you construct and interpret two-way frequency tables?

Objectives
Construct and interpret two-way frequency tables of data when two categories are associated with each object being classified.

Vocabulary
joint relative frequency
marginal relative frequency
conditional relative frequency

Who uses this?
Commuters can use two-way tables to determine the best route to work. (See Example 3.)

A *two-way table* is a useful way to organize data that can be categorized by two variables. Suppose you asked 20 children and adults whether they liked broccoli. The table shows one way to arrange the data.

The **joint relative frequencies** are the values in each category divided by the total number of values, shown by the shaded cells in the table. Each value is divided by 20, the total number of individuals.

The **marginal relative frequencies** are found by adding the joint relative frequencies in each row and column.

	Yes	No
Children	3	8
Adults	7	2

	Yes	No	Total
Children	0.15	0.4	0.55
Adults	0.35	0.1	0.45
Total	0.5	0.5	1

COMMON CORE GPS
EXAMPLE
MCC9-12.S.ID.5
1

Finding Joint and Marginal Relative Frequencies

my.hrw.com

Online Video Tutor

The table shows the results of a poll of 80 randomly selected high school students who were asked if they prefer math or English. Make a table of the joint and marginal relative frequencies.

	9th grade	10th grade	11th grade	12th grade
Math	10	12	11	8
English	12	11	8	8

Divide each value by the total of 80 to find the joint relative frequencies, and add each row and column to find the marginal relative frequencies.

	9th grade	10th grade	11th grade	12th grade	Total
Math	0.125	0.15	0.1375	0.1	0.5125
English	0.15	0.1375	0.1	0.1	0.4875
Total	0.275	0.2875	0.2375	0.2	1

 CHECK IT OUT!

1. The table shows the number of books sold at a library sale. Make a table of the joint and marginal relative frequencies.

	Fiction	Nonfiction
Hardcover	28	52
Paperback	94	36

To find a **conditional relative frequency**, divide the joint relative frequency by the marginal relative frequency. Conditional relative frequencies can be used to find conditional probabilities.

Using Conditional Relative Frequency to Find Probability

A sociologist collected data on the types of pets in 100 randomly selected households, and summarized the results in a table.

		Owns a cat	
		Yes	No
Owns a dog	Yes	15	24
	No	18	43

A Make a table of the joint and marginal relative frequencies.

		Owns a cat		
		Yes	No	Total
Owns a dog	Yes	0.15	0.24	0.39
	No	0.18	0.43	0.61
	Total	0.33	0.67	1

B If you are given that a household has a dog, what is the probability that the household also has a cat?

Use the conditional relative frequency for the row with the condition "Owns a dog." The total for households with dogs is 0.39, or 39%. Out of these, 0.15, or 15%, also have cats. The conditional relative frequency is $\frac{0.15}{0.39} \approx 0.38$.

Given that a household has a dog, there is a probability of about 0.38 that the household also has a cat.

CHECK IT OUT! The classes at a dance academy include ballet and tap dancing. Enrollment in these classes is shown in the table.

		Ballet	
		Yes	No
Tap	Yes	38	52
	No	86	24

2a. Copy and complete the table of the joint relative frequencies and marginal relative frequencies.

		Ballet		
		Yes	No	Total
Tap	Yes			
	No			
	Total			1

2b. If you are given that a student is taking ballet, what is the probability that the student is not taking tap?

Notice that in Example 2, the conditional relative frequency could have been found from the original data:

$$\frac{0.15}{0.39} = \frac{15}{39} \approx 0.38$$

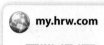
EXAMPLE **3**
MCC9-12.S.CP.4

Comparing Conditional Probabilities

Tomas is trying to decide on the best possible route to drive to work. He has a choice of three possible routes. On each day, he randomly selects a route and keeps track of whether he is late. After a 40-day trial, his notes look like this.

	Late	Not Late
Route A	IIII	HHT HHT
Route B	II	HHT II
Route C	IIII	HHT HHT II

Use conditional probabilities to determine the best route for Tomas to take to work.

Create a table of joint and marginal relative frequencies. There are 40 data values, so divide each frequency by 40.

	Late	Not late	Total
Route A	0.1	0.25	0.35
Route B	0.075	0.175	0.25
Route C	0.1	0.3	0.4
Total	0.275	0.725	1

To find the conditional probabilities, divide the joint relative frequency of being late by the marginal relative frequency in each row.

$P(\text{being late if driving Route A}) = \dfrac{0.1}{0.35} \approx 0.29$

$P(\text{being late if driving Route B}) = \dfrac{0.075}{0.25} = 0.3$

$P(\text{being late if driving Route C}) = \dfrac{0.1}{0.4} = 0.25$

The probability of being late is least for Route C. Based on the sample, Tomas is least likely to be late if he takes Route C.

 CHECK IT OUT!

3. Francine is evaluating three driving schools. She asked 50 people who attended the schools whether they passed their driving tests on the first try.

Use conditional probabilities to determine which is the best school.

	Pass	Fail
Al's Driving	HHT HHT IIII	HHT III
Drive Time	HHT HHT I	HHT II
Crash Course	HHT	HHT

THINK AND DISCUSS

1. Describe the relationship between joint relative frequencies and marginal relative frequencies.

2. Explain how to find the conditional relative frequencies from a two-way table showing joint and marginal relative frequencies.

3. GET ORGANIZED Copy and complete the graphic organizer at right. In each column, explain how to find the relative frequency from a two-way table.

Relative Frequencies		
Joint	Marginal	Conditional

GUIDED PRACTICE

Vocabulary Apply the vocabulary from this lesson to answer each question.

1. The ___?___ relative frequencies are the sums of each row and column in a two-way table. (*joint, marginal,* or *conditional*)

2. You can compare ___?___ probabilities to evaluate the best one out of a number of options. (*joint, marginal,* or *conditional*)

SEE EXAMPLE 1

3. The table shows the results of a poll of randomly selected high school students who were asked if they prefer to hear all-school announcements in the morning or afternoon.

	Underclassmen	Upperclassmen
Morning	8	14
Afternoon	18	10

Make a table of the joint and marginal relative frequencies.

4. **Customer Service** The table shows the results of a customer satisfaction survey for a cellular service provider, by location of the customer. In the survey, customers were asked whether they would recommend a plan with the provider to a friend.

	Arlington	Towson	Parkville
Yes	40	35	41
No	18	10	6

Make a table of the joint and marginal relative frequencies. Round to the nearest hundredth where appropriate.

SEE EXAMPLE 2

5. **School** Pamela has collected data on the number of students in the sophomore class who play a sport or play a musical instrument.

		Plays a sport	
		Yes	No
Plays an instrument	Yes	47	38
	No	51	67

a. Copy and complete the table of the joint and marginal relative frequencies. Round to the nearest hundredth where appropriate.

		Play Sport		
		Yes	No	Total
Play instrument	Yes			
	No			
	Total			

b. If you are given that a student plays an instrument, what is the probability that the student also plays a sport? Round your answer to the nearest hundredth.

c. If you are given that a student plays a sport, what is the probability that the student also plays an instrument? Round your answer to the nearest hundredth.

Artville/Getty Images

SEE EXAMPLE 3

6. **Business** Roberto is the owner of a car dealership. He is assessing the success rates of his top three salespeople in order to offer one of them a promotion. Over two months, for each attempted sale, he records whether the salesperson made a successful sale or not. The results are shown in the chart below.

	Successful	Unsuccessful
Becky	6	6
Raul	4	5
Darrell	6	9

a. Make a table of the joint relative frequencies and marginal relative frequencies. Round to the nearest hundredth where appropriate.

b. Find the probability that each salesperson will make a successful sale. Round to the nearest hundredth where appropriate.

c. Determine which salesperson has the highest success rate.

PRACTICE AND PROBLEM SOLVING

Independent Practice

For Exercises	See Example
7–8	1
9–12	2
13	3

my.hrw.com

Online Extra Practice

7. **Fundraising** The table shows the number of T-shirts and sweatshirts sold at a fundraiser during parent visitation night at Preston High School.

	Students	Adults
T-Shirts	16	23
Sweatshirts	7	14

Make a table of the joint relative frequencies and marginal relative frequencies.

8. **Write About It** Describe in your own words the process you use to write marginal relative frequencies for data given in a two-way table.

9. **Customer Service** The claims handlers at a car insurance company help customers with insurance issues when there has been an accident, so their customer service skills are very important.

The claims handlers at the Trust Auto Insurance Company are divided into three teams. For one month, a customer satisfaction survey was given for each team. The results of the surveys are shown below.

	Satisfied	Dissatisfied
Team 1	20	8
Team 2	34	12
Team 3	34	10

a. Make a table of the joint relative frequencies and marginal relative frequencies. Round to the nearest hundredth where appropriate.

b. Find the probability that a customer will be satisfied after working with each team. Round to the nearest hundredth where appropriate.

c. Determine which team has the highest rate of customer satisfaction.

10. **Critical Thinking** What do you notice about the value that always falls in the cell to the lower right of a two-way table when marginal relative frequencies have been written in? What does this value represent?

H.O.T. **11.** ///ERROR ANALYSIS/// One hundred adults and children were randomly selected and asked whether they spoke more than one language fluently. The data were recorded in a two-way table. Maria and Brennan each used the data to make the tables of joint relative frequencies shown below, but their results are slightly different. The difference is shaded. Can you tell by looking at the tables which of them made an error? Explain.

Maria's table

	Yes	No
Children	0.15	0.25
Adults	0.1	0.6

Brennan's table

	Yes	No
Children	0.15	0.25
Adults	0.1	0.5

H.O.T. **12. Estimation** A total of 107 brownies and muffins was sold at a school bake sale. The joint relative frequency representing muffins sold to seniors was 0.48. Use mental math to find approximately how many muffins were sold to seniors.

13. Public Transit A town planning committee is considering a new system for public transit. Residents of the town were randomly selected to answer two questions: "Do you work within 5 miles of your home?" and "Would you use the new system to get to work, if it were available?"
The results are shown below.

		Work less than 5 miles from home?	
		Yes	No
Use new system?	Yes	24	32
	No	44	20

a. Make a table of the joint relative frequencies and marginal relative frequencies. Round to the nearest hundredth where appropriate.

b. If residents work less than 5 miles from home, what is the probability that they would use the new system? Round to the nearest hundredth.

c. If residents are willing to use the new system, what is the probability that they don't work less than 5 miles from home? Round to the nearest hundredth.

TEST PREP

14. Students and teachers at a school were polled to see if they were in favor of extending the parking lot into part of the athletic fields. The results of the poll are shown in the two-way table.

	In Favor	Not in Favor
Students	16	23
Teachers	9	14

Which of the following statements is false?

Ⓐ Thirty-nine students were polled in all.

Ⓑ Fourteen teachers were polled in all.

Ⓒ Twenty-three students are not in favor of extending the parking lot.

Ⓓ Nine teachers are in favor of extending the parking lot.

15. A group of students were polled to find out how many were planning to major in a scientific field of study in college. The results of the poll are shown in the two-way table.

		Majoring in a science field	
		Yes	No
Class	Junior	150	210
	Senior	112	200

Which of the following statements is true?

(A) Three hundred sixty students were polled in all.

(B) A student in the senior class is more likely to be planning on a scientific major than a nonscientific major.

(C) A student planning on a scientific major is more likely to be a junior than a senior.

(D) More seniors than juniors plan to enter a scientific field of study.

16. Gridded Response A group of children and adults were polled about whether they watch a particular TV show. The survey results, showing the joint relative frequencies and marginal relative frequencies, are shown in the two-way table.

	Yes	No	Total
Children	0.3	0.4	0.7
Adults	0.25	x	0.3
Total	0.55	0.45	1

What is the value of x?

CHALLENGE AND EXTEND

The table shows the joint relative frequencies for data on how many children and teenagers attended a fair in one evening, and whether each bought a booklet of tickets for rides at the entrance gate.

	Yes	No
Children	0.125	0.1
Teenagers	0.725	0.05

Use the table to answer questions 17–20. Round answers to the nearest hundredth where appropriate.

17. Find the marginal relative frequencies for the data.

18. Based on this data, use a percentage to express how likely it is that tomorrow evening a teenager at the fair will buy a ticket booklet at the entrance. Round your answer to the nearest whole percent, if necessary.

19. If the data represent 80 teenagers and children altogether, how many children will have bought a ticket booklet at the entrance?

20. If 12 children did not buy ticket booklets at the entrance, then how many children and teenagers altogether does the data represent?

21. A poll with the options of 'yes' and 'no' was given. If the marginal relative frequency of 'yes' is 1.0, what was the marginal relative frequency of 'no'?

	Yes	No	Total
Group 1	0.24	?	?
Group 2	0.76	?	?
Total	1.0	?	?

22. Short Response What is the maximum a marginal relative frequency can be, and why?

FOCUS ON MATHEMATICAL PRACTICES

H.O.T. **23. Problem Solving** A survey of a sheep farm reveals that 27% of the sheep have long white wool, 8% have short black wool, and 3% have short white wool.

  a. Draw a two-way relative frequency table to show this information. Include marginal relative frequencies in your table.

  b. What percent of the sheep have black wool?

  c. If the farm has a total of 300 sheep, how many of them have short black wool or long white wool?

H.O.T. **24. Reasoning** The table shows the relative frequencies of the results of a survey of whether children and adults have recently used crayons. If 2 of the adults surveyed have recently used crayons, how many children were surveyed in all?

	Child	Adult	Total
Yes	0.55	0.05	0.6
No	0.1	0.30	0.4
Total	0.65	0.35	1

H.O.T. **25. Analysis** The partial frequency table compares the class year of students in a high school to where they like to eat lunch. Is enough information given to complete the table? If so, complete it. If not, complete as much as possible and explain what further information is needed.

	Freshman	Sophomore	Junior	Senior	Total
Cafeteria	75				
Library	20			10	65
Outside		30	50	55	
Total	125	110	140	100	475

14-4 # Data Distributions

? *Essential Question:* How can you describe data using measures of central tendency and spread, including displaying data on box-and-whisker plots?

Objectives
Describe the central tendency of a data set.

Create and interpret box-and-whisker plots.

Vocabulary
mean
median
mode
range
outlier
first quartile
third quartile
interquartile range (IQR)
box-and-whisker plot

Who uses this?

Sports analysts examine data distributions to make predictions. (See Example 4.)

A *measure of central tendency* describes the center of a set of data. Measures of central tendency include the *mean, median,* and *mode.*

- The **mean** is the average of the data values, or the sum of the values in the set divided by the number of values in the set.

- The **median** is the middle value when the values are in numerical order, or the mean of the two middle numbers if there are an even number of values.

- The **mode** is the value or values that occur most often. A data set may have one mode or more than one mode. If no value occurs more often than another, the data set has no mode.

The **range** of a set of data is the difference between the greatest and least values in the set. The range is one measure of the spread of a data set.

 EXAMPLE Prep. for MCC9-12.S.ID.2 **1**

 my.hrw.com

Online Video Tutor

Finding Mean, Median, Mode, and Range of a Data Set

The numbers of hours Isaac did homework on six days are 3, 8, 4, 6, 5, and 4. Find the mean, median, mode, and range of the data set.

3, 4, 4, 5, 6, 8   *Write the data in numerical order.*

mean: $\dfrac{3+4+4+5+6+8}{6} = \dfrac{30}{6} = 5$ *Add all the values and divide by the number of values.*

median: 3, 4, (4, 5) 6, 8

The median is 4.5.   *There is an even number of values. Find the mean of the two middle values.*

mode: 4   *4 occurs more than any other value.*

range: 8 − 3 = 5   *Subtract the least value from the greatest value.*

 1. The weights in pounds of five cats are 12, 14, 12, 16, and 16. Find the mean, median, mode, and range of the data set.

A value that is very different from the other values in a data set is called an **outlier**. In the data set below, one value is much greater than the other values.

Most of data   Mean   Much different value

Determining the Effects of Outliers

Identify the outlier in the data set {7, 10, 54, 9, 12, 8, 5}, and determine how the outlier affects the mean, median, mode, and range of the data.

5, 7, 8, 9, 10, 12, 54   *Write the data in numerical order.*

The outlier is 54.   *Look for a value much greater or less than the rest.*

With the Outlier:

mean: $\dfrac{5 + 7 + 8 + 9 + 10 + 12 + 54}{7}$

$= 15$

median: 5, 7, 8, ⑨ 10, 12, 54
The median is 9.

mode: Each value occurs once.
There is no mode.

range: $54 - 5 = 49$

Without the Outlier:

mean: $\dfrac{5 + 7 + 8 + 9 + 10 + 12}{6}$

$= 8.5$

median: 5, 7, ⑧|⑨ 10, 12
The median is 8.5.

mode: Each value occurs once.
There is no mode.

range: $12 - 5 = 7$

The outlier increases the mean by 6.5, the median by 0.5, and the range by 42. It has no effect on the mode.

2. Identify the outlier in the data set {21, 24, 3, 27, 30, 24}, and determine how the outlier affects the mean, median, mode, and range of the data.

As you can see in Example 2, an outlier can strongly affect the mean of a data set, while having little or no impact on the median and mode. Therefore, the mean may not be the best measure to describe a data set that contains an outlier. In such cases, the median or mode may better describe the center of the data set.

Choosing a Measure of Central Tendency

Niles scored 70, 74, 72, 71, 73, and 96 on his six geography tests. For each question, choose the mean, median, or mode, and give its value.

A **Which measure gives Niles's test average?**
The average of Niles's scores is the mean.

mean: $\dfrac{70 + 74 + 72 + 71 + 73 + 96}{6} = 76$

B **Which measure best describes Niles's typical score? Explain.**
The outlier of 96 causes the mean to be greater than all but one of the test scores, so it is not the best measure in this situation.

The data set has no mode.

The median best describes the typical score.

median: 70, 71, ⑦②, ⑦③ 74, 96   *Find the mean of the two middle values.*
The median is 72.5.

Josh scored 75, 75, 81, 84, and 85 on five tests. For each question, choose the mean, median, or mode, and give its value.

3a. Which measure describes the score Josh received most often?

3b. Which measure should Josh use to convince his parents that he is doing well in school? Explain.

Measures of central tendency describe how data cluster around one value. Another way to describe a data set is by its spread—how the data values are spread out from the center.

Quartiles divide a data set into four equal parts. Each quartile contains one-fourth of the values in the set. The **first quartile** is the median of the lower half of the data set. The second quartile is the median of the data set, and the **third quartile** is the median of the upper half of the data set.

Reading Math

The first quartile is sometimes called the lower quartile, and the third quartile is sometimes called the upper quartile.

The **interquartile range (IQR)** of a data set is the difference between the third and first quartiles. It represents the range of the middle half of the data.

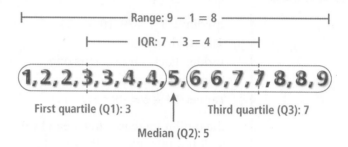

A **box-and-whisker plot** can be used to show how the values in a data set are distributed. You need five values to make a box-and-whisker plot: the minimum (or least value), first quartile, median, third quartile, and maximum (or greatest value).

EXAMPLE 4
COMMON CORE GPS
MCC9-12.S.ID.1

Sports Application

The numbers of runs scored by a softball team in 20 games are given. Use the data to make a box-and-whisker plot.

my.hrw.com

Online Video Tutor

3, 4, 8, 12, 7, 5, 4, 12, 3, 9, 11, 4, 14, 8, 2, 10, 3, 10, 9, 7

Step 1 Order the data from least to greatest.

2, 3, 3, 3, 4, 4, 4, 5, 7, 7, 8, 8, 9, 9, 10, 10, 11, 12, 12, 14

Step 2 Identify the five needed values.

2, 3, 3, 3, 4, 4, 4, 5, 7, 7, 8, 8, 9, 9, 10, 10, 11, 12, 12, 14

Minimum	Q1	Q2	Q3	Maximum
2	4	7.5	10	14

Step 3 Draw a number line and plot a point above each of the five needed values. Draw a box through the first and third quartiles and a vertical line through the median. Draw lines from the box to the minimum and maximum.

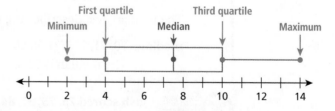

CHECK IT OUT!

4. Use the data to make a box-and-whisker plot.

13, 14, 18, 13, 12, 17, 15, 12, 13, 19, 11, 14, 14, 18, 22, 23

EXAMPLE **5**
MCC9-12.S.ID.2

Reading and Interpreting Box-and-Whisker Plots

The box-and-whisker plots show the ticket sales, in millions of dollars, of the top 25 movies in 2000 and 2007 (for the United States only).

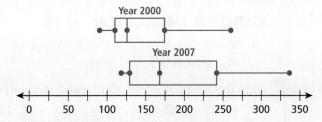

A **Which data set has a greater median? Explain.**

The vertical line in the box for 2007 is farther to the right than the vertical line in the box for 2000.

The data set for 2007 has a greater median.

B **Which data set has a greater interquartile range? Explain.**

The length of the box for 2007 is greater than the length of the box for 2000.

The data set for 2007 has a greater interquartile range.

C **About how much more were the ticket sales for the top movie in 2007 than for the top movie in 2000?**

2007 maximum: **about $335 million**   *Read the maximum values from*
2000 maximum: **about $260 million**   *the box-and-whisker plots.*
$335 - 260 = 75$ *Subtract the maximum values.*

The ticket sales for the top movie in 2007 were about $75 million more than for the top movie in 2000.

CHECK IT OUT!

Use the box-and-whisker plots above to answer each question.

5a. Which data set has a smaller range? Explain.

5b. About how much more was the median ticket sales for the top 25 movies in 2007 than in 2000?

MCC.MP.1, MCC.MP.6   **MATHEMATICAL PRACTICES**

THINK AND DISCUSS

1. Explain when the median is a value in the data set.

2. Give an example of a data set for which the mean is twice the median. Explain how you determined your answer.

3. Suppose the minimum in a data set is the same as the first quartile. How would this affect a box-and-whisker plot of the data?

4. GET ORGANIZED Copy and complete the graphic organizer. Tell which measure of central tendency answers each question.

Measures of Central Tendency	
Measure	**Used to Answer**
	What is the average?
	What is the halfway point of the data?
	What is the most common value?

GUIDED PRACTICE

1. **Vocabulary** What is the difference between the *range* and the *interquartile range* of a data set?

SEE EXAMPLE 1 **Find the mean, median, mode, and range of each data set.**

2. 85, 83, 85, 82

3. 12, 22, 33, 34, 44, 44

4. 10, 26, 25, 10, 20, 22, 25, 20

5. 71, 73, 75, 78, 78, 80, 85, 86

SEE EXAMPLE 2 **Identify the outlier in each data set, and determine how the outlier affects the mean, median, mode, and range of the data.**

6. 10, 96, 12, 17, 15

7. 64, 75, 72, 13, 64

SEE EXAMPLE 3 **Adrienne scored 82, 54, 85, 91, and 83 on her last five science tests. For each question, choose the mean, median, or mode, and give its value.**

8. Which measure best describes Adrienne's typical score? Explain.

9. Which measure should Adrienne use to convince her soccer coach she is doing well in science? Explain.

SEE EXAMPLE 4 **Use the data to make a box-and-whisker plot.**

10. 21, 31, 26, 24, 28, 26

11. 12, 13, 42, 62, 62, 82

SEE EXAMPLE 5 **The box-and-whisker plots show the scores, in thousands of points, of two players on a video game. Use the box-and-whisker plots to answer each question.**

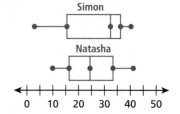

12. Which player has a higher median score? Explain.

13. Which player had the lowest score? Estimate this score.

PRACTICE AND PROBLEM SOLVING

Find the mean, median, mode, and range of each data set.

Independent Practice

For Exercises	See Example
14–17	1
18–19	2
20–21	3
22–23	4
24-26	5

14. 75, 63, 89, 91

15. 1, 2, 2, 2, 3, 3, 3, 4

16. 19, 25, 31, 19, 34, 22, 31, 34

17. 58, 58, 60, 60, 60, 61, 63

Identify the outlier in each data set, and determine how the outlier affects the mean, median, mode, and range of the data.

18. 42, 8, 54, 37, 29

19. 3, 8, 3, 3, 23, 8

my.hrw.com

Online Extra Practice

Lamont bowled 153, 145, 148, and 166 in four games. For each question, choose the mean, median, or mode, and give its value.

20. Which measure gives Lamont's average score?

21. Which measure should Lamont use to convince his parents to let him join a bowling league? Explain.

Use the data to make a box-and-whisker plot.

22. 62, 63, 62, 64, 68, 62, 62

23. 85, 90, 81, 100, 92, 85

The box-and-whisker plots show the prices, in dollars, of athletic shoes at two sports apparel stores. Use the box-and-whisker plots to answer each question.

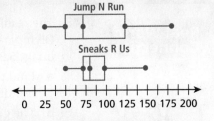

24. Which store has the greater median price? About how much greater?

25. Which store has the smaller interquartile range? What does this tell you about the data sets?

26. Estimate the difference in price between the most expensive shoe type at Jump N Run and the most expensive shoe at Sneaks R Us.

Find the mean, median, mode, and range of each data set.

27. 1, 2, 3, 4, 5, 6, 7, 8, 9, 10

28. 5, 6, 6, 5, 5

29. 2.1, 4.3, 6.5, 1.2, 3.4

30. 0, $\frac{1}{4}$, $\frac{1}{2}$, $\frac{3}{4}$, 1

31. 23, 25, 26, 25, 23

32. –3, –3, –3, –2, –2, –1

33. 1, 4, 9, 16, 25, 36

34. 1, 0, 0, 1, 1, 4

35. **Estimation** Estimate the mean of $16\frac{7}{8}$, $12\frac{1}{4}$, $22\frac{1}{10}$, $18\frac{5}{7}$, $19\frac{1}{3}$, $13\frac{8}{11}$, and $13\frac{8}{11}$.

Tell whether each statement is sometimes, always, or never true.

36. The mean is a value in the data set.

37. The median is a value in the data set.

38. If a data set has one mode, the mode is a value in the data set.

39. The mean is affected by including an outlier.

40. The mode is affected by including an outlier.

H.O.T. 41. **Sports** The table shows the attendance at six football games at Jefferson High School. Which measure of central tendency best indicates the typical attendance at a football game? Why?

Attendance at Football Games	
Eagles vs. Bulldogs	743
Eagles vs. Panthers	768
Eagles vs. Coyotes	835
Eagles vs. Bears*	1218
Eagles vs. Colts	797
Eagles vs. Mustangs	854

*Homecoming Game

42. **Weather** The high temperatures in degrees Fahrenheit on 11 consecutive days were 68, 71, 75, 74, 75, 71, 73, 71, 72, 74, and 79. Find the mean, median, mode, and range of the temperatures. Describe the effect on the mean, median, mode, and range if the next day's temperature was 70 °F.

H.O.T. 43. **Advertising** A home-decorating store sells five types of candles, which are priced at $3, $2, $2, $2, and $15. If the store puts an ad in the paper titled "Best Local Candle Prices," which measure of central tendency should it advertise? Justify your answer.

Use the data to make a box-and-whisker plot.

44. 25, 28, 26, 16, 18, 15, 25, 28, 26, 16

45. 2, 3, 5, 7, 11, 13, 17, 19, 23, 29, 31

46. 1, 1, 1, 1, 2, 2, 2, 2, 3, 3, 4, 4, 4, 4, 4

47. 50, 52, 45, 62, 36, 55, 40, 50, 65, 33

48. The results in Olympic pole-vaulting are given as heights in meters. In the 2008 Olympic Games in Beijing, the following results occurred for the men's pole-vault finals: 5.96, 5.85, 5.70, 5.70, 5.70, 5.70, 5.60, 5.60, 5.60, 5.45, 5.45.

   a. Find the mean, median, mode, and range of this data set. Round to the nearest hundredth if needed.

   b. The gold medal was won by Steve Hooker of Australia. What was his height in the pole-vault finals?

49. Business The salaries for the eight employees at a small company are shown in the stem-and-leaf plot. Find the mean and median of the salaries. Which measure better describes the typical salary of an employee at this company? Explain.

Salaries ($1000)

Stem	Leaves
2	0 0 3 5 5
3	0 5
4	
5	
6	
7	8

Key: 2|0 means $20,000

50. Critical Thinking Use the data set {1, 2, 3, 5, 8, 13, 21, 34} to complete the following.

   a. Find the mean of the data set.

   b. What happens to the mean of the data set if every number is increased by 2?

   c. What happens to the mean of the data set if every number is multiplied by 2?

51. Allison has taken 5 tests worth 100 points each. Her scores are shown in the grade book below. What score does she need on her next test to have a mean of 90%?

Student	Test 1	Test 2	Test 3	Test 4	Test 5	Test 6	Average
Allison	88	85	89	92	90		

52. Astronomy The table shows the number of moons of the planets in our solar system. What is the mean number of moons per planet? Is Earth's value of one moon typical for the solar system? Explain.

Planet	Mercury	Venus	Earth	Mars	Jupiter	Saturn	Uranus	Neptune
Moons	0	0	1	2	63	60	27	13

H.O.T. **53. Write About It** Explain how an outlier with a large value will affect the mean. Explain how an outlier with a small value will affect the mean.

TEST PREP

54. Which value is always represented on a box-and-whisker plot?

   Ⓐ Mean   Ⓑ Median   Ⓒ Mode   Ⓓ Range

55. The lengths in feet of the alligators at a zoo are 9, 7, 12, 6, and 10. The lengths in feet of the crocodiles at the zoo are 13, 10, 8, 19, 18, and 16. What is the difference between the mean length of the crocodiles and the mean length of the alligators?

   Ⓕ 0.5 foot   Ⓖ 5.2 feet   Ⓗ 8 feet   Ⓙ 11.4 feet

56. The mean score on a test is 50. Which CANNOT be true?

    (A) Half the scores are 0, and half the scores are 100.

    (B) The range is 50.

    (C) Half the scores are 25, and half the scores are 50.

    (D) Every score is 50.

57. Short Response The table shows the weights in pounds of six dogs. How does the mean weight of the dogs change if Rex's weight is not included in the data set?

Weights of Dogs (lb)			
Duffy	23	Rex	62
Rocky	15	Skipper	34
Pepper	21	Sunny	19

CHALLENGE AND EXTEND

58. List a set of data values with the following measures of central tendency:

    mean: 8   median: 7   mode: 6

59. Collect a set of data about your classmates or your school. For example, you might collect data about the number of points per game scored by your school's basketball team. Use the data you collect to make a box-and-whisker plot.

60. A *weighted average* is an average in which each data value has an importance, or weight, assigned to it. A teacher uses the following weights when determining course grades: homework 25%, tests 30%, and final exam 45%. The table shows Nathalie's scores in the class.

Homework	78, 83, 95, 82, 79, 93
Tests	88, 92, 81
Final exam	90

    a. Find the mean of Nathalie's homework scores and the mean of her test scores.

    b. Find Nathalie's weighted average for the class. To do so, multiply the homework mean, the test mean, and the final exam score by their corresponding weights. Then add the products.

    c. What if...? What would Nathalie's mean score for the class be if her teacher did not use a weighted average?

FOCUS ON MATHEMATICAL PRACTICES

H.O.T. **61. Precision** A data set has an even number of values. What do you know about the median?

H.O.T. **62. Problem Solving** The table shows the teams with the most World Series appearances as of 2011. It is missing the number of Yankee appearances.

    a. The article with the table states that the mean of the data is 21.6. Find the missing data value. Show your work.

    b. What is the range of the data?

    c. Do you think the number of Yankee appearances is an outlier for this data set? Explain.

MLB Team	World Series Appearances
Yankees	
Cardinals	18
Giants	18
Dodgers	18
Athletics	14

H.O.T. **63. Communication** Can a data set have two outliers? Can removing the two outliers not have an effect on the mean? Justify your responses.

Essential Question: How can you use dot plots to describe the shape of a data distribution?

A **dot plot** is a data representation that uses a number line and x's, dots, or other symbols to show frequency. Dot plots are sometimes called line plots.

EXAMPLE MCC9-12.S.ID.1

1 **Making a Dot Plot**

Objectives
Create dot plots.

Use a dot plot to describe the shape of a data distribution.

Vocabulary
dot plot
uniform distribution
symmetric distribution
skewed distribution

Mrs. Montoya asked her junior and senior students how many minutes each of them spent studying math in one day, rounded to the nearest five minutes. The results are shown below. Make a dot plot showing the data for juniors and a dot plot showing the data for seniors.

Time Spent Studying Math (min)	Frequency (Juniors)	Frequency (Seniors)
5	2	0
10	1	1
15	3	2
20	4	3
25	5	4
30	5	4
35	4	6
40	3	5
45	2	4

Find the least and greatest values in each data set. Then use these values to draw a number line for each graph. For each student, place a dot above the number line for the number of minutes he or she spent studying.

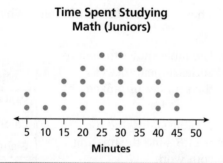

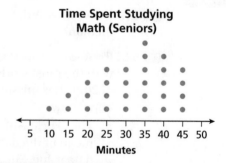

 1. The cafeteria offers items at six different prices. John counted how many items were sold at each price for one week. Make a dot plot of the data.

Price ($)	1.50	2.00	2.50	3.00	3.50	4.00	4.50
Items	3	3	5	8	6	5	3

A dot plot gives a visual representation of the distribution, or "shape", of the data. The dot plots in Example 1 have different shapes because the data sets are distributed differently.

Types of Distributions

UNIFORM DISTRIBUTION	SYMMETRIC DISTRIBUTION	SKEWED DISTRIBUTION
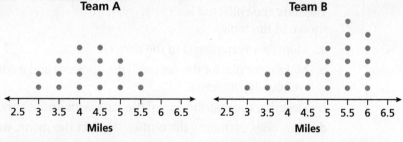		
In a **uniform distribution**, all data points have an approximately equal frequency.	In a **symmetric distribution**, a vertical line can be drawn and the result is a graph divided in two parts that are approximate mirror images of each other.	In a **skewed distribution**, the data is not uniform or symmetric. The data may be skewed to the right or skewed to the left.

EXAMPLE 2

MCC9-12.S.ID.3

Shapes of Data Distributions

The data table shows the number of miles run by members of two track teams during one day. Make a dot plot and determine the type of distribution for each team. Explain what the distribution means for each.

Miles	3	3.5	4	4.5	5	5.5	6
Team A	2	3	4	4	3	2	0
Team B	1	2	2	3	4	6	5

Make dot plots of the data.

Team A

Team B

2.5 3 3.5 4 4.5 5 5.5 6 6.5
Miles

2.5 3 3.5 4 4.5 5 5.5 6 6.5
Miles

The data for team A show a symmetric distribution. The distances run are evenly distributed about the mean.

The data for team B show a skewed left distribution. Most team members ran a distance greater than the mean.

2. Data for team C members are shown below. Make a dot plot and determine the type of distribution. Explain what the distribution means.

Miles	3	3.5	4	4.5	5	5.5	6
Team C	3	2	2	2	3	2	2

1. **Biology** Michael is collecting data for the growth of plants after one week. He planted nine seeds for each of three different types of plants and recorded his data in the table below.

Growth of Plants (in.)		
Type A	**Type B**	**Type C**
0.9	2.1	1.9
0.9	2.2	2.0
1.0	2.2	2.0
1.0	2.2	2.1
1.1	2.3	2.1
1.2	2.3	2.1
1.2	2.4	2.2
1.3	2.5	2.2
1.4	2.6	2.3

   a. Create a dot plot for each type of plant.

   b. Describe the distributions.

   c. Which data value(s) occur(s) the most often in each dot plot? the least often?

   d. For each dot plot, list the heights in order from least frequent to most frequent.

2. **Nutrition** Julia researched grape juice brands to determine how many grams of sugar each brand contained per serving (8 fluid ounces = 1 serving). The data she collected is shown in the table.

Grams of Sugar in Grape Juice (per serving)					
15	0	36	18	30	10
30	15	35	30	36	30
36	30	38	16	35	16

   a. Identify any outlier(s) in the data set.

   b. Make a dot plot for the data with the outlier(s) and a dot plot for the data without the outlier(s).

   c. Describe the distribution of the data with and without the outlier(s).

   d. How does excluding the outlier(s) affect the mean, median, and mode of the data set?

3. The frequency table shows the number of siblings of each student in a class. Use the table to make a dot plot of the data, and describe the distribution.

Number of Siblings	Frequency
0	7
1	9
2	5
3	1
4	1

4. School The list below shows which grade each member of a high school marching band belongs to.

9, 12, 9, 10, 9, 12, 9, 9, 11, 12, 12, 10, 10, 9, 9, 11, 9, 10, 10, 12, 9, 12, 11, 9, 12, 11, 10, 9, 12, 12, 9, 9, 11, 12

   a. Make a dot plot of the data.

   b. Explain how you can use the dot plot to find the mean, median, and mode of the data set. Then find each of these values.

Use the dot plot for Exercises 5 and 6.

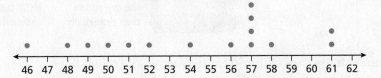

5. Write About It Compare stem-and-leaf plots and dot plots.

   a. How are they similar and how are they different?

   b. What information can you get from each graph?

   c. Can you make a dot plot given a stem-and-leaf plot? Explain.

   d. Can you make a stem-and-leaf plot given a dot plot? If so, make a stem-and-leaf plot of the data in the dot plot at right. If not, explain why not.

6. Write About It Compare histograms and dot plots.

   a. How are they similar and how are they different?

   b. What information can you get from each graph?

   c. Can you make a dot plot given a histogram? Explain.

   d. Can you make a histogram given a dot plot? If so, make a histogram of the data in the dot plot at right. If not, explain why not.

7. Multi-Step Gather data on the heights of people in your classroom. Separate the data for males from the data for females. Make two dot plots representing the data collected for each group. Compare the dot plots and the distributions of the data.

8. The dot plot at right shows an example of a *bimodal distribution*. Why is this an appropriate name for this type of distribution?

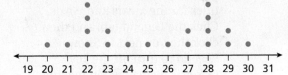

9. Critical Thinking Magdalene and Peter conducted the same experiment. Both of their data sets had the same mean. Both made dot plots of their data that showed symmetric distributions, but Peter's dot plot shows a greater range than Magdalene's dot plot. Identify which plot below belongs to Peter and which belongs to Magdalene.

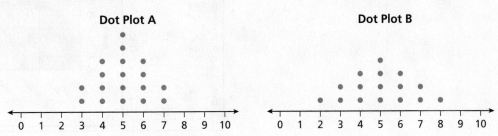

Dot Plot A   **Dot Plot B**

14-4
Technology
TASK

Use Technology to Make Graphs

You can use a spreadsheet program to create bar graphs, line graphs, and circle graphs. You can also use a graphing calculator to make a box-and-whisker plot.

Use with Data Distributions

Activity 1

MATHEMATICAL PRACTICES

Use appropriate tools strategically.

MCC9-12.S.ID.1 Represent data with plots on the real number line (… box plots).

Many colors are used on the flags of the 50 United States. The table shows the number of flags that use each color. Use a spreadsheet program to make a bar graph to display the data.

Color	Black	Blue	Brown	Gold	Green	Purple	Red	White
Number	27	46	20	36	24	4	34	42

1. Enter the data from the table in the first two columns of the spreadsheet.

2. Select the cells containing the titles and the data.

   Then click the Chart Wizard icon, . Click Column from the list on the left, and then choose the small picture of a vertical bar graph. Click Next.

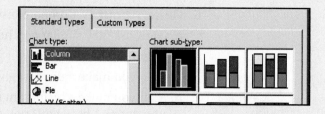

3. The next screen shows the range of cells used to make the graph. Click Next.

4. Give the chart a title and enter titles for the *x*-axis and *y*-axis. Click the Legend tab, and then click the box next to Show Legend to turn off the key. (A key is needed when making a double-bar graph.) Click Next.

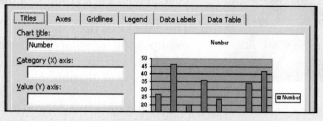

5. Click Finish to place the chart in the spreadsheet.

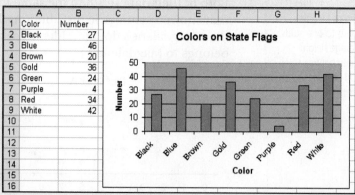

1. The table shows the average number of hours of sleep people at different ages get each night. Use a spreadsheet program to make a bar graph to display the data.

Age (yr)	3–9	10–13	14–18	19–30	31–45	46–50	51+
Sleep (h)	11	10	9	8	7.5	6	5.5

Activity 2

Adrianne is a waitress at a restaurant. The amounts Adrianne made in tips during her last 15 shifts are listed below. Use a graphing calculator to make a box-and-whisker plot to display the data. Give the minimum, first quartile, median, third quartile, and maximum values.

$58, $63, $40, $44, $57, $59, $61, $53, $54, $58, $57, $57, $58, $58, $56

1 To make a list of the data, press **STAT**, select **Edit**, and enter the values in List 1 **(L1)**. Press **ENTER** after each value.

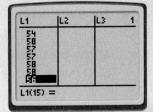

2 To use the **STAT PLOT** editor to set up the box-and-whisker plot, press **2nd** **Y=** , and then **ENTER**.

Press **ENTER** to select **Plot 1**.

3 Select **On**. Then use the arrow keys to choose the fifth type of graph, a box-and-whisker plot.

Xlist should be **L1** and **Freq:** should be 1.

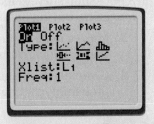

4 Press **ZOOM** and select **9: ZoomStat** to see the graph in the statistics window.

5 Use **TRACE** and the arrow keys to move the cursor along the graph to the five important values: minimum **(MinX)**, first quartile **(Q1)**, median **(MED)**, third quartile **(Q3)**, and maximum **(MaxX)**.

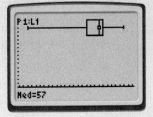

minimum: 40

first quartile: 54

median: 57

third quartile: 58

maximum: 63

Try This

2. The average length in inches of the ten longest bones in the human body are listed. Use a graphing calculator to make a box-and-whisker plot to display the data. What are the minimum, first quartile, median, third quartile, and maximum values of the data set?

19.88, 16.94, 15.94, 14.35, 11.10, 10.40, 9.45, 9.06, 7.28, 6.69

Ready to Go On?

my.hrw.com
Assessment and Intervention

✔ 14-1 Organizing and Displaying Data

1. The table shows the total proceeds for a fund-raiser at various times during the day. Choose a type of graph to display the given data. Make the graph, and explain why you chose that type of graph.

Time	Total Proceeds (thousand $)	Time	Total Proceeds (thousand $)
3:00 P.M.	1.5	6:00 P.M.	6.5
4:00 P.M.	2	7:00 P.M.	8
5:00 P.M.	4	8:00 P.M.	9.5

✔ 14-2 Frequency and Histograms

2. The number of people at a caterer's last 12 parties are given below.

    16, 18, 17, 19, 15, 25, 18, 17, 18, 16, 17, 19

    a. Use the data to make a frequency table with intervals.

    b. Use your frequency table from part a to make a histogram.

✔ 14-3 Two-Way Tables

A bookshop surveys its customers about their magazine-buying habits, summarized in the table.

3. Make a table of the joint relative frequencies and the marginal relative frequencies.

4. Given that a customer reads *Super News,* what is the probability that he or she also reads *Look Around?*

		Reads *Look Around*	
		Yes	No
Reads *Super News*	Yes	62	15
	No	21	136

✔ 14-4 Data Distributions

5. The daily high temperatures on 14 consecutive days in one city were 59 °F, 49 °F, 48 °F, 46 °F, 47 °F, 51 °F, 49 °F, 43 °F, 45 °F, 52 °F, 51 °F, 51 °F, 51 °F, and 38 °F.

    a. Find the mean, median, and mode of the temperatures.

    b. Which value describes the average high temperature for the 14 days?

    c. Which value best describes the high temperatures? Explain.

6. Use the temperature data above to make a box-and-whisker plot.

✔ 14-5 Misleading Graphs and Statistics

7. The graph shows the value of a company's stock over time. Explain why the graph is misleading. What might people be influenced to believe because of the graph? Who might want to use this graph?

8. The results of an online survey of 230 people showed that 92% of the population felt very comfortable using technology. Explain why this statistic is misleading.

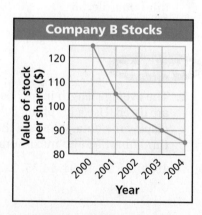

PARCC Assessment Readiness

Selected Response

1. How many more victories did the 8th grade basketball team have than the 10th grade team? Use the graph to answer the question.

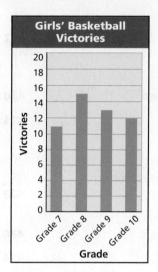

Girls' Basketball Victories

Ⓐ 2

Ⓑ 3

Ⓒ 1

Ⓓ 27

2. The cumulative frequencies of each interval have been given. Use this information to complete the frequency column.

Interval	Frequency	Cumulative Frequency
45–52	?	6
53–60	?	23
61–68	?	32
69–76	?	41
77–84	?	75
85–92	?	134

Ⓕ 7, 16, 16, 25, 50, 84

Ⓖ 6, 17, 6, 26, 15, 60, 74

Ⓗ 7, 30, 39, 48, 82, 141

Ⓙ 6, 17, 9, 9, 34, 59

3. A researcher surveys people at a train station about whether they favor a tax increase to improve railroad service. Explain why the following statement is misleading: "75% of commuters support a railroad tax increase."

Ⓐ The sample is biased because the researcher did not say how large the tax increase would be.

Ⓑ The statement is misleading because not enough people were surveyed.

Ⓒ The sample is biased because train riders are more likely to favor better railroad service than commuters who drive or use other types of transportation.

Ⓓ The data includes outliers, so the mean percentage is not a fair measure.

Mini-Tasks

4. Identify the sample space and the outcome shown for spinning the game spinner.

5. The table shows the numbers of points scored by the top three scorer's in a basketball tournament that were made as 1-point (free throws), 2-point, and 3-point shots.

	1-point	2-point	3-point
Tina	11	38	21
Stella	7	24	42
Misha	17	46	6

a. What is the joint relative frequency that represents points scored by Misha as 2-point shots?

b. What is the marginal relative frequency of the points that were made as 3-point shots?

15 Linear and Exponential Models

COMMON
CORE GPS

Contents

MATHEMATICAL
PRACTICES   The Common Core Georgia Performance Standards for Mathematical Practice
describe varieties of expertise that all students should seek to develop.
Opportunities to develop these practices are integrated throughout this program.

1 Make sense of problems and persevere in
solving them.

2 Reason abstractly and quantitatively.

3 Construct viable arguments and critique the
reasoning of others.

4 Model with mathematics.

5 Use appropriate tools strategically.

6 Attend to precision.

7 Look for and make use of structure.

8 Look for and express regularity in repeated
reasoning.

Unpacking the Standards

Understanding the standards and the vocabulary terms in the standards will help you know exactly what you are expected to learn in this chapter.

 MCC9-12.F.LE.1

Distinguish between situations that can be modeled with linear functions and with exponential functions.

Key Vocabulary

linear function (función lineal)
A function that can be written in the form $y = mx + b$, where x is the independent variable and m and b are real numbers. Its graph is a line.

What It Means For You

A linear function models a *constant amount* of change for equal intervals. An exponential function models a *constant factor*, or *constant ratio* of change for equal intervals.

EXAMPLE   **Exponential model**

Value of a car	
Car's Age (yr)	**Value ($)**
0	20,000
1	17,000
2	14,450
3	12,282.50

+1 ⟶ ×0.85
+1 ⟶ ×0.85
+1 ⟶ ×0.85

Ratio is constant.

NON-EXAMPLE   **Nonlinear, non-exponential model**

Height of Bridge Suspension Cables	
Cable's Distance from Tower (ft)	**Cable's Height (ft)**
0	400
100	256
200	144
300	64

+100 ⟶ −144, ×0.64
+100 ⟶ −112, ×0.56
+100 ⟶ −80, ×0.44

Neither difference nor ratio is constant.

Scatter Plots and Trend Lines

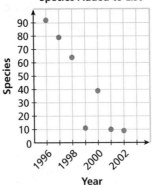

? **Essential Question:** How can you represent data on a scatter plot and use trend lines to make predictions?

Objectives
Create and interpret scatter plots.

Use trend lines to make predictions.

Vocabulary
scatter plot
correlation
positive correlation
negative correlation
no correlation
trend line

Who uses this?
Ecologists can use scatter plots to help them analyze data about endangered species, such as ocelots. (See Example 1.)

In this chapter, you have examined relationships between sets of ordered pairs, or data. Displaying data visually can help you see relationships.

A **scatter plot** is a graph with points plotted to show a possible relationship between two sets of data. A scatter plot is an effective way to display some types of data.

COMMON CORE GPS EXAMPLE **1**
MCC9-12.S.ID.6

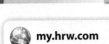
my.hrw.com

Online Video Tutor

Animated Math

Graphing a Scatter Plot from Given Data

The table shows the number of species added to the list of endangered and threatened species in the United States during the given years. Graph a scatter plot using the given data.

Increase in List							
Calendar Year	1996	1997	1998	1999	2000	2001	2002
Species	91	79	62	11	39	10	9

Source: U.S. Fish and Wildlife Service

Species Added to List

Use the table to make ordered pairs for the scatter plot.

The x-value represents the calendar year and the y-value represents the number of species added.

Plot the ordered pairs.

Helpful Hint

The point (2000, 39) tells you that in the year 2000, the list increased by 39 species.

CHECK IT OUT!

1. The table shows the number of points scored by a high school football team in the first four games of a season. Graph a scatter plot using the given data.

Game	1	2	3	4
Score	6	21	46	34

A **correlation** describes a relationship between two data sets. A graph may show the correlation between data. The correlation can help you analyze trends and make predictions. There are three types of correlations between data.

Correlations

Positive Correlation	Negative Correlation	No Correlation
Both sets of data values increase.	One set of data values increases as the other set decreases.	There is no relationship between the data sets.

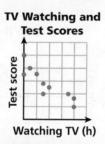

In the endangered species graph, as time increases, the number of new species added decreases. So the correlation between the data is negative.

EXAMPLE 2 Describing Correlations from Scatter Plots

Describe the correlation illustrated by the scatter plot.

TV Watching and Test Scores

Test score

Watching TV (h)

As the number of hours spent watching TV increased, test scores decreased.

There is a negative correlation between the two data sets.

CHECK IT OUT!

2. Describe the correlation illustrated by the scatter plot.

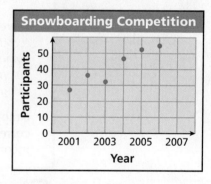

Snowboarding Competition

EXAMPLE 3 Identifying Correlations

Identify the correlation you would expect to see between each pair of data sets. Explain.

A the number of empty seats in a classroom and the number of students seated in the class

You would expect to see a negative correlation. As the number of students increases, the number of empty seats decreases.

B the number of pets a person owns and the number of books that person read last year

You would expect to see no correlation. The number of pets a person owns has nothing to do with how many books the person has read.

Identify the correlation you would expect to see between each pair of data sets. Explain.

C the monthly rainfall and the depth of water in a reservoir

You would expect to see a positive correlation. As more rain falls, there is more water in the reservoir.

 CHECK IT OUT! Identify the correlation you would expect to see between each pair of data sets. Explain.

3a. the temperature in Houston and the number of cars sold in Boston

3b. the number of members in a family and the size of the family's grocery bill

3c. the number of times you sharpen your pencil and the length of your pencil

COMMON CORE GPS **EXAMPLE 4** MCC9-12.S.ID.6

my.hrw.com

Online Video Tutor

Matching Scatter Plots to Situations

Choose the scatter plot that best represents the relationship between the number of days since a sunflower seed was planted and the height of the plant. Explain.

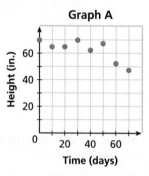

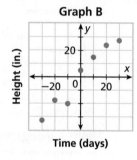

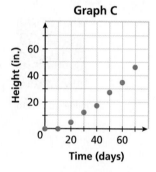

There will be a positive correlation between the number of days and the height because the plant will grow each day.

Graph A has a negative correlation, so it is incorrect.

Neither the number of days nor the plant heights can be negative.

Graph B shows negative values, so it is incorrect.

This graph shows all positive coordinates and a positive correlation, so it could represent the data sets.

Graph C is the correct scatter plot.

 CHECK IT OUT! **4.** Choose the scatter plot that best represents the relationship between the number of minutes since a pie has been taken out of the oven and the temperature of the pie. Explain.

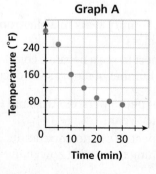

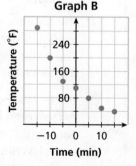

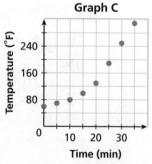

You can graph a line on a scatter plot to help show a relationship in the data. This line, called a **trend line,** helps show the correlation between data sets more clearly. It can also be helpful when making predictions based on the data.

 EXAMPLE 5
MCC9-12.S.ID.6c

Fund-raising Application

The scatter plot shows a relationship between the total amount of money collected and the total number of rolls of wrapping paper sold as a school fund-raiser. Based on this relationship, predict how much money will be collected when 175 rolls have been sold.

Draw a trend line and use it to make a prediction.

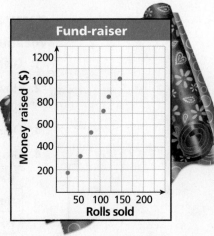

Fund-raiser

Fund-raiser

Draw a line that has about the same number of points above and below it. Your line may or may not go through data points.

Find the point on the line whose x-value is 175. The corresponding y-value is 1200.

Based on the data, $1200 is a reasonable prediction of how much money will be collected when 175 rolls have been sold.

CHECK IT OUT! 5. Based on the trend line above, predict how many wrapping paper rolls need to be sold to raise $500.

THINK AND DISCUSS

1. Is it possible to make a prediction based on a scatter plot with no correlation? Explain your answer.

2. GET ORGANIZED Copy and complete the graphic organizer with either a scatter plot, a real-world example, or both.

	Graph	Example
Positive Correlation		
Negative Correlation		The amount of water in a watering can and the number of flowers watered
No Correlation		

GUIDED PRACTICE

Vocabulary Apply the vocabulary from this lesson to answer each question.

1. Give an example of a graph that is not a *scatter plot*.

2. How is a scatter plot that shows *no correlation* different from a scatter plot that shows a *negative correlation*?

3. Does a *trend line* always pass through every point on a scatter plot? Explain.

SEE EXAMPLE 1
4. Graph a scatter plot using the given data.

Garden Statue	Cupid	Gnome	Lion	Flamingo	Wishing well
Height (in.)	32	18	35	28	40
Price ($)	50	25	80	15	75

SEE EXAMPLE 2
Describe the correlation illustrated by each scatter plot.

5.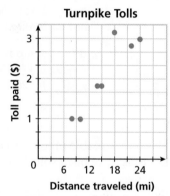

6.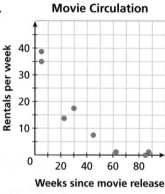

SEE EXAMPLE 3
Identify the correlation you would expect to see between each pair of data sets. Explain.

7. the volume of water poured into a container and the amount of empty space left in the container

8. a person's shoe size and the length of the person's hair

9. the outside temperature and the number of people at the beach

SEE EXAMPLE 4
Choose the scatter plot that best represents the described relationship. Explain.

10. age of car and number of miles traveled

11. age of car and sales price of car

12. age of car and number of states traveled to

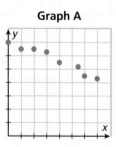

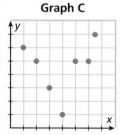

Graph A   Graph B   Graph C

13. **Transportation** The scatter plot shows the total number of miles passengers flew on U.S. domestic flights in the month of April for the years 1997–2004. Based on this relationship, predict how many miles passengers flew in April 2008.

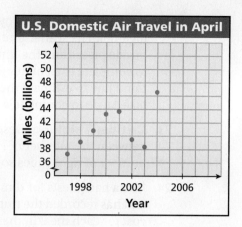

U.S. Domestic Air Travel in April

PRACTICE AND PROBLEM SOLVING

Independent Practice

For Exercises	See Example
14	1
15–16	2
17–18	3
19–20	4
21	5

my.hrw.com

Online Extra Practice

14. Graph a scatter plot using the given data.

Train Arrival Time	6:45 A.M.	7:30 A.M.	8:15 A.M.	9:45 A.M.	10:30 A.M.
Passengers	160	148	194	152	64

Describe the correlation illustrated by each scatter plot.

15. **Nascar**

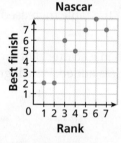

16. **Concert Ticket Costs**

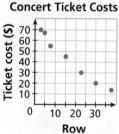

Identify the correlation you would expect to see between each pair of data sets. Explain.

17. the speed of a runner and the distance she can cover in 10 minutes

18. the year a car was made and the total mileage

Ecology

The ocelot population in Texas is dwindling due in part to their habitat being destroyed. The ocelot population at Laguna Atascosa National Wildlife Refuge is monitored by following 5–10 ocelots yearly by radio telemetry.

Choose the scatter plot that best represents the described relationship. Explain.

19. the number of college classes taken and the number of roommates

20. the number of college classes taken and the hours of free time.

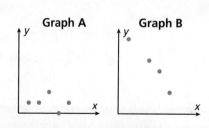

Graph A   Graph B

21. **Ecology** The scatter plot shows a projection of the average ocelot population living in Laguna Atascosa National Wildlife Refuge near Brownsville, Texas. Based on this relationship, predict the number of ocelots living at the wildlife refuge in 2014 if nothing is done to help manage the ocelot population.

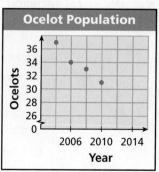

Ocelot Population

22. Estimation Angie enjoys putting jigsaw puzzles together. The scatter plot shows the number of puzzle pieces and the time in minutes it took her to complete each of her last six puzzles. Use the trend line to estimate the time in minutes it will take Angie to complete a 1200-piece puzzle.

23. Critical Thinking Describe the correlation between the number of left shoes sold and the number of right shoes sold.

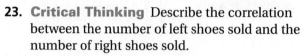

Puzzle Completion

24. Roma had guests for dinner at her house eight times and has recorded the number of guests and the total cost for each meal in the table.

Guests	3	4	4	6	6	7	8	8
Cost ($)	30	65	88	90	115	160	150	162

a. Graph a scatter plot of the data.

b. Describe the correlation.

c. Draw a trend line.

d. Based on the trend line you drew, predict the cost of dinner for 11 guests.

e. **What if...?** Suppose that each cost in the table increased by $5. How will this affect the cost of dinner for 11 guests?

25. ///ERROR ANALYSIS/// Students graphed a scatter plot for the temperature of hot bath water and time if no new water is added. Which graph is incorrect? Explain the error.

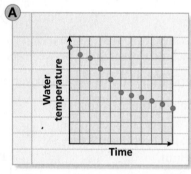

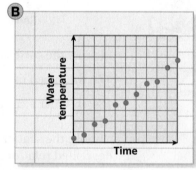

H.O.T. **26. Critical Thinking** Will more people or fewer people buy an item if the price goes up? Explain the relationship and describe the correlation.

Real-World Connections

27. Juan and his parents are visiting a university 205 miles from their home. As they travel, Juan uses the car odometer and his watch to keep track of the distance.

a. Make a scatter plot for this data set.

b. Describe the correlation. Explain.

c. Draw a trend line for the data and predict the distance Juan would have traveled going to a university 4 hours away.

Time (min)	Distance (mi)
0	0
30	28
60	58
90	87
120	117
150	148
180	178
210	205

28. Write About It Conduct a survey of your classmates to find the number of siblings they have and the number of pets they have. Predict whether there will be a positive, negative, or no correlation. Then graph the data in a scatter plot. What is the relationship between the two data sets? Was your prediction correct?

TEST PREP

29. Which graph is the best example of a negative correlation?

Ⓐ 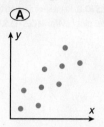 Ⓑ 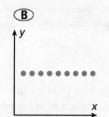 Ⓒ 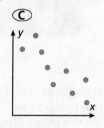 Ⓓ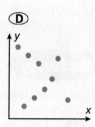

30. Which situation best describes a positive correlation?

Ⓕ The amount of rainfall on Fridays

Ⓖ The height of a candle and the amount of time it stays lit

Ⓗ The price of a pizza and the number of toppings added

Ⓙ The temperature of a cup of hot chocolate and the length of time it sits

31. Short Response Write a real-world situation for the graph. Explain your answer.

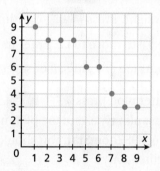

CHALLENGE AND EXTEND

32. Describe a situation that involves a positive correlation. Gather data on the situation. Make a scatter plot showing the correlation. Use the scatter plot to make a prediction. Repeat for a negative correlation and for no correlation.

33. Research an endangered or threatened species in your state. Gather information on its population for several years. Make a scatter plot using the data you gather. Is there a positive or negative correlation? Explain. Draw a trend line and make a prediction about the species population over the next 5 years.

FOCUS ON MATHEMATICAL PRACTICES

H.O.T. **34. Patterns** Gigi draws a scatter plot for a table that compares the weight of a bird to its wingspan. Would you expect this plot to show a positive correlation, no correlation, or a negative correlation? Why?

H.O.T. **35. Analysis** When you graph the function $y = x + 3$, you make a table with pairs of values, graph those ordered pairs, and then draw a line with arrows that joins the points. Contrast this to the way you draw the trend line for a scatter plot. How do the two lines differ?

Technology TASK
Interpret Scatter Plots and Trend Lines

You can use a graphing calculator to graph a trend line on a scatter plot.

Use with Scatter Plots and Trend Lines

Use appropriate tools strategically.

MCC9-12.S.ID.6 Represent data on two quantitative variables on a scatter plot, ... *Also* **MCC9-12.S.ID.6a, MCC9-12.S.ID.6c**

Activity

The table shows the recommended dosage of a particular medicine as related to a person's weight. Graph a scatter plot of the given data. Draw the trend line. Then predict the dosage for a person weighing 240 pounds.

Weight (lb)	90	100	110	125	140	155	170	180	200
Dosage (mg)	20	25	30	35	40	53	60	66	75

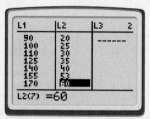

1 First enter the data. Press **STAT** and select **1: Edit**. In **L1**, enter the first weight. Press **ENTER**. Continue entering all weights. Use ▶ to move to **L2**. Enter the first dosage. Press **ENTER**. Continue entering all dosages.

2 To view the scatter plot, press **2nd** **Y=**. Select **Plot 1**. Select **On**, the first plot type, and the plot mark **+**. Press **ZOOM**. Select **9: ZoomStat**. You should see a scatter plot of the data.

3 To find the trend line, press **STAT** and select the **CALC** menu. Select **LinReg (ax+b)**. Press **ENTER**. This gives you the values of *a* and *b* in the trend line.

4 To enter the equation for the trend line, press **Y=**, and then input **.5079441502x − 26.78767453**. Press **GRAPH**.

5 Now predict the dosage for a weight of 240 pounds. Press **VARS**. Select **Y-VARS** menu and select **1:Function**. Select **1:Y1**. Enter **(240)**. Press **ENTER**. The dosage is about 95 milligrams.

Try This

1. The table shows the price of a stock over an 8-month period. Graph a scatter plot of the given data. Draw the trend line. Then predict what the price of one share of stock will be in the twelfth month.

Month	1	2	3	4	5	6	7	8
Price ($)	32	35	37	41	46	50	54	59

15-2 Line of Best Fit

Essential Question: How can you use residuals and linear regression to determine the line of best fit?

Objectives
Determine a line of best fit for a set of linear data.

Determine and interpret the correlation coefficient.

Vocabulary
residual
least-squares line
line of best fit
linear regression
correlation coefficient

Who uses this?
Climate scientists can use a least-squares line to study temperature-latitude relationships. (See Example 2.)

Recall that a scatter plot shows two data sets as one set of ordered pairs. A trend line, or line of fit, is a model for the data.

Some trend lines will fit a data set better than others. One way to evaluate how well a line fits a data set is to use *residuals*. A **residual** is the signed vertical distance between a data point and a line of fit. The closer the sum of the squared residuals is to 0, the better the line fits the data.

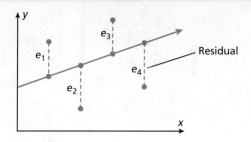

COMMON CORE GPS

EXAMPLE 1
MCC9-12.S.ID.6b

my.hrw.com

Online Video Tutor

Calculating Residuals

The data in the table are graphed along with two lines of fit. For each line, find the sum of the squares of the residuals. Which line is a better fit?

x	2	4	6	8
y	6	3	7	5

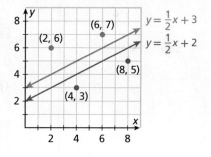

Find the residuals.

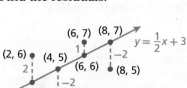

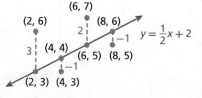

Sum of squared residuals:

$(2)^2 + (-2)^2 + (1)^2 + (-2)^2$

$4 + 4 + 1 + 4 = 13$

The line $y = \frac{1}{2}x + 3$ is a better fit for the data.

Sum of squared residuals:

$(3)^2 + (-1)^2 + (2)^2 + (-1)^2$

$9 + 1 + 4 + 1 = 15$

Helpful Hint

By using *squares* of residuals, positive and negative residuals do not "cancel out," and residuals with squares greater than 1 have a magnified effect on the sum.

©Gordon Wiltsie/National Geographic/Getty Images

1. Two lines of fit for this data are $y = -\frac{1}{2}x + 6$ and $y = -x + 8$. For each line, find the sum of the squares of the residuals. Which line is a better fit?

x	2	4	6	8
y	3	6	1	4

The **least-squares line** for a data set is the line of fit for which the sum of the squares of the residuals is as small as possible. So, the least-squares line is a *line of best fit*. A **line of best fit** is the line that comes closest to all of the points in the data set, using a given process. **Linear regression** is a process of finding the least-squares line.

EXAMPLE 2

MCC9-12.S.ID.6a

my.hrw.com

Online Video Tutor

Finding the Least-Squares Line

The table shows the latitudes and average temperatures of several cities.

City	Latitude	Average Temperature (°C)
Barrow, Alaska, USA	71.2° N	−12.7
Yakutsk, Russia	62.1° N	−10.1
London, England	51.3° N	10.4
Chicago, Illinois, USA	41.9° N	10.3
San Francisco, California, USA	37.5° N	13.8
Yuma, Arizona, USA	32.7° N	22.8
Tindouf, Algeria	27.7° N	22.8
Dakar, Senegal	14.0° N	24.5
Mangalore, India	12.5° N	27.1

A **Find an equation for a line of best fit.**

Use your calculator. To enter the data, press **STAT** and select **1:Edit**. Enter the latitudes in the **L1** column and the average temperatures in the **L2** column.

Then press **STAT** and choose **CALC**. Choose **4:LinReg(ax+b)** and press **ENTER**. An equation for a line of best fit is $y \approx -0.69x + 39.11$.

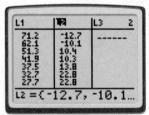

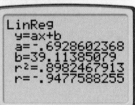

B **Interpret the meaning of the slope and *y*-intercept.**

The slope, −0.69, means that for each 1-degree increase in latitude, the average temperature decreases 0.69 °C. The *y*-intercept, 39.11, means that the average temperature is 39.11 °C at 0° N latitude.

C **The approximate latitude of Vancouver, Canada, is 49.1° N. Use your equation to predict Vancouver's average temperature.**

$y \approx -0.69x + 39.11$

$y \approx -0.69(49.1) + 39.11 \approx 5.23$

The average temperature of Vancouver should be close to 5 °C.

2. The table shows the prices and the lengths in yards of several balls of yarn at Knit Mart.

Length (yd)	1680	100	153	99	109	109	176	100	1440	61
Price ($)	65.85	7.85	9.80	10.85	8.35	7.85	19.85	5.35	65.85	14.85

a. Find an equation for a line of best fit.

b. Interpret the meaning of the slope and *y*-intercept.

c. Knit Mart also sells yarn in a 1000-yard ball. Use your equation to predict the cost of this yarn.

In Example 2, you may have noticed the last value the calculator gave you, *r*. This is the *correlation coefficient*. The **correlation coefficient** is a number *r*, where $-1 \leq r \leq 1$, that describes how closely the points in a scatter plot cluster around a line of best fit.

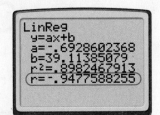

Properties of the Correlation Coefficient *r*

r is a value in the range $-1 \leq r \leq 1$.

If $r = 1$, the data set forms a straight line with a positive slope.

If $r = 0$, the data set has no correlation.

If $r = -1$, the data set forms a straight line with a negative slope.

Helpful Hint

r-values close to 1 or −1 indicate a very strong correlation. The closer *r* is to 0, the weaker the correlation.

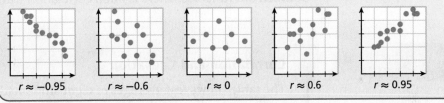

$r \approx -0.95$ $r \approx -0.6$ $r \approx 0$ $r \approx 0.6$ $r \approx 0.95$

COMMON CORE GPS
MCC9-12.S.ID.8

EXAMPLE 3

my.hrw.com

Online Video Tutor

Correlation Coefficient

The table shows a relationship between a city's population and the average time the city's citizens spend commuting to work each day.

City	Population (thousands)	Average Commute Time (min)
Albuquerque, NM	505	21.5
Atlanta, GA	486	31.1
Austin, TX	710	23.2
Charlotte, NC	630	25.1
Chicago, IL	2833	30.6
Eugene, OR	146	17.9
Houston, TX	2144	27.7
Las Vegas, NV	553	25.2
New York, NY	8496	34.0
New Orleans, LA	223	24.2

Find an equation for a line of best fit. How well does the line represent the data?

Use your calculator.

Enter the data into the lists **L1** and **L2**.

Then press ████ and choose **CALC**. Choose

4:LinReg(ax+b) and press ████ . An equation for a line of best fit is $y \approx 0.001x + 23.8$. The value of r is about 0.71, which indicates a moderate positive correlation.

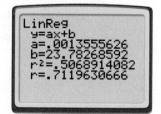

```
LinReg
 y=ax+b
 a=.0013555626
 b=23.78268592
 r²=.5068914082
 r=.7119630666
```

3. Kylie and Marcus designed a quiz to measure how much information adults retain after leaving school. The table below shows the quiz scores of several adults, matched with the number of years each person had been out of school. Find an equation for a line of best fit. How well does the line represent the data?

Time Out of School (yr)	1	1	1	2	2	3	5	7	10	10	14	25
Quiz Score	85	94	98	75	80	77	63	56	45	50	34	33

Causation refers to cause-and-effect. If a change in one variable directly causes a change in the other variable, then there is a cause-and-effect relationship between the variables. There is often correlation without causation.

COMMON CORE GPS
EXAMPLE 4
MCC9-12.S.ID.9

my.hrw.com

Online Video Tutor

Correlation and Causation

The table shows test averages of eight students. The equation of the least-squares line for the data is $y \approx 0.77x + 18.12$ and $r \approx 0.87$. Discuss correlation and causation for the data set.

U.S. History Test Average	90	70	75	100	90	85	80	90
Science Test Average	80	75	72	95	92	82	80	92

There is a strong positive correlation between the U.S. history test average and the science test average for these students. There is *not* a likely cause-and-effect relationship because there is no apparent reason why test scores in one subject would directly affect test scores in the other subject.

Caution!

Notice in Example 4, there is a strong correlation, but no causation. Two variables can be strongly correlated without having a direct cause-and-effect relationship.

4. Eight adults were surveyed about their education and earnings. The table shows the survey results. The equation of the least-squares line for the data is $y \approx 5.59x - 30.28$ and $r \approx 0.86$. Discuss correlation and causation for the data set.

Years of Education		12	16	20	14	18	16	16	18
Earnings Last Year (thousand $)		40	65	75	44	70	50	54	86

THINK AND DISCUSS

1. What is the residual for a data point that lies on the line of best fit?

2. **GET ORGANIZED** Copy and complete the graphic organizer. For each *r*-value, sketch a possible scatter plot and describe the correlation, choosing from the following: strong positive, weak positive, none, strong negative, weak negative.

r-value	−0.9	−0.4	0	0.4	0.9
Scatter Plot					
Description of Correlation					

15-2 Exercises

my.hrw.com
Homework Help

GUIDED PRACTICE

Vocabulary Apply the vocabulary from this lesson to answer each question.

1. A signed vertical distance between a data point and its corresponding model point is called a _____?_____ (*residual* or *correlation coefficient*)

2. A _____?_____ (*least squares line* or *correlation coefficient*) is a measure of how well a line of best fit models a data set.

SEE EXAMPLE 1

3. The data in the table are graphed along with two lines of fit. For each line, find the sum of the squares of the residuals. Which line is a better fit for the data?

x	2	3	4	5
y	2	5	6	2

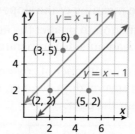

SEE EXAMPLE 2

4. The table shows numbers of books read by students in an English class over a summer and the students' grades for the following semester.

Books	0	0	0	0	1	1	1	2	3	5	6	8	10	12	20
Grade	65	69	70	73	70	75	78	77	86	85	89	90	95	99	98

a. Find an equation for a line of best fit.

b. Interpret the meaning of the slope and *y*-intercept.

c. Use your equation to predict the grade of a student who reads 15 books.

SEE EXAMPLE 3

5. A negative correlation exists between the time Shawnda spends on homework during an evening and the amount of sleep she gets that night. The table shows data for several nights. Find an equation for a line of best fit. How well does the line represent the data?

Homework (h)	0.5	0.5	1	1	1.5	2	2	2.5	3	3	3	4	4.5	5
Sleep (h)	8	9	8	8.5	8	7.5	8	7.5	7	7	8	6.5	6.5	6

SEE EXAMPLE 4

6. Some students were surveyed about how much time they spent playing video games last week and their overall test average. The equation of the least-squares line for the data is $y \approx -2.93x + 89.70$ and $r \approx -0.92$. Discuss correlation and causation for the data set.

Hours Playing Video Games	1	3	3	6	2	1	9	10
Test Average for all Subjects	80	85	78	70	86	92	60	64

PRACTICE AND PROBLEM SOLVING

Independent Practice

For Exercise	See Example
7	1
8	2
9	3
10	4

my.hrw.com

Online Extra Practice

7. The data in the table are graphed along with two lines of fit. For each line, find the sum of the squares of the residuals. Which line is a better fit for the data?

x	2	4	6	8
y	5	6	1	1

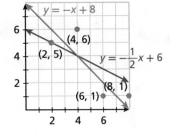

8. The table shows the mean outside temperature for each of six months and the amount of heating oil used by a family for each of those months.

Mean Outside Temperature (°F)	30	28	44	56	62	76
Heating Oil Used (gal)	112	115	94	60	35	12

a. Find an equation for a line of best fit.

b. Interpret the meaning of the slope and y-intercept.

c. Use your equation to predict the amount of heating oil used in a month in which the mean outside temperature is 20 °F.

9. The table shows the number of customers at a coffee shop and the number of cookies sold for several days. Find an equation for a line of best fit. How well does the line represent the data?

Customers	10	12	25	27	40	55	67	109
Cookies Sold	2	6	5	9	10	11	20	22

10. Some students were surveyed about how much time they spent watching television one week and how much time they spent playing video games the next week. The equation of the least-squares line for the data is $y \approx 0.76x + 1.63$ and $r \approx 0.77$. Discuss correlation and causation for the data set.

Week 1: Hours Watching Television	4	2	0	1	3	1	8	10
Week 2: Hours Playing Video Games	1	3	3	6	2	1	9	10

Sports

The New York Yankees opened a new stadium in 2009. Although the new stadium seats fewer fans than the old stadium (50,287 versus 56,886), the seats in the new stadium are wider, and there is more legroom between rows.

H.O.T. **11. Write About It** Tell which correlation coefficient, $r = 0.65$ or $r = -0.78$, indicates a stronger linear relationship between two variables. Explain your answer.

12. Critical Thinking What can you conclude if the sum of the squared residuals is 0? Explain why the same conclusion might not apply when the sum of the residuals is 0.

13. Sports The table shows hits and runs scored by eight New York Yankees in the 2009 baseball season.

a. Find the equation of the least-squares line.

b. Interpret the meaning of the slope.

c. Interpret the meaning of the y-intercept mathematically.

d. Describe any possible correlation for the data set. Use the correlation coefficient to support your answer.

e. Use the equation of the least-squares line from part **a** to predict how many runs a player will score if he gets 100 hits.

Player	Hits	Runs
Jorge Posada	109	55
Mark Teixeira	178	103
Robinson Cano	204	103
Derek Jeter	212	107
Johnny Damon	155	107
Melky Cabrera	133	66
Nick Swisher	124	84
Hideki Matsui	125	62

14. Community The table shows data about temperature and how much bottled water was sold at an annual summer festival in past years. The high temperature for the day of this year's festival is predicted to be 89 °F. The festival organizer must order bottled water in cases of 100. Find the equation of the least-squares line. Use the equation to decide how many cases the organizer should order.

Midtown Summer Fest						
Year	1	2	3	4	5	6
Daily High Temperature (°F)	75	82	95	92	80	84
Bottled Waters Sold	465	517	1052	940	611	625

Use the table for Exercises 15 and 16.

Regional Historical Museum						
Year	0	2	4	6	8	10
Visitors	980	1,251	1,667	1,785	2,110	2,056
Gift Shop Sales ($)	8,890	12,365	15,100	18,060	20,650	22,600

15. Complete parts **a–d** for the relationship between the year and the number of visitors.

a. Find the equation of the least-squares line and the correlation coefficient.

b. Interpret the meaning of the slope and the y-intercept.

c. Is it reasonable to use your equation to make predictions? Explain.

d. Is it reasonable to say there is a cause-and-effect relationship? Explain.

16. Complete parts **a–d** above for the relationship between the number of visitors and the gift shop sales.

TEST PREP

17. Which could be the correlation coefficient of this graph?

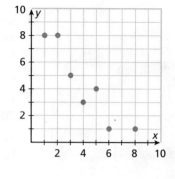

- (A) −1.00
- (B) −0.93
- (C) 0.93
- (D) 1.00

18. The table shows how much time five students studied for a test and their test scores. The equation of a line of fit for the data is $y = 5x + 60$. What is the sum of the squares of the residuals for the line of fit?

Hours Studying	0	2	4	6	8
Test Score	60	70	90	80	100

- (F) 0
- (G) 20
- (H) 40
- (J) 200

CHALLENGE AND EXTEND

H.O.T. 19. The heights and weights of eight basketball players are graphed along with a line of fit.

a. Find the sum of the squares of the residuals.

b. Find the *mean absolute deviation*. (The mean absolute deviation is the mean of the absolute values of the residuals.) Explain why the mean absolute deviation might be more useful than the sum of the squares of the residuals in some cases.

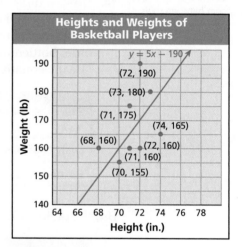

20. Use these facts to complete the data table:
The equation of a line of fit is $y = 2x - 3$.
The sum of the residuals is 0.
The sum of the squares of the residuals is 14.

x	1	3	4	5
y	1	▪	▪	8

FOCUS ON MATHEMATICAL PRACTICES

H.O.T. 21. Error Analysis Lainey calculated the correlation coefficient between the prices of items at two stores as −0.97, and found the line of best fit to be $y = 1.02x - 0.15$. Explain why Lainey must have made a mistake in her calculations.

H.O.T. 22. Analysis Examine the data in the table.

x	2	5	6	8	11
y	9	7	4	3	4

a. Find the line of best fit and the correlation coefficient.

b. Suppose each value of y is increased by 5. Find the new line of best fit and correlation coefficient. How did they change?

Interpreting Trend Lines

Previously, you learned how to draw trend lines on scatter plots. Now you will learn how to find the equations of trend lines and write them in slope-intercept form.

Example

Write an equation for the trend line on the scatter plot.

Two points on the trend line are (30, 75) and (60, 90).

To find the slope of the line that contains (**30**, **75**) and (**60**, **90**), use the slope formula.

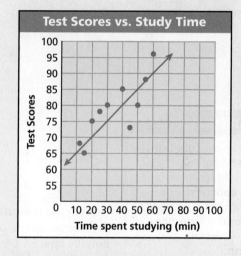

Test Scores vs. Study Time

$$m = \frac{y_2 - y_1}{x_2 - x_1}$$ *Use the slope formula.*

$$m = \frac{90 - 75}{60 - 30}$$ *Substitute (30, 75) for (x_1, y_1) and (60, 90) for (x_2, y_2).*

$$m = \frac{15}{30}$$ *Simplify.*

$$m = \frac{1}{2}$$

Use the slope and the point (30, 75) to find the *y*-intercept of the line.

$$y = mx + b$$ *Slope-intercept form*

$$75 = \frac{1}{2}(30) + b$$ *Substitute $\frac{1}{2}$ for m, 30 for x, and 75 for y.*

$$75 = 15 + b$$ *Solve for b.*

$$60 = b$$

Write the equation.

$$y = \frac{1}{2}x + 60$$ *Substitute $\frac{1}{2}$ for m and 60 for b.*

Try This

1. In the example above, what is the meaning of the slope?

2. What does the *y*-intercept represent?

3. Use the equation to predict the test score of a student who spent 25 minutes studying.

4. Use the table to create a scatter plot. Draw a trend line and find the equation of your trend line. Tell the meaning of the slope and *y*-intercept. Then use your equation to predict the race time of a runner who ran 40 miles in training.

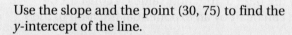

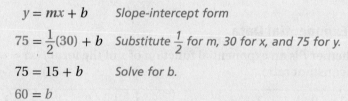

Distance Run in Training (mi)	12	15	16	18	21	23	24	25	33
Race Time (min)	65	64	55	58	55	50	50	47	36

EXTENSION

Curve Fitting with Exponential Models

Essential Question: How can you use exponential regression to fit a curve to data?

Objectives
Model data by using exponential functions.

Use exponential models to analyze and predict.

Vocabulary
exponential regression

Analyzing data values can identify a pattern, or repeated relationship, between two quantities.

Look at this table of values for the exponential function $f(x) = 2(3^x)$.

 Remember!

For linear functions (first degree), first differences are constant. For quadratic functions, second differences are constant, and so on.

x	−1	0	1	2	3
f(x)	$\frac{2}{3}$	2	6	18	54

$\times 3 \quad \times 3 \quad \times 3 \quad \times 3$

Notice that the *ratio* of each y-value and the previous one is constant. Each value is three times the one before it, so the ratio of function values is constant for equally spaced x-values. This data can be fit by an exponential function of the form $f(x) = ab^x$.

 COMMON CORE GPS
MCC9-12.F.LE.1

EXAMPLE 1 Identifying Exponential Data

Determine whether f is an exponential function of x of the form $f(x) = ab^x$. If so, find the constant ratio.

A
x	−1	0	1	2	3
f(x)	−3	−1	1	3	5

$+2 \ +2 +2 +2$ *First differences*

y is a linear function of x.

B
x	−1	0	1	2	3
f(x)	$\frac{1}{2}$	1	2	4	8

$+\frac{1}{2} \ +1 +2 \ +4$

Ratios $\frac{1}{\frac{1}{2}} = \frac{2}{1} = \frac{4}{2} = \frac{8}{4} = 2$

This data set is exponential, with a constant ratio of 2.

 CHECK IT OUT! Determine whether y is an exponential function of x of the form $f(x) = ab^x$. If so, find the constant ratio.

1a.
x	−1	0	1	2	3
f(x)	2.$\overline{6}$	4	6	9	13.5

1b.
x	−1	0	1	2	3
f(x)	−3	2	7	12	17

You have used a graphing calculator to perform *linear regressions* and *quadratic regressions* to make predictions. You can also use an *exponential model,* which is an exponential function that represents a real data set.

Once you know that data are exponential, you can use **ExpReg** (exponential regression) on your calculator to find a function that fits. This method of using data to find an exponential model is called an **exponential regression**. The calculator fits exponential functions to ab^x, so translations cannot be modeled.

COMMON CORE GPS

EXAMPLE **2**

MCC9-12.F.LE.2

Gemology Application

The table gives the approximate values of diamonds of the same quality. Find an exponential model for the data. Use the model to estimate the weight of a diamond worth $2325.

Diamond Values

Weight (carats)	Value ($)
0.5	920
1.0	1160
2.0	1580
3.0	2150
4.0	2900

Step 1 Enter the data into two lists in a graphing calculator. Use the exponential regression feature.

An exponential model is $V(w) \approx 814.96(1.38)^w$, where V is the diamond value and w is the weight in carats.

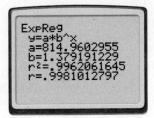

Remember!

If you do not see r^2 and r when you calculate regression, use

CATALOG

2nd   0   and

turn these features on by selecting **DiagnosticOn**.

Step 2 Graph the data and the function model to verify that it fits the data.

To enter the regression equation as **Y1** from the **Y=** screen, press **VARS**, choose **5:Statistics**, press **ENTER**, scroll to the **EQ** menu and select **1:RegEQ**.

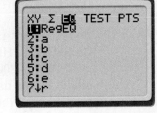

Enter 2325 as **Y2**. Use the intersection feature. You may need to adjust the window dimensions to find the intersection.

A diamond weighing about 3.26 carats will have a value of $2325.

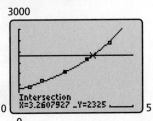

CHECK IT OUT!

2. Use exponential regression to find a function that models this data. When will the number of bacteria reach 2000?

Time (min)	0	1	2	3	4	5
Bacteria	200	248	312	390	489	610

Determine whether f is an exponential function of x of the form $f(x) = ab^x$. If so, find the constant ratio.

1.

x	−1	0	1	2	3
$f(x)$	$-2\frac{5}{7}$	−1	11	95	683

2.

x	−1	0	1	2	3
$f(x)$	27	18	12	8	$5\frac{1}{3}$

3.

x	−1	0	1	2	3
$f(x)$	5	1	−3	−7	−11

4.

x	−1	0	1	2	3
$f(x)$	$2\frac{1}{4}$	3	4	$5\frac{1}{3}$	$7\frac{1}{9}$

5. Physics The table gives the approximate number of degrees Fahrenheit above room temperature of a cup of tea as it cools. Find an exponential model for the data. Use the model to estimate how long it will take the tea to reach a temperature that is less than 40 degrees above room temperature.

Cooling Tea					
Time (min)	0	1	2	3	4
Degrees above room temperature (°F)	132	120	110	101	93

Determine whether f is an exponential function of x of the form $f(x) = ab^x$. If so, find the constant ratio.

6.

x	−1	0	1	2	3
$f(x)$	1.25	1	0.75	0.5	0.25

7.

x	−5	−3	1	3	5
$f(x)$	20	6	2	12	30

8.

x	−1	0	1	2	3
$f(x)$	0.667	1	1.5	2.25	3.375

9.

x	−1	0	1	2	3
$f(x)$	−16	−8	−4	−2	−1

10. Social Studies The table gives the United States Hispanic population from 1980 to 2000. Find an exponential model for the data. Use the model to predict when the Hispanic population will exceed 120 million.

United States Hispanic Population			
Years After 1970	10	20	30
Population (millions)	14.6	22.5	35.3

Source: Census 2000

11. Telecommunication The table gives the number of telecommuters in the United States from 1990 to 2000. Find an exponential model for the data. Use the model to estimate when the number of telecommuters will exceed 100 million.

U.S. Telecommuters											
Years After 1990	0	1	2	3	4	5	6	7	8	9	10
Telecommuters (millions)	4.4	5.5	6.6	7.3	9.1	8.5	8.7	11.1	15.7	19.6	23.6

Source: Federal Highway Administration

Decide whether the data set is exponential, and if it is, use exponential regression to find a function that models the data.

12.

x	1	2	3	4
f(x)	11	95	683	4799

13.

x	−1	0	2	3
f(x)	4	2	0.5	0.25

American alligator, Everglades National Park

14. **Critical Thinking** According to one source, the population of nesting wading birds in the wetlands of the Florida Everglades Park System has decreased from more than a half-million in the 1930s to less than 15,000 today. What do you need to know to determine whether this decrease in numbers is exponential? Explain.

15. **Ecology** One research study showed that the rate of calf survival in Yellowstone elk herds depends on spring snow depths. At snow depths of about 5000 mm, the rate of survival is about 0.9 per hundred cows; at 6700 mm it is about 0.3; and at 8250 mm, it is about 0.17. Find an exponential function to model the data. Use the model to predict the calf survival rate per hundred cows at snow depths of 4000 mm.

16. **Technology** Holiday season sales of a portable digital music player are shown in the graph. Assume that growth rate continues in the same way. Write an exponential function to model the data. Use the model to predict sales in three years.

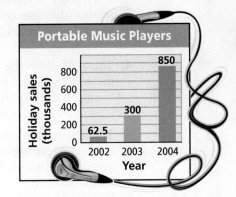

17. **Make a Conjecture** Make a table of values for an exponential function with $x = 1, 2, 3, \ldots 8$. Find the first differences, second differences, and third differences. Make a conjecture about the nth differences, assuming that the domain of the function is all natural numbers.

18. The table shows the total amount of farmland in Vermont since 1970.

   a. Use exponential regression to find a function that models the data.

   b. According to the model, by what percent does the amount of farmland decrease each year?

   c. Predict the amount of farmland in 2010.

Farmland in Vermont	
Year	Farmland (thousands of acres)
1970	2010
1980	1740
1990	1440
2000	1270

Ready to Go On?

my.hrw.com
Assessment and Intervention

15-1 Scatter Plots and Trend Lines

The table shows the time it takes different people to read a given number of pages.

Pages Read	2	6	6	8	8	10	10
Time (min)	10	15	20	15	30	25	30

1. Graph a scatter plot using the given data.

2. Describe the correlation illustrated by the scatter plot.

3. The scatter plot shows the estimated annual sales for an electronics and appliance chain of stores for the years 2004–2009. Based on this relationship, predict the annual sales in 2012.

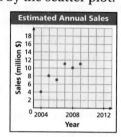

4. The table shows the value of a car for the given years. Graph a scatter plot using the given data. Describe the correlation illustrated by the scatter plot.

Year	2000	2001	2002	2003
Value (thousand $)	28	25	23	20

5. The graph shows the results of a 2003–2004 survey on class size at the given grade levels. Based on this relationship, predict the class size for the 9th grade.

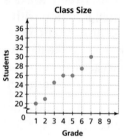

15-2 Line of Best Fit

6. A street vendor noted the daily high temperature and the number of ice cream cones she sold each day for one week. Find an equation for a line of best fit. How well does the line represent the data?

Temperature (°F)	80	73	65	90	96	100	82
Ice Cream Cones Sold	32	27	22	38	45	48	35

7. Two lines of fit for the data in the table are $y = 0.5x$ and $y = x - 1$. For each line, find the sum of the squares of the residuals. Which line is a better fit?

x	1	2	4	5
y	2	0	1	3

8. The lengths and weights of 6 koi in a pond are shown in the table. Find an equation of a line of best fit. How well does the line fit the data?

Length (in.)	9	12	11	15	8	10
Weight (oz)	5	11	9	20	4	7

9. Four friends recorded the numbers of CDs and video games their families purchased in the last month, as shown in the table. Find an equation of a line of best fit. How well does the line fit the data?

CDs	2	3	5	6
Games	2	5	4	6

Selected Response

1. Make a scatter plot using the given data.

x	3	6	5	2	7	4	8	1
y	4.5	6.5	6.5	3.5	6.5	4.5	8	4

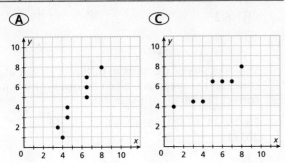

Ⓐ

Ⓒ

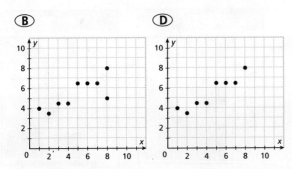

Ⓑ

Ⓓ

2. The table and accompanying scatter plot show forearm lengths *f* and heights *h* from a randomly selected sample of people. Find an equation of the line of best fit. Then use your equation to predict how tall a person is if the forearm length is 27.5 centimeters.

Forearm length (cm)	24	27	24	26	32	30	29	28
Body height (cm)	157	177	164	175	195	178	180	172

Ⓕ *h* = 3.64*f* + 74.57

about 175 centimeters tall

Ⓖ *h* = −1.16*f* + 203.24

about 171 centimeters tall

Ⓗ *h* = 2.34*f* + 116.23

about 181 centimeters tall

Ⓙ *h* = 0.23*f* + 152.49

about 159 centimeters tall

3. Describe the correlation illustrated by the scatter plot.

Ⓐ positive correlation

Ⓑ negative correlation

Ⓒ no correlation

Ⓓ cannot determine

Mini-Task

4. The table shows the relationship between typical weight and typical lifespan for several dog breeds. Find an equation of the line of best fit, and the correlation coefficient. How well does the line represent the data?

Breed	Weight (pounds)	Lifespan (years)
Yorkshire Terrier	5.5	15
Shih Tzu	12.5	13
Pug	16	13.5
Boston Terrier	20	13
Welsh Corgi (Pembroke)	26	13
Bulldog	45	7
Siberian Husky	47.5	12
Golden Retriever	65	12
German Shepherd	72.5	11
Rottweiler	107.5	10
Great Dane	135	8.5

PARCC Assessment Readiness

Selected Response

1. How many total victories did the four teams have?

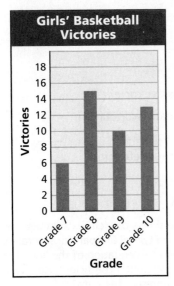

(A) 42 (C) 31

(B) 41 (D) 44

2. The graph shows the profit made at a family yard sale that lasted 8 hours. Between which hours did the profit increase at the slowest rate?

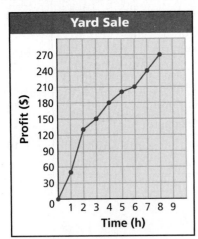

(F) 0–1 (H) 5–6

(G) 1–2 (J) 7–8

3. Which of the following is one of the five values needed to make a box-and-whisker plot?

(A) Mean (C) Mode

(B) Median (D) Average

4. What is the median of the data presented in this stem-and-leaf plot?

Stem	Leaves
6	0 2 2 2 5 8
7	3 4 4 6 7
8	2 5 8 9

Key: 8 | 2 means 0.82

(F) 0.62

(G) 0.74

(H) 6.2

(J) 7.4

5. The numbers of students in different classes at a community college are given below. Which is a correct histogram of these data?

25, 15, 28, 52, 22, 38, 42, 44, 24, 32, 19, 28, 29, 20, 31

(A)

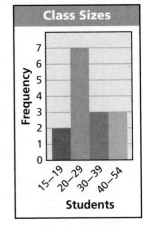

(B)

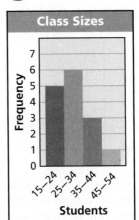

(C)

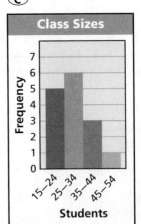

(D)

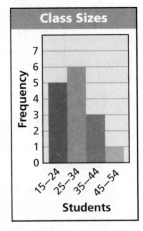

If you are allowed to write in your test booklet, you may want to add additional information to a given diagram. Be sure to mark your answer on the answer sheet since your marks on the test booklet will not be graded.

6. The cumulative frequencies of each interval have been given. What numbers should be placed in the frequency column?

Interval	Frequency	Cumulative Frequency
6–15	?	1
16–25	?	11
26–35	?	64
36–45	?	112
46–55	?	127
56–65	?	131

Ⓕ 10, 53, 48, 15, 4, 0

Ⓖ 0, 1, 12, 76, 188, 315

Ⓗ 1, 10, 53, 48, 15, 4

Ⓙ 1, 12, 76, 188, 315, 446

7. The table shows the number of stars that make up various constellations. What are the mean, median, mode, and range of the data set?

Constellation Number	Number of Stars in Constellation
Constellation 1	17
Constellation 2	35
Constellation 3	49
Constellation 4	17
Constellation 5	24

Ⓐ mean = 42.5; median = 24;
mode = 23; range = 32

Ⓑ mean = 28.4; median = 24;
mode = 17; range = 32

Ⓒ mean = 28.4; median = 49;
mode = 17; range = 49

Ⓓ mean = 42.5; median = 49;
mode = 17; range = 32

8. Which set of data values can be represented by the box-and-whisker plot shown?

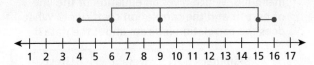

Ⓕ 4, 5, 6, 9, 11, 15, 16

Ⓖ 4, 5, 6, 7, 8, 9, 11, 13, 14, 15, 16

Ⓗ 4, 6, 8, 11, 15, 16

Ⓙ 4, 6, 7, 11, 15, 16

9. What is the outlier in the data set {42, 13, 23, 24, 5, 5, 13, 8}, and how does it affect the mean, median, mode(s), and range of the data?

Ⓐ The outlier is 42. The outlier increases the mean by 3.6 and the range by 18. The outlier has no effect on the median or the modes.

Ⓑ The outlier is 42. The outlier increases the mean by 3.6, the median by 5, and the range by 18. The outlier has no effect on the modes.

Ⓒ The outlier is 42. The outlier increases the mean by 5.2 and the range by 18. The outlier has no effect on the median and the modes.

Ⓓ The outlier is 42. The outlier increases the median by 3.6 and the range by 18. The outlier has no effect on the mean and the modes.

10. Between which of the following variables would you expect there to be a negative correlation?

Ⓕ A person's height and weight

Ⓖ The amount of time spent studying and a test grade

Ⓗ The outside temperature and the number of layers of clothing a person wears

Ⓙ The number of years spent in school and salary

11. Which of the following data sets has the greatest interquartile range?

Ⓐ 3, 4, 6, 5, 7, 5, 7

Ⓑ 8, 8, 8, 8, 8, 8, 8

Ⓒ 10, 3, 11, 11, 12, 11, 11

Ⓓ 2, 1, 2, 6, 4, 5, 6

12. The table shows the relationship between the typical weight and typical lifespan for several mammals. Which gives an equation of the line of best fit and the correlation coefficient? What does the correlation indicate about the data?

Mammal	Weight (pounds)	Lifespan (years)
African Elephant	9500	70
Hippopotamus	6500	40
Grizzly bear	800	25
Water buffalo	2075	25
Red panda	16	8
Kangaroo	120	10
Cottontail rabbit	3	3
Spotted hyena	200	25
Wolf	110	8
Skunk	1	3
Leopard seal	840	11.5

(F) $y \approx 0.006x + 10$
The value of r is about 0.93, which indicates a strong positive correlation.

(G) $y \approx -0.006x + 10$
The value of r is about -0.93, which indicates a strong positive correlation.

(H) $y \approx 0.006x + 10$
The value of r is about -0.07, which indicates a weak negative correlation.

(J) $y \approx -0.006x + 10$
The value of r is about 0.934, which indicates that weight and lifespan are not correlated.

13. Will has the following quiz scores in his Geography class.

86, 90, 80, 75, 80, 95, 97, 80

Will takes a ninth quiz, and his median score increases by 1. What score did he get on the ninth quiz?

(A) 82
(B) 83
(C) 84
(D) 85

14. Lionel observes that traffic is getting worse and it's taking him longer to get to work. He records the following data for several weeks. Which scatter plot shows Lionel's data?

Week	1	2	3	4	5	6	7	8
Time (min)	8.2	8.9	8.6	8.3	9	9.7	8.4	10.1

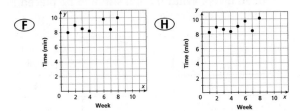

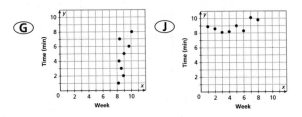

Mini-Tasks

15. The numbers of people who attended two different plays are shown in the table below. Make a back-to-back stem-and-leaf plot.

Play Attendance	
Comedy Camp	**Days and Days**
104 62 83 102	103 105 80 135
104 120 81	109 128 82
126 122	132 139

16. The capacities of the gas tanks on several new vehicles are shown below. Use the data to make a frequency table with intervals.

Gas Tank Capacity (gal)
15 12 12 15 18 26 25 12 15 18 11
10 12 16 15 16 18 25 21 18 20 21

A teacher collected data on the activities the class performed on their summer break and summarized the data in a table.

		Went to Beach	
		Yes	No
Joined a sports team	Yes	10	9
	No	11	6

17. Make a table of the joint and marginal relative frequencies.

18. Given that a student went to the beach, what is the probability he or she joined a sports team?

19. Given that a student did not go to the beach, what is the probability he or she did not join a sports team?

20. The table shows the number of Atlantic hurricanes for the years 1997–2004.

Atlantic Hurricanes			
Year	Number	Year	Number
1997	3	2001	9
1998	10	2002	4
1999	8	2003	7
2000	8	2004	9

a. Make a box-and-whisker plot of the hurricane data.

b. What is the mean number of hurricanes per year for the time period shown in the table?

21. On four math tests, Clark scored 90, 94, 97, and 93. Give an example of a score Clark could receive on his next test that would raise his mean test score but have no effect on the range or mode of his scores. Justify your answer.

Performance Tasks

22. Gustavo is comparing his basketball statistics for the current year with those from the previous year when he won the conference scoring championship. The points he has scored through the first ten games this year are given in this table.

22	17	10	23	31
3	18	26	18	18

The points Gustavo scored last year in all 12 games are given in this table.

23	35	19	11	28	21
25	17	18	15	24	28

a. Make a double box-and-whisker plot for the two sets of data.

b. Find the ranges and interquartile ranges of the two data sets.

c. Identify any outliers in each set of data.

d. The school newspaper reported that Gustavo's performance this year has been less consistent than and not as good as last year. Is this accurate? Use your results from parts a–c to explain why or why not.

23. The table shows the number of sales of a popular hybrid car in the U.S. for the first four years it was on sale.

Year	1	2	3	4
Number of cars sold	21,386	17,173	14,787	11,182

a. Graph the data in a scatter plot with year number on the x-axis and number of cars on the y-axis.

b. Graph a trend line for the data and write an equation for your trend line.

c. If the trend continues into year 5, how many cars should the manufacturer expect to sell? Include this point on your graph.

d. The manufacturer expects that rising gas prices and some upgrades to the car will help increase sales. They predict that after year 5, their sales will increase by 1,000 cars per year. Graph the data for years 6 through 8 based on their prediction, and write the equation of a trend line that models the data from year 5 on.

my.hrw.com
Online Assessment

Go online for updated, PARCC-aligned assessment readiness.

Are You Ready?

my.hrw.com
Assessment and Intervention

✓ Vocabulary

Match each term on the left with a definition on the right.

1. image

2. preimage

3. transformation

4. *y*-coordinate

A. a mapping of a figure from its original position to a new position

B. the first number in an ordered pair

C. a shape that undergoes a transformation

D. the second number in an ordered pair

E. the shape that results from a transformation of a figure

✓ Ordered Pairs

Graph each ordered pair.

5. $(0, 4)$

6. $(-3, 2)$

7. $(4, 3)$

8. $(3, -1)$

9. $(-1, -3)$

10. $(-2, 0)$

✓ Identify Similar Figures

Can you conclude that the given figures are similar? If so, explain why.

11. $\triangle JKL$ and $\triangle JMN$

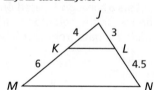

12. rectangle *PQRS* and rectangle *UVWX*

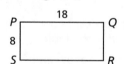

✓ Find Missing Measures in Similar Figures

13. $\triangle PQR \sim \triangle XYZ$. $m\angle PQR = 48°$ and $m\angle PRQ = 52°$. What is $m\angle XZY$?

14. $\square ABCD \sim \square JKLM$. $AD = 16$, $DC = 12$, and $JM = 24$. What is ML?

15. $\square WXYZ \sim \square CDEF$. $XY = 84$, $ZY = 54$, and $DE = 14$. What is FE?

Career Readiness Fabric Designers

Fabric designers create designs for all sorts of fabrics. Fabric designers may use the latest computer design methods or traditional hand-printing techniques. Both may involve using transformations and tessellations to produce designs. Fabric designers must be artistic and have good design skills. They may have a college degree in fine art or design. Some fabric designers work with clothing or furniture manufacturers or with fashion designers. Others work as artists, creating fabrics as art.

UNIT

5

Transformations in the Coordinate Plane

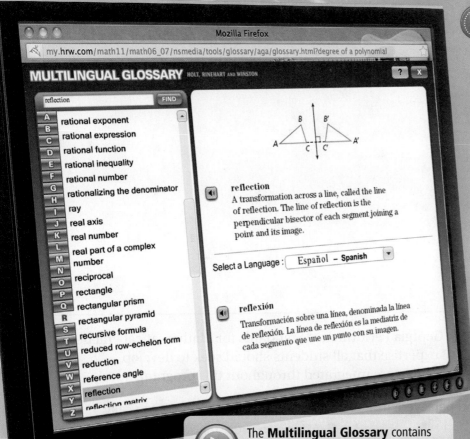

The **Multilingual Glossary** contains illustrated definitions and translations of chapter vocabulary words.

Unit Contents

COMMON CORE GPS

Module 16 Transformations
MCC9-12.G.CO.1, MCC9-12.G.CO.2, MCC9-12.G.CO.4, MCC9-12.G.CO.5

Module 17 Combined Transformations and Symmetry
MCC9-12.G.CO.3, MCC9-12.G.CO.5

UNIT 5

Module

16 Transformations

COMMON CORE GPS

Contents

MATHEMATICAL PRACTICES

The Common Core Georgia Performance Standards for Mathematical Practice describe varieties of expertise that all students should seek to develop. Opportunities to develop these practices are integrated throughout this program.

1. Make sense of problems and persevere in solving them.
2. Reason abstractly and quantitatively.
3. Construct viable arguments and critique the reasoning of others.
4. Model with mathematics.
5. Use appropriate tools strategically.
6. Attend to precision.
7. Look for and make use of structure.
8. Look for and express regularity in repeated reasoning.

Unpacking the Standards

Understanding the standards and the vocabulary terms in the standards will help you know exactly what you are expected to learn in this chapter.

 MCC9-12.G.CO.2

Represent transformations in the plane using, e.g., transparencies and geometry software; describe transformations as functions that take points in the plane as inputs and give other points as outputs. Compare transformations that preserve distance and angle to those that do not (e.g., translation versus horizontal stretch).

Key Vocabulary

transformation (transformación)
A change in the position, size, or shape of a figure or graph.

function (función) A relation in which every input is paired with exactly one output.

What It Means For You

Representing transformations as functions of points in the plane lets you use algebra tools such as the distance formula to investigate the results of transformations.

EXAMPLE　　　**Translation and Rotation**

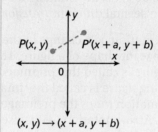

$(x, y) \rightarrow (x + a, y + b)$

$(x, y) \rightarrow (-y, x)$

The function $P(x, y)$ slides the point (x, y) by a units horizontally and b units vertically to the point $(x + a, y + b)$.

The function $P(x, y)$ rotates the point (x, y) by 90° in a counterclockwise direction about the origin to the point $(-y, x)$.

 MCC9-12.G.CO.5

Given a geometric figure and a rotation, reflection, or translation, draw the transformed figure using, e.g., graph paper, tracing paper, or geometry software. Specify a sequence of transformations that will carry a given figure onto another.

Key Vocabulary

rotation (rotación) A transformation that rotates or turns a figure about a point called the center of rotation.

reflection (reflexión) A transformation that reflects, or "flips," a graph or figure across a line, called the line of reflection, such that each reflected point is the same distance from the line of reflection but is on the opposite side of the line.

translation (traslación) A transformation that shifts or slides every point of a figure or graph the same distance in the same direction.

What It Means For You

Rotations, reflections, and translations do not change the shape or size of a figure. You can move a figure onto another of the same size by one or more of these transformations.

EXAMPLE

The diagram represents the whirling pockets of air that form behind a fast-moving truck.

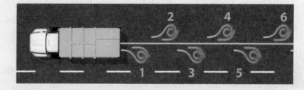

To carry whirl **1** onto whirl **2**: translate right and reflect up.

To carry whirl **2** onto whirl **3**: translate right and reflect down.

In the same way, you can carry each whirl onto the next.

Transformations in the Coordinate Plane

Essential Question: How can you define rotations, reflections, and translations of geometric figures?

Objectives
Identify reflections, rotations, and translations.

Graph transformations in the coordinate plane.

Vocabulary
transformation
preimage
image
reflection
rotation
translation

Animated Math

Who uses this?

Artists use transformations to create decorative patterns. (See Example 4.)

The Alhambra, a 13th-century palace in Granada, Spain, is famous for the geometric patterns that cover its walls and floors. To create a variety of designs, the builders based the patterns on several different *transformations*.

A **transformation** is a change in the position, size, or shape of a figure. The original figure is called the **preimage** . The resulting figure is called the **image** . A transformation *maps* the preimage to the image. Arrow notation (→) is used to describe a transformation, and primes (′) are used to label the image.

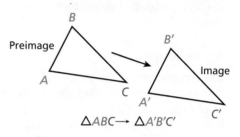

$\triangle ABC \rightarrow \triangle A'B'C'$

Transformations

REFLECTION	ROTATION	TRANSLATION
	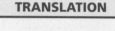	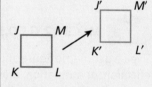
A **reflection** (or *flip*) is a transformation across a line, called the line of reflection. Each point and its image are the same distance from the line of reflection.	A **rotation** (or *turn*) is a transformation about a point *P*, called the center of rotation. Each point and its image are the same distance from *P*.	A **translation** (or *slide*) is a transformation in which all the points of a figure move the same distance in the same direction.

COMMON CORE GPS MCC9-12.G.CO.4

EXAMPLE 1 **Identifying Transformations**

Identify the transformation. Then use arrow notation to describe the transformation.

A

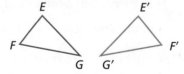

The transformation cannot be a translation because each point and its image are not in the same position.

The transformation is a reflection. $\triangle EFG \rightarrow \triangle E'F'G'$

Identify the transformation. Then use arrow notation to describe the transformation.

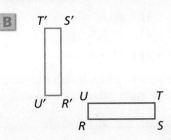

B

The transformation cannot be a reflection because each point and its image are not the same distance from a line of reflection.

The transformation is a 90° rotation. $RSTU \rightarrow R'S'T'U'$

Identify each transformation. Then use arrow notation to describe the transformation.

1a.

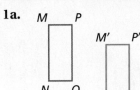

1b.

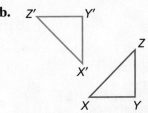

Drawing and Identifying Transformations

A figure has vertices at $A(-1, 4)$, $B(-1, 1)$, and $C(3, 1)$. After a transformation, the image of the figure has vertices at $A'(-1, -4)$, $B'(-1, -1)$, and $C'(3, -1)$. Draw the preimage and image. Then identify the transformation.

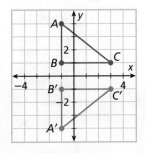

Plot the points. Then use a ruler to connect the vertices.

The transformation is a reflection across the *x*-axis because each point and its image are the same distance from the *x*-axis.

2. A figure has vertices at $E(2, 0)$, $F(2, -1)$, $G(5, -1)$, and $H(5, 0)$. After a transformation, the image of the figure has vertices at $E'(0, 2)$, $F'(1, 2)$, $G'(1, 5)$, and $H'(0, 5)$. Draw the preimage and image. Then identify the transformation.

To find coordinates for the image of a figure in a translation, add *a* to the *x*-coordinates of the preimage and add *b* to the *y*-coordinates of the preimage. Translations can also be described by a rule such as $(x, y) \rightarrow (x + a, y + b)$.

Translations in the Coordinate Plane

Find the coordinates for the image of $\triangle ABC$ after the translation $(x, y) \rightarrow (x + 3, y - 4)$. Draw the image.

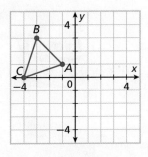

Step 1 Find the coordinates of $\triangle ABC$.

The vertices of $\triangle ABC$ are $A(-1, 1)$, $B(-3, 3)$, and $C(-4, 0)$.

Step 2 Apply the rule to find the vertices of the image.

$$A'(-1 + 3, 1 - 4) = A'(2, -3)$$
$$B'(-3 + 3, 3 - 4) = B'(0, -1)$$
$$C'(-4 + 3, 0 - 4) = C'(-1, -4)$$

Step 3 Plot the points. Then finish drawing the image by using a ruler to connect the vertices.

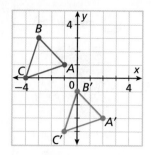

 **3.** Find the coordinates for the image of *JKLM* after the translation $(x, y) \rightarrow (x - 2, y + 4)$. Draw the image.

 EXAMPLE 4

COMMON CORE GPS MCC9-12.G.CO.2

Art History Application

The pattern shown is similar to a pattern on a wall of the Alhambra. Write a rule for the translation of square 1 to square 2.

Step 1 Choose 2 points

Choose a point *A* on the preimage and a corresponding point *A'* on the image. *A* has coordinates $(3, 1)$, and *A'* has coordinates $(1, 3)$.

Step 2 Translate

To translate *A* to *A'*, 2 units are subtracted from the *x*-coordinate and 2 units are added to the *y*-coordinate. Therefore, the translation rule is $(x, y) \rightarrow (x - 2, y + 2)$.

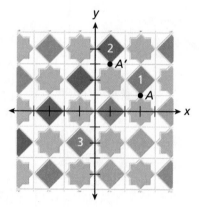

4. Use the diagram to write a rule for the translation of square 1 to square 3.

MCC.MP.6 | MATHEMATICAL PRACTICES

THINK AND DISCUSS

1. Explain how to recognize a reflection when given a figure and its image.

2. GET ORGANIZED Copy and complete the graphic organizer. In each box, sketch an example of each transformation.

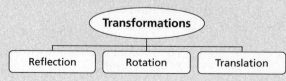

GUIDED PRACTICE

Vocabulary Apply the vocabulary from this lesson to answer each question.

1. Given the transformation $\triangle XYZ \rightarrow \triangle X'Y'Z'$, name the preimage and image of the transformation.

2. The types of transformations of geometric figures in the coordinate plane can be described as a slide, a flip, or a turn. What are the other names used to identify these transformations?

SEE EXAMPLE 1 Identify each transformation. Then use arrow notation to describe the transformation.

3.

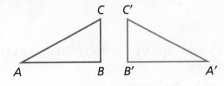

4.

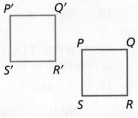

SEE EXAMPLE 2 5. A figure has vertices at $A(-3, 2)$, $B(-1, -1)$, and $C(-4, -2)$. After a transformation, the image of the figure has vertices at $A'(3, 2)$, $B'(1, -1)$, and $C'(4, -2)$. Draw the preimage and image. Then identify the transformation.

SEE EXAMPLE 3 6. **Multi-Step** The coordinates of the vertices of $\triangle DEF$ are $D(2, 3)$, $E(1, 1)$, and $F(4, 0)$. Find the coordinates for the image of $\triangle DEF$ after the translation $(x, y) \rightarrow (x - 3, y - 2)$. Draw the preimage and image.

SEE EXAMPLE 4 7. **Animation** In an animated film, a simple scene can be created by translating a figure against a still background. Write a rule for the translation that maps the rocket from position 1 to position 2.

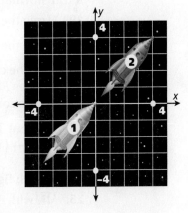

PRACTICE AND PROBLEM SOLVING

Identify each transformation. Then use arrow notation to describe the transformation.

my.hrw.com

Online Extra Practice

8.

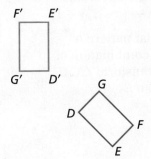

9.

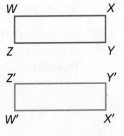

10. A figure has vertices at $J(-2, 3)$, $K(0, 3)$, $L(0, 1)$, and $M(-2, 1)$. After a transformation, the image of the figure has vertices at $J'(2, 1)$, $K'(4, 1)$, $L'(4, -1)$, and $M'(2, -1)$. Draw the preimage and image. Then identify the transformation.

11. **Multi-Step** The coordinates of the vertices of rectangle $ABCD$ are $A(-4, 1)$, $B(1, 1)$, $C(1, -2)$, and $D(-4, -2)$. Find the coordinates for the image of rectangle $ABCD$ after the translation $(x, y) \rightarrow (x + 3, y - 2)$. Draw the preimage and the image.

12. **Travel** Write a rule for the translation that maps the descent of the hot air balloon.

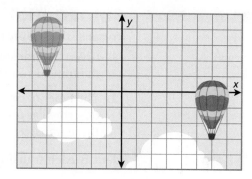

Which transformation is suggested by each of the following?

13. mountain range and its image on a lake

14. straight line path of a band marching down a street

15. wings of a butterfly

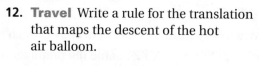

Given points $F(3, 5)$, $G(-1, 4)$, and $H(5, 0)$, draw $\triangle FGH$ and its reflection across each of the following lines.

16. the x-axis   17. the y-axis

18. Find the vertices of one of the triangles on the graph. Then use arrow notation to write a rule for translating the other three triangles.

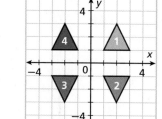

A transformation maps A onto B and C onto D.

19. Name the image of A.   20. Name the preimage of B.

21. Name the image of C.   22. Name the preimage of D.

23. Find the coordinates for the image of $\triangle RST$ with vertices $R(1, -4)$, $S(-1, -1)$, and $T(-5, 1)$ after the translation $(x, y) \rightarrow (x - 2, y - 8)$.

24. **Critical Thinking** Consider the translations $(x, y) \rightarrow (x + 5, y + 3)$ and $(x, y) \rightarrow (x + 10, y + 5)$. Compare the two translations.

Graph each figure and its image after the given translation.

25. $\overline{MN}$ with endpoints $M(2, 8)$ and $N(-3, 4)$ after the translation $(x, y) \rightarrow (x + 2, y - 5)$

26. $\overline{KL}$ with endpoints $K(-1, 1)$ and $L(3, -4)$ after the translation $(x, y) \rightarrow (x - 4, y + 3)$

H.O.T. 27. **Write About It** Given a triangle in the coordinate plane, explain how to draw its image after the translation $(x, y) \rightarrow (x + 1, y + 1)$.

28. Greg wants to rearrange a triangular pattern of colored stones on his patio. What combination of transformations could he use to transform $\triangle CAE$ to the image on the coordinate plane?

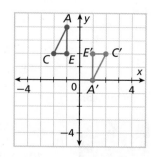

29. Which type of transformation maps $\triangle XYZ$ to $\triangle X'Y'Z'$?

    (A) Reflection   (C) Translation

    (B) Rotation   (D) Not here

30. $\triangle DEF$ has vertices at $D(-4, 2)$, $E(-3, -3)$, and $F(1, 4)$. Which of these points is a vertex of the image of $\triangle DEF$ after the translation $(x, y) \rightarrow (x - 2, y + 1)$?

    (F) $(-2, 1)$ (H) $(-5, -2)$

    (G) $(3, 3)$ (J) $(-6, -1)$

31. Consider the translation $(1, 4) \rightarrow (-2, 3)$. What number was added to the x-coordinate?

    (A) -3 (B) -1 (C) 1 (D) 7

32. Consider the translation $(-5, -7) \rightarrow (-2, -1)$. What number was added to the y-coordinate?

    (F) -3 (G) 3 (H) 6 (J) 8

CHALLENGE AND EXTEND

33. $\triangle RST$ with vertices $R(-2, -2)$, $S(-3, 1)$, and $T(1, 1)$ is translated by $(x, y) \rightarrow (x - 1, y + 3)$. Then the image, $\triangle R'S'T'$, is translated by $(x, y) \rightarrow (x + 4, y - 1)$, resulting in $\triangle R''S''T''$.

    a. Find the coordinates for the vertices of $\triangle R''S''T''$.

    b. Write a rule for a single translation that maps $\triangle RST$ to $\triangle R''S''T''$.

34. Find the angle through which the minute hand of a clock rotates over a period of 12 minutes. (*Hint:* There are 360° in a circle.)

35. A triangle has vertices $A(1, 0)$, $B(5, 0)$, and $C(2, 3)$. The triangle is rotated 90° counterclockwise about the origin. Draw and label the image of the triangle.

Determine the coordinates for the reflection image of any point $A(x, y)$ across the given line.

36. x-axis   37. y-axis

MATHEMATICAL PRACTICES

FOCUS ON MATHEMATICAL PRACTICES

H.O.T. 38. **Reasoning** A figure has vertices at $(1, 3)$, $(1, 5)$, $(3, 5)$, and $(3, 3)$. After a transformation, the image has vertices at $(1, -5)$, $(1, -3)$, $(3, -3)$, and $(3, -5)$. Sylvia says this transformation is a translation that is described by $(x, y) \rightarrow (x, y - 8)$. Helene says it is a reflection across the x-axis. Who is correct? Why?

H.O.T. 39. **Problem Solving** A circle with its center at $(-3, -4)$ is reflected across the x-axis. What is the center of the image?

H.O.T. 40. **Analysis** A point (x, y) undergoes the translation $(x + 6, y)$. This image is then translated again by $(x - 2, y)$. Write a rule for a single translation that has the same effect as these two translations.

H.O.T. 41. **Problem Solving** The graph of triangle ABC is within the first quadrant. Describe a transformation that would result in an image $A'B'C'$ that is within the second quadrant.

H.O.T. 42. **Communication** Under what circumstances is the image of a preimage also a preimage?

16-2
Technology TASK

Explore Transformations

A transformation is a movement of a figure from its original position (preimage) to a new position (image). In this lab, you will use geometry software to perform transformations and explore their properties.

Use with Transformations in the Coordinate Plane

 Use appropriate tools strategically.

MCC9-12.G.CO.2 Represent transformations in the plane using... geometry software... *Also* **MCC9-12.G.C0.5**

Activity 1

1. Construct a triangle using the segment tool. Use the text tool to label the vertices *A*, *B*, and *C*.

2. Select points *A* and *B* in that order. Choose Mark Vector from the Transform menu.

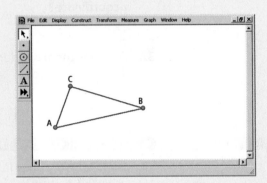

3. Select △*ABC* by clicking on all three segments of the triangle.

4. Choose Translate from the Transform menu, using *Marked* as the translation vector. What do you notice about the relationship between your preimage and its image?

5. What happens when you drag a vertex or a side of △*ABC*?

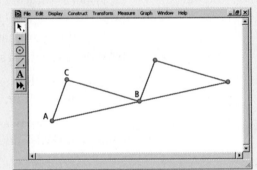

Try This

For Problems 1 and 2 choose New Sketch from the File menu.

1. Construct a triangle and a segment outside the triangle. Mark this segment as a translation vector as you did in Step 2 of Activity 1. Use Step 4 of Activity 1 to translate the triangle. What happens when you drag an endpoint of the new segment?

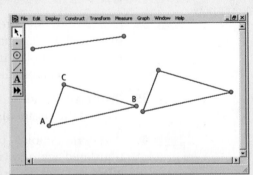

2. Instead of translating by a marked vector, use *Rectangular* as the translation vector and translate by a horizontal distance of 1 cm and a vertical distance of 2 cm. Compare this method with the marked vector method. What happens when you drag a side or vertex of the triangle?

3. Select the angles and sides of the preimage and image triangles. Use the tools in the Measure menu to measure length, angle measure, perimeter, and area. What do you think is true about these two figures?

Activity 2

1 Construct a triangle. Label the vertices *G*, *H*, and *I*.

2 Select point *H* and choose Mark Center from the Transform menu.

3 Select ∠*GHI* by selecting points *G*, *H*, and *I* in that order. Choose Mark Angle from the Transform menu.

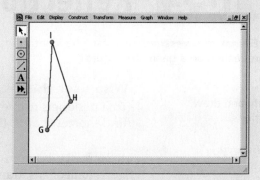

4 Select the entire triangle △*GHI* by dragging a selection box around the figure.

5 Choose Rotate from the Transform menu, using *Marked Angle* as the angle of rotation.

6 What happens when you drag a vertex or a side of △*GHI*?

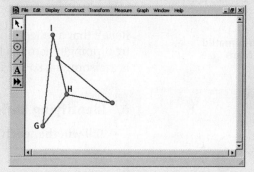

Try This

For Problems 4–6 choose New Sketch from the File menu.

4. Instead of selecting an angle of the triangle as the rotation angle, draw a new angle outside of the triangle. Mark this angle. Mark ∠*GHI* as Center and rotate the triangle. What happens when you drag one of the points that form the rotation angle?

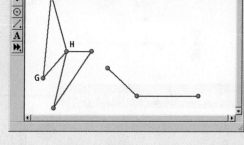

5. Construct △*QRS*, a new rotation angle, and a point *P* not on the triangle. Mark *P* as the center and mark the angle. Rotate the triangle. What happens when you drag *P* outside, inside, or on the preimage triangle?

6. Instead of rotating by a marked angle, use *Fixed Angle* as the rotation method and rotate by a fixed angle measure of 30°. Compare this method with the marked angle method.

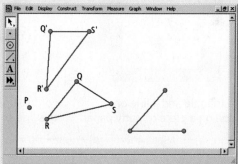

7. Using the fixed angle method of rotation, can you find an angle measure that will result in an image figure that exactly covers the preimage figure?

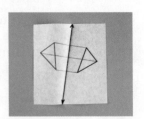

16-2 Reflections

Essential Question: How can you identify the effect of a reflection on a geometric figure?

Objective
Identify and draw reflections.

Vocabulary
isometry

Animated Math

Who uses this?

Trail designers use reflections to find shortest paths. (See Example 3.)

An **isometry** is a transformation that does not change the shape or size of a figure. Reflections, translations, and rotations are all isometries. Isometries are also called *congruence transformations* or *rigid motions.*

Recall that a reflection is a transformation that moves a figure (the preimage) by flipping it across a line. The reflected figure is called the image. A reflection is an isometry, so the image is always congruent to the preimage.

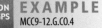
COMMON CORE GPS **EXAMPLE** **1**
MCC9-12.G.CO.4

Identifying Reflections

Tell whether each transformation appears to be a reflection. Explain.

my.hrw.com

Online Video Tutor

A

Yes; the image appears to be flipped across a line.

B

No; the figure does not appear to be flipped.

CHECK IT OUT!

Tell whether each transformation appears to be a reflection.

1a.

1b.

Reflect a Figure Using Patty Paper

 1
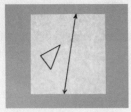

Draw a triangle and a line of reflection on a piece of patty paper.

 2

Fold the patty paper back along the line of reflection.

3

Trace the triangle. Then unfold the paper.

Remember!

A perpendicular bisector is a line perpendicular to a segment that passes through its midpoint.

Draw a segment from each vertex of the preimage to the corresponding vertex of the image. Your drawing should show that the line of reflection is the perpendicular bisector of every segment connecting a point and its image.

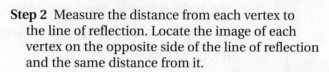

Reflections

A reflection is a transformation across a line, called the line of reflection, so that the line of reflection is the perpendicular bisector of each segment joining each point and its image.

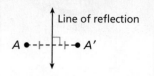

Line of reflection

$A \bullet \mathrel{-} \mathrel{+} \mathrel{-} \mathrel{+} \mathrel{-} \bullet A'$

MCC9-12.G.CO.5

EXAMPLE 2

Online Video Tutor

Drawing Reflections

Copy the quadrilateral and the line of reflection. Draw the reflection of the quadrilateral across the line.

Step 1 Through each vertex draw a line perpendicular to the line of reflection.

Step 2 Measure the distance from each vertex to the line of reflection. Locate the image of each vertex on the opposite side of the line of reflection and the same distance from it.

Step 3 Connect the images of the vertices.

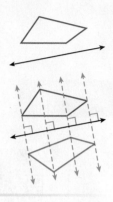

2. Copy the quadrilateral and the line of reflection. Draw the reflection of the quadrilateral across the line.

EXAMPLE 3

COMMON CORE GPS
MCC9-12.G.CO.5

Online Video Tutor

Problem-Solving Application

A trail designer is planning two trails that connect campsites A and B to a point on the river. He wants the total length of the trails to be as short as possible. Where should the trail meet the river?

$A \bullet$　　$\bullet B$

River

1 Understand the Problem

The problem asks you to locate point X on the river so that $AX + XB$ has the least value possible.

2 Make a Plan

Let B' be the reflection of point B across the river. For any point X on the river, $\overline{XB'} \cong \overline{XB}$, so $AX + XB = AX + XB'$. $AX + XB'$ is least when A, X, and B' are collinear.

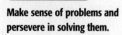

MATHEMATICAL PRACTICES

Make sense of problems and persevere in solving them.

3 Solve

Reflect B across the river to locate B'. Draw $\overline{AB'}$ and locate X at the intersection of $\overline{AB'}$ and the river.

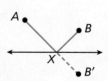

4 Look Back

To verify your answer, choose several possible locations for X and measure the total length of the trails for each location.

Remember!

The symbol $\cong$ is read as "is congruent to".

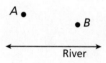

3. What if...? If A and B were the same distance from the river, what would be true about $\overline{AX}$ and $\overline{BX}$?

16-2 Reflections **453**

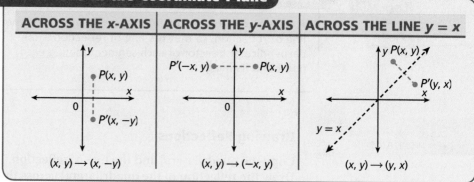

Reflections in the Coordinate Plane

ACROSS THE x-AXIS	ACROSS THE y-AXIS	ACROSS THE LINE y = x
$(x, y) \rightarrow (x, -y)$	$(x, y) \rightarrow (-x, y)$	$(x, y) \rightarrow (y, x)$

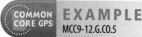

my.hrw.com

Online Video Tutor

EXAMPLE 4 — Drawing Reflections in the Coordinate Plane

MCC9-12.G.CO.5

Reflect the figure with the given vertices across the given line.

A $M(1, 2), N(1, 4), P(3, 3); y$-axis

The reflection of (x, y) is $(-x, y)$.

$M(1, 2) \rightarrow M'(-1, 2)$

$N(1, 4) \rightarrow N'(-1, 4)$

$P(3, 3) \rightarrow P'(-3, 3)$

Graph the preimage and image.

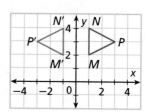

B $D(2, 0), E(2, 2), F(5, 2), G(5, 1); y = x$

The reflection of (x, y) is (y, x).

$D(2, 0) \rightarrow D'(0, 2)$

$E(2, 2) \rightarrow E'(2, 2)$

$F(5, 2) \rightarrow F'(2, 5)$

$G(5, 1) \rightarrow G'(1, 5)$

Graph the preimage and image.

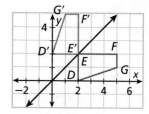

4. Reflect the rectangle with vertices $S(3, 4)$, $T(3, 1)$, $U(-2, 1)$, and $V(-2, 4)$ across the x-axis.

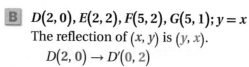

MCC.MP.6 — MATHEMATICAL PRACTICES

THINK AND DISCUSS

1. Acute scalene $\triangle ABC$ is reflected across $\overline{BC}$. Classify quadrilateral $ABA'C$. Explain your reasoning.

2. Point A' is a *reflection* of point A across line ℓ. What is the relationship of ℓ to $\overline{AA'}$?

3. GET ORGANIZED Copy and complete the graphic organizer.

Line of Reflection	Image of (a, b)	Example
x-axis		
y-axis		
y = x		

GUIDED PRACTICE

1. **Vocabulary** If a transformation is an *isometry*, how would you describe the relationship between the preimage and the image?

SEE EXAMPLE 1 **Tell whether each transformation appears to be a reflection.**

2.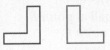

3.

4.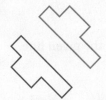

5.

SEE EXAMPLE 2 **Multi-Step** Copy each figure and the line of reflection. Draw the reflection of the figure across the line.

6.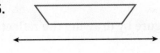

7.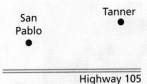

SEE EXAMPLE 3 8. **City Planning** The towns of San Pablo and Tanner are located on the same side of Highway 105. Two access roads are planned that connect the towns to a point *P* on the highway. Draw a diagram that shows where point *P* should be located in order to make the total length of the access roads as short as possible.

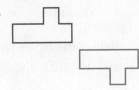

SEE EXAMPLE 4 **Reflect the figure with the given vertices across the given line.**

9. $A(-2, 1)$, $B(2, 3)$, $C(5, 2)$; x-axis

10. $R(0, -1)$, $S(2, 2)$, $T(3, 0)$; y-axis

11. $M(2, 1)$, $N(3, 1)$, $P(2, -1)$, $Q(1, -1)$; $y = x$

12. $A(-2, 2)$, $B(-1, 3)$, $C(1, 2)$, $D(-2, -2)$; $y = x$

PRACTICE AND PROBLEM SOLVING

Independent Practice	
For Exercises	See Example
13–16	1
17–18	2
19	3
20–23	4

Tell whether each transformation appears to be a reflection.

13.

14.

15.

16.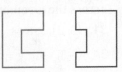

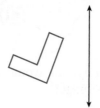
Multi-Step Copy each figure and the line of reflection. Draw the reflection of the figure across the line.

17.

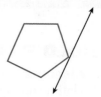

18.

19. Recreation Cara is playing pool. She wants to hit the ball at point *A* without hitting the ball at point *B*. She has to bounce the cue ball, located at point *C*, off the side rail and into her ball. Draw a diagram that shows the exact point along the rail that Cara should aim for.

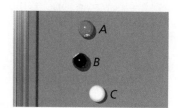

Reflect the figure with the given vertices across the given line.

20. $A(-3, 2)$, $B(0, 2)$, $C(-2, 0)$; *y*-axis

21. $M(-4, -1)$, $N(-1, -1)$, $P(-2, -2)$; $y = x$

22. $J(1, 2)$, $K(-2, -1)$, $L(3, -1)$; *x*-axis

23. $S(-1, 1)$, $T(1, 4)$, $U(3, 2)$, $V(1, -3)$; $y = x$

Copy each figure. Then complete the figure by drawing the reflection image across the line.

24.

25.

26.

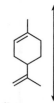

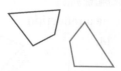
27. Chemistry In chemistry, *chiral* molecules are mirror images of each other. Although they have similar structures, chiral molecules can have very different properties. For example, the compound R-(+)-limonene smells like oranges, while its mirror image, S-(−)-limonene, smells like lemons. Use the figure and the given line of reflection to draw S-(−)-limonene.

R-(+)-limonene

Each figure shows a preimage and image under a reflection. Copy the figure and draw the line of reflection.

28.

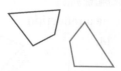

29.

30.

Use arrow notation to describe the mapping of each point when it is reflected across the given line.

31. $(5, 2)$; *x*-axis

32. $(-3, -7)$; *y*-axis

33. $(0, 12)$; *x*-axis

34. $(-3, -6)$; $y = x$

35. $(0, -5)$; $y = x$

36. $(4, 4)$; $y = x$

Real-World Connections

37. The figure shows one hole of a miniature golf course.

    a. Is it possible to hit the ball in a straight line from the tee *T* to the hole *H*?

    b. Find the coordinates of *H'*, the reflection of *H* across $\overline{BC}$.

    c. The point at which a player should aim in order to make a hole in one is the intersection of $\overline{TH'}$ and $\overline{BC}$. What are the coordinates of this point?

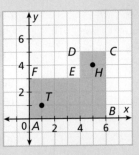

H.O.T. **38. Critical Thinking** Sketch the next figure in the sequence below.

Μ ℒ 83 М4 ᑐ ᕱᕱ ᐁ

H.O.T. **39. Critical Thinking** Under a reflection in the coordinate plane, the point $(3, 5)$ is mapped to the point $(5, 3)$. What is the line of reflection? Is this the only possible line of reflection? Explain.

Draw the reflection of the graph of each function across the given line.

40. *x*-axis

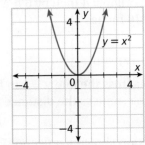

41. *y*-axis

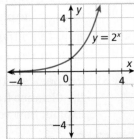

H.O.T. **42. Write About It** Imagine reflecting all the points in a plane across line ℓ. Which points remain fixed under this transformation? That is, for which points is the image the same as the preimage? Explain.

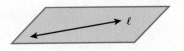

TEST PREP

43. Daryl is using a coordinate plane to plan a garden. He draws a flower bed with vertices $(3, 1)$, $(3, 4)$, $(-2, 4)$, and $(-2, 1)$. Then he creates a second flower bed by reflecting the first one across the *x*-axis. Which of these is a vertex of the second flower bed?

    Ⓐ $(-2, -4)$ Ⓒ $(2, 1)$
    Ⓑ $(-3, 1)$ Ⓓ $(-3, -4)$

44. In the reflection shown, the shaded figure is the preimage. Which of these represents the mapping?

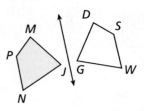

    Ⓕ $MJNP \rightarrow DSWG$ Ⓗ $JMPN \rightarrow GWSD$

    Ⓖ $DGWS \rightarrow MJNP$ Ⓙ $PMJN \rightarrow SDGW$

45. What is the image of the point $(-3, 4)$ when it is reflected across the *y*-axis?

    Ⓐ $(4, -3)$ Ⓒ $(3, 4)$

    Ⓑ $(-3, -4)$ Ⓓ $(-4, -3)$

CHALLENGE AND EXTEND

Find the coordinates of the image when each point is reflected across the given line.

46. $(4, 2); y = 3$ **47.** $(-3, 2); x = 1$ **48.** $(3, 1); y = x + 2$

FOCUS ON MATHEMATICAL PRACTICES

H.O.T **49. Analysis** Selina draws a pattern for the quilt she is going to make. As part of the pattern, she reflects a triangle with vertices at (3, 1), (6, 1), and (6, 4) across the line $x = y$ and then reflects this image across the *y*-axis. What are the coordinates of the final image?

H.O.T **50. Draw Conclusions** Henri takes an original 4 inch by 6 inch photo and enlarges it to be a new photo that is 8 inches by 10 inches.

    a. Is this a transformation? Explain.

    b. Is this an example of an isometry? Explain.

H.O.T **51. Properties** Triangle *JKL* is reflected across the line $y = x$ to form the image $J'K'L'$. Is the distance from *J* to the line $y = x$ the same as the distance from the line $y = x$ to J'? Explain how you know.

H.O.T **52. Communication** Is the transformation shown a reflection? Explain.

H.O.T **53. Make a Conjecture** An isosceles trapezoid is reflected across a line.

    a. What type of quadrilateral is the image? Classify it without drawing the figure.

    b. How can you be sure without drawing the image?

H.O.T **54. Draw Conclusions** A figure in Quadrant II is reflected across the *x*-axis.

    a. In what quadrant is the image?

    b. What conclusion can you draw about the signs of the coordinates of the vertices of the image?

16-3 Translations

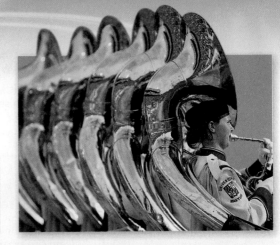

Essential Question: How can you identify the effect of a translation on a geometric figure?

Objective
Identify and draw translations.

Vocabulary
translation vector

Who uses this?
Marching band directors use translations to plan their bands' field shows. (See Example 4.)

A translation is a transformation where all the points of a figure are moved the same distance in the same direction. The distance and direction are indicated by a ray called the **translation vector**. A vector is a quantity that has both length and direction, and can be thought of as a line segment with a starting point and an endpoint. A translation is an isometry, so the image of a translated figure is congruent to the preimage.

COMMON CORE GPS MCC9-12.G.CO.4

EXAMPLE 1 Identifying Translations

 my.hrw.com

Online Video Tutor

Tell whether each transformation appears to be a translation. Explain.

A

No; not all of the points have moved the same distance.

B

Yes; all of the points have moved the same distance in the same direction.

CHECK IT OUT!

Tell whether each transformation appears to be a translation.

1a.

1b.

Translate a Figure Using Patty Paper

1
Draw a triangle and a translation vector on a sheet of paper.

2
Place a sheet of patty paper on top of the diagram. Trace the triangle and vector.

3
Slide the bottom paper in the direction of the vector until the head of the top vector aligns with the tail of the bottom vector. Trace the triangle.

Draw a segment from each vertex of the preimage to the corresponding vertex of the image. Your drawing should show that every segment connecting a point and its image is the same length as the translation vector. These segments are also parallel to the translation vector.

Translations

A translation is a transformation along a vector such that each segment joining a point and its image has the same length as the vector and is parallel to the vector.

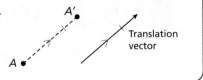

Translation vector

EXAMPLE **2**

Drawing Translations

Copy the triangle and the translation vector. Draw the translation of the triangle along $\vec{v}$.

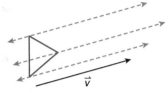

my.hrw.com

Online Video Tutor

Step 1 Draw a line parallel to the vector through each vertex of the triangle.

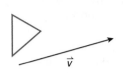

A vector v can be represented by the symbol $\vec{v}$.

Step 2 Measure the length of the vector. Then, from each vertex mark off this distance in the same direction as the vector, on each of the parallel lines.

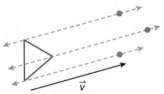

Step 3 Connect the images of the vertices.

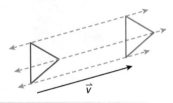

CHECK IT OUT!

2. Copy the quadrilateral and the translation vector. Draw the translation of the quadrilateral along $\vec{w}$.

The vector form $\langle a, b \rangle$ is called component form.

A vector in the coordinate plane can be written as $\langle a, b \rangle$, where a is the horizontal change and b is the vertical change from the initial point to the terminal point.

Translations in the Coordinate Plane

HORIZONTAL TRANSLATION ALONG VECTOR ⟨a, 0⟩	VERTICAL TRANSLATION ALONG VECTOR ⟨0, b⟩	GENERAL TRANSLATION ALONG VECTOR ⟨a, b⟩
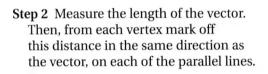		
$(x, y) \rightarrow (x + a, y)$	$(x, y) \rightarrow (x, y + b)$	$(x, y) \rightarrow (x + a, y + b)$

EXAMPLE 3
MCC9-12.G.CO.2

my.hrw.com

Online Video Tutor

Drawing Translations in the Coordinate Plane

Translate the triangle with vertices $A(-2, -4)$, $B(-1, -2)$, and $C(-3, 0)$ along the vector $\langle 2, 4 \rangle$.

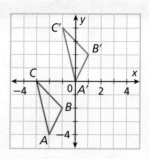

The image of (x, y) is $(x + 2, y + 4)$.

$$A(-2, -4) \rightarrow A'(-2 + 2, -4 + 4) = A'(0, 0)$$

$$B(-1, -2) \rightarrow B'(-1 + 2, -2 + 4) = B'(1, 2)$$

$$C(-3, 0) \rightarrow C'(-3 + 2, 0 + 4) = C'(-1, 4)$$

Graph the preimage and image.

3. Translate the quadrilateral with vertices $R(2, 5)$, $S(0, 2)$, $T(1, -1)$, and $U(3, 1)$ along the vector $\langle -3, -3 \rangle$.

EXAMPLE 4
MCC9-12.G.CO.5

my.hrw.com

Online Video Tutor

Entertainment Application

In a marching drill, it takes 8 steps to march 5 yards. A drummer starts 8 steps to the left and 8 steps up from the center of the field. She marches 16 steps to the right to her second position. Then she marches 24 steps down the field to her final position. What is the drummer's final position? What single translation vector moves her from the starting position to her final position?

The drummer's starting coordinates are $(-8, 8)$.

Her second position is $(-8 + 16, 8) = (8, 8)$.

Her final position is $(8, 8 - 24) = (8, -16)$.

The vector that moves her directly from her starting position to her final position is $\langle 16, 0 \rangle + \langle 0, -24 \rangle = \langle 16, -24 \rangle$.

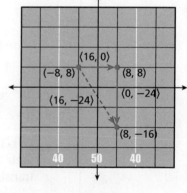

4. What if...? Suppose another drummer started at the center of the field and marched along the same vectors as above. What would this drummer's final position be?

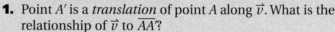

MCC.MP.1, MCC.MP.6

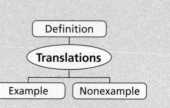
MATHEMATICAL PRACTICES

THINK AND DISCUSS

1. Point A' is a *translation* of point A along $\vec{v}$. What is the relationship of $\vec{v}$ to $\overline{AA'}$?

2. $\overline{AB}$ is translated to form $\overline{A'B'}$. Classify quadrilateral $AA'B'B$. Explain your reasoning.

3. GET ORGANIZED Copy and complete the graphic organizer.

Definition

Translations

Example | Nonexample

GUIDED PRACTICE

SEE EXAMPLE 1   Tell whether each transformation appears to be a translation.

1.

2.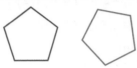

3.

4.

SEE EXAMPLE 2   **Multi-Step** Copy each figure and the translation vector. Draw the translation of the figure along the given vector.

5.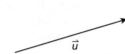

6.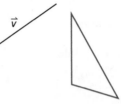

SEE EXAMPLE 3   Translate the figure with the given vertices along the given vector.

7. $A(-4, -4)$, $B(-2, -3)$, $C(-1, 3)$; $\langle 5, 0 \rangle$

8. $R(-3, 1)$, $S(-2, 3)$, $T(2, 3)$, $U(3, 1)$; $\langle 0, -4 \rangle$

9. $J(-2, 2)$, $K(-1, 2)$, $L(-1, -2)$, $M(-3, -1)$; $\langle 3, 2 \rangle$

SEE EXAMPLE 4   **10. Art** The Zulu people of southern Africa are known for their beadwork. To create a typical Zulu pattern, translate the polygon with vertices $(1, 5)$, $(2, 3)$, $(1, 1)$, and $(0, 3)$ along the vector $\langle 0, -4 \rangle$. Translate the image along the same vector. Repeat to generate a pattern. What are the vertices of the fourth polygon in the pattern?

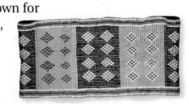

PRACTICE AND PROBLEM SOLVING

Tell whether each transformation appears to be a translation.

Independent Practice	
For Exercises	See Example
11–14	1
15–16	2
17–19	3
20	4

11.

12.

13.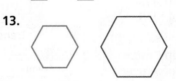

14.

Multi-Step Copy each figure and the translation vector. Draw the translation of the figure along the given vector.

15.

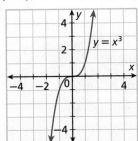

16.

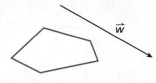

Translate the figure with the given vertices along the given vector.

17. $P(-1, 2)$, $Q(1, -1)$, $R(3, 1)$, $S(2, 3)$; $\langle -3, 0 \rangle$

18. $A(1, 3)$, $B(-1, 2)$, $C(2, 1)$, $D(4, 2)$; $\langle -3, -3 \rangle$

19. $D(0, 15)$, $E(-10, 5)$, $F(10, -5)$; $\langle 5, -20 \rangle$

20. **Animation** An animator draws the ladybug shown and then translates it along the vector $\langle 1, 1 \rangle$, followed by a translation of the new image along the vector $\langle 2, 2 \rangle$, followed by a translation of the second image along the vector $\langle 3, 3 \rangle$.

   a. Sketch the ladybug's final position.

   b. What single vector moves the ladybug from its starting position to its final position?

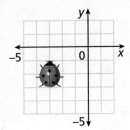

Draw the translation of the graph of each function along the given vector.

21. $\langle 3, 0 \rangle$

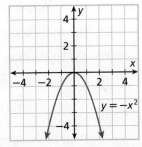

22. $\langle -1, -1 \rangle$

23. **Probability** The point $P(3, 2)$ is translated along one of the following four vectors chosen at random: $\langle -3, 0 \rangle$, $\langle -1, -4 \rangle$, $\langle 3, -2 \rangle$, and $\langle 2, 3 \rangle$. Find the probability of each of the following.

   a. The image of P is in the fourth quadrant.

   b. The image of P is on an axis.

   c. The image of P is at the origin.

24. The figure shows one hole of a miniature golf course and the path of a ball from the tee T to the hole H.

   a. What translation vector represents the path of the ball from T to $\overline{DC}$?

   b. What translation vector represents the path of the ball from $\overline{DC}$ to H?

   c. Show that the sum of these vectors is equal to the vector that represents the straight path from T to H.

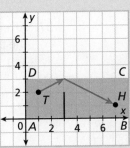

Each figure shows a preimage (blue) and its image (red) under a translation. Copy the figure and draw the vector along which the polygon is translated.

25.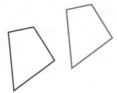

26.

27. Critical Thinking The points of a plane are translated along the given vector $\overrightarrow{AB}$. Do any points remain fixed under this transformation? That is, are there any points for which the image coincides with the preimage? Explain.

28. Carpentry Carpenters use a tool called *adjustable parallels* to set up level work areas and to draw parallel lines. Describe how a carpenter could use this tool to translate a given point along a given vector. What additional tools, if any, would be needed?

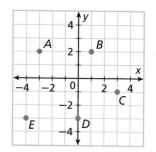

Find the vector associated with each translation. Then use arrow notation to describe the mapping of the preimage to the image.

29. the translation that maps point A to point B

30. the translation that maps point B to point A

31. the translation that maps point C to point D

32. the translation that maps point E to point B

33. the translation that maps point C to the origin

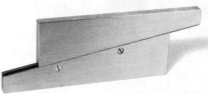

34. Multi-Step The rectangle shown is translated two-thirds of the way along one of its diagonals. Find the area of the region where the rectangle and its image overlap.

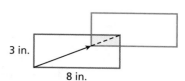

3 in.

8 in.

35. Write About It Point P is translated along the vector $\langle a, b \rangle$. Explain how to find the distance between point P and its image.

TEST PREP

36. What is the image of $P(1, 3)$ when it is translated along the vector $\langle -3, 5 \rangle$?

  Ⓐ $(-2, 8)$ Ⓑ $(0, 6)$ Ⓒ $(1, 3)$ Ⓓ $(0, 4)$

37. After a translation, the image of $A(-6, -2)$ is $B(-4, -4)$. What is the image of the point $(3, -1)$ after this translation?

  Ⓕ $(-5, 1)$ Ⓖ $(5, -3)$ Ⓗ $(5, 1)$ Ⓙ $(-5, -3)$

38. Which vector translates point Q to point P?

(A) $\langle -2, -4 \rangle$ (C) $\langle -2, 4 \rangle$

(B) $\langle 4, -2 \rangle$ (D) $\langle 2, -4 \rangle$

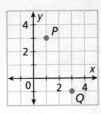

CHALLENGE AND EXTEND

39. The point $M(1, 2)$ is translated along a vector that is parallel to the line $y = 2x + 4$. The translation vector has magnitude $\sqrt{5}$. What are the possible images of point M?

40. A cube has edges of length 2 cm. Point P is translated along $\vec{u}$, $\vec{v}$, and $\vec{w}$ as shown.

a. Describe a single translation vector that maps point P to point Q.

b. Find the magnitude of this vector to the nearest hundredth.

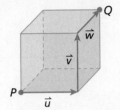

FOCUS ON MATHEMATICAL PRACTICES

MATHEMATICAL PRACTICES

H.O.T. 41. Analysis Does this transformation appear to be a translation? Explain why or why not.

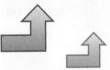

H.O.T. 42. Problem Solving Shelly graphs the line $y = x$ and then translates it along the vector $\langle 0, 3 \rangle$.

a. What are the slopes of the preimage and the image?

b. What are the y-intercepts of the preimage and the image?

c. Is this an isometry? How do you know?

H.O.T. 43. Justify Harold draws a translation of triangle ABC where the measure of angle B is 56°. He says that the measure of angle B' is also 56°. Justify his conclusion.

H.O.T. 44. Draw Conclusions The red parabola is the image of the blue parabola.

a. If the image was created by a translation followed by a reflection, describe the transformations that could have taken place.

b. If the image was created by a reflection followed by a translation, describe the transformations that could have taken place.

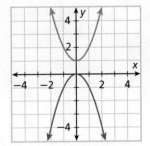

H.O.T. 45. Error Analysis The graph of the equation $y = |x|$ is translated so that the V-shape of the graph is moved up 3 units. Deb says the equation of the image is $y = |x| + 3$. Sara says it is $y = |x + 3|$. Who is correct? Use a point on the graph to justify your answer.

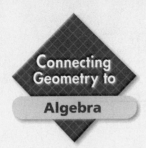

Transformations of Functions

Transformations can be used to graph complicated functions by using the graphs of simpler functions called *parent functions*. The following are examples of parent functions and their graphs.

$y = |x|$

$y = \sqrt{x}$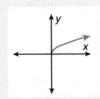

$y = x^2$

Transformation of Parent Function $y = f(x)$		
Reflection	**Vertical Translation**	**Horizontal Translation**
Across x-axis: $y = -f(x)$ Across y-axis: $y = f(-x)$	$y = f(x) + k$ Up k units if $k > 0$ Down k units if $k < 0$	$y = f(x - h)$ Right h units if $h > 0$ Left h units if $h < 0$

Example

For the parent function $y = x^2$, write a function rule for the given transformation and graph the preimage and image.

A a reflection across the x-axis
function rule: $y = -x^2$

graph:

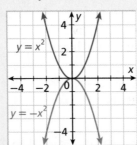

B a translation up 2 units and right 3 units
function rule: $y = (x - 3)^2 + 2$

graph:

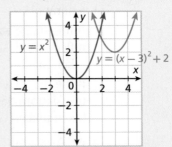

Try This

For each parent function, write a function rule for the given transformation and graph the preimage and image.

1. parent function: $y = x^2$
   transformation: a translation down 1 unit and right 4 units

2. parent function: $y = \sqrt{x}$
   transformation: a reflection across the x-axis

3. parent function: $y = |x|$
   transformation: a translation up 2 units and left 1 unit

Rotations

Essential Question: How can you identify the effect of a rotation on a geometric figure?

Objective
Identify and draw rotations.

Who uses this?
Astronomers can use properties of rotations to analyze photos of star trails. (See Exercise 35.)

Remember that a rotation is a transformation that turns a figure around a fixed point, called the center of rotation. A rotation is an isometry, so the image of a rotated figure is congruent to the preimage.

COMMON CORE GPS
EXAMPLE
MCC9-12.G.CO.4

1

Identifying Rotations

Tell whether each transformation appears to be a rotation. Explain.

my.hrw.com

Online Video Tutor

 A

Yes; the figure appears to be turned around a point.

 B

No; the figure appears to be flipped, not turned.

CHECK IT OUT!

Tell whether each transformation appears to be a rotation.

 1a.

1b.
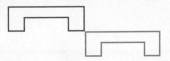

Rotate a Figure Using Patty Paper

1

On a sheet of paper, draw a triangle and a point. The point will be the center of rotation.

2
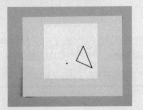

Place a sheet of patty paper on top of the diagram. Trace the triangle and the point.

3

Hold your pencil down on the point and rotate the bottom paper counterclockwise. Trace the triangle.

Remember!

An angle is a figure formed by two rays with a common endpoint.

Draw a segment from each vertex to the center of rotation. Your drawing should show that a point's distance to the center of rotation is equal to its image's distance to the center of rotation. The angle formed by a point, the center of rotation, and the point's image is the angle by which the figure was rotated.

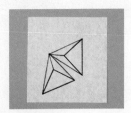

 **Know it! Note**

Rotations

A rotation is a transformation about a point P, called the center of rotation, such that each point and its image are the same distance from P, and such that all angles with vertex P formed by a point and its image are congruent. In the figure, $\angle APA'$ is the angle of rotation.

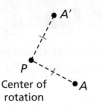

Center of rotation

COMMON CORE GPS **EXAMPLE 2** MCC9-12.G.CO.5

 **my.hrw.com**

Online Video Tutor

Helpful Hint

Unless otherwise stated, all rotations in this book are counterclockwise.

Drawing Rotations

Copy the figure and the angle of rotation. Draw the rotation of the triangle about point P by m$\angle A$.

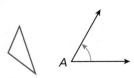

Step 1 Draw a segment from each vertex to point P.

Step 2 Draw an angle congruent to $\angle A$ onto each segment. Measure the distance from each vertex to point P and mark off this distance on the corresponding ray to locate the image of each vertex.

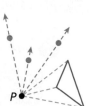

Step 3 Connect the images of the vertices.

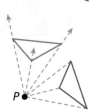

CHECK IT OUT!

2. Copy the figure and the angle of rotation. Draw the rotation of the segment about point Q by m$\angle X$.

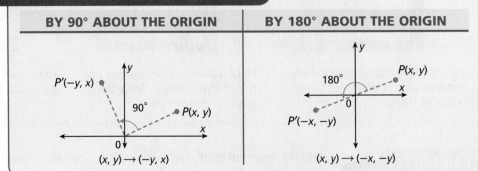 **Know it! Note**

Rotations in the Coordinate Plane

BY 90° ABOUT THE ORIGIN	BY 180° ABOUT THE ORIGIN
$(x, y) \rightarrow (-y, x)$	$(x, y) \rightarrow (-x, -y)$

Drawing Rotations in the Coordinate Plane

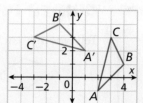

A Rotate $\triangle ABC$ with vertices $A(2, -1)$, $B(4, 1)$, and $C(3, 3)$ by 90° about the origin.

The rotation of (x, y) is $(-y, x)$.

$A(2, -1) \rightarrow A'(1, 2)$

$B(4, 1) \rightarrow B'(-1, 4)$

$C(3, 3) \rightarrow C'(-3, 3)$

Graph the preimage and image.

B The London Eye observation wheel has a radius of 67.5 m and takes 30 minutes to make a complete rotation. A car starts at position (34, 59). What are the coordinates of the car's location after 15 minutes?

Step 1 Find the angle of rotation. Fifteen minutes is $\frac{15}{30} = \frac{1}{2}$ of a complete rotation, or $\frac{1}{2}(360°) = 180°$.

Step 2 Draw a diagram to represent the car's starting location at (34, 59).

Step 3 Use the formula for the 180° rotation in the coordinate plane about the origin to find the new coordinates of the car's location.

The rotation of (x, y) is $(-x, -y)$.

$(34, 59) \rightarrow (-34, -59)$

The car's location after 15 minutes is $(-34, -59)$.

3a. Rotate $\triangle ABC$ by 180° about the origin.

3b. Find the coordinates of the location of the observation car after 7.5 minutes.

MCC.MP.1

 MATHEMATICAL PRACTICES

THINK AND DISCUSS

1. Describe the image of a rotation of a figure by an angle of 360°.

2. Point A' is a rotation of point A about point P. What is the relationship of $\overline{AP}$ to $\overline{A'P}$?

3. GET ORGANIZED Copy and complete the graphic organizer.

	Reflection	Translation	Rotation
Definition			
Example			

GUIDED PRACTICE

SEE EXAMPLE **1** Tell whether each transformation appears to be a rotation.

1.

2.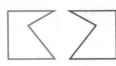

3.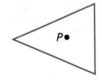

4.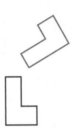

SEE EXAMPLE **2** Copy each figure and the angle of rotation. Draw the rotation of the figure about point *P* by m∠*A*.

5.

6.

SEE EXAMPLE **3** Rotate the figure with the given vertices about the origin using the given angle of rotation.

7. $A(1, 0)$, $B(3, 2)$, $C(5, 0)$; 90°

8. $J(2, 1)$, $K(4, 3)$, $L(2, 4)$, $M(-1, 2)$; 90°

9. $D(2, 3)$, $E(-1, 2)$, $F(2, 1)$; 180°

10. $P(-1, -1)$, $Q(-4, -2)$, $R(0, -2)$; 180°

PRACTICE AND PROBLEM SOLVING

Independent Practice

For Exercises	See Example
11–14	1
15–16	2
11–21	3

my.hrw.com

Online Extra Practice

Tell whether each transformation appears to be a rotation.

11.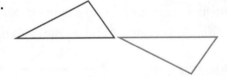

12.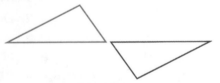

13.

14.

Copy each figure and the angle of rotation. Draw the rotation of the figure about point P by $m\angle A$.

15.

16.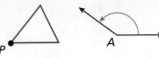

Rotate the figure with the given vertices about the origin using the given angle of rotation.

17. $E(-1, 2)$, $F(3, 1)$, $G(2, 3)$; 90°

18. $A(-1, 0)$, $B(-1, -3)$, $C(1, -3)$, $D(1, 0)$; 90°

19. $P(0, -2)$, $Q(2, 0)$, $R(3, -3)$; 180°

20. $L(2, 0)$, $M(-1, -2)$, $N(2, -2)$; 180°

21. **Architecture** The CN Tower in Toronto, Canada, features a revolving restaurant that takes 72 minutes to complete a full rotation. A table that is 50 feet from the center of the restaurant starts at position $(50, 10)$. What are the coordinates of the table after 18 minutes?

Copy each figure. Then draw the rotation of the figure about the red point using the given angle measure.

22. 90°

23. 180°

24. 180°

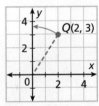

25. Point Q has coordinates $(2, 3)$. After a rotation about the origin, the image of point Q lies on $(-2, -3)$.

a. Find the angle of rotation.

b. Find the coordinates of the image of point Q after a 90° rotation about the origin.

Rectangle *RSTU* is the image of rectangle *LMNP* under a 180° rotation about point A. Name each of the following.

26. the image of point N

27. the preimage of point S

28. the image of $\overline{MN}$

29. the preimage of $\overline{TU}$

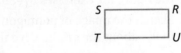

30. A miniature golf course includes a hole with a windmill. Players must hit the ball through the opening at the base of the windmill while the blades rotate.

a. The blades take 20 seconds to make a complete rotation. Through what angle do the blades rotate in 5 seconds?

b. Find the coordinates of point A after 5 seconds. (*Hint:* $(4, 3)$ is the center of rotation.)

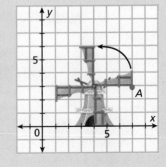

Each figure shows a preimage and its image under a rotation. Copy the figure and locate the center of rotation.

31. 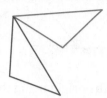   **32.** 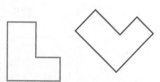   **33.**

H.O.T. 34. Astronomy The photograph was made by placing a camera on a tripod and keeping the camera's shutter open for a long time. Because of Earth's rotation, the stars appear to rotate around Polaris, also known as the North Star.

a. Estimation Estimate the angle of rotation of the stars in the photo.

b. Estimation Use your result from part **a** to estimate the length of time that the camera's shutter was open. (*Hint:* If the shutter was open for 24 hours, the stars would appear to make one complete rotation around Polaris.)

H.O.T. 35. Estimation In the diagram, $\triangle ABC \rightarrow \triangle A'B'C'$ under a rotation about point P.

a. Estimate the angle of rotation.

b. Explain how you can draw two segments and can then use a protractor to measure the angle of rotation.

c. Copy the figure. Use the method from part **b** to find the angle of rotation. How does your result compare to your estimate?

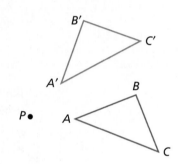

H.O.T. 36. Critical Thinking A student wrote the following in his math journal. "Under a rotation, every point moves around the center of rotation by the same angle measure. This means that every point moves the same distance." Do you agree? Explain.

Use the figure for Exercises 37–39.

37. Sketch the image of pentagon *ABCDE* under a rotation of 90° about the origin. Give the vertices of the image.

38. Sketch the image of pentagon *ABCDE* under a rotation of 180° about the origin. Give the vertices of the image.

H.O.T. 39. Write About It Is the image of *ABCDE* under a rotation of 180° about the origin the same as its image under a reflection across the *x*-axis? Explain your reasoning.

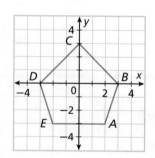

40. What is the image of the point $(-2, 5)$ when it is rotated about the origin by 90°?

(A) $(-5, 2)$ (B) $(5, -2)$ (C) $(-5, -2)$ (D) $(2, -5)$

41. The six cars of a Ferris wheel are located at the vertices of a regular hexagon. Which rotation about point P maps car A to car C?

(F) 60° (G) 90° (H) 120° (J) 135°

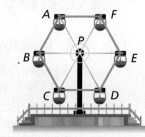

42. Gridded Response Under a rotation about the origin, the point $(-3, 4)$ is mapped to the point $(3, -4)$. What is the measure of the angle of rotation?

CHALLENGE AND EXTEND

H.O.T. **43. Engineering** Gears are used to change the speed and direction of rotating parts in pieces of machinery. In the diagram, suppose gear B makes one complete rotation in the counterclockwise direction. Give the angle of rotation and direction for the rotation of gear A. Explain how you got your answer.

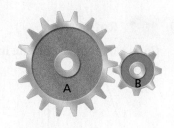

FOCUS ON MATHEMATICAL PRACTICES

H.O.T. **44. Reasoning** Cole rotates the point $(3, 4)$ about the origin by 270°. What is the image of this point? Explain how you found your answer.

H.O.T. **45. Make a Conjecture** Tell whether each figure appears to be a rotation. Explain. If it is not, name the translation it appears to be.

a.    b.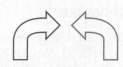

H.O.T. **46. Problem Solving** Rotate the figure with vertices $(1, 1)$, $(5, 1)$, $(4, 3)$ 90° about the origin. What are the coordinates of the image?

H.O.T. **47. Communication** What are the formal mathematical terms for flips, turns, and slides?

H.O.T. **48. Error Analysis** Landon says this figure has been rotated about the origin 90°. Garrett says that it has been rotated 270°. Who is correct? Explain.

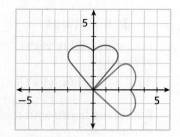

H.O.T. **49. Number Sense** The figure $ABCD$ is rotated about point P to form the image $A'B'C'D'$. Which distance is equal to PA?

H.O.T. **50. Modeling** To make the design for a tile border, Alexie rotates this figure 180° about the red point. Copy the figure and then draw the image.

Ready to Go On?

my.hrw.com
Assessment and Intervention

16-1 Transformations in the Coordinate Plane

1. A graphic designer used the translation $(x, y) \rightarrow (x - 3, y + 2)$ to transform square *HJKL*. Find the coordinates and graph the image *H'J'K'L'* of square *HJKL*.

2. A figure has vertices at $X(1, 1)$, $Y(3, 1)$, and $Z(3, 4)$. After a transformation, the image of the figure has vertices at $X'(-1, -1)$, $Y'(-3, -1)$, and $Z'(-3, -4)$. Graph the preimage and image. Then identify the transformation.

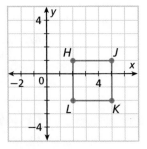

16-2 Reflections

Copy each figure and the line of reflection. Draw the reflection of the figure across the line.

3.

4.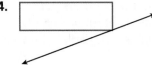

Reflect the figure with the given vertices across the given line.

5. $E(-3, 2)$, $F(0, 2)$, $G(-2, 5)$; *x*-axis

6. $J(2, -1)$, $K(4, -2)$, $L(4, -3)$, $M(2, -3)$; *y*-axis

16-3 Translations

7. A landscape architect represents a flower bed by a polygon with vertices $(1, 0)$, $(4, 0)$, $(4, 2)$, and $(1, 2)$. She decides to move the flower bed to a new location by translating it along the vector $\langle -4, -3 \rangle$. Draw the flower bed in its final position.

Translate the figure with the given vertices along the given vector.

8. $R(1, -1)$, $S(1, -3)$, $T(4, -3)$, $U(4, -1)$; $\langle -5, 2 \rangle$

9. $A(-4, -1)$, $B(-3, 2)$, $C(-1, -2)$; $\langle 6, 0 \rangle$

16-4 Rotations

Rotate the figure with the given vertices about the origin using the given angle of rotation.

10. $A(1, 0)$, $B(4, 1)$, $C(3, 2)$; 180°

11. $R(-2, 0)$, $S(-2, 4)$, $T(-3, 4)$, $U(-3, 0)$; 90°

Rotate the figure with the given vertices about the origin using the given angle of rotation.

12. $A(1, 3)$, $B(4, 1)$, $C(4, 4)$; 90°

13. $A(1, 3)$, $B(4, 1)$, $C(4, 4)$; 180°

Selected Response

1. A designer used the translation $(x, y) \rightarrow (x + 3, y - 3)$ to transform a triangular-shaped pin *ABC*. Find the coordinates and draw the image of △*ABC*. Which point is a vertex of the image?

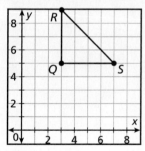

Ⓐ (−4, 4)

Ⓑ (−5, 1)

Ⓒ (1, 1)

Ⓓ (1, −1)

2. △*QRS* has vertices at *Q*(3, 5), *R*(3, 9), and *S*(7, 5). Which of these points is a vertex of the image of △*QRS* after the translation $(x, y) \rightarrow (x - 7, y - 6)$?

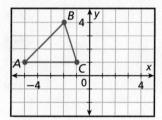

Ⓕ (−4, 3)   Ⓗ (4, 1)

Ⓖ (0, 0)   Ⓙ (4, −3)

3. △*ABC* is reflected across the *x*-axis. Then its image is rotated 180° about the origin. What are the coordinates of the image of point *B* after the reflection?

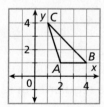

Ⓐ (−4, −1)   Ⓒ (1, −4)

Ⓑ (−1, 4)   Ⓓ (4, −1)

4. What is the image of the following figure after rotating it clockwise by 90°?

Ⓕ

Ⓖ

Ⓗ

Ⓙ

Mini-Task

5. The picture below shows half of a stenciled design. The full design should resemble a sun. Name two transformations that can be performed on the image so that the image and its preimage form a complete picture. Be as specific as possible, referring to *L* and *P*.

17 Combined Transformations and Symmetry

COMMON
CORE GPS

Contents

MCC9-12.G.CO.5

MCC9-12.G.CO.3

MCC9-12.G.CO.5

The Common Core Georgia Performance Standards for Mathematical Practice describe varieties of expertise that all students should seek to develop. Opportunities to develop these practices are integrated throughout this program.

1 Make sense of problems and persevere in solving them.

2 Reason abstractly and quantitatively.

3 Construct viable arguments and critique the reasoning of others.

4 Model with mathematics.

5 Use appropriate tools strategically.

6 Attend to precision.

7 Look for and make use of structure.

8 Look for and express regularity in repeated reasoning.

Unpacking the Standards

Understanding the standards and the vocabulary terms in the standards will help you know exactly what you are expected to learn in this chapter.

 MCC9-12.G.CO.3

Given a rectangle, parallelogram, trapezoid, or regular polygon, describe the rotations and reflections that carry it onto itself.

Key Vocabulary

rectangle (rectángulo)
A quadrilateral with four right angles.

parallelogram (paralelogramo)
A quadrilateral with two pairs of parallel sides.

trapezoid (trapecio)
A quadrilateral with exactly one pair of parallel sides.

regular polygon (polígono regular)
A polygon that is both equilateral and equiangular.

What It Means For You

The rotations and reflections that carry a figure onto itself determine what kind of symmetry, if any, that the figure has. Reflections determine line symmetry, and rotations determine rotational symmetry.

EXAMPLE   **Line symmetry and rotational symmetry**

 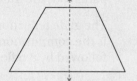

Parallelogram:

no line symmetry

180° rotational symmetry

Isosceles Trapezoid:

1 line of symmetry

no rotational symmetry

Square:

4 lines of symmetry

90° rotational symmetry

Compositions of Transformations

 Essential Question: How can you identify the effect of a composition of transformations on a geometric figure?

Objectives
Apply theorems about isometries.

Identify and draw compositions of transformations, such as glide reflections.

Vocabulary
composition of
  transformations
glide reflection

Why learn this?

Compositions of transformations can be used to describe chess moves. (See Exercise 11.)

A **composition of transformations** is one transformation followed by another. For example, a **glide reflection** is the composition of a translation and a reflection across a line parallel to the translation vector.

The glide reflection that maps $\triangle JKL$ to $\triangle J'K'L'$ is the composition of a translation along $\vec{v}$ followed by a reflection across line ℓ.

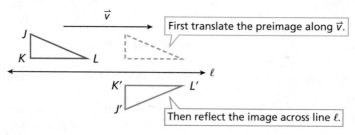

First translate the preimage along $\vec{v}$.

Then reflect the image across line ℓ.

The image after each transformation is congruent to the previous image. By the Transitive Property of Congruence, the final image is congruent to the preimage. This leads to the following theorem.

 Know it! *Note*

Theorem 17-1-1

A composition of two isometries is an isometry.

COMMON CORE GPS **EXAMPLE** 1
MCC9-12.G.CO.5

Drawing Compositions of Isometries

Draw the result of the composition of isometries.

A Reflect $\triangle ABC$ across line ℓ and then translate it along $\vec{v}$.

 **my.hrw.com**

Online Video Tutor

Step 1 Draw $\triangle A'B'C'$, the reflection image of $\triangle ABC$.

Step 2 Translate $\triangle A'B'C'$ along $\vec{v}$ to find the final image, $\triangle A''B''C''$.

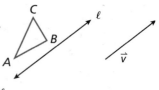

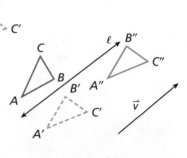

B $\triangle RST$ has vertices $R(1, 2)$, $S(1, 4)$, and $T(-3, 4)$. Rotate $\triangle RST$ 90° about the origin and then reflect it across the y-axis.

Step 1 The rotation image of (x, y) is $(-y, x)$.
$R(1, 2) \rightarrow R'(-2, 1)$, $S(1, 4) \rightarrow S'(-4, 1)$, and $T(-3, 4) \rightarrow T'(-4, -3)$.

Step 2 The reflection image of (x, y) is $(-x, y)$.
$R'(-2, 1) \rightarrow R''(2, 1)$, $S'(-4, 1) \rightarrow S''(4, 1)$, and $T'(-4, -3) \rightarrow T''(4, -3)$.

Step 3 Graph the preimage and images.

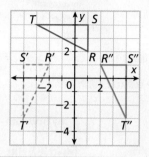

 1. $\triangle JKL$ has vertices $J(1, -2)$, $K(4, -2)$, and $L(3, 0)$. Reflect $\triangle JKL$ across the x-axis and then rotate it 180° about the origin.

 **Theorem 17-1-2**

The composition of two reflections across two parallel lines is equivalent to a translation.

- The translation vector is perpendicular to the lines.
- The length of the translation vector is twice the distance between the lines.

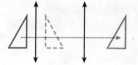

The composition of two reflections across two intersecting lines is equivalent to a rotation.

- The center of rotation is the intersection of the lines.
- The angle of rotation is twice the measure of the angle formed by the lines.

COMMON CORE GPS MCC9-12.G.CO.5

EXAMPLE 2

Art Application

 my.hrw.com

Online Video Tutor

Tabitha is creating a design for an art project. She reflects a figure across line ℓ and then reflects the image across line m. Describe a single transformation that moves the figure from its starting position to its final position.

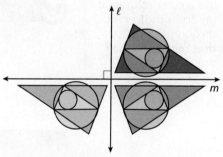

By Theorem 17-1-2, the composition of two reflections across intersecting lines is equivalent to a rotation about the point of intersection. Since the lines are perpendicular, they form a 90° angle. By Theorem 17-1-2, the angle of rotation is $2 \cdot 90° = 180°$.

 2. What if...? Suppose Tabitha reflects the figure across line n and then the image across line p. Describe a single transformation that is equivalent to the two reflections.

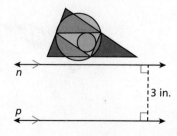

Theorem 17-1-3

Any translation or rotation is equivalent to a composition of two reflections.

Describing Transformations in Terms of Reflections

Copy each figure and draw two lines of reflection that produce an equivalent transformation.

my.hrw.com

Online Video Tutor

A translation: △ABC → △A'B'C'

Step 1 Draw $\overline{AA'}$ and locate the midpoint M of $\overline{AA'}$.

Step 2 Draw the perpendicular bisectors of $\overline{AM}$ and $\overline{A'M}$.

Remember!

To draw the perpendicular bisector of a segment, use a ruler to locate the midpoint, and then use a right angle to draw a perpendicular line. To draw the angle bisector of an angle, use a protractor to find the measure of the angle and then use a ruler to draw a ray from the vertex through the point that represents half the measure.

B rotation with center P: △DEF → △D'E'F'

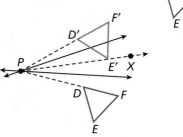

Step 1 Draw ∠DPD'. Draw the angle bisector $\overrightarrow{PX}$.

Step 2 Draw the bisectors of ∠DPX and ∠D'PX.

CHECK IT OUT!

3. Copy the figure showing the translation that maps $LMNP → L'M'N'P'$. Draw the lines of reflection that produce an equivalent transformation.

THINK AND DISCUSS

1. Which theorem explains why the image of a rectangle that is translated and then rotated is congruent to the preimage?

2. Point A' is a glide reflection of point A along $\vec{v}$ and across line ℓ. What is the relationship between $\vec{v}$ and ℓ? Explain the steps you would use to draw a glide reflection.

3. GET ORGANIZED Copy and complete the graphic organizer. In each box, describe an equivalent transformation and sketch an example.

Know it!
.Note

Composition of Two Reflections

Across parallel lines   Across intersecting lines

17-1 Exercises

GUIDED PRACTICE

1. **Vocabulary** Explain the steps you would use to draw a *glide reflection*.

SEE EXAMPLE 1 **Draw the result of each composition of isometries.**

2. Translate △DEF along $\vec{u}$ and then reflect it across line ℓ.

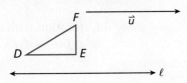

3. Reflect rectangle PQRS across line m and then translate it along $\vec{v}$.

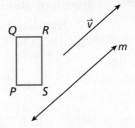

4. △ABC has vertices A(1, −1), B(4, −1), and C(3, 2). Reflect △ABC across the y-axis and then translate it along the vector ⟨0, −2⟩.

SEE EXAMPLE 2

5. **Sports** To create the opening graphics for a televised football game, an animator reflects a picture of a football helmet across line ℓ. She then reflects its image across line m, which intersects line ℓ at a 50° angle. Describe a single transformation that moves the helmet from its starting position to its final position.

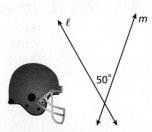

SEE EXAMPLE 3 **Copy each figure and draw two lines of reflection that produce an equivalent transformation.**

6. translation:
△EFG → △E'F'G'

7. rotation with center P:
△ABC → △A'B'C'

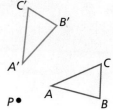

PRACTICE AND PROBLEM SOLVING

Independent Practice	
For Exercises	See Example
8–10	1
11	2
12–13	3

Draw the result of each composition of isometries.

8. Translate △RST along $\vec{u}$ and then translate it along $\vec{v}$.

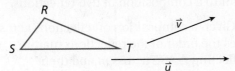

9. Rotate △ABC 90° about point P and then reflect it across line ℓ.

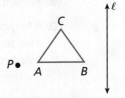

10. △GHJ has vertices G(1, −1), H(3, 1), and J(3, −2). Reflect △GHJ across the line y = x and then reflect it across the x-axis.

11. **Games** In chess, a knight moves in the shape of the letter L. The piece moves two spaces horizontally or vertically. Then it turns 90° in either direction and moves one more space.

   a. Describe a knight's move as a composition of transformations.

   b. Copy the chessboard with the knight. Label all the positions the knight can reach in one move.

   c. Label all the positions the knight can reach in two moves.

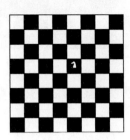

Copy each figure and draw two lines of reflection that produce an equivalent transformation.

12. translation:
   $ABCD \rightarrow A'B'C'D'$

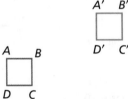

13. rotation with center Q:
   $\triangle JKL \rightarrow \triangle J'K'L'$

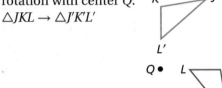

H.O.T. 14. ///**ERROR ANALYSIS**/// The segment with endpoints $A(4, 2)$ and $B(2, 1)$ is reflected across the y-axis. The image is reflected across the x-axis. What transformation is equivalent to the composition of these two reflections? Which solution is incorrect? Explain the error.

A
The image of $\overline{AB}$ reflected across the y-axis has endpoints $(-2, 1)$ and $(-4, 2)$. The image of $\overline{A'B'}$ reflected across the x-axis has endpoints $(-2, -1)$ and $(-4, -2)$. The reflections are equivalent to a translation along the vector $\langle -6, -3 \rangle$.

B
The angle between the x-axis and the y-axis is 90°. Therefore the composition of the two reflections is equivalent to a rotation about the origin by an angle measure of twice 90°, or 180°.

15. Equilateral $\triangle ABC$ is reflected across $\overline{AB}$. Then its image is translated along $\overrightarrow{BC}$. Copy $\triangle ABC$ and draw its final image.

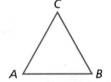

Tell whether each statement is sometimes, always, or never true.

16. The composition of two reflections is equivalent to a rotation.

17. An isometry changes the size of a figure.

18. The composition of two isometries is an isometry.

19. A rotation is equivalent to a composition of two reflections.

H.O.T. 20. Critical Thinking Given a composition of reflections across two parallel lines, does the order of the reflections matter? For example, does reflecting $\triangle ABC$ across m and then its image across n give the same result as reflecting $\triangle ABC$ across n and then its image across m? Explain.

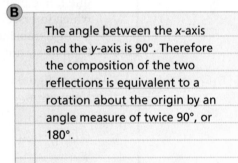

21. **Write About It** Under a glide reflection, $\triangle RST \rightarrow \triangle R'S'T'$. The vertices of $\triangle RST$ are $R(-3, -2)$, $S(-1, -2)$, and $T(-1, 0)$. The vertices of $\triangle R'S'T'$ are $R'(2, 2)$, $S'(4, 2)$, and $T'(4, 0)$. Describe the reflection and translation that make up the glide reflection.

Real-World Connections

22. The figure shows one hole of a miniature golf course where *T* is the tee and *H* is the hole.

  a. Yuriko makes a hole in one as shown by the red arrows. Write the ball's path as a composition of translations.

  b. Find a different way to make a hole in one, and write the ball's path as a composition of translations.

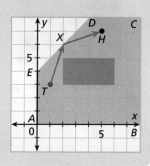

TEST PREP

23. △*ABC* is reflected across the *y*-axis. Then its image is rotated 90° about the origin. What are the coordinates of the final image of point *A* under this composition of transformations?

  Ⓐ $(-1, -2)$ Ⓑ $(-2, 1)$ Ⓒ $(1, 2)$ Ⓓ $(-2, -1)$

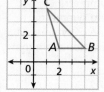

24. Which composition of transformations maps △*ABC* into the fourth quadrant?

  Ⓕ Reflect across the *x*-axis and then reflect across the *y*-axis.

  Ⓖ Rotate about the origin by 180° and then reflect across the *y*-axis.

  Ⓗ Translate along the vector $\langle -5, 0 \rangle$ and then rotate about the origin by 90°.

  Ⓙ Rotate about the origin by 90° and then translate along the vector $\langle 1, -2 \rangle$.

25. Which is equivalent to the composition of two translations?

  Ⓐ Reflection   Ⓑ Rotation   Ⓒ Translation   Ⓓ Glide reflection

CHALLENGE AND EXTEND

26. The point $A(3, 1)$ is rotated 90° about the point $P(-1, 2)$ and then reflected across the line $y = 5$. Find the coordinates of the image A'.

27. For any two congruent figures in a plane, one can be transformed to the other by a composition of no more than three reflections. Copy the figure. Show how to find a composition of three reflections that maps △*MNP* to △*M'N'P'*.

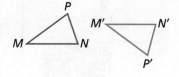

28. A figure in the coordinate plane is reflected across the line $y = x + 1$ and then across the line $y = x + 3$. Find a translation vector that is equivalent to the composition of the reflections. Write the vector in component form.

FOCUS ON MATHEMATICAL PRACTICES

H.O.T. 29. Communication Describe the two transformations that make up a glide reflection.

H.O.T. 30. Problem Solving A figure is reflected across the *x*-axis and the resulting image is then reflected across the *y*-axis. Describe a single transformation that is equivalent to the composition of these two reflections. Explain.

H.O.T. 31. Draw Conclusions A figure is reflected across the line $x = 2$ and the resulting image is then reflected across the line $x = 5$. Where is the image in comparison to the preimage? How do you know?

17-2 Symmetry

Essential Question: How can you identify and describe symmetry in a geometric figure?

Objective
Identify and describe symmetry in geometric figures.

Vocabulary
symmetry
line symmetry
line of symmetry
rotational symmetry

Who uses this?
Marine biologists use symmetry to classify diatoms.

Diatoms are microscopic algae that are found in aquatic environments. Scientists use a system that was developed in the 1970s to classify diatoms based on their *symmetry*.

A figure has **symmetry** if there is a transformation of the figure such that the image coincides with the preimage.

Line Symmetry

A figure has **line symmetry** (or reflection symmetry) if it can be reflected across a line so that the image coincides with the preimage. The **line of symmetry** (also called the axis of symmetry) divides the figure into two congruent halves.

COMMON CORE GPS | **EXAMPLE** | **1**
MCC9-12.G.CO.3

my.hrw.com

Online Video Tutor

Identifying Line Symmetry

Tell whether each figure has line symmetry. If so, copy the shape and draw all lines of symmetry.

A    yes; one line of symmetry

B   no line symmetry

C    yes; five lines of symmetry

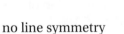

 Tell whether each figure has line symmetry. If so, copy the shape and draw all lines of symmetry.

1a.   1b. **B**   1c.

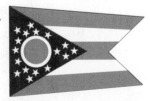

---

484 *Module 17 Combined Transformations and Symmetry*

Rotational Symmetry

A figure has **rotational symmetry** (or *radial symmetry*) if it can be rotated about a point by an angle greater than 0° and less than 360° so that the image coincides with the preimage.

The *angle of rotational symmetry* is the smallest angle through which a figure can be rotated to coincide with itself. The number of times the figure coincides with itself as it rotates through 360° is called the *order* of the rotational symmetry.

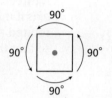

Angle of rotational symmetry: 90° Order: 4

COMMON CORE GPS
MCC9-12.G.CO.3

EXAMPLE 2 · Identifying Rotational Symmetry

my.hrw.com

Online Video Tutor

Tell whether each figure has rotational symmetry. If so, give the angle of rotational symmetry and the order of the symmetry.

A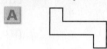

yes; 180°; order: 2

B

no rotational symmetry

C

yes; 60°; order: 6

CHECK IT OUT! Tell whether each figure has rotational symmetry. If so, give the angle of rotational symmetry and the order of the symmetry.

2a.

2b.

2c.

COMMON CORE GPS
MCC9-12.G.CO.3

EXAMPLE 3 · Biology Application

my.hrw.com

Online Video Tutor

Describe the symmetry of each diatom. Copy the shape and draw any lines of symmetry. If there is rotational symmetry, give the angle and order.

A

line symmetry and rotational symmetry; angle of rotational symmetry: 180°; order: 2

B

line symmetry and rotational symmetry; angle of rotational symmetry: 120°; order: 3

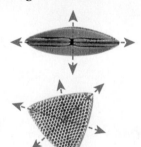

CHECK IT OUT! Describe the symmetry of each diatom. Copy the shape and draw any lines of symmetry. If there is rotational symmetry, give the angle and order.

3a.

3b.

(c-purple diatoms) Alfred Pasieka/Photo Researchers, Inc.; (bl) John Burbidge/Photo Researchers, Inc.; (bc) Eric Grave/Photo Researchers, Inc.; (br) John Burbidge/Photo Researchers, Inc.

A three-dimensional figure has *plane symmetry* if a plane can divide the figure into two congruent reflected halves.

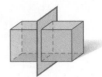

Plane symmetry

A three-dimensional figure has *symmetry about an axis* if there is a line about which the figure can be rotated (by an angle greater than 0° and less than 360°) so that the image coincides with the preimage.

Symmetry about an axis

EXAMPLE 4
Ext. of MCC9-12.CO.3

my.hrw.com

Online Video Tutor

Identifying Symmetry in Three Dimensions

Tell whether each figure has plane symmetry, symmetry about an axis, or neither.

A trapezoidal prism

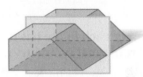

plane symmetry

B equilateral triangular prism

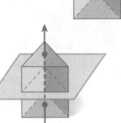

plane symmetry and symmetry about an axis

CHECK IT OUT! Tell whether each figure has plane symmetry, symmetry about an axis, or no symmetry.

4a. cone

4b. pyramid

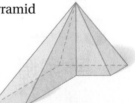

MCC.MP.6

MATHEMATICAL PRACTICES

THINK AND DISCUSS

1. Explain how you could use scissors and paper to cut out a shape that has line symmetry.

2. Describe how you can find the angle of rotational symmetry for a regular polygon with *n* sides.

3. GET ORGANIZED Copy and complete the graphic organizer. In each region, draw a figure with the given type of symmetry.

Know it! Note

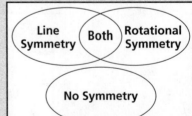
Line Symmetry — Both — Rotational Symmetry

No Symmetry

my.hrw.com
Homework Help

GUIDED PRACTICE

Vocabulary Apply the vocabulary from this lesson to answer each question.

1. Describe the *line of symmetry* of an isosceles triangle.

2. The capital letter T has ___?___ . (*line symmetry* or *rotational symmetry*)

SEE EXAMPLE 1 — Tell whether each figure has line symmetry. If so, copy the shape and draw all lines of symmetry.

3.

4.

5.

SEE EXAMPLE 2 — Tell whether each figure has rotational symmetry. If so, give the angle of rotational symmetry and the order of the symmetry.

6.

7.

8.

SEE EXAMPLE 3 — 9. **Architecture** The Pentagon in Alexandria, Virginia, is the world's largest office building. Copy the shape of the building and draw all lines of symmetry. Give the angle and order of rotational symmetry.

SEE EXAMPLE 4 — Tell whether each figure has plane symmetry, symmetry about an axis, or neither.

10. prism

11. cylinder

12. rectangular prism

PRACTICE AND PROBLEM SOLVING

Independent Practice	
For Exercises	See Example
13–15	1
16–18	2
19	3
20–22	4

Tell whether each figure has line symmetry. If so, copy the shape and draw all lines of symmetry.

13.

14.

15.

Tell whether each figure has rotational symmetry. If so, give the angle of rotational symmetry and the order of the symmetry.

16.

17.

18.

19. Art *Op art* is a style of art that uses optical effects to create an impression of movement in a painting or sculpture. The painting at right, *Vega-Tek*, by Victor Vasarely, is an example of op art. Sketch the shape in the painting and draw any lines of symmetry. If there is rotational symmetry, give the angle and order.

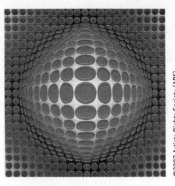

©2007 Artists Rights Society (ARS), New York/ADAGP, Paris

Tell whether each figure has plane symmetry, symmetry about an axis, or neither.

20. sphere

21. triangular pyramid

22. torus

Draw a triangle with the following number of lines of symmetry. Then classify the triangle.

23. exactly one line of symmetry

24. three lines of symmetry

25. no lines of symmetry

Data Analysis The graph shown, called the *standard normal curve*, is used in statistical analysis. The area under the curve is 1 square unit. There is a vertical line of symmetry at $x = 0$. The areas of the shaded regions are indicated on the graph.

26. Find the area under the curve for $x > 0$.

27. Find the area under the curve for $x > 2$.

28. If a point under the curve is selected at random, what is the probability that the *x*-value of the point will be between -1 and 1?

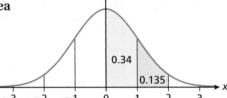

Tell whether the figure with the given vertices has line symmetry and/or rotational symmetry. Give the angle and order if there is rotational symmetry. Draw the figure and any lines of symmetry.

29. $A(-2, 2)$, $B(2, 2)$, $C(1, -2)$, $D(-1, -2)$

30. $R(-3, 3)$, $S(3, 3)$, $T(3, -3)$, $U(-3, -3)$

31. $J(4, 4)$, $K(-2, 2)$, $L(2, -2)$

32. $A(3, 1)$, $B(0, 2)$, $C(-3, 1)$, $D(-3, -1)$, $E(0, -2)$, $F(3, -1)$

33. Art The Chokwe people of Angola are known for their traditional sand designs. These complex drawings are traced out to illustrate stories that are told at evening gatherings. Classify the symmetry of the Chokwe design shown.

(tr), (c) ARS, NY/Art Resource, NY

Graph each function. Tell whether the graph has line symmetry and/or rotational symmetry. If there is rotational symmetry, give the angle and order. Write the equations of any lines of symmetry.

34. $y = x^2$

35. $y = (x - 2)^2$

36. $y = x^3$

Real-World Connections

37. This woodcut, entitled *Circle Limit III*, was made by Dutch artist M. C. Escher.

   a. Does the woodcut have line symmetry? If so, describe the lines of symmetry. If not, explain why not.

   b. Does the woodcut have rotational symmetry? If so, give the angle and order of the symmetry. If not, explain why not.

   c. Does your answer to part **b** change if color is not taken into account? Explain.

Classify the quadrilateral that meets the given conditions. First make a conjecture and then verify your conjecture by drawing a figure.

38. two lines of symmetry perpendicular to the sides and order-2 rotational symmetry

39. no line symmetry and order-2 rotational symmetry

40. two lines of symmetry through opposite vertices and order-2 rotational symmetry

41. four lines of symmetry and order-4 rotational symmetry

42. one line of symmetry through a pair of opposite vertices and no rotational symmetry

43. Physics High-speed photography makes it possible to analyze the physics behind a water splash. When a drop lands in a bowl of liquid, the splash forms a crown of evenly spaced points. What is the angle of rotational symmetry for a crown with 24 points?

44. Critical Thinking What can you conclude about a rectangle that has four lines of symmetry? Explain.

45. Geography The Isle of Man is an island in the Irish Sea. The island's symbol is a *triskelion* that consists of three running legs radiating from the center. Describe the symmetry of the triskelion.

46. Critical Thinking Draw several examples of figures that have two perpendicular lines of symmetry. What other type of symmetry do these figures have? Make a conjecture based on your observation.

Each figure shows part of a shape with a center of rotation and a given rotational symmetry. Copy and complete each figure.

47. order 4

48. order 6

49. order 2

50. Write About It Explain the connection between the angle of rotational symmetry and the order of the rotational symmetry. That is, if you know one of these, explain how you can find the other.

TEST PREP

51. What is the order of rotational symmetry for the hexagon shown?

    (A) 2   (B) 3   (C) 4   (D) 6

52. Which of these figures has exactly four lines of symmetry?

    (F) Regular octagon   (H) Isosceles triangle

    (G) Equilateral triangle   (J) Square

53. Consider the graphs of the following equations. Which graph has the y-axis as a line of symmetry?

    (A) $y = (x - 3)^2$ (B) $y = x^3$ (C) $y = x^2 - 3$ (D) $y = |x + 3|$

54. Donnell designed a garden plot that has rotational symmetry, but not line symmetry. Which of these could be the shape of the plot?

    (F)   (G)   (H)   (J)

CHALLENGE AND EXTEND

55. A regular polygon has an angle of rotational symmetry of 5°. How many sides does the polygon have?

H.O.T. 56. A polygon with n sides is called an n-gon. How many lines of symmetry does a regular n-gon have if n is even? if n is odd? Explain your reasoning.

Give the number of axes of symmetry for each regular solid. Describe all axes of symmetry.

57. cube   **58.** tetrahedron   **59.** octahedron

FOCUS ON MATHEMATICAL PRACTICES

H.O.T. 60. Make a Conjecture Describe any lines of symmetry in this design for the state flag of Colorado. What changes could be made to this design in order for it to have more types of symmetry?

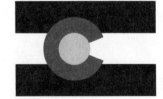

H.O.T. 61. Analysis Give the angle of rotational symmetry and the order of the symmetry for this letter. How many lines of symmetry does the letter have?

H.O.T. 62. Analysis Tell whether the figure with vertices at $(-1, -1)$, $(-4, -1)$, $(-4, -4)$, $(-1, -4)$ has line symmetry, rotational symmetry, or both, and describe any symmetry.

H.O.T. 63. Modeling Describe any symmetry of the graph of $y = |x|$.

H.O.T. 64. Make a Conjecture A certain figure has an order of rotational symmetry of 9. What would you predict for the angle of rotational symmetry? Explain.

H.O.T. 65. Properties A bass drum has a cylindrical shape, as shown. Does it have plane symmetry, symmetry about an axis, both, or neither?

17-3 Tessellations

Essential Question: How can you use transformations to draw tessellations?

Objectives
Use transformations to draw tessellations.

Identify regular and semiregular tessellations and figures that will tessellate.

Vocabulary
translation symmetry
frieze pattern
glide reflection symmetry
tessellation
regular tessellation
semiregular tessellation

Who uses this?
Repeating patterns play an important role in traditional Native American art.

A pattern has **translation symmetry** if it can be translated along a vector so that the image coincides with the preimage. A **frieze pattern** is a pattern that has translation symmetry along a line.

Both of the frieze patterns shown below have translation symmetry. The pattern on the right also has *glide reflection symmetry*. A pattern with **glide reflection symmetry** coincides with its image after a glide reflection.

COMMON CORE GPS

EXAMPLE 1 MCC9-12.G.CO.5

Art Application

Identify the symmetry in each frieze pattern.

my.hrw.com

Online Video Tutor

A

translation symmetry and glide reflection symmetry

B

translation symmetry

 CHECK IT OUT!

Identify the symmetry in each frieze pattern.

1a.    1b.

A **tessellation**, or *tiling*, is a repeating pattern that completely covers a plane with no gaps or overlaps. The measures of the angles that meet at each vertex must add up to 360°.

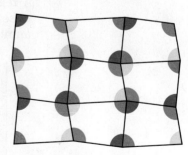

In the tessellation shown, each angle of the quadrilateral occurs once at each vertex. Because the angle measures of any quadrilateral add to 360°, any quadrilateral can be used to tessellate the plane. Four copies of the quadrilateral meet at each vertex.

The angle measures of any triangle add up to 180°. This means that any triangle can be used to tessellate a plane. Six copies of the triangle meet at each vertex, as shown.

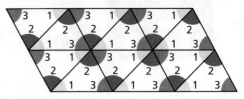

$$m\angle 1 + m\angle 2 + m\angle 3 = 180°$$
$$m\angle 1 + m\angle 2 + m\angle 3 + m\angle 1 + m\angle 2 + m\angle 3 = 360°$$

EXAMPLE 2 Using Transformations to Create Tessellations

Copy the given figure and use it to create a tessellation.

A

Step 1 Rotate the triangle 180° about the midpoint of one side.

Step 2 Translate the resulting pair of triangles to make a row of triangles.

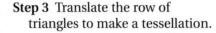

Step 3 Translate the row of triangles to make a tessellation.

B

Step 1 Rotate the quadrilateral 180° about the midpoint of one side.

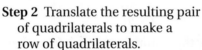

Step 2 Translate the resulting pair of quadrilaterals to make a row of quadrilaterals.

Step 3 Translate the row of quadrilaterals to make a tessellation.

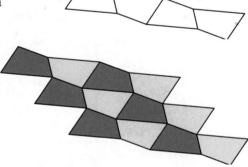

CHECK IT OUT!

2. Copy the given figure and use it to create a tessellation.

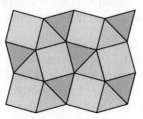

A **regular tessellation** is formed by congruent regular polygons. A **semiregular tessellation** is formed by two or more different regular polygons, with the same number of each polygon occurring in the same order at every vertex.

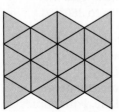

Regular tessellation   Semiregular tessellation

Every vertex has two squares and three triangles in this order: square, triangle, square, triangle, triangle.

Student to Student

Ryan Gray
Sunset High School

Tessellations

When I need to decide if given figures can be used to tessellate a plane, I look at angle measures. To form a regular tessellation, the angle measures of a regular polygon must be a divisor of 360°. To form a semiregular tessellation, the angle measures around a vertex must add up to 360°.

For example, regular octagons and equilateral triangles cannot be used to make a semiregular tessellation because no combination of 135° and 60° adds up to exactly 360°.

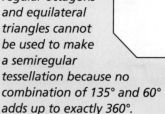

COMMON CORE GPS
CC.MP.7

EXAMPLE 3

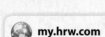
my.hrw.com

Online Video Tutor

Classifying Tessellations

Classify each tessellation as regular, semiregular, or neither.

A

Two regular octagons and one square meet at each vertex. The tessellation is semiregular.

B

Only squares are used. The tessellation is regular.

C

Irregular hexagons are used in the tessellation. It is neither regular nor semiregular.

 Classify each tessellation as regular, semiregular, or neither.

3a.   **3b.**   **3c.**

COMMON CORE GPS
CC.MP.7

EXAMPLE 4

my.hrw.com

Online Video Tutor

Determining Whether Polygons Will Tessellate

Determine whether the given regular polygon(s) can be used to form a tessellation. If so, draw the tessellation.

A

No; each angle of the pentagon measures 108°, and 108 is not a divisor of 360.

B

Yes; two octagons and one square meet at each vertex.
135° + 135° + 90° = 360°

 Determine whether the given regular polygon(s) can be used to form a tessellation. If so, draw the tessellation.

4a.   **4b.**

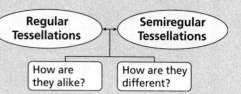
THINK AND DISCUSS

1. Explain how you can identify a frieze pattern that has glide reflection symmetry.

2. Is it possible to tessellate a plane using circles? Why or why not?

3. **GET ORGANIZED** Copy and complete the graphic organizer.

17-3 Exercises

GUIDED PRACTICE

Vocabulary Apply the vocabulary from this lesson to answer each question.

1. Sketch a pattern that has *glide reflection symmetry*.

2. Describe a real-world example of a *regular tessellation*.

SEE EXAMPLE 1

Transportation The tread of a tire is the part that makes contact with the ground. Various tread patterns help improve traction and increase durability. Identify the symmetry in each tread pattern.

3. **4.** **5.**

SEE EXAMPLE 2

Copy the given figure and use it to create a tessellation.

6. **7.** **8.**

SEE EXAMPLE 3

Classify each tessellation as regular, semiregular, or neither.

9. **10.** **11.**

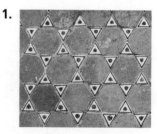

SEE EXAMPLE 4

Determine whether the given regular polygon(s) can be used to form a tessellation. If so, draw the tessellation.

12. **13.** **14.**

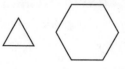
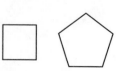

PRACTICE AND PROBLEM SOLVING

Independent Practice

For Exercises	See Example
15–17	1
18–20	2
21–23	3
24–26	4

my.hrw.com

Online Extra Practice

Interior Decorating Identify the symmetry in each wallpaper border.

15.

16.

17.

Copy the given figure and use it to create a tessellation.

18.

19.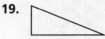

20.

Classify each tessellation as regular, semiregular, or neither.

21.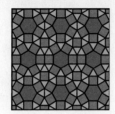

22.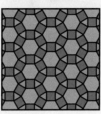

23.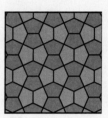

Determine whether the given regular polygon(s) can be used to form a tessellation. If so, draw the tessellation.

24.

25.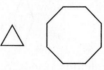

26.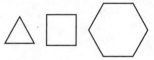

27. Physics A truck moving down a road creates whirling pockets of air called a *vortex train*. Use the figure to classify the symmetry of a vortex train.

Identify all of the types of symmetry (translation, glide reflection, and/or rotation) in each tessellation.

28.

29.

30.

Tell whether each statement is sometimes, always, or never true.

31. A triangle can be used to tessellate a plane.

32. A frieze pattern has glide reflection symmetry.

33. The angles at a vertex of a tessellation add up to 360°.

34. It is possible to use a regular pentagon to make a regular tessellation.

35. A semiregular tessellation includes scalene triangles.

36. Many of the patterns in M. C. Escher's works are based on simple tessellations. For example, the pattern at right is based on a tessellation of equilateral triangles. Identify the figure upon which each pattern is based.

a.

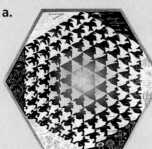

b.

Use the given figure to draw a frieze pattern with the given symmetry.

37. translation symmetry

38. glide reflection symmetry

39. translation symmetry

40. glide reflection symmetry

41. Optics A kaleidoscope is formed by three mirrors joined to form the lateral surface of a triangular prism. Copy the triangular faces and reflect it over each side. Repeat to form a tessellation. Describe the symmetry of the tessellation.

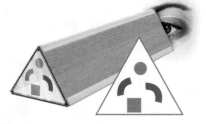

H.O.T. **42. Critical Thinking** The pattern on a soccer ball is a tessellation of a sphere using regular hexagons and regular pentagons. Can these two shapes be used to tessellate a plane? Explain your reasoning.

43. Chemistry A *polymer* is a substance made of repeating chemical units or molecules. The *repeat unit* is the smallest structure that can be repeated to create the chain. Draw the repeat unit for polypropylene, the polymer shown below.

$$- CH_2 - CH - CH_2 - CH - CH_2 - CH - CH_2 - CH -$$
$$\qquad\ \ \ | \qquad\qquad\quad | \qquad\qquad\quad | \qquad\qquad\quad |$$
$$\qquad\ \ CH_3 \qquad\quad\ CH_3 \qquad\quad\ CH_3 \qquad\quad\ CH_3$$

44. The *dual* of a tessellation is formed by connecting the centers of adjacent polygons with segments. Copy or trace the semiregular tessellation shown and draw its dual. What type of polygon makes up the dual tessellation?

H.O.T. **45. Write About It** You can make a regular tessellation from an equilateral triangle, a square, or a regular hexagon. Explain why these are the only three regular tessellations that are possible.

46. Which frieze pattern has glide reflection symmetry?

Ⓐ

Ⓑ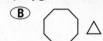

Ⓒ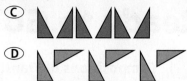

Ⓓ

47. Which shape CANNOT be used to make a regular tessellation?

Ⓕ Equilateral triangle   Ⓗ Regular pentagon

Ⓖ Square   Ⓙ Regular hexagon

48. Which pair of regular polygons can be used to make a semiregular tessellation?

Ⓐ    Ⓑ   Ⓒ   Ⓓ

CHALLENGE AND EXTEND

49. Some shapes can be used to tessellate a plane in more than one way. Three tessellations that use the same rectangle are shown. Draw a parallelogram and draw at least three tessellations using that parallelogram.

Determine whether each figure can be used to tessellate three-dimensional space.

50. **51.** **52.**

FOCUS ON MATHEMATICAL PRACTICES

H.O.T. 53. Reasoning Explain why the measures of the angles that meet at each vertex of a tessellation must add to 360°.

H.O.T. 54. Error Analysis Fred says this tiling is a tessellation. Hari says it is not. Who is correct? Explain.

H.O.T. 55. Problem Solving Can a non-isosceles trapezoid be used to tessellate a plane? Explain.

H.O.T. 56. Justify Can you form a regular tessellation using regular hexagons? Regular octagons? Justify your answers.

H.O.T. 57. Draw Conclusions Is this tiling a regular tessellation, a semiregular tessellation, or neither? Explain.

H.O.T. 58. Problem Solving Can a triangle with three different side lengths be used to tessellate a plane? If so, give a method. If not, explain why not.

Ready to Go On?

my.hrw.com
Assessment and Intervention

✓ 17-1 Compositions of Transformations

1. Draw the result of the following composition of transformations. Translate *GHJK* along $\vec{v}$, and then reflect it across line *m*.

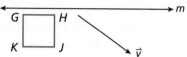

2. $\triangle ABC$ with vertices $A(1, 0)$, $B(1, 3)$, and $C(2, 3)$ is reflected across the *y*-axis, and then its image is reflected across the *x*-axis. Describe a single transformation that moves the triangle from its starting position to its final position.

✓ 17-2 Symmetry

Explain whether each figure has line symmetry. If so, copy the figure and draw all lines of symmetry.

3.

4.

5.

Explain whether each figure has rotational symmetry. If so, give the angle of rotational symmetry and the order of the symmetry.

6.

7.

8.

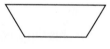...

✓ 17-3 Tessellations

Copy the given figure and use it to create a tessellation.

9.

10.

11.

...

Classify each tessellation as regular, semiregular, or neither.

12.

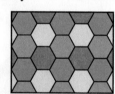

13.

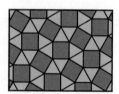

14.

15. Determine whether it is possible to tessellate a plane with regular octagons. If so, draw the tessellation. If not, explain why.

PARCC Assessment Readiness

Selected Response

1. Ann wants to create a design to decorate her Geometry binder. She draws a figure on a coordinate grid and reflects the figure across the *y*-axis. She then reflects the image across the *x*-axis. Describe a single transformation that moves the part of the design from its starting position to its final position.

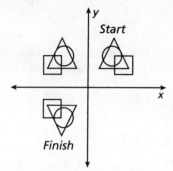

- Ⓐ rotation of 180° about the origin
- Ⓑ rotation of 90° about the origin
- Ⓒ translation along the line *y* = *x*
- Ⓓ reflection across the line *y* = *x*

2. Tell whether the figure has rotational symmetry. If so, give the angle of rotational symmetry and the order of the symmetry.

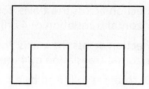

- Ⓕ The figure has no rotational symmetry.
- Ⓖ Yes, the figure has rotational symmetry. The angle of rotational symmetry is 180°, and the order of the symmetry is 2.
- Ⓗ Yes, the figure has rotational symmetry. The angle of rotational symmetry is 90°, and the order of the symmetry is 4.
- Ⓙ Yes, the figure has rotational symmetry. The angle of rotational symmetry is 45°, and the order of the symmetry is 8.

3. Identify the symmetry in the pattern. Assume that the pattern continues forever in both directions.

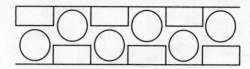

- Ⓐ Both translation symmetry and glide reflection symmetry
- Ⓑ Only translation symmetry
- Ⓒ Only glide reflection symmetry
- Ⓓ No symmetry

4. After a composition of transformations, the line segment from *A*(1, 4) to *B*(4, 2) maps to the line segment from *C*(−1, −2) to *D*(−4, −4). Which of the following describes the composition that is applied to $\overline{AB}$ to obtain $\overline{CD}$?

- Ⓕ Translate 5 units to the left and then reflect across the *y*-axis.
- Ⓖ Reflect across the *y*-axis and then reflect across the *x*-axis.
- Ⓗ Reflect across the *y*-axis and then translate 6 units down.
- Ⓙ Translate 6 units down and then reflect across the *x*-axis.

Mini-Task

5. Copy the given figure and use it to create a tessellation.

PARCC Assessment Readiness

Selected Response

1. The change in position from the solid figure to the dashed figure is best described as a _____.

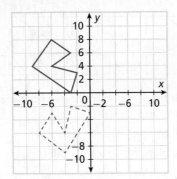

   (A) transmission

   (B) translation

   (C) rotation

   (D) reflection

2. The image of point A under a 90° rotation about the origin is $A'(10, -4)$. What are the coordinates of point A?

   (F) $(-10, -4)$

   (G) $(-10, 4)$

   (H) $(-4, -10)$

   (J) $(4, 10)$

3. Which are the angle of rotation and the order of rotational symmetry for the figure?

   (A) 90°; 2

   (B) 180°; 2

   (C) 90°; 4

   (D) 180°; 4

Use the graph for items 4–6.

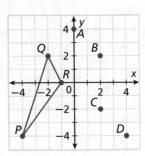

4. What are the coordinates of the image of point C under the same translation that maps point D to point B?

   (F) $(4, 4)$

   (G) $(0, 4)$

   (H) $(0, 8)$

   (J) $(4, -8)$

5. $\triangle PQR$ is rotated 180° about the origin. Which point is the image of point Q?

   (A) A **(C)** C

   (B) B **(D)** D

6. For which of the following combinations of transformations of $\triangle PQR$ would point A NOT be the image of point P?

   (F) Reflection across the x-axis, followed by a horizontal translation of 4 units

   (G) Reflection across the y-axis, followed by a horizontal translation of 4 units

   (H) 180° rotation followed by a horizontal translation of -4 units

   (J) Reflection across the line $x = -2$ followed by a vertical translation of 8 units

7. Which mapping represents three successive rotations of 90° about the origin?

   (A) $(x, y) \rightarrow (-x, -y)$

   (B) $(x, y) \rightarrow (x, -y)$

   (C) $(x, y) \rightarrow (-y, -x)$

   (D) $(x, y) \rightarrow (y, -x)$

8. Which regular polygon can be used with an equilateral triangle to tessellate a plane?

(F) Heptagon

(G) Octagon

(H) Nonagon

(J) Dodecagon

When problems involve geometric figures in the coordinate plane, it may be useful to describe properties of the figures algebraically. For example, you can use slope to verify that sides of a figure are parallel or perpendicular, or you can use the Distance Formula to find side lengths of the figure.

9. Which shows the image of △*EFG* after the translation $(x, y) \rightarrow (x - 6, y + 2)$?

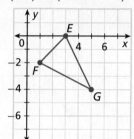

(A)

(B)

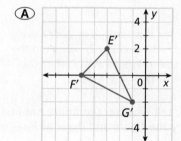

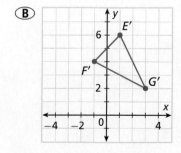

(C)

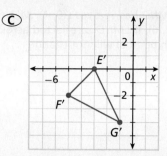

(D)

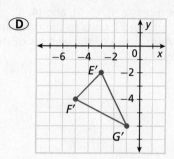

10. What are the coordinates of the image of the point (5, 5) when it is reflected across the line $y = 8$?

(F) (5, 13)

(G) (5, −3)

(H) (5, 11)

(J) (5, −5)

11. The point $G(6, 7)$ is rotated 90° about point $M(-9, -3)$ and then reflected across the line $y = 9$. What are the coordinates of the image *G'*?

(A) (37, 6)

(B) (−24, 11)

(C) (−7, 12)

(D) (−19, 6)

12. How many lines of symmetry does a regular hexagon have?

(F) 1

(G) 3

(H) 6

(J) 12

13. What is the *x*-coordinate of the image of the point $A(12, -7)$ after *A* is reflected across the *x*-axis?

(A) −12

(B) −7

(C) 7

(D) 12

14. Quadrilateral *LMNO* has vertices *L*(0, 4), *M*(3, 6), *N*(5, 4), and *O*(3, 0). If *LMNO* is reflected across the *x*-axis, which point(s) will not change location?

(F) *L* and *O*

(G) *L*

(H) *O*

(J) *L* and *N*

15. A triangle has vertices (0, 3), (0, 5), and (4, 5). The triangle is translated 2 units to the right and 2 units down. Which is one of the vertices of the translated triangle?

(A) (2, 3)

(B) (0, 1)

(C) (4, 2)

(D) (−2, 1)

16. Which of the following represents a reflection across the line $y = 0$?

(F) $(x, y) \rightarrow (-x, y)$

(G) $(x, y) \rightarrow (x, -y)$

(H) $(x, y) \rightarrow (-x, -y)$

(J) $(x, y) \rightarrow (y, x)$

17. What would be the coordinates of *M*(4, 3) after a rotation of 90° about the origin?

(A) (0, 5)

(B) (−2, 6)

(C) (−3, 4)

(D) (−1, 0)

18. A triangle has vertices *A*(1, 1), *B*(4, 1), and *C*(4, 3). After a transformation, the image has vertices *A'*(−1, 1), *B'*(−4, 1), and *C'*(−4, 3). Which of the following describes the transformation?

(F) A rotation of 180° about the origin

(G) A reflection across the *x*-axis

(H) A reflection across the *y*-axis

(J) A translation 2 units to the left

19. The vertices of triangle *JKL* are *J*(−3, −1), *K*(−1, −3), and *L*(−4, −4). Triangle *JKL* is reflected across the *x*-axis. What are the coordinates of *K'*?

(A) (1, −3)

(B) (−1, 3)

(C) (−1, −3)

(D) (1, 3)

20. Triangle *PQR* has vertices at *P*(2, 3), *Q*(3, 5), and *R*(5, 1). The triangle will be translated 4 units up. What will be the coordinates of point *R'*?

(F) (2, 7)

(G) (7, 5)

(H) (9, 5)

(J) (5, 5)

Mini-Tasks

21. △*ABC* is reflected across line *m*. What observations can be made about △*ABC* and its reflected image △*A'B'C'* regarding the following properties: collinearity, betweenness, angle measure, triangle congruence, and orientation? Explain.

For items 22 and 23, identify the transformation. Then use arrow notation to describe the transformation.

22.

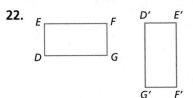

23.

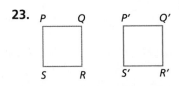

24. The coordinates for the vertices of △*XYZ* are *X*(−5, −4), *Y*(−3, −1), and *Z*(−2, −2). Find the coordinates for the image of △*XYZ* after the translation $(x, y) \rightarrow (x + 4, y + 5)$.

For items 25 and 26, tell whether the figure has line symmetry. If so, copy the figure and draw all lines of symmetry.

25.

26.

For items 27 and 28, tell whether the figure has rotational symmetry. If so, give the angle of rotational symmetry and the order of symmetry.

27.

28.

For items 29 and 30, copy the given figure and use it to create a tessellation.

29.

30.

31. The coordinates of the vertices of rectangle *HJKL* are *H*(2, −1), *J*(5, −1), *K*(5, −3), and *L*(2, −3).

   a. Graph *HJKL* in the coordinate plane.

   b. Graph *H′J′K′L′* by applying the translation $(x, y) \rightarrow (x - 4, y + 1)$ to *HJKL*.

32. A triangle has vertices at (−1, 1), (1, 3), and (4, −2). After a reflection and a translation, the coordinates of the image are (5, 3), (3, 5), and (0, 0). Describe the reflection and the translation.

For items 33–36, reflect the figure with the given vertices across the given line.

33. *E*(−3, 2), *F*(0, 2), *G*(−2, 5); *x*-axis

34. *J*(2, −1), *K*(4, −2), *L*(4, −3), *M*(2, −3); *y*-axis

35. *P*(2, −2), *Q*(4, −2), *R*(3, −4); *y = x*

36. *A*(2, 2), *B*(−2, 2), *C*(−1, 4); *y = x*

37. Many of the capital letters in our alphabet have horizontal or vertical lines of symmetry.

   a. Make a list of the capital letters that have horizontal lines of symmetry.

   b. Make a list of the capital letters that have vertical lines of symmetry.

   c. Which capital letters have both horizontal and vertical lines of symmetry?

Performance Tasks

38. Archeologists examine digital images of their excavations on a computer screen. They have the ability to move the image left, right, up, or down. They can also rotate the image. Suppose a computer screen has a coordinate grid transposed over it, and a bone fragment is in the shape of a rectangle that has the vertices *A*(4, −6), *B*(4, −8), *C*(8, −6) and *D*(8, −8). Determine the effects that an archeologist's actions will have on the bone fragment's position on the screen.

   a. First, the archeologist moves the bone fragment up 5 units on the screen. Find its new vertices.

   b. Next, the archeologist moves the bone fragment left 4 units on the screen. What are its vertices now?

39. Square *ABCD* was transformed using the rule $(x, y \rightarrow x + 5, y - 5)$ to produce the image *A′B′C′D′*.

   a. Is the transformation a reflection, a rotation, or a translation? How do you know?

   b. The vertices of square *ABCD* are *A*(−3 −7), *B*(−1, −5), *C*(1, −7), and *D*(−1, −9). What are the coordinates of *A′B′C′D′*?

   c. Right triangle *QRS* is transformed using the rule to produce the image *Q′R′S′*. Will △*Q′R′S′* be a right triangle? Explain.

 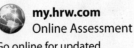

Are You Ready?

my.hrw.com
Assessment and Intervention

✓ Vocabulary

Match each term on the left with a definition on the right.

1. coefficient

2. coordinate plane

3. transformation

4. perpendicular

   A. a change in the size or position of a figure

   B. forming right angles

   C. a two-dimensional system formed by the intersection of a horizontal number line and a vertical number line

   D. an ordered pair of numbers that gives the location of a point

   E. a number that is multiplied by a variable

✓ Solve for a Variable

Solve each equation for the indicated variable.

5. $2x + y = 8; y$

6. $5y = 5x - 10; y$

7. $2y = 6x - 8; y$

8. $10x + 25 = 5y; y$

✓ Evaluate Expressions

Evaluate each expression for the given value of the variable.

9. $4g - 3; g = -2$

10. $8p - 12; p = 4$

11. $4x + 8; x = -2$

12. $-5t - 15; t = 1$

✓ Connect Words and Algebra

13. The value of a stock begins at \$0.05 and increases by \$0.01 each month. Write an equation representing the value of the stock v in any month m.

14. Write a situation that could be modeled by the equation $b = 100 - s$.

Career Readiness **Personal Trainers**

Personal trainers are fitness professionals who motivate and provide feedback to their clients. They use fitness assessments that may involve formulas for the following:

- Body Mass Index, or BMI
- Basal Metabolic Rate, or BMR
- Maximum Heart Rate, or MHR
- Training Zone Heart Rate

Personal trainers must be certified. Most trainers have college degrees and many of them are employed by gyms or health clubs.

Connecting Algebra and Geometry Through Coordinates

Online Edition

my.hrw.com

Access the complete online textbook, interactive features, and additional resources.

Homework Help

Get instant help with tutorial videos, practice problems, and step-by-step solutions.

TI-Nspire™ Activities

Enhance your learning with cutting edge technology from Texas Instruments.

Portable Devices

eTextbook

Access your full textbook on your tablet or e-reader.

On the Spot

Watch video tutorials anywhere, anytime with this app for iPhone® and iPad®.

Chapter Resources

Scan with your smart phone to jump directly to the online edition.

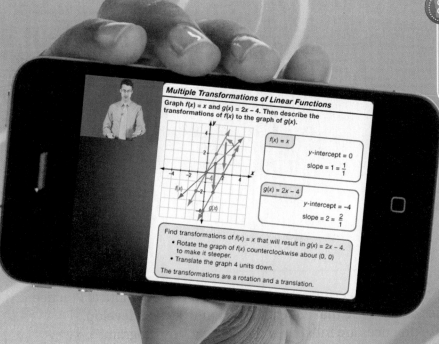

 Use **On the Spot** videos to see linear functions and transformations in action.

18 Coordinate Geometry

COMMON
CORE GPS

Contents

MATHEMATICAL
PRACTICES
The Common Core Georgia Performance Standards for Mathematical Practice describe varieties of expertise that all students should seek to develop. Opportunities to develop these practices are integrated throughout this program.

1 Make sense of problems and persevere in solving them.

2 Reason abstractly and quantitatively.

3 Construct viable arguments and critique the reasoning of others.

4 Model with mathematics.

5 Use appropriate tools strategically.

6 Attend to precision.

7 Look for and make use of structure.

8 Look for and express regularity in repeated reasoning.

Unpacking the Standards

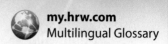
my.hrw.com
Multilingual Glossary

Understanding the standards and the vocabulary terms in the standards will help you know exactly what you are expected to learn in this chapter.

Use coordinates to prove simple geometric theorems algebraically.

Key Vocabulary

coordinate (coordenada) A number used to identify the location of a point. On a number line, one coordinate is used. On a coordinate plane, two coordinates are used, called the *x*-coordinate and the *y*-coordinate. In space, three coordinates are used, called the *x*-coordinate, the *y*-coordinate, and the *z*-coordinate.

What It Means For You

You can prove some properties of geometric figures by using coordinates and algebra. These proofs sometimes involve the distance formula or the midpoint formula.

EXAMPLE

The midpoint of $\overline{AB}$, point M, has coordinates $M\left(\frac{0+x}{2}, \frac{0+y}{2}\right)$.

Area $\triangle AMC = \frac{1}{2}(x)\left(\frac{y}{2}\right) = \frac{xy}{4}$.

Area $\triangle ABC = \frac{1}{2}(x)(y) = \frac{xy}{2}$.

The area of triangle AMC is half the area of triangle ABC.

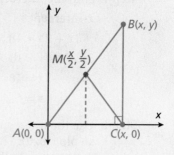

Prove the slope criteria for parallel and perpendicular lines and use them to solve geometric problems (e.g., find the equation of a line parallel or perpendicular to a given line that passes through a given point).

Key Vocabulary

slope (pendiente) A measure of the steepness of a line. If (x_1, y_1) and (x_2, y_2) are any two points on the line, the slope of the line, known as *m*, is represented by the equation $m = \dfrac{y_2 - y_1}{x_2 - x_1}$.

What It Means For You

Parallel lines have the same slope. Perpendicular lines have slopes whose product is –1. You can use these facts to conclude that lines are parallel or perpendicular, or to identify slopes of lines.

EXAMPLE

The slope of $\overleftrightarrow{AB}$ is –4.

The slope of $\overleftrightarrow{CD}$ is –4.

The slopes are the same.

So, $\overleftrightarrow{AB} \parallel \overleftrightarrow{CD}$.

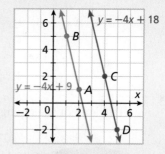

The slope of $\overleftrightarrow{FG}$ is 1.

The slope of $\overleftrightarrow{JH}$ is –1.

The product of the slopes is –1.

So, $\overleftrightarrow{FG} \perp \overleftrightarrow{JH}$.

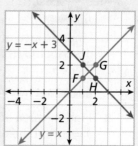

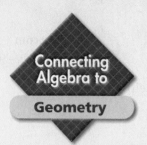

Area in the Coordinate Plane

Lines in the coordinate plane can form the sides of polygons. You can use points on these lines to help you find the areas of these polygons.

Example

Find the area of the triangle formed by the *x*-axis, the *y*-axis, and the line described by $3x + 2y = 18$.

Step 1 Find the intercepts of $3x + 2y = 18$.

x-intercept:	*y*-intercept:
$3x + 2y = 18$	$3x + 2y = 18$
$3x + 2(0) = 18$	$3(0) + 2y = 18$
$3x = 18$	$2y = 18$
$x = 6$	$y = 9$

Step 2 Use the intercepts to graph the line. The *x*-intercept is 6, so plot $(6, 0)$. The *y*-intercept is 9, so plot $(0, 9)$. Connect with a straight line. Then shade the triangle formed by the line and the axes, as described.

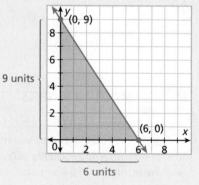

Step 3 Recall that the area of a triangle is given by $A = \frac{1}{2}bh$.

- The length of the base is 6.
- The height is 9.

Step 4 Substitute these values into the formula.

$A = \frac{1}{2}bh$

$A = \frac{1}{2}(6)(9)$ *Substitute into the area formula.*

$= \frac{1}{2}(54)$ *Simplify.*

$= 27$

The area of the triangle is 27 square units.

Try This

1. Find the area of the triangle formed by the *x*-axis, the *y*-axis, and the line described by $3x + 2y = 12$.

2. Find the area of the triangle formed by the *x*-axis, the *y*-axis, and the line described by $y = 6 - x$.

3. Find the area of the polygon formed by the *x*-axis, the *y*-axis, the line described by $y = 6$, and the line described by $x = 4$.

Slopes of Parallel and Perpendicular Lines

Essential Question: How can you use the relationships between the slopes of parallel and perpendicular lines to solve problems?

Objectives
Identify and graph parallel and perpendicular lines.

Write equations to describe lines parallel or perpendicular to a given line.

Vocabulary
parallel lines
perpendicular lines

Animated Math

Why learn this?

Parallel lines and their equations can be used to model costs, such as the cost of a booth at a farmers' market.

To sell at a particular farmers' market for a year, there is a $100 membership fee. Then you pay $3 for each hour that you sell at the market. However, if you were a member the previous year, the membership fee is reduced to $50.

- The **red** line shows the total cost if you are a new member.

- The **blue** line shows the total cost if you are a returning member.

These two lines are *parallel*. **Parallel lines** are lines in the same plane that have no points in common. In other words, they do not intersect.

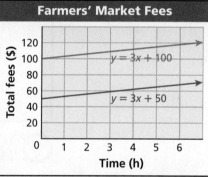

Farmers' Market Fees

Parallel Lines

Know it!
Note

WORDS	Two different nonvertical lines are parallel if and only if they have the same slope.	All different vertical lines are parallel.
GRAPH	$y = \frac{1}{2}x + 5$ $y = \frac{1}{2}x + 1$	$x = -2$ $x = 4$

COMMON CORE GPS
MCC9-12.G.GPE.5

EXAMPLE 1

Identifying Parallel Lines

Identify which lines are parallel.

A $y = \frac{4}{3}x + 3$; $y = 2$; $y = \frac{4}{3}x - 5$; $y = -3$

The lines described by $y = \frac{4}{3}x + 3$ and $y = \frac{4}{3}x - 5$ both have slope $\frac{4}{3}$. These lines are parallel. The lines described by $y = 2$ and $y = -3$ both have slope 0. These lines are parallel.

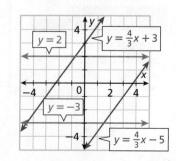

my.hrw.com

Online Video Tutor

Identify which lines are parallel.

B $y = 3x + 2$; $y = -\dfrac{1}{2}x + 4$; $x + 2y = -4$; $y - 5 = 3(x - 1)$

Write all equations in slope-intercept form to determine the slopes.

$y = 3x + 2$	$y = -\dfrac{1}{2}x + 4$
slope-intercept form ✓	slope-intercept form ✓
$x + 2y = -4$	$y - 5 = 3(x - 1)$
$\underline{-x \qquad\qquad -x}$	$y - 5 = 3x - 3$
$2y = -x - 4$	$\underline{+5 \qquad\qquad +5}$
$\dfrac{2y}{2} = \dfrac{-x - 4}{2}$	$y = 3x + 2$
$y = -\dfrac{1}{2}x - 2$	

The lines described by $y = 3x + 2$ and $y - 5 = 3(x - 1)$ have the same slope, but they are not parallel lines. They are the same line.

The lines described by $y = -\dfrac{1}{2}x + 4$ and $x + 2y = -4$ represent parallel lines. They each have slope $-\dfrac{1}{2}$.

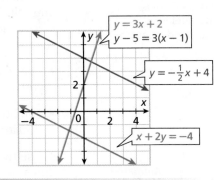

 **Identify which lines are parallel.**

1a. $y = 2x + 2$; $y = 2x + 1$; $y = -4$; $x = 1$

1b. $y = \dfrac{3}{4}x + 8$; $-3x + 4y = 32$; $y = 3x$; $y - 1 = 3(x + 2)$

COMMON CORE GPS
MCC9-12.G.GPE.5

EXAMPLE **2**

Geometry Application

Show that *ABCD* is a parallelogram.

Use the ordered pairs and the slope formula to find the slopes of $\overline{AB}$ and $\overline{CD}$.

$$\text{slope of } \overline{AB} = \frac{7 - 5}{4 - (-1)} = \frac{2}{5}$$

$$\text{slope of } \overline{CD} = \frac{3 - 1}{4 - (-1)} = \frac{2}{5}$$

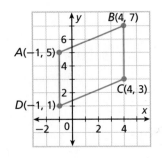

$\overline{AB}$ is parallel to $\overline{CD}$ because they have the same slope.

$\overline{AD}$ is parallel to $\overline{BC}$ because they are both vertical.

Therefore, *ABCD* is a parallelogram because both pairs of opposite sides are parallel.

my.hrw.com

Online Video Tutor

Remember!

In a parallelogram, opposite sides are parallel.

---

 2. Show that the points $A(0, 2)$, $B(4, 2)$, $C(1, -3)$, and $D(-3, -3)$ are the vertices of a parallelogram.

Perpendicular lines are lines that intersect to form right angles (90°).

Perpendicular Lines

WORDS	Two nonvertical lines are perpendicular if and only if the product of their slopes is −1.	Vertical lines are perpendicular to horizontal lines.
GRAPH	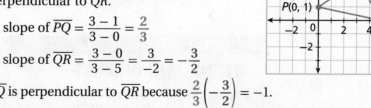	

EXAMPLE 3
MCC9-12.G.GPE.5

Identifying Perpendicular Lines

Identify which lines are perpendicular: $x = -2$; $y = 1$; $y = -4x$; $y + 2 = \frac{1}{4}(x + 1)$.

The graph described by $x = -2$ is a vertical line, and the graph described by $y = 1$ is a horizontal line. These lines are perpendicular.

The slope of the line described by $y = -4x$ is −4. The slope of the line described by $y + 2 = \frac{1}{4}(x - 1)$ is $\frac{1}{4}$.

$(-4)\left(\frac{1}{4}\right) = -1$

These lines are perpendicular because the product of their slopes is −1.

Online Video Tutor

 3. Identify which lines are perpendicular: $y = -4$; $y - 6 = 5(x + 4)$; $x = 3$; $y = -\frac{1}{5}x + 2$.

EXAMPLE 4
MCC9-12.G.GPE.4

Geometry Application

Show that *PQR* is a right triangle.

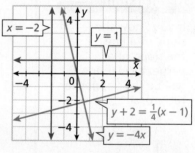

If *PQR* is a right triangle, $\overline{PQ}$ will be perpendicular to $\overline{QR}$.

$$\text{slope of } \overline{PQ} = \frac{3 - 1}{3 - 0} = \frac{2}{3}$$

$$\text{slope of } \overline{QR} = \frac{3 - 0}{3 - 5} = \frac{3}{-2} = -\frac{3}{2}$$

$\overline{PQ}$ is perpendicular to $\overline{QR}$ because $\frac{2}{3}\left(-\frac{3}{2}\right) = -1$.

Therefore, *PQR* is a right triangle because it contains a right angle.

Online Video Tutor

 4. Show that $P(1, 4)$, $Q(2, 6)$, and $R(7, 1)$ are the vertices of a right triangle.

COMMON CORE GPS · EXAMPLE 5 · MCC9-12.G.GPE.5

Writing Equations of Parallel and Perpendicular Lines

my.hrw.com

Online Video Tutor

A Write an equation in slope-intercept form for the line that passes through $(4, 5)$ and is parallel to the line described by $y = 5x + 10$.

Step 1 Find the slope of the line.

$y = 5x + 10$ ... *The slope is 5.*

The parallel line also has a slope of 5.

Step 2 Write the equation in point-slope form.

$y - y_1 = m(x - x_1)$ ... *Use point-slope form.*

$y - 5 = 5(x - 4)$ ... *Substitute 5 for m, 4 for x_1, and 5 for y_1.*

Step 3 Write the equation in slope-intercept form.

$y - 5 = 5(x - 4)$

$y - 5 = 5x - 20$ ... *Distributive Property*

$y = 5x - 15$ ... *Addition Property of Equality*

B Write an equation in slope-intercept form for the line that passes through $(3, 2)$ and is perpendicular to the line described by $y = 3x - 1$.

Step 1 Find the slope of the line.

$y = 3x - 1$ ... *The slope is 3.*

The perpendicular line has a slope of $-\frac{1}{3}$, because $3\left(-\frac{1}{3}\right) = -1$.

Step 2 Write the equation in point-slope form.

$y - y_1 = m(x - x_1)$ ... *Use point-slope form.*

$y - 2 = -\frac{1}{3}(x - 3)$ ... *Substitute $-\frac{1}{3}$ for m, 3 for x_1, and 2 for y_1.*

Step 3 Write the equation in slope-intercept form.

$y - 2 = -\frac{1}{3}(x - 3)$

$y - 2 = -\frac{1}{3}x + 1$ ... *Distributive Property*

$y = -\frac{1}{3}x + 3$ ... *Addition Property of Equality*

Helpful Hint

If you know the slope of a line, the slope of a perpendicular line will be the "opposite reciprocal."

$\frac{2}{3} \rightarrow -\frac{3}{2}$

$\frac{1}{5} \rightarrow -5$

$-7 \rightarrow \frac{1}{7}$

CHECK IT OUT!

5a. Write an equation in slope-intercept form for the line that passes through $(5, 7)$ and is parallel to the line described by $y = \frac{4}{5}x - 6$.

5b. Write an equation in slope-intercept form for the line that passes through $(-5, 3)$ and is perpendicular to the line described by $y = 5x$.

MCC.MP.6, MCC.MP.7 · MATHEMATICAL PRACTICES

THINK AND DISCUSS

1. Are the lines described by $y = \frac{1}{2}x$ and $y = 2x$ perpendicular? Explain.

2. Describe the slopes and y-intercepts when two nonvertical lines are parallel.

3. **GET ORGANIZED** Copy and complete the graphic organizer. In each box, sketch an example and describe the slopes.

| Parallel lines | Perpendicular lines |

GUIDED PRACTICE

1. Vocabulary ____?____ lines have the same slope. (*Parallel* or *Perpendicular*)

SEE EXAMPLE 1 Identify which lines are parallel.

2. $y = 6$; $y = 6x + 5$; $y = 6x - 7$; $y = -8$

3. $y = \frac{3}{4}x - 1$; $y = -2x$; $y - 3 = \frac{3}{4}(x - 5)$; $y - 4 = -2(x + 2)$

SEE EXAMPLE 2 **4. Geometry** Show that *ABCD* is a trapezoid. (*Hint:* In a trapezoid, exactly one pair of opposite sides is parallel.)

SEE EXAMPLE 3 Identify which lines are perpendicular.

5. $y = \frac{2}{3}x - 4$; $y = -\frac{3}{2}x + 2$; $y = -1$; $x = 3$

6. $y = -\frac{3}{7}x - 4$; $y - 4 = -7(x + 2)$;

$y - 1 = \frac{1}{7}(x - 4)$; $y - 7 = \frac{7}{3}(x - 3)$

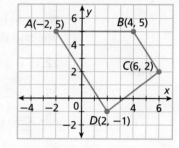

SEE EXAMPLE 4 **7. Geometry** Show that *PQRS* is a rectangle. (*Hint:* In a rectangle, all four angles are right angles.)

SEE EXAMPLE 5 **8.** Write an equation in slope-intercept form for the line that passes through (5, 0) and is perpendicular to the line described by $y = -\frac{5}{2}x + 6$.

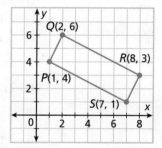

PRACTICE AND PROBLEM SOLVING

For Exercises	See Example
9–11	1
12	2
13–15	3
16	4
17	5

Independent Practice

my.hrw.com

Online Extra Practice

Identify which lines are parallel.

9. $x = 7$; $y = -\frac{5}{6}x + 8$; $y = -\frac{5}{6}x - 4$; $x = -9$

10. $y = -x$; $y - 3 = -1(x + 9)$; $y - 6 = \frac{1}{2}(x - 14)$; $y + 1 = \frac{1}{2}x$

11. $y = -3x + 2$; $y = \frac{1}{2}x - 1$; $-x + 2y = 17$; $3x + y = 27$

12. Geometry Show that *LMNP* is a parallelogram.

Identify which lines are perpendicular.

13. $y = 6x$; $y = \frac{1}{6}x$; $y = -\frac{1}{6}x$; $y = -6x$

14. $y - 9 = 3(x + 1)$; $y = -\frac{1}{3}x + 5$; $y = 0$; $x = 6$

15. $x - 6y = 15$; $y = 3x - 2$; $y = -3x - 3$; $y = -6x - 8$; $3y = -x - 11$

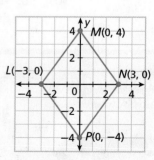

16. Geometry Show that ABC is a right triangle.

17. Write an equation in slope-intercept form for the line that passes through $(0, 0)$ and is parallel to the line described by $y = -\frac{6}{7}x + 1$.

Without graphing, tell whether each pair of lines is parallel, perpendicular, or neither.

18. $x = 2$ and $y = -5$

19. $y = 7x$ and $y - 28 = 7(x - 4)$

20. $y = 2x - 1$ and $y = \frac{1}{2}x + 2$

21. $y - 3 = \frac{1}{4}(x - 3)$ and $y + 13 = \frac{1}{4}(x + 1)$

Write an equation in slope-intercept form for the line that is parallel to the given line and that passes through the given point.

22. $y = 3x - 7; (0, 4)$

23. $y = \frac{1}{2}x + 5; (4, -3)$

24. $4y = x; (4, 0)$

25. $y = 2x + 3; (1, 7)$

26. $5x - 2y = 10; (3, -5)$

27. $y = 3x - 4; (-2, 7)$

28. $y = 7; (2, 4)$

29. $x + y = 1; (2, 3)$

30. $2x + 3y = 7; (4, 5)$

31. $y = 4x + 2; (5, -3)$

32. $y = \frac{1}{2}x - 1; (0, -4)$

33. $3x + 4y = 8; (4, -3)$

Write an equation in slope-intercept form for the line that is perpendicular to the given line and that passes through the given point.

34. $y = -3x + 4; (6, -2)$

35. $y = x - 6; (-1, 2)$

36. $3x - 4y = 8; (-6, 5)$

37. $5x + 2y = 10; (3, -5)$

38. $y = 5 - 3x; (2, -4)$

39. $-10x + 2y = 8; (4, -3)$

40. $2x + 3y = 7; (4, 5)$

41. $4x - 2y = -6; (3, -2)$

42. $-2x - 8y = 16; (4, 5)$

43. $y = -2x + 4; (-2, 5)$

44. $y = x - 5; (0, 5)$

45. $x + y = 2; (8, 5)$

46. Write an equation describing the line that is parallel to the y-axis and that is 6 units to the right of the y-axis.

47. Write an equation describing the line that is perpendicular to the y-axis and that is 4 units below the x-axis.

48. Critical Thinking Is it possible for two linear functions whose graphs are parallel lines to have the same y-intercept? Explain.

49. Estimation Estimate the slope of a line that is perpendicular to the line through $(2.07, 8.95)$ and $(-1.9, 25.07)$.

H.O.T 50. Write About It Explain in words how to write an equation in slope-intercept form that describes a line parallel to $y - 3 = -6(x - 3)$.

Real-World Connections

51. a. Flora walks from her home to the bus stop at a rate of 50 steps per minute. Write a rule that gives her distance from home (in steps) as a function of time.

b. Flora's neighbor Dan lives 30 steps closer to the bus stop. He begins walking at the same time and at the same pace as Flora. Write a rule that gives Dan's distance from *Flora's* house as a function of time.

c. Will Flora meet Dan along the walk? Use a graph to help explain your answer.

52. Which describes a line parallel to the line described by $y = -3x + 2$?

　Ⓐ $y = -3x$ 　　　 Ⓑ $y = \frac{1}{3}x$ 　　　 Ⓒ $y = 2 - 3x$ 　　　 Ⓓ $y = \frac{1}{3}x + 2$

53. Which describes a line passing through $(3, 3)$ that is perpendicular to the line described by $y = \frac{3}{5}x + 2$?

Ⓕ
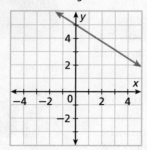

Ⓗ
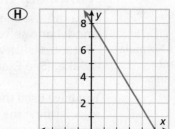

　Ⓖ $y = \frac{5}{3}x - 2$ 　　　　　　　　　 Ⓙ $y = \frac{3}{5}x + \frac{6}{5}$

54. Gridded Response The graph of a linear function $f(x)$ is parallel to the line described by $2x + y = 5$ and contains the point $(6, -2)$. What is the y-intercept of $f(x)$?

CHALLENGE AND EXTEND

 55. Three or more points that lie on the same line are called *collinear points*. Explain why the points A, B, and C must be collinear if the line containing A and B has the same slope as the line containing B and C.

56. The lines described by $y = (a + 12)x + 3$ and $y = 4ax$ are parallel. What is the value of a?

57. The lines described by $y = (5a + 3)x$ and $y = -\frac{1}{2}x$ are perpendicular. What is the value of a?

58. Geometry The diagram shows a square in the coordinate plane. Use the diagram to show that the diagonals of a square are perpendicular.

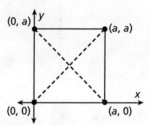

FOCUS ON MATHEMATICAL PRACTICES

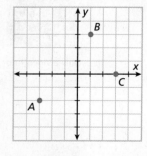

59. Error Analysis Trent found that both the lines shown had the same slope and concluded that the equations represent parallel lines. Is Trent correct? Explain.

$$5x + 2y = 12$$
$$4(y - 6) = -10x$$

60. Problem Solving Three points are shown.

　a. Write an equation of a line that contains two of the points.

　b. Write an equation of a line through the third point that is parallel to your line.

　c. Write an equation of the line through the third point that is perpendicular to your line.

18-2 The Midpoint and Distance Formulas

Essential Question: How can you apply the Midpoint and Distance Formulas?

Objectives
Apply the formula for midpoint.

Use the Distance Formula to find the distance between two points.

Vocabulary
midpoint

Remember!

A segment is a part of a line consisting of two endpoints and all points between them. A segment is named by its endpoints. The notation $\overline{CD}$ is read "segment CD."

Why learn this?

You can use the coordinate plane to model and solve problems involving distances, such as the distance across a lake. (See Example 4.)

You have used the coordinates of points to determine the slope of lines. You can also use coordinates to determine the *midpoint* of a line segment on the coordinate plane.

The **midpoint** of a line segment is the point that divides the segment into two congruent segments. *Congruent segments* are segments that have the same length.

You can find the midpoint of a segment by using the coordinates of its endpoints. Calculate the average of the x-coordinates and the average of the y-coordinates of the endpoints.

Midpoint Formula

The midpoint M of $\overline{AB}$ with endpoints $A(x_1, y_1)$ and $B(x_2, y_2)$ is

$$M\left(\frac{x_1 + x_2}{2}, \frac{y_1 + y_2}{2}\right).$$

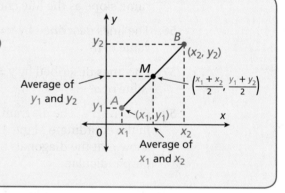

COMMON CORE GPS
MCC9-12.G.GPE.6

EXAMPLE 1 Finding the Coordinates of a Midpoint

Find the coordinates of the midpoint of $\overline{CD}$ with endpoints $C(-2, -1)$ and $D(4, 2)$.

$M\left(\dfrac{x_1 + x_2}{2}, \dfrac{y_1 + y_2}{2}\right)$ *Write the formula.*

$M\left(\dfrac{-2 + 4}{2}, \dfrac{-1 + 2}{2}\right)$ *Substitute.*

$M\left(\dfrac{2}{2}, \dfrac{1}{2}\right) = M\left(1, \dfrac{1}{2}\right)$ *Simplify.*

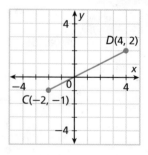

my.hrw.com

Online Video Tutor

 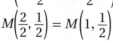 **1.** Find the coordinates of the midpoint of $\overline{EF}$ with endpoints $E(-2, 3)$ and $F(5, -3)$.

EXAMPLE 2
Ext. of MCC9-12.G.GPE.6

Finding the Coordinates of an Endpoint

M is the midpoint of $\overline{AB}$. *A* has coordinates (2, 2), and *M* has coordinates (4, −3). Find the coordinates of *B*.

my.hrw.com

Online Video Tutor

Step 1 Let the coordinates of *B* equal (x, y).

Step 2 Use the Midpoint Formula.

$$(4, -3) = \left(\frac{2 + x}{2}, \frac{2 + y}{2} \right)$$

Step 3 Find the *x*-coordinate.   Find the *y*-coordinate.

$4 = \dfrac{2 + x}{2}$	*Set the coordinates equal.*	$-3 = \dfrac{2 + y}{2}$
$2(4) = 2\left(\dfrac{2 + x}{2}\right)$	*Multiply both sides by 2.*	$2(-3) = 2\left(\dfrac{2 + y}{2}\right)$
$8 = 2 + x$	*Simplify.*	$-6 = 2 + y$
$\underline{-2 \quad -2}$	*Subtract 2 from both sides.*	$\underline{-2 \quad -2}$
$6 = \quad x$	*Simplify.*	$-8 = \quad y$

The coordinates of *B* are (6, –8).

Check   Graph points *A* and *B* and midpoint *M*.

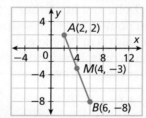

Point M appears to be the midpoint of $\overline{AB}$.

2. *S* is the midpoint of $\overline{RT}$. *R* has coordinates (−6, −1), and *S* has coordinates (−1, 1). Find the coordinates of *T*.

You can also use coordinates to find the distance between two points or the length of a line segment. To find the length of segment *PQ*, draw a horizontal segment from *P* and a vertical segment from *Q* to form a right triangle.

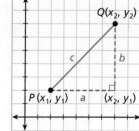

Remember!

The *Pythagorean Theorem* states that if a right triangle has legs of lengths *a* and *b* and a hypotenuse of length *c*, then $a^2 + b^2 = c^2$.

$c^2 = a^2 + b^2$ *Pythagorean Theorem*

$c = \sqrt{a^2 + b^2}$ *Solve for c. Use the positive square root to represent distance.*

$PQ = \sqrt{\underbrace{(x_2 - x_1)^2}_{\text{Length of horizontal segment}} + \underbrace{(y_2 - y_1)^2}_{\text{Length of vertical segment}}}$

This equation represents the Distance Formula.

Distance Formula

Know it!
Note

In a coordinate plane, the distance *d* between two points (x_1, y_1) and (x_2, y_2) is
$$d = \sqrt{(x_2 - x_1)^2 + (y_2 - y_1)^2}.$$

COMMON CORE GPS
Prep. for MCC9-12.G.GPE.7

EXAMPLE 3 Finding Distance in the Coordinate Plane

Use the Distance Formula to find the distance, to the nearest hundredth, from $A(-2, 3)$ to $B(2, -2)$.

$$d = \sqrt{(x_2 - x_1)^2 + (y_2 - y_1)^2}$$ *Distance Formula*

$$d = \sqrt{[2 - (-2)]^2 + (-2 - 3)^2}$$ *Substitute $(-2, 3)$ for (x_1, y_1) and $(2, -2)$ for (x_2, y_2).*

$$d = \sqrt{4^2 + (-5)^2}$$ *Subtract.*

$$d = \sqrt{16 + 25}$$ *Simplify powers.*

$$d = \sqrt{41}$$ *Add.*

$$d \approx 6.40$$ *Find the square root to the nearest hundredth.*

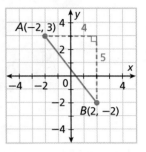

CHECK IT OUT!   **3.** Use the Distance Formula to find the distance, to the nearest hundredth, from $R(3, 2)$ to $S(-3, -1)$.

EXAMPLE 4 Geography Application

COMMON CORE GPS
MCC9-12.A.CED.2

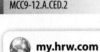

Each unit on the map of Lake Okeechobee represents 1 mile. Delia and her father plan to travel from point A near the town of Okeechobee to point B at Pahokee. To the nearest tenth of a mile, how far do Delia and her father plan to travel?

$$d = \sqrt{(x_2 - x_1)^2 + (y_2 - y_1)^2}$$

$$d = \sqrt{(33 - 22)^2 + (13 - 39)^2}$$ *Substitute.*

$$d = \sqrt{11^2 + (-26)^2}$$ *Subtract.*

$$d = \sqrt{121 + 676}$$ *Simplify powers.*

$$d = \sqrt{797}$$ *Add.*

$$d \approx 28.2$$ *Find the square root to the nearest tenth.*

Delia and her father plan to travel about 28.2 miles.

CHECK IT OUT!   **4.** Jacob takes a boat from Pahokee to Clewiston. To the nearest tenth of a mile, how far does he travel?

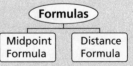
MCC.MP.3   MATHEMATICAL PRACTICES

THINK AND DISCUSS

1. If you use the formula $M\left(\dfrac{x_2 + x_1}{2}, \dfrac{y_2 + y_1}{2}\right)$ to find the midpoint of a segment, will you get the correct coordinates for the midpoint? Explain.

2. GET ORGANIZED Copy and complete the graphic organizer. In each box, write a formula. Then make a sketch that will illustrate the formula.

Formulas
— Midpoint Formula
— Distance Formula

GUIDED PRACTICE

1. **Vocabulary** In your own words, describe the *midpoint* of a line segment.

SEE EXAMPLE 1 Find the coordinates of the midpoint of each segment.

2. $\overline{AB}$ with endpoints $A(4, -6)$ and $B(-4, 2)$

3. $\overline{CD}$ with endpoints $C(0, -8)$ and $D(3, 0)$

4. $\overline{EF}$ with endpoints $E(-8, 17)$ and $F(-12, -16)$

SEE EXAMPLE 2 5. M is the midpoint of $\overline{LN}$. L has coordinates $(-3, -1)$, and M has coordinates $(0, 1)$. Find the coordinates of N.

6. B is the midpoint of $\overline{AC}$. A has coordinates $(-3, 4)$, and B has coordinates $\left(-1\frac{1}{2}, 1\right)$. Find the coordinates of C.

SEE EXAMPLE 3 Use the Distance Formula to find the distance, to the nearest hundredth, between each pair of points.

7. $A(1, -2)$ and $B(-4, -4)$

8. $X(-2, 7)$ and $Y(-2, -8)$

9. $V(2, -1)$ and $W(-4, 8)$

SEE EXAMPLE 4 10. **Recreation** Each unit on the map of a public park represents 1 kilometer. To the nearest tenth of a kilometer, what is the distance from the campground to the waterfall?

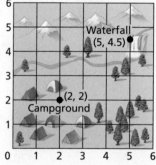

PRACTICE AND PROBLEM SOLVING

Independent Practice	
For Exercises	See Example
11–12	1
13–15	2
16–19	3
20	4

my.hrw.com

Online Extra Practice

Find the coordinates of the midpoint of each segment.

11. $\overline{XY}$ with endpoints $X(-3, -7)$ and $Y(-1, 1)$

12. $\overline{MN}$ with endpoints $M(12, -7)$ and $N(-5, -2)$

13. M is the midpoint of $\overline{QR}$. Q has coordinates $(-3, 5)$, and M has coordinates $(7, -9)$. Find the coordinates of R.

14. D is the midpoint of $\overline{CE}$. E has coordinates $(-3, -2)$, and D has coordinates $\left(2\frac{1}{2}, 1\right)$. Find the coordinates of C.

15. Y is the midpoint of $\overline{XZ}$. X has coordinates $(0, -1)$, and Y has coordinates $\left(1, -4\frac{1}{2}\right)$. Find the coordinates of Z.

Use the Distance Formula to find the distance, to the nearest hundredth, between each pair of points.

16. $U(0, 1)$ and $V(-3, -9)$

17. $M(10, -1)$ and $N(2, -5)$

18. $P(-10, 1)$ and $Q(5, 5)$

19. $F(6, 15)$ and $G(4, 24)$

20. **Astronomy** Each unit on the map of a section of a moon represents 1 kilometer. To the nearest tenth of a kilometer, what is the distance between the two craters?

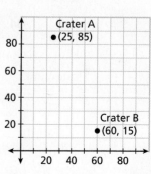

For Exercises 21 and 22, use the map, and round your answers to the nearest tenth of a mile. Each unit on the map represents 1 mile.

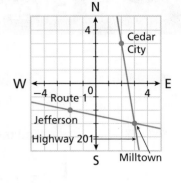

21. How far is it from Cedar City to Milltown along Highway 201?

22. A car breaks down on Route 1 halfway between Jefferson and Milltown. A tow truck is sent out from Jefferson. How far does the truck travel to reach the car?

H.O.T. 23. Estimation Estimate the distance between the points $(-5.21, 1.84)$ and $(16.62, -23.19)$. Explain how you determined your answer.

24. Geometry The coordinates of the vertices of $\triangle ABC$ are $A(1, 4)$, $B(-2, -1)$, and $C(3, -2)$. Find the perimeter of $\triangle ABC$ to the nearest whole number.

Find the distance, to the nearest hundredth, between each pair of points.

25. $J(0, 3)$ and $K(-6, -9)$ **26.** $L(-5, 2)$ and $M(-8, 10)$ **27.** $N(4, -6)$ and $P(-2, 7)$

28. Aviation A Coast Guard helicopter receives a distress signal from a boat. The units on the map represent miles. To the nearest minute, how long will it take the helicopter to reach the boat if the helicopter travels at an average speed of 75 miles per hour?

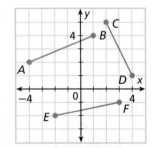

29. Geometry A diameter of a circle has endpoints $(-2, -5)$ and $(2, 1)$.

  a. Find the length of the diameter to the nearest tenth.

  b. Find the coordinates of the center of the circle.

  c. Find the circumference of the circle to the nearest whole number.

30. Travel A group of tourists is traveling by camel in the desert. They are following a straight path from point $(2, 4)$ to point $(8, 12)$ on a map. Each unit on the map represents 1 mile. An oasis lies at the midpoint of the path. The group has already traveled 3.2 miles. How much farther do they need to go to reach the oasis?

31. Multi-Step Use the Distance Formula to order $\overline{AB}$, $\overline{CD}$, and $\overline{EF}$ from shortest to longest.

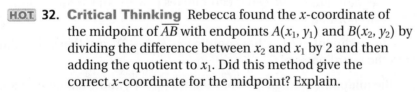

H.O.T. 32. Critical Thinking Rebecca found the x-coordinate of the midpoint of $\overline{AB}$ with endpoints $A(x_1, y_1)$ and $B(x_2, y_2)$ by dividing the difference between x_2 and x_1 by 2 and then adding the quotient to x_1. Did this method give the correct x-coordinate for the midpoint? Explain.

H.O.T. 33. Write About It Explain why the Distance Formula is not needed to find the distance between two points that lie on a horizontal or vertical line.

34. On a map of a city park, the ordered pairs $(3, 5)$ and $(8, 17)$ mark the starting and ending points of a straight jogging trail. Each unit on the map represents 0.1 mile.

  a. What is the length of the trail in miles?

  b. How many back-and-forth trips would Marisol need to make on the trail in order to run at least 7 miles?

35. Which segment has a length closest to 4 units?

   Ⓐ $\overline{EF}$ Ⓒ $\overline{JK}$

   Ⓑ $\overline{GH}$ Ⓓ $\overline{LM}$

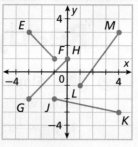

36. What is the distance between the points $(7, -3)$ and $(-5, 6)$?

   Ⓕ 4   Ⓗ 15

   Ⓖ 9   Ⓙ 21

37. A coordinate plane is placed over the map of a town. A library is located at $(-5, 1)$, and a museum is located at $(3, 5)$. What is the distance, to the nearest tenth, from the library to the museum?

   Ⓐ 4.5 units   Ⓑ 5.7 units   Ⓒ 6.3 units   Ⓓ 8.9 units

H.O.T. 38. Short Response Brian is driving along a straight highway. His truck can travel 22 miles per gallon of gasoline, and it has 2 gallons of gas remaining. On a map, the truck's current location is $(7, 12)$, and the nearest gas station on the highway is located at $(16, 52)$. Each unit on the map represents 1 mile. Will the truck reach the gas station before running out of gas? Support your answer.

CHALLENGE AND EXTEND

39. Geometry Find the area of a trapezoid with vertices $A(-4, 2)$, $B(0, 4)$, $C(3, 3)$, and $D(-3, 0)$. (*Hint*: The formula for the area of a trapezoid is $A = \frac{1}{2}h(b_1 + b_2)$.)

40. X has coordinates $(a, 3a)$, and Y has coordinates $(-5a, 0)$. Find the coordinates of the midpoint of $\overline{XY}$.

41. The coordinates of P are $(a - 5, 0)$. The coordinates of Q are $(a + 1, a)$. The distance between P and Q is 10 units. Find the value of a.

42. Find two points on the y-axis that are a distance of 5 units from $(4, 2)$.

43. The coordinates of S are $(4, 5)$. The coordinates of the midpoint of $\overline{ST}$ are $(-1, -7)$. Find the length of $\overline{ST}$.

FOCUS ON MATHEMATICAL PRACTICES

H.O.T. 44. Reasoning Two line segments on a graph are parallel and congruent.

   a. Will they have the same midpoint? Explain.

   b. Are the distances between the endpoints of each segment the same? Explain.

H.O.T. 45. Analysis On a graph, $\overline{DF}$ is a line segment and point E is equidistant from D and F. Is E the midpoint of $\overline{DF}$? Justify your answer.

H.O.T. 46. Reasoning Carmen says she can find the distance between two points on a graph by using this formula: $d = \sqrt{(x_1 - x_2)^2 + (y_2 - y_1)^2}$. Is she correct? Explain your answer.

H.O.T. 47. Draw Conclusions Alex graphs the line segment from $(0, 0)$ to $(5, 5)$ and labels it $\overline{AB}$. He graphs segment $\overline{AC}$ from $(0, 0)$ to $(-5, -5)$. Without calculating, determine whether $\overline{AB}$ or $\overline{AC}$ is longer, or if they are the same length. Explain.

Ready to Go On?

18-1 Slopes of Parallel and Perpendicular Lines

Identify which lines are parallel.

1. $y = -\frac{1}{3}x$; $y = 3x + 2$; $y = -\frac{1}{3}x - 6$; $y = 3$

2. $y - 2 = -4(x - 1)$; $y = 4x - 4$; $y = \frac{1}{4}x$; $y = -4x - 2$

3. $y = -2x$; $y = 2x + 1$; $y = 2x$; $y = 2(x + 5)$

4. $-3y = x$; $y = -\frac{1}{3}x + 1$; $y = -3x$; $y + 2 = x + 4$

Identify which lines are perpendicular.

5. $y = -4x - 1$; $y = \frac{1}{4}x$; $y = 4x - 6$; $x = -4$

6. $y = -\frac{3}{4}x$; $y = \frac{3}{4}x - 3$; $y = \frac{4}{3}x$; $y = 4$; $x = 3$

7. $y - 1 = -5(x - 6)$; $y = \frac{1}{5}x + 2$; $y = 5$; $y = 5x + 8$

8. $y = 2x$; $y - 2 = 3(x + 1)$; $y = \frac{2}{3}x - 4$; $y = -\frac{1}{3}x$

9. Write an equation in slope-intercept form for the line that passes through $(1, -1)$ and is parallel to the line described by $y = 2x - 4$.

18-2 The Midpoint and Distance Formulas

Find the coordinates of the midpoint of each segment.

10. $\overline{EF}$ with endpoints $E(9, 12)$ and $F(21, 18)$

11. $\overline{GH}$ with endpoints $G(-5, -7)$ and $H(4, -11)$

12. Find the coordinates of the midpoint of $\overline{XY}$ with endpoints $X(-4, 6)$ and $Y(3, 8)$.

Use the Distance Formula to find the distance, to the nearest hundredth, between each pair of points.

13. $J(3, 10)$ and $K(-2, 4)$

14. $L(-6, 0)$ and $M(8, -7)$

15. Each unit on a map of a forest represents 1 mile. To the nearest tenth of a mile, what is the distance from a ranger station at $(1, 2)$ on the map to a river crossing at $(2, 4)$?

16. On a treasure map, the coordinates of a crooked palm tree are $(3, 6)$, and the coordinates of a buried treasure chest are $(12, 18)$. Each unit on the map represents 10 feet. What is the distance in feet between the palm tree and the treasure chest?

PARCC Assessment Readiness

Selected Response

1. The equations of four lines are given. Identify which lines are parallel.

Line 1: $y = 8x - 3$

Line 2: $y - 6 = \frac{1}{8}(x - 4)$

Line 3: $y = 3x + 4$

Line 4: $x - \frac{1}{3}y = -4$

Ⓐ Lines 2 and 3 are parallel.

Ⓑ Lines 3 and 4 are parallel.

Ⓒ All four lines are parallel.

Ⓓ None of the lines are parallel.

2. Identify the lines that are perpendicular:
$y = 4; y = \frac{1}{5}x - 5; x = 8; y + 5 = -5(x + 1)$

Ⓕ Only $y = \frac{1}{5}x - 5$ and $y + 5 = -5(x + 1)$ are perpendicular.

Ⓖ Only $y = 4$ and $x = 8$ are perpendicular.

Ⓗ $y = 4$ and $x = 8$ are perpendicular; $y = \frac{1}{5}x - 5$ and $y + 5 = -5(x + 1)$ are perpendicular.

Ⓙ None of the lines are perpendicular.

3. M is the midpoint of $\overline{AN}$, A has coordinates $(-2, 6)$, and M has coordinates $(1, 2)$. Find the coordinates of N.

Ⓐ $(4, -2)$

Ⓒ $(-1, 8)$

Ⓑ $\left(4\frac{1}{2}, -\frac{1}{2}\right)$

Ⓓ $\left(-\frac{1}{2}, 4\right)$

4. What is the area of the square?

Ⓕ 16

Ⓖ 25

Ⓗ 32

Ⓙ 36

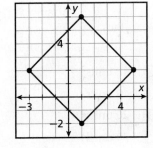

5. The line segment between the points $(4, 0)$ and $(2, -2)$ forms one side of a rectangle. Which of the following coordinates could determine another vertex of that rectangle?

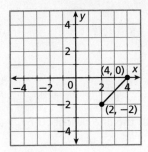

Ⓐ $(-2, 6)$

Ⓑ $(-2, -2)$

Ⓒ $(0, 6)$

Ⓓ $(1, 2)$

6. Find CD and EF. Then determine if $\overline{CD} \cong \overline{EF}$.

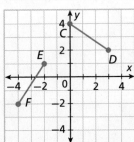

Ⓕ $CD = \sqrt{13}, EF = \sqrt{13}, \overline{CD} \cong \overline{EF}$

Ⓖ $CD = \sqrt{5}, EF = \sqrt{13}, \overline{CD} \not\cong \overline{EF}$

Ⓗ $CD = \sqrt{13}, EF = 3\sqrt{5}, \overline{CD} \not\cong \overline{EF}$

Ⓙ $CD = \sqrt{5}, EF = \sqrt{5}, \overline{CD} \cong \overline{EF}$

Mini-Task

7. Sketch the polygon with vertices $D(-1, 3)$, $E(2, 3)$, and $F(2, -5)$. Then find the area.

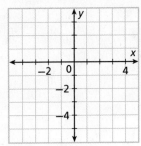

PARCC Assessment Readiness

Selected Response

1. A line passes through point A at $(2, 3)$ and point B at $(4, 7)$. Which is the equation of $\overleftrightarrow{BC}$ if $\overleftrightarrow{AB} \perp \overleftrightarrow{BC}$?

   Ⓐ $y = -2x + 5$

   Ⓑ $y = -\dfrac{1}{2}x + 5$

   Ⓒ $y = -\dfrac{1}{2}x + 9$

   Ⓓ $y = \dfrac{1}{2}x + 5$

2. Which line is parallel to the line described by $2x + 3y = 6$?

   Ⓕ $3x + 2y = 6$

   Ⓖ $3x - 2y = -6$

   Ⓗ $2x + 3y = -6$

   Ⓙ $2x - 3y = 6$

3. Which function's graph is NOT perpendicular to the line described by $4x - y = -2$?

   Ⓐ $y + \dfrac{1}{4}x = 0$

   Ⓑ $\dfrac{1}{2}x = 10 - 2y$

   Ⓒ $3y = \dfrac{3}{4}x + 3$

   Ⓓ $y = -\dfrac{1}{4}x + \dfrac{3}{2}$

4. Which equation describes a line perpendicular to $y = 8x - 9$ that passes through the point $(9, -9)$?

   Ⓕ $y = 8x - 81$

   Ⓖ $y = -\dfrac{1}{8}x - \dfrac{63}{8}$

   Ⓗ $y = 8x - 9$

   Ⓙ $y = -\dfrac{1}{8}x + \dfrac{585}{8}$

5. Point P is on the line segment from point $A(-11, 4)$ to point $B(-1, -6)$ and divides the segment in the ratio 1 to 3. Which could be the coordinates of P?

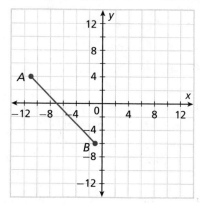

   Ⓐ $P(-6, -1)$

   Ⓑ $P(-3, -4)$

   Ⓒ $P\left(-\dfrac{7}{2}, -\dfrac{7}{2}\right)$

   Ⓓ $P\left(-\dfrac{9}{5}, \dfrac{2}{5}\right)$

6. What is the area of the polygon?

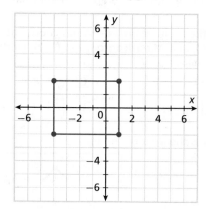

   Ⓕ 18 units^2

   Ⓖ 18 units

   Ⓗ 20 units^2

   Ⓙ 20 units

7. Which are the vertices of a polygon with a perimeter of $10\sqrt{5}$ units?

Ⓐ $A(5, -1)$, $B(-1, -4)$, $C(-3, 1)$

Ⓑ $K(-4, 1)$, $L(0, 4)$, $M(4, 0)$, $N(-2, -3)$

Ⓒ $P(-4, 1)$, $Q(2, 4)$, $R(4, 0)$, $S(-2, -3)$

Ⓓ $T(5, -1)$, $U(-1, -4)$, $V(0, 3)$

8. What are the coordinates of the midpoint of $\overline{BL}$ with endpoints $B(-7, -4)$ and $L(2, 3)$?

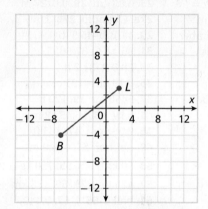

Ⓕ $\left(-3\frac{1}{2}, -1\frac{1}{2}\right)$　　Ⓗ $\left(-1\frac{1}{2}, 0\right)$

Ⓖ $\left(-2\frac{1}{2}, -\frac{1}{2}\right)$　　Ⓙ $(-5, -1)$

9. Jocelyn writes the equation of a line that passes through the point $(4, 0)$ and is perpendicular to the line $y = 2x + 1$. Jocelyn writes her equation in the form $y = mx + b$. What are the values of m and b?

Ⓐ $m = 2$, $b = 1$　　Ⓒ $m = -\frac{1}{2}$, $b = 2$

Ⓑ $m = 2$, $b = 2$　　Ⓓ $m = -\frac{1}{2}$, $b = 4$

10. Nadine graphs a line using the tables of values shown. Mei graphs a line that is parallel to Nadine's line. Which of these could be the equation of Mei's line?

x	y
−2	6
−1	4
2	−2
4	6

Ⓕ $-x + 2y = 8$　　Ⓗ $2x + y = 8$

Ⓖ $x + 2y = 8$　　Ⓙ $-2x + y = -8$

11. Ricardo plots the points $(0, 0)$, $(6, 0)$, and $(0, 8)$. Then he connects the points to form a right triangle. What is the length of the triangle's hypotenuse?

Ⓐ 5 units　　　　Ⓒ 14 units

Ⓑ 10 units　　　Ⓓ 100 units

Mini-Tasks

12. Find the coordinates of the midpoint of each side of the parallelogram.

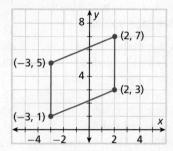

13. Each unit on a coordinate map of a bay represents 1 kilometer. Two buoys are located at $(1, 5)$ and $(3, 6)$. To the nearest tenth of a kilometer, what is the distance between the two buoys?

Performance Task

14. Show that LMN is a right triangle.

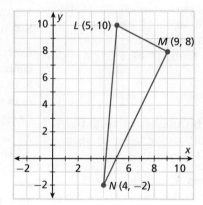

1-1

Check It Out! 1a. 4 decreased by n; n less than 4 **1b.** the quotient of t and 5; t divided by 5 **1c.** the sum of 9 and q; q added to 9 **1d.** the product of 3 and h; 3 times h **2a.** $65t$ **2b.** $m + 5$ **2c.** $32d$ **3a.** 6 **3b.** 7 **3c.** 3 **4. a.** $63s$, **b.** 756 bottles; 1575 bottles; 3150 bottles

Exercises 1. variable **3.** the quotient of f and 3; f divided by 3 **5.** 9 decreased by y; y less than 9 **7.** the sum of t and 12; t increased by 12 **9.** x decreased by 3; the difference of x and 3 **11.** $w + 4$ **13.** 12 **15.** 6 **17.** the product of 5 and p; 5 groups of p **19.** the sum of 3 and x; 3 increased by x **21.** negative 3 times s; the product of negative 3 and s **23.** 14 decreased by t; the difference of 14 and t **25.** $t + 20$ **27.** 1 **29.** 2 **31a.** $h - 40$, **b.** 0; 4; 8; 12 **33.** $2x$ **35.** $y + 10$ **37.** $9w$; 9 in^2; 72 in^2; 81 in^2; 99 in^2 **39.** 13; 14; 15; 16 **41.** 6; 10; 13; 15 **43a.** $47.84 + m$; **b.** $58.53 - s$ **45.** $x + 7$; 19; 21 **47.** $x + 3$; 15; 17 **49.** F **51.** 36 **53.** 1.

1-2

Check It Out! 1a. 8.8 **1b.** 0 **1c.** 25 **2a.** $\frac{1}{2}$ **2b.** -10 **2c.** 8 **3a.** 9.3 **3b.** 2 **3c.** 44 **4.** 35 years old

Exercises 3. 21 **5.** 16.3 **7.** $\frac{1}{2}$ **9.** 0 **11.** 2.3 **13.** 1.2 **15.** 32 **17.** 3.7 **19.** $\frac{17}{6}$ **21.** 9 **23.** 17 **25.** $\frac{4}{7}$ **27.** 10.5 **29.** 9 **31.** 0 **33.** -17 **35.** -3100 **37.** -0.5 **39.** 0.05 **41.** 15 **43.** 1545 **45.** 30 **47.** $\frac{1}{3}$ **49.** $a + 500 = 4732$; \$4232 **51.** $x - 10 = 12$; $x = 22$ **53.** $x + 8 = 16$; $x = 8$ **55.** $5 + x = 6$; $x = 1$ **57.** $x - 4 = 9$; $x = 13$ **59.** $m + 560 = 1680$; \$1120 **61.** $63 + x = 90$; $x = 27$ **63.** $x + 15 = 90$; $x = 75$ **65.** $h - 47 = 28$; 75 **69.** J **71.** $-\frac{12}{5}$ **73.** $-\frac{13}{12}$ **75.** 10 **77.** 90

1-3

Check It Out! 1a. 50 **1b.** -39 **1c.** 56 **2a.** 4 **2b.** -20 **2c.** 5 **3a.** $-\frac{5}{4}$ **3b.** 1 **3c.** 612 **4.** 15,000 ft

Exercises 1. 32 **3.** 14 **5.** 19 **7.** 7 **9.** 5 **11.** 2.5 **13.** 14 **15.** -9 **17.** $\frac{1}{8}$ **19.** $16c = 192$; \$12 **21.** 24 **23.** -36 **25.** -150 **27.** 55 **29.** -3 **31.** 1 **33.** 13 **35.** 0.3 **37.** 2 **39.** -16 **41.** -3.5 **43.** -2 **45.** $\frac{7}{10}s = 392$; \$560 **49.** $4s = 84$; 21 in. **51.** $4s = 16.4$; 4.1 cm **53.** $-3x = 12$; $x = -4$ **55.** $\frac{x}{3} = -8$; $x = -24$ **57.** $6.25h = 50$; 8 h **59.** $0.05m = 13.80$; 276 min **61.** -2 **63.** 0; $8y = 0$; 0 **65a.** number of data values **c.** 185,300 acres **67.** 7 **69.** 605 **71.** $\frac{3}{16}$ **73.** 5.7 **75.** $\frac{2}{3}g = 2$; 3 g **77.** D **79.** B **81a.** $6c = 4.80$ **b.** $c = \$0.80$ **83.** 2 **85.** 9 **87.** 2 **89.** -20 **91.** -132 **93.** Multiply both sides by a.

2-1

Check It Out! 1. 12 **2.** \$7.50/h **3.** 20.5 ft/s **4a.** -20 **4b.** 5.75 **5.** 6 in.

Exercises 1. The ratios are equivalent. **3.** 682 trillion **5.** 18,749 lb/cow **7.** 0.075 page/min **9.** 18 mi/gal **11.** $\frac{3}{5}$ **13.** 39 **15.** 6.5 **17.** 23 **19.** $\frac{3}{5} = \frac{h}{4.9}$; 2.94 m **21.** 72 **23.** \$403.90/oz **25.** 2498.4 km/h **27.** 10 **29.** -1 **31.** 13 **33.** 1.2 **35.** $\frac{1}{9}$ **37.** 45 **39.** \$84 **43.** 1.625 **45.** 3 **47.** $-\frac{2}{7}$ **49.** $\frac{11}{3}$ **51.** 3 **53.** 24 **55.** -120 **59.** A **61.** D **63.** 40°; 50° **65.** 0.0006722 people/m^2

2-2

Check It Out! 1. 2.8 in. **2a.** $\frac{150}{x} = \frac{45}{195}$; 650 cm **2b.** $\frac{5.5}{x} = \frac{3.5}{28}$; 44 ft **3.** The ratio of the perimeters is equal to the ratio of the corresponding sides.

Exercises 3. 10 ft **7.** 7 in. **11.** 480 ft^2 **13.** 4 **15.** 2.8 ft **17.** 4 cm **21.** $\frac{1.5}{x} = \frac{4.5}{36}$; 12 m **23.** k^2 **25.** G **27.** $w = 4$; $x = 7.5$; $y = 8$ **29.** 16.6 cm

2-3

Check It Out! 1a. 17 oz **1b.** 7.85 m **1c.** 6000 g **2a.** C **2b.** C **3.** no; C **4a.** 3.89 cm–4.31 cm **4b.** 463.12 m–486.88 m **4c.** 84.57 mg–85.43 mg

Exercises 1. precise **3.** 4.3 mL **5.** 2.37 mg **7.** 47.3 ft **9a.** 1 **9b.** 1 **11.** no; ball 4 **13.** 49 lb–51 lb **15.** 24 cm–26 cm **17.** 240 mm–260 mm **19.** 4337 mg **21.** 11,000 lb **23.** 6.83 cm **25.** 0.0127 m **27a.** Chandra **27b.** Lucy **29.** 44.1 lb–45.9 lb **31.** 36.44°C–37.56°C **33.** 28.8 ft–31.2 ft **35.** 0.19 cm–0.21 cm **37.** 5456 mi **39.** 120 ft **41.** 6 kg **43.** 16,453.2 mL **45.** 0.265 cm **47.** 165 ft **49.** neither **51.** 475.0 mL **53.** 50 kg ± 4% **55.** 750 kg ± 2% **57.** 425 lb ± 2% **59.** 175 km ± 3% **61.** ball 4 **65.** J **67.** 0.04% **69.** 384,326 km–384,480 km

3-1

Check It Out! 1a. 1 1b. 6 1c. 0
2a. $\frac{55}{4}$ 2b. $\frac{1}{2}$ 2c. 15 3a. $-\frac{5}{6}$ 3b. 5
3c. 8 4. $60 5. -42

Exercises 1. 2 3. -18 5. 2 7. 66
9. $\frac{5}{4}$ 11. -12 13. 16 15. -3.2 17. 4
19. 15 passes 21. 4 23. -4 25. 4
27. 5 29. -9 31. $\frac{1}{4}$ 33. 1 35. 3
37. $\frac{28}{5}$ 39. 3 41. 8 43. 7 45. $-\frac{1}{2}$
47. $x = 40$ 49. $x = 35$
51. $8 - 3n = 2$; $n = 2$
53a. $1963 - 5s = 1863$; $s = 20$ 53b. 3
55. 8 57. 4.5 59. -10 61. 10
63. $5k - 70 = 60$; 26 in. 65. Stan: 36;
Mark: 37; Wayne: 38 67a. 45,000;
112,500; 225,000; 337,500; $225n$
67b. $c = 225n$ 71. H 73. 27 75. $6\frac{1}{5}$
77. 14.5 79. -6

3-2

Check It Out! 1a. -2 1b. 2
2a. 4 2b. -2 3a. no solution
3b. all real numbers 4. 10 years old

Exercises 3. 1 5. 40 7. $-\frac{2}{3}$
9. 3 11. no solution 13. all real
numbers 15. 6 17. 6 19. 2.85
21. 10 23. 6 25. 14 27. $\frac{3}{4}$
29. -4 31. no solution 33a. 15 weeks
33b. 180 lb 35. $x - 30 = 14 - 3x$;
$x = 11$ 37. -4 39. 7 41. -3 43. 2
45. 1 47. $-\frac{7}{5}$ 49. 4 51. no solution
53. 9 59. F 61. H 63. 2 65. no
solution 67. -20 69. 6, 7, 8 71. $1.68

3-3

Check It Out! 1. about 1.46 h
2. $i = f + gt$ 3a. $t = \frac{5-b}{2}$ 3b. $V = \frac{m}{D}$

Exercises 3. $w = \frac{V}{\ell h}$ 5. $m = 4n + 8$
7. $a = \frac{10}{b+c}$ 9. $I = A - P$
11. $x = \frac{k+5}{y}$ 13. $\frac{x-2}{z} = y$
15. $x = 5(a + g)$ 17. $x = \frac{y-b}{m}$
19. $T = \frac{PV}{nR}$ 21. $T = M + R$
23. $b = \frac{c-2a}{2}$ 25. $r = 7 - ax$
27. $x = \frac{5-4y}{3}$ 31. $a = \frac{t-g}{-0.0035}$
35. C 37. D 39. $a = \frac{5}{2}\left(c + \frac{3}{4}b\right)$
41. $d = 500\left(t - \frac{1}{2}\right)$ 43. $s = \frac{v^2 - u^2}{2a}$
45. 120 s

4-1

Check It Out! 1. all real numbers
greater than 4

2a.

2b.

2c.

3. $x < 2.5$ 4. $d =$ amount employee
can earn per hour; $d \geq 8.25$

Exercises 1. A solution of an
inequality makes the inequality
true when substituted for the
variable. 3. all real numbers greater
than -3 5. all real numbers greater
than or equal to 3 11. $b > -8\frac{1}{2}$
13. $d < -7$ 15. $f \leq 14$ 17. $r < 140$
where r is positive 19. all real
numbers less than 2 21. all real
numbers less than or equal to 12
27. $v < -11$ 29. $x > -3.3$ 31. $z \geq$
9 33. $y =$ years of experience;
$y \geq 5$ 35. h is less than -5. 37. r is
greater than or equal to -2.
39. $p \leq 17$ 41. $f > 0$ 43. $p =$ profits;
$p < 10,000$ 45. $e =$ elevation;
$e \leq 5000$ 51. D 53. C 59. D 61. C
65. $<$

4-2

Check It Out! 1a. $s \leq 9$

1b. $t < 5\frac{1}{2}$

1c. $q < 11$

2. $11 + m \leq 15$; $m \leq 4$ where m is
nonnegative; Sarah can consume
4 mg or less without exceeding the
RDA. 3. $250 + p > 282$; $p > 32$; Josh
needs to bench press more than
32 additional pounds to break the
school record.

Exercises 1. $p > 6$ 3. $x \leq -15$
5. $102 + t \leq 104$; $t \leq 2$ where t is

nonnegative 7. $a \geq 5$ 9. $x < 15$
11. $1400 + 243 + w \leq 2000$;
$w \leq 357$ where w is nonnegative
13. $x - 10 > 32$; $x > 42$
15. $r - 13 \leq 15$; $r \leq 28$ 17. $q > 51$
19. $p \leq 0.8$ 21. $c > -202$ 23. $x \geq 0$
25. $21 + d \leq 30$; $d \leq 9$ where d is
nonnegative 27. $x < 3$; B
29. $x \leq 3$; D 31. $p \leq 40,421$ where p
is nonnegative 35. a. $411 + 411 =$
882 miles b. $822 + m \leq 1000$
c. $m \leq 178$, but m cannot be negative.
37. F 39. J 41. $r \leq 5\frac{1}{10}$
43. sometimes 45. always

4-3

Check It Out! 1a. $k > 6$

1b. $q \leq -10$

1c. $g > 36$

2a. $x \geq -10$

2b. $h > -17$

3. 0, 1, 2, 3, 4, 5, 6, 7, 8, 9, 10, 11, or
12 servings

Exercises 1. $b > 9$ 3. $d > 18$
5. $m \leq 1.1$ 7. $s > -2$ 9. $x > 5$
11. $n > -0.4$ 13. $d > -3$ 15. $t > -72$
17. 0, 1, 2, 3, 4, 5, or 6 nights 19. $j \leq$
12 21. $d < 7$ 23. $h \leq \frac{8}{7}$ 25. $c \leq$
-12 27. $b \geq \frac{1}{10}$ 29. $b \leq -16$
31. $r < -\frac{3}{2}$ 33. $y < 2$ 35. $t > 4$
37. $z < -11$ 39. $k \leq -7$ 41. $p \geq$
-12 43. $x > -3$ 45. $x < 20$
47. $p \leq -6$ 49. $b < 2$ 51. $7x \geq 21$;
$x \geq 3$ 53. $-\frac{4}{5}b \leq -16$; $b \geq 20$ 57. C
59. A 67. B 71. $g \leq -\frac{14}{5}$ 73. $m > \frac{4}{15}$
75. $x = 5$

5-1

Check It Out! 1a. $x \leq -6$

1b. $x < -11$

1c. $n \leq -10$

2a. $m > 10$

2b. $x > -4$

2c. $x > 2\frac{1}{3}$

3. $\frac{95 + x}{2} \geq 90$; $95 + x \geq 180$; $x \geq 85$; Jim's score must be at least 85.

Exercises 1. $m > 6$ **3.** $x \leq -2$ **5.** $x > -16$ **7.** $x \geq -9$ **9.** $x > -\frac{1}{2}$ **11.** $x \leq 19$ **13.** $x > 1$ **15.** sales of more than \$9000 **17.** $x \leq 1$ **19.** $w < -2$ **21.** $x < -6$ **23.** $f < -4.5$ **25.** $w > 0$ **27.** $v > \frac{2}{3}$ **29.** $x > -5$ **31.** $x < -2$ **33.** $a \geq 11$ **35.** $x > 3$ **37.** starting at 29 min **39.** $x \leq 2$ **41.** $x < 4$ **43.** $x < -6$ **45.** $r < 8$ **47.** $x < 7$ **49.** $p \geq 18$ **51.** $\frac{1}{2}x + 9 < 33$; $x < 48$ **53.** $4(x + 12) \leq 16$; $x \leq -8$ **55.** B **57.** A **59.** 24 months or more **61a.**

Number	Process	Cost
1	$350 + 3$	353
2	$350 + 3(2)$	356
3	$350 + 3(3)$	359
10	$350 + 3(10)$	380
n	$350 + 3n$	$350 + 3n$

b. $c = 350 + 3n$ **c.** $350 + 3n \leq 500$; $n \leq 50$; 50 CDs or fewer **65.** G **67.** 59 **69.** $x > 5$ **71.** $x > 0$ **73.** $x \geq 0$ **75.** $-3x > 0$

5-2

Check It Out! 1a. $x \leq -2$

1b. $t < -1$

2. more than 160 flyers

3a. $r \leq 2$

3b. $x < 3$

4a. no solutions **4b.** all real numbers

Exercises 1. $x < 3$ **3.** $x < 2$ **5.** $c < -2$ **7.** at least 34 pizzas **9.** $p < -17$ **11.** $x > 3$ **13.** $t < 6.8$ **15.** no solutions **17.** all real numbers **19.** no solutions **21.** $y > -2$ **23.** $b \geq -7$ **25.** $m > 5$ **27.** $x \geq 2$ **29.** $w \geq 6$ **31.** $r \geq -4$ **33.** no solutions **35.** all real numbers **37.** all real numbers **39.** $t < -7$ **41.** $x > 3$ **43.** $x < 2$ **45.** $x > -2$ **47.** $x \leq -6$ **49.** 27 s **51a.** $400 + 4.50n$ **b.** $12n$ **c.** $400 + 4.50n < 12n$; $n > 53\frac{1}{3}$; 54 CDs or more **53.** $5x - 10 < 6x - 8$; $x > -2$ **55.** $\frac{3}{4}x \geq x - 5$; $x \leq 20$ **59.** x can never be greater than itself plus 1. **61.** D **63.** A **67.** $x < -3$ **69.** $w \geq -1\frac{6}{7}$

5-3

Check It Out! 1. $1.0 < c < 3.0$

2a. $1 < x < 5$

2b. $-3 \leq n < 2$

3a. $r < 10$ OR $r > 14$

3b. $x \geq 3$ OR $x < -1$

4a. $-9 < y < -2$

4b. $x \leq -13$ OR $x \geq 2$

Exercises 1. intersection **3.** $-5 < x < 5$ **5.** $0 < x < 3$ **7.** $x < -8$ OR $x > 4$ **9.** $n < 1$ OR $n > 4$ **11.** $-5 \leq a \leq -3$ **13.** $c < 1$ OR $c \geq 9$ **15.** $16 \leq k \leq 50$ **17.** $3 \leq n \leq 6$ **19.** $2 < x < 6$ **21.** $x < 0$ OR $x > 3$ **23.** $x < -3$ OR $x > 2$ **25.** $q < 0$ OR $q \geq 2$ **27.** $-2 < s < 1$ **29a.** $225 + 80n$ gives the cost of the studio and technicians; the band will spend between \$200 and \$550.

b. $-0.3125 \leq n \leq 4.0625$; n cannot be a negative number **c.** \$155 **31.** $1 \leq x \leq 2$ **33.** $-10 \leq x \leq 10$ **35.** $t < 0$ OR $t > 100$ **37.** $-2 < x < 5$ **39.** $a < 0$ OR $a > 1$ **41.** $n < 2$ OR $n > 5$ **43.** $7 \leq m \leq 60$ **47.** D **49.** B **51.** $0.5 < c < 3$ **53.** $s \leq 6$ OR $s \geq 9$ **55.** $-1 \leq x \leq 3$mm

6-1

Check It Out! 1a. yes **1b.** no **2a.** $(-2, 3)$ **2b.** $(3, -2)$ **3.** 5 movies; \$25

Exercises 1. an ordered pair that satisfies both equations **3.** yes **5.** $(2, 1)$ **7.** $(-4, 7)$ **9.** no **11.** yes **13.** $(3, 3)$ **15.** $(3, -1)$

17a. $\begin{cases} y = 2x \\ y = 16 + 0.50x \end{cases}$

b.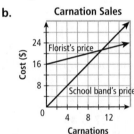

Carnation Sales

It represents how many carnations need to be sold to break even.
c. No, because the solution is not a whole number of carnations; 11 carnations. **19.** $(-2.4, -9.3)$ **21.** $(0.3, -0.3)$ **23.** 45 white; 120 pink **25.** 8 yr **29.** C **31.** month 11; 400

6-2

Check It Out! 1a. $(-2, 1)$ **1b.** $(0, 2)$ **1c.** $(3, -10)$ **2.** $(-1, 6)$ **3.** 10 months; \$860; the first option; the first option is cheaper for the first 9 months; the second option is cheaper after 10 months.

Exercises 1. $(9, 35)$ **3.** $(3, 8)$ **5.** $(-3, -9)$ **7a.** 3 months; \$136 **b.** Green Lawn **9.** $(-4, 2)$ **11.** $(-1, 2)$ **13.** $(1, 5)$ **15.** $(3, -2)$ **17.** 6 months; \$360; the second option **19.** $(2, -2)$ **21.** $(8, 6)$ **23.** $(-9, -14.8)$ **25.** 12 nickels; 8 dimes

27. $\begin{cases} x + y = 1000 \\ 0.05x + 0.06y = 58 \end{cases}$; $200 at 5%; $800 at 6%

29. $x = 60°; y = 30°$
35. Possible estimate: $(1.75, -2.5)$; $(1.8, -2.4)$ **37.** F **39.** $r = 5; s = -2$; $t = 4$ **41.** $a = 9; b = 5; c = 0$

6-3

Check It Out! 1. $(-2, 4)$ **2.** $(4, 1)$
3a. $(2, 0)$ **3b.** $(3, 4)$ **4.** 9 lilies; 4 tulips

Exercises 1. $(-4, 1)$ **3.** $(-2, -4)$
5. $(-6, 30)$ **7.** $(3, 2)$ **9.** $(4, -3)$
11. $(-1, -2)$ **13.** $(1, 5)$ **15.** $\left(6, -\frac{1}{2}\right)$
17. $(-1, 2)$ **19.** $(-1, 2)$

21. $\begin{cases} \ell - w = 2 \\ 2\ell + 2w = 40 \end{cases}$; length: 11 units; width: 9 units

25. $(3, 3)$ **27.** $\left(\frac{46}{7}, \frac{8}{7}\right)$ **29.** $\left(\frac{15}{7}, \frac{9}{7}\right)$

31a. $\begin{cases} 3A + 2B = 16 \\ 2A + 3B = 14 \end{cases}$ **b.** $A = 4; B = 2$
c. Buying the first package will save $8; buying the second package will save $7. **33.** A **35a.** $s =$ number of student tickets; $n =$ number of nonstudent tickets;
$\begin{cases} s + n = 358 \\ 1.50s + 3.25n = 752.25 \end{cases}$
b. $s = 235; n = 123$; 235 student tickets, 123 nonstudent tickets

7-1

Check It Out! 1. Possible answer: Substitute $-2x + 5$ for y in the second equation: $2x + (-2x + 5) = 1; 5 = 1$ ✘ **2.** Possible answer: Substitute $x - 3$ for y in the second equation: $x - (x - 3) - 3 = 0; 3 - 3 = 0; 0 = 0$ ✔
3a. consistent, dependent; infinitely many solutions
3b. consistent, independent; one solution **3c.** inconsistent; no solution **4.** Yes; the graphs of the two equations have different slopes so they intersect.

Exercises 1. consistent **3.** Possible answer: Substitute $-3x + 2$ for y in the first equation: $3x + (-3x + 2) = 6; 2 = 6$ ✘ **5.** Possible answer: Substitute $-x + 3$ for y in the

second equation: $x + (-x + 3) - 3 = 0; 0 = 0$ ✔ **7.** Possible answer: Add the two equations:

$$\begin{array}{r} -7x + y = -2 \\ +7x - y = 2 \\ \hline 0 + 0 = 0 \\ 0 = 0 \text{ ✔} \end{array}$$

9. inconsistent; no solutions
11. yes **13.** Possible answer: Substitute $-x - 1$ for y in the first equation: $x + (-x - 1) = 3; -1 = 3$ ✘ **15.** Possible answer: Compare slopes and intercepts. $-6 + y = 2x \rightarrow y = 2x - 6; y = 2x - 36$; the lines have the same slope and different y-intercepts. Therefore the lines are parallel. **17.** Possible answer: Substitute $x - 2$ for y in the second equation: $x - (x - 2) - 2 = 0; 2 - 2 = 0; 0 = 0$ ✔
19. Possible answer: Compare slopes and intercepts. $-9x - 3y = -18 \rightarrow y = -3x + 6; 3x + y = 6 \rightarrow y = -3x + 6$; the lines have the same slope and the same y-intercepts. Therefore the graphs are one line. **21.** consistent, independent; one solution **23.** Yes; the graphs of the two equations have different slopes, so they intersect. **27.** They will always have the same number; both started with 2 and add 4 every year. **29.** The graph will be 2 parallel lines. **31.** A **33.** D
35. $p = q; p \neq q$

7-2

Check It Out! 1a. no **1b.** yes
2a.
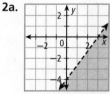
2b.
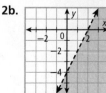

2c.

3a. $2.5b + 2g \leq 6$
3b.

Olive Combinations

Green olives vs Black olives

3c. Possible answer: (1 lb black, 1 lb green), (0.5 lb black, 2 lb green)
4a. $y < -x$ **4b.** $y \geq -2x - 3$

Exercises 3. yes
5.

7.

9a. $r + p \leq 16$
b.

Punch Combinations

Pineapple juice (c) vs Orange juice (c)

c. Possible answer: (2 c orange, 2 c pineapple), (4 c orange, 10 c pineapple) **11.** $y \geq x + 5$ **13.** yes
15.

19a. $3x + 2y \leq 30$

b.

Food Combinations

Hot dogs (lb) / Hamburger meat (lb)

c. Possible answer: (3 lb hamburger, 2 lb hot dogs), (5 lb hamburger, 6 lb hot dogs) **21.** $y \leq -\frac{1}{5}x + 3$

23.

25.

29.

31.

33.

35.

37. $7a + 4s \geq 280$ **41.** A **43.** B **45.** C

47.

49. $y \geq \frac{1}{2}x + 3$

7-3

Check It Out! **1a.** yes **1b.** no

2a.

Possible answer: solutions: $(3, 3)$, $(4, 4)$; not solutions: $(-3, 1)$, $(-1, -4)$

2b.

Possible answer: solutions: $(0, 0)$, $(3, -2)$; not solutions: $(4, 4)$, $(1, -6)$

3a.

no solutions

3b.

all points between and on the parallel lines

3c.

same as solutions of $y > -2x + 3$

4.

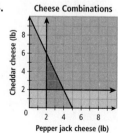

Cheese Combinations

Cheddar cheese (lb) / Pepper jack cheese (lb)

Possible answer: (3 lb pepper jack, 2 lb cheddar), (2.5 lb pepper jack, 4 lb cheddar)

Exercises **1.** all **3.** yes

5.

Possible answer: solutions: $(3, 3)$, $(4, 3)$; not solutions: $(0, 0)$, $(2, 1)$

7.

Possible answer: solutions: $(0, 4)$, $(1, 4)$; not solutions: $(2, -1)$, $(3, 1)$

9.

no solutions

11.

all points between the parallel lines and on the solid line

13.

same solutions as $y > 2x - 1$

15.

Sales Goals

Cupcakes / Lemonade (c)

(6, 13)   (10, 10)

Possible answer: (6 lemonade, 13 cupcakes), (10 lemonade, 10 cupcakes) **17.** yes

19.

Possible answer: solutions: $(-2, 0)$, $(-3, 1)$; not solutions: $(0, 0)$, $(1, 4)$

21.

Possible answer: solutions: $(-1, 3)$, $(0, 5)$; not solutions: $(0, 0)$, $(1, 4)$

23.

no solutions

25.

All points are solutions.

27.

same solutions as $y > 2$

29.

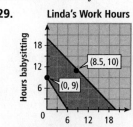

Linda's Work Hours

Possible answer:
$(0$ h at pharmacy, 9 h babysitting$)$,
$(8.5$ h at pharmacy, 10 h babysitting$)$

31.

33.

35. $\begin{cases} y > x + 1 \\ y < x + 3 \end{cases}$

37. $\begin{cases} y < 2 \\ x \geq -2 \end{cases}$

39. Student B **45.** G

47. about 12 square units

49.

8-1

Check It Out! 1. C
2a. discrete;

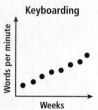

Keyboarding

2b. continuous;

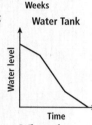

Water Tank

3. Possible answer: When the number of students reaches a certain point, the number of pizzas bought increases.

Exercises 1. continuous **3.** B
5. C **11.** A **13.** continuous **19.** The point of intersection represents the time of day when you will be the same distance from the base of the mountain on both the hike up and the hike down. **23.** C

8-2

Check It Out! 1.

x	y
1	3
2	4
3	5

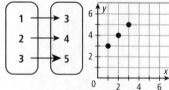

2a. D: $\{6, 5, 2, 1\}$; R: $\{-4, -1, 0\}$
2b. D: $\{1, 4, 8\}$; R: $\{1, 4\}$
3a. D: $\{-6, -4, 1, 8\}$; R: $\{1, 2, 9\}$; yes; each domain value is paired with exactly one range value.
3b. D: $\{2, 3, 4\}$; R: $\{-5, -4, -3\}$; no; the domain value 2 is paired with both −5 and −4.

Exercises

3.

x	y
1	1
1	2

5.

x	y
−7	7
−3	3
−1	1
5	−5

7. D: $\{-5, 0, 2, 5\}$; R: $\{-20, -8, 0, 7\}$ **9.** D: $\{2, 3, 5, 6, 8\}$; R: $\{4, 9, 25, 36, 81\}$ **11.** D: $\{1\}$; R: $\{-2, 0, 3, 8\}$; no **13.** D: $\{-2, -1, 0, 1, 2\}$; R: $\{1\}$; yes

15.

x	y
−2	−4
−1	−1
0	0
1	−1
2	−4

17. D: $\{3\}$; R: $1 \leq y \leq 5$
19. D: $-2 \leq x \leq 2$; R: $0 \leq y \leq 2$; yes **21.** yes **23.** yes **25.** yes
27. no **29a.** D: $0 \leq t \leq 5$; R: $0 \leq v \leq 750$ **b.** yes **c.** $(2, 300)$; $(3.5, 525)$
33. G **35a.** $\{(-3, 5), (-1, 7), (0, 9), (1, 11), (3, 13)\}$ **b.** D: $\{-3, -1, 0, 1, 3\}$; R: $\{5, 7, 9, 11, 13\}$ **c.** yes
37. all real numbers

8-3

Check It Out! 1. $y = 3x$
2a. independent: time; dependent: cost **2b.** independent: pounds; dependent: cost **3a.** independent: pounds; dependent: cost; $f(x) = 1.69x$ **3b.** independent: people; dependent: cost; $f(x) = 6 + 29.99x$
4a. 1; −7 **4b.** −5; 101 **5.** $f(x) = 500x$; D: $\{0, 1, 2, 3\}$; R: $\{0, 500, 1000, 1500\}$

Exercises 1. dependent
3. $y = x - 2$ **5.** independent: size of bottle; dependent: cost of water
7. independent: hours; dependent: cost; $f(h) = 75h$ **9.** 2; 9 **11.** −1; −15
13. $y = -2x$ **15.** independent: size of lawn; dependent: cost
17. independent: days late; dependent: total cost; $f(x) = 3.99 + 0.99x$ **19.** independent: gallons of gas; dependent: miles; $f(x) = 28x$

21. 7; 10 **23.** $f(n) = 2n + 5$; D: $\{1, 2, 3, 4\}$; R: $\{\$7, \$9, \$11, \$13\}$
25.

z	1	2	3	4
g(z)	−3	−1	1	3

27. $f(-6.89) \approx -16$; $f(1.01) \approx 8$; $f(4.67) \approx 20$ **33.** D **35.** 3.5
37. 44.1 m

9-1

Check It Out! 1a.

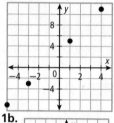

1b.

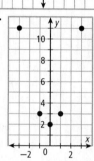

2a.

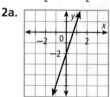

2b.

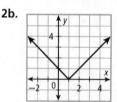

3. $x = 3$ **4.** Possible answer: about 32.5 mi

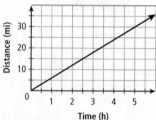

Average Speed of Lava Flow

Exercises

1.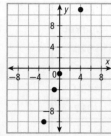

3.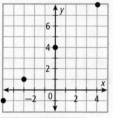

5.

7.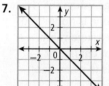

9.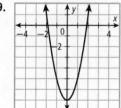

11. $y = -1$

13.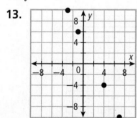

15.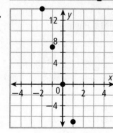

17.

19.

21.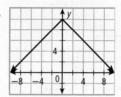

23.

25. $y = 5$

29.

31.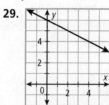

33.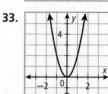

35.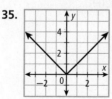

37. $x = 1$ **39.** $y = -8$ **41.** yes; yes **43.** no; yes **45.** no; yes; yes

47. yes; no; yes **55a.** $v = 10,000 - 1500h$ **b.** 8500 gal

c.

Time (h)	Volume (gal)
0	10,000
1	8,500
2	7,000
3	5,500
4	4,000

59. J **61.** J **63.** $y = 4x + 64$

9-2

Check It Out!
1a. $(3, 3)$ **b.** $(-2, 1)$
2a.

$x + 3$	x	y
1	−2	4
2	−1	0
3	x	2
5	x	2

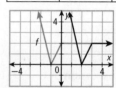

b.

x	y	$-y$
−2	4	−4
−1	0	x
x	2	−2
x	2	−2

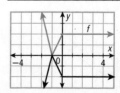

3.

x	y	$2y$
−1	3	6
0	0	0
2	2	4
4	2	4

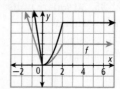

4. vertical compression by a factor of $\frac{3}{4}$

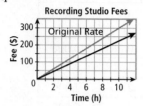

Recording Studio Fees

Exercises 1. compression
3. $(4, -1)$

5.
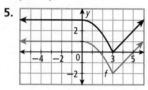

7.
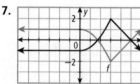

9.
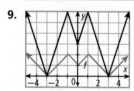

11. vertical compression by a factor of $\frac{1}{2}$ **13.** horizontal shift right 5 units **15.** $(3, 5)$

17.
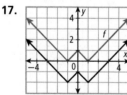

21.
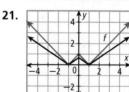

25. vertical shift down 5 units
27. horizontal stretch by a factor of 2 **29.** 10 square units; the same as the original **31.** 7 square units; smaller than the original
33. 10 square units; the same as the original **35.** 30 square units; larger than the original
37a. vertical translation
b. horizontal compression

c. the increase in the per-hour labor rate

39.
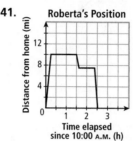
Roberta's Position

41.
Roberta's Position

43. The library is half as far from Roberta's house. **47.** H
49. H **53a.** $c(n) = 0.37n$
b. vertical stretch **c.** 15 in 1999 and 13 in 2002 **d.** The number of letters that can be mailed for $5.00 must be rounded down to the nearest whole number.

9-3

Check It Out! 1a. yes; $\frac{1}{2}, \frac{5}{4}, \frac{7}{4}, \frac{9}{4}$
1b. no **2a.** -343 **2b.** 19.6 **3.** 750 lb
Exercises 1. common difference
3. yes; -0.7; $-0.7, -1.4, -2.1$
5. no **7.** -53 **9.** no **11.** yes; -9; $-58, -67, -76$ **13.** 5.9 **15.** 9500 mi **17.** $\frac{1}{4}$ **19.** -2.2 **21.** 0.07
23. $-\frac{3}{8}, -\frac{1}{2}, -\frac{5}{8}, -\frac{3}{4}$ **25.** -0.2, $-0.7, -1.2, -1.7$ **27.** $-0.3, -0.1$, $0.1, 0.3$ **29.** 22 **31.** 122 **33b.** $9, $11, $13, $15; $a_n = 2n + 7$ **c.** $37
d. no **35.** -104.5 **37.** $\frac{20}{3}$ **39a.** $a_n = 6 + 3(n - 1)$ **b.** 48 **c.** $7800 **d.** $a_n = 7 + 3(n - 1)$; $8200

41a.

Time Interval	Mile Marker
1	520
2	509
3	498
4	487
5	476
6	465

b. $a_n = 520 + (n - 1)(-11)$
c. number of miles per interval
d. 421 **43.** F **45.** 173 and 182; 20th and 21st terms **47a.** session 16; yes
b. Thursday

10-1

Check It Out! 1a. Yes; each domain value is paired with exactly one range value; yes **1b.** Yes; each domain value is paired with exactly one range value; yes **1c.** No; each domain value is not paired with exactly one range value.
2. Yes; a constant change of $+2$ in x corresponds to a constant change of -1 in y.
3a. yes

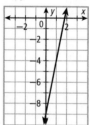

3b. yes
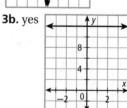

3c. no
4.
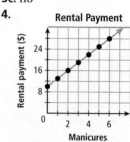
Rental Payment

D: {0, 1, 2, 3, …}
R: {$10, $13, $16, $19, …}

Exercises 1. No; it is not in the form $Ax + By = C$. **3.** yes; yes
5. yes **7.** yes **9.** yes **11.** no **15.** yes; no **17.** yes; no **19.** yes **23.** no
27. yes; yes **29.** yes; yes
31. yes; $-4x + y = 2$; $A = -4$; $B = 1$; $C = 2$ **33.** no **35.** yes; $x = 7$; $A = 1$; $B = 0$; $C = 7$ **37.** yes; $3x - y = 1$; $A = 3$; $B = -1$; $C = 1$ **39.** yes; $5x - 2y = -3$; $A = 5$, $B = -2$, $C = -3$ **41.** no **55.** no **57.** C
63. not linear

Check It Out! 1a. x-intercept: -2; y-intercept: 3 **1b.** x-intercept: -10; y-intercept: 6 **1c.** x-intercept: 4; y-intercept: 8

2a.

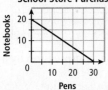

School Store Purchases

x-intercept: 30; y-intercept: 20
2b. x-intercept: number of pens that can be purchased if no notebooks are purchased; y-intercept: number of notebooks that can be purchased if no pens are purchased

3a.

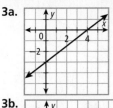

3b.

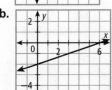

Exercises 1. y-intercept
3. x-intercept: 2; y-intercept: -4
5. x-intercept: 2; y-intercept: -1
7. x-intercept: 2; y-intercept: 8
13. x-intercept: -1; y-intercept: 3
15. x-intercept: -4; y-intercept: 2
17. x-intercept: -4; y-intercept: 2
19. x-intercept: 2; y-intercept: 8

21. x-intercept: $\frac{1}{8}$; y-intercept: -1
35. A **37.** B **41.** F **47.** x-intercept: 950; y-intercept: -55

 10-3

Check It Out! 1. day 1 to day 6: -53; day 6 to day 16: -7.5; day 16 to day 22: 0; day 22 to day 30: -4.375; from day 1 to day 6

2.

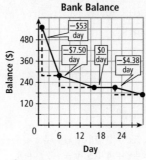

Bank Balance

3. $-\frac{2}{5}$ **4a.** undefined **4b.** 0
5a. undefined **5b.** positive

Exercises 1. constant **5.** $-\frac{3}{4}$
7. undefined **9.** undefined
11. positive **15.** 1 **17.** 0
19. positive **23.** $\frac{17}{18}$ **29.** C **31.** G

10-4

Check It Out! 1a. $m = 0$ **1b.** $m = 3$
1c. $m = 2$ **2a.** $m = \frac{1}{2}$ **2b.** $m = -3$
2c. $m = 2$ **2d.** $m = -\frac{3}{2}$ **3.** $m = \frac{1}{2}$; the height of the plant is increasing at a rate of 1 cm every 2 days.
4. $m = -\frac{2}{3}$

Exercises 1. 1 **3.** $-\frac{1}{2}$ **5.** 10 **7.** $\frac{1}{540}$
9. $-\frac{5}{9}$ **11.** -4 **13.** undefined
15. $-\frac{3}{4}$ **17.** $-\frac{9}{5000}$ **19.** $-\frac{13}{5}$
23a. Car 1; 20 mi/h **b.** The speed and the slope are both equal to the distance divided by time. **c.** 20 mi/h
25a. $y = 220 - x$ **27.** G **29.** $-\frac{b}{a}$
31. $\frac{3}{2} - y$ **33.** $x = \frac{1}{2}$ **35.** $x = -3$
37. $x = 0$

11-1

Check It Out! 1a. no **1b.** yes; $-\frac{3}{4}$
1c. yes; -3 **2a.** No; possible answer: the value of $\frac{y}{x}$ is not the same for each ordered pair. **2b.** Yes; possible answer: the value of $\frac{y}{x}$ is the same for each ordered pair.
2c. No; possible answer: the value

of $\frac{y}{x}$ is not the same for each ordered pair. **3.** 90

4. $y = 4x$

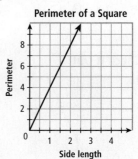

Perimeter of a Square

Exercises 1. direct variation
3. yes; -4 **5.** no **7.** 18 **9.** $y = 7x$
11. yes; $\frac{1}{4}$ **13.** yes **15.** -16
17. $y = 2.50x$ **19.** no **21.** $y = -3x$

The value of k is -3, and the graph shows that the slope of the line is -3.
25. $y = 2x$

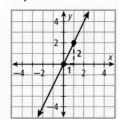

The value of k is 2, and the graph shows that the slope of the line is 2.
29. $y = -\frac{2}{9}x$

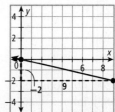

The value of k is $-\frac{2}{9}$, and the graph shows that the slope of the line is $-\frac{2}{9}$.
33. $y = -6x$

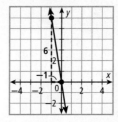

The value of k is -6, and the graph shows that the slope of the line is -6. **41.** C **43.** B

11-2

Check It Out!

1a.

1b.

2a. $y = -12x - \frac{1}{2}$ **2b.** $y = x$
2c. $y = 8x - 25$
3a. $y = \frac{2}{3}x$

3b. $y = -3x + 5$

3c. $y = -4$

4a. $y = 18x + 200$ **4b.** slope: 18; cost per person; y-intercept: 200; fee **4c.** \$3800

Exercises

1.

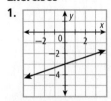

5. $y = x - 2$ **7.** $y = -3$

9. $y = -2x - 1$ **11.** $y = 3x - 1$
13a. $y = 18x + 10$ **b.** slope: 18; Helen's speed; y-intercept: 10; distance she has already biked
c. 46 mi

15.

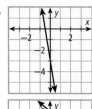

17.

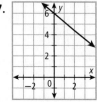

19. $y = 5x - 9$ **21.** $y = -\frac{1}{2}x + 7$
23. $y = \frac{1}{2}x + 4$ **25.** $y = -2x + 8$
29. possible **31.** impossible
33. C **37.** B **39.** B **41.** $y = \frac{1}{3}x - 3$
43. -6

11-3

Check It Out!
1a. $y - 1 = 2\left(x - \frac{1}{2}\right)$
1b. $y + 4 = 0(x - 3)$

2a.

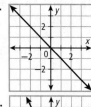

2b.

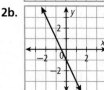

3a. $y = \frac{1}{3}x + 2$ **3b.** $y = 6x - 8$
4. x-intercept: -3; y-intercept: 9
5. $y = 2.25x + 6$; \$53.25

Exercises 1. $y + 6 = \frac{1}{5}(x - 2)$
3. $y + 7 = 0(x - 3)$ **7.** $y = -\frac{1}{3}x + 7$
9. $y = -x$ **11.** $y = -\frac{1}{2}x + 4$
13. x-intercept: 3; y-intercept: -3
15. x-intercept: -1; y-intercept: 3
17. $y - 5 = \frac{2}{9}(x + 1)$ **19.** $y - 8 = 8(x - 1)$ **23.** $y = -\frac{2}{7}x + 1$ **25.** $y = -6x + 57$ **27.** $y = -\frac{11}{2}x + 18$
29. $y = 2x - 6$ **31.** x-intercept: 1; y-intercept: -2 **33.** x-intercept: -6;

y-intercept: 9 **35.** $y = -\frac{1}{500}x + 212$; 200 °F **41.** never **43a.** $y - 11 = 2.5$ $(x - 2)$ **b.** 6 in. **c.** $16\frac{5}{8}$ in.
47. $y = -8$; $x = 4$ **49.** A **53a.** (0, 12) and (6, 8) **b.** $y = -\frac{2}{3}x + 12$
c. 18 min **55.** H **57.** $y = -3x + \frac{11}{4}$

11-4

Check It Out!
1a. $g(x) = 3(x - 2) + 1$
b. $g(x) = -(x + 2)$
2. $g(x) = \frac{1}{4}(3x + 2)$

3. $g(x) = \frac{1}{2}(x + 8)$
4a. $S(n) = 25n - 75$
b.

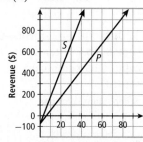

4c. horizontal compression by a factor of $\frac{1}{2}$

Exercises **1.** $g(x) = -\frac{3}{2}x + 2$

3. $g(x) = x - 6$

5. $g(x) = \frac{2}{3}x - 6$
7a. $D(n) = 0.60n + 5.00$
b.

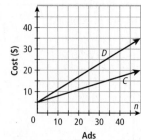

c. horizontal compression by a factor of $\frac{1}{2}$
9. $g(x) = \frac{1}{2}x - 4$
11. $g(x) = 1.2(-0.5x + 0.5)$
13. $g(x) = \frac{1}{2.75}(x + 1)$

15a. $g(x) = 0.15x + 0.35$

b.

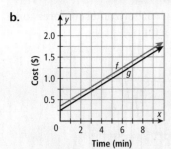

c. vertical shift up 0.1 unit

17. $g(x) = 2x$

19. $T(n) = 0.10\left(\dfrac{n}{15}\right) = \dfrac{n}{150}$; vertical

stretch by a factor of 1.6

21a. $g(x) = -x - 2$

b. $h(x) = -x + 2$

23a. 22.125; 20; 23; 59 **b.** Mean, median, and mode are increased by 7. Range stays the same.

c. All are multiplied by 4.

d. Mean, median, and mode are multiplied by 2, and 5 is added. Range is multiplied by 2. **25.** H

27. F

12-1

Check It Out! 1a. 80, −160, 320
1b. 216, 162, 121.5 **2.** 7.8125
3. $1342.18

Exercises 3. 25, 12.5, 6.25
5. 1,000,000,000 **7.** 4 **9.** 162, 243, 364.5 **11.** 2058; 14,406; 100,842
13. $\dfrac{5}{32}, \dfrac{5}{128}, \dfrac{5}{512}$ **15.** 0.0000000001, or
1×10^{-10} **17.** 80; 160 **19.** $\dfrac{1}{3}$ **21.** $\dfrac{1}{7}; \dfrac{1}{49}$
23. 6; −48 **25.** 4913 **27.** yes; $\dfrac{1}{3}$ **29.** no
31. no **33a.** 1.28 cm **b.** 40.96 cm
35. −2, −8, −32, −128
37. 2, 4, 8, 16 **39.** 12, 3, $\dfrac{3}{4}, \dfrac{3}{16}$
43a. $3993; $4392.30 **b.** 1.1
c. $2727.27 **45.** J **47.** x^4, x^5, x^6
49. 1, y, y^2 **51.** −400 **53.** the 7th term

12-2

Check It Out! 1. 3.375 in. **2a.** no
2b. yes

3a.

3b.

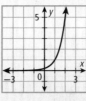

4a.

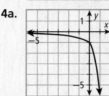

4b.

5a.

5b.

6. after about 13 yr

Exercises 1. no **3.** no **17.** about 2023 **19.** 289 ft **21.** yes **23.** no
35. $y = 4.8(2)^x$ **41.** −0.125
43a. $2000 **b.** 8% **c.** $2938.66
45. C **45.** C **47.** D **49.** 3 **51.** The value of a is the y-intercept.

12-3

Check It Out! 1. $y = 1200(1.08)^t$;
$1904.25 **2a.** $A = 1200(1.00875)^{4t}$;
$1379.49 **2b.** $A = 4000(1.0025)^{12t}$;
$5083.47 **3.** $y = 48,000(0.97)^t$; 38,783
4a. 1.5625 mg **4b.** 0.78125 g

Exercises 1. exponential growth
3. $y = 300(1.08)^t$; 441 **5.** $A =$
$4200(1.007)^{4t}$; $4965.43 **7.** $y =$
$10(0.84)^t$; 4.98 mg **9.** 5.5 g **11.** $y =$
$1600(1.03)^t$; 2150 **13.** $A = 30(1.078)^t$;
47 members **15.** $A = 7000(1.0075)^{4t}$;
$9438.44 **17.** $A = 12,000(1.026)^t$;
$17,635.66 **19.** $y = 58(0.9)^t$; $24.97

21. growth; 61% **23.** decay; $33\frac{1}{3}$%
25. growth; 10% **27.** growth; 25%
29. $y = 58,000,000(1.001)^t$;
58,174,174 **31.** $y = 8200(0.98)^t$;
$7118.63 **33.** $y = 970(1.012)^t$; 1030
35. B **37.** 18 yr **39.** A; B **45.** D **47.** D
49. about 20 yr **51.** 100 min, or 1 h
40 min **53.** $225,344

13-1

Check It Out!

1a.

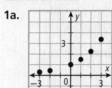

exponential

1b.

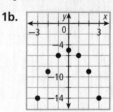

quadratic

2. quadratic **3.** The oven temperature decreases by 50 °F every 10 min; $y = -5x + 375$; 75 °F

Exercises 1. exponential
3. linear **5.** exponential **7.** Grapes cost $1.79/lb; $y = 1.79x$; $10.74
11. linear **13.** exponential
15. $\ell = 6k$; linear **17.** linear
19. $y = 0.2(4)^x$ **21.** linear **27.** C
29. C

13-2

Check It Out! 1. Slope: Dave is saving at a higher rate ($12/wk) than Arturo ($8/wk); y-int.: Dave started with more money ($30) than Arturo ($24). **2.** A increased about $1.67/yr; B increased about $1.13/yr. **3.** A: $y = 100x + 850$; B: $y = 850(1.08)^x$; school A's enrollment will exceed school B's enrollment at first, but school B will have more students by the end of the 11th year. After that, school B's enrollment exceeds school A's enrollment by ever-increasing amounts each year.

Exercises 1. Slope: Kara is withdrawing at a higher rate ($75/wk) than Fay ($50/wk); y-int.: Kara started with more money ($500) than Fay ($425). **3.** Plan A will result in more bicycles at first, but plan B surpasses plan A by the end of the 8th year. After that, B exceeds A by ever-increasing amounts each year.

5. A: 6.3 people per square mile; **B:** about 5.25 people per square mile **7a.** about 120 **b.** $5

13-2 Extension

Check It Out!

1.

x	-2	-1	0	1	2
$j(x)$	$\frac{1}{16}$	$\frac{1}{8}$	$\frac{1}{4}$	$\frac{1}{2}$	1

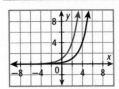

$y = 0$; $j(x) = 2^x$ translation 2 units right

2a.

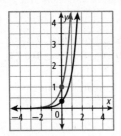

$\frac{1}{3}$; $y = 0$; $f(x) = 5^x$ vertical compression by a factor of 3

b.

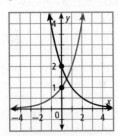

2; $y = 0$; $j(x) = 2^x$ reflection across y-axis and vertical stretch by a factor of 2

Exercises

1.

x	-2	-1	0	1	2
$g(x)$	2.1	2.3	3	5	11

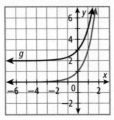

$y = 2$; translation 2 units up; R: $\{y \mid y > 2\}$

3.

x	-3	-2	-1	0	1
$j(x)$	0.11	0.33	1	3	9

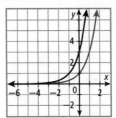

$y = 0$; translation 1 unit left

5. $\frac{1}{3}$; $y = 0$; vertical compression by a factor of $\frac{1}{3}$

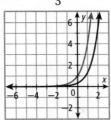

7. -2; $y = 0$; vertical stretch by a factor of 2 and reflection across the x-axis; R: $\{y \mid y < 0\}$

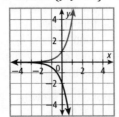

9. 1; $y = 0$; horizontal compression by a factor of $\frac{1}{2}$

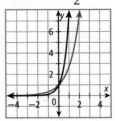

11.

x	-2	-1	0	1	2
$h(x)$	1	5	25	125	625

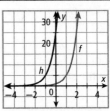

$y = 0$; translation 2 units left

13. 4; $y = 0$; vertical stretch by a factor of 4 **15.** -0.25; $y = 0$; vertical compression by a factor of 0.25 and reflection across the x-axis; R: $\{y \mid y < 0\}$ **17.** 4; $y = 0$; vertical stretch by a factor of 4 and reflection across the y-axis

14-1

Check It Out! **1a.** bread
1b. cheese and mayonnaise
2. 2001, 2002, and 2005; about
13,000 **3.** about 18 °F **4.** Prices
increased from January through
July or August, and then prices
decreased through November.
5. 31.25%
6.

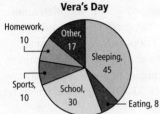

Vera's Day

Homework, 10; Other, 17; Sleeping, 45; Sports, 10; School, 30; Eating, 8

A circle graph shows parts of a
whole.

Exercises **1.** one part of a whole
3. 82 animals **5.** $15 **7.** Prices at
stadium A are greater than prices at
stadium B. **9.** between weeks 4 and
5 **11.** 18% **13.** purple **15.** blue and
green **17.** 225,000 **19.** Friday
21. 3.5 times **23.** games 3, 4, and 5
25. Stock Y changed the most
between April and July of 2004.
27. $8\frac{1}{3}$% **31.** double line **33.** circle
35a. Greece; about 40% **b.** United
States; about 15% **37.** D **41.** 19
girls

14-2

Check It Out!

1.

Temperature (°C)

Stem	Leaves
0	7
1	9
2	23679
3	01124566

Key: 1|9 means 19

2.

Interval	Frequency
4–6	5
7–9	4
10–12	4
13–15	2

3.

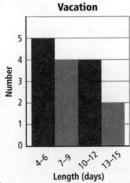

Vacation

Number vs. Length (days): 4–6: 5; 7–9: 4; 10–12: 4; 13–15: 2

4a.

Interval	Frequency	Cumulative Frequency
28–31	2	2
32–35	7	9
36–39	5	14
40–43	3	17

4b. 9

Exercises **1.** stem-and-leaf plot

3.

Austin	Stem	New York
999	1	
4321	2	
65320	3	13336679
	4	1122

5.

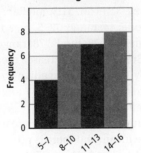

Breathing Intervals

Frequency vs. Time (min.): 5–7: 4; 8–10: 7; 11–13: 7; 14–16: 8

7.

Summer	Stem	Winter
	0	499
	1	123499
9776553322	2	17
	3	035
	4	
9743	5	

Key: |2|1 means 21
7|2| means 27

9.

Interval	Frequency
2.0–2.4	2
2.5–2.9	7
3.0–3.4	5
3.5–3.9	3

11a.

Interval	Frequency	Cumulative Frequency
36–38	4	4
39–41	6	10
42–44	5	15
45–47	1	16

b. 10

15a.

Interval	Frequency
160–169.9	2
170–179.9	4
180–189.9	3
190–199.9	1
200–209.9	2
210–219.9	1

19. G **21.** 8; 8; 41; 66

14-3

Check It Out!

1.

	Fiction	Nonfiction	Total
Hardcover	0.133	0.248	0.381
Paperback	0.448	0.171	0.619
Total	0.581	0.419	1

2a.

		Ballet		
		Yes	No	Total
Tap	**Yes**	0.19	0.26	0.45
	No	0.43	0.12	0.55
	Total	0.62	0.38	1

b. 0.69 or 69%

3. Al's Driving has the best pass
rate, about 64%, versus 61% for
Drive Time and 50% for Crash
Course.

Exercises 1. marginal

3.

	Under-classmates	Upper-classmates	Total
Morning	0.16	0.28	0.44
Afternoon	0.36	0.2	0.56
Total	0.52	0.48	1

5a.

Play Sport

Play instrument		Yes	No	Total
	Yes	0.23	0.19	0.42
	No	0.25	0.33	0.58
	Total	0.48	0.52	1

b. 0.55

c. 0.48

7.

	Students	Adults	Total
T-Shirts	0.267	0.383	0.65
Sweatshirts	0.117	0.233	0.35
Total	0.384	0.616	1

9a.

	Satisfied	Dissatisfied	Total
Team 1	0.17	0.07	0.24
Team 2	0.29	0.1	0.39
Team 3	0.29	0.08	0.37
Total	0.75	0.25	1

b. Team 1: 0.71; Team 2: 0.74; Team 3: 0.78

c. Team 3 has the highest rate of customer satisfaction.

11. Maria made an error; Possible answer: You can tell because the four relative frequencies have a sum of 1.1, rather than 1.

13a.

Work less than 5 miles from home?

Use new system?		Yes	No	Total
	Yes	0.2	0.27	0.47
	No	0.37	0.17	0.54
	Total	0.57	0.44	1

b. 0.35

c. 0.57

15. C

17.

	Yes	No	Total
Children	0.125	0.1	0.225
Teenagers	0.725	0.05	0.775
Total	0.85	0.15	1

19. 10 children

21. 0

14-4

Check It Out! 1. mean: 14 lb; median: 14 lb; modes: 12 lb and 16 lb; range: 4 lb **2.** 3; the outlier decreases the mean by 3.7 and increases the range by 18. It has no effect on the median and mode. **3a.** mode: 7 **3b.** Median: 81; the median is greater than either the mean or the mode.

4.

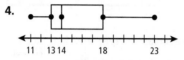

5a. The data set for 2000; the distance between the points for the least and greatest values is less for 2000 than for 2007. **5b.** about $40 million

Exercises 3. mean: 31.5; median: 33.5; mode: 44; range: 32 **5.** mean: 78.25; median: 78; mode: 78; range: 15 **7.** 13; the outlier decreases the mean by 11.15 and the median by 4. It increases the range by 51 and has no effect on the mode. **9.** Median: 83; the median is greater than the mean, and there is no mode. **13.** Simon; about 3000 points **15.** mean: 2.5; median: 2.5; modes: 2 and 3; range: 3 **17.** mean: 60; median: 60; mode: 60; range: 5 **19.** 23; the outlier increases the mean by 3, the median by 2.5, and the range by 15. It has no effect on the mode. **21.** Mean: 153; the mean is greater than the median, and there is no mode. **25.** Sneaks R Us; the middle half of the data doesn't vary as much at Sneaks R Us as at Jump N Run. **27.** mean: 5.5; median: 5.5; mode: none; range: 9 **29.** mean: 3.5; median: 3.4; mode: none; range: 5.3

31. mean: 24.4; median: 25; modes: 23 and 25; range: 3 **33.** mean: $15\frac{1}{2}$; median: $12\frac{1}{2}$; mode: none; range: 35 **37.** sometimes **39.** always **41.** Median; the mean is affected by the outlier of 1218, and there is no mode. **43.** Median or mode; the store wants their prices to seem low, and the median and mode are both $2.80 less than the mean. **49.** Mean: $32,000; median: $25,000; median; the outlier of $78,000 increases the mean significantly. **51.** 96 **53.** increase the mean; decrease the mean **55.** G **57.** The mean decreases by 6.6 lb.

15-1

Check It Out!

1. Football Team Score

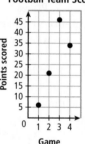

2. positive **3a.** No correlation; the temperature in Houston has nothing to do with the number of cars sold in Boston. **3b.** Positive; as the number of family members increases, more food is needed, so the grocery bill increases too. **3c.** Negative; as the number of times you sharpen your pencil increases, the length of the pencil decreases. **4.** Graph A; it cannot be graph B because graph B shows negative minutes; it cannot be graph C because graph C shows the temperature of the pie increasing, a positive correlation. **5.** about 75 rolls

Exercises 3. no **5.** positive **7.** negative **9.** positive **11.** A **15.** positive **17.** positive **19.** A **23.** positive **25.** B

27a.

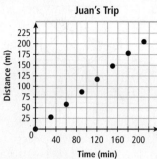

Juan's Trip

b. positive **29.** C

Check It Out! 1. $y = -\frac{1}{2}x + 6$: 16; $y = -x + 8$: 30; $y = -\frac{1}{2}x + 6$ is better. **2a.** $y < 0.04x + 6.38$
2b. slope: cost is $0.04/yd; y-int.: $6.38 is added to the cost of every ball of yarn. **2c.** $46.38
3. $y < -2.74x + 84.32$; very well ($r < -0.88$) **4.** strong positive correlation; likely cause-and-effect (more education often contributes to higher earnings)

Exercises 1. residual **3.** $y = x + 1$: 19; $y = x - 1$: 23; $y = x + 1$ is better. **5.** $y < -0.53x + 8.8$; very well ($y < -0.91$) **7.** $y = -x + 8$: 7; $y = -\frac{1}{2}x + 6$: 9; $y = -x + 8$ is better. **9.** $y < 0.2x + 2$; very well ($r < 0.94$) **13a.** $y < 0.48x + 12.03$
13b. A player will score 0.48 run for every hit. **13c.** A player with no hits will score 12.03 runs. **13d.** There is a strong correlation between the number of hits and the number of runs, since the correlation cofficient is $r < 0.84$. **13e.** <60 runs
15a. $y < 115.36x + 1065$; $r < 0.96$
15b. Slope: each year there will be 115.36 more visitors than the previous year; y-intercept: there were 1065 visitors in year 0.
15c. yes; $r < 0.96$, which is very close to 1. **15d.** No; the passage of time likely does not cause changes in the number of visitors. **17.** B
19a. 1000

15-2 Extension

Check It Out!
1a. yes; 1.5 **b.** no
2. $B(t) \approx 199(1.25)^t$; ≈ 10.3 min

Exercises
1. no **3.** no
5. $T(t) \approx 131(0.92)^t$; ≈ 13.6 min
7. no **9.** yes; $\frac{1}{2}$
11. $T(t) \approx 4.45(1.165)^t$; ≈ 2011
13. yes; $f(x) = 2(0.5)^x$
15. $r(d) \approx 10.99(0.9995)^d$; 1.40 per 100 cows

16-1

Check It Out! 1a. translation;
$MNOP \rightarrow M'N'O'P'$ **1b.** rotation;
$\triangle XYZ \rightarrow \triangle X'Y'Z'$ **2.** rotation; 90°
3. $J'(-1, -5); K'(1, 5); L'(1, 0);$
$M'(-1, 0)$ **4.** $(x, y) \rightarrow (x - 4, y - 4)$

Exercises 1. Preimage is $\triangle XYZ$;
image is $\triangle X'Y'Z'$ **3.** reflection;
$\triangle ABC \rightarrow \triangle A'B'C'$ **5.** reflection
across the y-axis **7.** $(x, y) \rightarrow$
$(x + 4, y + 4)$ **9.** reflection; $WXYZ$
$\rightarrow W'X'Y'Z'$ **11.** $A'(-1, -1),$
$B'(4, -1), C'(4, -4), D'(-1, -4)$
13. reflection **15.** reflection
17.

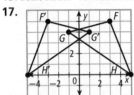

19. B **21.** D **23.** $R'(-1, -12);$
$S'(-3, -9); T'(-7, -7)$
25.

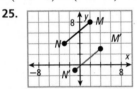

29. A **31.** A **33a.** $R''(1, 0); S''(0, 3);$
$T''(4, 3)$ **b.** $(x, y) \rightarrow (x + 3, y + 2)$
35.

37. $(-x, y)$

16-2

Check It Out! 1a. no **1b.** yes
2.

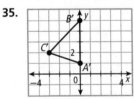

3. $\overline{AX}$ and $\overline{BX}$ would be $\cong$.

4.

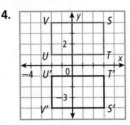

Exercises 1. They are $\cong$. **3.** no
5. no
7.

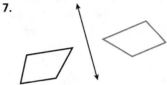

9.

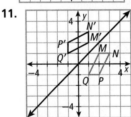

11.

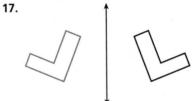

13. no **15.** yes
17.

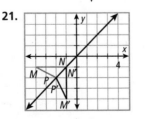

19.

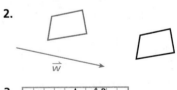

21.

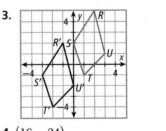

23.

27.

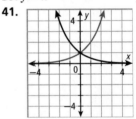

R-(+)-limonene S-(−)-limonene

29.

31. $(5, 2) \rightarrow (5, -2)$ **33.** $(0, 12) \rightarrow$
$(0, -12)$ **35.** $(0, -5) \rightarrow (-5, 0)$
37a. no **b.** $(7, 4)$ **c.** $(6, 3.5)$
39. $y = x$
41.

43. A **45.** C **47.** $(5, 2)$

16-3

Check It Out! 1a. Yes **1b.** no
2.

3.

4. $(16, -24)$

Exercises 1. no **3.** yes

7.
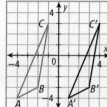
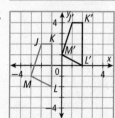

9.
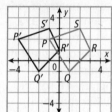

11. yes **13.** no

17.
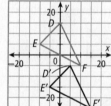

19.
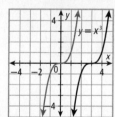

21.
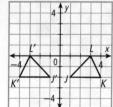

23a. $\frac{1}{4}$ **b.** $\frac{1}{2}$. **c.** 0 **27.** No; there are no fixed pts. because, by def. of a translation, every pt. must move by the same distance.
29. $\langle 4, 0 \rangle$, $(-3, 2) \rightarrow (1, 2)$
31. $\langle -3, -2 \rangle$, $(3, -1) \rightarrow (0, -3)$
33. $\langle -3, 1 \rangle$, $(3, -1) \rightarrow (0, 0)$
37. G **39.** $(0, 0)$ and $(2, 4)$

16-4

Check It Out! 1a. no **1b.** yes

2.
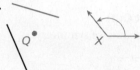

3a.
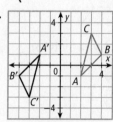

3b. $(-59, 34)$

Exercises 1. yes **3.** no

5.
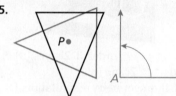

7.
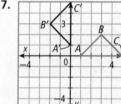

9.
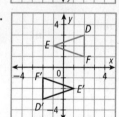

11. no **13.** yes

15.

17.
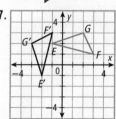

19.
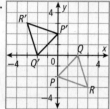

21. $(-10, 50)$
25a. 180°
b. $(-3, 2)$
27. M
29. $\overrightarrow{NP}$
35a. Possible answer: about 45°
b. Draw $\overrightarrow{AP}$ and $\overrightarrow{AQ}$ and use the protractor to measure $\angle AQA$.
c. 50°
37. $A'(3, 2)$, $B'(0, 3)$, $C'(3, 0)$, $D'(0, -3)$, $E'(3, -2)$
41. H
43. 160°; clockwise; gear B has 8 teeth, so one complete rotation of gear B in the counterclockwise direction will move gear A by 8 teeth in the clockwise direction. Gear A has 18 teeth, so 8 teeth is $\frac{4}{9}$ of a complete rotation, or $\frac{4}{9}(360°) = 160°$.

17-1

Check It Out!

1.
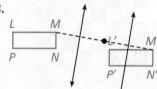

2. a translation in direction $\perp$ to n and p, by distance of 6 in.
3.

L ____ M   ____
| | | | L' ____ M'
P ____ N | | | |
                   P' ____ N'

Exercises 1. Draw a figure and translate it along a vector. Then reflect the image across a line.

3.
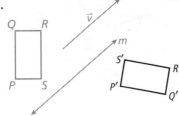

5. a rotation of 100° about the pt. of intersection of the lines

7.
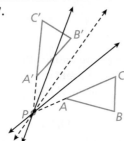

9.

11a. The move is a horiz. or vert. translation by 2 spaces followed by a vert. or horiz. translation by 1 space.

11b.
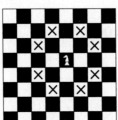

11c.
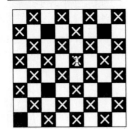

13.
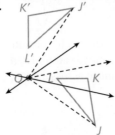

17. never **19.** always **23.** A

25. C

17-2

Check It Out!
1a. yes; 2 lines of symmetry

1b. yes; 1 line of symmetry

1c. yes; 1 line of symmetry

2a. yes; 120°; order: 3 **2b.** yes; 180°; order: 2° **2c.** no
3a. line symmetry and rotational symmetry; 72°; order: 5

3b. line symmetry and rotational symmetry; 51.4°; order: 7
4a. both **4b.** neither

Exercises 1. The line of symmetry is the ⊥ bisector of the base.
3. yes; 2 lines of symmetry
5. no **7.** no
9. 72°; order: 5
11. both
13. yes; 1 line of symmetry
15. no **17.** yes; 72°; order: 5
19. 90; order: 4 **21.** neither
23. isosc. **25.** scalene **27.** 0

29. line symmetry
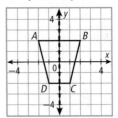

31. line symmetry
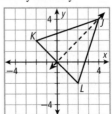

33. rotational symmetry of order 4
35. line symmetry; $x = 2$ **37a.** no
b. yes; 180°; 2. **c.** Yes; if color is not taken into account the ∠ of rotational symmetry is 90.
39. parallelogram **41.** square
43. 15° **45.** It has rotational symmetry of order 3, with an ∠ of rotational symmetry of 120°.

47.

49.

51. A **53.** C **55.** 72 **57.** 13
59. 13

17-3

Check It Out! 1a. translation symmetry **1b.** translation symmetry and glide reflection symmetry

2.

3a. regular **3b.** neither.
3c. semiregular
4a. yes

4b. no

Exercises 3. translation symmetry and glide reflection symmetry
5. translation symmetry and glide reflection symmetry **9.** regular
11. semiregular
13. yes; possible answer

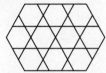

15. translation symmetry
17. translation symmetry
19.

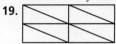

21. neither **23.** neither **25.** no
27. translation symmetry and glide reflection symmetry
29. translation, glide reflection, rotation **31.** always **33.** always
35. never **41.** The tessellation has translation symmetry, reflection symmetry, and order 3 rotation symmetry.
43. $CH_2 - CH$
           $|$
           CH_3

47. H **51.** yes

18-1

Check It Out! 1a. $y = 2x + 2$ and $y = 2x + 1$ **1b.** $y = 3x$ and $y - 1 = 3(x + 2)$

2. slope of $\overline{AB} = 0$; slope of $\overline{BC} = \frac{5}{3}$; slope of $\overline{CD} = 0$; slope of $\overline{AD} = \frac{5}{3}$; $\overline{AB}$ is parallel to $\overline{CD}$ because they have the same slope. $\overline{AD}$ is parallel to $\overline{BC}$ because they have the same slope. Since opposite sides are parallel, $ABCD$ is a parallelogram. **3.** $y = -4$ and $x = 3$; $y - 6 = 5(x + 4)$ and $y = -\frac{1}{5}x + 2$
4. slope of $\overline{PQ} = 2$; slope of $\overline{QR} = -1$; slope of $\overline{PR} = -\frac{1}{2}$; $\overline{PQ}$ is perpendicular to $\overline{PR}$ because the product of their slopes is -1. Since PQR contains a right angle, PQR is a right triangle. **5a.** $y = \frac{4}{5}x + 3$
5b. $y = -\frac{1}{5}x + 2$

Exercises 1. parallel **3.** $y = \frac{3}{4}x - 1$ and $y - 3 = \frac{3}{4}(x - 5)$ **5.** $y = \frac{2}{3}x - 4$ and $y = -\frac{3}{2}x + 2$; $y = -1$ and $x = 3$
9. $x = 7$ and $x = -9$; $y = -\frac{5}{6}x + 8$ and $y = -\frac{5}{6}x - 4$ **11.** $y = -3x + 2$ and $3x + y = 27$; $y = \frac{1}{2}x - 1$ and $-x + 2y = 17$ **13.** $y = 6x$ and $y = -\frac{1}{6}x$; $y = \frac{1}{6}x$ and $y = -6x$ **15.** $x - 6y = 15$ and $y = -6x - 8$; $y = 3x - 2$ and $3y = -x - 11$ **17.** $y = -\frac{6}{7}x$ **19.** neither
21. parallel **23.** $y = \frac{1}{2}x - 5$
25. $y = 2x + 5$ **27.** $y = 3x + 13$
29. $y = -x + 5$ **31.** $y = 4x - 23$
33. $y = -\frac{3}{4}x$ **35.** $y = -x + 1$
37. $y = \frac{2}{5}x - \frac{31}{5}$ **39.** $y = -\frac{1}{5}x - \frac{11}{5}$
41. $y = -\frac{1}{2}x - \frac{1}{2}$ **43.** $y = \frac{1}{2}x + 6$
45. $y = x - 3$ **47.** $y = -4$ **51a.** $y = 50x$ **b.** $y = 50x + 30$ **53.** H **57.** $-\frac{1}{5}$

18-2

Check It Out! 1. $\left(\frac{3}{2}, 0\right)$ **2.** $(4, 3)$
3. 6.71 **4.** 17.7 mi

Exercises 3. $\left(1\frac{1}{2}, -4\right)$ **5.** $(3, 3)$
7. 5.39 **9.** 10.82 **11.** $(-2, -3)$
13. $(17, -23)$ **15.** $(2, -8)$ **17.** 8.94
19. 9.22 **21.** 6.1 mi **25.** 13.42
27. 14.32 **29a.** 7.2 **b.** $(0, -2)$ **c.** 23
31. $\overline{CD}$, $\overline{EF}$, $\overline{AB}$ **35.** B **37.** D
39. 12.5 square units **41.** ± 8
43. 26

Glossary/Glosario

Learn It Online
Multilingual Glossary

 A

ENGLISH	SPANISH	EXAMPLES
absolute value The absolute value of x is the distance from zero to x on a number line, denoted $\lvert x \rvert$. $$\lvert x \rvert = \begin{cases} x & \text{if } x \geq 0 \\ -x & \text{if } x < 0 \end{cases}$$	**valor absoluto** El valor absoluto de x es la distancia de cero a x en una recta numérica, y se expresa $\lvert x \rvert$. $$\lvert x \rvert = \begin{cases} x & \text{si } x \geq 0 \\ -x & \text{si } x < 0 \end{cases}$$	$\lvert 3 \rvert = 3$ $\lvert -3 \rvert = 3$
absolute-value equation An equation that contains absolute-value expressions.	**ecuación de valor absoluto** Ecuación que contiene expresiones de valor absoluto.	$\lvert x + 4 \rvert = 7$
absolute-value function A function whose rule contains absolute-value expressions.	**función de valor absoluto** Función cuya regla contiene expresiones de valor absoluto.	$y = \lvert x + 4 \rvert$
absolute-value inequality An inequality that contains absolute-value expressions.	**desigualdad de valor absoluto** Desigualdad que contiene expresiones de valor absoluto.	$\lvert x + 4 \rvert > 7$
accuracy The closeness of a given measurement or value to the actual measurement or value.	**exactitud** Cercanía de una medida o un valor a la medida o el valor real.	
acute angle An angle that measures greater than 0° and less than 90°.	**ángulo agudo** Ángulo que mide más de 0° y menos de 90°.	
acute triangle A triangle with three acute angles.	**triángulo acutángulo** Triángulo con tres ángulos agudos.	
Addition Property of Equality For real numbers a, b, and c, if $a = b$, then $a + c = b + c$.	**Propiedad de igualdad de la suma** Dados los números reales a, b y c, si $a = b$, entonces $a + c = b + c$.	$\begin{array}{r} x - 6 = 8 \\ +6 \;\; +6 \\ \hline x \;\;\;\;\; = 14 \end{array}$
Addition Property of Inequality For real numbers a, b, and c, if $a < b$, then $a + c < b + c$. Also holds true for $>$, $\leq$, $\geq$, and $\neq$.	**Propiedad de desigualdad de la suma** Dados los números reales a, b y c, si $a < b$, entonces $a + c < b + c$. Es válido también para $>$, $\leq$, $\geq$ y $\neq$.	$\begin{array}{r} x - 6 < 8 \\ +6 \;\; +6 \\ \hline x \;\;\;\;\; < 14 \end{array}$
additive inverse The opposite of a number. Two numbers are additive inverses if their sum is zero.	**inverso aditivo** El opuesto de un número. Dos números son inversos aditivos si su suma es cero.	The additive inverse of 5 is −5. The additive inverse of −5 is 5.

Glossary/Glosario

ENGLISH	SPANISH	EXAMPLES
AND A logical operator representing the intersection of two sets.	**Y** Operador lógico que representa la intersección de dos conjuntos.	$A = \{2, 3, 4, 5\}$ $B = \{1, 3, 5, 7\}$ The set of values that are in A AND B is $A \cap B = \{3, 5\}$.
angle A figure formed by two rays with a common endpoint.	**ángulo** Figura formada por dos rayos con un extremo común.	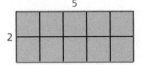
area The number of nonoverlapping unit squares of a given size that will exactly cover the interior of a plane figure.	**área** Cantidad de cuadrados unitarios de un determinado tamaño no superpuestos que cubren exactamente el interior de una figura plana.	5 2 The area is 10 square units.
arithmetic sequence A sequence whose successive terms differ by the same nonzero number d, called the *common difference*.	**sucesión aritmética** Sucesión cuyos términos sucesivos difieren en el mismo número distinto de cero d, denominado *diferencia común*.	4, 7, 10, 13, 16, … $+3 +3 +3 +3$ $d = 3$
Associative Property of Addition For all numbers a, b, and c, $(a + b) + c = a + (b + c)$.	**Propiedad asociativa de la suma** Dados tres números cualesquiera a, b y c, $(a + b) + c = a + (b + c)$.	$(5 + 3) + 7 = 5 + (3 + 7)$
Associative Property of Multiplication For all numbers a, b, and c, $(a \cdot b) \cdot c = a \cdot (b \cdot c)$.	**Propiedad asociativa de la multiplicación** Dados tres números cualesquiera a, b y c, $(a \cdot b) \cdot c = a \cdot (b \cdot c)$.	$(5 \cdot 3) \cdot 7 = 5 \cdot (3 \cdot 7)$
asymptote A line that a graph gets closer to as the value of a variable becomes extremely large or small.	**asíntota** Línea recta a la cual se aproxima una gráfica a medida que el valor de una variable se hace sumamente grande o pequeño.	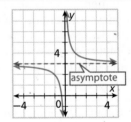
average *See* mean.	**promedio** *Ver* media.	
axis of a coordinate plane One of two perpendicular number lines, called the *x*-axis and the *y*-axis, used to define the location of a point in a coordinate plane.	**eje de un plano cartesiano** Una de las dos rectas numéricas perpendiculares, denominadas eje *x* y eje *y*, utilizadas para definir la ubicación de un punto en un plano cartesiano.	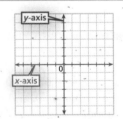
axis of symmetry A line that divides a plane figure or a graph into two congruent reflected halves.	**eje de simetría** Línea que divide una figura plana o una gráfica en dos mitades reflejadas congruentes.	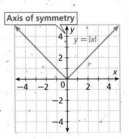

	ENGLISH	SPANISH	EXAMPLES

back-to-back stem-and-leaf plot (A graph used to organize and compare two sets of data so that the frequencies can be compared. *See also* stem-and-leaf plot.)

diagrama doble de tallo y hojas Gráfica utilizada para organizar y comparar dos conjuntos de datos para poder comparar las frecuencias. *Ver también* diagrama de tallo y hojas.

Data set A: 9, 12, 14, 16, 23, 27
Data set B: 6, 8, 10, 13, 15, 16, 21

Set A		Set B
9	0	6 8
6 4 2	1	0 3 5 6
7 3	2	1

Key: |2|1 means 21
7|2| means 27

---

bar graph A graph that uses vertical or horizontal bars to display data.

gráfica de barras Gráfica con barras horizontales o verticales para mostrar datos.

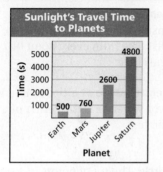

---

base of a power The number in a power that is used as a factor.

base de una potencia Número de una potencia que se utiliza como factor.

$3^4 = 3 \cdot 3 \cdot 3 \cdot 3 = 81$
3 is the base.

---

base of an exponential function The value of b in a function of the form $f(x) = ab^x$, where a and b are real numbers with $a \neq 0$, $b > 0$, and $b \neq 1$.

base de una función exponencial Valor de b en una función del tipo $f(x) = ab^x$, donde a y b son números reales con $a \neq 0$, $b > 0$ y $b \neq 1$.

In the function $f(x) = 5(2)^x$, the base is 2.

---

biased sample A sample that does not fairly represent the population.

muestra no representativa Muestra que no representa adecuadamente una población.

To find out about the exercise habits of average Americans, a fitness magazine surveyed its readers about how often they exercise. The population is all Americans and the sample is readers of the fitness magazine. This sample will likely be biased because readers of fitness magazines may exercise more often than other people do.

---

binomial A polynomial with two terms.

binomio Polinomio con dos términos.

$x + y$
$2a^2 + 3$
$4m^3n^2 + 6mn^4$

---

boundary line A line that divides a coordinate plane into two half-planes.

línea de límite Línea que divide un plano cartesiano en dos semiplanos.

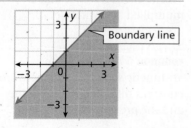

ENGLISH	SPANISH	EXAMPLES
box-and-whisker plot A method of showing how data are distributed by using the median, quartiles, and minimum and maximum values; also called a *box plot*.	**gráfica de mediana y rango** Método para mostrar la distribución de datos utilizando la mediana, los cuartiles y los valores mínimo y máximo; también llamado *gráfica de caja*.	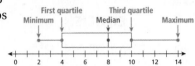

C

ENGLISH	SPANISH	EXAMPLES
Cartesian coordinate system *See* coordinate plane.	**sistema de coordenadas cartesianas** *Ver* plano cartesiano.	
center of a circle The point inside a circle that is the same distance from every point on the circle.	**centro de un círculo** Punto dentro de un círculo que se encuentra a la misma distancia de todos los puntos del círculo.	
central angle of a circle An angle whose vertex is the center of a circle.	**ángulo central de un círculo** Ángulo cuyo vértice es el centro de un círculo.	
circle The set of points in a plane that are a fixed distance from a given point called the center of the circle.	**círculo** Conjunto de puntos en un plano que se encuentran a una distancia fija de un punto determinado denominado centro del círculo.	
circle graph A way to display data by using a circle divided into non-overlapping sectors.	**gráfica circular** Forma de mostrar datos mediante un círculo dividido en sectores no superpuestos.	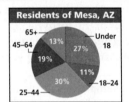
circumference The distance around a circle.	**circunferencia** Distancia alrededor de un círculo.	
closure A set of numbers is said to be closed, or to have closure, under a given operation if the result of the operation on any two numbers in the set is also in the set.	**cerradura** Se dice que un conjunto de números es cerrado, o tiene cerradura, respecto de una operación determinada, si el resultado de la operación entre dos números cualesquiera del conjunto también está en el conjunto.	The natural numbers are closed under addition because the sum of two natural numbers is always a natural number.
coefficient A number that is multiplied by a variable.	**coeficiente** Número que se multiplica por una variable.	In the expression $2x + 3y$, 2 is the coefficient of x and 3 is the coefficient of y.
common difference In an arithmetic sequence, the nonzero constant difference of any term and the previous term.	**diferencia común** En una sucesión aritmética, diferencia constante distinta de cero entre cualquier término y el término anterior.	In the arithmetic sequence 3, 5, 7, 9, 11, …, the common difference is 2.

ENGLISH	SPANISH	EXAMPLES
common factor A factor that is common to all terms of an expression or to two or more expressions.	**factor común** Factor que es común a todos los términos de una expresión o a dos o más expresiones.	Expression: $4x^2 + 16x^3 - 8x$ Common factor: $4x$ Expressions: 12 and 18 Common factors: 2, 3, and 6
common ratio In a geometric sequence, the constant ratio of any term and the previous term.	**razón común** En una sucesión geométrica, la razón constante entre cualquier término y el término anterior.	In the geometric sequence 32, 16, 8, 4, 2, . . ., the common ratio is $\frac{1}{2}$.
Commutative Property of Addition For any two numbers a and b, $a + b = b + a$.	**Propiedad conmutativa de la suma** Dados dos números cualesquiera a y b, $a + b = b + a$.	$3 + 4 = 4 + 3 = 7$
Commutative Property of Multiplication For any two numbers a and b, $a \cdot b = b \cdot a$.	**Propiedad conmutativa de la multiplicación** Dados dos números cualesquiera a y b, $a \cdot b = b \cdot a$.	$3 \cdot 4 = 4 \cdot 3 = 12$
complement of an event The set of all outcomes that are not the event.	**complemento de un suceso** Todos los resultados que no están en el suceso.	In the experiment of rolling a number cube, the complement of rolling a 3 is rolling a 1, 2, 4, 5, or 6.
complementary angles Two angles whose measures have a sum of 90°.	**ángulos complementarios** Dos ángulos cuyas medidas suman 90°.	
completing the square A process used to form a perfect-square trinomial. To complete the square of $x^2 + bx$, add $\left(\frac{b}{2}\right)^2$.	**completar el cuadrado** Proceso utilizado para formar un trinomio cuadrado perfecto. Para completar el cuadrado de $x^2 + bx$, hay que sumar $\left(\frac{b}{2}\right)^2$.	$x^2 + 6x + \blacksquare$ Add $\left(\frac{6}{2}\right)^2 = 9$. $x^2 + 6x + 9$
complex fraction A fraction that contains one or more fractions in the numerator, the denominator, or both.	**fracción compleja** Fracción que contiene una o más fracciones en el numerador, en el denominador, o en ambos.	$\dfrac{\frac{1}{2}}{1 + \frac{2}{3}}$
composite figure A plane figure made up of triangles, rectangles, trapezoids, circles, and other simple shapes, or a three-dimensional figure made up of prisms, cones, pyramids, cylinders, and other simple three-dimensional figures.	**figura compuesta** Figura plana compuesta por triángulos, rectángulos, trapecios, círculos y otras figuras simples, o figura tridimensional compuesta por prismas, conos, pirámides, cilindros y otras figuras tridimensionales simples.	
composition of transformations One transformation followed by another transformation.	**composición de transformaciones** Una transformación seguida de otra transformación.	

ENGLISH	SPANISH	EXAMPLES
compound event An event made up of two or more simple events.	**suceso compuesto** Suceso formado por dos o más sucesos simples.	In the experiment of tossing a coin and rolling a number cube, the event of the coin landing heads and the number cube landing on 3.
compound inequality Two inequalities that are combined into one statement by the word *and* or *or*.	**desigualdad compuesta** Dos desigualdades unidas en un enunciado por la palabra *y* u *o*.	$x \geq 2$ AND $x < 7$ (also written $2 \leq x < 7$) $x < 2$ OR $x > 6$
compound interest Interest earned or paid on both the principal and previously earned interest. The formula for compound interest is $A = P\left(1 + \frac{r}{n}\right)^{nt}$, where A is the final amount, P is the principal, r is the interest rate expressed as a decimal, n is the number of times interest is compounded, and t is the time.	**interés compuesto** Intereses ganados o pagados sobre el capital y los intereses ya devengados. La fórmula de interés compuesto es $A = P\left(1 + \frac{r}{n}\right)^{nt}$, donde A es la cantidad final, P es el capital, r es la tasa de interés expresada como un decimal, n es la cantidad de veces que se capitaliza el interés y t es el tiempo.	If \$100 is put into an account with an interest rate of 5% compounded monthly, then after 2 years, the account will have $100\left(1 + \frac{0.05}{12}\right)^{12 \cdot 2} = \$110.49$.
compound statement Two statements that are connected by the word *and* or *or*.	**enunciado compuesto** Dos enunciados unidos por la palabra *y* u *o*.	The sky is blue and the grass is green. I will drive to school or I will take the bus.
compression A transformation that pushes the points of a graph horizontally toward the *y*-axis or vertically toward the *x*-axis.	**compresión** Transformación que desplaza los puntos de una gráfica horizontalmente hacia el eje *y* o verticalmente hacia el eje *x*.	
conditional relative frequency The ratio of a joint relative frequency to a related marginal relative frequency in a two-way table.	**frecuencia relativa condicional** Razón de una frecuencia relativa conjunta a una frecuencia relativa marginal en una tabla de doble entrada.	
cone A three-dimensional figure with a circular base and a curved surface that connects the base to a point called the vertex.	**cono** Figura tridimensional con una base circular y una superficie lateral curva que conecta la base con un punto denominado vértice.	
congruent Having the same size and shape, denoted by $\cong$.	**congruente** Que tiene el mismo tamaño y la misma forma, expresado por $\cong$.	$\overline{PQ} \cong \overline{RS}$
consistent system A system of equations or inequalities that has at least one solution.	**sistema consistente** Sistema de ecuaciones o desigualdades que tiene por lo menos una solución.	$\begin{cases} x + y = 6 \\ x - y = 4 \end{cases}$ solution: $(5, 1)$

ENGLISH	SPANISH	EXAMPLES
constant A value that does not change.	**constante** Valor que no cambia.	$3, 0, \pi$
constant of variation The constant k in direct and inverse variation equations.	**constante de variación** La constante k en ecuaciones de variación directa e inversa.	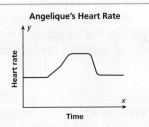
continuous graph A graph made up of connected lines or curves.	**gráfica continua** Gráfica compuesta por líneas rectas o curvas conectadas.	**Angelique's Heart Rate**
convenience sample A sample based on members of the population that are readily available.	**muestra de conveniencia** Una muestra basada en miembros de la población que están fácilmente disponibles.	A reporter surveys people he personally knows.
conversion factor The ratio of two equal quantities, each measured in different units.	**factor de conversión** Razón entre dos cantidades iguales, cada una medida en unidades diferentes.	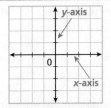 $\dfrac{12 \text{ inches}}{1 \text{ foot}}$
coordinate plane A plane that is divided into four regions by a horizontal line called the x-axis and a vertical line called the y-axis.	**plano cartesiano** Plano dividido en cuatro regiones por una línea horizontal denominada eje x y una línea vertical denominada eje y.	
correlation A measure of the strength and direction of the relationship between two variables or data sets.	**correlación** Medida de la fuerza y dirección de la relación entre dos variables o conjuntos de datos.	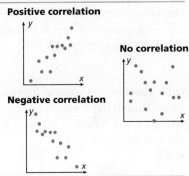
correlation coefficient A number r, where $-1 \le r \le 1$, that describes how closely the points in a scatter plot cluster around the least-squares line.	**coeficiente de correlación** Número r, donde $-1 \le r \le 1$, que describe a qué distancia de la recta de mínimos cuadrados se agrupan los puntos de un diagrama de dispersión.	An r-value close to 1 describes a strong positive correlation. An r-value close to 0 describes a weak correlation or no correlation. An r-value close to -1 describes a strong negative correlation.
corresponding angles of polygons Angles in the same relative position in polygons with an equal number of angles.	**ángulos correspondientes de los polígonos** Ángulos que se ubican en la misma posición relativa en polígonos que tienen el mismo número de ángulos.	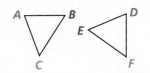 $\angle A$ and $\angle D$ are corresponding angles.

ENGLISH	SPANISH	EXAMPLES
corresponding sides of polygons Sides in the same relative position in polygons with an equal number of sides.	**lados correspondientes de los polígonos** Lados que se ubican en la misma posición relativa en polígonos que tienen el mismo número de lados.	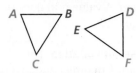 $\overline{AB}$ and $\overline{DE}$ are corresponding sides.
cosine In a right triangle, the cosine of angle A is the ratio of the length of the leg adjacent to angle A to the length of the hypotenuse.	**coseno** En un triángulo rectángulo, el coseno del ángulo A es la razón entre la longitud del cateto adyacente al ángulo A y la longitud de la hipotenusa.	$\cos A = \dfrac{\text{adjacent}}{\text{hypotenuse}}$
cross products In the statement $\frac{a}{b} = \frac{c}{d}$, bc and ad are the cross products.	**productos cruzados** En el enunciado $\frac{a}{b} = \frac{c}{d}$, bc y ad son productos cruzados.	$\dfrac{1}{2} = \dfrac{3}{6}$ Cross products: $2 \cdot 3 = 6$ and $1 \cdot 6 = 6$
Cross Product Property For any real numbers a, b, c, and d, where $b \neq 0$ and $d \neq 0$, if $\frac{a}{b} = \frac{c}{d}$, then $ad = bc$.	**Propiedad de productos cruzados** Dados los números reales a, b, c y d, donde $b \neq 0$ y $d \neq 0$, si $\frac{a}{b} = \frac{c}{d}$, entonces $ad = bc$.	If $\dfrac{4}{6} = \dfrac{10}{x}$, then $4x = 60$, so $x = 15$.
cube A prism with six square faces.	**cubo** Prisma con seis caras cuadradas.	
cube in numeration The third power of a number.	**cubo en numeración** Tercera potencia de un número.	8 is the cube of 2.
cube root A number, written as $\sqrt[3]{x}$, whose cube is x.	**raíz cúbica** Número, expresado como $\sqrt[3]{x}$, cuyo cubo es x.	$\sqrt[3]{64} = 4$, because $4^3 = 64$; 4 is the cube root of 64.
cubic equation An equation that can be written in the form $ax^3 + bx^2 + cx + d = 0$, where a, b, c, and d are real numbers and $a \neq 0$.	**ecuación cúbica** Ecuación que se puede expresar como $ax^3 + bx^2 + cx + d = 0$, donde a, b, c, y d son números reales y $a \neq 0$.	$4x^3 + x^2 - 3x - 1 = 0$
cubic function A function that can be written in the form $f(x) = ax^3 + bx^2 + cx + d$, where a, b, c, and d are real numbers and $a \neq 0$.	**función cúbica** Función que se puede expresar como $f(x) = ax^3 + bx^2 + cx + d$, donde a, b, c, y d son números reales y $a \neq 0$.	$f(x) = x^3 + 2x^2 - 6x + 8$
cubic polynomial A polynomial of degree 3.	**polinomio cúbico** Polinomio de grado 3.	$x^3 + 4x^2 - 6x + 2$
cumulative frequency The frequency of all data values that are less than or equal to a given value.	**frecuencia acumulativa** Frecuencia de todos los valores de los datos que son menores que o iguales a un valor dado.	For the data set 2, 2, 3, 5, 5, 6, 7, 7, 8, 8, 8, 9, the cumulative frequency table is shown below.

Data	Frequency	Cumulative Frequency
2	2	2
3	1	3
5	2	5
6	1	6
7	2	8
8	3	11
9	1	12

ENGLISH	SPANISH	EXAMPLES
cylinder A three-dimensional figure with two parallel congruent circular bases and a curved surface that connects the bases.	**cilindro** Figura tridimensional con dos bases circulares congruentes paralelas y una superficie lateral curva que conecta las bases.	

ENGLISH	SPANISH	EXAMPLES
data Information gathered from a survey or experiment.	**datos** Información reunida en una encuesta o experimento.	
degree measure of an angle A unit of angle measure; one degree is $\frac{1}{360}$ of a circle.	**medida en grados de un ángulo** Unidad de medida de los ángulos; un grado es $\frac{1}{360}$ de un círculo.	
degree of a monomial The sum of the exponents of the variables in the monomial.	**grado de un monomio** Suma de los exponentes de las variables del monomio.	$4x^2y^5z^3$ Degree: $2 + 5 + 3 = 10$ $5 = 5x^0$ Degree: 0
degree of a polynomial The degree of the term of the polynomial with the greatest degree.	**grado de un polinomio** Grado del término del polinomio con el grado máximo.	$3x^2y^2 + 4xy^5 - 12x^3y^2$ ↑ ↑ ↑ Degree 4 Degree 6 Degree 5 Degree 6
dependent events Events for which the occurrence or nonoccurrence of one event affects the probability of the other event.	**sucesos dependientes** Dos sucesos son dependientes si el hecho de que uno de ellos ocurra o no afecta la probabilidad del otro suceso.	From a bag containing 3 red marbles and 2 blue marbles, draw a red marble, and then draw a blue marble without replacing the first marble.
dependent system A system of equations that has infinitely many solutions.	**sistema dependiente** Sistema de ecuaciones que tiene infinitamente muchas soluciones.	$\begin{cases} x + y = 2 \\ 2x + 2y = 4 \end{cases}$
dependent variable The output of a function; a variable whose value depends on the value of the input, or independent variable.	**variable dependiente** Salida de una función; variable cuyo valor depende del valor de la entrada, o variable independiente.	For $y = 2x + 1$, y is the dependent variable. input: x output: y
diameter A segment that has endpoints on the circle and that passes through the center of the circle; also the length of that segment.	**diámetro** Segmento que atraviesa el centro de un círculo y cuyos extremos están sobre la circunferencia; longitud de dicho segmento.	
difference of two cubes A polynomial of the form $a^3 - b^3$, which may be written as the product $(a - b)(a^2 + ab + b^2)$.	**diferencia de dos cubos** Polinomio del tipo $a^3 - b^3$, que se puede expresar como el producto $(a - b)(a^2 + ab + b^2)$.	$x^3 - 8 = (x - 2)(x^2 + 2x + 4)$
difference of two squares A polynomial of the form $a^2 - b^2$, which may be written as the product $(a + b)(a - b)$.	**diferencia de dos cuadrados** Polinomio del tipo $a^2 - b^2$, que se puede expresar como el producto $(a + b)(a - b)$.	$x^2 - 4 = (x + 2)(x - 2)$

Glossary/Glosario

Glossary/Glosario

ENGLISH	SPANISH	EXAMPLES
dilation A transformation in which the lines connecting every point P with its preimage P' all intersect at a point C known as the center of dilation, and $\frac{CP'}{CP}$ is the same for every point P; a transformation that changes the size of a figure but not its shape.	**dilatación** Transformación en la cual las líneas que conectan cada punto P con su imagen original P' se cruzan en un punto C conocido como centro de dilatación, y $\frac{CP'}{CP}$ es igual para cada punto P; transformación que cambia el tamaño de una figura pero no su forma.	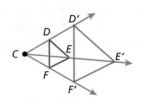
dimensional analysis A process that uses rates to convert measurements from one unit to another.	**análisis dimensional** Un proceso que utiliza tasas para convertir medidas de unidad a otra.	$12 \text{ pt} \cdot \dfrac{1 \text{ qt}}{2 \text{ pt}} = 6 \text{ qt}$
direct variation A linear relationship between two variables, x and y, that can be written in the form $y = kx$, where k is a nonzero constant.	**variación directa** Relación lineal entre dos variables, x e y, que puede expresarse en la forma $y = kx$, donde k es una constante distinta de cero.	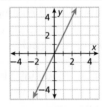 $y = 2x$
discontinuous function A function whose graph has one or more jumps, breaks, or holes.	**función discontinua** Función cuya gráfica tiene uno o más saltos, interrupciones u hoyos.	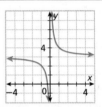
discrete graph A graph made up of unconnected points.	**gráfica discreta** Gráfica compuesta de puntos no conectados.	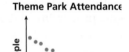
Distance Formula In a coordinate plane, the distance from (x_1, y_1) to (x_2, y_2) is $d = \sqrt{(x_2 - x_1)^2 + (y_2 - y_1)^2}$.	**Fórmula de distancia** En un plano cartesiano, la distancia desde (x_1, y_1) hasta (x_2, y_2) es $d = \sqrt{(x_2 - x_1)^2 + (y_2 - y_1)^2}$.	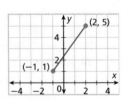 The distance from $(2, 5)$ to $(-1, 1)$ is $d = \sqrt{(-1 - 2)^2 + (1 - 5)^2}$ $= \sqrt{(-3)^2 + (-4)^2} = \sqrt{25} = 5.$
Distributive Property For all real numbers a, b, and c, $a(b + c) = ab + ac$, and $(b + c)a = ba + ca$.	**Propiedad distributiva** Dados los números reales a, b y c, $a(b + c) = ab + ac$, y $(b + c)a = ba + ca$.	$3(4 + 5) = 3 \cdot 4 + 3 \cdot 5$ $(4 + 5)3 = 4 \cdot 3 + 5 \cdot 3$
Division Property of Equality For real numbers a, b, and c, where $c \neq 0$, if $a = b$, then $\frac{a}{c} = \frac{b}{c}$.	**Propiedad de igualdad de la división** Dados los números reales a, b y c, donde $c \neq 0$, si $a = b$, entonces $\frac{a}{c} = \frac{b}{c}$.	$4x = 12$ $\dfrac{4x}{4} = \dfrac{12}{4}$ $x = 3$

ENGLISH	SPANISH	EXAMPLES
Division Property of Inequality If both sides of an inequality are divided by the same positive quantity, the new inequality will have the same solution set. If both sides of an inequality are divided by the same negative quantity, the new inequality will have the same solution set if the inequality symbol is reversed.	**Propiedad de desigualdad de la división** Cuando ambos lados de una desigualdad se dividen entre el mismo número positivo, la nueva desigualdad tiene el mismo conjunto solución. Cuando ambos lados de una desigualdad se dividen entra el mismo número negativo, la nueva desigualdad tiene el mismo conjunto solución si se invierte el símbolo de desigualdad.	$4x \geq 12$ $$\frac{4x}{4} \geq \frac{12}{4}$$ $x \geq 3$ $-4x \geq 12$ $$\frac{-4x}{-4} \leq \frac{12}{-4}$$ $x \leq -3$
domain The set of all first coordinates (or x-values) of a relation or function.	**dominio** Conjunto de todos los valores de la primera coordenada (o valores de x) de una función o relación.	The domain of the function $\{(-5, 3), (-3, -2), (-1, -1), (1, 0)\}$ is $\{-5, -3, -1, 1\}$.

E

ENGLISH	SPANISH	EXAMPLES
element Each member in a set or matrix. *See also* entry.	**elemento** Cada miembro en un conjunto o matriz. *Ver también* entrada.	
elimination method A method used to solve systems of equations in which one variable is eliminated by adding or subtracting two equations of the system.	**eliminación** Método utilizado para resolver sistemas de ecuaciones por el cual se elimina una variable sumando o restando dos ecuaciones del sistema.	
empty set A set with no elements.	**conjunto vacío** Conjunto sin elementos.	The solution set of $|x| < 0$ is the empty set, $\{\ \}$, or $\varnothing$.
entry Each value in a matrix; also called an element.	**entrada** Cada valor de una matriz, también denominado elemento.	3 is the entry in the first row and second column of $A = \begin{bmatrix} 2 & 3 \\ 0 & 1 \end{bmatrix}$, denoted a_{12}.
equally likely outcomes Outcomes are equally likely if they have the same probability of occurring. If an experiment has n equally likely outcomes, then the probability of each outcome is $\frac{1}{n}$.	**resultados igualmente probables** Los resultados son igualmente probables si tienen la misma probabilidad de ocurrir. Si un experimento tiene n resultados igualmente probables, entonces la probabilidad de cada resultado es $\frac{1}{n}$.	If a fair coin is tossed, then $P(\text{heads}) = P(\text{tails}) = \frac{1}{2}$. So the outcome "heads" and the outcome "tails" are equally likely.
equation A mathematical statement that two expressions are equivalent.	**ecuación** Enunciado matemático que indica que dos expresiones son equivalentes.	$x + 4 = 7$ $2 + 3 = 6 - 1$ $(x - 1)^2 + (y + 2)^2 = 4$
equilateral triangle A triangle with three congruent sides.	**triángulo equilátero** Triángulo con tres lados congruentes.	
equivalent ratios Ratios that name the same comparison.	**razones equivalentes** Razones que expresan la misma comparación.	$\frac{1}{2}$ and $\frac{2}{4}$ are equivalent ratios.

ENGLISH	SPANISH	EXAMPLES
evaluate To find the value of an algebraic expression by substituting a number for each variable and simplifying by using the order of operations.	**evaluar** Calcular el valor de una expresión algebraica sustituyendo cada variable por un número y simplificando mediante el orden de las operaciones.	Evaluate $2x + 7$ for $x = 3$. $2x + 7$ $2(3) + 7$ $6 + 7$ 13
event An outcome or set of outcomes of an experiment.	**suceso** Resultado o conjunto de resultados en un experimento.	In the experiment of rolling a number cube, the event "an odd number" consists of the outcomes 1, 3, and 5.
excluded values Values of x for which a function or expression is not defined.	**valores excluidos** Valores de x para los cuales no está definida una función o expresión.	The excluded values of $$\frac{(x + 2)}{(x - 1)(x + 4)}$$ are $x = 1$ and $x = -4$, which would make the denominator equal to 0.
experiment An operation, process, or activity in which outcomes can be used to estimate probability.	**experimento** Una operación, proceso o actividad en la que se usan los resultados para estimar una probabilidad.	Tossing a coin 10 times and noting the number of heads
experimental probability The ratio of the number of times an event occurs to the number of trials, or times, that an activity is performed.	**probabilidad experimental** Razón entre la cantidad de veces que ocurre un suceso y la cantidad de pruebas, o veces, que se realiza una actividad.	Kendra attempted 27 free throws and made 16 of them. The experimental probability that she will make her next free throw is $P(\text{free throw}) =$ $$\frac{\text{number made}}{\text{number attempted}} = \frac{16}{27} \approx 0.59.$$
exponent The number that indicates how many times the base in a power is used as a factor.	**exponente** Número que indica la cantidad de veces que la base de una potencia se utiliza como factor.	$3^4 = 3 \cdot 3 \cdot 3 \cdot 3 = 81$ 4 is the exponent.
exponential decay An exponential function of the form $f(x) = ab^x$ in which $0 < b < 1$. If r is the rate of decay, then the function can be written $y = a(1 - r)^t$, where a is the initial amount and t is the time.	**decremento exponencial** Función exponencial del tipo $f(x) = ab^x$ en la cual $0 < b < 1$. Si r es la tasa decremental, entonces la función se puede expresar como $y = a(1 - r)^t$, donde a es la cantidad inicial y t es el tiempo.	$f(x) = 3\left(\frac{1}{2}\right)^x$ 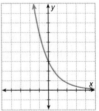
exponential expression An algebraic expression in which the variable is in an exponent with a fixed number as the base.	**expresión exponencial** Expresión algebraica en la que la variable está en un exponente y que tiene un número fijo como base.	2^{x+1}
exponential function A function of the form $f(x) = ab^x$, where a and b are real numbers with $a \neq 0$, $b > 0$, and $b \neq 1$.	**función exponencial** Función del tipo $f(x) = ab^x$, donde a y b son números reales con $a \neq 0$, $b > 0$ y $b \neq 1$.	$f(x) = 3 \cdot 4^x$ 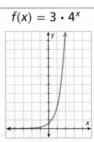

Glossary/Glosario

	ENGLISH	SPANISH	EXAMPLES

exponential growth An exponential function of the form $f(x) = ab^x$ in which $b > 1$. If r is the rate of growth, then the function can be written $y = a(1 + r)^t$, where a is the initial amount and t is the time.

crecimiento exponencial Función exponencial del tipo $f(x) = ab^x$ en la que $b > 1$. Si r es la tasa de crecimiento, entonces la función se puede expresar como $y = a(1 + r)^t$, donde a es la cantidad inicial y t es el tiempo.

$f(x) = 2^x$

---

exponential regression A statistical method used to fit an exponential model to a given data set.

regresión exponencial Método estadístico utilizado para ajustar un modelo exponencial a un conjunto de datos determinado.

---

expression A mathematical phrase that contains operations, numbers, and/or variables.

expresión Frase matemática que contiene operaciones, números y/o variables.

$6x + 1$

---

extraneous solution A solution of a derived equation that is not a solution of the original equation.

solución extraña Solución de una ecuación derivada que no es una solución de la ecuación original.

To solve $\sqrt{x} = -2$, square both sides; $x = 4$.

Check $\sqrt{4} = -2$ is false; so 4 is an extraneous solution.

---

factor A number or expression that is multiplied by another number or expression to get a product. *See also* factoring.

factor Número o expresión que se multiplica por otro número o expresión para obtener un producto. *Ver también* factoreo.

$12 = 3 \cdot 4$
3 and 4 are factors of 12.

$x^2 - 1 = (x - 1)(x + 1)$
$(x - 1)$ and $(x + 1)$ are factors of $x^2 - 1$.

---

factorial If n is a positive integer, then n factorial, written $n!$, is $n \cdot (n - 1) \cdot (n - 2) \cdot \ldots \cdot 2 \cdot 1$. The factorial of 0 is defined to be 1.

factorial Si n es un entero positivo, entonces el factorial de n, expresado como $n!$, es $n \cdot (n - 1) \cdot (n - 2) \cdot \ldots \cdot 2 \cdot 1$. Por definición, el factorial de 0 será 1.

$7! = 7 \cdot 6 \cdot 5 \cdot 4 \cdot 3 \cdot 2 \cdot 1 = 5040$

---

factoring The process of writing a number or algebraic expression as a product.

factorización Proceso por el que se expresa un número o expresión algebraica como un producto.

$x^2 - 4x - 21 = (x - 7)(x + 3)$

---

fair When all outcomes of an experiment are equally likely.

justo Cuando todos los resultados de un experimento son igualmente probables.

When tossing a fair coin, heads and tails are equally likely. Each has a probability of $\frac{1}{2}$.

---

family of functions A set of functions whose graphs have basic characteristics in common. Functions in the same family are transformations of their parent function.

familia de funciones Conjunto de funciones cuyas gráficas tienen características básicas en común. Las funciones de la misma familia son transformaciones de su función madre.

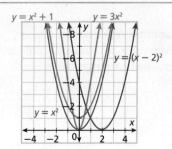

ENGLISH	SPANISH	EXAMPLES

first differences The differences between y-values of a function for evenly spaced x-values.

primeras diferencias Diferencias entre los valores de y de una función para valores de x espaciados uniformemente.

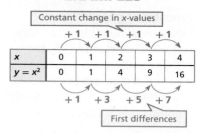

---

first quartile The median of the lower half of a data set, denoted Q_1. Also called *lower quartile*.

primer cuartil Mediana de la mitad inferior de un conjunto de datos, expresada como Q_1. También se llama *cuartil inferior*.

Lower half   **Upper half**
18, ⓔ23, 28,   29, 36, 42
First quartile

FOIL A mnemonic (memory) device for a method of multiplying two binomials:

Multiply the **First** terms.
Multiply the **Outer** terms.
Multiply the **Inner** terms.
Multiply the **Last** terms.

FOIL Regla mnemotécnica para recordar el método de multiplicación de dos binomios:

Multiplicar los términos **Primeros** (*First*).
Multiplicar los términos **Externos** (*Outer*).
Multiplicar los términos **Internos** (*Inner*).
Multiplicar los términos **Últimos** (*Last*).

$$(x + 2)(x - 3) = x^2 - 3x + 2x - 6$$
$$= x^2 - x - 6$$

---

formula A literal equation that states a rule for a relationship among quantities.

fórmula Ecuación literal que establece una regla para una relación entre cantidades.

$$A = \pi r^2$$

---

fractional exponent *See* rational exponent.

exponente fraccionario *Ver* exponente racional.

---

frequency The number of times the value appears in the data set.

frecuencia Cantidad de veces que aparece el valor en un conjunto de datos.

In the data set 5, 6, 6, 7, 8, 9, the data value 6 has a frequency of 2.

---

frequency table A table that lists the number of times, or frequency, that each data value occurs.

tabla de frecuencia Tabla que enumera la cantidad de veces que ocurre cada valor de datos, o la frecuencia.

Data set: 1, 1, 2, 2, 3, 4, 5, 5, 5, 6, 6, 6, 6
Frequency table:

Data	Frequency
1	2
2	2
3	1
4	1
5	3
6	4

---

function A relation in which every domain value is paired with exactly one range value.

función Relación en la que a cada valor de dominio corresponde exactamente un valor de rango.

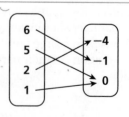

ENGLISH	SPANISH	EXAMPLES

function notation If x is the independent variable and y is the dependent variable, then the function notation for y is $f(x)$, read "f of x," where f names the function.

notación de función Si x es la variable independiente e y es la variable dependiente, entonces la notación de función para y es $f(x)$, que se lee "f de x," donde f nombra la función.

equation: $y = 2x$
function notation: $f(x) = 2x$

---

function rule An algebraic expression that defines a function.

regla de función Expresión algebraica que define una función.

$$f(x) = \underset{\uparrow}{\underline{2x^2 + 3x - 7}}$$
function rule

Fundamental Counting Principle If one event has m possible outcomes and a second event has n possible outcomes after the first event has occurred, then there are mn total possible outcomes for the two events.

Principio fundamental de conteo Si un suceso tiene m resultados posibles y otro suceso tiene n resultados posibles después de ocurrido el primer suceso, entonces hay mn resultados posibles en total para los dos sucesos.

If there are 4 colors of shirts, 3 colors of pants, and 2 colors of shoes, then there are $4 \cdot 3 \cdot 2 = 24$ possible outfits.

geometric sequence A sequence in which the ratio of successive terms is a constant r, called the common ratio, where $r \neq 0$ and $r \neq 1$.

sucesión geométrica Sucesión en la que la razón de los términos sucesivos es una constante r, denominada razón común, donde $r \neq 0$ y $r \neq 1$.

1, 2, 4, 8, 16, …
$\cdot 2 \cdot 2 \cdot 2 \cdot 2$ $r = 2$

---

glide reflection A composition of a translation and a reflection across a line parallel to the translation vector.

deslizamiento con inversión Composición de una traslación y una reflexión sobre una línea paralela al vector de traslación.

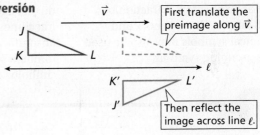

First translate the preimage along $\vec{v}$.

Then reflect the image across line ℓ.

---

graph of a function The set of points in a coordinate plane with coordinates (x, y), where x is in the domain of the function f and $y = f(x)$.

gráfica de una función Conjunto de los puntos de un plano cartesiano con coordenadas (x, y), donde x está en el dominio de la función f e $y = f(x)$.

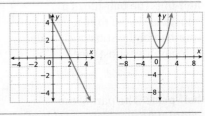

---

graph of a system of linear inequalities The region in a coordinate plane consisting of points whose coordinates are solutions to all of the inequalities in the system.

gráfica de un sistema de desigualdades lineales Región de un plano cartesiano que consta de puntos cuyas coordenadas son soluciones de todas las desigualdades del sistema.

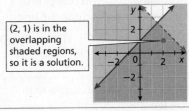

(2, 1) is in the overlapping shaded regions, so it is a solution.

---

graph of an inequality in one variable The set of points on a number line that are solutions of the inequality.

gráfica de una desigualdad en una variable Conjunto de los puntos de una recta numérica que representan soluciones de la desigualdad.

$x \geq 2$

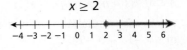

Glossary/Glosario

ENGLISH	SPANISH	EXAMPLES

graph of an inequality in two variables The set of points in a coordinate plane whose coordinates (x, y) are solutions of the inequality.

gráfica de una desigualdad en dos variables Conjunto de los puntos de un plano cartesiano cuyas coordenadas (x, y) son soluciones de la desigualdad.

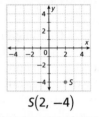
$y \leq x + 1$

---

graph of an ordered pair For the ordered pair (x, y), the point in a coordinate plane that is a horizontal distance of x units from the origin and a vertical distance of y units from the origin.

gráfica de un par ordenado Dado el par ordenado (x, y), punto en un plano cartesiano que está a una distancia horizontal de x unidades desde el origen y a una distancia vertical de y unidades desde el origen.

$S(2, -4)$

---

greatest common factor (monomials) (GCF) The product of the greatest integer and the greatest power of each variable that divide evenly into each monomial.

máximo común divisor (monomios) (MCD) Producto del entero mayor y la potencia mayor de cada variable que divide exactamente cada monomio.

The GCF of $4x^3y$ and $6x^2y$ is $2x^2y$.

---

greatest common factor (numbers) (GCF) The largest common factor of two or more given numbers.

máximo común divisor (números) (MCD) El mayor de los factores comunes compartidos por dos o más números dados.

The GCF of 27 and 45 is 9.

---

grouping symbols Symbols such as parentheses ( ), brackets [ ], and braces { } that separate part of an expression. A fraction bar, absolute-value symbols, and radical symbols may also be used as grouping symbols.

símbolos de agrupación Símbolos tales como paréntesis ( ), corchetes [ ] y llaves { } que separan parte de una expresión. La barra de fracciones, los símbolos de valor absoluto y los símbolos de radical también se pueden utilizar como símbolos de agrupación.

$6 + \{3 - [(4 - 3) + 2] + 1\} - 5$
$6 + \{3 - [1 + 2] + 1\} - 5$
$6 + \{3 - 3 + 1\} - 5$
$6 + 1 - 5$
2

H

half-life The half-life of a substance is the time it takes for one-half of the substance to decay into another substance.

vida media La vida media de una sustancia es el tiempo que tarda la mitad de la sustancia en desintegrarse y transformarse en otra sustancia.

Carbon-14 has a half-life of 5730 years, so 5 g of an initial amount of 10 g will remain after 5730 years.

---

half-plane The part of the coordinate plane on one side of a line, which may include the line.

semiplano La parte del plano cartesiano de un lado de una línea, que puede incluir la línea.

Heron's Formula A triangle with side lengths a, b, and c has area $A = \sqrt{s(s - a)(s - b)(s - c)}$, where s is one-half the perimeter, or $s = \frac{1}{2}(a + b + c)$.

fórmula de Herón Un triángulo con longitudes de lado a, b y c tiene un área $A = \sqrt{s(s - a)(s - b)(s - c)}$, donde s es la mitad del perímetro ó $s = \frac{1}{2}(a + b + c)$.

ENGLISH	SPANISH	EXAMPLES
histogram A bar graph used to display data grouped in intervals.	**histograma** Gráfica de barras utilizada para mostrar datos agrupados en intervalos de clases.	
horizontal line A line described by the equation $y = b$, where b is the y-intercept.	**línea horizontal** Línea descrita por la ecuación $y = b$, donde b es la intersección con el eje y.	$y = 4$
hypotenuse The side opposite the right angle in a right triangle.	**hipotenusa** Lado opuesto al ángulo recto de un triángulo rectángulo.	hypotenuse

identity An equation that is true for all values of the variables.	**identidad** Ecuación verdadera para todos los valores de las variables.	$3 = 3$ $2(x - 1) = 2x - 2$
inclusive events Events that have one or more outcomes in common.	**sucesos inclusivos** Sucesos que tienen uno o más resultados en común.	In the experiment of rolling a number cube, rolling an even number and rolling a number less than 3 are inclusive events because both contain the outcome 2.
inconsistent system A system of equations or inequalities that has no solution.	**sistema inconsistente** Sistema de ecuaciones o desigualdades que no tiene solución.	$\begin{cases} x + y = 0 \\ x + y = 1 \end{cases}$
independent events Events for which the occurrence or nonoccurrence of one event does not affect the probability of the other event.	**sucesos independientes** Dos sucesos son independientes si el hecho de que se produzca o no uno de ellos no afecta la probabilidad del otro suceso.	From a bag containing 3 red marbles and 2 blue marbles, draw a red marble, replace it, and then draw a blue marble.
independent system A system of equations that has exactly one solution.	**sistema independiente** Sistema de ecuaciones que tiene sólo una solución.	$\begin{cases} x + y = 7 \\ x - y = 1 \end{cases}$ Solution: $(4, 3)$
independent variable The input of a function; a variable whose value determines the value of the output, or dependent variable.	**variable independiente** Entrada de una función; variable cuyo valor determina el valor de la salida, o variable dependiente.	For $y = 2x + 1$, x is the independent variable.

ENGLISH	SPANISH	EXAMPLES
index In the radical $\sqrt[n]{x}$, which represents the nth root of x, n is the index. In the radical $\sqrt{x}$, the index is understood to be 2.	**índice** En el radical $\sqrt[n]{x}$, que representa la enésima raíz de x, n es el índice. En el radical $\sqrt{x}$, se da por sentado que el índice es 2.	The radical $\sqrt[3]{8}$ has an index of 3.
indirect measurement A method of measurement that uses formulas, similar figures, and/or proportions.	**medición indirecta** Método de medición en el que se usan fórmulas, figuras semejantes y/o proporciones.	
inequality A statement that compares two expressions by using one of the following signs: $<$, $>$, $\leq$, $\geq$, or $\neq$.	**desigualdad** Enunciado que compara dos expresiones utilizando uno de los siguientes signos: $<$, $>$, $\leq$, $\geq$, o $\neq$.	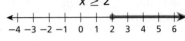 $x \geq 2$
input A value that is substituted for the independent variable in a relation or function.	**entrada** Valor que sustituye a la variable independiente en una relación o función.	For the function $f(x) = x + 5$, the input 3 produces an output of 8.
input-output table A table that displays input values of a function or expression together with the corresponding outputs.	**tabla de entrada y salida** Tabla que muestra los valores de entrada de una función o expresión junto con las correspondientes salidas.	Input / Output table: x: 1, 2, 3, 4; y: 4, 7, 10, 13
integer A member of the set of whole numbers and their opposites.	**entero** Miembro del conjunto de números cabales y sus opuestos.	..., -3, -2, -1, 0, 1, 2, 3, ...
intercept *See* x-intercept and y-intercept.	**intersección** *Ver* intersección con el eje x e intersección con el eje y.	
interquartile range (IQR) The difference of the third (upper) and first (lower) quartiles in a data set, representing the middle half of the data.	**rango entre cuartiles** Diferencia entre el tercer cuartil (superior) y el primer cuartil (inferior) de un conjunto de datos, que representa la mitad central de los datos.	Lower half: Upper half: 18, ⟨23⟩, 28, 29, ⟨36⟩, 42. First quartile, Third quartile. Interquartile range: $36 - 23 = 13$
intersection The intersection of two sets is the set of all elements that are common to both sets, denoted by $\cap$.	**intersección de conjuntos** La intersección de dos conjuntos es el conjunto de todos los elementos que son comunes a ambos conjuntos, expresado por $\cap$.	$A = \{1, 2, 3, 4\}$ $B = \{1, 3, 5, 7, 9\}$ $A \cap B = \{1, 3\}$
inverse function The function that results from exchanging the input and output values of a one-to-one function. The inverse of $f(x)$ is denoted $f^{-1}(x)$.	**función inversa** Función que resulta de intercambiar los valores de entrada y salida de una función uno a uno. La función inversa de $f(x)$ se expresa $f^{-1}(x)$.	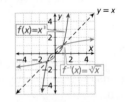
inverse operations Operations that undo each other.	**operaciones inversas** Operaciones que se anulan entre sí.	Addition and subtraction of the same quantity are inverse operations: $5 + 3 = 8$, $8 - 3 = 5$ Multiplication and division by the same quantity are inverse operations: $2 \cdot 3 = 6$, $6 \div 3 = 2$

ENGLISH	SPANISH	EXAMPLES
inverse variation A relationship between two variables, x and y, that can be written in the form $y = \frac{k}{x}$, where k is a nonzero constant and $x \neq 0$.	**variación inversa** Relación entre dos variables, x e y, que puede expresarse en la forma $y = \frac{k}{x}$, donde k es una constante distinta de cero y $x \neq 0$.	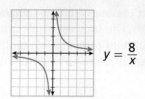 $y = \frac{8}{x}$
irrational number A real number that cannot be expressed as the ratio of two integers.	**número irracional** Número real que no se puede expresar como una razón de enteros.	$\sqrt{2}$, π, e
isolate the variable To isolate a variable in an equation, use inverse operations on both sides until the variable appears by itself on one side of the equation and does not appear on the other side.	**despejar la variable** Para despejar la variable de una ecuación, utiliza operaciones inversas en ambos lados hasta que la variable aparezca sola en uno de los lados de la ecuación y no aparezca en el otro lado.	$10 = 6 - 2x$ $\frac{-6 \quad -6}{4 = \quad -2x}$ $\frac{4}{-2} = \frac{-2x}{-2}$ $-2 = x$
isometry A transformation that does not change the size or shape of a figure.	**isometría** Transformación que no cambia el tamaño ni la forma de una figura.	Reflections, translations, and rotations are all examples of isometries.
isosceles triangle A triangle with at least two congruent sides.	**triángulo isósceles** Triángulo que tiene al menos dos lados congruentes.	

joint relative frequency The ratio of the frequency in a particular category divided by the total number of data values.	**frecuencia relativa conjunta** La razón de la frecuencia en una determinada categoría dividida entre el número total de valores.	

leading coefficient The coefficient of the first term of a polynomial in standard form.	**coeficiente principal** Coeficiente del primer término de un polinomio en forma estándar.	$3x^2 + 7x - 2$ Leading coefficient: 3
least common denominator (LCD) The least common multiple of the denominators of two or more given fractions or rational expressions.	**mínimo común denominador (MCD)** Mínimo común múltiplo de los denominadores de dos o más fracciones dadas o expresionnes racionales.	The LCD of $\frac{3}{4}$ and $\frac{5}{6}$ is 12.
least common multiple (monomials) (LCM) The product of the smallest positive number and the lowest power of each variable that divide evenly into each monomial.	**mínimo común múltiplo (monomios) (MCM)** El producto del número positivo más pequeño y la menor potencia de cada variable que divide exactamente cada monomio.	The LCM of $6x^2$ and $4x$ is $12x^2$.

ENGLISH	SPANISH	EXAMPLES
least common multiple (numbers) (LCM) The smallest whole number, other than zero, that is a multiple of two or more given numbers.	**mínimo común múltiplo (números) (MCM)** El menor de los números cabales, distinto de cero, que es múltiplo de dos o más números dados.	The LCM of 10 and 18 is 90.
least-squares line The line of fit for which the sum of the squares of the residuals is as small as possible.	**línea de mínimos cuadrados** La línea de ajuste en que la suma de cuadrados de los residuos es la menor.	
line of best fit The line that comes closest to all of the points in a data set.	**línea de mejor ajuste** Línea que más se acerca a todos los puntos de un conjunto de datos.	
linear equation in one variable An equation that can be written in the form $ax = b$ where a and b are constants and $a \neq 0$.	**ecuación lineal en una variable** Ecuación que puede expresarse en la forma $ax = b$ donde a y b son constantes y $a \neq 0$.	$x + 1 = 7$
linear equation in two variables An equation that can be written in the form $Ax + By = C$ where A, B, and C are constants and A and B are not both 0.	**ecuación lineal en dos variables** Ecuación que puede expresarse en la forma $Ax + By = C$ donde A, B y C son constantes y A y B no son ambas 0.	$2x + 3y = 6$
linear function A function that can be written in the form $y = mx + b$, where x is the independent variable and m and b are real numbers. Its graph is a line.	**función lineal** Función que puede expresarse en la forma $y = mx + b$, donde x es la variable independiente y m y b son números reales. Su gráfica es una línea.	$y = x - 1$
linear inequality in one variable An inequality that can be written in one of the following forms: $ax < b$, $ax > b$, $ax \leq b$, $ax \geq b$, or $ax \neq b$, where a and b are constants and $a \neq 0$.	**desigualdad lineal en una variable** Desigualdad que puede expresarse de una de las siguientes formas: $ax < b$, $ax > b$, $ax \leq b$, $ax \geq b$ o $ax \neq b$, donde a y b son constantes y $a \neq 0$.	$3x - 5 \leq 2(x + 4)$
linear inequality in two variables An inequality that can be written in one of the following forms: $Ax + By < C$, $Ax + By > C$, $Ax + By \leq C$, $Ax + By \geq C$, or $Ax + By \neq C$, where A, B, and C are constants and A and B are not both 0.	**desigualdad lineal en dos variables** Desigualdad que puede expresarse de una de las siguientes formas: $Ax + By < C$, $Ax + By > C$, $Ax + By \leq C$, $Ax + By \geq C$ o $Ax + By \neq C$, donde A, B y C son constantes y A y B no son ambas 0.	$2x + 3y > 6$
linear regression A statistical method used to fit a linear model to a given data set.	**regresión lineal** Método estadístico utilizado para ajustar un modelo lineal a un conjunto de datos determinado.	
line symmetry A figure that can be reflected across a line so that the image coincides with the preimage.	**simetría axial** Figura que puede reflejarse sobre una línea de forma tal que la imagen coincida con la imagen original.	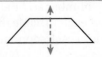

Glossary/Glosario

ENGLISH	SPANISH	EXAMPLES
literal equation An equation that contains two or more variables.	**ecuación literal** Ecuación que contiene dos o más variables.	$d = rt$ $A = \frac{1}{2}h(b_1 + b_2)$
lower quartile *See* first quartile.	**cuartil inferior** *Ver* primer cuartil.	

mapping diagram A diagram that shows the relationship of elements in the domain to elements in the range of a relation or function.	**diagrama de correspondencia** Diagrama que muestra la relación entre los elementos del dominio y los elementos del rango de una función.	 **Mapping Diagram**
marginal relative frequency The sum of the joint relative frequencies in a row or column of a two-way table.	**frecuencia relativa marginal** La suma de las frecuencias relativas conjuntas en una fila o columna de una tabla de doble entrada.	
maximum of a function The *y*-value of the highest point on the graph of the function.	**máximo de una función** Valor de *y* del punto más alto en la gráfica de la función.	 The maximum of the function is 2.
mean The sum of all the values in a data set divided by the number of data values. Also called the *average*.	**media** Suma de todos los valores de un conjunto de datos dividida entre el número de valores de datos. También llamada *promedio*.	Data set: 4, 6, 7, 8, 10 Mean: $\dfrac{4 + 6 + 7 + 8 + 10}{5}$ $= \dfrac{35}{5} = 7$
measure of an angle Angles are measured in degrees. A degree is $\frac{1}{360}$ of a complete circle.	**medida de un ángulo** Los ángulos se miden en grados. Un grado es $\frac{1}{360}$ de un círculo completo.	*M* 26.8°
measure of central tendency A measure that describes the center of a data set.	**medida de tendencia dominante** Medida que describe el centro de un conjunto de datos.	mean, median, or mode
median For an ordered data set with an odd number of values, the median is the middle value. For an ordered data set with an even number of values, the median is the average of the two middle values.	**mediana** Dado un conjunto de datos ordenado con un número impar de valores, la mediana es el valor medio. Dado un conjunto de datos con un número par de valores, la mediana es el promedio de los dos valores medios.	8, 9, (9,) 12, 15 Median: 9 4, 6, (7, 10,) 10, 12 Median: $\dfrac{7 + 10}{2} = 8.5$
midpoint The point that divides a segment into two congruent segments.	**punto medio** Punto que divide un segmento en dos segmentos congruentes.	*A* *B* *C* Point *B* is the midpoint of $\overline{AC}$.

ENGLISH	SPANISH	EXAMPLES

minimum of a function The *y*-value of the lowest point on the graph of the function.

mínimo de una función Valor de *y* del punto más bajo en la gráfica de la función.

(0, −2)

The minimum of the function is −2.

---

mode The value or values that occur most frequently in a data set; if all values occur with the same frequency, the data set is said to have no mode.

moda El valor o los valores que se presentan con mayor frecuencia en un conjunto de datos. Si todos los valores se presentan con la misma frecuencia, se dice que el conjunto de datos no tiene moda.

Data set: 3, 6, 8, 8, 10 Mode: 8

Data set: 2, 5, 5, 7, 7 Modes: 5 and 7

Data set: 2, 3, 6, 9, 11 No mode

---

monomial A number or a product of numbers and variables with whole-number exponents, or a polynomial with one term.

monomio Número o producto de números y variables con exponentes de números cabales, o polinomio con un término.

$3x^2y^4$

Multiplication Property of Equality If *a*, *b*, and *c* are real numbers and $a = b$, then $ac = bc$.

Propiedad de igualdad de la multiplicación Si *a*, *b* y *c* son números reales y $a = b$, entonces $ac = bc$.

$$\frac{1}{3}x = 7$$
$$(3)\left(\frac{1}{3}x\right) = (3)(7)$$
$$x = 21$$

Multiplication Property of Inequality If both sides of an inequality are multiplied by the same positive quantity, the new inequality will have the same solution set.
If both sides of an inequality are multiplied by the same negative quantity, the new inequality will have the same solution set if the inequality symbol is reversed.

Propiedad de desigualdad de la multiplicación Si ambos lados de una desigualdad se multiplican por el mismo número positivo, la nueva desigualdad tendrá el mismo conjunto solución.
Si ambos lados de una desigualdad se multiplican por el mismo número negativo, la nueva desigualdad tendrá el mismo conjunto solución si se invierte el símbolo de desigualdad.

$$\frac{1}{3}x > 7$$
$$(3)\left(\frac{1}{3}x\right) > (3)(7)$$
$$x > 21$$

$$-x \leq 2$$
$$(-1)(-x) \geq (-1)(2)$$
$$x \geq -2$$

---

multiplicative inverse The reciprocal of the number.

inverso multiplicativo Recíproco de un número.

The multiplicative inverse of 5 is $\frac{1}{5}$.

---

mutually exclusive events Two events are mutually exclusive if they cannot both occur in the same trial of an experiment.

sucesos mutuamente excluyentes Dos sucesos son mutuamente excluyentes si ambos no pueden ocurrir en la misma prueba de un experimento.

In the experiment of rolling a number cube, rolling a 3 and rolling an even number are mutually exclusive events.

---

natural number A counting number.

número natural Número que se utiliza para contar.

1, 2, 3, 4, 5, 6, …

---

negative correlation Two data sets have a negative correlation if one set of data values increases as the other set decreases.

correlación negativa Dos conjuntos de datos tienen una correlación negativa si un conjunto de valores de datos aumenta a medida que el otro conjunto disminuye.

ENGLISH	SPANISH	EXAMPLES
negative exponent For any nonzero real number x and any integer n, $x^{-n} = \frac{1}{x^n}$.	**exponente negativo** Para cualquier número real distinto de cero x y cualquier entero n, $x^{-n} = \frac{1}{x^n}$.	$x^{-2} = \dfrac{1}{x^2}$; $3^{-2} = \dfrac{1}{3^2}$
negative number A number that is less than zero. Negative numbers lie to the left of zero on a number line.	**número negativo** Número menor que cero. Los números negativos se ubican a la izquierda del cero en una recta numérica.	-2 is a negative number. 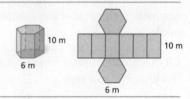
net A diagram of the faces of a three-dimensional figure arranged in such a way that the diagram can be folded to form the three-dimensional figure.	**plantilla** Diagrama de las caras de una figura tridimensional que se puede plegar para formar la figura tridimensional.	
no correlation Two data sets have no correlation if there is no relationship between the sets of values.	**sin correlación** Dos conjuntos de datos no tienen correlación si no existe una relación entre los conjuntos de valores.	
nonlinear system of equations A system in which at least one of the equations is not linear.	**sistema no lineal de ecuaciones** Sistema en el cual por lo menos una de las ecuaciones no es lineal.	A system that contains one quadratic equation and one linear equation is a nonlinear system.
nth root The nth root of a number a, written as $\sqrt[n]{a}$ or $a^{\frac{1}{n}}$, is a number that is equal to a when it is raised to the nth power.	**enésima raíz** La enésima raíz de un número a, que se escribe $\sqrt[n]{a}$ o $a^{\frac{1}{n}}$, es un número igual a a cuando se eleva a la enésima potencia.	$\sqrt[5]{32} = 2$, because $2^5 = 32$.
number line A line used to represent the real numbers.	**recta numérica** Línea utilizada para representar los números reales.	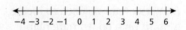

ENGLISH	SPANISH	EXAMPLES
obtuse angle An angle that measures greater than 90° and less than 180°.	**ángulo obtuso** Ángulo que mide más de 90° y menos de 180°.	
obtuse triangle A triangle with one obtuse angle.	**triángulo obtusángulo** Triángulo con un ángulo obtuso.	
odds A comparison of favorable and unfavorable outcomes. The odds in favor of an event are the ratio of the number of favorable outcomes to the number of unfavorable outcomes. The odds against an event are the ratio of the number of unfavorable outcomes to the number of favorable outcomes.	**probabilidades a favor y en contra** Comparación de los resultados favorables y desfavorables. Las probabilidades a favor de un suceso son la razón entre la cantidad de resultados favorables y la cantidad de resultados desfavorables. Las probabilidades en contra de un suceso son la razón entre la cantidad de resultados desfavorables y la cantidad de resultados favorables.	The odds in favor of rolling a 3 on a number cube are $1:5$. The odds against rolling a 3 on a number cube are $5:1$.

Glossary/Glosario

ENGLISH	**SPANISH**	**EXAMPLES**
opposite The opposite of a number a, denoted $-a$, is the number that is the same distance from zero as a, on the opposite side of the number line. The sum of opposites is 0.	**opuesto** El opuesto de un número a, expresado $-a$, es el número que se encuentra a la misma distancia de cero que a, del lado opuesto de la recta numérica. La suma de los opuestos es 0.	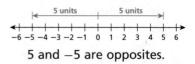 5 and −5 are opposites.
opposite reciprocal The opposite of the reciprocal of a number. The opposite reciprocal of any nonzero number a is $-\frac{1}{a}$.	**recíproco opuesto** Opuesto del recíproco de un número. El recíproco opuesto de a es $-\frac{1}{a}$.	The opposite reciprocal of $\frac{2}{3}$ is $-\frac{3}{2}$.
OR A logical operator representing the union of two sets.	**O** Operador lógico que representa la unión de dos conjuntos.	$A = \{2, 3, 4, 5\}$ $B = \{1, 3, 5, 7\}$ The set of values that are in A OR B is $A \cup B = \{1, 2, 3, 4, 5, 7\}$.
order of operations A process for evaluating expressions: First, perform operations in parentheses or other grouping symbols. Second, simplify powers and roots. Third, perform all multiplication and division from left to right. Fourth, perform all addition and subtraction from left to right.	**orden de las operaciones** Regla para evaluar las expresiones: Primero, realizar las operaciones entre paréntesis u otros símbolos de agrupación. Segundo, simplificar las potencias y las raíces. Tercero, realizar todas las multiplicaciones y divisiones de izquierda a derecha. Cuarto, realizar todas las sumas y restas de izquierda a derecha.	$2 + 3^2 - (7 + 5) \div 4 \cdot 3$ $2 + 3^2 - 12 \div 4 \cdot 3$ Add inside parentheses. $2 + 9 - 12 \div 4 \cdot 3$ Simplify the power. $2 + 9 - 3 \cdot 3$ Divide. $2 + 9 - 9$ Multiply. $11 - 9$ Add. 2 Subtract.
ordered pair A pair of numbers (x, y) that can be used to locate a point on a coordinate plane. The first number x indicates the distance to the left or right of the origin, and the second number y indicates the distance above or below the origin.	**par ordenado** Par de números (x, y) que se pueden utilizar para ubicar un punto en un plano cartesiano. El primer número, x, indica la distancia a la izquierda o derecha del origen y el segundo número, y, indica la distancia hacia arriba o hacia abajo del origen.	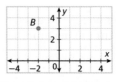 The ordered pair $(-2, 3)$ can be used to locate B.
origin The intersection of the x- and y-axes in a coordinate plane. The coordinates of the origin are $(0, 0)$.	**origen** Intersección de los ejes x e y en un plano cartesiano. Las coordenadas de origen son $(0, 0)$.	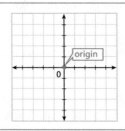
outcome A possible result of a probability experiment.	**resultado** Resultado posible de un experimento de probabilidad.	In the experiment of rolling a number cube, the possible outcomes are 1, 2, 3, 4, 5, and 6.
outlier A data value that is far removed from the rest of the data.	**valor extremo** Valor de datos que está muy alejado del resto de los datos.	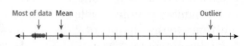
output The result of substituting a value for a variable in a function.	**salida** Resultado de la sustitución de una variable por un valor en una función.	For the function $f(x) = x^2 + 1$, the input 3 produces an output of 10.

parabola The shape of the graph of a quadratic function.

parábola Forma de la gráfica de una función cuadrática.

parallel lines Lines in the same plane that do not intersect.

líneas paralelas Líneas en el mismo plano que no se cruzan.

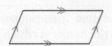

parallelogram A quadrilateral with two pairs of parallel sides.

paralelogramo Cuadrilátero con dos pares de lados paralelos.

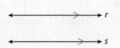

parent function The simplest function with the defining characteristics of the family. Functions in the same family are transformations of their parent function.

función madre La función más básica que tiene las características distintivas de una familia. Las funciones de la misma familia son transformaciones de su función madre.

$f(x) = x^2$ is the parent function for $g(x) = x^2 + 4$ and $h(x) = (5x + 2)^2 - 3$.

Pascal's triangle A triangular arrangement of numbers in which every row starts and ends with 1 and each other number is the sum of the two numbers above it.

triángulo de Pascal Arreglo triangular de números en el cual cada fila comienza y termina con 1 y los demás números son la suma de los dos valores que están arriba de cada uno.

```
      1
     1 1
    1 2 1
   1 3 3 1
  1 4 6 4 1
```

percent A ratio that compares a number to 100.

porcentaje Razón que compara un número con 100.

$\dfrac{17}{100} = 17\%$

percent change An increase or decrease given as a percent of the original amount. *See also* percent decrease, percent increase.

porcentaje de cambio Incremento o disminución dada como un porcentaje de la cantidad original. *Ver también* porcentaje de disminución, porcentaje de incremento.

percent decrease A decrease given as a percent of the original amount.

porcentaje de disminución Disminución dada como un porcentaje de la cantidad original.

If an item that costs $8.00 is marked down to $6.00, the amount of the decrease is $2.00, so the percent decrease is $\dfrac{2.00}{8.00} = 0.25 = 25\%$.

percent increase An increase given as a percent of the original amount.

porcentaje de incremento Incremento dado como un porcentaje de la cantidad original.

If an item's wholesale cost of $8.00 is marked up to $12.00, the amount of the increase is $4.00, so the percent increase is $\dfrac{4.00}{8.00} = 0.5 = 50\%$.

perfect square A number whose positive square root is a whole number.

cuadrado perfecto Número cuya raíz cuadrada positiva es un número cabal.

36 is a perfect square because $\sqrt{36} = 6$.

ENGLISH	SPANISH	EXAMPLES
perfect-square trinomial A trinomial whose factored form is the square of a binomial. A perfect-square trinomial has the form $a^2 - 2ab + b^2 = (a - b)^2$ or $a^2 + 2ab + b^2 = (a + b)^2$.	**trinomio cuadrado perfecto** Trinomio cuya forma factorizada es el cuadrado de un binomio. Un trinomio cuadrado perfecto tiene la forma $a^2 - 2ab + b^2 = (a - b)^2$ o $a^2 + 2ab + b^2 = (a + b)^2$.	$x^2 + 6x + 9$ is a perfect-square trinomial, because $x^2 + 6x + 9 = (x + 3)^2$.
perimeter The sum of the side lengths of a closed plane figure.	**perímetro** Suma de las longitudes de los lados de una figura plana cerrada.	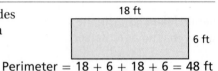 Perimeter = $18 + 6 + 18 + 6 = 48$ ft
permutation An arrangement of a group of objects in which order is important.	**permutación** Arreglo de un grupo de objetos en el cual el orden es importante.	For objects A, B, C, and D, there are 12 different permutations of 2 objects. AB, AC, AD, BC, BD, CD BA, CA, DA, CB, DB, DC
perpendicular Intersecting to form 90° angles.	**perpendicular** Que se cruza para formar ángulos de 90°.	
perpendicular lines Lines that intersect at 90° angles.	**líneas perpendiculares** Líneas que se cruzan en ángulos de 90°.	
plane A flat surface that has no thickness and extends forever.	**plano** Una superficie plana que no tiene grosor y se extiende infinitamente.	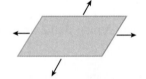
point A location that has no size.	**punto** Ubicación exacta que no tiene ningún tamaño.	$P \bullet$ point P
point-slope form The point-slope form of a linear equation is $y - y_1 = m(x - x_1)$, where m is the slope and (x_1, y_1) is a point on the line.	**forma de punto y pendiente** La forma de punto y pendiente de una ecuación lineal es $y - y_1 = m(x - x_1)$, donde m es la pendiente y (x_1, y_1) es un punto en la línea.	$y - 3 = 2(x - 3)$
polygon A closed plane figure formed by three or more segments such that each segment intersects exactly two other segments only at their endpoints and no two segments with a common endpoint are collinear.	**polígono** Figura plana cerrada formada por tres o más segmentos tal que cada segmento se cruza únicamente con otros dos segmentos sólo en sus extremos y ningún segmento con un extremo común a otro es colineal con éste.	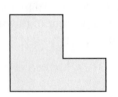
polynomial A monomial or a sum or difference of monomials.	**polinomio** Monomio o suma o diferencia de monomios.	$2x^2 + 3xy - 7y^2$

ENGLISH	SPANISH	EXAMPLES
polynomial long division A method of dividing one polynomial by another.	**división larga polinomial** Método por el que se divide un polinomio entre otro.	$$\begin{array}{r} x+1 \\ x+2\overline{)\;x^2+3x+5} \\ -(x^2+2x) \\ \hline x+5 \\ -(x+2) \\ \hline 3 \end{array}$$ $$\frac{x^2+3x+5}{x+2}=x+1+\frac{3}{x+2}$$
population The entire group of objects or individuals considered for a survey.	**población** Grupo completo de objetos o individuos que se desea estudiar.	In a survey about the study habits of high school students, the population is all high school students.
positive correlation Two data sets have a positive correlation if both sets of data values increase.	**correlación positiva** Dos conjuntos de datos tienen correlación positiva si los valores de ambos conjuntos de datos aumentan.	
positive number A number greater than zero.	**número positivo** Número mayor que cero.	2 is a positive number. $$\xleftarrow[\;-4\;-3\;-2\;-1\;\;0\;\;1\;\;2\;\;3\;\;4\;]{}$$
Power of a Power Property If a is any nonzero real number and m and n are integers, then $\left(a^m\right)^n=a^{mn}$.	**Propiedad de la potencia de una potencia** Dado un número real a distinto de cero y los números enteros m y n, entonces $\left(a^m\right)^n=a^{mn}$.	$$\left(6^7\right)^4=6^{7\cdot4}$$ $$=6^{28}$$
Power of a Product Property If a and b are any nonzero real numbers and n is any integer, then $(ab)^n=a^nb^n$.	**Propiedad de la potencia de un producto** Dados los números reales a y b distintos de cero y un número entero n, entonces $(ab)^n=a^nb^n$.	$$(2\cdot4)^3=2^3\cdot4^3$$ $$=8\cdot64$$ $$=512$$
Power of a Quotient Property If a and b are any nonzero real numbers and n is an integer, then $\left(\frac{a}{b}\right)^n=\frac{a^n}{b^n}$.	**Propiedad de la potencia de un cociente** Dados los números reales a y b distintos de cero y un número entero n, entonces $\left(\frac{a}{b}\right)^n=\frac{a^n}{b^n}$.	$$\left(\frac{3}{5}\right)^4=\frac{3}{5}\cdot\frac{3}{5}\cdot\frac{3}{5}\cdot\frac{3}{5}$$ $$=\frac{3\cdot3\cdot3\cdot3}{5\cdot5\cdot5\cdot5}$$ $$=\frac{3^4}{5^4}$$
precision The level of detail of a measurement, determined by the unit of measure.	**precisión** Detalle de una medición, determinado por la unidad de medida.	A ruler marked in millimeters has a greater level of precision than a ruler marked in centimeters.
prediction An estimate or guess about something that has not yet happened.	**predicción** Estimación o suposición sobre algo que todavía no ha sucedido.	
prime factorization A representation of a number or a polynomial as a product of primes.	**factorización prima** Representación de un número o de un polinomio como producto de números primos.	The prime factorization of 60 is $2\cdot2\cdot3\cdot5$.

prime number A whole number greater than 1 that has exactly two positive factors, itself and 1.

número primo Número cabal mayor que 1 que es divisible únicamente entre sí mismo y entre 1.

5 is prime because its only positive factors are 5 and 1.

---

principal An amount of money borrowed or invested.

capital Cantidad de dinero que se pide prestado o se invierte.

---

prism A polyhedron formed by two parallel congruent polygonal bases connected by faces that are parallelograms.

prisma Poliedro formado por dos bases poligonales congruentes y paralelas conectadas por caras laterales que son paralelogramos.

---

probability A number from 0 to 1 (or 0% to 100%) that is the measure of how likely an event is to occur.

probabilidad Número entre 0 y 1 (o entre 0% y 100%) que describe cuán probable es que ocurra un suceso.

A bag contains 3 red marbles and 4 blue marbles. The probability of randomly choosing a red marble is $\frac{3}{7}$.

Product of Powers Property If a is any nonzero real number and m and n are integers, then $a^m \cdot a^n = a^{m+n}$.

Propiedad del producto de potencias Dado un número real a distinto de cero y los números enteros m y n, entonces $a^m \cdot a^n = a^{m+n}$.

$$6^7 \cdot 6^4 = 6^{7+4}$$
$$= 6^{11}$$

Product Property of Square Roots For $a \geq 0$ and $b \geq 0$, $\sqrt{ab} = \sqrt{a} \cdot \sqrt{b}$.

Propiedad del producto de raíces cuadradas Dados $a \geq 0$ y $b \geq 0$, $\sqrt{ab} = \sqrt{a} \cdot \sqrt{b}$.

$$\sqrt{9 \cdot 25} = \sqrt{9} \cdot \sqrt{25}$$
$$= 3 \cdot 5 = 15$$

---

proportion A statement that two ratios are equal; $\frac{a}{b} = \frac{c}{d}$.

proporción Ecuación que establece que dos razones son iguales; $\frac{a}{b} = \frac{c}{d}$.

$$\frac{2}{3} = \frac{4}{6}$$

---

pyramid A polyhedron formed by a polygonal base and triangular lateral faces that meet at a common vertex.

pirámide Poliedro formado por una base poligonal y caras laterales triangulares que se encuentran en un vértice común.

Pythagorean Theorem If a right triangle has legs of lengths a and b and a hypotenuse of length c, then $a^2 + b^2 = c^2$.

Teorema de Pitágoras Dado un triángulo rectángulo con catetos de longitudes a y b y una hipotenusa de longitud c, entonces $a^2 + b^2 = c^2$.

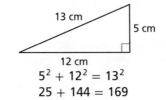

$$5^2 + 12^2 = 13^2$$
$$25 + 144 = 169$$

Pythagorean triple A set of three positive integers a, b, and c such that $a^2 + b^2 = c^2$.

Tripleta de Pitágoras Conjunto de tres enteros positivos a, b y c tal que $a^2 + b^2 = c^2$.

The numbers 3, 4, and 5 form a Pythagorean triple because $3^2 + 4^2 = 5^2$.

---

quadrant One of the four regions into which the x- and y-axes divide the coordinate plane.

cuadrante Una de las cuatro regiones en las que los ejes x e y dividen el plano cartesiano.

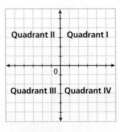

ENGLISH	SPANISH	EXAMPLES
quadratic equation An equation that can be written in the form $ax^2 + bx + c = 0$, where a, b, and c are real numbers and $a \neq 0$.	**ecuación cuadrática** Ecuación que se puede expresar como $ax^2 + bx + c = 0$, donde a, b y c son números reales y $a \neq 0$.	$x^2 + 3x - 4 = 0$ $x^2 - 9 = 0$
Quadratic Formula The formula $x = \frac{-b \pm \sqrt{b^2 - 4ac}}{2a}$, which gives solutions, or roots, of equations in the form $ax^2 + bx + c = 0$, where $a \neq 0$.	**fórmula cuadrática** La fórmula $x = \frac{-b \pm \sqrt{b^2 - 4ac}}{2a}$, que da soluciones, o raíces, para las ecuaciones del tipo $ax^2 + bx + c = 0$, donde $a \neq 0$.	The solutions of $2x^2 - 5x - 3 = 0$ are given by $x = \frac{-(-5) \pm \sqrt{(-5)^2 - 4(2)(-3)}}{2(2)}$ $= \frac{5 \pm \sqrt{25 + 24}}{4} = \frac{5 \pm 7}{4}$ $x = 3$ or $x = -\frac{1}{2}$
quadratic function A function that can be written in the form $f(x) = ax^2 + bx + c$, where a, b, and c are real numbers and $a \neq 0$.	**función cuadrática** Función que se puede expresar como $f(x) = ax^2 + bx + c$, donde a, b y c son números reales y $a \neq 0$.	$f(x) = x^2 - 6x + 8$
quadratic polynomial A polynomial of degree 2.	**polinomio cuadrático** Polinomio de grado 2.	$x^2 - 6x + 8$
quartile The median of the upper or lower half of a data set. *See also* first quartile, third quartile.	**cuartil** La mediana de la mitad superior o inferior de un conjunto de datos. *Ver también* primer cuartil, tercer cuartil.	First quartile / Third quartile — Minimum, Median, Maximum 0 2 4 6 8 10 12 14
Quotient of Powers Property If a is a nonzero real number and m and n are integers, then $\frac{a^m}{a^n} = a^{m-n}$.	**Propiedad del cociente de potencias** Dado un número real a distinto de cero y los números enteros m y n, entonces $\frac{a^m}{a^n} = a^{m-n}$.	$\frac{6^7}{6^4} = 6^{7-4} = 6^3$
Quotient Property of Square Roots For $a \geq 0$ and $b > 0$, $\sqrt{\frac{a}{b}} = \frac{\sqrt{a}}{\sqrt{b}}$.	**Propiedad del cociente de raíces cuadradas** Dados $a \geq 0$ y $b > 0$, $\sqrt{\frac{a}{b}} = \frac{\sqrt{a}}{\sqrt{b}}$.	$\sqrt{\frac{9}{25}} = \frac{\sqrt{9}}{\sqrt{25}} = \frac{3}{5}$

ENGLISH	SPANISH	EXAMPLES
radical equation An equation that contains a variable within a radical.	**ecuación radical** Ecuación que contiene una variable dentro de un radical.	$\sqrt{x + 3} + 4 = 7$
radical expression An expression that contains a radical sign.	**expresión radical** Expresión que contiene un signo de radical.	$\sqrt{x + 3} + 4$
radical symbol The symbol $\sqrt{}$ used to denote a root. The symbol is used alone to indicate a square root or with an index, $\sqrt[n]{}$, to indicate the nth root.	**símbolo de radical** Símbolo $\sqrt{}$ que se utiliza para expresar una raíz. Puede utilizarse solo para indicar una raíz cuadrada, o con un índice, $\sqrt[n]{}$, para indicar la enésima raíz.	$\sqrt{36} = 6$ $\sqrt[3]{27} = 3$

Glossary/Glosario

| --- | --- | --- |
radicand The expression under a radical sign.	**radicando** Número o expresión debajo del signo de radical.	Expression: $\sqrt{x+3}$ Radicand: $x+3$
radius A segment whose endpoints are the center of a circle and a point on the circle; the distance from the center of a circle to any point on the circle.	**radio** Segmento cuyos extremos son el centro de un círculo y un punto de la circunferencia; distancia desde el centro de un círculo hasta cualquier punto de la circunferencia.	
random sample A sample selected from a population so that each member of the population has an equal chance of being selected.	**muestra aleatoria** Muestra seleccionada de una población tal que cada miembro de ésta tenga igual probabilidad de ser seleccionada.	Mr. Hansen chose a random sample of the class by writing each student's name on a slip of paper, mixing up the slips, and drawing five slips without looking.
range of a data set The difference of the greatest and least values in the data set.	**rango de un conjunto de datos** La diferencia del mayor y menor valor en un conjunto de datos.	The data set {3, 3, 5, 7, 8, 10, 11, 11, 12} has a range of $12 - 3 = 9$.
range of a function or relation The set of all second coordinates (or y-values) of a function or relation.	**rango de una función o relación** Conjunto de todos los valores de la segunda coordenada (o valores de y) de una función o relación.	The range of the function {(−5, 3), (−3, −2), (−1, −1), (1, 0)} is {−2, −1, 0, 3}.
rate A ratio that compares two quantities measured in different units.	**tasa** Razón que compara dos cantidades medidas en diferentes unidades.	$\dfrac{55\ \text{miles}}{1\ \text{hour}} = 55\ \text{mi/h}$
rate of change A ratio that compares the amount of change in a dependent variable to the amount of change in an independent variable.	**tasa de cambio** Razón que compara la cantidad de cambio de la variable dependiente con la cantidad de cambio de la variable independiente.	The cost of mailing a letter increased from 22 cents in 1985 to 25 cents in 1988. During this period, the rate of change was $\dfrac{\text{change in cost}}{\text{change in year}} = \dfrac{25-22}{1988-1985} = \dfrac{3}{3}$ $= 1$ cent per year.
ratio A comparison of two quantities by division.	**razón** Comparación de dos cantidades mediante una división.	$\dfrac{1}{2}$ or 1 : 2
rational equation An equation that contains one or more rational expressions.	**ecuación racional** Ecuación que contiene una o más expresiones racionales.	$\dfrac{x+2}{x^2+3x-1} = 6$
rational exponent An exponent that can be expressed as $\frac{m}{n}$ such that if m and n are integers, then $b^{\frac{m}{n}} = \sqrt[n]{b^m} = \left(\sqrt[n]{b}\right)^m$.	**exponente racional** Exponente que se puede expresar como $\frac{m}{n}$ tal que si m y n son números enteros, entonces $b^{\frac{m}{n}} = \sqrt[n]{b^m} = \left(\sqrt[n]{b}\right)^m$.	$64^{\frac{1}{6}} = \sqrt[6]{64}$
rational expression An algebraic expression whose numerator and denominator are polynomials and whose denominator has a degree ≥ 1.	**expresión racional** Expresión algebraica cuyo numerador y denominador son polinomios y cuyo denominador tiene un grado ≥ 1.	$\dfrac{x+2}{x^2+3x-1}$

Glossary/Glosario

ENGLISH	SPANISH	EXAMPLES
rational function A function whose rule can be written as a rational expression.	**función racional** Función cuya regla se puede expresar como una expresión racional.	$f(x) = \dfrac{x+2}{x^2 + 3x - 1}$
rational number A number that can be written in the form $\frac{a}{b}$, where a and b are integers and $b \neq 0$.	**número racional** Número que se puede expresar como $\frac{a}{b}$, donde a y b son números enteros y $b \neq 0$.	$3, \ 1.75, \ 0.\overline{3}, \ -\dfrac{2}{3}, \ 0$
rationalizing the denominator A method of rewriting a fraction by multiplying by another fraction that is equivalent to 1 in order to remove radical terms from the denominator.	**racionalizar el denominador** Método que consiste en escribir nuevamente una fracción multiplicándola por otra fracción equivalente a 1 a fin de eliminar los términos radicales del denominador.	$\dfrac{1}{\sqrt{2}} \cdot \dfrac{\sqrt{2}}{\sqrt{2}} = \dfrac{\sqrt{2}}{2}$
ray A part of a line that starts at an endpoint and extends forever in one direction.	**rayo** Parte de una recta que comienza en un extremo y se extiende infinitamente en una dirección.	
real number A rational or irrational number. Every point on the number line represents a real number.	**número real** Número racional o irracional. Cada punto de la recta numérica representa un número real.	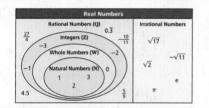
reciprocal For a real number $a \neq 0$, the reciprocal of a is $\frac{1}{a}$. The product of reciprocals is 1.	**recíproco** Dado el número real $a \neq 0$, el recíproco de a es $\frac{1}{a}$. El producto de los recíprocos es 1.	Number / Reciprocal table

Number	Reciprocal
2	$\frac{1}{2}$
1	1
−1	−1
0	No reciprocal

ENGLISH	SPANISH	EXAMPLES
rectangle A quadrilateral with four right angles.	**rectángulo** Cuadrilátero con cuatro ángulos rectos.	
rectangular prism A prism whose bases are rectangles.	**prisma rectangular** Prisma cuyas bases son rectángulos.	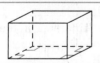
rectangular pyramid A pyramid whose base is a rectangle.	**pirámide rectangular** Pirámide cuya base es un rectángulo.	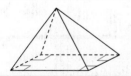
reflection A transformation that reflects, or "flips," a graph or figure across a line, called the line of reflection.	**reflexión** Transformación en la que una gráfica o figura se refleja o se invierte sobre una línea, denominada la línea de reflexión.	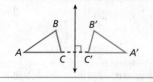
regular polygon A polygon that is both equilateral and equiangular.	**polígono regular** Polígono equilátero de ángulos iguales.	

ENGLISH	SPANISH	EXAMPLES
relation A set of ordered pairs.	**relación** Conjunto de pares ordenados.	$\{(0, 5), (0, 4), (2, 3), (4, 0)\}$
repeating decimal A rational number in decimal form that has a nonzero block of one or more digits that repeat continuously.	**decimal periódico** Número racional en forma decimal que tiene un bloque de uno o más dígitos que se repite continuamente.	$1.\overline{3},\ 0.\overline{6},\ 2.\overline{14},\ 6.77\overline{3}$
replacement set A set of numbers that can be substituted for a variable.	**conjunto de reemplazo** Conjunto de números que pueden sustituir una variable.	
residual The signed vertical distance between a data point and a line of fit.	**residuo** La diferencia vertical entre un dato y una línea de ajuste.	
rhombus A quadrilateral with four congruent sides.	**rombo** Cuadrilátero con cuatro lados congruentes.	
right angle An angle that measures 90°.	**ángulo recto** Ángulo que mide 90°.	
rise The difference in the *y*-values of two points on a line.	**distancia vertical** Diferencia entre los valores de *y* de dos puntos de una línea.	For the points $(3, -1)$ and $(6, 5)$, the rise is $5 - (-1) = 6$.
rotation A transformation that rotates or turns a figure about a point called the center of rotation.	**rotación** Transformación que rota o gira una figura sobre un punto llamado centro de rotación.	
rotational symmetry A figure that can be rotated about a point by an angle less than 360° so that the image coincides with the preimage has rotational symmetry.	**simetría de rotación** Una figura que puede rotarse alrededor de un punto en un ángulo menor de 360° de forma tal que la imagen coincide con la imagen original tiene simetría de rotación.	Order of rotational symmetry: 4
run The difference in the *x*-values of two points on a line.	**distancia horizontal** Diferencia entre los valores de *x* de dos puntos de una línea.	For the points $(3, -1)$ and $(6, 5)$, the run is $6 - 3 = 3$.

S

sample A part of the population.	**muestra** Una parte de la población.	In a survey about the study habits of high school students, a sample is a survey of 100 high school students.
sample space The set of all possible outcomes of a probability experiment.	**espacio muestral** Conjunto de todos los resultados posibles de un experimento de probabilidad.	In the experiment of rolling a number cube, the sample space is $\{1, 2, 3, 4, 5, 6\}$.
scale The ratio between two corresponding measurements.	**escala** Razón entre dos medidas correspondientes.	1 cm : 5 mi

Glossary/Glosario

ENGLISH	SPANISH	EXAMPLES
scale drawing A drawing that uses a scale to represent an object as smaller or larger than the actual object.	**dibujo a escala** Dibujo que utiliza una escala para representar un objeto como más pequeño o más grande que el objeto original.	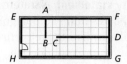 A blueprint is an example of a scale drawing.
scale factor The multiplier used on each dimension to change one figure into a similar figure.	**factor de escala** El multiplicador utilizado en cada dimensión para transformar una figura en una figura semejante.	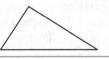 Scale factor: $\frac{3}{2} = 1.5$
scale model A three-dimensional model that uses a scale to represent an object as smaller or larger than the actual object.	**modelo a escala** Modelo tridimensional que utiliza una escala para representar un objeto como más pequeño o más grande que el objeto real.	
scalene triangle A triangle with no congruent sides.	**triángulo escaleno** Triángulo sin lados congruentes.	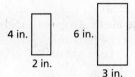
scatter plot A graph with points plotted to show a possible relationship between two sets of data.	**diagrama de dispersión** Gráfica con puntos que se usa para demostrar una relación posible entre dos conjuntos de datos.	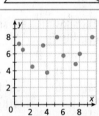
second differences Differences between first differences of a function.	**segundas diferencias** Diferencias entre las primeras diferencias de una función.	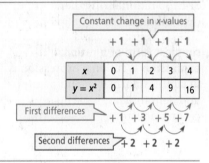
sequence A list of numbers that often form a pattern.	**sucesión** Lista de números que generalmente forman un patrón.	1, 2, 4, 8, 16, …
set A collection of items called elements.	**conjunto** Grupo de componentes denominados elementos.	{1, 2, 3}
set-builder notation A notation for a set that uses a rule to describe the properties of the elements of the set.	**notación de conjuntos** Notación para un conjunto que se vale de una regla para describir las propiedades de los elementos del conjunto.	$\{x \mid x > 3\}$ is read "The set of all x such that x is greater than 3."
similar Two figures are similar if they have the same shape but not necessarily the same size.	**semejantes** Dos figuras con la misma forma pero no necesariamente del mismo tamaño.	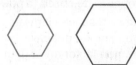

ENGLISH	SPANISH	EXAMPLES

similarity statement A statement that indicates that two polygons are similar by listing the vertices in the order of correspondence.

enunciado de semejanza Enunciado que indica que dos polígonos son semejantes enumerando los vértices en orden de correspondencia.

quadrilateral $ABCD \sim$
quadrilateral $EFGH$

---

simple event An event consisting of only one outcome.

suceso simple Suceso que tiene sólo un resultado.

In the experiment of rolling a number cube, the event consisting of the outcome 3 is a simple event.

---

simple interest A fixed percent of the principal. For principal P, interest rate r, and time t in years, the simple interest is $I = Prt$.

interés simple Porcentaje fijo del capital. Dado el capital P, la tasa de interés r y el tiempo t expresado en años, el interés simple es $I = Prt$.

If $100 is put into an account with a simple interest rate of 5%, then after 2 years, the account will have earned $I = 100 \cdot 0.05 \cdot 2 = \$10$ in interest.

---

simplest form of a square root expression A square root expression is in simplest form if it meets the following criteria:
1. No perfect squares are in the radicand.
2. No fractions are in the radicand.
3. No square roots appear in the denominator of a fraction.

See also rationalizing the denominator.

forma simplificada de una expresión de raíz cuadrada Una expresión de raíz cuadrada está en forma simplificada si reúne los siguientes requisitos:
1. No hay cuadrados perfectos en el radicando.
2. No hay fracciones en el radicando.
3. No aparecen raíces cuadradas en el denominador de una fracción.

Ver también racionalizar el denominador.

Not Simplest Form	Simplest Form
$\sqrt{180}$	$6\sqrt{5}$
$\sqrt{216a^2b^2}$	$6ab\sqrt{6}$
$\dfrac{\sqrt{7}}{\sqrt{2}}$	$\dfrac{\sqrt{14}}{2}$

---

simplest form of a rational expression A rational expression is in simplest form if the numerator and denominator have no common factors.

forma simplificada de una expresión racional Una expresión racional está en forma simplificada cuando el numerador y el denominador no tienen factores comunes.

$$\frac{x^2 - 1}{x^2 + x - 2} = \frac{(x-1)(x+1)}{(x-1)(x+2)}$$
$$= \frac{x+1}{x+2}$$
↑
Simplest form

---

simplest form of an exponential expression An exponential expression is in simplest form if it meets the following criteria:
1. There are no negative exponents.
2. The same base does not appear more than once in a product or quotient.
3. No powers, products, or quotients are raised to powers.
4. Numerical coefficients in a quotient do not have any common factor other than 1.

forma simplificada de una expresión exponencial Una expresión exponencial está en forma simplificada si reúne los siguientes requisitos:
1. No hay exponentes negativos.
2. La misma base no aparece más de una vez en un producto o cociente.
3. No se elevan a potencias productos, cocientes ni potencias.
4. Los coeficientes numéricos en un cociente no tienen ningún factor común que no sea 1.

Not Simplest Form	Simplest Form
$7^8 \cdot 7^4$	7^{12}
$(x^2)^{-4} \cdot x^5$	$\dfrac{1}{x^3}$
$\dfrac{a^5b^9}{(ab)^4}$	ab^5

Glossary/Glosario

ENGLISH	SPANISH	EXAMPLES
simplify To perform all indicated operations.	**simplificar** Realizar todas las operaciones indicadas.	$13 - 20 + 8$ $-7 + 8$ 1
simulation A model of an experiment, often one that would be too difficult or time-consuming to actually perform.	**simulación** Modelo de un experimento; generalmente se recurre a la simulación cuando realizar dicho experimento sería demasiado difícil o llevaría mucho tiempo.	
sine In a right triangle, the ratio of the length of the leg opposite $\angle A$ to the length of the hypotenuse.	**seno** En un triángulo rectángulo, razón entre la longitud del cateto opuesto a $\angle A$ y la longitud de la hipotenusa.	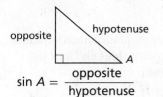 $\sin A = \dfrac{\text{opposite}}{\text{hypotenuse}}$
slope A measure of the steepness of a line. If (x_1, y_1) and (x_2, y_2) are any two points on the line, the slope of the line, known as m, is represented by the equation $m = \frac{y_2 - y_1}{x_2 - x_1}$.	**pendiente** Medida de la inclinación de una línea. Dados dos puntos (x_1, y_1) y (x_2, y_2) en una línea, la pendiente de la línea, denominada m, se representa con la ecuación $m = \frac{y_2 - y_1}{x_2 - x_1}$.	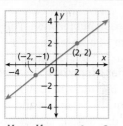 $m = \dfrac{y_2 - y_1}{x_2 - x_1} = \dfrac{-1 - 2}{-2 - 2} = \dfrac{3}{4}$
slope-intercept form The slope-intercept form of a linear equation is $y = mx + b$, where m is the slope and b is the y-intercept.	**forma de pendiente-intersección** La forma de pendiente-intersección de una ecuación lineal es $y = mx + b$, donde m es la pendiente y b es la intersección con el eje y.	$y = -2x + 4$ The slope is -2. The y-intercept is 4.
solution of a linear equation in two variables An ordered pair or ordered pairs that make the equation true.	**solución de una ecuación lineal en dos variables** Un par ordenado o pares ordenados que hacen que la ecuación sea verdadera.	$(4, 2)$ is a solution of $x + y = 6$.
solution of a linear inequality in two variables An ordered pair or ordered pairs that make the inequality true.	**solución de una desigualdad lineal en dos variables** Un par ordenado o pares ordenados que hacen que la desigualdad sea verdadera.	$(3, 1)$ is a solution of $x + y < 6$.
solution of a system of linear equations Any ordered pair that satisfies all the equations in a system.	**solución de un sistema de ecuaciones lineales** Cualquier par ordenado que resuelva todas las ecuaciones de un sistema.	$\begin{cases} x + y = -1 \\ -x + y = -3 \end{cases}$ Solution: $(1, -2)$
solution of a system of linear inequalities Any ordered pair that satisfies all the inequalities in a system.	**solución de un sistema de desigualdades lineales** Cualquier par ordenado que resuelva todas las desigualdades de un sistema.	$\begin{cases} y \leq x + 1 \\ y < -x + 4 \end{cases}$ $(2, 1)$ is in the overlapping shaded regions, so it is a solution.

solution of an equation in one variable A value or values that make the equation true.

solución de una ecuación en una variable Valor o valores que hacen que la ecuación sea verdadera.

Equation: $x + 2 = 6$
Solution: $x = 4$

---

solution of an inequality in one variable A value or values that make the inequality true.

solución de una desigualdad en una variable Valor o valores que hacen que la desigualdad sea verdadera.

Inequality: $x + 2 < 6$
Solution: $x < 4$

---

solution set The set of values that make a statement true.

conjunto solución Conjunto de valores que hacen verdadero un enunciado.

Inequality: $x + 3 \geq 5$
Solution set: $\{x \mid x \geq 2\}$

---

square A quadrilateral with four congruent sides and four right angles.

cuadrado Cuadrilátero con cuatro lados congruentes y cuatro ángulos rectos.

---

square in numeration The second power of a number.

cuadrado en numeración La segunda potencia de un número.

16 is the square of 4.

---

standard form of a linear equation $Ax + By = C$, where A, B, and C are real numbers and A and B are not both 0.

forma estándar de una ecuación lineal $Ax + By = C$, donde A, B y C son números reales y A y B no son ambos cero.

$2x + 3y = 6$

---

standard form of a polynomial A polynomial in one variable is written in standard form when the terms are in order from greatest degree to least degree.

forma estándar de un polinomio Un polinomio de una variable se expresa en forma estándar cuando los términos se ordenan de mayor a menor grado.

$4x^5 - 2x^4 + x^2 - x + 1$

---

standard form of a quadratic equation $ax^2 + bx + c = 0$, where a, b, and c are real numbers and $a \neq 0$.

forma estándar de una ecuación cuadrática $ax^2 + bx + c = 0$, donde a, b y c son números reales y $a \neq 0$.

$2x^2 + 3x - 1 = 0$

---

stem-and-leaf plot A graph used to organize and display data by dividing each data value into two parts, a stem and a leaf.

diagrama de tallo y hojas Gráfica utilizada para organizar y mostrar datos dividiendo cada valor de datos en dos partes, un tallo y una hoja.

Stem	Leaves
3	2 3 4 4 7 9
4	0 1 5 7 7 7 8
5	1 2 2 3

Key: 3|2 means 3.2

---

stratified random sample A sample in which a population is divided into distinct groups and members are selected at random from each group.

muestra aleatoria estratificada Muestra en la que la población está dividida en grupos diferenciados y los miembros de cada grupo se seleccionan al azar.

Ms. Carter chose a stratified random sample of her school's student population by randomly selecting 30 students from each grade level.

---

stretch A transformation that pulls the points of a graph horizontally away from the y-axis or vertically away from the x-axis.

estiramiento Transformación que desplaza los puntos de una gráfica en forma horizontal alejándolos del eje y o en forma vertical alejándolos del eje x.

Glossary/Glosario

subset A set that is contained entirely within another set. Set B is a subset of set A if every element of B is contained in A, denoted $B \subset A$.

subconjunto Conjunto que se encuentra dentro de otro conjunto. El conjunto B es un subconjunto del conjunto A si todos los elementos de B son elementos de A; se expresa $B \subset A$.

The set of integers is a subset of the set of rational numbers.

---

substitution method A method used to solve systems of equations by solving an equation for one variable and substituting the resulting expression into the other equation(s).

sustitución Método utilizado para resolver sistemas de ecuaciones resolviendo una ecuación para una variable y sustituyendo la expresión resultante en las demás ecuaciones.

Subtraction Property of Equality If a, b, and c are real numbers and $a = b$, then $a - c = b - c$.

Propiedad de igualdad de la resta Si a, b y c son números reales y $a = b$, entonces $a - c = b - c$.

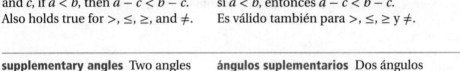

$$\begin{array}{rcl} x + 6 &=& 8 \\ -6 & & -6 \\ \hline x &=& 2 \end{array}$$

Subtraction Property of Inequality For real numbers a, b, and c, if $a < b$, then $a - c < b - c$. Also holds true for $>$, $\leq$, $\geq$, and $\neq$.

Propiedad de desigualdad de la resta Dados los números reales a, b y c, si $a < b$, entonces $a - c < b - c$. Es válido también para $>$, $\leq$, $\geq$ y $\neq$.

$$\begin{array}{rcl} x + 6 &<& 8 \\ -6 & & -6 \\ \hline x &<& 2 \end{array}$$

---

supplementary angles Two angles whose measures have a sum of 180°.

ángulos suplementarios Dos ángulos cuyas medidas suman 180°.

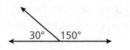
30° 150°

---

surface area The total area of all faces and curved surfaces of a three-dimensional figure.

área total Área total de todas las caras y superficies curvas de una figura tridimensional.

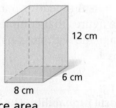
12 cm
6 cm
8 cm

Surface area
$= 2(8)(12) + 2(8)(6) + 2(12)(6)$
$= 432 \text{ cm}^2$

---

symmetry In the transformation of a figure such that the image coincides with the preimage, the image and preimage have symmetry.

simetría En la transformación de una figura tal que la imagen coincide con la imagen original, la imagen y la imagen original tienen simetría.

---

system of linear equations A system of equations in which all of the equations are linear.

sistema de ecuaciones lineales Sistema de ecuaciones en el que todas las ecuaciones son lineales.

$$\begin{cases} 2x + 3y = -1 \\ x - 3y = 4 \end{cases}$$

---

system of linear inequalities A system of inequalities in which all of the inequalities are linear.

sistema de desigualdades lineales Sistema de desigualdades en el que todas las desigualdades son lineales.

$$\begin{cases} 2x + 3y > -1 \\ x - 3y \leq 4 \end{cases}$$

ENGLISH	SPANISH	EXAMPLES
systematic random sample A sample based on selecting one member of the population at random and then selecting other members by using a pattern.	**muestra sistemática** Muestra en la que se elige a un miembro de la población al azar y luego se elige a otros miembros mediante un patrón.	Mr. Martin chose a systematic random sample of customers visiting a store by selecting one customer at random and then selecting every tenth customer after that.

T

ENGLISH	SPANISH	EXAMPLES
tangent In a right triangle, the ratio of the length of the leg opposite $\angle A$ to the length of the leg adjacent to $\angle A$.	**tangente** En un triángulo rectángulo, razón entre la longitud del cateto opuesto a $\angle A$ y la longitud del cateto adyacente a $\angle A$.	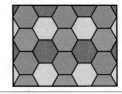 $$\tan A = \frac{opposite}{adjacent}$$
term of an expression The parts of the expression that are added or subtracted.	**término de una expresión** Parte de una expresión que debe sumarse o restarse.	$3x^2 + 6x - 8$ Term Term Term
term of a sequence An element or number in the sequence.	**término de una sucesión** Elemento o número de una sucesión.	5 is the third term in the sequence 1, 3, 5, 7, …
terminating decimal A decimal that ends, or terminates.	**decimal finito** Decimal con un número determinados de posiciones decimales.	1.5, 2.75, 4.0
tessellation A repeating pattern of plane figures that completely covers a plane with no gaps or overlaps.	**teselado** Patrón que se repite formado por figuras planas que cubren completamente un plano sin dejar espacios libres y sin superponerse.	
theoretical probability The ratio of the number of equally likely outcomes in an event to the total number of possible outcomes.	**probabilidad teórica** Razón entre el número de resultados igualmente probables de un suceso y el número total de resultados posibles.	In the experiment of rolling a number cube, the theoretical probability of rolling an odd number is $\frac{3}{6} = \frac{1}{2}$.
third quartile The median of the upper half of a data set. Also called *upper quartile*.	**tercer cuartil** La mediana de la mitad superior de un conjunto de datos. También se llama *cuartil superior*.	Lower half Upper half 18, 23, 28, 29, (36), 42 **Third quartile**
tolerance The amount by which a measurement is permitted to vary from a specified value.	**tolerancia** La cantidad por que una medida se permite variar de un valor especificado.	
transformation A change in the position, size, or shape of a figure or graph.	**transformación** Cambio en la posición, tamaño o forma de una figura o gráfica.	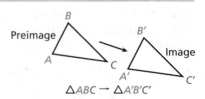 $\triangle ABC \rightarrow \triangle A'B'C'$

Glossary/Glosario

ENGLISH	SPANISH	EXAMPLES
translation A transformation that shifts or slides every point of a figure or graph the same distance in the same direction.	**traslación** Transformación en la que todos los puntos de una figura o gráfica se mueven la misma distancia en la misma dirección.	
translation symmetry A figure has translation symmetry if it can be translated along a vector so that the image coincides with the preimage.	**simetría de traslación** Una figura tiene simetría de traslación si se puede trasladar a lo largo de un vector de forma tal que la imagen coincida con la imagen original.	
trapezoid A quadrilateral with exactly one pair of parallel sides.	**trapecio** Cuadrilátero con sólo un par de lados paralelos.	
tree diagram A branching diagram that shows all possible combinations or outcomes of an experiment.	**diagrama de árbol** Diagrama con ramificaciones que muestra todas las combinaciones o resultados posibles de un experimento.	H T 1 2 3 4 5 6 1 2 3 4 5 6 The tree diagram shows the possible outcomes when tossing a coin and rolling a number cube.
trend line A line on a scatter plot that helps show the correlation between data sets more clearly.	**línea de tendencia** Línea en un diagrama de dispersión que sirve para mostrar la correlación entre conjuntos de datos más claramente.	**Fund-raiser**
trial Each repetition or observation of an experiment.	**prueba** Una sola repetición u observación de un experimento.	In the experiment of rolling a number cube, each roll is one trial.
triangular prism A prism whose bases are triangles.	**prisma triangular** Prisma cuyas bases son triángulos.	Bases
triangular pyramid A pyramid whose base is a triangle.	**pirámide triangular** Pirámide cuya base es un triángulo.	
trigonometric ratio Ratio of the lengths of two sides of a right triangle.	**razón trigonométrica** Razón entre dos lados de un triángulo rectángulo.	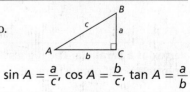 $\sin A = \dfrac{a}{c}$, $\cos A = \dfrac{b}{c}$, $\tan A = \dfrac{a}{b}$
trinomial A polynomial with three terms.	**trinomio** Polinomio con tres términos.	$4x^2 + 3xy - 5y^2$

Glossary/Glosario

union The union of two sets is the set of all elements that are in either set, denoted by ∪.

unión La unión de dos conjuntos es el conjunto de todos los elementos que se encuentran en ambos conjuntos, expresado por ∪.

$A = \{1, 2, 3, 4\}$
$B = \{1, 3, 5, 7, 9\}$
$A \cup B = \{1, 2, 3, 4, 5, 7, 9\}$

---

unit rate A rate in which the second quantity in the comparison is one unit.

tasa unitaria Tasa en la que la segunda cantidad de la comparación es una unidad.

$\dfrac{30 \text{ mi}}{1 \text{ h}} = 30 \text{ mi/h}$

---

unlike radicals Radicals with a different quantity under the radical.

radicales distintos Radicales con cantidades diferentes debajo del signo de radical.

$2\sqrt{2}$ and $2\sqrt{3}$

---

unlike terms Terms with different variables or the same variables raised to different powers.

términos distintos Términos con variables diferentes o las mismas variables elevadas a potencias diferentes.

$4xy^2$ and $6x^2y$

---

upper quartile *See* third quartile.

cuartil superior *Ver* tercer cuartil.

V

value of a function The result of replacing the independent variable with a number and simplifying.

valor de una función Resultado de reemplazar la variable independiente por un número y luego simplificar.

The value of the function $f(x) = x + 1$ for $x = 3$ is 4.

---

value of a variable A number used to replace a variable to make an equation true.

valor de una variable Número utilizado para reemplazar una variable y hacer que una ecuación sea verdadera.

In the equation $x + 1 = 4$, the value of x is 3.

---

value of an expression The result of replacing the variables in an expression with numbers and simplifying.

valor de una expresión Resultado de reemplazar las variables de una expresión por un número y luego simplificar.

The value of the expression $x + 1$ for $x = 3$ is 4.

---

variable A symbol used to represent a quantity that can change.

variable Símbolo utilizado para representar una cantidad que puede cambiar.

In the expression $2x + 3$, x is the variable.

Venn diagram A diagram used to show relationships between sets.

diagrama de Venn Diagrama utilizado para mostrar la relación entre conjuntos.

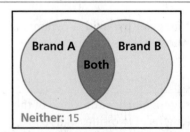

---

vertex of a parabola The highest or lowest point on the parabola.

vértice de una parábola Punto más alto o más bajo de una parábola.

The vertex is $(0, -2)$.

vertex of an absolute-value graph The point on the axis of symmetry of the graph.

vértice de una gráfica de valor absoluto Punto en el eje de simetría de la gráfica.

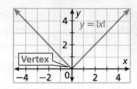

vertical angles The nonadjacent angles formed by two intersecting lines.

ángulos opuestos por el vértice Ángulos no adyacentes formados por dos líneas que se cruzan.

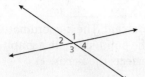

∠1 and ∠3 are vertical angles.
∠2 and ∠4 are vertical angles.

vertical line A line whose equation is $x = a$, where a is the x-intercept.

línea vertical Línea cuya ecuación es $x = a$, donde a es la intersección con el eje x.

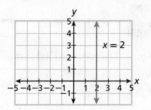

vertical-line test A test used to determine whether a relation is a function. If any vertical line crosses the graph of a relation more than once, the relation is not a function.

prueba de la línea vertical Prueba utilizada para determinar si una relación es una función. Si una línea vertical corta la gráfica de una relación más de una vez, la relación no es una función.

Function   Not a function

volume The number of nonoverlapping unit cubes of a given size that will exactly fill the interior of a three-dimensional figure.

volumen Cantidad de cubos unitarios no superpuestos de un determinado tamaño que llenan exactamente el interior de una figura tridimensional.

Volume = (3)(4)(12) = 144 ft³

voluntary response sample A sample in which members choose to be in the sample.

muestra de respuesta voluntaria Una muestra en la que los miembros eligen participar.

A store provides survey cards for customers who wish to fill them out.

whole number A member of the set of natural numbers and zero.

número cabal Miembro del conjunto de los números naturales y cero.

0, 1, 2, 3, 4, 5, …

_x_-axis The horizontal axis in a coordinate plane.

eje _x_ Eje horizontal en un plano cartesiano.

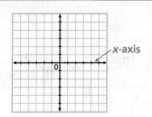

Glossary/Glosario

ENGLISH	SPANISH	EXAMPLES
x-coordinate The first number in an ordered pair, which indicates the horizontal distance of a point from the origin on the coordinate plane.	**coordenada x** Primer número de un par ordenado, que indica la distancia horizontal de un punto desde el origen en un plano cartesiano.	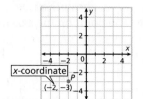
x-intercept The x-coordinate(s) of the point(s) where a graph intersects the x-axis.	**intersección con el eje x** Coordenada(s) x de uno o más puntos donde una gráfica corta el eje x.	 The x-intercept is 2.

ENGLISH	SPANISH	EXAMPLES
y-axis The vertical axis in a coordinate plane.	**eje y** Eje vertical en un plano cartesiano.	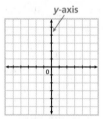
y-coordinate The second number in an ordered pair, which indicates the vertical distance of a point from the origin on the coordinate plane.	**coordenada y** Segundo número de un par ordenado, que indica la distancia vertical de un punto desde el origen en un plano cartesiano.	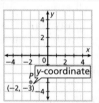
y-intercept The y-coordinate(s) of the point(s) where a graph intersects the y-axis.	**intersección con el eje y** Coordenada(s) y de uno o más puntos donde una gráfica corta el eje y.	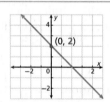 The y-intercept is 2.

Z

ENGLISH	SPANISH	EXAMPLES
zero exponent For any nonzero real number x, $x^0 = 1$.	**exponente cero** Dado un número real distinto de cero x, $x^0 = 1$.	$5^0 = 1$
zero of a function For the function f, any number x such that $f(x) = 0$.	**cero de una función** Dada la función f, todo número x tal que $f(x) = 0$.	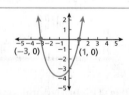 The zeros are −3 and 1.
Zero Product Property For real numbers p and q, if $pq = 0$, then $p = 0$ or $q = 0$.	**Propiedad del producto cero** Dados los números reales p y q, si $pq = 0$, entonces $p = 0$ o $q = 0$.	If $(x - 1)(x + 2) = 0$, then $x - 1 = 0$ or $x + 2 = 0$, so $x = 1$ or $x = -2$.

Index

Index

Index

Index

Index

Index

O

Oceanography, 33, 218
ocelots, 417
Online Resources
  Career Resources Online, 76, 120, 138
  Chapter Project Online, 42
  Homework Help Online
    Homework Help Online is available for every lesson. Refer to the box at the beginning of each exercise set. Some examples: 9, 16, 23, 66, 75
  Lab Resources Online, 12, 69, 132, 139, 221, 420, 450
  Parent Resources Online
    Parent Resources Online are available for every lesson. Refer to the box at the beginning of each exercise set. Some examples: 9, 16, 23, 66, 75
op art, 488
operations, inverse, 13, 20, 62, 70, 77, 92
opposite coefficients, 147
orangutans, 102
ordered pairs
  identifying exponential functions by using, 342
  identifying linear functions by using, 241, 342
  identifying quadratic functions by using, 315, 342
  showing relations by, 194
organizing data, 370, 371, 372, 373, 374
outliers, 394, 395
output, 203

P

paella, 274
parallel lines
  slopes of, 509, 510, 511, 512
parallels adjustable, 464
PARCC Assessment Readiness, 29, 53–57, 83, 105, 129, 155, 179–183, 211, 271, 305, 337, 361–365, 409, 435–439, 475, 499–503, 523–525
parent functions
  horizontal translations of, 466
  reflections of, 466
  vertical translations of, 466
Parent Resources Online
  Parent Resources Online are available for every lesson. Refer to the box at the beginning of each exercise set. Some examples:, 9, 16, 23, 66, 75

Pasteur, Louis, 456
patterns
  in choosing a model, 342
  identifying, 332
Pentagon building, 487
Performance Tasks, 57, 183, 365, 439, 503, 525
perpendicular lines
  slopes of, 509, 510, 511, 512
Personal Finance, 251, 330
Pet Care, 347
Physical Science, 246, 311, 350
Physics, 318, 432, 489
Pimlico Race Course, 192
plane symmetry, 486
point-slope form of linear equations, 287, 288, 289, 290, 291
Population, 38
positive correlation, 413
positive slope, 256
precision of measurements, 45, 46, 47, 48
preimage, 444
primes, 444
probability, 463
  conditional relative frequency to find, 387
Problem-Solving Applications, 64, 93, 94, 135, 217, 290, 343, 344, 453
Properties, 229
  of equality, 15, 22
  of inequality, 92, 98, 99
proportions
  applications of, 39, 40, 41
  cross products in, 33
  definition of, 32
  rates, ratios and, 32, 33, 34, 35

Q

Qin Jiushao, 152
quadratic models, 341, 342, 343, 344

R

range, 18, 194, 195, 196, 197, 198, 199, 200, 206, 207, 208, 209, 218
range of a data set, 394, 395
rate of change
  constant and variable, 348, 349
  decrease, 321
  definition of, 254, 348
  identifying linear and nonlinear functions from, 349, 350
  increase, 321
  slope and, 254, 255, 256, 257
rates, 32, 33, 34, 35

ratio(s)
  equivalent, 32
  rates and proportions, 32, 33, 34, 35
Reading and Writing Math. *See also* **Reading Strategies; Study Strategies; Writing Strategies,** 381
Reading Math, 32, 34, 39, 88, 160, 205, 230, 264, 324, 353, 372, 396
Reading Strategies
  Read and Interpret Graphics, 381
Ready to Go On?. *See also* **Assessment,** 28, 52, 82, 104, 128, 154, 178, 210, 270, 304, 336, 360, 408, 434, 474, 498, 522
Real Estate, 43
reasonable answer, 15, 16, 17, 18, 24, 25, 33, 35, 36, 38, 40, 42, 65, 74, 88, 94, 100, 135, 136, 166, 173, 189, 217, 314, 323, 325
reasonable domain, 206, 207, 208, 209, 217, 243, 248
reasonable range, 206, 207, 208, 209, 217, 243, 248
reasonableness, 15, 16, 17, 18, 24, 25, 65, 74, 35, 36, 38, 40, 42, 208, 209, 217, 415
reasoning, 303, 393, 521
Recreation, 23, 118, 144, 175, 192, 198, 226, 234, 261, 456, 480, 519
rectangles, area of, 19
recursive patterns, 332
Recycling, 8
Reflecting functions, 223, 297
reflections, 223, 444, 452, 453, 454
  constructing, 457
  describing transformations in terms of, 480
  exponential functions, 359
  glide, 478, 481
  in the coordinate plane, 454
  of figures constructing, 452
regression
  linear, 422, 423
relations
  functions and, 194, 195, 196
relationships
  graphing, 188, 189, 190
  variable model, 202
Remember!, 78, 108, 122, 148, 171, 242, 243, 342, 354, 370, 430, 431, 459, 469, 510, 516, 517
replacement set, 8
representations
  multiple, 12, 15, 22, 69, 71, 87, 92, 98, 99, 116, 121, 122, 123, 139, 194, 221, 258, 264, 280, 509, 511
residual, 421
rigid motions, 452
rise, 255
rotational symmetry, 485
  angle of, 485
  order of, 485

Index

Index

Index

Index *(side tab)*